D1189675

LAWRENCE HENRY GIPSON

AUTHOR

JARED INGERSOLL: A STUDY OF AMERICAN LOYALISM IN RELATION TO BRITISH COLONIAL GOVERNMENT

STUDIES IN CONNECTICUT COLONIAL TAXATION

THE MORAVIAN INDIAN MISSION ON WHITE RIVER

LEWIS EVANS

THE COMING OF THE REVOLUTION, 1763–1775

THE BRITISH EMPIRE BEFORE THE AMERICAN REVOLUTION

VOLUME I. THE BRITISH ISLES AND THE AMERICAN COLONIES: GREAT BRITAIN AND IRELAND, 1748–1754

VOLUME II. THE BRITISH ISLES AND THE AMERICAN COLONIES: THE SOUTHERN PLANTATIONS, 1748–1754

VOLUME III. THE BRITISH ISLES AND THE AMERICAN COLONIES: THE NORTHERN PLANTATIONS, 1748–1754

VOLUME IV: ZONES OF INTERNATIONAL FRICTION: NORTH AMERICA, SOUTH OF THE GREAT LAKES REGION, 1748–1754

VOLUME V. ZONES OF INTERNATIONAL FRICTION: THE GREAT LAKES FRONTIER, CANADA, THE WEST INDIES, INDIA, 1748–1754

VOLUME VI. THE GREAT WAR FOR THE EMPIRE: THE YEARS OF DEFEAT, 1754–1757

VOLUME VII. THE GREAT WAR FOR THE EMPIRE: THE VICTORIOUS YEARS, 1758–1760

VOLUME VIII. THE GREAT WAR FOR THE EMPIRE: THE CULMINATION, 1760–1763

VOLUME IX. THE TRIUMPHANT EMPIRE: NEW RESPONSIBILITIES WITHIN THE ENLARGED EMPIRE, 1763–1766

VOLUME X. THE TRIUMPHANT EMPIRE: THUNDER-CLOUDS GATHER IN THE WEST, 1763–1766

VOLUME XI. THE TRIUMPHANT EMPIRE: THE RUMBLING OF THE COMING STORM, 1766–1770

VOLUME XII. THE TRIUMPHANT EMPIRE: BRITAIN SAILS INTO THE STORM, 1770–1776

VOLUME XIII. THE TRIUMPHANT EMPIRE: PART I, THE EMPIRE BEYOND THE STORM, 1770–1776; PART II, A SUMMARY OF THE SERIES; PART III, HISTORIOGRAPHY

VOLUME XIV. BIBLIOGRAPHY (in preparation)

THE BRITISH EMPIRE

BEFORE THE AMERICAN REVOLUTION

VOLUME XI

THE TRIUMPHANT EMPIRE:

THE RUMBLING OF THE COMING STORM

1766–1770

THE BRITISH EMPIRE
BEFORE THE AMERICAN REVOLUTION
VOLUME XI

THE TRIUMPHANT EMPIRE:

THE RUMBLING OF THE COMING STORM, 1766–1770

BY

LAWRENCE HENRY GIPSON

MCMLXVII
ALFRED A. KNOPF
NEW YORK

L. C. catalog card number: 58–9670

THIS IS A BORZOI BOOK,
PUBLISHED BY ALFRED A. KNOPF, INC.

PUBLISHED, DECEMBER 1965
SECOND PRINTING, APRIL 1967

To the memory of a distinguished American pioneer and descendant of eighteenth-century Ohio Valley pioneers,

WILLIAM JUDSON BOONE,

founder and first President of the College of Idaho, Minister of the Gospel, Botanist, lover of nature and mankind, whose guiding hand helped to send me along the path of academic life.

Preface

In the Preface to Volume X of this series I wrote that Volume XI would bring my series to completion with accounts of the coming of the Revolution in the thirteen older North American colonies and of events in those areas of the Empire which did not rebel. The jacket of that volume also announced that Volume XII would include a Historiography and a Bibliography of the period 1748 to 1775 along with a General Index. Once again my plans have been changed by the wealth of the available material and the demands of scholarship that my work should more nearly encompass the full measure of the imperial problems in order to live up to its title—one which, with hindsight, I could wish to amend to read *The British Empire before the American Declaration of Independence,* for I have long been convinced, along with John Adams, that the Revolution was completed before the outbreak of what should properly be called the War for American Independence. Thus, what was to have been one work has developed into two companion volumes—the present one and Volume XII, *Britain Sails into the Storm* —now published simultaneously. Volume XIII will follow, with the section *The Empire beyond the Storm* (already written) together with a summary chapter on the series forming the first part, and with the second part comprehending sections on the Historiography (now in the writing) and Bibliography (in preparation) of the period 1748 to 1776. There will, however, be no General Index to the series, as it has been the consensus of many scholars that the indexes to the various volumes are thoroughly serviceable and adequate, especially when taken together with the detailed tables of contents and chronologies.

The present volume picks up the thread of events following the repeal of the Stamp Act and carries forward to the end of the 1760's, with continued emphasis upon the relations between the government of Great Britain and the thirteen older North American colonies. It is particularly concerned with the growing colonial discontent resulting from the Townshend legislation and with the domestic discontent in the British Isles that saw the rise to power of John Wilkes and the beginnings of the reform and urban radical movements, as the various opposition factions proved inadequate to change the policies of the Ministry supported by the King.

Nor is it possible, in rounding out the history of the Empire during the twenty-five years before the outbreak of the War for American Independence, to ignore the bitter intercolonial rivalries that characterized the period in North America. To treat them all adequately would demand far more space than is possible to assign to them in this series. Therefore it has seemed best to highlight these conflicts of interest by concentrating upon the more important intercolonial disputes over charter rights and boundaries that centred in the provinces of New York and Pennsylvania, since these involved most of the Northern colonies. Among other matters of deep concern to Americans were the struggles among the inhabitants of some of the colonies for political equality. Nowhere were these contests more vivid or dramatic than in North Carolina and South Carolina. These two colonies have therefore been selected to illustrate the intracolonial rivalries of the period.

There were, too, the vastly important problems of establishing equitable land and Indian policies to govern the future disposition of the vast trans-Appalachian area with the gradual breaking down of the Proclamation Line of 1763 by a series of treaties. Thus two chapters of this volume are devoted to picking up the story (begun in Volume IV and carried forward in Volume IX) of the westward movement of land speculators, settlers, and veterans of the Great War for the Empire and to dealing with the attendant problems of Indian-white relations. For the obsessive lure of lands claimed by the Indians beckoned not only to colonials who formed companies and abortive plans for new colonies to settle the eastern part of the Mississippi basin, but also to men in the British Isles, even some in high places.

While a great deal of thought has been given to the proper arrangement of chapters in this volume and the one to follow, in order that they might possess unity and coherence, I am still not completely satisfied with it. Nevertheless, the plan adopted is the best that could be devised in view of the need to move from one point of vantage to the next—now to Great Britain, now to one or another of the Atlantic seaboard colonies, and now again to the largely unsettled trans-Appalachian area.

Because of the related nature of the subject matter of Volumes XI and XII, acknowledgment of the sources drawn upon for the writing of both volumes follows, as does my tribute to the individuals who have contributed in such full measure to my project. The materials utilized have been consulted in many depositories of manuscripts and rare printed works. Among them are the following: in London, the Public Record Office, the British Museum, and the Library of the United East India Company, located in what was earlier the Company's impressive headquarters and is now the Commonwealth Building; in Oxford, the Bodleian Library; in Sheffield, the Central Library, where rest great collections of Rockingham and Burke manuscripts; in Washington, the Library of Congress with its vast collection of reproductions of British manuscripts; in Boston, the Massachusetts Archives and the Massachusetts Historical Society; in Cambridge, Massachusetts, the Houghton Library of Harvard University, in which, among other collections, are the Sir Francis Bernard Papers and Arthur Lee Papers; in Providence, the John Carter Brown Library; in New Haven, the Sterling Library of Yale University; in New York City, the Manuscript Division of the Public Library and the New-York Historical Society; in Albany, the State Archives; in Philadelphia, the American Philosophical Society, the Historical Society of Pennsylvania, and the Library Company of Philadelphia; in Harrisburg, the Pennsylvania Archives; in Baltimore, the Maryland Historical Society; in Annapolis, the Maryland Archives; in Richmond, the Virginia Historical Society and the Virginia Archives; in Raleigh, the North Carolina Archives; in Chapel Hill, the University of North Carolina Library; in Columbia, the South Carolina Archives Department and the University of South Carolina Carolinian Library; in Charleston, the Historical Society of South Carolina; in Atlanta, the Georgia Archives; in Ottawa, the Canadian Archives; in Ann Arbor, Michigan, the Clements Library with the Shelburne, Gage, and other great collections of papers; and at San Marino, California, the Huntington Library with its Stowe Americana manuscripts.

The Lehigh University Library not only has freely placed its resources at my disposal but throughout the years has rendered many important services, in addition to providing very generous quarters for my project. I am under particular obligation therefore to the Librarian, Mr. James D. Mack, and his staff, especially the Order Librarian, Mrs. Ruth Pace, the Reference Librarian, Miss Margaret Dennis, and her assistant in charge of inter-library loans, Mrs. Polly Orsagh. While the Lehigh Library holdings in eighteenth-century history are excellent and include the *Journals of the House of Commons* in microprint, special acknowledgment must be made to Beaver College in Jenkintown, Pennsylvania, for the loan of the printed volumes of the *Journals* over an extended period of time. Nor must I fail to mention the excellent work done on the illustrative material for the final volumes of the series by photographer Miles E. Raudenbush of the Lehigh University Printery and by J. Carroll Tobias of Bethlehem, Pennsylvania.

With respect to the financial support that enabled me to complete the series, some of which has been acknowledged in previous prefaces, I must again express my great indebtedness to the Rockefeller Foundation for its very generous aid covering a decade. But even greater is my sense of obligation to Lehigh University, which, from the inception of my undertaking down to the present, has seen to it that the many material needs involved in my project have been generously met. Nor must the congenial environment resulting from the constant encouragement and stimulation provided by members of the University's Administration and my colleagues on the Faculty go without tribute.

My Research Associate, Mrs. Jere Knight, has given to me, as she did in the preparation of Volume X, the most invaluable aid at every stage in the writing of this volume and the one to follow. Without this dedicated collaboration these books would have fallen far short of the completeness and standard of scholarship that, I trust, they possess. Acknowledgment is also due to her part-time assistants, Miss Michele Reis, Mr. Paul Minnich, and Mrs. Linda L. Schwarz, in the research work involved in preparing the manuscripts for the press. Nor must I fail to mention the important services rendered by my late secretary, Mrs. Rosabelle Harrison, and my present secretary, Mrs. Evelyn J. Evans. Professor John H. Cary, Head of the Lehigh Department of History, very kindly read over much of the manuscript, and I am indebted to him for many helpful suggestions.

Last, but most important, I must express my gratitude to Alfred A. Knopf for his enduring faith in my multi-volume enterprise and for bringing out each volume in such aesthetically pleasing and impressively functional format.

Lawrence Henry Gipson

The Library
Lehigh University
Bethlehem, Pennsylvania
December 4, 1964

Contents

Chapter I

EFFORTS TO HEAL THE BREACH

Chapter II

NEW YORK AND THE QUARTERING ACT

Chapter III

CHARLES TOWNSHEND MOVES TO THE FRONT

CHAPTER IV

THE IMPLEMENTATION OF THE TOWNSHEND ACTS

CHAPTER V

MASSACHUSETTS BAY AND RESISTANCE TO THE TOWNSHEND PROGRAM

Chapter VI

OTHER COLONIES FOLLOW THE LEAD OF MASSACHUSETTS BAY

Chapter VII

THE DISCONTENTED—"WILKES AND LIBERTY"

Chapter VIII

THE BRITISH MINISTRY AT SEA

Chapter IX

"THE UNIVERSAL DISCONTENT AND THE INFLAMED STATE OF AMERICA"

Chapter X

INTERCOLONIAL CONFLICTS: NEW YORK AND ITS RIVALS

Chapter XI

INTERCOLONIAL CONFLICTS: PENNSYLVANIA AND ITS RIVALS

The Rivalry between the Penns and the Baltimores

Chapter XII

TRANS-APPALACHIAN DEVELOPMENTS: BRITISH POLICIES AND PLANS FOR THE MANAGEMENT OF WESTERN LANDS AND INDIAN AFFAIRS

Chapter XIII

TRANS-APPALACHIAN DEVELOPMENTS: THE BRITISH MINISTRY FACES THE FAILURE OF IMPERIAL REGULATION

CONTENTS

CHAPTER XIV

THE STRUGGLE FOR POLITICAL EQUALITY: NORTH CAROLINA

Chapter XV

STRUGGLE FOR POLITICAL EQUALITY: SOUTH CAROLINA

Maps, Views, and Plans

CHRONOLOGY

Background to Intercolonial Rivalries

1634: establishment of the proprietary of Maryland; 1662: Connecticut's sea-to-sea charter; 1680: granting of the charter for the proprietary of Pennsylvania; 1681: Lord Baltimore challenges the Pennsylvania-Maryland line; 1684: The Privy Council considers the Pennsylvania-Maryland dispute; 1718: New York and New Jersey appoint commissioners to determine a boundary line; 1738: an order in council attempts to alleviate the Pennsylvania-Maryland boundary dispute; 1740: the New Hampshire southern boundary is fixed by an order in council; 1750: a boundary line between Pennsylvania and Maryland is determined by a decision in Chancery; 1753: formation of the Susquehannah Company in Connecticut; 1754: the Susquehannah Company purchases land in the Wyoming Valley already claimed by Pennsylvania; 1754: riots break out on the New York-New Jersey border; 1757: the Board of Trade representation to the King in Council on the New York-Massachusetts Bay land dispute; 1760: the Penn and Baltimore families reach an agreement on boundaries; 1762: the problem of the area disputed by New York and Massachusetts Bay becomes acute; 1763: an order in council attempts to settle the Pennsylvania-Connecticut land dispute; 1764: the Privy Council fixes the western boundary of New Hampshire.

Background to the Westward Movement and Land Speculation in the West

1747: the Ohio Company of Virginia is informally organized; 1749: an order in council favours plans for settlements in the trans-Appalachian West by the Ohio Company of Virginia; 1754: the Albany Congress treats with the Indians on western lands and recommends creation of the Indian superintendencies; 1755: Sir William Johnson is appointed Indian Superintendent for the Northern Department; 1756: creation of the office of Indian Superintendent for the Southern Department; Edmund Atkin is appointed; 1757: formulation of the Yorke-Pratt decision relating to

India, later used as precedent for American land Company purchases; 1763: royal proclamation lays down an Indian demarcation line; formation of the Mississippi Company and of plans for the western colonies of Charlotina and New Wales; formation of the Indiana Company to further the claims of the "Suffering Traders"; 1765: expansion of the Indiana Company plans; the Ohio Company of Virginia petition to the Crown is delivered in London by George Mercer with his own memorial.

General Background

1696 Creation of a vice-admiralty court system for the colonies.
1701 Founding of the Society for the Propagation of the Gospel in Foreign Parts.
1754 Outbreak of the Great War for the Empire.
1757 Passage of the Massachusetts Bay Quartering Act.
1763 The Peace of Paris terminates the Great War for the Empire.
1764 Passage of the Sugar Act and the Legal Tender Act.
1765 Passage of the Stamp Act and the Quartering Act.

1766

Jan. 28 The great debate over the repeal of the Stamp Act begins in the House of Commons.
March 18 The act to repeal the Stamp Act and the new Declaratory Act becomes effective.
April–May Changes in the British Ministry evidence the coming end of the Rockingham administration.
May–June General celebrations in the American colonies over the Stamp Act repeal; first reactions against the Declaratory Act.
Speculation in East India Company stock increases.
June 3 The Massachusetts Bay General Court objects to voting compensation to sufferers from the Stamp Act riots.
6 Parliament enacts a bill for liberalizing trade relations with the American colonies.
The boundary dispute between New York and New Hampshire over the New Hampshire grants area flares up.
23 The New York Assembly resolves not to comply with all the requirements of the Quartering Act passed by Parliament in 1765.
New York authorities appeal for British regulars to help quell tenant riots.

July 3 The New York Assembly raises the question of Parliament's right to interfere in colonial fiscal affairs.

23 The formation of the new administration, with Grafton succeeding Rockingham at the Treasury and Pitt replacing Newcastle as Lord Privy Seal.

30 Charles Townshend assumes the post of Chancellor of the Exchequer.

Aug. 4 William Pitt is created Viscount Pitt of Burton Pynsent, Earl of Chatham, and enters the House of Lords.

7 Protests in Massachusetts Bay against the customs service become overt at Falmouth.

Sept. Corn riots take place in England.

The East India Company financial crisis produces a parliamentary inquiry.

Sept. 23 The "Malcom affair" in Boston reveals the resentment of that town toward Parliament's control of trade.

26 An order in council attempts to ease the shortage of wheat in England and to prevent further corn riots.

Oct. Major General Phineas Lyman petitions the King on behalf of the Company of Military Adventurers.

Nov. 11 Parliament reconvenes; debates the corn crisis.

24 The introduction of an indemnity bill causes extended debate in both Houses of Parliament and a near constitutional crisis.

28 New York merchants adopt a petition to the King protesting trade restrictions.

Dec. 9 Governor Bernard signs the Massachusetts Bay indemnity act to make compensation for the Stamp Act riots.

1767

Jan. 26 Parliament reconvenes to debate the problem of securing American revenue to help finance the defence of British North America.

Feb. 6 The East India Company seeks to extend its charter.

Lieutenant Governor Hutchinson is removed from the Massachusetts Bay Council and Board.

17–19 The administration defeats opposition proposals on the services in America and the Commons approves a bill to defray such costs.

22 The question of redistribution of the British forces in North America is raised.

	27	Townshend's proposal to retain the four-shilling land tax is defeated.
March		Crisis mounts in the affairs of the East India Company.
		Chatham withdraws from public affairs after a brief return to London on the 2nd.
	12	At a Cabinet Council meeting Townshend forces the issue on voting supplies for the troops in America.
April	28	General Gage, Commander-in-Chief of the British Forces in North America, recommends to Secretary of State Shelburne methods of controlling smuggling.
May	13	Townshend presents his plan for an American revenue to Parliament, and quashes attempts to repeal the American Currency Act of 1764.
		The Privy Council disallows the Massachusetts Bay provincial indemnity act.
June	2	The New York provincial government appoints commissioners to settle the boundary line disputed by Massachusetts Bay.
	3	Presentation to the House of Commons of Townshend's bill for an American Board of Customs Commissioners.
	10	Townshend's second revenue bill comes before Parliament.
	11	Townshend's third revenue bill is submitted to Parliament.
	29	The King signs the first and second Townshend revenue bills, and approves the bill regulating the dividends of joint stock companies, thus establishing parliamentary supremacy over the East India Company.
July	2	The King signs into law the third Townshend revenue bill, the New York restraining bill, and a bill relating to East India Company revenue.
	24	The Privy Council intervenes in the New York-New Hampshire land dispute.
Sept.	4	The death of Charles Townshend.
	10	Lord North succeeds Townshend as Chancellor of the Exchequer.
Oct.		The South Carolina Regulator movement attempts to stop lawlessness in the backcountry.
	8	An impasse ends negotiations between New York and Massachusetts Bay boundary commissioners.
	28	A Boston town meeting resolves in favour of domestic manufacturers and non-consumption of foreign luxury goods.
Nov.		The American Customs Commissioners' first meeting in Boston.
Dec.	2	The first of John Dickinson's "Farmer" letters appears in the colonial press.

1768

Jan.		The Ministry is reorganized.
	20	The office of Secretary of State for the Colonies is created; the Earl of Hillsborough appointed.
		The Massachusetts Bay House of Representatives petitions the King to repeal the Townshend Acts.
Feb.	6	John Wilkes returns to England from exile in France.
	11	The Massachusetts Bay House of Representatives approves a circular letter to go to each colonial Assembly as an effort to gain colonial unity of action against the Townshend Acts.
	20	The Pennsylvania Assembly instructs its London agent to join with others to press for repeal of the Townshend Acts.
	24	Lord North presents to Parliament a bill for enforcing the trade and revenue acts in the American colonies by prosecuting violations in the courts of vice-admiralty.
	29	The Rhode Island Assembly acts in line with the Massachusetts Bay circular letter.
March	16	Boston merchants seek the cooperation of other colonial merchants in a non-importation association.
	16–18	Wilkes defeated as candidate for a London seat in Parliament.
	28	Wilkes elected to Parliament for Middlesex County.
April	4	The Regulator movement begins in North Carolina.
	11	The Speaker of the Georgia Assembly writes to the colony's London agent to seek repeal of the Townshend Acts.
	14	The Virginia House of Burgesses acts on the Massachusetts Bay circular letter by voting to address the King and Parliament on the Townshend Acts and the New York Restraining Act.
	21	The South Carolina Commons House of Asssembly authorizes its London agent to seek repeal of the Townshend Acts.
		Coal heavers in England riot at Wapping and Stepney.
	22	Lord Hillsborough directs the colonial Governors to demand that their assemblies ignore the Massachussetts Bay circula-letter.
	27	John Wilkes is committed to the King's Bench prison.
May	6	The New Jersey Assembly votes action in line with the Massachusetts Bay circular letter.
	9	The Virginia House of Burgesses sends a circular letter to the other colonial assemblies urging them to follow its lead.
	10	Supporters of John Wilkes riot at St. George's Fields.
June	10	The seizure by customs officers of John Hancock's sloop *Liberty*.

		The Connecticut Assembly, backed by the Governor, resolves to send a conservative petition to the King.
	13	Sons of Liberty gather in Boston to petition the Governor for respect of their rights as Englishmen.
	14	The Governor of New Jersey dissolves the Assembly on the issue of the Massachusetts Bay circular letter.
	15	The Board of Customs Commissioners appeals to General Gage for support by British regulars.
	18	Wilkes is sentenced to twenty-two months' imprisonment.
	24	The Speaker of the Maryland Assembly sends a letter to the Massachusetts Bay Speaker approving the means taken for redress.
	30	Massachusetts Bay representatives refuse to rescind the resolutions that produced the circular letter and seek means to remove the Governor.
		Governor Bernard adjourns the Massachusetts Assembly.
July–Sept.		Disunity in the Cabinet Council; efforts to oust Shelburne.
July	6	An order in council authorizes revision of the vice-admiralty system.
	30	A meeting of Philadelphia freemen protests the New York Restraining Act, the Declaratory Act, the Townshend Acts, and Hillsborough's directive to the Governor.
Aug.	4	Royal letters patent create the four new vice-admiralty courts to complete the implementation of Townshend's American program.
	27	The New Hampshire Assembly approves a petition to the King in protest against the Townshend Acts.
Sept.	12	General Gage informs Governor Bernard that by command of the King he has ordered two regiments to Boston.
	12–14	Boston town meetings seek to prevent the arrival of troops and call a provincial convention to debate the unconstitutionality of taxation by Parliament and of a standing army in Massachusetts Bay.
	17	Rhode Island's Governor upholds the Assembly's decision to send an address to the King protesting taxation.
	22	The Pennsylvania Assembly addresses the King and Parliament and urges the London agents to join in seeking repeal of the Townshend legislation.
		A convention of delegates from 96 towns and 8 districts of Massachusetts Bay petitions the Governor to call an Assembly.
	30	British warships land troops at Boston Harbour.
Oct.	14	Chatham's resignation as Lord Privy Seal; Grafton becomes the King's chief minister.

The Treaty of Hard Labour is negotiated with the Cherokee.
19 Shelburne resigns his office.
24 The Delaware Assembly resolves to address the King for repeal of the Townshend legislation.
Nov. 6 The Treaty of Fort Stanwix and the Indian land cession.
17 South Carolina Commons House resolutions on grievances cause the Governor to dissolve the Assembly.
Dec. 5 The Governor prorogues the North Carolina Assembly upon its resolution to send the King an address of protest against taxation without representation.
15 Hillsborough's resolutions to punish Massachusetts Bay approved by the House of Lords.
24 The Georgia Governor dissolves the Assembly when it votes an address to the King seeking relief from the Townshend Acts.
31 The New York Assembly passes resolutions of protest over currency regulation and other infringements of colonial rights.

1769

Parliament is faced with issues over the controverted elections of John Wilkes, arrears in the King's Civil List, and American grievances over the Townshend Acts.
The "Junius" letters attacking the Grafton administration appear in the London press.
The Grand Ohio Company (also known as the Walpole or Vandalia Company) is formed from the Indiana Company.
The New York Assembly seeks permission to issue paper money as legal tender at the provincial loan office.
The Regulator movement gains momentum in North Carolina.
Jan. 11 An order in council confirms the Mason-Dixon line to end the disputed boundary between Pennsylvania and Maryland.
20 Parliament begins consideration of the situation in Massachusetts Bay.
27 John Wilkes is elected a London alderman.
Jan.–Feb. The urban reform program and London radical movement in support of Wilkes get under way.
Feb. Philadelphia merchants join the Boston and New York nonimportation agreement of 1768.
3 John Wilkes denounced and expelled by the House of Commons.

	8	The House of Commons supports the House of Lords resolutions for bringing radical Boston leaders to England for trial.
	14–15	Wilkes's re-election to the House of Commons is disallowed by Parliament.
March	16	Wilkes is again elected to Parliament for Middlesex and again denied a seat.
April	13	Wilkes's fourth election to Parliament is repudiated by the House of Commons.
	19	Thomas Pownall proposes repeal of the Townshend Acts, but advocates parliamentary supremacy.
May	1	Grafton, defeated in his attempt to seek complete repeal of the Townshend Acts, plans to resign.
	8	The House of Commons seats Luttrell in the place of Wilkes.
	9	Parliament is prorogued.
	13	Hillsborough's circular letter informing the colonial Governors of the proposed partial repeal of the Townshend American Revenue Acts stirs the Cabinet Council.
June	16	The Governor dissolves the Virginia House of Burgesses over the non-importation issue.
	22	Maryland reaches a general agreement on non-importation.
July	22	South Carolina merchants agree on a compromise non-importation plan.
Aug.	28	Delaware's New Castle County takes non-importation action.
Oct.	2	A resolution by the Connecticut House of Representatives approves the non-importation stand of the merchants.
	7	Commissioners decide the New York-New Jersey boundary dispute.
	18	The New Jersey Assembly endorses the non-importation policy of its neighbouring colonies.
	19	New Hampshire land patentees arm to resist New York authority over disputed lands.
	24	Providence merchants come to a limited non-importation agreement.
	30	Newport merchants follow the lead of those in Providence.
Nov.	29	The Privy Council approves the South Carolina Circuit Court Act.
Dec.	27	Grand Ohio Company members in London seek authorization to purchase twenty million acres to set up the Vandalia Colony in the trans-Appalachian West.

1770

Jan. 4 The Grand Ohio Company petitions the Lords of the Treasury.

9 Parliament reconvenes.

The Earl of Chatham condemns the House of Commons for the unconstitutionality of its action in disallowing the Wilkes elections.

11 The report in Parliament on the King's Civil List fails to uncover the anticipated scandal.

17 The Great Seal taken from Lord Camden.

27 The Duke of Grafton resigns from the Cabinet Council.

29 Lord North becomes First Lord of the Treasury and the King's chief minister.

31 The London agent for Virginia files a counter petition to that of the Grand Ohio Company.

Feb.–March Debates in the House of Commons on controverted elections, removal of "evil ministers," and partial repeal of the Townshend Revenue Act.

Feb. 19 The House of Commons approves the resolution declaring its constitutional right to exclude Wilkes from Parliament.

March 5 London merchants trading to North America petition Parliament on the distressed state of their trade.

Boston townsmen and British regulars clash in the so-called Boston Massacre.

April 12 The King signs the bill repealing the Townshend Act except the duty on tea and the enabling clause.

14 An instruction issued by the King in Council limits the powers of the South Carolina Commons House of Assembly to disburse public funds.

17 John Wilkes is released from prison.

19 The King signs the bill amending the Currency Act of 1764 to permit the emission of bills of credit as legal tender at the provincial loan office in New York.

May News of the repeal of the Townshend Acts reaches America.

The colonial non-importation movement begins to break down.

7 George Mercer takes unauthorized steps to merge the Ohio Company of Virginia in the Grand Ohio Company.

June 11 Inhabitants of New York City vote to import goods in contravention of the non-importation agreement.

22 Virginia merchants belatedly agree upon non-importation measures.

July–Oct. Disintegration of the non-importation movement in the New England and Middle colonies.

July 31 The Earl of Hillsborough attempts to protect the Indian demarcation line from further encroachment.

Oct. 24–30 The trial and acquittal of Captain Preston for his part in the Boston Massacre.

Oct.–Dec. The collapse of the non-importation movement in the Southern colonies.

Nov. 27 The trial of the soldiers involved in the Boston Massacre.

Dec. Ethan Allen leads the Green Mountain Boys in opposing New York authority in the disputed land area.

Post-1770

1771 An issue over the right of newspapers to report parliamentary debates is raised in Parliament; a riot act is passed in North Carolina against the Regulators; commemoration ceremonies are held in Boston to memorialize the Boston Massacre; Thomas Hutchinson succeeds as Governor of Massachusetts Bay; the War of the Regulators begins in North Carolina and is climaxed by the Battle of the Alamance; the Virginia clergy resist proposals for an American episcopate; the Paxton Boys help the Connecticut men of the Susquehannah Company gain control in the Wyoming Valley; the Bill of Rights Society meets in London to resolve that all candidates for Parliament pledge support to a reform program.

1772 The Government crisis over the Grand Ohio Company; Massachusetts Bay appoints commissioners to settle the boundary dispute with New York; the Pennsylvania Governor takes action to expel Connecticut settlers from the Wyoming Valley; the Earl of Dartmouth assumes the office of Secretary of State for the Colonies; the Green Mountain Boys begin to oust New Yorkers from lands at Otter Creek.

1773 The Privy Council acts on the New York-New Hampshire land dispute; New York appoints commissioners to settle the boundary line with Massachusetts Bay; the land commissioners agree on a New York-Massachusetts Bay boundary line; passage of the Loan Act and the Regulating Act governing the affairs of the East India Company; a Currency Act is passed to permit the colonies to issue bills of credit as legal tender at the provincial loan offices; the Privy Council approves a final agreement on the New York-New Jersey border dispute; the Connecticut Assembly backs the Susquehannah Company claims in the Wyoming Valley; the collapse of the Grand Ohio Company's Vandalia Colony scheme.

1774 The organization of the Louisa (later called the Transylvania) Land Company; Board of Trade instructions lay down conditions for the acquisition of lands in America; the New York Assembly denounces the actions of the Green Mountain Boys; Dunmore's War against the Ohio Valley Indians; John Wilkes becomes Lord Mayor of London and takes his seat in Parliament; passage of the Coercive Acts; the gathering of the First Continental Congress.

1775 New Hampshire patentees riot against New York authority; the Pennamite War continues in the Wyoming Valley; the Continental Congress intervenes in the Pennamite War; the capture of Fort Ticonderoga and Crown Point by the "Bennington Mob."

The Period of the War for American Independence

1777 The disputed New Hampshire grants area becomes the state of Vermont.

1782 The Decree of Trenton gives the Susquehannah Company lands to Pennsylvania.

THE BRITISH EMPIRE
BEFORE THE AMERICAN REVOLUTION

VOLUME XI

THE TRIUMPHANT EMPIRE:
THE RUMBLING OF THE COMING STORM
1766–1770

CHAPTER I

Efforts to Heal the Breach

WHEN George III came to the House of Lords on March 18, 1766, and, in the presence of the peers of the realm and members of the House of Commons, gave his royal assent to the repeal of the American Stamp Act, there was great rejoicing among the people of the trading and manufacturing towns of Great Britain.[1] On that day fifty coaches, filled with London merchants trading to North America, went in solemn procession from the King's Arms Tavern in Cornhill to Westminster to pay their respects to His Majesty and to express their gratification at the happy outcome of the great debate; the bells in many of the London parishes continued to peal the greater part of the day; "an universal joy appeared in people's countenances, . . . and at night . . . houses were illuminated." Local merchantmen that had lain in the Thames—some of them since November 1—were now given orders to proceed immediately to North America with their cargoes.[2] This also was true in other ports such as Bristol. The King's chief minister, the Marquess of Rockingham, was overwhelmed with addresses and commendatory letters, as were William Pitt and others who had taken leading parts in the repeal legislation.[3]

---

[1] *Journals of the House of Commons,* XXX, 667.

[2] Westminster, March 19, *Pennsylvania Gazette,* May 22, 1766; see also *Gentleman's Magazine,* XXXVI, 148–9, which gave the date as March 19, and *Annual Register, 1766,* p. 77, which reported: "On this occasion the American merchants made a most numerous appearance, to express their gratitude and joy; ships in the river displayed their colours; houses at night were illuminated all over the city; and every decent and orderly method was observed to demonstrate the just sense they entertained of his Majesty's goodness, and the wisdom of parliament, in conciliating the minds of the people on this critical occasion.—An express was dispatched immediately to Falmouth, with letters to the different provinces, to acquaint them with the news of the repeal."

[3] Dora M. Clark: *British Opinion and the American Revolution* (New Haven, 1930), pp. 42–6.

The first authentic news of the repeal of the Stamp Act reached Boston on May 16, 1766, when John Hancock's brig the *Harrison,* six weeks and two days from London, dropped anchor in the harbour. "It is impossible to express the Joy the Town is now in, "declared the *Glorious News,* a broadside published simultaneously (and distributed without charge) by agreement of the four Boston printers.[4] The official intelligence reached Philadelphia, now the chief North American population centre, on the 19th, when Captain Wise of the *Minerva,* "from Poole, in Eight weeks," brought with him a copy of the act of Parliament. It was read aloud at the London Coffee House "in Transports of our Joy," as the *Pennsylvania Gazette* expressed it. That night the houses of Philadelphia were alight and the populace was entertained with a great bonfire and "many Barrels of Beer."[5] Two days later, as a fitting climax to the celebrations of the glad tidings, a banquet with places for three hundred gentlemen was held at the State House. In the presence of Deputy Governor John Penn, some twenty-one toasts were drunk in "flowing Glasses," starting with "The King!" and significantly ending with "The Liberty of the Press in America!"[6]

On June 3 Deputy Governor Penn sent the Pennsylvania Assembly a letter from Secretary of State Conway giving official notifica-

---

[4] These printers were Richard Draper of the *Boston News-Letter,* John Fleet of the *Boston Evening-Post,* John Green and Joseph Russell of the *Boston Post-Boy,* and Benjamin Edes and John Gill of the *Boston Gazette.* The Newport, Rhode Island, publisher Samuel Hall published the same broadside "for the Benefit of the Public in general," adding to the title "Just received from Boston, brought by Messrs. Jonathan Lowder and Thomas Brackett." An express also carried the news from Boston to New York and Philadelphia. Hugh Gaine, publisher of the *New-York Mercury,* followed the example of the printers to the northward and issued the broadside *Joy to America!* in which he congratulated "the friends of America"; Anthony Armbruster of Philadelphia issued his notice as *Good News for America. To the Sons of Liberty.* For an excellent account of the demonstrations, celebrations, and other reactions to the news of repeal, not only during 1766 but up to the anniversary celebrated in 1775, see P. G. Davidson: *Propaganda and the American Revolution, 1763–1783* (Chapel Hill, N.C., 1941), pp. 178–82. For subsequent anniversary celebrations in Newport, Rhode Island, of the King's signing the repeal of the Stamp Act on March 18, see *The Literary Diary of Ezra Stiles* (ed. F. B. Dexter, 3 vols., New York, 1901), I, 6–7, 42, and *passim.*

[5] *Pennsylvania Gazette,* May 22, 1766.

[6] *Ibid.* The above happy scene was duplicated in most towns, both large and small, of every colony, with the Sons of Liberty taking the lead. See, for example, the account of the celebration at Woodbridge, New Jersey, in *New-York Gazette; or, the Weekly Post-Boy,* June 19, 1766. For the celebrations at New Haven on May 19 see *Connecticut Gazette,* May 24, 1776. At Hartford the celebration that took place on May 23 was less happy in its termination. According to an account left by the Rev. Ezra Stiles, "the large Brick School house was blown up with twenty-four white persons, two molattos, & two negro Boys," several of whom lost their lives. See Ezra Stiles Papers (Yale University Library) as quoted in L. H. Gipson: *Jared Ingersoll . . .* (New Haven, 1920), p. 225.

tion of the passing of both the act for securing "the just Dependency of the Colonies on the Mother Country" and the act repealing the Stamp Act; it also contained the King's "Approbation of the wise and prudent, as well as dutiful Behaviour, which the Province of *Pennsylvania* has held amidst the too prevailing Distractions, which have so generally agitated the other Colonies."[7] A committee was immediately appointed to draft a letter to His Majesty. This letter, approved on the 6th, was the model of loyalty, as the following excerpts indicate:

> "The paternal Concern for the Welfare and Prosperity of all your Majesty's Subjects, however remote, which your Majesty has demonstrated on this very important Occasion, cannot fail of fixing, in the Hearts of the good People of this Province, the most inviolable Affection and Loyalty to your Royal Person and Government, and exciting their sincerest Prayers for the long Continuance of your Majesty on the Throne of those extensive Dominions, whose Happiness and Glory have been the invariable Objects of your Care and Attention. . . . [Therefore] . . . no Care or Endeavours shall be wanting, on our Part, to promote and establish that Union of Affections and Interests, so essential to the Welfare of both, and to preserve that Loyalty and Affection to your Majesty's Person and Government, which we esteem to be one of their first and most important Duties."[8]

That same day the Assembly resolved that the Pennsylvania inhabitants would at all times in the future, when requested in a properly constitutional manner, provide such aid as the safety of the colonies might require and the circumstances of the province would permit.[9] There was no quibbling about the force of "requisitions" that the King might make on the people of Pennsylvania for the common good; no setting forth of colonial rights.[10] These communications from Pennsylvania represented everything that Rockingham, Conway, and Pitt (still outside the government) had hoped for in the way of a loyal colonial attitude to the government at home.

In Charleston, South Carolina, where the general celebration was equally enthusiastic,[11] the members of the Commons House of As-

[7] Conway to Penn, March 31, 1766, *Pennsylvania Archives*, 8th ser., VII, 5878–9. In this connection see Penn's letter to Conway, dated February 19, 1766, *ibid.*, 4th ser., III, 311–13.

[8] *Ibid.*, 8th ser., VII, 5884–5.

[9] *Ibid.*

[10] *Ibid.*

[11] *South-Carolina Gazette*, May 13, 1766. For the correspondence between the South Carolina committee of correspondence and their London agent, Charles Garth,

sembly voted to provide for the painting of likenesses of the three men who had represented them at the Stamp Act Congress—Thomas Lynch, Christopher Gadsden, and John Rutledge—so that the portraits might be hung in the assembly room of the State House. They also agreed to defray the expense of procuring from England a marble statue of William Pitt, as a "Testimony of the great Veneration and Respect they have for his Person, and the Obligation they lye under in Common with the Rest of his Majesty's American Subjects . . . for his noble, disinterested, and generous Assistance afforded them toward obtaining the Repeal of the Stamp Act. . . ."[12] But when a motion was made that a statue should likewise be erected to George III "the mover had not the honour of a second, on the contrary was derided for his presumption."[13]

Countless sermons of thanksgiving for the great deliverance of the people from the financial burdens that Parliament had placed upon them were presented in churches throughout North America. Some of these also appeared in print, as did special broadsides and pamphlets confirming the "Glorious News."[14] Nor did the newspapers fail to give due space to the welcome event.

But all was not rejoicing. A Virginian pointed out that there was no occasion for gratitude on the part of the American people for repeal of the Stamp Act since it was done, as the act itself indicated, at the desire of the British merchants and was therefore "professedly for their own sakes, not ours."[15] Moreover, the news of repeal was accompanied by notice of the passing of the Declaratory

---

during the period 1766 to 1770, over the purchase of a statue of Pitt to celebrate the repeal of the Stamp Act, see *South Carolina Historical and Genealogical Magazine,* XXVIII, 79–93. The statue is still standing.

[12] *Ibid.*

[13] Henry Laurens to John Lewis Gervais, May 12, 1766, Laurens Letter Book, Historical Society of Pennsylvania, pp. 417–19.

[14] See, for instance, *A Thanksgiving Sermon on the total repeal of the Stamp-Act* . . . (Boston, 1766), delivered on May 20, by the Rev. Nathaniel Appleton, and *A Discourse On "the good News from a far Country"* (Boston, 1766), delivered by the Rev. Charles Chauncy on July 24, a day of thanksgiving appointed by the Governor at the desire of the House of Representatives of Massachusetts Bay. In all some seven sermons and discourses (one of which had been delivered at Hallifax in Plymouth County) were printed in Boston, two in Providence, and one, *The Stamp-Act Repealed* by John Joachim Zubly, in Georgia. This last was so popular it went into a second edition at Savannah and was reprinted later in 1766 both in Charleston and in Philadelphia. For the various orations, pamphlets, broadsides, and poems honouring the event published during the same period in Boston, Philadelphia, Providence, New York, Charleston, and Savannah, see also Charles Evans: *American Bibliography* (New York, 1941), IV.

[15] *Rind's Virginia Gazette,* May 30, 1766.

Act, asserting the sovereign right of Parliament "to make Laws . . . of sufficient Force and Validity to bind the Colonies and People of America, Subjects of the Crown of Great Britain, in all Cases whatsoever."[16] The Declaratory Statute was printed in full in some papers, for example in the *Pennsylvania Gazette,* but it received only casual reference in such papers as the *Maryland Gazette*, where under the title "An Act for securing the Dependencies of the British Colonies in America, on the Crown and Parliament of Great-Britain," it was simply listed among other routine measures of Parliament. What did this mean, if anything? Richard Jackson, in a letter to Thomas Hutchinson, reminded him that the repeal act was accompanied by another declaring the right of Parliament to make laws binding the colonies *"in all Cases whatsoever,"* and added, "I hope no ill use will be made of this by alarming ye People in America, believing as I do that our future Rule in America may be that we have used in Ireland."[17] As is quite clear, Jackson properly expressed himself with due caution. A writer in the *Virginia Gazette* took a view that were the Declaratory Act laid before the colonial assemblies they should "enter on their own journals as strong declarations of their own rights as words can express."[18] This was the mood of the Virginia House of Burgesses when it at last reassembled.

The House had been dissolved by Governor Fauquier on June 1, 1765, on account of the adoption of the Stamp Act resolutions on May 29, 30, and 31.[19] If the Governor expected to have a more dutiful body to deal with as the result of the elections, he was disappointed. Nevertheless, he determined not to permit the Burgesses to meet until their heads had had an opportunity to cool. By a series of five proclamations he prorogued them to the first Thursday

[16] Geo. III, c. 12, *Statutes at Large* (Eyre and Strahan), VII, 571. The *Statutes at Large* cited throughout this volume will be assumed to be the Eyre and Strahan edition unless otherwise indicated. It may be noted that the Declaratory Act of 1766 was modelled upon that of 1719 relating to Ireland, "An Act for the better securing the Dependency of the Kingdom of *Ireland* upon the Crown of *Great Britain*" (6 Geo. I, c. 5). But for the first statement of legislative supremacy of Parliament over the colonies one must go back to the Act of 1696 declaring the supremacy of all laws of Parliament.

[17] Jackson to Hutchinson, March 3, 1766, Hutchinson Correspondence, Massachusetts Archives, 25:64–5. Jackson was London agent for Connecticut, Massachusetts Bay, and Pennsylvania.

[18] *Virginia Gazette* (Purdie & Co.), May 2, 1766.

[19] See Francis Fauquier to the Board of Trade, June 5, 1765, *Journals of the House of Burgesses of Virginia* (eds. J. P. Kennedy and H. R. McIlwaine, 13 vols., Richmond, 1905–13), *1761–1765,* p. lxvii.

in November 1766 before they were finally permitted to meet and organize.[20] Fauquier thereupon placed before them all the papers he had received from Secretary of State Conway, including the resolutions adopted by the House of Commons and the acts adopted by Parliament.[21] In his speech before the General Assembly he declared:

> "Your Grievances have been redressed, the Act you thought oppressive repealed, and every Indulgence in Commerce which you could with Reason expect, or even desire, been granted you. Your Mother Country has on this Occasion not only acted with her usual Prudence, but also the greatest Kindness and Affection towards you her Children; and as an indulgent Parent has a Right to expect a Return of Duty, Obedience, and Gratitude, from her natural Children, she has a Right to claim the same from you, her political Ones."[22]

The address of the House—adopted on November 12, after an opportunity had been afforded to examine the papers Fauquier had placed before it—showed no retreat from the position assumed in May 1765, although it declared:

> "As we have ever been truly sensible of the tender Regard shown by his Majesty to the Rights and Liberties of his People, every where, we cannot but think we should, . . . be wanting in our Duty to the best of Kings if we did not embrace the Opportunity offered to us by your Honor of gratefully acknowledging that benign Virtue so distinguishable in him, that of protecting the constitutional Privileges of his Subjects, . . . so lately exemplified to us in his Majesty's gracious Assent to the Repeal of that oppressive Act; . . .
>
> "We are so convinced of an immediate Connexion between Great Britain and the Colonies, that we cannot but wish that no future Accident may ever interrupt that Union so essential to the Well-being of each of them; and . . . we hope we have Reason now to conclude that the Parliament of Great Britain . . . was actuated by the true Principles of Fellow Subjects with us. . . ."

The appeal emphasized that the people of Virginia—during the "Period rendered unhappy by the precarious situation that their Liberties were thrown into"—had not committed the least act of violence, but added that it should not be concluded from this pru-

[20] The prorogations by the Governor were initially to the first Tuesday in March 1766, then to the last Thursday in May, further to the last Thursday in July, next to the last Thursday in September, and finally, on August 11, to the first Thursday in November. See *ibid., 1766–1769,* pp. 5–9.

[21] *Ibid.*, pp. 11–12.

[22] *Ibid.*

dence that any inference might be drawn when it came to the "Preservation of their Rights and Liberties."[23]

The address was in the firm, dignified, but latently suspicious language of a mature person referring to a parent with whom he has quarrelled—it spoke the language of equality. Writing to the Earl of Shelburne on November 18, Fauquier, however, called the address "an Extraordinary one in Every Light, and shews great Weakness and want of Judgment, but much Heat in the Composers." The Governor also mentioned having information that the Burgesses were preparing an appeal to His Majesty and expressed the hope that it would contain "nothing of the same Spirit of Justification of their former proceedings [that is, the resolutions of May 1765]" as was "strongly insinuated in their address. . . ."[24] But the same firm position toward colonial rights characterized the wording of the resolution passed by the Virginia House on November 20: "That a Statute [statue] be raised to his Majesty, as a grateful Acknowledgment for repealing the Stamp Act, and thereby restoring the Rights and Privileges of his *American* Subjects, and consequently the Ease and Happiness of this Colony,"[25] as well as the later vote for erecting an obelisk as an expression of gratitude to those in both houses of Parliament who had procured repeal of the Stamp Act.[26] Yet these manifestations of appreciation failed to materialize in Virginia. This was, perhaps, the result of the chaotic state of the provincial finances—which had gradually come to light after the death of the provincial treasurer, John Robinson, the preceding May—and the subsequent bitterness that developed between the more conservative and the more radical factions in the province.[27]

Such were the attitudes expressed in the assemblies of Pennsylvania, South Carolina, and Virginia in reactions typical of the general rejoicing in most colonies, which significantly ignored the

---

[23] *Ibid.*, p. 23.

[24] P.R.O., C.O. 5:1345, pp. 314–15, and Shelburne Papers, 52:22–3, Clements Library, Ann Arbor, Michigan. In writing to the Board of Trade on September 4, 1766, Fauquier was obliged to admit that "the People are Sour, occasioned by their Distresses, & by being spirited up by the News Papers; . . . and that a Spirit of Discontent & cavil runs thro' the Colony" (Enclosure in the letter to Shelburne, November 10, 1766, *ibid.*, 52:37–40).

[25] *Journals of the House of Burgesses, 1766–1769*, p. 33.

[26] *Ibid.*, pp. 53, 56, 59.

[27] See Volume X in this series, pp. 99–100, 136, 289; see also Governor Fauquier to the Board of Trade, September 4, 1766, Shelburne Papers, 52:37–40. For the importance of John Robinson, one of the most powerful politicians in colonial Virginia, see J. P. Greene: "The Attempt to Separate the Offices of Speaker and Treasurer in Virginia, 1758–1766," *Virginia Magazine of History and Biography*, LXXI, 11–18.

Declaratory Act and its implications. Before examining the developments in Massachusetts Bay, however, it is important to review the events that took place in the mother country in 1766 after the repeal of the Stamp Act. For it should be made clear that before the Rockingham Ministry went out of office it took other steps to remove any real basis of complaint on the part of the colonial merchants and ship masters who had been charging the government with certain crippling restraints of their trade. The ministers were most anxious to see good relations restored within the Empire, but they also sought to maintain the financial integrity of the government by upholding the trade laws. In accordance with this policy, they secured House of Commons approval on May 9 for certain resolutions. One of these favoured the elimination of all special duties on foreign-produced molasses carried to any British colony that had been imposed by any previous act of Parliament; another recommended the levy of a mere penny sterling on all molasses imported into a colony from whatever source;[28] a third called for the dropping of the special duty on sugar exported from any British plantation that had been provided for by the act passed in the 25th year of the reign of Charles II; a fourth provided for dropping the duty on all foreign sugar, coffee, and indigo[29] imported into any colony, with the proviso that it should (if intended for re-exportation) be deposited and secured in a warehouse in order to be re-exported under proper restrictions. Further recommendations were to drop all import duties on the fabrics of Persia, China, and India entering the colonies; also to drop the import

---

[28] In this connection it should be noted that a committee representing the merchants with interests and trade in both North America and the British West Indies, meeting on March 10, 1766, at the King's Arms Tavern in London, came to a unanimous agreement to recommend to the government that a duty of only a penny sterling per gallon be levied on all molasses imported into the North American colonies—a duty "which should be enforced"; that foreign-produced sugar, coffee, and cocoa, designed for re-exportation should be imported into these colonies only at ports where custom houses were established, there to be warehoused until carried to Europe under regulations that the government might think proper; that indigo and cotton were to be imported to these places only for re-exportation; finally, that foreign-produced sugar imported into the colonies for consumption there should carry a duty of five shillings sterling per hundredweight. For these resolutions see the Shelburne Papers, 49:521–2; see also "A Short Sketch of the Transactions that led to the new Regulations of Commerce that have lately been agitated in Favour of the Colonies," *Gentleman's Magazine,* XXXVI, 228–31. See further Dora Mae Clark: *The Rise of the British Treasury: Colonial Administration in the Eighteenth Century* (Yale Historical Studies, No. 20, New Haven, 1960), pp. 151–4.

[29] It will be noted that the agreement reached by the North American and British West Indies committee of merchants had specified sugar, coffee, and cocoa, but that the last item was dropped in favour of indigo.

duties on foreign cambrics and French lawns going into the colonies in favour of other duties; to place a duty of seven shillings sterling on each hundredweight only on foreign-produced coffee imported into any colony and one of a halfpenny per pound weight only on foreign pimento (unless said coffee and pimento were secured in a warehouse for re-exportation); and, finally, to free from all export duties cotton sent from any colony to Great Britain, where it should then enter free of duty. It was further resolved that whatever sums were secured by duties raised in the colonies should, upon being paid into His Majesty's Exchequer, be reserved in a separate fund to be disposed of from time to time by Parliament "towards defraying the necessary Expences of defending, protecting and securing the said Colonies and Plantations."[30] A bill in harmony with these features for liberalizing the trade relations of the colonies was framed and, after passing through the two houses of Parliament, received the royal approval on June 6, 1766.[31]

In a letter written in behalf of the merchants of London trading to North America and sent to John Hancock, Esq., and the rest of the merchants of Boston, reference was made to the above statute for liberalizing trade as well as to two other acts—one, which had been given royal approval (6 George III, c. 51), providing for indemnifying persons who had incurred certain penalties as a result of the late Stamp Act and for making valid all instruments executed on unstamped paper, and another (6 George III, c. 49) for establishing certain free ports on the islands of Jamaica and Domi-

---

[30] The above resolutions are printed in the *Pennsylvania Gazette* of July 10, 1766, preceded by the following statement: "Extract of a Letter from London, May 10, 1766. The inclosed are the Resolutions agreed to last night by the House of Commons, and a Bill ordered in accordingly, which will doubtless be the greatest Acquisition to the Trade and Navigation of these Kingdoms that has ever been obtained since the Act of Navigation [of 1696]; and at the same time, we hope will effectually cement the Affections of the Colonists to their Mother Country."

[31] *Journals of the House of Commons*, XXX, 844. For the act, 6 Geo. III, c. 52, "An Act for repealing certain Duties, in the British Colonies and Plantations granted by several Acts of Parliament; and also the Duties imposed by an Act made in the last Session of Parliament upon certain East India Goods exported from Great Britain; and for granting other Duties instead thereof; and for further encouraging, regulating, and securing, several Branches of the Trade of this Kingdom, and the British Dominions in America," See *Statutes at Large*, VII, 619–24. Indicative of the importance Americans attached to the act is the fact that it was printed in full in the *Pennsylvania Gazette*, September 4, 1766, where it covered the entire first page and two-thirds of the last. It may be noted that, as finally passed, the act made no reference to setting up, out of the duties raised, a special fund to provide for the defence of America. But, since the act included taxes on East Indian, Persian, and Chinese fabrics brought to England by the East India Company to be sold there, such a reference would have been inappropriate.

nica.[32] These acts, the letter went on to state, should provide "the basis of an extensive system of trade between Great-Britain and her colonies, framed [as they were] on liberal principles of reciprocal advantage, relieving the colonies from injudicious restrictions, and severe duties, [and] enlarging old and opening . . . new channels of commerce. . ."[33]

The great efforts made by the government to reclaim the loyalty of Americans are also revealed in a letter written later in the year by Richard Jackson, a staunch friend of the colonies and London agent for several of them. Referring to the distress of the common people in England and the riots that had taken place over the high price of corn, he stated that the "Enemies of the Colonies, Observe the wide difference between the Conduct of [the] Administration on the 2 Sides of the Water, their Lenity in America & comparative Cruelty in England. . . ."[34] In other words, the government was, as he saw it, applying a double standard in its policy of leniency toward the colonials with respect to general laws binding them, as against a policy of rigid enforcement for the laws binding the people of England. This anxiety to restore harmony within the Empire was further indicated by the action of the House of Commons on June 3 before it was prorogued.[35] On that day a motion made by the opposition to the Ministry was defeated. It read as follows:

> "That an humble address be presented to his Majesty, to express the earnest wish and desire of this House, that his Majesty would be graciously pleased to suspend any Prorogation of his Parliament, until positive assurance shall be received, from the several governors of the respective provinces in North America, that the people are returned to a due sense of their duty and obedience to the laws. That this House is the more earnest in their pressing solicitations to his Majesty, to grant this their humble request, as they apprehend many of the fatal consequences of the *rebellious* disposition of his Majesty's subjects in those parts, might have been prevented, if the Parliament had been called last year, as soon as accounts of the disorderly and tumultuous conduct of the Americans came to the knowledge of his Majesty's ministers. To assure his Majesty, that this House is deter-

[32] *Journals of the House of Commons*, XXX, 844.

[33] This letter was printed in the September 1, 1766, issue of the *Boston Evening-Post;* see also the identical letter, but addressed to the Committee of the Merchants of Philadelphia, that appeared in the *Pennsylvania Gazette*, August 21, 1766.

[34] Jackson to Hutchinson, November 18, 1766, Hutchinson Correspondence, Massausetts Archives 25:101–7.

[35] For the prorogation of June 6, 1766, see *Parliamentary History*, XVI, 228–35.

mined to support the legal authority of the Crown, and the just rights of the British legislature over all parts of his Majesty's dominions, And, when permitted, to offer their advice, to guard the honour and dignity of the Crown and government from any insult whatsoever."[36]

By rejecting this motion the Rockingham Ministry undoubtedly sought to impress upon the colonials its belief in their loyalty and to affirm binding ties of friendship with them. However, colonial loyalty had been so shaken that it was never to be manifested again as it had been before 1763. This was nowhere more apparent than in Massachusetts Bay—the province destined to lead the other colonies step by step into open resistance to the mother country.

The day before Governor Bernard appeared before the Massachusetts Bay General Court to congratulate the members on the repeal of the Stamp Act, certain things had occurred which had brought him deep dismay. For, on the morning of May 28, 1766, when convening the House of Representatives after the general election, the members had chosen James Otis as Speaker and Samuel Adams as Clerk. Both men were considered by the administration to be most dangerous opponents of the established form of constitutional government. The choice of Speaker could be and was immediately rejected by Bernard, who was nevertheless impelled to accept Otis's strong supporter, Thomas Cushing, for the post.[37] In the afternoon, the House turned to the choice of members of the Council. As might have been anticipated, in view of the morning proceedings, the House had already determined to retire from the

[36] "Extract of the Votes of the British House of Commons, June 3, 1766," *Boston Evening-Post,* September 29, 1766.

[37] For the election of Otis as Speaker and the subsequent election of Cushing see *Journal of the Honourable House of Representatives of . . . Massachusetts-Bay . . .* (Boston, 1766–7), p. 5. The journals for 1715–59 have been reprinted by the Massachusetts Historical Society (35 vols., Boston, 1919–63) with the original pagination; however, in the interest of consistency, they will be cited throughout this volume as *Journal of the House of Representatives,* with place and date of publication as it appears on the originals, which may be found in *Early American Imprints, 1639–1800* (ed. C. K. Shipton) a microprint project based on, and numbered according to, Charles Evans: *American Bibliography.* For the Governor's message rejecting Otis see *ibid.* and General Court Records, 1765–1767, Vol. 26:198, Massachusetts Archives. In rejecting Otis as Speaker, Bernard was acting under the terms of an explanatory charter—issued in 1725 to supplement that of 1691—which upheld the right of the Governor to negative the choice of a Speaker. See *Acts of the Privy Council, Col. Ser., 1720–1745,* pp. 94–5, 103. Hutchinson apparently advised the Governor to permit Otis to retain the office of Speaker, in view of the fact that he later wrote: "Some of the governor's friends thought Mr. Otis would be of less importance in the chair than out of it, and advised against a negative" (*The History of the Colony and Province of Massachusetts-Bay* [ed. L. S. Mayo, 3 vols., Cambridge, Mass., 1936], III, 107). The Mayo edition of Hutchinson's *History* will be used throughout this volume.

Council every firm supporter of the Governor. Lieutenant Governor Hutchinson, Secretary Andrew Oliver (who had also been appointed Stamp Distributor), Attorney General Edmund Trowbridge, and Judge Peter Oliver of the Superior Court—Bernard's chief advisers on provincial matters—were thus passed over. In place of them the House elected men who shared what, in the Governor's opinion, were the radical tendencies of the House of Representatives. John Adams recorded in his *Diary:* "Thus the Triumph of Otis and his Party are compleat."[38] It is true that Bernard, as was his right under the authority granted him, rejected six of the twenty-eight newly elected councillors, including Otis's father, Colonel Otis. But nothing could disguise the fact that a revolutionary step had been taken in the organization of the provincial government of Massachusetts Bay. From the day of this election onward, the Council no longer acted as a prop for the Governor, but was now available to the House as a lever to weaken his authority. Writing to London agent Dennys (Dennis) De Berdt on December 2, 1766, Samuel Adams countered what he quoted to be the Governor's opinion—namely, "that they [the Council members] were turned out for their Deferrence to Acts of y[e] British legislature"—by stating that there had "been for many years past a great uneasiness, that the Lieut. Govr. of the Province & the Judges of the Superior Court sh[d] sit at the Council Board, as part of the legislative Power," for it was such uniting of too many powers in the same person that the House viewed as dangerous to liberty. Adams hoped the agent could make this position clear to the King and "to our friends at home."[39]

Bernard's speech to the General Court on the 29th indicated that he fully realized what had actually taken place. "When the government is attacked in form; when there is a profest intention to deprive it of its best and most able servants, whose only crime is their fidelity to the Crown, I cannot be indifferent; . . ."[40] But

---

[38] *Adams Papers,* 1st ser., *Diary and Autobiography of John Adams* (eds. L. H. Butterfield *et al.*, 4 vols., Cambridge, Mass., 1961), I, 313; cited hereafter as *Adams Papers* (Butterfield), 1st ser.

[39] Samuel Adams Papers, Adams Out-letters, pp. 225–6, New York Public Library. See, in this connection, Ellen E. Brennan: *Plural Office-Holding in Massachusetts, 1760–1780 . . .* (Chapel Hill, N.C., 1945). It should be pointed out that the practice of multiple office-holding prevailed in other colonies and was characteristic of the Council of Virginia, the members of which also formed the highest judicial body in the colony and acted as itinerant judges of gaol-delivery.

[40] *Speeches of the Governors of Massachusetts 1765–1775 . . . and other Public Papers* (ed. [Alden Bradford], Boston, 1818), pp. 74–6; cited subsequently as *Massachusetts State Papers.* For the reply of the House of Representatives to this charge

he was, in fact, helpless to retrieve what had been taken away from him. Thus the radical party of Massachusetts Bay celebrated the repeal of the Stamp Act with a victory over the office of Governor of the province. As Hutchinson later wrote in his *History:* "An experiment had been made, which persuaded them, that, by union and firmness, the colonies would be able to carry every point they wished for. Power, once acquired, is seldom voluntarily parted with."[41] Nor were the radicals to relinquish the power they had gained over the Council.

The revolutionary movement in Massachusetts Bay arose chiefly from the bitter opposition of the province's trading interests to Pitt's policy of trying to suppress trade with the enemy during the course of the Great War for the Empire through strict enforcement of the trade and navigation acts. The province had sought to deny the power of Parliament to pass laws making these acts more effective. The passing of the Sugar Act and the Stamp Act had given the movement greater impetus and nowhere else in the British colonies had the violence of the Sons of Liberty reached the level manifested in the Boston Stamp Act riots.[42]

Against the resistance movement were ranged the forces of conservatism entrenched in the office of the Governor and in the Council, the courts, and the customs service. No one more fully symbolized this conservatism than native-born, Harvard-educated Thomas Hutchinson, who was both Lieutenant Governor and Chief Justice. It was largely through his influence that the legality of the granting of writs of assistance within the colony had been sustained against the efforts of the merchants. He had earlier stood for a hard money policy against those favouring a policy of permitting bills of credit to become legal tender. Through his influence the resolution of the House of Representatives challenging the authority of Parliament to pass the Sugar Act was rejected by the Council in favour of a much more moderate and consitutional petition, which he himself framed. Finally, it was through his influence, despite great pressure, that the Superior Court remained closed after November 1, 1765. Therefore, it is not surprising that he should have been

see *ibid.*, pp. 76–81. Refuting the Governor's charge that "the government is attacked in form," the representatives declared: "It seems to us to be little short, if any thing, of a direct impeachment of the two Houses of high treason" (*ibid.*). Further, Joseph Warren in a series of articles signed "True Patriot" that appeared in the *Boston Gazette* castigated Bernard as an enemy of the colony. For an excellent and balanced treatment of these letters see John Cary: *Joseph Warren, Physician, Politician, Patriot* (Urbana, Ill., 1961), pp. 64–8.

[41] Hutchinson: *op. cit.*, III, 107.

[42] See Volume X of this series.

marked for early attention by the more radical elements, that his Boston mansion should have fallen victim to the fury of the mob in the summer of 1765 when it could not lay hands on him, and that, under the influence of Otis and others, he should have been deprived of his seat on the Council.[43]

Hutchinson, who had never been a friend of the Stamp Act and, to the contrary, had pointed out its serious implications for Amercans, very naturally felt that he should be reimbursed for his great losses. Yet neither the General Court nor the town of Boston took any steps toward that end or appeared likely to do so. As Samuel Adams, Clerk of the House, later put the matter in a letter to London agent De Berdt, referring to the request for restitution made in Governor Bernard's speech to the House in September 1765: ". . . till some good reason could be assign'd why those losses sh^{d} be made good, rather than any damage wch other persons on any different occasions w^{d} suffer, they [the members of the House] could not see their way clear, etc., withal adding that they c^{d} not conceive who had any right to require it of them."[44] It was therefore obvious that unless outside pressure were brought to bear this would not be done.

The fourth resolution of the House of Commons relating to Stamp Act commotions in America (passed without a division or protest on February 24, 1766) stated that persons who had been prepared to comply with any act of Parliament relating to the colonies and who had thereby "suffered any injury or damage, ought to have full and ample compensation made to them . . . by the respective colonies in which such injuries or damages were sustained."[45] The Lieutenant Governor had been singled out in Great Britain as one especially deserving of recognition in this regard. Writing to Hutchinson on April 19, William Bollan stated that he had been assured by certain of the British officials that, if need be, an indemnifying bill would be brought into the House of Commons containing a clause providing relief for him and others who had suffered by "the late outrages."[46] In extension of this Bollan made clear that Rose

[43] See Volume II in this series, p. 12, and X, 121–30, 233–4, 295, 355–7.

[44] Adams to De Berdt, November 15, 1766, Samuel Adams Papers.

[45] *Parliamentary History*, XVI, 161–2.

[46] A native of England, Bollan was educated for the law in Boston, acted as legal counsel for Harvard College, became advocate general of the vice-admiralty court in the province, and in 1745 was sent to London as its colonial agent. Although he was dismissed from that post by the House of Representatives, he continued to act as agent for the Council. In 1769 he regained his popularity with the House by securing and sending to the Speaker certain letters written by Governor Bernard and General Gage and by writing pamphlets favourable to the colonies.

Fuller—who had been a key figure in the House of Commons at the time of the repeal of the Stamp Act and who, clearly, had the closest relations with the Rockingham Ministry—had assured him that Hutchinson and Oliver would be provided for, even if the General Court of the province should fail to vote them reimbursement. According to Fuller this would be by way of a bill in Parliament imposing a tax on the province for this specific purpose.[47] That this was not mere idle talk is indicated by similar statements made later to Hutchinson's son not only by Richard Jackson, another influential member of Parliament and a great friend of the colonies, but also by the Marquess of Rockingham, the King's chief minister.[48] In other words, there is every reason to believe that the power claimed under the Declaratory Act, as recently enacted, would have been utilized had the colony failed to take action. As cited earlier in this chapter, this statute gave Parliament full authority to make laws binding upon the colonies in all cases whatsoever.[49]

Arrayed against the provisions of the Declaratory Act involving the principle of forced payment of reimbursement money by requisition of the Crown, were the resolves of the House of Representatives passed in October of the preceding year, the leading one of which had affirmed: "That all Acts made, by any Power whatever, other than the General Assembly of this Province, imposing Taxes on the Inhabitants are infringements of our *inherent* and *unalienable* Rights, as *Men* and *British Subjects;* and render void the most valuable Declarations of our *Charter.*"[50]

Before considering the steps finally taken by the Massachusetts Bay General Court to compensate those who had suffered from the Stamp Act riots, it would be well to point out that when on June 19, 1766, the House of Representatives expressed its thanks to the King for assenting to the repeal of the Stamp Act, it also expressed "with the greatest grief and anxiety . . . our apprehension,

---

[47] Bollan to Hutchinson, April 19, 1766, Hutchinson Correspondence, Massachusetts Archives, 25:70.

[48] Thomas Hutchinson, Jr., to Hutchinson, London, May 29 and July 1–2, 1766, *ibid.,* 25:74 and 84. In the words of Hutchinson, Jr., in an earlier letter, Jackson "told me that he thot the Parliament would look upon themselves obliged to see your loss made up by laying a Tax on the province if they should refuse doing it. . . ." In his letter of July 1–2 he wrote that he had again been assured by Jackson that Parliament would see that compensation was made to his father, if the General Court did not act, "& that by a Tax on the province," and that he had been given the same encouragement from the Marquess of Rockingham, as well as from John Pownall, John Roberts, and Soame Jenyns, of the Board of Trade.

[49] *Statutes at Large,* VII, 571.

[50] *Journal of the House of Representatives* (Boston, 1765–6), pp. 151–7.

that your American subjects may have been represented to your Parliament as having manifested some kind of disaffection to their constitutional dependence on the parent country; and as disposed . . . to abate of their respect and submission to the supreme legislative authority of Great Britain." The "great injustice" of such a charge, the representatives of the province stated, they could only regard with "abhorrence." [51] The following day votes of thanks were extended to William Pitt and to twenty-four other members of Parliament for their successful efforts in bringing about the repeal. Among those singled out for special praise, it may be noted, was Charles Townshend, later author of the so-called Townshend Acts.[52]

But, to return to the question of the reimbursement of Hutchinson for his losses. On June 3 the Governor appeared before the General Court to announce, among other things, that he had received a letter from Secretary of State Conway,[53] ordering him to recommend that the legislature make "full and ample compensation . . . to the late sufferers by the madness of the people," accompanied by a resolution of the House of Commons, "expressing their sense upon that subject." In this context Bernard asserted: "The justice and humanity of this requisition is so forcible, that it cannot be controverted. The authority, with which it is introduced, should preclude all disputation about complying with it." He thereupon expressed the hope that the legislature would set "the first example of gratitude and dutiful affection to the King and Parliament, by giving those proofs of it, which are now pointed out to you."[54]

The members of the House of Representatives, taking great exception to the term "requisition," replied: "If 'the authority with which it is introduced should preclude all disputation about complying with it,' we should be glad to know what freedom we have in the case."[55] Yet is appears from the records that the House itself first made use of the word "requisition" in the course of the late war, when on April 4, 1761, it had recorded the following

---

[51] *Massachusetts State Papers,* pp. 91–2.

[52] *Ibid.,* pp. 92–3. For a copy of the letter of thanks to Pitt signed by Thomas Cushing, Speaker, and dated June 21, 1766, see Arthur Lee Papers, 1:10, Harvard College Library. Dennys De Berdt, acting for the House of Representatives in London, was instructed to see that a copy of the vote of thanks was transmitted to each of the twenty-four other persons. See Cushing to De Berdt, June 28, 1766, *ibid.,* 1:12.

[53] For Conway's circular letter to the Governors in America, dated March 31, 1766, see *Documents Relative to the Colonial History of the State of New York* (eds. E. B. O'Callaghan and B. Fernow, 15 vols., Albany, 1853–87), VII, 823–4; cited hereafter as *New York Colonial Documents.*

[54] *Massachusetts State Papers,* pp. 81–4.

[55] *Ibid.,* pp. 90–1.

comment in its journal: "The House taking into consideration . . . a Requisition from His Majesty to this government to raise a number of Forces. . . ." From then on the term was commonly used without repercussion until the exception taken to Bernard's use of it.[56]

Not until the 24th of the month did the House of Representatives appoint a committee to reply to the Governor's message. Two prominent members were Thomas Cushing, the Speaker, and Samuel Adams, both from Boston. The committee's report, adopted the next day, referred to those who had suffered from "the madness and barbarity" of certain people and pledged that nothing would be omitted "to bring the perpetrators of so horrid a fact to exemplary justice; and if it be in their power, to a pecuniary restitution of all damages." As to the Assembly making good the losses, that appeared to the House "not as an act of justice, but rather of generosity"; yet they doubted that they had the authority to do this without first consulting their constituents. They therefore requested leave to refer the matter to the next General Court so that the members might have an opportunity to secure instructions from their towns.[57]

In his message of June 27, acknowledging the answer of the House, the Governor raised the question of whether he was to understand that "a detection of the perpetrators of the late mischiefs is necessary to entitle the sufferers to a compensation for their losses." He went on to say that while it appeared to be "the gracious intention of the King and Parliament, that a veil should be cast over the late disturbances, . . . it is certainly no less their firm and resolute purpose, that the sufferers . . . shall have a full and ample indemnification made to them." Pointing out his fears that the King and Parliament would think their wishes disregarded by the proposal of an inquiry after a nine months' delay, he concluded:

> "I, therefore, wish for the sake of the province, . . . that you would remove this disgrace without the least delay, by ordering the indemnification immediately to be made upon the credit of those whom you shall hereafter judge to be chargeable with it. When this is done, there can be no objection to your postponing the consideration, on whom this money ought ultimately to be laid, to what time you please."[58]

[56] Instances of prior use of the term "requisition" were collected by Bernard and enclosed in his letter to the Earl of Shelburne of December 24, 1766; see Shelburne Papers, 58:567–74.

[57] *Massachusetts State Papers,* 93–4.

[58] *Ibid.,* pp. 94–5.

But the House remained firm in its stand that no action should be taken on the matter of paying for the losses until the fall session. It did, however, appoint a committee to make enquiry into the outrages of the preceding summer in order to determine who the leaders were. Such an assignment was manifestly a dangerous one, if the committee were really to do its work. Writing from Boston on June 28 to Hutchinson, then at Ipswich, Andrew Oliver stated:

> "Cap^{n}. Sheaffe was one, who excused himself this morning, on account of some Insults he had rec^{d}. on the occasion as he went home last evening. . . . Mr. Hall was another of the Com^{te} but has also got excused. He tells me He could not be upon it for £1000. . . ."[59]

On June 29 the Governor dismissed the Assembly without receiving any indication from it that satisfaction would be provided for Hutchinson and the other sufferers when it met again in the fall.[60] The position of most members was that if the indemnification were to be considered strictly an act of justice it ought to come from the town of Boston.[61] But the Boston members were opposed to providing any reimbursement, even out of the provincial treasury, lest it should afterwards be charged against the town.[62]

On October 29 the General Court reassembled. In his speech delivered the following day, the Governor declared he had called the Assembly solely to give the members an opportunity to return a positive answer to his earlier recommendation made on order of His Majesty.[63] Ignoring this limitation on its activities, the House of Representatives on the 30th appointed two committees on grievances: one to determine whether any acts of Parliament had been inserted in the province law books by order of the Governor and Council; the other "to inquire at large into the Practice of issuing Proclamations from the Governor and Council with promise of Reward from the Province Treasury, for enforcing Acts of Parliament."[64] Never-

---

[59] Hutchinson Correspondence, Massachusetts Archives 25:38. Captain Edward Sheaffe represented Charlestown and Stephen Hall, Medford.

[60] Bernard to Conway, June 29, 1766, Shelburne Papers, 58:1–4.

[61] Bernard to Conway, July 19, 1766, *ibid.*, 58:12–18.

[62] Bernard to Shelburne, November 14, 1766, *ibid.*, 58:21–3.

[63] *Journal of the House of Representatives* (Boston, 1766–7), p. 147–8.

[64] *Ibid.*, p. 152. As will be indicated later, the cause of the House's anger was the printing at the public expense of the Quartering Act passed by Parliament (5 Geo. III, c. 33) and the issuing of a proclamation offering a reward out of the public treasury to anyone who would give information leading to the conviction of those engaged in defying the customs officers at Falmouth while seeking to secure certain goods smuggled into that port.

theless, that same day the committee appointed to investigate the riots of August 1765 reported that it had been unable to secure any information as to the names of the rioters since many who were most active in the disorders "from their Habits appeared to be disguised. . . ."[65]

The House now received petitions from Thomas Hutchinson, Benjamin Hallowell, Jr., Andrew Oliver, and William Story praying for reimbursement for their losses as the result of the riots.[66] These petitions came to a vote on the 31st, when but 36 members of the House were disposed to grant compensation from the province to Hutchinson as against 44 opposed. The other petitions were also rejected.[67]

This was not, however, the end of the story. When reports were received from England that Parliament itself "was concerned to see that compensation was duly made," the people of Boston, according to Bernard, "began to grow uneasy" and, reversing their position in town meeting, instructed their local representatives in the Assembly "to use their utmost endeavours to get the money paid out of the [provincial] Treasury."[68] Doubtless this was due in part to the letters to the Speaker written in August and September by the London agent of the Assembly, Dennys De Berdt, emphasizing the unfavourable impression that a continued refusal would make upon all the colony's friends in England.[69] In addition, with the news that America's great hero, William Pitt, was now at the head of the Ministry and the feeling that he should not be embarrassed, came the realization that compensation for the riots must be made. It is therefore not surprising that the House agreed that a new committee, consisting of Speaker Thomas Cushing, James Otis, Joseph Hawley, John Hancock, and three other members, should be appointed "further to consider his Excellency's Speech, and of Ways and Means of making Compensation to the Sufferers. . . ."[70] On November 4 the new committee reported, recommending that the vote of October 31 against compensation be reconsidered. When this was agreed to, and it was further decided to vote by "Yeas & Nays" on the petitions severally, again the vote went against payment to

[65] *Ibid.*, pp. 153–4.

[66] *Ibid.*, pp. 155, 156, 158.

[67] *Ibid.*, p. 159.

[68] Bernard to Shelburne, November 14, 1766, Shelburne Papers, 58:21–3; see also the vote as certified by the town clerk in the *Boston Evening-Post*, October 13, 1766.

[69] For the De Berdt letters of August 6 and September 19, 1766, see *Massachusetts State Papers*, pp. 101–2.

[70] *Journal of the House of Representatives* (Boston, 1766–7), p. 159.

Hutchinson, this time by a majority of 51 to 43. Negative votes were likewise cast against the other claimants. Immediately thereafter it was agreed that the Governor's speech should be taken up the next morning. The committee reported on the 5th that it saw no other practicable way of providing compensation except out of the treasury and asked the House to reconsider the matter. But when a motion was made to this effect, and including a request for authorization for a lottery to replace the sum to be paid from the treasury, it was defeated by a vote of 54 to 35. Also lost was a second motion that an estimate should be made to determine the proportion of the total sum that might be levied on the towns in case agreement was reached that reimbursement be assumed by the province. But the supporters of the idea were not easily deflected in their determination that Boston should not bear the sole responsibility. A new committee to consider the Governor's speech was now moved and approved. It is significant that its chairman was Joseph Hawley, a leading lawyer of radical tendencies, who represented the western Massachusetts Bay towns of Northampton and Southampton.[71]

That Hawley, at least temporarily, took over leadership in the House of Representatives at this critical juncture seems manifest. In the course of the debate, with obvious reference to Hutchinson, he reportedly declared: "Of those seeking compensation, the chief is a person of unconstitutional principles, as one day or other he will be made appear." Then, in reply to those who urged the binding force of acts of Parliament, he is said to have retorted: "The Parliament of Great Britain has no right to legislate for us." At this revolutionary statement, James Otis purportedly rose and, bowing to Hawley, thanked him, with the comment that he "has gone further than I myself have yet done in this house."[72] In this connection it should be noted that as recently as January 27, 1761, the General Court in a message to the Governor emphasized the point "that we are far from apprehending that a resolve of this court can alter an act of parliament: . . . Every act we make, repugnant to an act of parlia-

---

[71] *Ibid.*, pp. 170–1.

[72] For the above statements attributed to Hawley and Otis see W. V. Wells: *The Life and Public Services of Samuel Adams . . .* (3 vols., Boston, 1865), I, 127. Writing to Judge Israel Williams on December 7, 1766, Hutchinson commented on the remarks in Hawley's speech relating to himself: "Some who were in the gallery told me he [Hawley] argued that the rioters who had been in error had a claim to favour as well as the sufferers, the chief of whom was a person of unconstitutional principles and that one time or other he might make it appear; others understood him that in [the] view of the people I was such a person" (Hutchinson Correspondence, 4, Bancroft transcripts, New York Public Library).

ment extending to the plantations is *ipso facto* null and void. . . ."[73] Now—according to Hawley, if he was quoted correctly—nothing that Parliament might seek to do could bind the colony against its will. This was a denial of the constitutional position occupied by Parliament since the Revolution of 1689 as well as a repudiation of the fundamental statute relating to the colonies passed by that body in 1696, 7 and 8 William III, c. 22, the 9th clause of which stated:

> "That all Laws, Bye-Laws, Usages, or Customs at this Time, or which hereafter shall be in Practice, . . . in any of the said Plantations, which are in any wise repugnant to the before mentioned Laws, . . . so far as they do relate to the said Plantations, . . . or which are any ways repugnant . . . to any other Law . . . made in this Kingdom, so far as such Law shall relate to . . . the said Plantations, are illegal, null, and void, to all Intents and Purposes whatsoever."[74]

Hawley now urged the granting of compensation by the province, but only on condition that the General Court give pardon and amnesty to all who were concerned in the riots against the Stamp Act.[75] This was in itself a revolutionary step in that it ignored one of the great prerogatives of the Crown—the power of pardon—and really constituted an extraordinary break with confirmed constitutional procedures.[76] Nevertheless, the House approved the proposal and, on November 6, agreed to appoint a committee to bring in an

---

[73] The message of January 27, 1761, is printed in Hutchinson's *History,* III, Appendix A, pp. 331–3.

[74] *Statutes at Large,* III, 587.

[75] Hutchinson, writing on November 22, 1766, to William Bollan, stated: "Towns whose members are firmly attached to me, had given instructions not to grant the money . . . unless a tax for it should be laid on the town of Boston. Still there would have been enough force to have carried the vote, if Mr. Hawley who always before had shewn himself well disposed, had not strangely appeared in opposition, & carried divers others with him who have a great opinion of his understanding & integrity. By this means thirty-six only were for it, & forty against it. . . . At the superior court for Berkshire one of his clients was tried upon an appeal from the court of sessions, when he with divers others had been convicted of . . . opposing the stamp act. Only one appealed & the fact being fully proved, the jury could not avoid finding him guilty, & . . . fined him but moderately, yet it had such effect upon this lawyer that he came down to the general court, determined to oppose a compensation, unless not only they who had been injured . . . but all others guilty of riots since the first disorder occasioned by the Stamp Act, should be pardoned—and such as had been fined, have their money if paid restored" (Hutchinson Correspondence, 2:98, Bancroft transcripts).

[76] For the earlier exercise of the pardoning power on the part of the Crown there is to be found among the Shelburne Papers (58:227–57) "An account of several Acts of Grace" in which the King granted his pardon. Among the precedents cited were Bacon's rebellion in Virginia in 1676, the Jacob Leisler uprising in New York in 1690, the disturbances on the island of St. Christopher in 1711, and the New Jersey land riots in 1747.

omnibus bill for both compensation and pardon with the proviso that it should be printed for the consideration of the towns. This was done. When published the title of the bill read "An Act for granting Compensation to the Sufferers, and of free and general Pardon, Indemnity, and Oblivion to the Offenders in the late Times."[77] Thereupon the House sought a recess,[78] and Bernard agreed to adjourn the Court until December 3.

Although many disapproved of the bill,[79] the conviction that compensation must be made carried the day, even in the face of its unconstitutional nature. On December 4, after the reassembling of the House, the bill was read a second time. An attempt to substitute another bill, freed of the unconstitutional feature, that would simply read "An Act for granting Compensation to certain Sufferers in the late Times," was voted down, as was the question "Whether this House will make a Compensation to the Sufferers without an Act of Indemnity to the Offenders in the late Times." After this the way was clear for a third reading of the bill and a vote on its engrossment which was carried by 53 yeas to 35 nays on December 5.[80] It then went to the Council, where it passed by a vote of 14 to 1, and on December 9 Governor Bernard signed it—undoubtedly feeling under great pressure to see that compensation was provided—and in spite of doubts that he was justified in doing so.[81] The act provided for the payment of definite sums to the four chief sufferers at

[77] *Journal of the House of Representatives* (Boston, 1766–7), p. 198.

[78] For the request for a recess see the reply of the House of November 11 to the Governor's speech of October 29, 1766, in *Massachusetts State Papers,* pp. 97–8.

[79] On November 29, 1766, Judge Israel Williams wrote to Hutchinson from Hatfield: "I have heard of Majr. Hawley's Bill of indemnity or whatever it is called. That I perceive is generally disapproved and must be bad policy. . . . The general voice here is that reparation ought to be made, and paid out of the Treasury, but refunded in a reasonable time" (Hutchinson Correspondence, Vol. 2, Bancroft transcripts).

[80] *Journal of the House of Representatives* (Boston, 1766–7), pp. 207–10. As is to be assumed, among the yeas were the Boston representatives, James Otis, Samuel Adams, and John Hancock, as well as Joseph Hawley of Northhampton. After the approval of the bill, which thereupon was sent to the Council, the House in a resolution gave the reasons for it, as influenced "by a loyal and grateful Regard to His Majesty's most mild and gracious Recommendation; by a Deference to the Opinion of the illustrious Patrons of the Colonies in Great-Britain; and for the sake of internal Peace and Order: Without Regard to any Interpretation of His Majesty's Recommendation into a Requisition, precluding all Debate and Controversy; and under a full Perswasion that the Sufferers had no just Claim or Demand on the Province. And that this Compliance ought not hereafter to be drawn into a Precedent" (*ibid.,* pp. 210–11).

[81] *Ibid.,* p. 221. Hutchinson in his *History* (III, 114–15) writes with reference to the indemnity bill: "The council concurred, but it was a doubt with the governor, whether he could be justified in giving his assent to it."

the hands of the rioters,[82] and then recited, "That all Riots, Routs and unlawful Assemblies" between August 1, 1765, and May 1, 1766, and "all Burglaries, Felonies, Rescues and Breaches of the Peace whatsoever . . . are pardoned . . . and put in utter Oblivion. . . . That any Person indited . . . for any of the Offenses by this Act pardoned, may plead the general Issue, and give this Act in Evidence, which shall be sufficient to acquit him."[83]

When a copy of the Indemnity Act, transmitted to London as required by the charter, came before the Board of Trade for examination on March 12, 1767, it appeared to that body "to be of a new and extraordinary nature and importance. . . ."[84] This was also the view of both the Attorney General and the Solicitor General, who reported on April 10, 1767: "That the Governor, Council, and Assembly of the Massachusetts Bay have not by the Constitution of that Province, any original Power to enact a Law of General Pardon, Indemnity and Oblivion . . . without previous Communication of the Grace and Pleasure of the Crown." Concurring with this opinion, the Board made a representation on the 13th to His Majesty in Council.[85]

The importance of the potential effect of this indemnity act upon the integrity of the constitution of the Empire did not escape Parliament. The two houses called for all papers relating to the act.[86] The House of Lords addressed the King, humbly asking him

---

[82] To Hutchinson was given as compensation £3,194.17.6, to Andrew Oliver, £172.4, to Hallowell, £385.6.10, and to Story, £67.8.10; see *Journal of the House of Representatives* (Boston, 1766–7), pp. 184–5, 189–90.

[83] For the act see *Acts and Laws . . . of the Massachusetts-Bay . . .* (Sessions of May 28–October 29, 1766, Boston, 1766), pp. 519–20. Judge Israel Williams, in a letter to Hutchinson dated January 5, 1767, wrote: "I heartily rejoice that your losses are in so great a measure repair'd, tho' I dislike the mode—Is not the Act an unprecedented Stretch of Power, does it not Teem with Injustice? Mayn't we hope it will be disallow'd?" (Hutchinson Correspondence, Massachusetts Archives, 25:140.)

[84] *Journal of the Commissioners for Trade and Plantations from . . . 1704 to . . . 1782 . . .* (14 vols., London, 1920–38), *1764–1767*, p. 375 (to be referred to hereafter as the Board of Trade *Journal*). One may indeed question the accuracy of the statement of Thomas Cushing, Speaker of the House of Representatives, in a letter dated June 24, 1767, to De Berdt, the London agent, when he wrote: "We observe by your letter of the 10th of April; that Exception had been taken to an Act passed by this Government for granting Compensation to the Sufferers, and of free and general Pardon, Indemnification and Oblivion to the Offenders in the late Times: We presume that the House who passed that Act had not the least Apprehension that they thereby made any Infraction of the Prerogative of his Majesty; and we think that the House if they had made any mistake in that Matter . . . have done it through Inadvertence . . . : As his Excellency our Governor gave his Assent to the said Bill, and never hinted to the House that he had any Suspicion that his Majesty would be displeased thereat . . ." (Arthur Lee Papers, 1:36, Harvard College Library).

[85] For this representation of April 13, 1767, see the Shelburne Papers, 58:605–7.

[86] Board of Trade *Journal, 1764–1767*, p. 388.

"to take under His Royal Consideration in His Privy Council the Validity of such part of an Act granting Compensation to the Sufferers lately pass'd by the Governor, Council, and Assembly of Massachusetts Bay, . . . as purports to be a free & general Pardon, Indemnity & Oblivion to the Offenders in the late times, tacked to the said Act from their own motion And by their own Authority. And what the said Governor, Council & Assembly had no Authority to enact, that His Majesty will take such measures as may be necessary thereupon . . . to assert ye inherent & inseparable Right of His Majesty's Crown alone to pardon Offenders, & to grant that mercy which His Majesty may be graciously pleased to extend to any of his subjects in America on the late Occasion, under the Great Seal, or in Parliament."[87]

In conformity with this position the Privy Council on May 13 issued an order repealing the law on the ground that it "unwarrantably incorporated an Act of Pardon, with an Act of Compensation, without having obtained Your Majesty's previous consent to such Act of Pardon."[88] The same order directed the Governor to "require the Assembly to pass an Act for compensating the sufferers, unmixed with any other matter, in case such compensation shall not have been already made."[89] But long before the news of the royal disapproval had reached the colony the money had been paid.[90]

Under the leadership of James Otis, the Massachusetts Bay House of Representatives—despite its submission on the question of compensation—was none the less determined to bend the government of the province to its will. It was now in a position to isolate the Governor and control the Council through its power of electing the members of that body. There was, however, one obstacle to total domination of the Board—the presence of Hutchinson, who, as Lieutenant Governor, continued to sit as a non-voting member. This became a leading issue when the General Court met in Jan-

[87] For this address see P.R.O., Treas. 1. 446:188.

[88] *Acts of the Privy Council, Col. Ser., 1766–1783*, p. 87.

[89] Board of Trade *Journal, 1764–1767*, p. 391. Hutchinson, in his *History* (III, 115), makes the following comment: "The act was disapproved, upon its being laid before the king, merely from the nature of it, and the danger of establishing a precedent; but the money was paid before the news arrived, and nothing further passed on the subject"—including, one may add, any further attempt to prosecute the Stamp Act offenders.

[90] Samuel Dexter, a member of the House of Representatives from Dedham, wrote to De Berdt on January 6, 1767, indicating that the money had already been paid to the sufferers out of the provincial treasury and that since this took place "every thing is quiet, & no dissention of a public Nature exists among us, saving only what immediately respects the Governor. Whether he & the People will ever be harmonious again, time must discover" (Shelburne Papers, 58:581–90). It may be added that Dexter was one of those elected to the Council who was disapproved by Bernard.

uary 1767. In his speech on the 28th Bernard urged upon the members "support of the authority of the government, . . . the honor of the province, and the . . . welfare of the people. . . ." The House assured him that its members would "sacredly adhere to their own rights as one branch of the legislature." Their reply further contended that the House considered the presence of Hutchinson in the Council "not only in itself an impropriety, but repugnant to the constitution, and the letter of the charter. . . ." What is more, this was given as "a new and additional instance of ambition, and a lust of power. . . ."[91]

The Governor, who felt that he needed Hutchinson at hand to advise him on weighty matters that came before the Council, stated in a letter to the Earl of Shelburne on February 7 "that so studied an Affront to the King's Commission should not pass unnoticed." He went on to declare that it had been "the uniform practice for the Lieu^{t}. Govr. when he was not elected a Councillor, to sit in Council next to the Governor, but without having a Voice." The only exception to this rule, Bernard affirmed, was during the administration of Governor Belcher, "who would not suffer Lieu^{t}. Govr. Phipps to sit in the Council"; he then added that therefore the present Lieutenant Governor, after being excluded from the Council, "frequently took his place at the Board, but without interfering in the Debate, except when desired to inform the Board or give his Opinion on matters within his Knowledge." Before closing his letter, the Governor referred to "the Impropriety & Indecency of the House of Representatives taking upon them to judge of the Order of Regulation of the Council," and also lamented the fact that the members of the Council were now "too dispirited to assert their Rights. . . ."[92] Indeed, when called upon by the House to answer the question of the legality of the presence of the Lieutenant Governor in their chamber, they meekly voted unanimously on March 7 that he had not "by the Charter, any Constitutional Right to a Seat at the Board, either with or without a Voice"; at the same time they excused his presence there by pointing to former precedents, one of them contemporaneous with the issuing of the charter.[93] As for the Lieutenant Governor, in the interests of restoring harmony, he announced to Governor Bernard that he would avoid all occasions of controversy with the present House of Representatives by wholly absenting himself

---

[91] For Bernard's speech and the House's reply see *Massachusetts State Papers*, pp. 102–5.

[92] Bernard to Shelburne, February 7, 1767, Shelburne Papers, 51:525–7.

[93] *Journal of the House of Representatives* (Boston, 1766–7), p. 368.

from the Council chamber, "unless your Excellency shall give Directions for my Attendance there for any Special Purpose."[94] This he did despite his feelings of being personally aggrieved that so heavy a judgment had been passed on his conduct without giving him an opportunity to defend himself.

Hutchinson's disappearance from the Council meant that the Board was no longer potent as a support to the Governor, at least against the House of Representatives.[95] For the radical leaders in the House, during the annual election of councillors, sought to take good care that the Governor—despite his power to reject those elected—should remain isolated. In defending the efforts of the House to bar Hutchinson from the Council, Samuel Adams expressed the surprise of the members that, despite the provisions made for his compensation, Hutchinson should "make an attack upon the charter, & endeavour to support a claim joyntly with his Exc^y [the Governor] which if they attain their ends has a manifest tendency very unduly to influence & alter if not totally to subdue the free legislation of the Province"[96]—a perhaps unwitting recognition of the great influence of Hutchinson in Massachusetts Bay public affairs.[97] In fact when the highly important matter came up

---

[94] See Hutchinson to Governor Bernard, February 20, 1767, Hutchinson Correspondence, Massachusetts Archives, 25:164–6. In this letter the Lieutenant Governor justified himself by stating that ever since the last election he had frequently been present in the Council without any evidence of dissatisfaction on the part of the members of the House and that he had always considered his presence there entirely justified by provisions of the charter and past precedent even though his immediate predecessor had been excluded from the Council, since that action had been taken by the Governor and "as a mere act of Power" (*ibid.*).

[95] Among the Shelburne Papers (Vol. 58) is a loose file without folio or page number with the following heading: "Minute, about the Right of the Lt Govr of Massachusetts Bay to sit in the Council—[and other questions involving the right of the Governor to negative members elected to the Council and the right of the House to appoint its own London agent] with the Attorney General's opinion on these Points." Attorney General William De Grey did not think the Lieutenant Governor had a right to a seat, or a vote in the Council unless elected except that "as the second in command he should have the right to be present to be instructed in everything that passes regarding Public Affairs." De Grey also gave the opinion on April 25, 1767 (*ibid.*, 61:701–3), that the Massachusetts Bay Assembly "is going much too far to say that his [the Lieutenant Governor's] presence at the Council is illegal & unconstitutional, whether he is there as attending the person of the Governor or is admitted out of respect to his character, while he forbears to interfere with the Business."

[96] Samuel Adams to Dennys De Berdt, London agent, March 16, 1767, Samuel Adams Papers. This is a very long letter that seeks to vindicate the constitutional position of the House in the interpretation of the charter of 1691.

[97] In the May 1767 election of councillors Hutchinson received 50 votes out of a total of 137 for membership on the Council. When the names of those elected to the Board were submitted to the Governor he found the names of six who had been negatived by him in the 1766 election; four of these Bernard again rejected. See Bernard to Shelburne, May 30, 1767, Shelburne Papers, 51:575–9.

of appointing commissioners to meet with representatives to be selected by New York to determine the Massachusetts Bay–New York boundary, the Lieutenant Governor was chosen to head the commission by a majority of votes of both houses, despite the opposition of Otis's friends.[98]

But the movement to free the legislature of Massachusetts Bay from the influence of the government of Great Britain in so far as was possible, did not stop with the determination to keep the Lieutenant Governor from a seat in the Council. This step was merely preparatory to "another exclusion of much greater Consequence"—that of the Governor himself from the Council. Writing to the Earl of Shelburne on February 21, 1767, Bernard pointed out that provincial councils in America had two functions: one was to act as a privy council to the Governor; the other, to serve as a part of the legislature. He then demonstrated that before the time of William Shirley it had been customary for the Governor to preside in the Council, even during its legislative sessions. This was discontinued upon a motion made in the Council itself that this body should take its legislative action "separately from the Governor." While Shirley agreed to this, he still, according to Bernard, continued to be present whenever he thought it proper, and that was quite frequently. The Governor went on to state that he had followed the Shirley practice, "which greatly conduces to the Ease and Facility of the publick Business." Yet this had now aroused complaints "without Doors" of an exercise of undue influence, and the leader in the House, James Otis, had made public the threat that when his "Faction shall get Possession of the Council by Garbelling it," the Governor would be excluded.[99] Indeed, the Council, even acting in its executive capacity, had already showed such a degree of independence that Bernard had been compelled to protest when its members proceeded without him in the "Business of Privy Council, in which they could not act separately from him."[100] As a leading modern authority has pointed out, "the practice of meeting without the governor became so common in Massachusetts during the next

[98] See the *Journal of the House of Representatives* (Boston, 1766–7) for March 13 and 17, pp. 385 and 408. Bernard, in referring to the selection of Hutchinson to head the boundary commission, wrote to Shelburne on March 23, 1767, that "no one in the province is so well acquainted with these matters as he is. His Appointment also gives great Pleasure to the Friends of Government . . . He happened, by the Form of Election used there [in the Assembly] to be singly opposed to *Otis* and carried it by a considerable Majority" (Shelburne Papers, 51:561–2).

[99] Bernard to Shelburne, February 21, 1767, *ibid.*, 51:533–7.

[100] Bernard to Shelburne, February 18, 1767, *ibid.*, 51:527–31.

few years [after 1767] and the council's pretensions to executive authority at these sessions grew so bold that an article was added to the instructions to Governor Hutchinson in 1771, forbidding such 'unjustifiable and unconstitutional proceedings'."[101]

This determination of the popular branch of the General Court to place the colonial government in an autonomous position with relation to the authority of the mother country was manifested in other respects. For example, as has already been indicated, a motion was carried in the House on October 30, 1766, that a committee, consisting of James Otis and two other members, be appointed "to inquire Whether any Acts of Parliament are inserted in the Province Law Book, by Order of the Governor and Council"; on that same day a committee consisting of the Speaker, Otis, Hancock, Captain Sheaffe, and Samuel Dexter was established "to inquire at large into the Practice of issuing Proclamations from the Governor and Council with promise of Reward from the Province Treasury, for enforcing Acts of Parliament."[102] Then, on December 8, Otis was appointed chairman of the separate committees that prepared and delivered the following message to the Council:

> "Mr. President,
> "The House having observed That an Act or Acts of the British Parliament have been printed and published among the Laws of this Province; they desire to be informed by what Authority said Act or Acts have been published: And whether they know of any Act requiring the Registry of Ordinances which this Legislature never consented to."[103]

That same day the Clerk of the House, Samuel Adams, was directed to go to the Board to inquire "whether the Board or the Governor and Council, have made any Provision for His Majesty's Troops lately arrived in this Harbour, and how?"[104] To this the Council replied that the orders for publishing certain acts of Parliament—the Quartering Act, the act setting up free ports in Dominica and Jamaica, and the provision made for the troops that had lately arrived—were given by the Governor "by the Advice of the Council, in the Recess of the General Court; and therefore the Honorable

---

[101] L. W. Labaree: *Royal Government in America* (New Haven and London, 1930), p. 159. For this instruction see *Royal Instructions to British Colonial Governors, 1670–1776* (ed. L. W. Labaree, 2 vols., New York and London, 1935), I, 48–9.

[102] *Journal of the House of Representatives* (Boston, 1766–7), pp. 151–2.

[103] *Ibid.*, p. 216.

[104] *Ibid.*, p. 218.

House will please be referred to His Excellency, for the Information they desire."[105]

This answer was not considered satisfactory. But on December 9 the General Court was given a recess until January 28, so no further immediate steps could be taken on the new issue that had arisen. However, on January 30 the House sent a message to the Governor asking him if any provision at the expense of the province had been made for the newly arrived troops, and if so, by whom. He was also asked if he had reason to expect the arrival of any more troops to be quartered in the colony.[106] In reply Bernard sent to the House a copy of the minutes of the Council "by which Provision for the Artillery Company at the Castle in pursuance of the late Act of Parliament [the Quartering Act] was made." He also stated that he was intending to lay the matter before them, and added that no advice had been received about any other troops to be quartered in the province.[107]

On February 4, under the chairmanship of Otis, a committee of the House sent a message to the Governor having to do with its right to pass on all expenditures, and stating:

> "it is still more grievous to us, to find your Excellency making mention of a late act of parliament, in pursuance of which your Excellency and the council have created this expence to the province. One great grievance in regard to the stamp-act was, that it deprived us of the advantage of a fundamental and most essential part of the British constitution, and unalienable right of freedom, from all taxation, but such as we shall voluntarily consent to and grant: . . . [Further,] we cannot but express a very deep concern, that an act of Parliament should yet be in being, which appears to us to be as real a grievance, as was that which so justly alarm'd this continent [that is, the Stamp Act]. Your Excellency and the Council, by taking this step, have unwarrantably and unconstitutionally subjected the people of this province to an expence, without giving this house an opportunity of passing their judgment upon it. . . ."[108]

The issue raised in Massachusetts Bay over the quartering of British troops might have surpassed in seriousness that which—as shall be seen in the chapter to follow—had by then arisen in New York, had it not been for Bernard's skill in clarifying the situation before the House. The barracks, he emphasized, had been built by

[105] *Ibid.*, pp. 219–20.
[106] *Ibid.*, p. 229.
[107] *Ibid.*, p. 230.
[108] *Ibid.*, pp. 242–4.

order of the General Court to receive the King's troops when they should arrive, so that "there might be no Occasion for quartering them upon the Inhabitants. Fuel and Candle are necessary to the Occupation of Barracks: Without them no Troops could go in or stay there, it being an Allowance always incidental to their living in Barracks." In authorizing the construction of the barracks, he reasoned, the General Court must have implied that incidental needs should be furnished; otherwise it must be supposed that the Assembly had not intended the barracks to be put to the use for which they were built. Indeed, the manner of making provision had followed early practice—furnishing items always allowed in these barracks—"and did not include several Articles prescribed by the Act of Parliament."[109] It therefore must come home to the majority of the House, Bernard concluded, that there was little real basis for attacking the Governor and Council for ignoring provincial rights.

Yet, rights of Americans, rather than their obligations, were kept foremost in public discussions led by the popular provincial leaders and, despite the Declaratory Act, these rights were asserted categorically, regardless of the pronouncements of Parliament. Moreover, those who disagreed with such assertions were denounced as enemies. For example, the *Boston Evening-Post,* one of the more moderate newspapers, printed a long article under the heading "*The Crisis* or a full Defence of the Colonies. In which it is incontestably proven that the British Constitution has been flagrantly violated in the late Stamp Act." At the beginning of his essay the writer made the following significant statement:

> "The main argument which the enemies of the colonies make use of to justify the act of parliament . . . is that the *British* legislature has an undoubted right of establishing whatever ordinances it may think proper for the regulation of all the *British* dominions,[110] . . . To this the *Americans* reply that as they are utterly unrepresented in the parliament of the mother country, a doctrine of this kind must inevitably rob them of the most valuable rights which they ought to possess, as *Englishmen,* and reduce them in an instant, from a nation of free born subjects, to a set of the most miserable slaves. Such is the state of the present question."

Nor did another item in the same paper suggest that the Sons of Liberty were disposed to pardon those Americans who had taken the position during the late crisis that the acts of Parliament con-

---

[109] The Governor's message of February 17, 1767, *ibid.,* pp. 298–300.

[110] This principle was embodied in the Declaratory Act (6 Geo. III, c. 12).

stituted the supreme law of the land in the colonies as well as in Great Britain. It read:

> "Thursday last being the Anniversary of the glorious 14th of August 1765 [the occasion of the great riot in Boston over the Stamp Act] when the noble Ardour of Liberty burst thro' its long Concealment, o'erleap'd the Barriers of Oppression, and lifted its awful Crest amid the Group of lowering Dastards, haughty Tyrants and merciless Paracides—the Patrons and Sons of Liberty avowed the illustrious Cause, and met, a numerous and truly respectable Circle of the most virtuous, most opulent and most sensible Part of this great Metropolis.—At the Hour of XII they convened at the sacred Tree of Liberty, every Bosom dilating with Joy, and every Eye sparkling with Satisfaction."[111]

To what extent this attitude of continued hostility toward the government of Great Britain can be attributed to the influence of any one man in Massachusetts Bay is not clear. Governor Bernard pointed to James Otis as the one who did most to promote it. Reviewing the situation in Massachusetts Bay during his administration, in a letter addressed to the Earl of Shelburne on December 22, 1766, Bernard insisted that he had maintained good relations with the House of Representatives until his refusal to appoint Otis's father chief justice of the province. It was then, according to the Governor, that Otis swore—as testified by two gentlemen of credit whose depositions had been sent home—that if his father was not appointed judge, "he would set the whole Province in a Flame. . . ." This Otis had proceeded to do. The Governor's letter set down in detail the various steps taken by that "passionate, violent, and desperate man" to overthrow the royal government of the colony.

According to Bernard's review of the situation, the following sequence of events had taken place. Thinking that Otis might be pacified by extending special favours to his father, the Governor had bestowed two offices on the senior Otis, thus putting him at the head of his county. Despite assurances that this would wipe away all ill feeling, as soon as the patents for these offices had been sealed the son renewed his hostility against the government with fresh vigour, initially by falsely accusing the Governor and his friends of devising the scheme for the stamp tax. Next he denounced the government of Great Britain in a speech before the House, declaring that "he wished that the island was sunk in the sea so that the King and his family was saved." In paying his compliments to the Gov-

[111] *Boston Evening-Post,* August 18, 1766.

ernors of the colonies, he had affirmed that "those who were appointed to the American governments were such as were obliged either by their crimes or their debts to fly their country." As to the Massachusetts Bay Council [before the year 1766], he had stated that it "was an infernal demon and deserved to be sent to the place from whence they derived their councils." Further, when any member of the House ventured to make a statement that seemed to support the established government, Otis would threaten that this person "would not sit in that House the next year," and, accordingly, a newspaper that he and "his junto" controlled listed the names of thirty-two members "who were proscribed as enemies to their country because they had given their testimony against the violences lately committed; and of these 32, 19 lost their elections." Finally, at a Boston meeting after the repeal of the Stamp Act, he had asserted that "the distinction between inland taxes and port duties was without foundation for whoever had a right to impose one had the right to impose the other: and therefore as the Parliament had given up the one (for he said the Act for securing the dependency [the Declaratory Act] had no relations to taxes), they had given up the other: and the merchants were great fools if they submitted any longer to the laws restraining their trade which ought to be free." This, according to the Governor, led people to take the position that there should be no more seizures by the customs officers.[112] Such was Bernard's indictment of Otis.

Those who acted first on the Otis principle that there should be no more seizures in Massachusetts Bay were not the people of Boston but those of Falmouth, York County (in what is now the state of Maine). On the morning of August 7, 1766, Francis Waldo, a collector, and Arthur Savage, the comptroller at this port of entry, went to the storehouse of Enoch Ilfley in search of uncustomed goods; by virtue of a writ of assistance, they were accompanied by Alexander Ross, a justice of the peace for this county. There they found a number of hogsheads of sugar and some three hogsheads of rum on which duties had not been paid. These they seized in the name of the King and marked for confiscation. As the officials were not provided with carriages to remove the smuggled goods immediately to a place of security, they put a lock on the door of the storehouse. That afternoon, hearing that a rescue had been planned, they called upon the justice of the peace to issue a warrant to the county sheriff and his deputies requiring them to assist the custom-

[112] For the Bernard letter see the Shelburne Papers, 51:507–16.

house officers. This was done. As the sheriff was at a distance, the warrant was given to Joseph Noyes, a deputy sheriff, who was enjoined to prevent a rescue and agreed to do so. However, by the time he had received the warrant night had come. A crowd had gathered about the home of the comptroller (where he and the collector were at the time) and pelted it with stones and beat upon it with clubs until about ten o'clock. During this interval the goods apparently were removed from Ilfley's store after the deputy sheriff had been carried away by the mob and the warrant rifled from his pocket. At any rate, the next morning the goods were missing and Ilfley stoutly denied that he knew who had taken them.

Upon receiving a report of the incident from the collector and comptroller—which indicated that "a considerable part of the town were active in the rescue"—and after submitting the matter to the Council, Bernard issued a proclamation offering a reward of £50 out of the public treasury to anyone who informed against those engaged "in these riotous and unlawful Proceedings." It is hardly necessary to note that no one ventured to supply the desired information.[113] In reporting the affair to the Lords Commissioners for Trade and Plantations, the Governor was obliged to admit the bald fact that "Government is become a mere Shadow, & is not like, by any Internal Powers of Its own, to recover itself from the great blow it has lately received."[114] He wrote in like terms to the Earl of Shelburne, now Secretary of State for the Southern Department. In his reply Shelburne expressed the hope that only a few people had been involved in this lawless activity and that these had been punished. Since "the Provinces in general have shewn the utmost Gratitude for the tender Regard of His Majesty and the Parliament of Great Britain, it is scarcely to be conceived," he declared, "that the Province of Massachusetts should countenance such a Spirit of Anarchy and Disobedience. . . ."[115]

But Shelburne was unaware of the strength of the forces bent on loosening the bonds that had tied the dynamic province to the mother country or of the deep resentment against all restrictions placed by the home government on Massachusetts Bay's trade with the outside world. The month following the Falmouth riot a much more serious incident occurred in Boston that only re-emphasized

---

[113] For the details of the Falmouth incident see the report of the collector and comptroller, dated August 11, 1766, *ibid.*, 51:461, and the proclamation printed in the *Boston Evening-Post,* August 25, 1766.

[114] Bernard to the Board of Trade, August 18, 1766, Shelburne Papers, 51:461.

[115] Shelburne to Bernard, December 11, 1766; *ibid,* 53:196–7.

the fact that the imperial arm was weak in the face of popular local resistance. It appears that very early on the morning of September 23—according to an alleged customs informer, Ebenezer Richardson—certain goods (barrels of brandy, other liqueurs, and wine) consigned to a man at Casco Bay were carted to the home of Captain Daniel Malcom (Malcolm, Malcome, Malcomb), where they were lodged in a cellar. As duties had not been paid on the goods and information was received by the custom house that they had been deposited at the Malcom home, two of its officers, William Sheaffe, deputy collector, and Benjamin Hallowell, comptroller, accompanied by the deputy sheriff, went there the following morning. Malcom, according to Hallowell's deposition made on the affair, "willingly showed us his outhouse and all his cellers, except one." When they insisted on viewing its contents he became abusive and threatened them with death after arming himself with a sword and two pistols. In the face of these threats the officers left the place, and reported the situation to the Governor and Council, then meeting. Bernard directed the high sheriff, Stephen Greenleaf, to attend the officers to the house and, if need be, to raise a *posse comitatus*. However, when the party arrived at the place that afternoon, they found the gate barred and a crowd of between three and four hundred people assembled in the neighbourhood of the house. Greenleaf testified later that it would have been impossible to secure the aid of a *posse comitatus* in the face of the mass of people assembled in the streets leading to the house. After having been informed that any attempt to enter by force "would cost some of them their lives [as] a signal would be given by Ringing the Bell of the Old North Meeting House as for Fire," the law-enforcement officers had withdrawn. However, it was intimated that they might still gain entry if the customs officials would give Malcom's friends the name of the person who had informed—something that could not be done.

This inability of the sheriff and customs officials to act was reported to the Governor in the evening. The charge of resisting the King's officers was a serious one, and depositions were taken.[116] When news spread that this testimony was to be sent to London,

[116] For the Malcom affair see Bernard to the Earl of Shelburne, October 4, 1766, *ibid.*, 51:469–70; for the depositions of September 24, 1766, with affidavits covering thirty folio pages, see P.R.O., Treas. 1, 446: 103–33; see also Hallowell to the Customs Commissioners, November 14, 1766, Treas. 1. 452:35. Copies of the depositions among the Arthur Lee Papers include not only those of September 24 but those taken later, including the last four pages only of the affidavit signed by Captain Malcom himself on October 21, 1766. See the Arthur Lee Papers, 1:15–23, Harvard College Library.

Bostonians became alarmed lest measures should be taken against the province by Parliament or the Crown, whereby regular troops might be sent to the colony as the only means of executing the trade acts.[117] A town meeting held at Faneuil Hall on October 8 heard that the Council had taken depositions of the activities at the time of the "search of contraband Goods pretended to be in the Dwelling House of Capt. Daniel Malcomb of this Town." The reaction of the meeting was that these depositions might contain opinions and assertions "which, . . . unaccompanied with a full and true Representation of that Affair, may . . . affect and prejudice the Trade, Commerce, and Reputation of this Metropolis, and of the Province in General." It was therefore voted that the moderator of the meeting, who was Otis, with eight others, including Samuel Adams and John Hancock, should wait upon the Governor with a request that the secretary of the province be ordered to furnish the town clerk with copies of all depositions "so the Town having Knowledge of their Accusers, and . . . of the Testimonies taken," might counteract "the Designs of any who would represent them in a disadvantageous Light to his Majesty's Ministers."[118]

Many reasons were doubtless weighed by Governor Bernard in his decision to minimize the real seriousness of the Malcom affair. Although the town meeting, it is true, did not utter a word condemning Malcom for his actions but did vote to request copies of the depositions "of their Accusers," it also voted unanimously that same day that the Boston representatives in the General Court should exert themselves to secure reimbursement to the sufferers from the great riot of the preceding year.[119] This the Governor had very much at heart. Again, with the Boston incident coming so soon after that at Falmouth, Bernard may well have felt that his prestige was at stake at home. Further, it was difficult for him to take steps

---

[117] It should be noted in this connection that from time to time it was necessary, in the interests of enforcing the trade laws in Great Britain, to use dragoons against rings of armed smugglers. Samuel Adams, Clerk of the House of Representatives, was aware that regular troops might also be used as an instrument for enforcing the laws in the colony. In writing to Christopher Gadsden of South Carolina on December 11, 1766, he mentioned, doubtless with irony, that George Grenville had been told "that he missed it in his politicks, for he should have stationed a sufficient number of Troops in America before he sent the Stamp Act among them." As a leading Boston politician, Adams may have had in mind the Falmouth and Malcom incidents and the inability of the civil authorities to enforce the law, which might have led to the sending of regulars to the province. See Samuel Adams Papers, New York Public Library.

[118] For this extract from the minutes of the town meeting, signed by the town clerk as a true copy, see *Boston Evening-Post,* October 13, 1766.

[119] See *ibid.* for this vote.

against Malcom since no positive evidence had been obtained of the existence of contraband goods on his premises—outside of the secret information supplied by the informer—and several depositions taken later before local justices of the peace testified to facts that could not be reconciled with the depositions of the customs officers.[120] Among these was Malcom's affidavit, which affirmed that he had not been the possessor of any contraband goods; that all he had sought was, for the good of the country, to determine the validity of the officers' powers; that he had never planned to use any violence if the officers attempted to force their way into his house, but only to seek legal redress; that he had asked only a few gentlemen to come to his home as witnesses of the distress of his family; and that he barred his gate and doors for fear the crowd outside would tear down his house.[121] Moreover, Samuel Adams framed a most adroit letter, signed by James Otis as moderator of the town meeting,[122] which, together with copies of the depositions, were sent to Dennys De Berdt, the London agent for the House of Representatives, to use as he might judge proper and expedient. The letter stressed the town's abhorrence of the disorderly conduct of irresponsible people and the devotion of its inhabitants to the King and the British connections.[123] For his part, Bernard wrote to the Secretary of State for the Southern Department about the affair and also sent copies of the depositions, but he did not press the matter. Shelburne in turn transferred these papers to the Lords Commissioners of the Treasury, who were responsible for the maintenance of the customs service, and they turned them over to the Attorney General and the Solicitor General for their advice on the proper proceedings to be instituted against Daniel Malcom. Doubtless the conflicting nature of the depositions, taken together with the important issue that had arisen in the neighbouring Province of New York, caused the matter to be allowed to rest. The question, however, still remained: could the trade laws be effectively enforced any longer within the bounds of the Province of Massachusetts Bay?

---

[120] These affidavits are among the Arthur Lee Papers, 1:22–3.

[121] A copy of Malcom's deposition (sworn before Edmund Quincy, a justice of the peace, on October 21) was turned over to Hallowell. In his letter to the Customs Commissioners in London, dated November 14, 1766, Hallowell pointed out numerous statements in the Malcom affidavit which he claimed were false. For this see P.R.O., Treas. 1. 452:35.

[122] See W. V. Wells: *The Life and Public Services of Samuel Adams . . .*, I, 130.

[123] For the letter of the Committee of the Town of Boston to De Berdt, October 26, 1766, see Arthur Lee Papers, 1:14.

CHAPTER II

New York and the Quartering Act

DURING the period from 1760 to 1775 Massachusetts Bay was destined to take the lead among the American colonies, if not always in declarations of local rights, certainly in actions resisting the measures of the home government that were considered to impinge upon the powers claimed by the colonial legislatures. One exception was the leadership shown by the Province of New York in contesting—prematurely and unsuccessfully, as it proved—the validity of the Act of Parliament passed in 1765 to provide for quartering troops that might be sent to a colony to carry out imperial policy in North America (5 Geo. III, c. 33).[1]

In the course of the Great War for the Empire the New York Assembly had been led to consider a billeting bill to provide accommodations for soldiers engaged in defending the northern frontiers of the province against the French and their Indian allies. In the fall of 1756 Governor Charles Hardy had brought the problem of securing winter quarters for these soldiers to the attention of the Assembly, and on October 9 a bill had been sent to the Council. But the Assembly delayed action on it, so that on November 4 he sent a message to the Assembly pointing out that the time was nearly at

[1] It should be noted, however, that Massachusetts Bay also took early action in protest against the Mutiny Act when, in January and February 1767, its House of Representatives objected to the request of the Governor and the Council that supplies be voted for the artillery troops who had been landed by ship in Boston the previous December as the result of a storm. See *Journal of the House of Representatives* (Boston, 1766–7), pp. 229, 230, 240; see also W. V. Wells: *The Life . . . of Samuel Adams . . .* (2 vols., Boston, 1865), I, 131–4, 139–40. Further, by 1768, the quartering of troops in Boston was, of course, to become a more serious issue; see *The Correspondence of General Thomas Gage with the Secretaries of State, 1763–1775* (ed. C. E. Carter, 2 vols., New Haven, 1931, 1933), II, 488; cited hereafter as *Gage Correspondence.*

hand when winter quarters simply must be found for the troops.[2] On November 15 the Governor informed the legislators that the Earl of Loudoun, Commander-in-Chief of the British Forces in North America, had demanded quarters in New York City for a battalion of Royal Americans (almost all of them recruited in America) who were coming down the Hudson from Albany.[3] In view of the urgency of the situation the Billeting Act, with certain amendments proposed by the Council, was approved by the Assembly and received the Governor's signature on December 1, 1756.

The "Act for billeting and quartering his Majesty's Forces within this Colony" emphasized the points that too many soldiers had been sent "for the defence of this colony" to be quartered in barracks erected therein; that, as a consequence, when troops were ordered to come to any city, borough, town, or manor, it would be lawful for the mayor and two aldermen or two justices of the peace to quarter the troops—in the absence of adequate barracks—in inns, livery stables, ale houses, or victualling houses; further, that, should these quarters be insufficient, then "in such private Houses . . . as the Mayor . . . and two Aldermen, in their Discretion shall see fit." The rates for this service were to be fixed by the magistrates, and persons unwilling to receive troops so billeted were to forfeit £5.[4]

In his interview with John Cruger, mayor of New York City, Lord Loudoun insisted that his officers receive quarters without expense to themselves just as if they were in barracks, stating "that this was every where the custom," and even threatening that if difficulties developed, he would concentrate all the troops within the province in New York City for the winter. The issue, therefore, centred on the matter of free quarters, which a committee of citizens asserted, in a memorial to the Governor, was "against the common law, and the petition of rights, . . . and the mutiny and desertion act; and that the colonists were entitled to all the rights of Englishmen."[5]

Despite their protest the citizens became aware that the troops were concentrated for a purpose most vital to the interests of all New Yorkers and the opposition to providing quarters faded away. By

[2] *Journal of the Legislative Council of the Colony of New-York . . . 8 December 1743–3 April 1775* (Albany, 1861), pp. 1274, 1276, 1277; cited hereafter as *Journal of the Legislative Council of New-York*.

[3] *Ibid.*, p. 1280.

[4] For the Billeting Act of 1756 see *Laws of New-York, from . . . 1752 to . . . 1762* (eds. William Livingston and William Smith, Jr., 2 vols., New York, 1752, 1762), II, 106–7.

[5] William Smith: *History of the Late Province of New-York . . . to . . . 1762*, Vols. IV and V of New-York Historical Society *Collections* (2 vols., New York, 1829), II, 241–2.

February 28, 1757, Hardy was able to write from New York to the Lords Commissioners for Trade and Plantations that little or no difficulties had "arisen in quartering the Forces in this City, the Townships near adjoining to it, and in others on Long Island."[6] In fact, the *New-York Mercury* of January 31, 1757, printed the full text of the Billeting Act, and neither in that issue nor in the preceding or succeeding issues was there any criticism of the measure. The need for making some such provision for the welfare of the soldiers seemed apparent and justified. In 1757, 1758, 1759, and 1760 the Act was renewed.[7] Although it was allowed to lapse after January 1, 1762, on November 16 of that year Governor Robert Monckton, in a speech to the Council and Assembly, declared: "Among the Laws which require your Consideration, I must point out to you, the Necessity of reviving those for billeting and quartering the King's Troops, and the impressing of Horses and Carriages: Experience having shewn the Impracticability of carrying on the public Service with Effect, without the Aid of these Laws."[8] On December 4 he repeated his request, pointing out that this was "a measure which cannot be left unprovided for, without prejudice to the Crown, and great inconvenience to the Subject."[9] With this additional urging a new billeting bill passed through its readings in the Assembly and Council without incident.[10]

As the Billeting Act ran for only one year—as had been true of the earlier billeting laws—at the beginning of 1764 there was no measure in force requiring that quarters, even temporary ones, be furnished for the needs of either the troops moving up from the city to the distant posts on the province frontiers or those returning from this service. Writing to the Earl of Halifax, Secretary of State for the Southern Department, on January 23, 1765, General Thomas Gage, Commander-in-Chief of the British Forces in North America, outlined some of the problems of quartering troops and other difficulties attendant upon his responsibilities for maintaining posts in upper New York:

> "It is declared generaly, that the Mutiny Act, does not extend to America, but in such Clauses only where it is particularly Specified

[6] *Documents Relative to the Colonial History of the State of New-York* (eds. E. B. O'Callaghan and B. Fernow, 15 vols., Albany, 1856–87), VII, 217; cited hereafter as *New York Colonial Documents*.

[7] *Laws of New-York, 1752–1762*, II, 118, 141, 167, 200.

[8] *Journal of the Legislative Council of New-York,* p. 1484.

[9] *Ibid.*, p. 1493.

[10] *Ibid.*, p. 1500; see also *The Colonial Laws of New York . . .* (eds. C. Z. Lincoln, W. H. Johnson, and A. J. Northrup, 5 vols., Albany, 1894–6), IV, 637.

> to extend . . . to His Majesty's Dominions beyond the Seas. Soldiers are seduced from the King's Service, Deserters protected and Secreted, Arms Cloaths etc. purchased. Quarters and Carriages refused, without incurring any Penalty. Officers have been prosecuted and fined for Seizing Deserters, Seduced from their Regiments, and indented as private Servants; sent to Jail for being in the Quarters which had been allotted for them, and prosecuted for getting Carriages on their March . . . and the People in general begin to be Sensible, that they are not obliged to do, what they submitted to, in Times of Danger. It will soon be difficult in the present Situation, to keep Soldiers in the Service; or possible to March and quarter them where the Service shall require, or however urgent the Occasion, without Numberless Prosecutions, or perhaps worse Consequences."[11]

Gage therefore submitted a memorial concerned with the proper quartering of soldiers, prepared by a member of his staff, Lieutenant Colonel James Robertson, Deputy Quartermaster-General, together with proposed additions to the Mutiny Act "calculated to Suit the particular Circumstances of North America."[12]

Later correspondence between Lord Halifax and Secretary at War Ellis resulted in a quartering bill that took the Robertson recommendations into consideration and conformed to the New York Billeting Act at least to the extent that, under certain circumstances, soldiers could be quartered in private homes.[13] When Grenville studied the problem he came to the conclusion that for the bill to carry a provision having general application in America would "create difficulties and uneasiness . . . especially as the quartering of soldiers upon the people against their wills is declared by the petition of right to be contrary to law."[14] This view was held by others.

---

[11] *Gage Correspondence,* I, 49.

[12] *Ibid.* Writing to the Earl of Shelburne on February 10, 1767, Welbore Ellis, the Secretary at War, gave a brief account of the background of the Quartering Act passed in 1765. Until the late war, he wrote, the few soldiers maintained in North America had remained fairly stationary at particular forts. During the war the colonists had allowed soldiers on the march to be quartered in private houses when necessary, while the great towns had provided barracks at their own expense to prevent that inconvenience. After the war, with no law existing to enforce making quarters available to soldiers, "the Americans" objected to resorting to the earlier practice. General Gage had made this clear to Ellis and had sent over plans for correcting the situation by making alterations in the annual Mutiny Bill, but it was thought best to have a separate bill for North America. See the Shelburne Papers, 58: 597–8, Clements Library.

[13] While Halifax took the position that the clamour over the practice of billeting soldiers in private homes in America might be disregarded, Ellis felt differently about it. George III also advised Grenville to weigh the matter carefully. See George III to Grenville, March 9, 1765, *The Grenville Papers . . .* (ed. W. J. Smith, 4 vols., London, 1853), III, 11–12.

[14] Grenville to the King, March 9, 1765, *ibid.,* III, 12–14.

The great Quaker merchant David Barclay, who had important connections in America, expressed the fear that the "clause in the Mutiny Act, now framing for that part of the King's dominions, making it lawful to billet soldiers on a march in *private* families, is, in the opinion of every well-wisher to America, and every friend to liberty, . . . an innovation upon the privileges of those who justly claim the natural rights of this country. . . ."[15] Thomas Pownall, who had served as Governor of Massachusetts Bay, also took the position that it was a "very wrong, & bad clause." What is more, as a man of influence, he did something about it. Writing to Thomas Hutchinson, he affirmed:

> "I drew up & gott inserted ye clause as it now stands [in the Quartering Act]—taken literally as far as general circumstances would suit, from ye Act we passed in ye Massachusetts, & for which the People were originally obliged to your forecast & prudence. This is known to Ben Franklin, is known to all ye ministers here & yet I dare say neither is nor would be believed in ye Colonies."[16]

In preparing the bill, care was also taken to list those articles that a colony in which soldiers were temporarily quartered during transit would be reasonably expected to furnish. Before Grenville was prepared to accept the clause that called upon a colony to provide soldiers quartered in barracks and hired houses with bedding, barrack utensils, firewood, candles, and small beer or rum mixed with water, he consulted two merchants with American interests and sympathies, Barlow Trecothick and Richard Glover. Neither of them questioned the propriety of these requirements.[17]

Out of these deliberations finally emerged a bill entitled "An Act to amend and render more effectual, in His Majesty's Dominions in America, an Act passed in this present Session of Parliament intituled, An Act for punishing Mutiny and Desertion, and for the better Payment of the Army and their Quarters." This followed as closely as possible both the content and the language of an "Act making Provision for the Quartering and Billeting [of] Recruiting

---

[15] Barclay to Lord Hyde, April 11, 1765, *ibid.*, III, 11*n.*

[16] Pownall to Hutchinson, December 3, 1765, Hutchinson Correspondence, Massachusetts Archives, 25:1, 2–3. That Pownall was correct in the above statement on his role in the framing of the bill is indicated by a letter that Grenville addressed to Charles Jenkinson on April 13, 1765, in which he said: "I approve extremely of Govr Pownall meeting with Mr. Franklyn in order to form a Clause for billeting Soldiers in America, for I own I have always thought it very disagreeable to put it upon the Footing it was proposed if it can be avoided . . . by makng Provisions of a less exceptionable Nature" (Grenville Letter Books, Vol. 2, Stowe Collection, Huntington Library).

[17] Grenville to Welbore Ellis, April 27, 1765, *ibid.*

Officers and Recruits in his Majesty's Regular Forces, employed for the Protection and Defence of his Majesty's Dominions in North-America," passed by the General Court of Massachusetts Bay, approved by Governor Pownall and published on December 1, 1757.[18] Framed to deal with the particular situation in North America, the Act of the Parliament laid down the principle that if barracks were either insufficient or lacking in any colony where it was necessary to send troops, the provincial or local officials should be charged with the responsibility of quartering the soldiers in inns, livery stables, victualling houses dispensing ale, wine, and distilled liquors, as well as in uninhabited houses and out-houses.[19] The payment for these temporary accommodations was to be made by the colony, which should also provide the soldiers with bedding, firewood, kitchen utensils, candles, vinegar, salt, and "small beer or cyder, not exceeding five pints, or half a pint of rum mixed with a quart of water, to each man."[20] The Act reflected the efforts of the colonial

---

[18] For the Massachusetts Bay Act see *Acts and Laws [Temporary] . . . of the Massachusetts-Bay in New-England* (Boston, 1758), pp. 319–20. Writing to Governor Pownall from New York on November 15, 1757, Lord Loudoun was fixed in his position that the troops sent over to operate against the enemy were not to be permitted at the end of every campaign "to Perish in the Snow in the Streets during the Winter. . . ." He was especially firm as to who should bear the charges. "Charity will not permitt me to believe . . . that the Mother Country should Pay for the quartering the Troops here, that are sent for their [the colonials'] Protection, who have Quarters in Great Britain without Payment." What is more—in view of the opposition that had developed in the Massachusetts Bay Assembly against making provision for any of the regular troops—the Commander-in-Chief warned Pownall that if arrangements were not immediately made for the care of the Highland Regiment he desired to quarter in Boston preparatory to the spring campaign, he would order three battalions of regulars, then quartered in New York, Long Island, and Connecticut, to Boston, "and if more are wanted, I have two in the Jerseys, at hand, besides those in Pennsylvania" (Loudoun Papers, No. 4838, Huntington Library). In view of this threat the Assembly gave way and passed the Quartering Act referred to above. See also S. M. Pargellis: *Lord Loudoun in North America* (Yale Historical *Publications,* VII, New Haven and London, 1933), Chap. 7, "Quartering."

[19] The Act placed limitations on the use of uninhabited houses, out-houses, barns, and other such buildings. These were to be used only if all the other means previously listed were insufficient to accommodate the troops and were to be requisitioned not by the military but by appointees of the Governor and Council. Any officer assuming to take quarters contrary to the Act was to be cashiered, and any person aggrieved by having soldiers quartered upon him could be given relief by the justices of the peace.

[20] The Act is listed as 5 Geo. III, c. 33, *Statutes at Large* (Pickering) XXVI, 305–18. On March 22, 1765, the regular annual renewal of the Mutiny Act was given royal assent; on the 29th of that month leave was given to bring in a bill which would render more effectual the foregoing act and the Secretary at War and Thomas Gore were designated to prepare and present the bill. While the bill was being framed Edward Montague, London agent for Virginia, petitioned by counsel to be heard against any parts of it that might authorize the quartering of soldiers in private homes. When the question was proposed in the House, it was moved that the entry in the

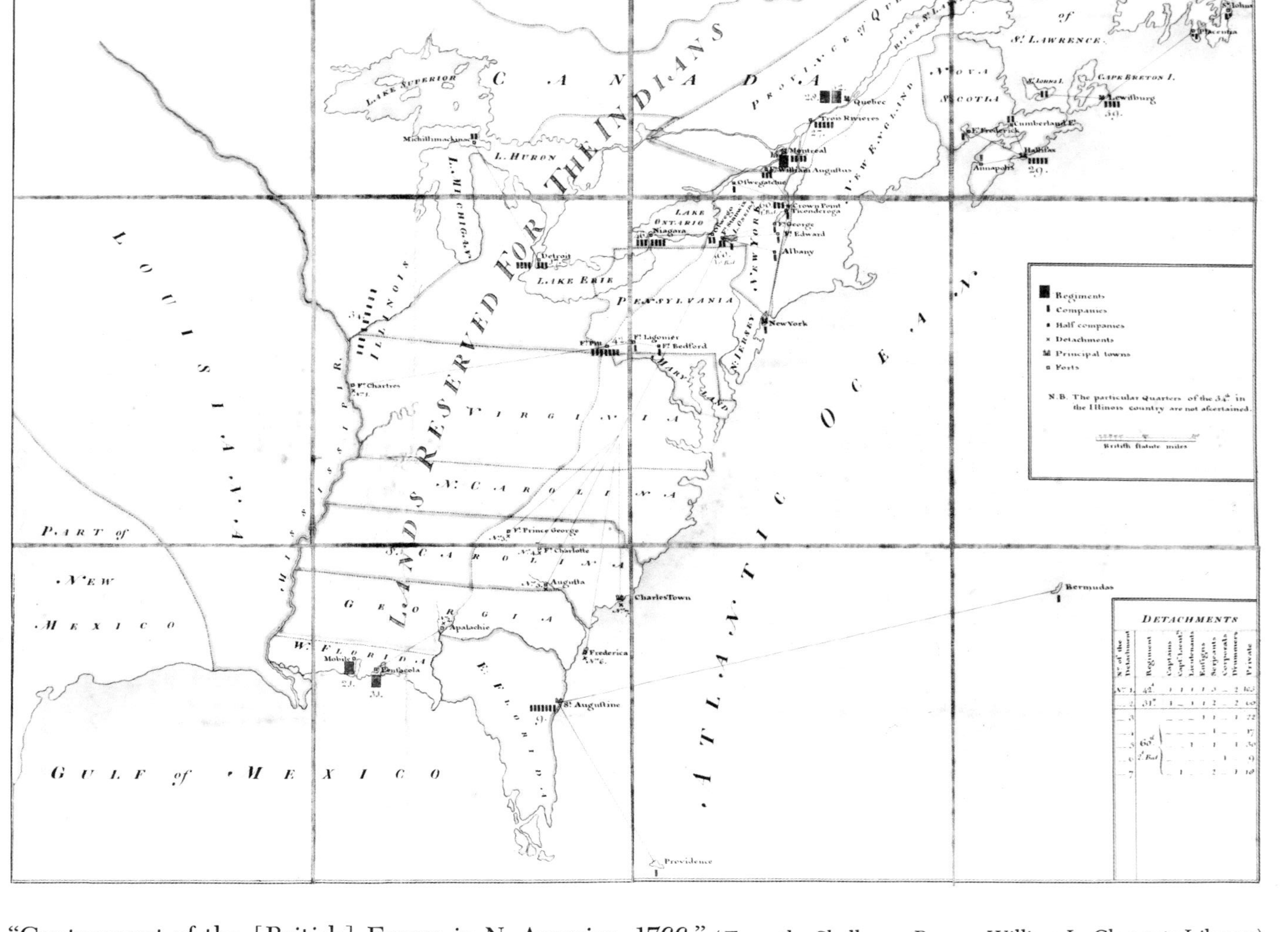

"Cantonment of the [British] Forces in N. America, 1766." (From the Shelburne Papers, William L. Clements Library)

agents—Benjamin Franklin, acting for Pennsylvania, Edward Montague for Virginia, and Jared Ingersoll[21] for Connecticut—as well as other friends of America. For it laid down elaborate rules for preventing abuses and for rectifying any that might occur, as the result either of quartering soldiers or of impressing horses and wagons. This may help to explain why, except in New York, there was comparatively little serious complaint over the billeting of troops. Actually the disposition of the fifteen regiments and ten companies of royal artillery stationed throughout North America resulted in no heavy concentration in the older provinces, as shown in Volume X of this series,[22] and will be discussed in Chapter IV of this volume.

The issue in New York over the Quartering Act arose in the midst of the Stamp Act crisis when, on December 1, 1765, General Gage applied to the new Governor, Sir Henry Moore, asking for immediate provision of quarters for the troops present in the province and those that might subsequently be stationed there or have occasion to march through in transit.[23] For, as is well known, the government of Great Britain esteemed it a matter of great strategic importance that certain posts in the area of the upper New York frontier be maintained. Gage had received copies of the Act in August, but had made no move to carry out the terms of the statute until the Assembly could meet and make provisions for reimbursing the magistrates for the expenses they would incur in quartering and supplying the troops.[24] On the 3rd the Governor forwarded the request to the Council and Assembly together with a copy of the Quartering Act. In an accompanying message he expressed the hope that the legisla-

Journal for December 16, 1754, relating to the petition of William Bollan, agent for Massachusetts Bay, be read, and this was done. The order of the day was thereupon read. The bill, at last freed of the clause permitting billeting in private homes, then made its way through the two houses and on May 15 received the royal approval. See *Journals of the House of Commons,* XXX, 293, 321, 343–4, 426.

[21] For Ingersoll's part in the shaping of the Quartering Act, see *Mr. Ingersoll's Letters Relating to the Stamp-Act* (New Haven, 1766), p. 3*n*.

[22] General Conway is reported to have stated during the Great Debate over the repeal of the Stamp Act on February 21, 1766, that there were but 5,000 British regulars in 3,000 miles of territory; see Walpole's *Memoirs of the Reign of George the Third* (ed. Sir Denis Le Marchant, 4 vols., London, 1845, and 2 vols., Philadelphia, 1845; the two-volume Philadelphia edition will be used throughout this volume, cited hereafter as Walpole's *Memoirs of George III),* I, 391, and Nathaniel Ryder's Parliamentary Notes, Doc. 64, Harrowby Manuscript Trust, Sandon Hall, Staffordshire, as cited in Volume X of this series, pp. 408–9. For the disposition of the regular troops in 1763 see *ibid.,* X, 200–2; for their proposed disposition in 1767 see *Gage Correspondence,* II, 408–10.

[23] Gage to Moore, December 1, 1765, Shelburne Papers, 58:2.

[24] *Gage Correspondence,* II, 296 and 328.

ture would "chearfully and readily comply with what is expected of the Colony."[25] When the Council met again on the 9th—following its adjournment on November 26—the Governor's request was entered into the minutes. There the matter ended.[26] As to the Assembly, on December 5 it adopted a resolution presented by a committee of the whole house granting £400 to provide firewood and candles for His Majesty's garrison at Fort George in New York City for the period September 1, 1765, to September 1, 1766.[27] With this accomplished, on the 13th the Assembly unanimously adopted three resolutions as a result of a report of the committee of the whole house that had met to consider the Governor's request and the papers accompanying his message. The first resolution asserted that when His Majesty's forces were quartered in barracks belonging to the King they had always been furnished with the necessaries required by the Quartering Act "without any expense to the Countries in which they are quartered. . . ." The second resolution pointed out that there were barracks in the cities of New York and Albany sufficient to accommodate twice the number of forces mentioned in General Gage's return and that any application to the Assembly appeared altogether unnecessary at that time. The third stated that if any expense should be necessary for quartering troops on the march and supplying them with what was required by the Act, "the House ought to consider thereof after the expense is incurred." With this done, two members of the Assembly were ordered to wait upon the Governor and present the resolves as a reply to his message.[28]

In transmitting the resolutions of the General Assembly to Secretary Conway, Gage remarked: "They have not directly rejected the Act, but Set the Demand aside by Evasions. What they call King's Barracks are some Buildings in Albany built by the Crown during the War, and others built long ago in this Town at the Expense of the Province, and constantly repaired at their Expence; But being Situated either within the Fort, or under it's Protection, they make use of that Pretence, to call them King's Barracks, and [to assume] that the Crown should be at the Expence of furnishing them

[25] *Journal of the Votes and Proceedings of the General Assembly of the Colony of New-York, Vol. II, 1743–1765* (publ. Hugh Gaine, New York, 1766), pp. 788–9, reproduced in *Early American Imprints, 1639–1800* (ed. C. K. Shipton, Readex Microprints), Evans No. 10418, cited hereafter as *New York Assembly Journals, 1743–1765* (Gaine); see also *Journal of the Legislative Council of New-York, 1743–1775*, p. 1568.

[26] *Ibid.*

[27] *New York Assembly Journals, 1743–1765* (Gaine), p. 791.

[28] *Ibid.*, pp. 802–8. These resolves were framed by Justice Robert R. Livingston (1718–75).

with Necessarys." The General went on to point out that no provision had been made for meeting the contingency of additional troops coming into the province or marching through it. And, he affirmed, the magistrates would not under the circumstances incur any expense, lest they should not be repaid. As to the various requirements of the Mutiny Act, he said that he had never heard any complaint except against the clause specifying that the soldiers be given an allowance of beer, cider, or rum. "Some pretend that this is an Extraordinary Imposition on America. . . ." In fact, in the face of the crisis over the Stamp Act, Gage felt he must advise the Secretary of State that there was little probability that anything effectual could be done immediately to implement the Quartering Act.[29] That he was right was borne out by the refusal of the Albany magistrates to honour Colonel Bradstreet's request for quarters made in January of the new year, since the Assembly had provided no fund for this purpose.[30] Writing to Conway on February 22, 1766, from New York, Gage again emphasized the fact that "the Assembly of this Province would make no Provision, to defray the Expence of quartering His Majesty's Troops, in Conformity to the Mutiny Act for America. . . ."[31]

On December 23, in view of the intense emotional pitch of the Assembly over the Stamp Act, Governor Moore thought it best to adjourn that body to March 4. By a series of subsequent prorogations he put off any further meeting until after the news of the Stamp Act repeal had arrived. Not until June 11 did the legislators reassemble. Meanwhile nothing could be done to implement the Quartering Act. Early in May, however, Gage had reached the decision that as soon as any new body of troops arrived in the province, he would renew his applications for quarters "in the strongest manner" to the Governor and the Council, as well as to the New York City magistrates. He also expressed the feeling that until the Act was altered so as to provide a more serious penalty than a mere £5 for refusal to implement it, the law would never answer the intended purpose.[32] Nevertheless, on May 26 he addressed from his New York headquarters a request to Governor Moore for "Bedding, Utensils etc agreeable to the Act of Parliament for His Majesty's Troops then

[29] Gage to Conway, December 21, 1765, *Gage Correspondence*, I, 77.

[30] The magistrates of Albany to Colonel Bradstreet, January 23, 1766, Shelburne Papers, 58:3, and Bradstreet to Gage, January 26, 1766, Gage Papers, Clements Library, Ann Arbor.

[31] *Gage Correspondence*, I, 84.

[32] Gage to Conway, May 6, 1766, *Gage Correspondence*, I, 89.

under orders of march for this city." But his request was in vain.[33] Although troops sent to New Jersey and Pennsylvania were provided quarters "without any Difficulty," when the contingent that was to be billeted in New York arrived in that city, nothing had been done to prepare for their reception. As a result, according to the Governor, the soldiers were put to "great Inconveniences."[34]

When Moore called upon the legislators to make proper provision for the troops, they took certain resolutions in the Assembly on June 19.[35] First, they resolved that the Assembly had always been ready to comply with requests and that no instance could be recalled of a request for aid ever being refused. Second, that the requisition was of such a nature and tendency that if granted the expense would probably soon exceed the ability of the province to meet it, since the number of troops that might from time to time require provisions was quite unknown and the articles demanded were for the greater part "unprecedented." Third, the requisition would amount to threepence per diem for each private soldier, exclusive of bedding. Fourth, ". . . the House upon a proper requisition from the Crown for that Purpose, should be at the Expence of furnishing Barracks, Bedding, Utensils for dressing Victuals, and Firewood and Candles, for a proportionate Part of the Troops with the Rest of the Colonies; which the Committee conceives is as much as reasonably can be requested." Fifth, that His Majesty's service would not suffer by the non-compliance of the Assembly with the requisitions, since the troops had hitherto subsisted very well without such provision being made for them, and if this were not the case there was £3,990 still in the treasury of the province subject to the order of the Commander-in-Chief, which had been left by Sir Jeffrey Amherst and could be drawn upon.[36]

When Gage applied to the Governor[37] to determine whether the fund thus specified might be available for reimbursing the magis-

---

[33] Gage to Moore, May 26, 1766, Gage Papers, and Moore to Conway, June 20, 1766, *New York Colonial Documents,* VII, 831.

[34] *Ibid.*

[35] Moore to the Assembly, June 12, 1766, *Journal of the General Assembly of New-York, June 11 to December 19, 1766* (publ. Weyman, New York, 1766), pp. 2–3, cited hereafter as *New York Assembly Journal, 1766* (Weyman). The only known copy of this journal is in the Public Record Office, C.O. 5:1217, but it may be found in Readex Microprint, *Early American Imprints, 1639–1800* (ed. C. K. Shipton), Evans No. 10419.

[36] For these resolves enclosed in Moore's letter to Conway of June 20, 1766, see *ibid.,* p. 9, and P.R.O., Treas. 1. 446:174–7.

[37] For an excerpt from Gage's letter see the *New York Assembly Journal, 1766* (Weyman), p. 13.

trates who would quarter the troops, the members of the Assembly on June 23 resolved:

> "That it is impossible for the General Assembly, in Justice to their Constituents, to raise or appropriate any Fund for furnishing His Majesty's Forces in the Manner required by his Excellency, for the Reasons given in the Resolutions of the House of the 19th Instant: But as the General Assembly have been always ready to promote His Majesty's Service . . . Provision should be made for furnishing the Barracks in . . . *New-York* and *Albany* with Beds and Bedding, Fire Wood, Candles, and Utensils for dressing of Victuals, for two Battalions, not exceeding Five Hundred Men each, and one Company of Artillery for One Year.
>
> "That the Expences [thereby] to accrue . . . be made payable out of the Money now remaining in the Treasury, by Virtue of an Act passed the 20th March 1762, entitled, *An Act directing the Treasurer of this Colony, to pay to the Commander in Chief of all His Majesty's Forces in North-America the Sum of Four Thousand Seven Hundred and Ninety Pounds for His Majesty's Service, to be repaid when His Majesty shall think proper.*"[38]

Gage had taken the precaution to "have some of the Leading Men of the Assembly talked to." At that time the Act had been explained and the "Care the Parliament had taken to adopt the quartering of the Troops in America to the Circumstances of the Country, in the Manner the least Burthensome to the Inhabitants," had also been emphasized.[39] Yet this had not influenced the legislators to accept the law's requirement. Nor were they, while "making use of every Evasion," at all impressed by the knowledge that Gage "sent Troops thro' the Jerseys and Pennsylvania, where they have been quartered without any Difficulty."[40]

It would be quite wrong to think that the presence in New York of British regular troops was distasteful to the Assembly and the more substantial people of the colony. In fact, as a result of the agrarian crisis that developed in Dutchess County—where between four and five hundred men, supported by others from Albany and Westchester counties, had banded together in June to refuse the payment of rents, to rescue those who had been imprisoned for the non-payment, and even to threaten a march on New York City—these soldiers were considered to be a perfect godsend. Unable to rely upon the militia, the civil officers of the county appealed for

---

[38] *Ibid.*, p. 15.

[39] Gage to Conway, December 21, 1765, *Gage Correspondence*, I, 77.

[40] Gage to Conway, June 24, 1766, Shelburne Papers, 58:9.

effective military aid. As a result, the 28th Regiment under Major Brown was, at the request of the Governor, sent by Gage into Dutchess County "to Assist the Civil Officers in putting the Laws [of the province] in Execution, and to quell some dangerous Riots. . . ." After a brief engagement the rioters were pursued and dispersed, notwithstanding their superior numbers.[41] In order to support the quelling of the riots, the Assembly resolved on June 23 to provide for payment of the rewards that Governor Moore's public proclamation had promised "for apprehending the most notorious and active of the Offenders."[42] The departure of the regulars from New York at this juncture would have indeed been considered a great misfortune.

It must be stressed that in the eyes of the New York Assembly the issue over quartering the King's troops had important political and constitutional implications in addition to those that were more strictly fiscal. For example, on July 2, 1766, the Assembly resolved that whenever His Majesty's forces should, at the request of the Governor and by the advice and consent of the Council—as had been the case when regulars marched into Dutchess County—march to any part of the colony, any extraordinary expense would be paid.[43] The next day, furthermore, Moore assented to a bill that had been approved by the Council on June 27, "An Act to furnish the Barracks in the Cities of New York and Albany, with Firewood and Candles, and the other necessaries therein mentioned for His Majesty's Forces."[44] This law was designed to guarantee that all financial arrangements for the quartering of troops would be controlled by the provincial Assembly itself. By it the principle was laid down that such funds were to be appropriated only upon a direct requisition of the Crown, and also that all funds thus made available by the Assembly for meeting the expenses of troops in barracks were to be issued by the treasurer of the colony on direct application from the magistrates of New York and Albany, where the barracks were located, thus barring the military and even the Governor and Council from any interference in the matter. Finally, the items that the colony agreed to furnish were specified and did not include the ration of small beer or rum in water as required by the Act of

---

[41] Gage to Conway, July 15, 1766, *Gage Correspondence*, I, 99; Moore to Conway, July 14, 1766, *New York Colonial Documents*, VII, 845–6.

[42] *New York Assembly Journal, 1766* (Weyman), p. 14.

[43] *Ibid.*, pp. 23–4.

[44] *Journal of the Legislative Council of New-York*, pp. 1593–4, 1596.

Parliament.[45] Although acknowledging the need of obedience when the Crown applied for aid, the law as framed ignored the Act of Parliament and, by implication, the right of Parliament to interfere in the matter. Loyalty to the King had already been emphasized, when on June 23 the Assembly had voted that "an Equestrian Statue of His present Majesty be erected in the City of *New York,"* as well as a statute "in brass" of William Pitt.[46]

Actually the colony was not overburdened in providing barracks and the specified necessities for the regular troops, since neither of the two regiments, the 28th and the 46th, was up to strength. By 1766 many old and infirm men had been discharged and a large number of other soldiers had completed their tour of enlistment; so that Gage, in order to rebuild the regiments to effective strength, had found it necessary to send recruiting parties back to Great Britain[47] It is true that Secretary of State Conway had been deeply concerned lest too many troops should be quartered in the Middle colonies, particularly New York, and these provinces thereby be burdened beyond their proper proportion.[48] Gage himself was fully alive to the need of distributing the troops. Writing to the Duke of Richmond, Conway's successor as Secretary of State for the Southern Department, he made clear that, although most of the troops were initially landed in New York, they were distributed to other colonies as soon as circumstances permitted. He cited the sending of the first battalion of Royal Americans to Quebec and the second battalion to posts in the Great Lakes region. As to the 28th and the 46th regiments, he also indicated that as soon as the riots in Dutchess and Albany counties were quieted, one of these units would be sent to New Jersey.[49]

The unwillingness of the New York Assembly to recognize the Quartering Act, which it seemed determined to circumvent, led the Earl of Shelburne, who (during the change of ministry in the

---

[45] *The Colonial Laws of New York . . .*, IV, 901. It may be noted that William Smith, whose influence in New York provincial affairs at this period was very powerful, took the view "that the Act of Parliament appeared to be designed to inable the Executive Power to raise the Money, & consequently the Requisition [of the Crown] should not lie to the Legislative Authority" (*Historical Memoirs . . . 1763–1776 . . .* [ed. W. H. W. Sabine, New York, 1956], p. 33). The provincial act, as has been noted, placed authority in the hands of the Assembly, the provincial treasurer, and the magistrates of the cities, thus by-passing the Governor and Council.

[46] *New York Assembly Journal, 1776* (Weyman), p. 16.

[47] Gage to Conway, July 15, 1766, *Gage Correspondence,* I, 99.

[48] See Conway to Gage, May 20, 1766, Gage Papers.

[49] Gage to Richmond, August 25, 1766, *Gage Correspondence,* I, 101.

summer of 1766) had become Secretary of State for the Southern Department, to write to Governor Moore on August 9 that it was

> "the indispensable Duty of His [Majesty's] Subjects in *America* to obey the Acts of the Legislature of *Great Britain*. The King both expects and requires a due and chearful Obedience to the same; and it cannot be doubted that His Majesty's Province of *New-York*, after the Lenity of *Great-Britain* so recently extended to *America* [with the repeal of the Stamp Act], will not fail duly to carry into Execution the Act of Parliament . . . for Quartering His Majesty's Troops, in the full Extent and Meaning of the Act, without referring to the Usage of other Parts of His Majesty's Dominions where the Legislature has thought fit to prescribe different Regulations, and which cannot be altered . . . except upon a respectful and well grounded Representation of the Hardship or Inconvenience."[50]

On November 18 Moore sent a copy of the letter to the Assembly. That same day a committee was ordered to consider it and to draw up an answer. When the committee finally reported on December 13, it was through its chairman, Mr. Justice Livingston. This in itself may have been an indication of the importance attached to the reply and the care taken in framing it. In its approach to the issue involved, the report was direct but distinctly courteous. After affirming that nothing would give the members greater pleasure than to be able to comply with every requisition tending in any manner to promote His Majesty's service, the address continued:

> "It is therefore with great Concern that we find it impossible to comply with what is now demanded, consistent with our Obligations to our Constituents. . . . We hope it will be considered that we are chosen [as representatives] to make such a Provision for the Support of His Majesty's Government in this Colony . . . as is most suitable to the Circumstances of the People we represent; and that we should be guilty of a Breach of that most sacred Trust, if we should load them with Burthens they are incapable of supporting."

The address thereupon asserted that in quartering the two battalions of foot soldiers and a company of artillery, the province loaded the people with a burden much greater than that carried in any of the neighbouring governments. Further, while the Act of Parliament appeared to provide quarters only for soldiers on the march, according to the construction placed upon it in New York, it required that all forces that might enter the colony should be quartered during the whole year

---

[50] Shelburne to Moore, August 9, 1766, P.R.O., Treas. 1. 446:174–7, and *New York Assembly Journal, 1766* (Weyman), p. 11.

"in a very unusual and Expensive Manner: . . . And therefore, we cannot, consistent with our Duty to our Constituents, put it in the Power of any person . . . to lay such a Burthen on them . . . and therefore we humbly intreat your Excellency to set our Conduct . . . in its true Light, by representing that our Non Compliance on this Occasion proceeds entirely from a just Sense of what our Duty requires."[51]

The Assembly voted that the address should be presented to His Excellency not by a small committee, as was the rule, but "by the whole House." On December 18 this was done. The Governor expressed concern over the disparity between the Assembly's sentiments and his own, but agreed to transmit the address to the Secretary of State at the earliest opportunity.[52] The following day, after consenting to certain bills—among them two bills to permit the mayor, recorder, and aldermen of New York City to raise in all some £2,400 "for the uses therein mentioned"—he adjourned the General Assembly until the 10th day of March.[53] In his letter to the Earl of Shelburne of the 19th, in which he enclosed the Assembly's address, Moore expressed his mortification that it had been presented in such terms. Anticipating that the Secretary of State would require an answer as to why he had not immediately dissolved the Assembly after its refusal to recognize the binding power of a British statute, he pointed out that the members of the House were unanimous in their views, which also reflected those of their constituents. "So that in case of a dissolution the same members would have been returned again, [and] a Flame would have lighted up throughout the Country, and not a single advantage derived from it. . . . "[54]

Gage, who also commented upon the address in a letter to Shelburne, stressed the fact that wherever troops were quartered, far from burdening the people, they carried "an Increase of Wealth wherever they go" and that New York particularly was "happy in the State of its Finances, for I am credibly informed that every Farthing of Debt will be paid off this year, and good Revenues coming in." No, Gage stated, it was not the inability of the colony to support the troops; "the Assembly had Reasons of another Nature for refusing Obedience to an Act of the Legislature of Great-Britain" and for using such methods to obtain redress, if indeed

[51] *Ibid.*, pp. 43–4.
[52] *Ibid.*, p. 45.
[53] *Ibid.*
[54] *New York Colonial Documents,* VII, 883–4.

there were grounds for a grievance.[55] In the return of troops which Gage enclosed, he pointed out that only 646 soldiers were being quartered in the provincial barracks.[56]

The refusal of the New York Assembly to recognize the binding power of the American Quartering Act had shortly before been preceded by a petition to the House of Commons from the merchants of the city of New York that seemed to strike at the whole trade and navigation system. This long petition, signed by 240 merchants, was presented to the Governor on November 28 with a request that it be forwarded.[57] As the matter concerned trade and as the colonial Governors had access only to the executive branch of the government at home, Moore very properly sent it to the Board of Trade so that this body might take appropriate action. On January 29, 1767, the petition came before the Lords Commissioners, who decided to transmit it to the Earl of Shelburne to be laid before the King in Council.[58] It was presented to the House of Commons on February 16, 1767, by the President of the Board of Trade, Robert Nugent, Viscount Clare, and immediately brought up for action. But after being read it was tabled.[59] Undoubtedly it was regarded by the members—as it had been by Governor Moore—as "a most extraordinary Petition."[60]

According to the petitioners: "the Commerce of the North American Colonies is so severely clogged and restricted by the Statutes of the Fourth and Sixth of His Present Majesty[61] as to afford a melancholy Presage of its Destruction, the fatal Effects of which, though first felt there, must finally be transferred to Great Britain, and center with her Merchants and Manufacturers." The petitioners then went on to show the unfavourable balance of trade and their need to seek markets which would "enable them to sustain their Credit with the Mother Country" and argued that the "Nature of the Petitioners Commerce when free from the late Restraints, ought to be understood." After detailing their current trade situation they

---

[55] Gage to Shelburne, January 17, 1767, *Gage Correspondence,* I, 118.

[56] For the troop return see Shelburne Papers, 51:62–3.

[57] Governor Moore to Shelburne, December 10, 1766, Shelburne Papers, 51:659–63.

[58] Shelburne to the Earl of Chatham, February 1, 1767, *Correspondence of William Pitt* . . . (eds. W. S. Taylor and J. H. Pringle, 4 vols., London, 1838–40), III, 186, cited hereafter as *Pitt Correspondence,* and Board of Trade *Journal, 1764–1767,* pp. 360–1.

[59] *Journals of the House of Commons,* XXXI, 158–60.

[60] Moore to the Board of Trade, December 11, 1766, Shelburne Papers, 53:149–50.

[61] The acts complained of were the Sugar Act of 1764 (4 Geo. III, c. 15) and the act of 1766 repealing certain duties and regulating several branches of trade (6 Geo. III, c. 52).

added: "it seems therefore consistent with sound Policy to indulge those colonies in a free and unrestrained Exportation of all the Lumber and Produce they raise and can spare, and an ample Importation of Sugar, Rum, and Molasses, to supply the various Branches of their Trade. . . ." In fact, "the Regulations prescribed by the two before-mentioned Acts . . . must . . . ruin the Trade, of the Colonies, and prove highly pernicious to . . . Great Britain. . . ." As for rum, the importation of which from foreign parts had been prohibited (by 4 George III, c. 15), the petitioners now made a surprising proposal, that the importation of such rum (French-produced rum excepted) be permitted; that Parliament by charging "a moderate Duty would add considerably to the Revenue, prevent Smuggling, promote the Petitioners Navigation, increase the Vent of their own Produce . . . and enable them to bring back the full Value of their Cargoes. . . ." The duties on foreign sugar and the regulations applied to it, the restrictions on trade with Ireland, the fisheries, the logwood trade, and the British West Indies free ports, with the extension of the jurisdiction of the courts of vice-admiralty, all came under attack.[62]

In the eyes of the Earl of Chatham the petition was "highly improper: in point of time, most absurd; in the extent of their pretensions, most excessive; and in the reasoning, most grossly fallacious and offensive."[63] According to Shelburne, the London merchants with American connections "unanimously disavow the New York petition," laying the blame for it on the New Yorker Kelly, "the demon who has kindled this fire, and who is the sole author of it."[64]

---

[62] For this petition see *Journals of the House of Commons*, XXXI, 158–60. According to John Watts, a member of the New York Council, the New York merchant William Kelly, who circulated the petition, "had or pretended to have Mr. C. Townshend's countenance in procuring such a thing for the Ministry's Information & as he Corresponds with him did actually convey him a particular Copy by Letter assuming . . . an air of merit; pity he sho[d] be disappointed & loose his patron in the bargain" (Watts to former Governor Monckton, April 30, 1767, George Chalmers Manuscript Collection, 25 vols., "Papers Relating to New York, 1608–1792," New York Public Library, 2:17, cited hereafter as Chalmers Collection). Kelly had also appeared at the bar of the House of Commons early in 1766 as a witness against the stamp tax.

[63] Chatham to Shelburne, February 3, 1767, *Pitt Correspondence*, III, 188–9. John Watts took the view with respect to the petition that it was "really beneath the Dignity of a great Government to be so much alarm'd & rous'd at it, be it ever so absurd or ill drawn, when it is considered as coming from only Some merchants of one single Trade Town in America. Is their request unreasonable & ridiculous, point it out & expose the folly—but my own opinion is, it contains too much truth. I never saw it till within these few days. Henry Cruger was prevailed on to espouse it, by Mr. Kelly" (Watts to Monckton, April 30, 1767, Chalmers Collection, 2:17).

[64] Shelburne to Chatham [February 6, 1767], *Pitt Correspondence*, III, 191.

By striking at the established trade and navigation system, the New York merchants' petition undoubtedly aroused the apprehensions of many members of Parliament who had been persuaded a year earlier that, with the repeal of the Stamp Act, the old harmony that had once subsisted between the provinces and the mother country would be restored. The demands of the petitioners for a removal of trade restrictions, combined with the refusal of the Assembly to recognize the binding power of the Quartering Act, led to a really fundamental change in the attitude of both the Ministry and Parliament toward American affairs by the spring of 1767. Israel Mauduit, who had been associated with his brother Jasper in the Massachusetts Bay agency, wrote to Thomas Hutchinson on April 11: "The open disobedience of the Assembly at N. York to the Act for Quartering the Soldiers, has raised a Spirit in parliament, wch I have not seen before. All now agree that Governm^t w^d be no more, if it suffer'd any of its Subjects to dispute its supreme Authority." He went on to report that Lord Camden, the Lord High Chancellor, who had championed the colonies so vigorously in the Stamp Act repeal debates, declared that the colony of New York "was in a State of Delinquency," and that the First Lord of the Treasury, the Duke of Grafton, and the Secretary of State for the Southern Department, the Earl of Shelburne, had recently assured the House of Lords that the Earl of Chatham, with the assistance of other ministers, was preparing a bill for the maintenance of the King's rights and planned to carry it into execution.[65] Indeed, to Chatham the disobedience of the New York Assembly was "a matter so weighty, and big with consequences, which may strike so deep and spread so wide, that it ought, on no account, to rest on the advice of meetings of the cabinet, ... but . . . ought, in the proper manner, be laid before parliament, in order that his Majesty may be . . . strengthened by the sense of his grand council, with regard to whatever steps shall be found necessary to be taken in this unfortunate business."[66]

David Hume doubtless reflected the attitude of many in Great Britain in 1766 who were conversant with American affairs when he stated that New York was now the chief centre of disaffection toward the whole system of colonial government. In a letter written in the spring of that year he mentioned the report then circulating concerning "the most extraordinary Votes and Resolutions" taken by the New York Assembly to the effect that "the Parliament . . .

[65] Hutchinson Correspondence, Massachusetts Archives, 25:177.

[66] Chatham to Shelburne, February 17, 1767, *Pitt Correspondence,* III, 215.

had no Right to impose on them any Taxes whatsoever; that they had no Right to make any Laws for them without their Consent; that the Colonies had a Right to trade freely to any Part of the World where they found their Advantage;[67] that they were determin'd to maintain these Principles to the last Drop of their Blood. . . ."[68]

This view of the recalcitrance in New York of a year earlier had only become intensified by the spring of 1767. On March 12 the Cabinet Council came to the conclusion that the matter should be dealt with by an act of Parliament, despite the doubts raised by Secretary of State Conway.[69] Undoubtedly the feeling of urgency that something should be done to bring New York back to an obedient attitude was heightened by a letter received by the Secretary at War, Lord Barrington, from General Gage. Writing on January 17, 1767, from his New York headquarters, the General affirmed that the colonies were "taking large strides toward Independency" and warned that some speedy action must be taken by the mother country to make it clear to them that they "are British colonies dependent on her, and that they are not independent States."[70] Accordingly, the New York Barracks Act of 1766 was repealed by an order in council on April 13, 1767.[71] At a meeting on the 26th, the Cabinet Council rejected Townshend's idea—namely, that the Crown be addressed to withhold approval of all

---

[67] For resolutions passed by the New York Assembly on October 18, 1764, against "all Impositions, whether they be internal Taxes, or Duties paid, . . . and [for] . . . a Freedom to drive all Kinds of Traffic . . . not inconsistent with the British Trade; and an Exemption from all Duties in such a Course of Commerce," see *New York Assembly Journals, 1743–1765* (Gaine), pp. 769–79. In the petition to the House of Commons of December 11, 1765, the principle was laid down by the Assembly: "That all Supplies to the Crown being in their Nature free Gifts, it would, as we humbly conceive, be unconstitutional for the People of *Great-Britain,* by their Representatives in Parliament, to dispose of the Property of Millions of his Majesty's Subjects, who are not, and cannot be there represented" (*ibid.,* p. 800).

[68] Hume to [the Earl of Hertford (?)], May 8, 1766, *The Letters of David Hume* (ed. J. Y. T. Greig, 2 vols., Oxford, 1932), II, 42–3.

[69] The Duke of Grafton to Chatham, March 13, 1767, and Shelburne to Chatham, of the same date, *Pitt Correspondence,* III, 231–6.

[70] Gage to Barrington, January 17, 1767, *Gage Correspondence,* II, 406.

[71] For the disallowance see *Acts of the Privy Council, Col. Ser., 1766–1783,* p. 581. The order in council recites that the New York act, having been considered by themselves and the Lords Commissioners, had been presented to His Majesty in Council for repeal. "His Majesty was thereupon this Day pleased with the advice of the Privy Council to Declare his Disallowance of the said Act; and . . . the said Act is hereby Repealed, Declared void and of non effect." For a copy of the order in council see Shelburne Papers, 58:609; see also Board of Trade *Journal, 1764–1767,* pp. 375, 376, 418. On October 24, 1767, Governor Moore acknowledged receipt of the order in council from Shelburne, who had forwarded it to him. For Moore's letter see Shelburne Papers, 51:761.

laws passed by the New York Assembly until the American Quartering Act had been fully obeyed by that province—in favour of seeking an act of Parliament to restrain the New York legislature.[72] In consequence of this resolution the papers relating to New York and other North American colonies were presented to the House of Commons on the 30th. The previous day Alderman Beckford had written to Pitt emphasizing that a former administration (Grenville's) had "made the Americans stark staring mad; and at present, the Devil seems to have taken possession of their understandings." He, nevertheless, opposed all strong measures to remedy the situation and favoured a "cool and temperate" approach to colonial problems. "Recall your troops from the old provinces in America, where they are not wanted," he counselled, "and the cause of anger, hatred, and malice is removed."[73] Thus Beckford, a member of Parliament with great interests in Jamaica, not only opposed the Stamp Act in 1765, but also stood against the enforcement of the Quartering Act in 1767. His opinion, however, seems to have carried little weight with Chatham and other members of the Ministry at this juncture.[74]

On May 13 the House of Commons met as a committee of the whole House to discuss American affairs, a decision taken on April 30. In the course of debate the situation in New York came under review. William Dowdeswell, Chancellor of the Exchequer under Rockingham, argued that if the Assembly would make no proper provision for troops, they should be billeted in private houses[75]—a feature that had been dropped from the American Quartering Act by Parliament. George Grenville then proposed that to implement the Act the treasurer of New York be ordered to pay the needed funds, without further resort to the Assembly.[76] A third suggestion made in the course of the debate was that a local tax be placed on all importations into the province to provide a fund for this service.[77] None of these proposals—all previously rejected by the Cabinet Council on April 26—found favour with a majority of

---

[72] Shelburne to Chatham, April 26, 1767, Chatham Mansucripts, Vol. 56, P.R.O.

[73] Beckford to Chatham, April 29, 1767, *Pitt Correspondence*, III, 251–2.

[74] *Journals of the House of Commons*, XXXI, 333 and 358.

[75] Thomas Bradshaw, a joint secretary of the Treasury, to the Duke of Grafton [May 14, 1767], *Autobiography and Political Correspondence of Augustus Henry, Third Duke of Grafton* (ed. Sir William R. Anson, London, 1898), p. 176, cited hereafter as Grafton's *Autobiography*.

[76] *Ibid.*, p. 177.

[77] Charles Garth to the committee of correspondence of the South Carolina Commons House of Assembly, May 17, 1767, *South Carolina Historical and Genealogical Magazine*, XXIX, 225–6.

the committee of the whole House. Its report, presented by Rose Fuller, came in the form of three resolutions that had been proposed by Charles Townshend, not as Chancellor of the Exchequer, but simply in his capacity as a member of Parliament.[78]

The first of these resolutions stated: "That it appears . . . the House of Representatives of . . . New York have, in direct Disobedience of the Authority of the Legislature of Great Britain, refused to make Provision for supplying with Necessaries His Majesty's Troops, in such Manner as is required by an Act of Parliament. . . ." The second indicated: "That . . . an Act of Assembly hath been passed in the said Province, for furnishing the Barracks in the cities of New York and Albany, with Firewood and Candles, and other Necessaries therein mentioned . . . inconsistent with the Provisions, and in Opposition to the Directions, of the said Act of Parliament." The third recommended: "That, . . . until Provisions shall have been made, by the said Assembly, for furnishing the King's Troops with all the Necessaries required by the said Act of Parliament, the Governor, Council, and Assembly, be respectively restrained and prohibited from passing or assenting to any Act of Assembly, for any other Purpose whatsoever."[79] Taken together, these resolves in fact represent a determination to make binding the fundamental principle underlying the Declaratory Act of 1766.

With the resolves now before the House of Commons, a motion was made that the first five resolutions passed on February 24, 1766, in the debate on the repeal of the Stamp Act, be read. This was done. After a request for the re-reading of the first of these five resolves—the resolution that became the basis for the Declaratory Act—George Grenville made a motion to amend the first of the three new resolutions. He proposed that the following be inserted after the word "appears":

> "to this House, that the Assemblies in some of the North American Colonies still persist in the open Denial of the Legislative Authority of the Crown and Parliament of Great Britain, to impose Duties and Taxes on the Subjects in the said Colonies, notwithstanding the Declaration of both Houses of Parliament, and the Act passed . . . for the better securing the Dependence of His Majesty's Dominions in America upon the Crown and Parliament of Great Britain. . . ."[80]

---

[78] Shelburne to Chatham, April 26, 1767, Chatham Manuscripts, Vol. 56, P.R.O.; Bradshaw to Grafton, May 14, 1767, Grafton's *Autobiography*, p. 176; Horace Walpole: *Memoirs of George III*, II, 26–30; and John Brooke: *The Chatham Administration, 1766–1768* (London, 1956), pp. 136–7.

[79] *Journals of the House of Commons*, XXXI, 358 and 364.

[80] *Ibid.;* Thomas Bradshaw to the Duke of Grafton, May 16, 1767, Grafton's *Autobiography*, pp. 179–80.

As the Ministry was most anxious to deal with the problem in New York as an isolated instance of resistance[81]—just as the North Ministry in 1774, as will be noted in Volume XII of this series, felt that it should concern itself solely with the conduct of Massachusetts Bay—the amendment was frowned upon by the leaders in the House and was defeated.[82] The House then moved that a bill be brought in to cover the last of the three resolutions.

This motion was the occasion for Thomas Pownall, one-time Governor of Massachusetts Bay, to deliver a major speech, the first time he had addressed the House. As the author of "An Act . . . for Quartering . . . his Majesty's Regular Forces . . . ,"[83] passed in that colony in 1757, he declared that this law was "adapted to the nature of the country, and to the circumstances of the people, so it was universally submitted to, and (during the war) constantly carried into execution." His opposition to the Quartering Act of Parliament, and therefore to any bill enforcing it, was that it did not allow the colonies a proper latitude in its execution. He asserted that his own position respecting it, at the time it was passed, was "totally misapprehended" in view of the fact that its "errors and defects" have "perverted every means of carrying the measure into execution" with no "effectual clause to enforce its execution, nor . . . sufficient provision for the expence incurred. . . ." He warned that as the Act stands "the people of the colonies, from one end of the continent to the other, do invariably consider the clause in the act of parliament, directing how that charge shall be supplied, as an internal tax imposed upon them. . . . And although you represent the assembly of the Province of New York alone, as having revolted against this power—believe me, there is not a . . . colony . . . that will submit to a tax thus imposed, more than New York will." He therefore recommended that the Act be amended to make any supply for the expense of the troops be an act of the local assembly, in which case an enforcing bill would be unnecessary, or let the provision for quarters be considered a service which the

---

[81] The Earl of Shelburne, Secretary of State for the Southern Department, writing to the Earl of Chatham, on February 6, 1767, of his interview with King George, reported that "I took the liberty to say to the King . . . that I hoped both he and parliament would distinguish between New York and America" (*Pitt Correspondence*, III, 192).

[82] For this action, showing the vote as 150 noes to but 51 yeas, see *Journals of the House of Commons*, XXXI, 364.

[83] For the Act see *Acts and Laws of . . . Massachusetts-Bay* . . . (Boston, 1758), pp. 319–20.

Crown requires of it and for which—without the interposition of Parliament—it makes the proper requisitions.[84]

But Chatham and Shelburne, as well as all other members of the Cabinet Council except General Conway, had determined on enforcement of the Quartering Act. A very strong committee was therefore appointed to frame a bill. The committee consisted, among others, of Charles Townshend, who was Chancellor of the Exchequer, Lord Clare, President of the Board of Trade, Lord North, as well as the Attorney General, the Solicitor General, and Colonel Barré, one of the great defenders of the Americans in the spring of 1765 when the bill to impose stamp taxes was before the House.[85]

Again, the opposition—which, unlike Pownall, favoured a much more rigid policy toward the colonies—sought to place the House of Commons on record to that end. As a result, Grenville moved on May 15:

> "That, for the better securing the Dependency of His Majesty's Dominions in America, upon the Crown and Parliament of Great Britain, all Persons within His Majesty's said Dominions, who shall be elected or appointed Governor, Member of the Council, General Assembly, House of Representatives, or General Court, of any Province within the same; and also all other Persons within the same, who, by any Charter, Act of Parliament, or Provincial Law, are required to take the Oaths of Allegiance and Abjuration, be required to subscribe a Declaration; [as follows:] 'That the Colonies and Plantations in America are, and of Right ought to be, subordinate unto, and dependent upon, the Imperial Crown and Parliament of Great Britain; and that the King's Majesty, by and with the Advice and Consent of the Lords Spiritual and Temporal, and Commons of Great Britain, in Parliament assembled, had, hath, and of Right ought to have, full Power and Authority to make Laws and Statutes, of sufficient Force and Validity to bind the Colonies, and People of America, Subjects of the Crown of Great Britain, in all Cases whatsoever.' "[86]

Again the House divided, with but 42 members voting for the motion and 141 against it.[87] Nevertheless, the opposition did enjoy one satisfaction. In line with Grenville's motion that had been

[84] *Parliamentary History,* XVI, 331–41; see also J. A. Schutz: *Thomas Pownall, British Defender of American Liberty. A Study of Anglo-American Relations in the Eighteenth Century* (Glendale, Calif., 1951), 215–17.

[85] *Journals of the House of Commons,* XXXI, 364.

[86] Thomas Bradshaw to Grafton, May 16, 1767, Grafton's *Autobiography,* p. 180.

[87] *Journals of the House of Commons,* XXXI, 364–5.

adopted as the fifth resolution on February 24 of the preceding year,[88] the House of Commons voted unanimously, also on his motion, the following resolution:

> "That an humble Address be presented to His Majesty, that he will be graciously pleased to confer some Marks of His Royal Favour on those Governors and Officers in the several Colonies, who distinguished themselves by their Zeal and Fidelity in supporting the Dignity of the Crown, the just Rights of Parliament, and the supreme Authority of Great Britain over the Colonies, during the Late Disturbances in America."[89]

It was thereupon ordered that those members of the House who were of His Majesty's Privy Council should present the address to the King.[90]

The bill for restraining the government of New York was the subject of careful attention. On May 27, the Solicitor General presented it to the House of Commons, where it was read a second time on June 1, and the following day was referred to a committee of the whole House. On the 11th the House ordered that the prohibition against the transaction of any business should extend to "Bills, Orders, Resolutions, or Votes, of either House of the Assembly. . . ." With the adoption of these amendments the engrossed bill was sent to the House of Lords, which returned it on that 30th with one clarifying amendment, to the effect that the intent of the Act was not meant to prevent the choice of a Speaker for the New York House of Representatives. This was agreed to in the Commons, and on July 2 the King gave the bill his royal assent.[91] When forwarding

[88] This resolution reads: "That the House . . . declare, that all His Majesty's Subjects, residing in the said Colonies, who have manifested their Desire to comply with, or to assist in carrying into execution, any Acts of the Legislature of Great Britain, relating to the British Colonies in North America, have acted as dutiful and loyal Subjects, and are therefore entitled to, and will assuredly have, the Protection of the House of Commons of Great Britain" (*ibid.*, XXX, 602).

[89] *Ibid.*, XXXI, 365.

[90] *Ibid.*

[91] *Ibid.*, XXXI, 387, 392, 395, 402, 417, 418. For the Act, listed as 7 Geo. III, c. 59, see *Statutes at Large*, VII, 242–3. As to the authorship of the Restraining Act, Dr. Nicholas Varga, in his interesting article "The New York Restraining Act: Its Passage and Some Effects, 1766–1768," *New York History*, XXXVII, 233–58, argues (pp. 245–6) in favour of the Earl of Shelburne rather than Charles Townshend. It is certain that after the bill had passed, Shelburne endorsed it to Governor Moore as a relatively mild measure; it is equally certain that Townshend introduced the resolution to the House in favour of restraining the province and that he was a member of the committee called upon to frame the bill. However, since the Solicitor General, Edward Willes, reported the bill from the special committee to the House, it may be presumed that he had a major role in its drafting, doubtless in consultation with Townshend and Shelburne, as Secretary of State for the Southern Department.

the statute to Governor Moore, the Earl of Shelburne tactfully pointed out that while its purpose was to enforce the Assembly's obedience to the terms of the Mutiny Act, the Act had been framed "with that singular Temper and Lenity as to offer that Assembly an opportunity of rectifying their Conduct, and this without involving them in any Disabilities only as the Consequence of further Disobedience. . . ."[92] In New York, Governor Moore made the Act public by proclamation on October 8.[93] But by that time the New York Assembly had reconsidered its position and it was no longer necessary to apply the statute.

On December 19, 1766, when the Governor had prorogued the Assembly upon the completion of its work, he designated March 10, 1767, as the date for it to reassemble. However, by further prorogations, the time was put off until May 27.[94] When the legislators met on that date, the Governor addressed them as follows:

> "As the Act for providing Fuel, Barracks etc. for his Majesty's Troops now quartered in this City, will expire in a few days, I am now to recommend a farther Provision for them, and on the Plan prescribed by the Act of Parliament. I am fully persuaded that on a due consideration, the Impropriety of the Limitations in the Act of Assembly pass'd last year will sufficiently appear; and that this House will with chearfulness provide for the Troops in the manner now expected from them, nor suffer . . . a Reflection on their Proceedings, as can any way be construed to represent them as undeserving of the Favours they have received from the Crown."[95]

Moore's surmise was correct. The Privy Council had on April 13 repealed the Barracks Act of 1766 and no act comparable to it could possibly have received the Governor's approval in view of the wording of the repeal order. Again, the formal action of the Assembly—in indicating that it was accountable solely to its constituents and not to Parliament for its manner of providing for the regular troops—stood alone; no other American assembly had followed its lead. Further, the province was held to be one of the most prosperous among the American colonies; for it was now virtually free of public debt, and its government in receipt of good revenues, as Gage had pointed out in his letter to Shelburne in January 1767, stating:

---

[92] Shelburne to Moore, July 18, 1767, Shelburne Papers, 54:55–7; see also *New York Colonial Documents*, VII, 945.

[93] Moore to Shelburne, October 24, 1767, *ibid.*, 51:761. The proclamation appeared in the *New-York Mercury* on October 19, 1767.

[94] *Journal of the Legislative Council of New York*, pp. 1613–15.

[95] *Ibid.*, pp. 1616–17.

". . . this Province has reaped very considerable Benefits from his Majesty's Troops beyond any other part of America; That it is to the Troops the Traders chiefly owe the Fortunes they have made, the Citizens of this Capital the great Increase of this City, and the Neighbouring Farmers their present opulent Circumstances."[96]

On June 3 the Assembly addressed the Governor in reply to his speech, declaring:

"All Requisitions from the Crown have ever been answered with ready and liberal Grants; and even for the Purpose your Excellency now demands a Supply, we have gone to the very Extent of what we are able to perform. We have last Year expended for quartering His Majesty's Forces in this Colony, above £3500; a Sum we imagine more than equal to the Charge all the Colonies on the Continent are put to on that Account, and we have voted, and are preparing a Bill for granting to His Majesty for quartering His Forces in this Province, £3000. . . ."

After referring to the distressed state of the colony for want of an adequate circulating medium, the address continued:

"In our former Bill we thought some Restrictions necessary in order to a faithful Discharge of the Trust reposed in us: But since these have been construed to our Prejudice, . . . we shall avoid all Manner of Restrictions, hoping, that long before this large Sum is expended, it will be evident that too great a Part of this Burthen is likely to fall on this Colony, and . . . that no more for the future than a due Proportion will be asked from this Colony."[97]

By June 6 the Assembly passed a bill granting "the Sum of three thousand pounds for furnishing Necessaries for the Troops Quartered within this Colony" and sent it to the Council for concurrence. This it received the following day along with the Governor's approval.[98] Thus, although the law made no reference to the Quar-

[96] Gage to Shelburne, January 17, 1767, *Gage Correspondence,* I, 118. Governor Moore's letter to the Earl of Shelburne of February 21, 1767, presented a fairly detailed statement of the public finances of the province. In it he indicated that even in 1767, a difficult year financially, there was a small surplus after all obligations had been met, and in previous years the surplus had been "very Considerable" (Shelburne Papers, 55:165–72).

[97] For this address see *Pennsylvania Gazette,* June 18, 1767. In his reply to the above address the Governor pointed out that "whenever the Demands of the Crown are thought burthensome, a respectful and well grounded Representation . . . cannot fail of obtaining that Relief, which from his Majesty's Justice, and paternal Regard for his People, has always been extended to his most distant Subjects" (*ibid.*).

[98] *Journal of the Legislative Council of New York,* pp. 1618–20; *Laws of New-York, 1691–1773* (2 vols., New York, 1774), II, 495.

tering Act passed by Parliament, it provided funds to furnish all the items specified by the parliamentary statute.[99] In its address the Assembly had made clear that it was not bowing to Parliament but was acceding to a requisition from the Crown, to which it acknowledged full loyalty. A great demonstration of this loyalty, in fact, occurred on June 4, when the anniversary of George III's birthday was celebrated in New York "with great Solemnity." In the morning General Gage reviewed a military parade involving the artillery and the 17th and 18th regiments; at the same time Governor Moore, the members of the Council, the Mayor and members of the Corporation of the City,

> "and most of the other Gentlemen of the City, were assembled in Fort George, where his Majesty's, and many other loyal Health's were drunk, under the Discharge of a Royal Salute from the Fort, which was immediately followed by a Salute of 21 Guns from the Liberty Pole, on which was suspended a Union . . . Elegant Entertainments were given at Fort George and Headquarters by their Excellencies Sir Henry Moore and General Gage. In the evening the most magnificent Fire-Works ever seen in America were played off before a greater Number of Spectators than ever were collected together here before at one Time, on the like or any other Occasion . . . There being also a general Illumination throughout the City."[100]

Despite the celebration it was apparent that the issue of quartering troops persisted in the minds of New Yorkers as well as other colonials and would require settlement at a later date. An unsigned letter on this subject, written by Benjamin Franklin in London, appeared in the colonial papers in June 1767.[101] In it the author, after raising certain questions, dealt as follows with the American Quartering Act:

> "The Act was a production of the same administration that made the stamp-act, and was probably intended to facilitate . . . submission to it. . . . This [act] is therefore to be considered as a law made

[99] For the Act see *The Colonial Laws of New York . . .*, IV, 947.

[100] *New-York Mercury,* June 8, 1767.

[101] The letter in question, first published in the *London Chronicle* of April 9, 1767, was reprinted in the *Pennsylvania Chronicle* on June 8 and in the *New-York Mercury* on June 22, 1767. In the first columns of the same issue of the *London Chronicle* (and also reprinted in the above-mentioned issue of the *Pennsylvania Chronicle*) is a letter to the printer signed "F.B.," also attributed to Franklin, which raised the question whether a "*bare letter* of a Governor of one of our provinces, accusing his People of rebellious *intentions*, is . . . sufficient ground for inflicting penalties on such province. . . ." See V. W. Crane: *Benjamin Franklin's Letters to the Press, 1758–1775* (Chapel Hill, N.C., 1950), pp. 81–6.

> here, directing that the assembly in America should make another law. The propriety of this proceeding has by some been doubted, they having been of opinion that an assembly is a kind of little parliament in America, not an *executive* officer of government, and as such oblig'd to obey and execute orders; that it is in its nature a *deliberative* body; its members are to consider such matters as come before them; and when a law is proposed, they are to weigh well its utility, . . . and determine . . . according to their judgments. If they were oblig'd to make laws right or wrong in obedience to a law made by a superior legislature, they would be of no use as a parliament, their nature would be changed, their constitution destroyed. Indeed the act of parliament itself seems sensible of this. . . . It was therefore look'd upon in America merely as a requisition, which the assemblies were to consider, and comply with or decline, in the whole or in part, as it might happen to suit the different circumstances and abilities of different colonies."

Although the news had reached London of the action being taken by the New York Assembly, the Earl of Shelburne insisted upon sending a copy of the Restraining Act to Governor Moore, as has been stated above, but he indicated that "the Prudent conduct of the Assembly has already rendered the Provisions contained in it unnecessary."[102] Nevertheless, he touched a tender spot when he declared in the same letter: "I entertain no doubt but that the same just spirit of subordination & constitutional obedience to that supreme Legislature . . . will render New York equally worthy with the Rest of His Majestys Provinces of His Majestys favor."[103]

It may be added that from 1767 to 1775 the Assembly made a yearly appropriation for supplying necessaries to the regular

---

[102] On August 23, 1767, Governor Moore wrote to the Board of Trade, enclosing the act making provision for the troops. On February 4, 1768, the Board considered the act of June 1767 and did not find it liable to the objections raised against the Barracks Act of 1766 and so stated in their representation to the Privy Council. On May 6 the Restraining Act of Parliament came under the consideration of the Board and a representation relating to it was agreed upon. This representation was referred to the Lords of the Committee on May 11 and on June 28 the New York Supply Act of 1767 was referred to the Attorney General and the Solicitor General to report upon. A report was issued by them on July 24 to the effect that the New York Assembly had made "such a compliance with the said Act of Parliament as can give validity to all Acts and Proceedings of the said Assembly subsequent to the first of October, 1767" [when the Restraining Act was to go into force]. On August 12, the Privy Council agreed that the New York Assembly by its conduct was restored to its former activity and no longer was under restraint. See Board of Trade *Journal, 1764–1767,* p. 417; *ibid., 1768–1775,* pp. 9 and 27, and *Acts of the Privy Council, Col. Ser.,* 1766–1783, pp. 137–9; for a copy of the report of the Attorney General and the Solicitor General, see Shelburne Papers, 61:713–14.

[103] Shelburne to Moore, July 18, 1767, *New York Colonial Documents,* VII, 945.

troops.[104] John Watts, New York merchant and member of the Governor's Council, writing to former Governor Monckton on January 23, 1768, declared: "This Colony is grown the quintessence of moderation, all its neighbours are writing inflamatory papers, while our poor printers would starve if it was not for the dirty trade of copying [articles from other papers] which they are forced to submit for want of originals."[105] But all was not serene in the Province of New York. The statement by Watts in no way reflected the economic problems there, nor the serious situation of the colony's finances due to a lack of paper money, the last of which was due to be called in by November 1768. When the new Assembly met in that month the temper of things had changed. On the 24th, in an open letter to their representatives in the General Assembly, the "Freeholders and Freemen of the city and county of New-York" charged that the "Act of Parliament laying you under this severe inhibition, is, we conceive, more oppressive and dangerous in its consequences, than was the pernicious Stamp-Act . . . nor can we comprehend the difference (as to taxation only) between a law compelling our Representatives to levy taxes on us, or by taxing us directly without the consent of such Representatives."[106]

By December the deputies to the Assembly were addressing petitions to the mother country voicing their general dissatisfaction over the attempts of Parliament to raise a revenue in the colonies, and over the threat to the integrity of the colonial legislature posed by the Restraining Act, among other inequities complained of, and were passing resolutions couched in the strongest terms objecting to these and other infringements upon their rights.[107] As a result

[104] For acts passed December 21, 1767; December 31, 1768; May 20, 1769; January 5, 1770; February 16, 1771; February 26, 1772; and March 8, 1773 see *Laws of New-York, 1691–1773*, II, 496, 514, 536, 554, 601, 633, 773; for January–March 1774 see *Journal of the Votes and Proceedings of the General Assembly of New-York* (New York, 1774; reprinted Albany, 1820), pp. 22, 23, 43–4, 47, 88.

[105] For this letter see the Chalmers Collection; it is printed in the "Aspinwall Papers," Part 2, Massachusetts Historical Society *Collections*, 4th ser., X, 600.

[106] For this letter see *Boston Chronicle*, December 5–12, 1768.

[107] For the representation of the New York General Assembly presented to the House of Commons on March 14, 1769, by Barlow Trecothick, but refused a hearing by the Commons, see *Parliamentary History*, XVI, 603–5, and *Journals of the House of Commons*, XXXII, 312. For a full treatment of the proceedings in the New York Assembly in December 1768, in connection with reaction to the Massachusetts Bay circular letter of that year, see Chapter 6 of this volume, which will serve to clarify Carl Becker's analysis of this situation as part of what he called "The Economic Crisis of 1768–1770" in his *History of Political Parties*, Chap. 3, and in which he further suggests that fears of "the substitution of arbitrary military rule for the existing government" helped to produce the revival of activities by the Sons of Liberty at this juncture.

of these resolutions Governor Moore dissolved the Assembly.[108] The new Assembly elected in 1769 did not reflect the coming split between radical and conservative, but it did not hesitate to use the threat of a refusal to vote provisions for the British troops as a means of trying to secure the approval of the Privy Council to a bill for issuing paper money redeemable at the provincial loan office of their issuance and at the colonial treasury in support of the provincial government. Although the New York act gave the bills limited legal-tender value, as redeemable only at the loan office or the treasury, the Privy Council refused its assent both in 1769 and in January 1770, when substantially the same bill was again submitted for approval. However, when the London agent for the province, Robert Charles, petitioned the House of Commons in April 1770 to permit the New York Assembly to issue such paper money, Parliament passed a bill to this effect, which became law on May 19. Thus, a British act of Parliament made possible the emission of legal tender in New York with which to satisfy the British Mutiny (or Quartering) Act—a concession on both sides whereby Parliament permitted the issuance of such money by a colony in return for recognition of its supreme authority.[109] But resentment in New York over the Quartering Act was not yet dead.

In December 1769 a handbill appeared in New York addressed *To the Betrayed Inhabitants of the City and Colony of New-York.* Signed "A Son of Liberty," it was written by the radical leader Alexander McDougall. This broadside denounced the "Minions of Tyranny and Despotism in the Mother Country, and the Colonies [who] are indefatigable in laying every Snare that their malevolent and corrupt Hearts can suggest, to enslave a free People." In particular his attack was directed against the de Lancey family for throwing its influence in the Assembly in favour of continuing to make grants for the troops.[110] This was followed by

[108] *New York Colonial Documents,* VIII, 143.

[109] The question of a colonial currency will be dealt with in part in Chapter 3 and in full at the end of Chapter 8 of this volume. For an excellent account of the currency problem in New York see J. M. Sosin: "Imperial Regulation of Colonial Paper Money, 1764–1773," *Pennsylvania Magazine of History and Biography,* LXXXVIII, 194–6, in which he points out (p. 196) that Thomas Hutchinson emphasized the importance of Parliament's taking the initiative in providing the authority for the New York currency as demonstration of its supremacy.

[110] A copy of this handbill (not listed by Evans) is in the New York Public Library; see also *Documentary History of the State of New York* (ed. E. B. O'Callaghan, 4 vols., Albany, 1849–51), III, 317–21. In reply to "A Son of Liberty" came *A Citizen's Address to the Public,* in which it was argued that it was for the interest of the province to co-operate with the mother country by helping with the support of the troops so that, among other benefits to be received, there might be a relaxa-

another broadside *By a Plebeian To the Public,* in which the writer contended that the New York City representatives in the Assembly went against the views of the majority of their constituents, whose real feelings were expressed by such leading Sons of Liberty as John Lamb and Isaac Sears, opposed as they were to making any provision for the troops.[111] Yet, the McDougall pamphlet, *To the Betrayed Inhabitants . . .* was denounced in resolutions passed *nemine contradicente* by the Assembly as "a false, seditious and infamous Libel," and Lieutenant Governor Colden was requested to issue a proclamation offering a reward of £100 for the discovery of the author of it.[112] This was done. As a result, McDougall, having refused bail upon his arrest, spent most of the time between the middle of February and the middle of April 1770 in gaol, was subsequently treated by his fellow Sons of Liberty as a martyr to a great and good cause, and was dubbed the "Wilkes of America."[113]

The stand of New Yorkers by the end of 1769 was only part of a trend against parliamentary controls which had its active focal point in Massachusetts Bay. However, the outbursts due to erupt against the Townshend legislation would not fail to make use of Parliament's passage of the Restraining Act for bringing New York to heel as an additional example of an oppressive measure. But before examining the colonial resistance that sprang up in 1767 to 1768, the part played by Charles Townshend in the Pitt-Grafton Ministry and the impact of his revenue program upon the North American colonies warrants investigation.

---

tion of the restrictions on paper currency. Its author referred to the "extreme and contemptable" charges by the "vile and infamous Author" and charged that he was "afraid to shew his Face." In defence of the New York City representatives he emphasized the fact that the Assembly voted "unanimously" to grant money to the troops and that the only difference was in the manner in which it should be done. A copy of this broadside is owned by the New-York Historical Society.

[111] A copy of this pamphlet is in the New-York Historical Society Library.

[112] For the resolution of the Assembly and the proclamation see *Documentary History of New York,* III, 321–2.

[113] For a contemporary account of the McDougall libel episode see *Historical Memoirs . . . 1763–1776 of William Smith . . .* pp. 71–6; see also *New York Colonial Documents,* VIII, 208. For a conservative view of the McDougall affair see E. P. Alexander: *A Revolutionary Conservative: James Duane of New York* (New York, 1938), pp. 95–6.

CHAPTER III

Charles Townshend Moves to the Front

BEFORE the outbreak of hostilities with France in 1754, one of the striking characteristics of the British Empire had been the basic harmony that existed between the mother country and the colonies. This had lasted almost to the close of the Great War for the Empire, but had been brought to an end by parliamentary legislation passed during the Grenville Ministry's period of power. One of the chief aims of the Rockingham administration in 1766—once it had accomplished the repeal of the Stamp Act—was to restore good relations within the Empire, but it was forced to devote as much effort to maintaining harmony within the administration itself.

The three men of weight in the Ministry were Charles Watson-Wentworth, 2nd Marquess of Rockingham, First Lord of the Treasury; Augustus Henry Fitzroy, 3rd Duke of Grafton, Secretary of State for the Northern Department; and Henry Seymour Conway, Secretary of State for the Southern Department and leader in the House of Commons. Although Conway was forty-five years of age when he took office, Rockingham was but thirty-five, Grafton thirty, and their King, George III, twenty-seven. These young and comparatively inexperienced men had to encounter in opposition such able veterans in public affairs as George Grenville, fifty-three; his brother Richard, Earl Temple, fifty-four; and John Russell, 4th Duke of Bedford, fifty-five.

Among the difficulties the Rockingham administration had to face from the beginning was its weakness in not having within the Ministry the man most admired and respected by the two Secretaries of State. The Secretaries held the view that any administration formed without William Pitt could be neither strong nor lasting. Their conviction was doubtless strengthened when, early in 1766, the Great Commoner took the lead in the House of Commons in openly advocating the repeal of the Stamp Act, while the King's chief minister, Rockingham, although receptive to the idea, remained inactive in the House of Lords. Grafton and Conway felt that, at this critical juncture, the country needed a dynamic leader, such as Pitt had been during most of the war years. Clearly Rockingham was not that type. Recognizing this himself, he began his attempts to turn over the leadership to Pitt,[1] making the overtures plain—provided that "a system might be previously settled" that would prevent the administration from "breaking to pieces."[2] Grafton and Conway naturally gave hearty support to his appeal. However, Pitt very properly replied to this overture that, while he felt highly honoured by the invitation, his duty to the King forbad him to engage in any negotiations without His Majesty's express commands.[3] Behind this reply was also the intimation that there would have to be certain changes in the Ministry before he could consider joining it.[4] Rockingham, his suspicions now aroused, turned against Pitt, especially as he was made to realize that he could no longer count on Grafton and Conway's loyalty and would be expected—were Pitt to join the Ministry—to relinquish the post of First Lord of the Treasury with its control of the Secret Service money. Although he and Pitt had agreed on the necessity for the repeal of the Stamp Act, he had differed fundamentally with the Great Commoner over the affirmation by the Declaratory Act of the authority of Parliament to make laws of sufficient force and validity to bind the colonies and inhabitants thereof "in all cases whatsoever"—a pronouncement which he felt must go hand in hand with the Stamp Act Repeal Act but which Pitt had consistently and vigorously opposed in the course of the debates. The negotiations, especially in view of the negative attitude of George III, were therefore dropped.[5]

---

[1] Grafton: *Autobiography and Political Correspondence of Augustus Henry Third Duke of Grafton* (ed. Sir William R. Anson, London, 1898), pp. 62–8, cited hereafter as Grafton's *Autobiography*, and *Pitt Correspondence*, II, 371–3.

[2] Memorandum of a conference held by Mr. Nuthall, Solicitor of the Treasury, with Lord Rockingham, February 26, 1766, *ibid.*, II, 397–8.

[3] For this reply see *ibid.* II, 398–401.

[4] Pitt laid down two conditions: one was that Newcastle must retire from the Ministry; the other, that Rockingham must give up the Treasury in favour of Lord Temple. See *A Narrative of the Changes in the Ministry, 1765–1767, told by the Duke of Newcastle in a Series of Letters to John White, M.P.* (ed. Mary Bateson, Royal Historical Society, London and New York, 1898), Camden Second Series, LIX, 44, cited hereafter as Newcastle's *Changes in the Ministry*.

[5] See *Memoirs of the Marquis of Rockingham . . .* (ed. George Thomas, Earl of Albemarle, 2 vols., London, 1852), I, 271; see also Lord Edmund Fitzmaurice:

With the passing of the Declaratory Act and the repeal of the Stamp Act, the Rockingham administration turned to self-analysis. It was clear that many of its members had openly fought the plan of repeal to which the Ministry had been committed. However, the King opposed any reprisals against them and they therefore remained in office. Rockingham hoped that with the disposal of this major issue these men would now support the government in other measures, as in the issue over general warrants. But, according to the Marquess, "the carrying of that measure produced no change in their conduct, and their opposition continued as systematic and violent as before."[6] All this seemed to indicate that the King, while theoretically giving the Ministry his support, was simultaneously offering protection to opposition office-holders. Late in April the Duke of Newcastle warned Rockingham that a movement seemed to be on foot to dissolve the administration.[7] That he was right is indicated by letters exchanged at this time by Conway and Grafton, in which the General urged the Duke not to give up his post. Grafton's reply revealed that he had quite lost sympathy with Rockingham after a conference at which it became apparent that there "was now no hesitation in him to declare that *he would never advise His Majesty to call Mr. Pitt into his closet, that this was a fixed resolution to which he would adhere.*"[8]

Pitt, at this juncture of affairs, displayed great bitterness in the House of Commons toward the Ministry. Even his staunch admirer Conway had to admit "the unprovoked violence with which Mr. Pitt is said to have arraign'd the Administration on the slightest occasion, . . . with as much passion, as if the highest provokation had been offerr'd him."[9] Pitt's aim was manifestly to topple the administration, and his first success in this direction was the Duke of Grafton's resignation on April 28.[10] The post was offered to Lord

---

Life of William, Earl of Shelburne . . . (3 vols., London, 1875–6), I, 375; Grafton's *Autobiography*, pp. 63–8; and *Pitt Correspondence*, II, 371–2.

[6] *Memoirs of the Marquis of Rockingham* . . . , I, 321.

[7] Newcastle, writing to Rockingham on April 22, referred to long conferences the preceding day carried on in the House of Lords between Lord Camden, Chancellor Northington, and the Duke of Grafton; see *ibid.*

[8] For Conway to Grafton, April 22, Grafton to Conway, of the same date, and Conway to Grafton, April 23, 1766, see Grafton's *Autobiography*, pp. 70–3. The words in italics are underlined in the *Autobiography*.

[9] Conway to Grafton, April 16, 1766, *ibid.*, pp. 86–7.

[10] The King to the Lord Chancellor, [April 28, 1766], *The Correspondence of King George The Third* . . . (ed. Sir John Fortescue, 6 vols., London, 1927–8), I, 295, to be cited hereafter as *Correspondence of George III* (Fortescue). In using this volume the student should have on hand Sir Lewis Namier: *Additions and Corrections to Sir John Fortescue's Edition of The Correspondence of King George The Third* (Manchester, 1937).

Hardwicke, who promptly declined it.[11] Although the King objected strongly to Rockingham's proposal to appoint the Duke of Richmond, he finally gave way when the Marquess asserted that he himself could not stay in office unless Conway kept one seal and the Duke of Richmond got the other.[12] Richmond took over the post of Secretary of State for the Northern Department on May 23.[13] On the 28th Grafton, now out of office, took part in the debate in the House of Lords over the window tax, which he defended. He took the occasion to stress the need of the government for "authority, dignity, and extension," adding that if Pitt would give his "assistance," and become a part of an administration formed with his concurrence, he (Grafton) would "with pleasure take up the spade and the pick-axe, and dig in the trenches. . . ."[14] Lord Chancellor Northington, although remaining in the Ministry, was equally unhappy over its weakness but did nothing to help strengthen it; rather, he encouraged the King in the view that it must soon terminate.[15]

The Duke of Richmond sought to strengthen the Ministry by of-

---

[11] Hardwicke to Charles Yorke (his brother), May 14, 1766, *Memoirs of the Marquis of Rockingham,* I, 330–1. The King was also favourable to giving the office to Charles Yorke but Hardwicke discouraged him. See *ibid.*, I, 331–3.

[12] The King to Lord Egmont, [May 16, 1766], *Correspondence of George III* (Fortescue), I, 307. It is of interest to note that both Secretaries of State now were professional soldiers—Richmond in 1761 obtained the rank of major general and in 1770 that of lieutenant general.

[13] The London *Gazetteer and New Daily Advertiser* in its May 3 edition stated: "It was yesterday very confidently asserted, . . . that the Duke of Grafton had resigned, and was to be succeeded by the Duke of Richmond"; in its edition of May 9 it indicated that, among other changes in the Ministry, the Earl of Egmont would take the post of the Duke of Grafton; then in its edition of May 19 it stated that the Duke of Richmond "is still confidently talked of, to succeed the late Duke of Grafton, as one of the Secretaries of State."

[14] T. Nuthall to Pitt, May 29, 1766, *Pitt Correspondence,* II, 421–2. Grafton, in his *Autobiography* (p. 74), says that in this speech he pleaded "for a junction of the ablest and most experienced statesmen" and that "if every one would join with me in declaring they would take up the mattock and spade in so good a cause, it would be soon accomplished."

[15] For example, when Jeremiah Dyson, a member of the Board of Trade and also a member of Parliament, attempted on June 3 to block a ministerial measuse and was defeated in the attempt, Rockingham went to the King to beg him to dismiss Dyson from his office. See *Memoirs of the Marquis of Rockingham,* I, 346. On Northington's recommendation of June 5 to His Majesty not to dismiss Dyson, the Lord Chancellor wrote: "I think with Regard to Mr. Dyson, that as Your Majesty seems to consider Your Ministry as not able to continue, It would not be a proper Chrisis to remove Him, for that may tend at the close of a Session, to imply an Approbation [of the Ministry] which Your Majesty doth not seem to entertain; But on the other Hand, if You intend them to go on with their present Business they must have, for they want, all Support. I return . . . the Papers, & have destroyed Your Note" (*Correspondence of George III* [Fortescue,] I, 356). Dyson continued in office.

fering appointments to a number of the Earl of Bute's friends. But Rockingham and Newcastle would have none of it.[16]

Another minister, the Earl of Egmont, First Lord of the Admiralty, appears to have been equally opposed to Rockingham's continuation at the head of the administration. According to Rockingham, it was not

> "by storms, but by hidden shoals and false beacons, that the Whig vessel was doomed to founder. Secret negociations for its destruction were set on foot immediately after the prorogation [of Parliament on June 6]. The first agent for this service was John Percival, Earl of Egmont."[17]

According to the Duke of Richmond's "Journal," Egmont's conversations with others disclosed that he held the Rockingham administration "very cheap,"[18] thus helping to lower its standing.

But it was the Lord High Chancellor, the Earl of Northington, a confidant of the King, who set off "the mine laid for the demolition of our weak Ministerial fabric."[19] The issue that arose within the Cabinet had to do with Canada. The government of the new Province of Quebec, as has been indicated in a preceding volume of this series,[20] was in need of reorganization. Theoretically based upon the Proclamation of 1763, the administration, manifestly defective, was in fact based upon *ordonnances* issued by the Governor and Council, to some of which the Board of Trade in England took exception. There was also (as will be discussed in a later volume of this series) much discontent within the province itself. The papers having to do with this discontent were therefore referred by the Ministry to Attorney General Charles Yorke and Solicitor General William de Grey to report upon, and to suggest a reorganization of this government. When the report, in the form of "a plan for the Civil Government of Quebec,"[21] was submitted to the Cabinet for consideration, Lord Chancellor Northington, according to Lord Hardwicke's "Memoriall," declared "his absolute dislike to it, . . . and was absolutely for doing nothing till we had a complete

[16] See the long "Memorandum," largely concerned with events in June, written by Richmond early in July 1766, which appears edited by A. G. Olson in the *English Historical Review*, LXXV, 475–82.

[17] Rockingham to Sir George Savile, "towards the . . . end of May," 1766, *Memoirs of the Marquis of Rockingham*, I, 347.

[18] Quoted in *ibid.*, I, 349.

[19] *Ibid.*, I, 350.

[20] See Volume IX of this series, pp. 162–76.

[21] The substance of the report was ultimately embodied in the Quebec Act of 1774.

code of the laws of Canada sent over." The meeting held toward the end of June in Northington's home broke up in great confusion. When the Lord Chancellor declared he would attend no more meetings of the Cabinet, the Ministry was doomed.[22]

While there seems to be little doubt that George III had lost faith in the Ministry and had been seeking to bring it to an end—although still seeming to support it—it was Lord Chancellor Northington, with the support of Chief Justice Lord Camden, who undertook, at the King's desire, to open the way for Pitt to come in.[23] On July 5 Northington announced to the King that he wished to give up the Great Seal, "declaring openly what he had done," but not giving the Ministers any formal notification of his intention.[24] The following day the King addressed a letter to the Lord Chancellor in which His Majesty recounted a conversation he had just had with Lord Rockingham about Northington's contemplated retirement from the Ministry unless it "could have a more enlarg'd foundation . . ."; mentioning the Earl of Egmont's feeling that the administration was "too feeble," he voiced his own that a new administration ought to be organized "on a more enlarged foot." With this letter the King also placed in the Lord Chancellor's hands a letter to Pitt requesting him to come to town in order to give his thoughts on "how an Able & Dignify'd Ministry may be form'd."[25] The Great Commoner responded with alacrity—"happy could I change Infirmity into Wings of Expedition, the sooner to be permitted The high Honour to lay at your Majesty's Feet the poor but sincere offering of the small Services of Your Majesty's most dutifull Subject and most devoted Servant."[26] Acting with equal alacrity, he arrived in London on the 11th and, in an interview with North-

[22] For the Hardwicke "Memoriall" see *Memoirs of the Marquis of Rockingham,* I, 350–1; see also the quotation from the Duke of Richmond's "Journal" under date-line of June 27, 1766, *ibid.,* I, 351–5, and Hardwicke to Rockingham, June 30, 1766, *ibid.,* I, 355–6, for additional light on the crisis meeting of the Cabinet. Attorney General Yorke was Hardwicke's brother.

[23] For confirmation of the above view see George III to Bute [July 12, 1766], *Letters from George III to Lord Bute, 1756–1766* (ed. Romney Sedgwick, London, 1939), pp. 250–4. Rockingham, after his return from the King's closet, wrote to Newcastle that it was "Lord Cambden and the Chancellor negotiated this affair" (Newcastle Papers, B.M., Add. Mss. 32976, folio 103).

[24] Horace Walpole: *Memoirs of the Reign of King George the Third* (ed. Sir. Denis Le Marchant, 2 vols., Philadelphia, 1845), I, 410. Although the pagination in the Philadelphia edition varies from that in the London first edition, it was published from the original manuscript and will be used throughout this volume, cited hereafter as Walpole's *Memoirs of George III.*

[25] *Correspondence of George III* (Fortescue), I, 367–8; see also Namier's *Additions and Corrections to . . . Fortescue's Edition of The Correspondence . . . ,* p. 59.

[26] *Pitt Correspondence,* II, 436 and 438.

ington, expressed his desire to have Lord Temple with him in any administration he might form, but not Grenville, and spoke of "preserving many of the present [ministers]."[27]

Meanwhile, earlier in the week, when the ministers severally appeared in the royal closet, each of them was informed by His Majesty that Pitt had been summoned. Both Rockingham and Newcastle, according to the King, were "thunderstruck" at the news. Apparently George III had words of appreciation only for Conway.[28]

But all was not immediately clear sailing for Pitt. At his desire Lord Temple, his brother-in-law, had—presumably at the command of the King—been summoned to London by Northington.[29] Whether or not Temple misread the true meaning of the royal invitation is not clear.[30] But he left no doubt that were he to take the office of First Lord of the Treasury, which the King now offered him,[31] he would expect to have the authority and influence which had customarily gone with it. Instead, he was—as he later complained to his brother George Grenville—set up as "a capital cypher, surrounded with cyphers of quite a different complexion, the whole under the guidance of that great Luminary, the great Commoner, with the Privy Seal in his hand."[32] Nor was this all that led him to decline office. For he was made to realize that he would be surrounded in the Ministry by those "most choice spirits who did in the last Session most eminently distinguish themselves in the sacrifice of the rights and honour of the whole Legislature and Kingdom of Great Britain"—referring of course to those reponsible for the repeal of the Stamp Act.[33] In fact, the question may be raised whether either Pitt or the King really wanted Temple in the government.[34] To the Earl his return home ended "this po-

[27] Northington to the King [July 11, 1766], *Correspondence of George III* (Fortescue), I, 371.

[28] George III to Bute [July 12, 1766], *op. cit.*, 250–4; see also Walpole's *Memoirs of George III*, I, 411. For additional details on the change of Ministers see *Horace Walpole's Correspondence with Sir Horace Mann* (ed. W. S. Lewis *et al.*, 6 vols., New Haven, 1954–60), VI, 431–4 (this is Vol. 22 of the Yale edition of *Horace Walpole's Correspondence* and is cited hereafter as *Walpole-Mann Correspondence*); see also *Letters of Horace Walpole* (ed. Mrs. Paget Toynbee, 16 vols., Oxford, 1903–5), VII, 13, and Newcastle's *Changes in the Ministry*, previously cited.

[29] The Lord Chancellor to Temple, July 13, 1766, *Grenville Papers*, III, 263.

[30] See Temple to the Lord Chancellor, July 14, 1766, *ibid.*, III, 263–4.

[31] See the King to Pitt, July 15, 1766, *Pitt Correspondence*, II, 443–4.

[32] Temple to Grenville, July 18, 1766, *Grenville Papers*, III, 267–8.

[33] *Ibid.*

[34] While Pitt was still negotiating with Temple, he had sent for the Duke of Grafton. See Conway to Pitt, July 15, 1766, *Pitt Correspondence*, II, 446–7.

litical farce of my journey to town, as it was always intended. . . ."[35]

With this family obligation accounted for, Pitt was now free to build an administration of men who would accept his authority, as he had already amply reason to believe Temple would not. Among those whom he desired to have in the government, none was more absolutely devoted to him than the young Duke of Grafton, although he was independently wealthy and not ambitious for power. Grafton had left the Rockingham administration in the spring without loss of prestige. It had been made clear to him shortly before reaching London in the middle of July 1766 from his country seat that he was Pitt's choice for the Treasury; he seems to have been equally convinced in his own mind that he should not accept that office. In his interview with Pitt he showed his unwillingness to assume such a responsibility. According to his account of the meeting, after he had stated his own position, Pitt rose and declared with evidence of deep disappointment "that his whole attempt to relieve the country and His Majesty was at an end. . . ." In the face of this Grafton felt compelled to give way, although "as firmly persuaded as ever, how little suited the post was to my inexperience and my feelings."[36] With the way now cleared for the establishment of the new Ministry, the King announced on July 23 to Rockingham and Newcastle that he had entered into "new arrangements" for carrying on the government.[37] On that same day it was agreed that Grafton should succeed Rockingham at the Treasury, Pitt replace Newcastle as Lord Privy Seal, Camden take over the Chancellorship held by Northington, with the latter despite ill health to become Lord President of the Council in place of the Earl of Winchilsea, and the Earl of Shelburne to displace Richmond as Secretary of State. Conway, remaining as the other Secretary of State,

---

[35] *Grenville Papers,* III, 268. The best account of the Pitt-Temple conference, undoubtedly from Earl Temple, is in [Humphrey Cotes:] *An Enquiry into the conduct of a late Right Honourable Commoner* (London, 1766). An "Extract" from this pamphlet covering the conference appeared in the 30th of October edition of the *Pennsylvania Gazette.* Temple sought to bring into the administration Lord Lyttelton, as Lord President, and Lord Gower as a Secretary of State. Lord Lyttelton in 1765 had refused the post of First Lord of the Treasury out of loyalty to Pitt. For an excellent life, written as a doctoral dissertation at Columbia University, see Rose Mary Davis: *The Good Lord Lyttelton. A Study in Eighteenth Century Politics and Culture* (Bethlehem, Penn., 1939). For the circumstances of Lyttleton's refusal of the Treasury see pp. 347–8.

[36] Grafton's *Autobiography,* p. 89–91. In view of the great responsibilities involved in the office of First Lord of the Treasury and Grafton's comparative youth, his love of pleasure, and his wealth, the views that he expressed to Pitt were doubtless sincere.

[37] Newcastle to Conway, July 23, 1766, Newcastle Papers, B.M., Add. Mss. 32976, folio 213.

was ordered by the King on July 28 to perform the embarrassing task of sending letters of dismissal to his colleagues, Rockingham, Newcastle, Richmond, Winchilsea, and Dowdeswell.[38]

The political immaturity of the Duke of Grafton—which he himself had recognized earlier—soon became evident; for it was he who persuaded Pitt, against the latter's better judgment, to appoint that dazzling figure Charles Townshend to fill the post of Chancellor of the Exchequer, vacated upon the dismissal of William Dowdeswell.[39] Yet Grafton may be pardoned in light of the fact that his friend Conway, who continued in the new Ministry as Secretary of State and was held in high esteem by Pitt, also held the view that Townshend was the only acceptable man with the requisite abilities to fill the duties of the office. It was also Conway who later, upon Townshend's death, delivered in the House of Commons a panegyric on his talents.[40] In fact, even Pitt himself seems to have been persuaded that, after all, it was better to have so formidable a figure within the Ministry than as an opponent of it. Writing to Townshend with a certain brusqueness and hauteur, yet in a vein designed to impress him favourably, Pitt declared: "Sir, you are of too great a magnitude not to be in a responsible place: I intend to propose you to the King to-morrow for Chancellor of the Exchequer, and must desire to have your answer to-night by nine o'clock."[41] At first Townshend refused to consider the change of posts—which meant that he would be obliged to surrender his office of Paymaster-General, yielding £7,000 a year, for one that brought but £2,500 to £2,700—but he finally yielded and on July 30, with the other chief appointees, kissed the King's hand. Respecting his talents yet fearing them, Pitt had determined that Townshend, although a minister, should not be of the Cabinet.[42]

[38] The King to Conway, July 28, 1766, *Correspondence of George III* (Fortescue), I, 384.

[39] See Grafton's *Autobiography*, p. 92.

[40] For Conway's tribute to Townshend see Debrett's *History, Debates and Proceedings of Both Houses of Parliament . . . 1743 to . . . 1774* (7 vols., London, 1792), IV, 474. The historian John Adolphus agreed with Conway on Townshend's talents in his *The History of England from the Accession . . . of King George the Third* (3rd edn., 7 vols., London, 1840–5), I, 304–5. The most penetrating studies of Townshend are by the late Sir Lewis Namier in his Leslie Stephen Lecture: *Charles Townshend. His Character and Career* (Cambridge, 1959), and his collaborations with John Brooke: *Charles Townshend* (London, 1964) and *History of Parliament: The House of Commons, 1754–1790* (3 vols., London and New York, 1964), III, 539–48.

[41] For this notification to Townshend see Walpole's *Memoirs of George III*, I, 416. The letter was undoubtedly written prior to July 21. See Grafton to Pitt, [July 21], and Townshend to Pitt, July 22, 1766, *Pitt Correspondence*, II. 452 and 456.

[42] See Grafton to Pitt, [July 25], Townshend to Grafton, [July 25], the King to Pitt, July 25, and Townshend to Pitt, July 26, 1766, *ibid.*, II, 459–65.

An event of equal importance to the inclusion of Charles Townshend in the Ministry was the following announcement:

> "St. James's, July 30. The King has been pleased to grant unto the right honourable William Pitt, Esq. and his heirs male, the dignity of a viscount and earl of Great Britain, by the titles of viscount Pitt of Burton Pynsent, and earl of Chatham, in the county of Kent."[43]

Writing on August 1 to his friend Horace Mann in Florence, Horace Walpole summed up the situation laconically: "Well! Europe must have done talking of Mr. Pitt; there is no longer such a man. He is lord privy seal and Earl of Chatham. I don't know how Europe will like it, but the City and the mob are very angry."[44] The Earl of Chesterfield, referring to Pitt's peerage, declared prophetically:

> "The joke here is, that he has had a *fall up stairs,* and has done himself so much hurt, that he will never be able to stand upon his legs again. . . . To withdraw, in the fullness of his power, and in the utmost gratification of his ambition, from the House of Commons, (which procured him his power, and which alone could insure it to him) . . . is a measure so unaccountable, that nothing but proof positive could have made me believe it."

Chesterfield was inclined to attribute this crucial error in judgment on the part of Pitt to the influence of the Earl of Bute.[45] The repercussions of the disgust at Pitt's action reached America. The *Boston Evening-Post* of September 29, 1766, printed the following biting "Intelligence Extraordinary" from London:

> "We hear that the new Chancellor [Lord Camden] will be applied to for a commission of Lunacy against the Earl of Chatham, and that the City of London are to sue it out.
>
> "The Pitt, a First Rate [ship] being much damaged in the Head in a late Cruise on the Coast of Scotland, is paid off and laid up at Chatham [shipyard], where she is to serve as a Storeship. On examination, her timbers, which were supposed to have been true English Heart of Oak, turn out to be nothing more than mere Scantlings of a rotten Scotch Fir, brought up by the Favourite from Mount Stuart in Bute-shire & Hewn out by him into a proper Form, at his Dock-Yard, near the Pay-Office, Westminster."

In justice to Pitt it should be pointed out that he was in no physi-

[43] *Ibid.*, III, 21*n.*

[44] *Walpole-Mann Correspondence,* VI, 442–3.

[45] Chesterfield to his son, August 1, 1766, *Letters of Phillip Dormer Stanhope, 4th Earl of Chesterfield* (ed. Bonamy Dobrée, 6 vols., London, 1932), VI, 2752–3. (This edition incorporates the two-volume 1774 edition of Chesterfield's *Letters . . . to His Son . . .*).

cal condition—without raising any question as to his mental condition—to bear the burden of any active office of great responsibility, much less leadership in the House of Commons, in the brilliant fashion that had characterized his preceding administration. It is also apparent that he counted heavily on his prestige and popularity throughout the Empire as a heroic figure. However, to give effective guidance to the affairs of state from the sidelines—by occupying an office which, as constituted, was largely a sinecure,[46] and by taking a seat in the House of Lords, a body isolated from the people—proved to be an impossibility, especially in view of the new Earl's precarious state of health and his consequent inaccessibility to his supporters.

The Chatham administration brought to Great Britain and the Empire none of the anticipated results—that it would produce a government wise in statecraft, permanent, and popular. In reflecting on the course of events the student of eighteenth-century British history soon realizes that those who advised the King to withdraw his confidence from the Marquess of Rockingham and to place it in Chatham were hopelessly deluded. For they were asking him to believe that a man who "knew nothing of financial or commercial matters," and who was by 1766 a confirmed invalid, was competent to lead the country in what seemed to be a rather prosaic yet important task, that of extricating the state from the huge load of debt, while continuing to strengthen the bonds that tied the colonies to the mother country. Nevertheless, it is understandable why Grafton, Northington, Camden, and others acted as they did. They still had before them the image of the man who had performed prodigies in the course of the Great War for the Empire; they still were under the spell of a person who had proved to be one of the greatest orators of all time, especially in his ability to sway and dominate an audience of highly sophisticated and educated men such as had faced him in the House of Commons for many years;[47] they still

[46] Thinking that some readers might not know about the functions of the Great Officers of Crown, the London *Gazetteer and New Daily Advertiser* in the issue of August 21, 1766, gave the following account of the office of the Lord Privy Seal among others: "The Lord Keeper of his Majesty's Privy Seal is a Privy Councellor by his office, which is to keep the King's Privy Seal, and to set it to all charters and grants of the King, and pardons signed by him, before they come to the Great Seal; and to other things of less concern, as, for the payment of money, etc. which do not pass by the great seal." It may be added that most of the work of the office was done by others although certain documents had to carry the signature of the Lord Privy Seal. The salary attached to it was £3,000, and not £4,000 as was reported at the time.

[47] The student is referred to the important study by G. P. Judd, IV: *Members of Parliament, 1734–1832* (Yale Historical *Publications, Miscellany,* 61, New Haven and London, 1955), Chaps, 6, 7, and 8.

"Wentworth House in Yorkshire, the Seat of the Marquis of Rockingham."

"The Cock Pit," engraved by G. Presbury from the original by William Hogarth.

had vividly in mind that it was Pitt who—despite his physical infirmities and the further fact that he was not in the Ministry—had early that same year exhibited his magic power of swaying the House of Commons to determine the line of action that Parliament would take on the grave issue of American taxation.

No one can say with assurance what would have been the fate of the Old British Empire had the Rockingham Ministry remained in power for the decade following the summer of 1766 and had it been permitted by George III to carry out its policies. Certainly it had at hand a handsome majority in the House of Commons and seemed to enjoy the confidence of the country, if not of the King; it was committed to a policy of reconciling the colonies to British rule; it was opposed to adventurous measures and, one may assume with confidence, neither Rockingham, as chief minister and First Lord of the Treasury, nor Dowdeswell, as Chancellor of the Exchequer,[48] or Conway, as Secretary of State for the Southern Department, which included the colonies, would have revived the issue of American taxation. They had secured the statement of the *right* of Parliament to levy taxes on the colonies in the Declaratory Act. But to them it was a right to be exercised only in exceptional cases, limited in objective and time—for example, the projected plan for placing import duties on one colony simply to provide a fund for the reimbursement of those who had suffered in Boston by the fury of the mob, should the Massachusetts Bay Assembly itself refuse to perform this act of justice.

This is not to say that the Rockingham Ministry or their supporters in and out of Parliament approved in any way the conduct of the colonials who resisted by acts of violence the program of the government of Great Britain requiring them to assist in paying the costs of providing security for North America. So far as the records show, the need for this security was never questioned by any British minister or member of Parliament from the time France had been

[48] Edmund Burke, in the epitaph which is inscribed on the monument of William Dowdeswell, who died in 1775, referred to him as "a man of unshaken constancy, inflexible integrity, unremitted industry: . . . rejecting all sorts of duplicity and disguise as useless to his designs and odious to his nature! . . . his knowledge of all things which concerned his duty, profound: he understood, beyond any man of his time, the revenues of his country; . . . all the proceedings which have weakened government, endangered freedom, and distracted the British empire, were by him strenuously opposed; and his last efforts, under which his health sunk, were to preserve his country from a civil war, which, being unable to prevent, he had not the misfortune to see" (for this see *Pitt Correspondence*, III, 22*n*). When displaced by Chatham as Chancellor of the Exchequer, Dowdeswell refused to accept another post in the new administration. See Dowdeswell to Chatham, July 31, 1766, *ibid.*, III, 22–3.

compelled to surrender her claims to Canada down to the colonial rebellion in 1775; nor were there many people in Great Britain, at the time of the passing of the Stamp Act, who doubted the propriety of an act of Parliament obligating the colonials to make some definite contribution to their own defence. But General Conway, who in 1765 had opposed the Stamp Act and who in 1766 was the minister most closely in touch with the colonial situation by reason of his position, was rightly persuaded that the colonials would not submit to being taxed, whether justly or unjustly, but would revolt and in doing so would seek an alliance with England's traditional enemies, the French and the Spaniards.

Unhappily, from the very beginning, the new administration was beset with frustrations. Not one of the policies that Chatham favoured was brought to fruition. For example, he had set his heart upon creating a triple alliance of Great Britain, Prussia, and Russia as a counterbalance to the Bourbon Family Compact of France and Spain.[49] To this end he appointed Hans Stanley, who had seen some diplomatic service in France in 1761, to be ambassador extraordinary to the Russian court and instructed him to work intimately with Sir Andrew Mitchell, British envoy to Prussia, in order to bring the alliance into existence. Unfortunately, Chatham had made the appointment in haste without taking into consideration many important aspects of the international situation and without prior consultation with Secretary of State Conway. The Secretary was therefore obliged, with great delicacy, to point out to Chatham that he himself had given solemn assurance to the Austrian ambassador in London that no changes were considered in the diplomatic relations of London and Berlin. Further, the displacing of Sir George Macartney, envoy extraordinary to the court of Russia, just after he had succeeded in concluding a commercial treaty with Russia—"the object of nine years' negotiations"—seemed an unusual way to recognize the achievements of a faithful and competent servant of the Crown.[50] After Stanley had talked over the whole matter with Conway he realized not only that the mission that Chatham had desired him to undertake would run "a great risk in compromising the King's honour" but that the government of Great Britain "stood upon much colder and worse terms" at Berlin than Chatham had led him

---

[49] See Chatham to Sir Andrew Mitchell, British envoy at the court of Frederick II of Prussia, August 8, 1766, and General Conway to Mitchell, August 8, 1766, *ibid.*, III, 29–32.

[50] See Conway to Chatham, July 29, 1766, *ibid.*, III, 15–19.

to believe was the case.[51] In fact the courts of Frederick II of Prussia and Catherine II of Russia had objectives in mind that were quite foreign to those of the British Ministry.[52] Stanley never ventured to fulfil his mission; rather, to save his reputation, he wisely resigned his post.

Nor did the Chatham Ministry add to its prestige by its handling of the issue that was presented in the fall of 1766 by the scarcity of corn, the consequent rise in price, and the wide-spread rioting over the high cost of provisions that followed. On September 10 the King, acting upon the advice of the Ministry, issued a proclamation against "forestallers, regraters, and engrossers." As this did not seem to afford adequate protection to the public, a committee of the Privy Council on the 24th recommended that His Majesty place an embargo on wheat and flour; an order in council to this effect was issued on the 26th, as was a second order in council prohibiting the making of wine or spirits from wheat products.[53] The crop situation in Europe was especially serious that year, with the result that famine prices were being offered for wheat and its products in a number of countries.[54] With the price of grain now mounting beyond the ability of the poor in England to pay, their discontent turned into violence. In Wiltshire, a correspondent wrote: "We have nothing but insurrections of the poor for bread, who are burning and pulling down the mills of those, whom they know to be concerned in sending meal to Bristol for exportation. . . ."[55] With corn selling at twelve shillings a bushel, the people of Salisbury, after pulling down the mill there, compelled the farmers to sell their wheat at five shillings and sixpence a bushel, and butter at sevenpence a

[51] Stanley to Pitt, July 30, 1766, *ibid.*, III, 19–20.

[52] The court of Prussia was by 1766 laying the groundwork of a close alliance with Russia for the partitioning of Poland, while the Russian court was at that time interested only in the creation of an alliance as the basis for a war against Turkey. See Grafton's *Autobiography*, pp. 97–8.

[53] For the proclamation see the September issues of the *London Gazette,* the organ used by the government for official announcements; see also the *Annual Register, 1766,* pp. 224–6; for the subsequent orders in council see *ibid.,* pp. 226–7.

[54] The London *Gazetteer and New Daily Advertiser* in its edition of September 27, 1766, stated that: ". . . by the last letters received from Italy, all agree that the corn has failed this year almost every where; particularly in Russia, Turkey, France, Spain, Portugal, and all over Italy, except the Kingdom of the two Sicilies, and there the corn runs thin, as in England; and that the Turks have felt the scarcity so much, as to order their galleys to seize on all corn ships wherever they can find them. That the orders are unlimited as to price, which must be a great temptation to export; for one gentleman, some time since, bought up corn to the amount of £2,000 for exportation, by which he got £4,000."

[55] London, September 21, *ibid.*

pound.[56] Many similar incidents were reported. It is therefore understandable that the Chatham administration felt it imperative to take the immediate steps it did to quiet the minds of the people.[57] Chatham's position at the time was unequivocal. Writing to Charles Townshend after the meeting of the Privy Council on September 24, he declared (using the formal third person): "that his mortification is extreme at not being able to go to council to-day, having nothing so much at heart as to give his opinion *publicly* for the embargo on corn, which he has strenuously advised in *private* . . ."[58]

When Parliament assembled on November 11 the principal theme of the King's speech from the throne was the vindication of the measures resulting from the corn crisis. In this connection he declared:

> "The urgency of the necessity called upon me . . . to exert my royal authority for the preservation of the public safety, against a growing calamity which could not admit of delay. I have, therefore, by and with the advice of my privy council, laid an Embargo on wheat and wheat flour going out of the Kingdom, until the advice of parliament could be taken thereupon."[59]

The opposition was critical of the fact that instead of summoning Parliament at an earlier date, on September 10—the very day that the proclamation against forestallers was issued—His Majesty, upon the advice of his ministers, had prorogued Parliament for sixty-two days.[60] The chief attack, however, was aimed against the view that the Crown still possessed the dispensing power. In the House of Commons debate over a motion to bring in a bill for protecting from prosecution those who had acted in obedience to the embargo, Alderman William Beckford declared: "Whenever the public is in danger, the King has a dispensing power." When George Grenville took exception to these words, Beckford explained that this power could be exercised "with the advice of council, when-

[56] *Ibid.* Under heading "Rising of the people on account of the high price of provisions," under date of September 23, 1766, a long list of towns and cities, including Oxford, where rioters took things in hand, is given in the *Gentleman's Magazine*, XXXVI, 436–7.

[57] That this decision of the Privy Council was voted "unanimously" is indicated by the King's letter to Secretary Conway of September 24 requesting that the proclamation for the embargo be prepared "for my signing on Friday" (*Correspondence of George III* [Fortescue], I, 398).

[58] *Pitt Correspondence*, III, 73.

[59] *Parliamentary History*, XVI, 235–6.

[60] For George Grenville's motion in the House of Commons to amend the Address see *Journals of the House of Commons*, XXXI, 4; for Lord Suffolk's similar motion in the House of Lords see *Journals of the House of Lords*, XXXI, 427–8.

ever the *salus populi* requires it." Upon further objection, he finally explained that "such exertion of power is excusable only by necessity, and justifiable by act of parliament."[61]

Because of the serious implications of this new-old doctrine of the dispensing power, Secretary Conway on November 24 presented an indemnity bill in the House of Commons, which provoked an extended debate in both Houses of Parliament. The issue was the legality of an embargo by mere order of the Privy Council. According to Newcastle, Lord High Chancellor Camden had argued in the Privy Council before the laying of the embargo that while the King's ordinary prerogative did not permit him by the constitution to declare an embargo, "there must be a power to save the whole . . . ; that, if this was the case, if there was such a necessity, then there was that power to do it."[62] By maintaining this position in the House of Lords on December 10, Camden aroused a long debate during which Lord Mansfield put forth one of his greatest exertions in the ensuing condemnation of the suspending and dispensing prerogative of the Crown.[63] Grenville's "Diary" for December 10 characterized the debate in the following terms:

> "The Chancellor [Camden] and Lord Northington stuck to their dispensing doctrine, and maintained it to be law. Lord Chatham

---

[61] *Ibid.*, XXXI, 15; see also *Parliamentary History,* XVI, 245. It was Grenville who moved that the clerk take down Beckford's words, which if not withdrawn "must remain on the books as an eternal blot upon that House of Commons which had let it pass without censure. Mr. Beckford was then advised by his friends to recant, which he did, and Mr. Grenville suffered the motion [of censure] to be withdrawn" (Grenville's "Diary," *Grenville Papers,* III, 387). In a letter to the Earl of Buckinghamshire, dated November 22, 1766, George Grenville wrote: "Mr. Alderman Beckford after 3 or 4 Hours Debate thought it safer to give way & to retract his opinion & that of his Friends in the House of Peers, which you will see done by his last explanation" (Grenville Letter Books, Vol. 2, Stowe Collection, Huntington Library).

It is of interest that Beckford's exposition of the doctrine of the dispensing power of the Crown was viewed by Grenville as being "exactly conformable to the Doctrines laid down by those enlighten'd Whig Ministers, the Earls of Northington & Chatham & L[d] Chancellor Camden in the House of Peers the first day of the Session" (*ibid.*).

[62] See B. M., Add. Mss. 32977, folio 160; see also Walpole's *Memoirs of George III,* I, 428–9, for this and the gist of Camden's defence of the embargo in the House of Lords.

[63] According to the editor of *Parliamentary History* (XVI, 251*n*), "This Speech was supposed to be penned by lord Mansfield, but was, in fact, written by Mr. Macintosh, assisted by lord Temple and lord Lyttelton"; he also states (*ibid.*, 250–1) that the "Speech" as printed (*ibid.*, 251–313) represents the combined arguments raised in the long debate, "the distinct speeches of which have not been preserved." First published as a pamphlet (by Almon, according to Grenville), *A Speech against the Suspending and Dispensing Prerogative* was appearing in a fifth edition with corrections and additions before the end of 1767.

> shuffled between necessity and law. Lord Shelburne attacked Lord Mansfield, who made the most eloquent speech, with the most spirited attack upon Lord Chatham and the two lawyers [Chancellor Camden and President of the Council Northington], that ever was heard."[64]

It would appear, nevertheless, that Mansfield as late as November 10 did not feel that the embargo was a serious breach of the constitution and only after Beckford in the House of Commons and Camden in the House of Lords had asserted the power of the King to dispense with law was he persuaded that a serious breach in the constitution had occurred.[65] What was more embarrassing for the Chatham Ministry was that the bill which finally became the Indemnity Act was expanded to cover the servants of the King, obviously including those ministerial servants who, as members of the Privy Council, issued the order.[66] Later, during the debate on the embargo, Chatham (according to Camden's subsequent recollection) repudiated his own views, as well as those of other members of his administration, when he took the position that "the proclamation was illegal."[67] If that had been his position on or before September 24, he surely would have advised that Parliament be summoned

[64] *Grenville Papers,* III, 397.

[65] See Mansfield to Grenville, November 10, 1766, *ibid.,* III, 337–9. In the reign of James I the question had been put to Sir Edward Coke, Chief Justice of the King's Bench, whether for the public welfare the King could by proclamation prohibit the manufacture of starch so as to provide a more abundant supply of food for the people of the kingdom. The opinion rendered by Coke and the three other judges was that the King could not create any new offence by his proclamation. Otherwise, he might alter the law of the land "in a high point." See T. P. Taswell-Langmead: *English Constitutional History* . . . (7th edn., London, 1911), pp. 403–4. Lord Camden, although doubtless familiar with this important opinion, reiterated his former position in defending the legality of the King's proclamation, when in 1778 he stated: "As soon as parliament met, an indemnity was proposed; for my part, I was against it; because I thought it unnecessary. . . . The issuing of the proclamation was a strictly justifiable act of prerogative, an act of prerogative not only warranted by particular necessity, but supported upon general principles" (*Parliamentary History,* XIX, 1248). This position, as Professor Holdsworth has pointed out, together with the claim in 1766 of the power possessed by the King to set aside laws, "was hardly reconcilable with the principles of constitutional law which had been established by the Revolution [of 1688]." See Sir William Holdsworth: *A History of English Law* (13 vols.+, London, 1903+), X, 365.

[66] The title of the so-called Indemnity Act (7 Geo. III, c. 7) reads: "An Act for indemnifying such Persons as have acted for the Service of the Publick, in advising or carrying into Execution the Order of Council of the twenty-sixth Day of September last, for laying an Embargo on all Ships laden with Wheat or Wheat Flour; and for preventing Suits in consequence of the said Embargo."

[67] For Camden's recollection twelve years later of Chatham's position in the debate in the House of Lords in 1766, see *Parliamentary History,* XIX, 1248. By contrast, for Grenville's contemporary report, previously cited, see *Grenville Papers,* III, 397.

without delay to deal with the emergency. Instead, however—despite the generally hostile attitude taken by both Houses of Parliament toward the doctrine that the King still enjoyed the power of dispensing with the law, as voiced by the Lord High Chancellor, the chief spokesman for the government on all constitutional matters—the Ministry, in order to clear itself, had been obliged "to stoop to a Bill of Indemnity."[68]

The Chatham administration, it is now clear, epitomized the new Toryism, in so far as any group did in 1766. By utilizing the principle embodied in Lord Bolingbroke's *The Idea of a Patriot King,* that the King should rise above all political factions in choosing his servants among those best capable of serving him, the Ministry was now excluding from the affairs of state the great, aristocratic Whig families which, ever since the end of Queen Anne's reign, had dominated the political scene.[69] This strategy went hand in hand with Chatham's abject self-abasement in the presence of George III and his emphasis on those who were His Majesty's real friends as against those who were not (some of whom had a design to "storm the closet" and deprive the King of freedom of action). Yet Chatham was unable to build a strong administration based on these theories of government; rather, he was to be faced with many frustrations.

When Chatham had agreed to re-enter the King's service he took the position that he must have as colleagues men prepared to carry out *his* policies rather than their own. Therefore, the King gave him the greatest possible degree of liberty in filling the offices. Nevertheless, it would appear that by the fall of 1766 Chatham was already being thwarted by the opposition of some of his ministers, in particular Charles Townshend. Certain items on this subject were even carried in the colonial press, among them the following:

> "It is rumoured that the Chancellor of the Exchequer hath strongly disapproved of some of the Earl of C[hatham]'s plans, relative to raising the funds for the service of the next year.
>
> "We are told, that the proposal (said to be the late great Commoner's) to dissolve the present parliament at the end of next session, has already caused great heat, animosity, and opposition amongst some of the noble and Right Hon. personages at the helm.
>
> ....
>
> "The scheme for dissolving the parliament next session, is the Earl

[68] Grafton's *Autobiography,* p. 99.

[69] The brief treatise by G. H. Guttridge: *English Whiggism and the American Revolution* (University of California *Publications in History,* Vol. 28, Berkeley and Los Angeles, 1942) offers a clear analysis of Chatham's position and his new Toryism; see particularly pp. 34–6.

of C[hatha]m's, but the Ch[ancello]r of the E[xcheque]r highly disapproves of it."[70]

The early days of the Chatham administration found the Ministry made up largely of men connected with, and having varying degrees of loyalty to, the Marquess of Rockingham. A conspicuous example was General Conway, a principal Secretary of State, who remained in office under Chatham. In view of this, the Rockingham Whigs who had been deprived of office restricted their open criticism for some months. But this truce soon ended. For reasons that are not clear, Chatham had promised John Shelley, the Duke of Newcastle's nephew (whose step in deserting to Pitt had been bitterly resented by his uncle), the post of Treasurer of the Household in the place of a staunch Rockingham supporter, George, 1st Lord Edgcumbe, after reducing the latter to the status of a Lord of the Bedchamber. Edgcumbe not only refused the office but brought about the resignation of several of his friends on November 27, when an ultimatum delivered to Chatham demanding satisfaction was ignored. Among those who now retired were the Lord Chamberlain of the Household, William Cavendish Bentinck, 3rd Duke of Portland, a man of immense wealth and later to be twice the King's chief minister; Admiral Augustus Keppel, Groom of the Bedchamber; Sir Charles Saunders, First Lord of the Admiralty; and others—some seven in all. General Conway, although openly distressed[71] remained in office, as did others equally displeased by the incident.[72] What is more, the new appointees—apart from Sir Edward Hawke, who filled the post of First Lord of the Admiralty —were by no means equal in influence to the previous incumbents. Thus, Chatham, instead of having a strong, harmonious, and effective administration, was heading one that proved to be weak, lacking unanimity on major questions, and vacillating under inadequate leadership. Feeling the need to strengthen the Ministry, Chatham sought an alliance with the Bedford Whigs and offered the post of First Lord of the Admiralty—which had become vacant upon the resignation in August of Lord Egmont—to Lord Gower, brother-in-law of the Duke of Bedford. But Gower, despite prolonged negoti-

[70] See London *Gazetteer and New Daily Advertiser* of September 20 and 22; see also London advices, September 20 and 22, *Pennsylvania Gazette,* November 27, 1766. This paper, founded by Benjamin Franklin, is one of the most reliable of colonial newspapers both in reporting events and in correcting reports that later proved to be unfounded.

[71] See Conway to Chatham November 22, 1766, *Pitt Correspondence,* III, 126–9.

[72] For an excellent treatment of the above episode see John Brooke: *The Chatham Administration, 1766–1768* (London, 1956), pp. 50–60.

ations, could not be prevailed upon to come in alone,[73] although he was to yield in the summer of 1767. What added to the perplexity of the active ministers was their inability during the winter of 1766 to 1767 to confer with Chatham on matters of the highest importance by reason of his physical, if not mental, incapacity, which kept him in seclusion at Bath until he was able to return to London in March of the new year.

One of the most difficult problems presented to the Chatham administration during this period was the question of the relationship that the United East India Company should have to the government, especially in view of the breakdown of the effective authority of the native rulers in India at the end of the Great War for the Empire. As has been stressed in a preceding volume of this series,[74] the Company had been the one stabilizing force in India by 1763. It had, under the peculiar circumstances, one of two choices: either to sacrifice its important capital investments in permanent improvements and leave the distracted country, or, if it were to continue in business, to extend its authority not only over all of Bengal but also over neighbouring Orissa and Behar. It was driven to the latter course.

Early in 1759 Clive had written to Pitt to indicate that a situation might well arise that would lead the Company "to take the sovereignty upon themselves" of the possessions of the Nabob of Bengal.[75] He had suggested in this connection that the revenues from this province, added to that of Orissa and Behar, would amount to £2,000,000 sterling. In August 1765, as the result of events already detailed in this series,[76] the Great Mogul by an imperial firman had confirmed the earlier treaty made by the Company servants in India with the Nabob whereby the *diwanni* (*diwani*), or financial administration, of Bengal, Behar, and Orissa should be

---

[73] Chatham seemed to put aside political principles when making his appointments. Gower, who refused office, was identified with the Bedford group which had aided Lord Bute and Henry Fox in ratifying the Treaty of Peace of 1763, negotiated by the Duke of Bedford and denounced by Pitt; Charles Jenkinson, now appointed to the Admiralty, had been a Secretary of the Treasury under Bute and under George Grenville, and as such one of the architects of the Stamp Act, also denounced by Pitt; the Earl of Hillsborough, who had been President of the Board of Trade under Grenville, now returned to this office. For the approach to Lord Gower see Grafton's *Autobiography*, pp. 99–102; *Correspondence of George III* (Fortescue), I, 417–20; and *Pitt Correspondence*, III, 54–5, 134–8.

[74] For the course of events in India in the early 1760's see Volume IX of this series, Chaps. 12 and 13.

[75] For this letter see Sir George Forrest: *The Life of Lord Clive* (2 vols., London and New York, 1918), II, Appendix.

[76] See Volume IX in this series, pp. 321–7.

the responsibility of the Company.[77] In writing to the Directors on September 30, Clive had indicated that the new revenues, after all expenses and obligations had been met, would provide "a clear gain to the Company of 122 lack [lakh] of Sicca Rupees, or £1,650,900 sterling. . . ."[78] At the end of the year 1766 the Company—according to a report on the public finances, apparently sent by Clive to George Grenville—was in receipt of an annual revenue from Bengal that amounted to £2,178,972.12 sterling, and from Behar it was £786,688; in addition, the revenue from the Company's own lands came to £990,383.6, making a total of £3,956,043.18 as its public revenues, without reference to trade. From this sum £980,000 had to be disbursed to cover the Company's civil and military expenditures, with £487,200 allotted to the Nabob of Bengal and £351,866.13 as "tribute" to the Great Mogul at Delhi, leaving theoretically a net balance to the Company's credit of £2,136,977.5.[79]

The news of the granting of the *diwanni* of three of the richest provinces of India to the Company did not fail to excite the cupidity of holders, or "proprietors," of its stock. Although this stock had long been considered a gilt-edge investment, paying an annual dividend of six per cent, and had stood steady on the market at 164 for some time, as indicated by stock quotations in the press, after the receipt of the information from Calcutta in the spring of 1766 the shares rapidly rose in value as the fever of speculation mounted, until they reached 273 in 1767.[80]

This was the situation that faced the Chatham administration when it took office. It became clear to the ministers that the character of the Company was being transformed, changing basically from a trading enterprise to a governing power, and that the public at

[77] For a copy of the firman see Harry Verelst: *View of the Rise, Progress, and Present State of the English Government in Bengal, including a Reply to the Misrepresentations of Mr. Bolts and other writers* (London, 1772), p. 167; for the administration of the *diwanni* after 1765 and up to 1776, see B. B. Misra: *The Central Administration of the East India Company, 1773–1834* (Manchester University Press, 1959), pp. 108–22.

[78] India Office (now Commonwealth Relations Office), Abstracts of letters received from Bengal, 1770–1774, 2:185.

[79] "East India Company. A State of the Company's Revenue for the Year 1766," Stowe Collection, Box 102, Huntington Library. It will be borne in mind that George Grenville and Lord Clive were on most intimate terms at this period and that this summary of receipts and expenditures of revenues was apparently prepared by Clive and reached Grenville sometime in 1767.

[80] The student should in this connection consult the exceedingly important study by Lucy S. Sutherland: *The East India Company in Eighteenth Century Politics* (Oxford, 1952), pp. 138–76.

large, as well as the Directors of the Company and its stockholders, had an interest and a responsibility in the matter. Therefore, in August 1766 discussions were entered into by the First Lord of the Treasury, the Chancellor of the Exchequer, and officials of the Company.[81] The probability of a parliamentary inquiry was raised. The attitude of the Directors against increasing the dividend, as demanded by speculators in the stock, was based on the fact that the Company had incurred great debts, the liquidation of which should have precedence over dividends. On September 26 a General Court of the proprietors was held. The problem became acute. As a result of the so-called splitting of stock on the part of those interested in profits (with the consequent increase by three hundred of those entitled to vote), the Directors could muster only 231 votes as against 340 in favour of a motion to increase the dividend from six to ten per cent.[82] When Chatham conferred with Lord Clive's agent, John Walsh (a member of Parliament), he realized that the Company interests were "of too extensive and too difficult a nature for [the] ministers to determine" and therefore decided that the matter must necessarily come before Parliament since the Crown "had nothing to do in the affair. . . ."[83]

An inquiry into the true situation of the Company—especially into the extent of its ability, by means of a public accounting to Parliament, to give finanical assistance to the country—occupied the chief attention of the administration by the end of 1766. The King's support of the idea is evident from his statement to First Lord of the Treasury Grafton that this seemed to be "the only safe method of extracting this country out of its lamentable situation owing to the load of debt it labours under."[84] Since Alderman William Beckford was not of the ministry—although in the confidence of Chatham, at whose behest he acted—it was somewhat surprising that he should make a motion on November 25 in the House of Commons calling for an examination of the Company's affairs.[85] That the Chancellor

---

[81] See Grafton to Chatham, August 27, 1766, *Pitt Correspondence,* III, 59.

[82] Lucy S. Sutherland: *op. cit.,* p. 146. Alexander Wedderburn, writing to George Grenville on September 25, gives the arguments advanced in opposition to those of the Directors at the General Court. See *Grenville Papers,* III, 323–5.

[83] *Pitt Correspondence,* III, 93–5.

[84] The King to Grafton, December 9, 1766, *The Letters of King George III* (ed. Bonamy Dobrée, London, 1935), p. 33.

[85] *Journals of the House of Commons,* XXXI, 25. This was not a surprise move; on December 18 Beckford also gave notice that he would move on East India Company matters. That this had been arranged by Chatham is evident in light of his statement on December 7 that "Mr. Beckford will move his questions, . . .

of the Exchequer was not called upon to perform this function, as one logically attached to his office, was due to the fact that Chatham was by this time convinced that Townshend's views on East India matters were so much in opposition to his own that he must replace him in office.[86]

Chatham's plan relating to India seems to have been limited to securing a declaration by Parliament that the "right" of possession of the territories secured by the East India Company lay in the Crown, with the inference that once this was established negotiations would follow with the Company over the conditions under which the new possessions would be administered. The debate in the House of Commons that followed Beckford's motion resulted only in the demand that the all-important papers bearing upon the finances of the Company should be presented. Soon afterwards Parliament adjourned for the Christmas holidays.

At the meeting of the General Court of the Company on December 31, the necessity of arriving at an understanding with the government was apparent in the approval of a motion empowering the Directors "to treat with administration upon all such points in the general affairs of the Company as they shall judge to be most requisite . . . to the extending their commerce, securing their possessions, and perpetuating the prosperity of the Company. . . ."[87] The use of the expression "their possessions" was significant. It was this statement that caused Chatham to reject the proposal as inadequate. As he wrote on January 6 to Charles Townshend, the first matter was to determine the "right" of the Company to claim as its "possessions" the concessions approved by the Nabob of Bengal and the Great Mogul; only after "deciding the question of right" should consideration be given to what "portion of the revenue shall be left by parliament to the Company as indulgence and matter of discretion"—implying that only after the Company had agreed that these revenue concessions were the property of the government, with all

---

and upon the issue . . . must turn the decision of the present system, whether to stand or make way for another scene of political revolution. . . . I hope Mr. Beckford will walk out of the House, and leave the name of an enquiry . . . in other hands, in case this question be not fully supported and carried" (Chatham to Grafton [December 7, 1766], Grafton's' *Autobiography*, pp. 110–11).

[86] Writing to Grafton early in December with reference to the Company, he stated: "If the enquiry is to be contracted within the ideas of Mr. Chancellor of the Exchequer . . . the whole becomes a *farce*, and the *Ministry a ridiculous phantom* . . . Mr. C. Townshend's fluctuations and incurable weaknesses cannot comport with his remaining in that critical office" *(ibid.)*. But the ousting of Townshend was never undertaken. He was to die the following year still occupying his important post.

[87] For a copy of the motion see *Pitt Correspondence*, III, 150.

that was to be involved in the transfer, would the latter be prepared to treat with the Company.[88] But Townshend had already arrived at the conclusion that were the government to press its "right" to these revenues, endless difficulties would accompany "every idea of substituting the public in the place of the Company, in collecting, investing and remitting the revenue to Great Britain"; therefore the sensible policy to pursue was for the government to reach an "amicable" arrangement with the Company without entering upon the question of right.[89] It was this position, also strongly held by Conway,[90] that was destined to prevail at the time.

Obviously what the Company wanted was that the government grant it the powers needed to regulate its affairs in India, either by providing a new charter or by extending the old one. Early in the year certain Company officials had made representations to government officials advising that the Company could not function adequately until the question of its right was determined.[91] After some earlier tentative proposals, the appropriate Company committee formally requested on February 6 that, "as the basis of a negotiation for settling all matters betwixt the public and the company," the late acquisitions, possessions, and revenues should be annexed to the exclusive trade of the Company by act of Parliament, that the charter be extended for a period of fifty years, that the cost of civil and military administration be paid out of the revenues, and that certain specified provisions be made for the Company income to compensate the proprietors adequately, with the final surplus to be divided between the government and the Company; finally, in consideration of the extended charter, the Company would pay £500,-000 a year.[92]

When informed of this offer Chatham insisted that it was quite inadmissible. Writing to the Duke of Grafton on February 9, he asserted: "If this be the project of the negotiation, I know one of the King's servants who will never give in to such a snare." Yet, he added—rather weakly and quite unlike the former Great Com-

---

[88] Chatham to Townshend, January 6, 1767, *ibid.*, III, 157–8.

[89] Townshend to Chatham, January 4, 1767, *ibid.*, III, 154–7.

[90] Grafton's *Autobiography*, p. 109.

[91] For the Earl of Shelburne's conference with the chairman and deputy-chairman of the Company as outlined in his letter to Chatham of February 1, 1767, see *Pitt Correspondence*, III, 182–4.

[92] For the formal memorandum of the treasury committee of the East India Company of the 6th of February to be presented to the government see *ibid.*, III, 196*n.* These proposals were handed to Grafton the following day. See Grafton to Chatham, February 8, 1767, *ibid.*, III 194–8; see also Lucy S. Sutherland: *op. cit.*, pp. 159–62.

moner—"In this case, parliament must finally decide, and fix the public lot."[93] The Cabinet Council, meeting on February 14 in his absence, instead of rejecting the propositions of the Company, asked for a clarification of them.[94] This the Directors provided on February 20.[95] Although still the faithful supporter of Chatham, whom he considered his master, Grafton, upon receipt of the Company's clarification, advised the absent Minister that the decision of the rights involved must be determined by Parliament.[96] This elicited a reply disclosing Chatham's fixed purpose with regard to East India regulations to be that he himself would not be "a proposer of plans" but, as one with a seat in Parliament, simply "an unbiassed judge of them."[97] Although the Earl returned to London from Bath on March 2, he did not attend the Cabinet Council meeting that apparently met the following day at Grafton's house, when an effort was made to formulate ministerial policy toward the Directors' propositions. At this meeting both Townshend and Conway, according to Horace Walpole, not only opposed pushing the inquiry into the Company's affairs but refused to be involved in any such attempt in the House of Commons; they also declined to go to any other meeting called by Grafton on this subject. What is more, "in that dilemma the Cabinet broke up in confusion. . . ."[98] Conway wrote to the King, defending his position that the Company's offer was a proper basis for negotiation.[99]

But it was against Townshend, the most outspoken among those opposed to his policy, rather than Conway, that Chatham and the ministers who supported him sought to vent their wrath. His place in the Ministry was now offered to Lord North, who, perhaps wisely under the circumstances, declined it.[100] With the two key members

---

[93] *Pitt Correspondence,* III, 199–201.

[94] For the minute of the Cabinet Council of February 14, 1767, see *ibid.,* III, 204–5.

[95] For the Directors' paper clarifying their proposals see *ibid.,* III, 216–17*n.*

[96] Grafton to Chatham, February 22, 1767, *ibid.,* III, 216–18.

[97] Chatham to Grafton, February 23, 1767, *ibid.,* III, 218–19. When Shelburne wrote to Chatham two days later that Earl Bathhurst—"a strenuous advocate of the right of the public"—was anxious to bring to a decision the question of the right of the Company to the concessions, Chatham replied that the offer "seems to require much consideration, and the expediency of it admitting of some doubt" (*ibid.,* III, 219–22).

[98] *Memoirs of George III,* I, 456. On any matter involving Conway, his close friend Walpole was well informed.

[99] For the memorandum of Conway to the King, endorsed by the King on March 4, 1767, see *Correspondence of George III* (Fortescue), I, 458–9; see also in Grafton's *Autobiography,* pp. 121–2.

[100] See North to Grafton [March 4, 1767], *ibid.,* p. 123; Grafton to the King, March 5, 1767, *Correspondence of George III* (Fortescue), I, 459–60.

of the Cabinet Council carrying the responsibility for leadership in the House of Commons in open opposition to his views, and with his health shattered, Chatham chose this juncture to withdraw from public affairs. This left another of his loyal adherents, the Earl of Shelburne, who had already been involved in East India Company affairs, the task of providing administrative leadership in the negotiations. But Shelburne was not a member of the House of Commons, nor was he a match as a speaker for either Charles Townshend or George Grenville.

On March 6 the House of Commons ordered that the file of the East India Company papers already presented in that session be printed.[101] Although the motion was approved, on the 9th Robert Jones, one of the Directors of the Company, presented a petition in their name arguing that a printing of *all* these papers would be "greatly to the Prejudice of the said Company. . . ." This led to a motion that the orders given for their printing "be discharged," or rescinded. It carried by a vote of 180 to 140.[102] When the matter came up again on the 11th, George Dudley and Thomas Rous, both close to Clive and representing the Company, appeared at the bar of the House and declared that "the printing of any of their papers, except the Charters and Firmans, might be prejudicial to their affairs. . . ."[103] This stand was accepted by Townshend, Conway, and Grenville, so that when a motion to that effect was made, it passed the House without a division.[104] Thus the basic features of the Chatham approach to the inquiry into the situation of the Company were repudiated by the House of Commons. In fact, his prestige as a national leader and hero, still quite high in the spring of 1766, had by the spring of the following year sunk to such a point that he was thought of by many one-time admirers as someone of the past rather than of the present.

From early March until May the Company expended much energy on reaching a peaceable accommodation with the government. A growing influence was manifested once again by Laurence Sulivan, who, as the leading opponent of Clive in the Court of Directors, had earlier been displaced as chairman in favour of Thomas Rous. In March he submitted a set of proposals designed to please both the

---

[101] *Journals of the House of Commons*, XXXI, 207; Walpole to Mann, March 8, 1767, *Walpole-Mann Correspondence*, VI, 493.

[102] *Journals of the House of Commons*, XXXI, 211.

[103] Walpole: *Memoirs of George III*, I, 459–60.

[104] *Journals of the House of Commons*, XXXI, 216; James West to Newcastle, March 11, 1767, Newcastle Papers, B.M., Add. Mss. 32980, folio 262.

government and the holders of stock. This proposition placed the revenues and the profits on trade in separate categories. To tempt the stockholders it provided dividends of fourteen per cent, an extension of the charter privileges to 1817, and an increase in the capitalization of the Company by £800,000 at 250 per cent. From these resources, £1,200,000 would be used to retire the Company's debts. To tempt the government, £800,000 was to be paid to it for these concessions and all revenues subsequently received were to go to His Majesty's Exchequer after deducting expenses and after creating a reserve fund to help support the increased dividend payments.[105] This plan, however, was rejected by the General Court on March 19 by a vote of 456 to 264.[106] Nevertheless, as Principal Lucy Sutherland has made clear,[107] when the Directors early in April again reshaped their proposals, the influence of Sulivan's plan was manifest; yet there was a fundamental difference between the two. For example, the dividend was to rise to sixteen per cent, while but £500,000 was offered to the government for the renewal of the charter. As for the revenues, after the deduction of expenses and the creation of a dividend reserve fund of £400,000, the balance was to be divided equally between the government and the Company.[108] While these proposals were in the course of negotiation with the Ministry, at a meeting of the General Court of the Company on May 6 the speculators got control and voted to raise the semi-annual dividends to six and a quarter per cent, or twelve and a half per cent a year.[109] The reaction to this advance of dividends, especially in view of the fact that this was done while the parliamentary inquiry into the Company was in process, was swift. The following day the House of Commons voted that the Company be required to lay before it an account of the proceedings of the 6th, together with copies of all papers laid before the General Court relating to them.[110] This was done.[111] On the 8th a motion was made to bring in a bill to

---

[105] India Office, Court Book, 75:443 (Commonwealth Relations Building, London).

[106] India Office, Court Book, 75:452. It may be noted that the pro-Clive anti-Sulivan forces in the Court of Directors was sufficiently strong to bring about, in a lengthy report dated March 24, 1767, an endorsement of Clive's work. See India Office, Home Misc. Ser., 191 (18):425–90.

[107] *Op. cit.*, pp. 163–9.

[108] India Office, Court Book, 75:480 and 76:6. According to Dr. Sutherland (*op. cit.*, pp. 167–9), no fewer than eleven proposals by various proprietors were sent to the Directors after Sulivan had offered his. For a digest of the Directors' proposal see *Gentleman's Magazine*, XXXVII, 101.

[109] India Office, Court Book, 76:36.

[110] *Journals of the House of Commons*, XXXI, 344.

[111] *Ibid.*, XXXI, 347.

regulate the announcing of dividends by the Company.[112] This so-called Dividend Bill, after prolonged hearings and amendment, was finally passed by Parliament and was approved by the King on June 29.[113] It not only provided safeguards against the calling of meetings of the Company for declaring dividends without proper notice and against hasty balloting but also declared that it would be unlawful for any General Court of the Company between May 8, 1767, and the beginning of the next session of Parliament to declare any dividend beyond the rate of "ten pounds per centum per annum, being the Rate at which the Dividend for the Half Year, ending the twenty-fourth Day of June one thousand seven hundred and sixty-seven, is made payable."[114] The statute was specifically designed to rescind the advance in the dividends that had been voted by stockholders on May 6—an advance, it may be noted, that had the approval of both Townshend, Chancellor of the Exchequer, and Conway, leader in the House of Commons as well as Secretary of State for the Northern Department.[115] In this connection it should be mentioned that another bill received the royal approval at the same time. The new act, while drawn in general terms, struck particularly at the practice of splitting stock for the purpose of creating a temporary increase in the number of voters who might influence the measures involving public interest that occasionally came before the Company.[116]

As for the proposals of the United East India Company, consultations continued between the Directors and ministers until May 20. On that date the Company submitted a petition to the House of Commons that sought to bring about at least a temporary settlement of the issue of the public interest as against private interest of stockholders in its affairs. This petition was manifestly prepared with great care so that the two "should mutually reap the Benefits arising from the Acquisitions and Revenues lately obtained in India."

The petition proposed a three-year agreement and offered a choice of two plans. One of the plans presented the following proposals: first, an alteration in the import duties on tea, not only to encourage

[112] *Ibid.*, XXXI, 348.

[113] *Ibid.*, XXXI, 415.

[114] 7 Geo. III, c. 49, "An act for regulating certain Proceedings of the General Courts of the United Company of Merchants of England trading to the East Indies," *Statutes at Large,* VIII, 45.

[115] Charles Jenkinson to Sir James Lowther, June 2, 1767, B.M., Add. Mss. 38205, folios 174–174ᵛ, quoted by Lucy S. Sutherland: *op. cit.*, p. 175.

[116] 7 Geo. III, c. 48, "An Act for regulating the Proceedings of certain Public Companies and Corporations carrying on Trade or Dealings with Joint Stocks," *Statutes at Large,* VIII, 44–5.

its consumption but also "to prevent the pernicious Practice of Smuggling," together with a drawback of duties paid on teas re-exported to Ireland and the American colonies, and alterations in the duties paid on certain textiles imported from India; second, that Parliament would provide effective methods for recruiting forces necessary to maintain order in India and for preventing the exportation there of all military stores not sent for the use of the Company; third, that from its total revenues there be deducted the cost of all security measures, with the rendering of annual accounts covering them; fourth, that the sum of £400,000 be deducted annually from the total receipts of the Company to support the payment of dividends; fifth, that the net surplus then be equally divided between the public and the Company; sixth, that that portion of the surplus going to the Company be appropriated solely to the payment of its debts; and seventh, that the agreement should be binding as of February 1, 1767, and continue for three years, provided that the *diwanni* of Bengal, Behar, and Orissa remain in the Company's hands. The second plan was identical with the one just outlined except in two respects. Instead of an equal division of the net revenues of the Company, the government was offered the annual sum of £400,000 for three years, the first half-yearly payment of which was to begin March 25, 1768. Also, the Company under this arrangement agreed to indemnify the public for the drawback on teas re-exported as well as for the reduction of the inland duty on tea to the amount of one shilling a pound—in case the anticipated increased consumption of legally imported tea would not be sufficient to make up the difference.[117] The second plan was the one finally accepted by Parliament, after amendment,[118] with the chief difference only that the agreement was limited to two years rather than three. On July 2 its features were embodied into the formal bills. One took off the inland duty of a shilling a pound on teas and provided for a drawback of duties paid on teas exported to Ireland and the colonies;[119] the other related to the revenues.[120] In line with the views of Townshend and Conway, as opposed to those of Chatham and Grafton, the question of "right" was not touched upon in this legislation,

[117] *Journals of the House of Commons,* XXXI, 377–8.

[118] On June 12 the House of Commons accepted for engrossment a bill after amendment. See *ibid.*, XXXI, 403.

[119] 7 Geo. III, c. 56, *Statutes at Large,* VIII, 48–50.

[120] 7 Geo. III, c. 57, "An Act for establishing an Agreement for the Payment of the Annual Sum of four hundred thousand Pounds, for a limited Time, by the East India Company, in respect of the territorial Acquisitions and Revenues lately obtained in the East Indies." *Ibid.*, VIII, 50–1.

which merely provided "a temporary Agreement . . . made in relation to the territorial Acquisitions and Revenues lately obtained there [in the East Indies]."

As for Chatham's basic theory on the freedom of the colonies from taxation by Parliament, it fared no better than his policy on the territorial acquisitions of the East India Company. On January 26, 1767, the House of Commons resolved itself into a committee of the whole House to consider the supplies to be granted to His Majesty for the next fiscal year. Among other items were estimates of the charges of supporting the armed forces stationed in North America, Africa, Minorca, and Gibraltar. According to George Grenville, there was some debate over

> "the enormous expense attending them, amounting [in the whole] to above £400,000, or near a shilling in the Pound on the land. This I propos'd should be all defrayed by America & the West Indies, after having reduced it near one half by striking off the unnecessary Articles. Mr. Townshend in answer to this, tho' he refused to consent to it, yet held a very strong Language that America ought to pay that expense, and disclaim'd in very strong Terms almost every word of Lord Chatham's Language on this Subject, treating his Lordship's distinction between *Internal* & *External* Taxes with the same Contempt that I did, & calling it *absurd, nonsensical,* & *ridiculous* to the highest degree, & determin'd as he said to assert his own opinions with regard to it etc. etc. Nor did Mr. Conway tho' he spoke on the same Subject say one word in support or vindication of Ld Chatham's Sentiments or measures nor any other Person, tho' they were strongly censur'd by your Humble Servant [that is, Grenville], and tho' the Division upon the Question yesterday was 126 to 35 [in support of the government]."[121]

Grenville the next day divided the House over his amendment to the report. This amendment was that "such Forces as shall be kept up and employed in and for the Defence and Service of any of His Majesty's Colonies in America, . . . except . . . in the new Settlements

[121] Grenville to the Earl of Buckinghamshire, January 27, 1767, Grenville Letter Book, Vol. 2, Huntington Library; see also *Report on the Manuscripts of the Marquess of Lothian . . . , Historical Manuscripts Commission,* Vol. 62 (London, 1905), p. 275. According to Horace Walpole, "Grenville proposed that the Colonies should pay the regiments quartered there. Beckford told him he was mad on the Stamp Act, and could think of nothing else; Charles Townshend ridiculed and exposed him infinitely on the same topic. Lord George Sackville blaming the disposition of the troops in that part of the world, Lord Granby told him the plan had been drawn by his own friend General Amherst; the Court had a majority of 106 to 35" (*Memoirs of George III,* I, 449). It will be noted that the two writers differ respecting the number voting with the majority. The *Journals of the House of Commons* shed no light on the actual vote.

of East and West Florida, and in the new ceded Islands of Tobago, Dominica, and Saint Vincent's, be maintained, and the expence thereof defrayed by a Revenue to be raised from said Colonies . . ." However, when the House divided but 19 voted for the amendment as against 71 who endorsed the report without it.[122]

Yet public sentiment in Great Britain was shifting strongly in favour of the Grenville position. Writing on February 17 to General Simon Fraser,[123] then in Portugal, Grenville declared: "Nothing has yet been done or is likely to be done . . . except voting vast Sums of money to be raised upon Great Britain in order to ease America from the Burthen of Contributing any thing to her own Support, but however we may look upon the Question within Doors [of Parliament] the Tide out of Doors seems very strongly & universally turning the other way."[124] When on February 18 the extraordinary military services not provided for by Parliament and covering the period January 1766 to February 1767 were considered,[125] Grenville again came to the attack with two motions. One was to concentrate the garrisons in America near the capital of each colony rather than on the frontiers; the other was to employ any money that might be received from the East India Company for the payment of the services in America. Although the vote in favour of each of these motions was 67, the administration rallied 131 votes against them.[126] It was equally successful on the 19th when defeating a motion (presumably made by Grenville) that

> "an humble Address be presented to His Majesty, to express the Concern of this House, at the grievous and heavy Charge, . . . lately brought upon this Country, for Services not authorized by Parlia-

[122] *Journals of the House of Commons,* XXXI, 76; see also Grenville to Buckinghamshire January 27, 1767 (*loc. cit.*), giving the nays as 75; and Walpole (*op. cit.,* I, 449), who gives the vote in favour of Grenville's motion as 16. The resolution presented to the House of Commons on January 27 which was the object of amendment was: "That it is the Opinion of this Committee, That a Sum, not exceeding Four hundred Five thousand Six hundred and Seven Pounds [£405,607.2.11] . . . be granted to His Majesty, for maintaining His Majesty's Forces and Garisons in the Plantations and Africa . . ." (*Journals of the House of Commons,* XXXI, 75).

[123] Simon Fraser (1726–82), sometimes called the Master of Lovat, after serving with the British forces in Portugal entered the Portuguese army and attained the rank of lieutenant general; later he returned to the British service.

[124] Grenville Letter Book, Vol. 2, Huntington Library.

[125] *Journals of the House of Commons,* XXXI, 168.

[126] Walpole: *Memoirs,* I, 451. In this connection Walpole writes: "Beckford was very abusive on George Grenville. Rigby reproached Colonel Barré with his *former* attacks on Lord Chatham, and with not defending him now; and he taxed Charles Townshend with his subjection to Lord Chatham, which drew a fine oration from Townshend on his own situation and on that of America" (*ibid.*).

ment; and which, before the Commencement of the last War, were constantly defrayed by the Colonies; and humbly to represent to His Majesty, that . . . an enormous and unprecedented Expence has been incurred, by maintaining a large Number of Troops in the Out Posts of North America, [and] humbly to submit to His Majesty's Wisdom, whether the greater Part of the said Troops may not now be stationed in such a Manner, as may reduce the Charge thereof within narrower Limits, and at the same Time be in every Respect more advantageous to His Service."[127]

That same day the House gave its approval to a bill providing for the payment of £315,917.16.5 "toward defraying the extraordinary expences of his majesty's land forces [in America] and other services" up to February 3.[128] However, on February 27, when the House resolved itself into a committee of the whole to consider ways and means for raising supplies,[129] the unexpected happened. Townshend, as Chancellor of the Exchequer, proposed a continuance of the four-shilling levy on land. His position, as reported, was that this heavy tax should remain still another year "to give room for the most brilliant operation of finance which this country ever saw, to ensure to us dignity abroad, stability at home, and enable us to enter with advantage into any future war."[130] Nevertheless, his predecessor in that office under Rockingham, William Dowdeswell, "with great strength of argument, moved for three shillings and carried it on a division. . . ."[131] As Horace Walpole, who supported the government, expressed it: "The late outed ministers, forgetting their actions and declarations against Grenville, in their new hatred to Chatham, joined in the cry. In short, when we came to a division we were but one hundred eighty-eight, they two hundred and six."[132] Thereupon, on March 2, approval was given to the following resolution submitted by the Committee on Ways and Means: "That 3s. in the pound, and no more, be raised within the space of one year . . . upon lands, tenements, hereditaments, pensions, offices and personal estates, in . . . England, Wales, and the town of Berwick upon Tweed: and that a proportionable cess, according to the 9th article

[127] *Journals of the House of Commons,* XXXI, 171.

[128] *Annual Register, 1767,* p. 217.

[129] *Journals of the House of Commons,* XXXI, 192.

[130] *Pitt Correspondence,* III, 223*n;* see also *Parliamentary History,* XVI, 362–3, which presents the arguments for and against the reduction of the land tax.

[131] Newcastle to Dr. Caryl, February 28, 1767, Newcastle Papers, B.M., Add. Mss. 32980, folio 191.

[132] Walpole to Horace Mann, March 2, 1767, *Walpole-Mann Correspondence,* VI, 487–8.

of the Treaty of Union, be laid upon that part of Great Britain called Scotland [to raise the sum of] £1,528,568.11s.11¾d."[133]

This repudiation of a major financial recommendation on the part of the Chancellor of the Exchequer was certainly something of a blow to his prestige and at the present writing would bring about his resignation, if not that of the whole Ministry.[134] But there was no thought of this, especially in the light of the King's strong support of the administration on this issue.[135] It would appear that in the debate on February 27, in which twenty-two speakers participated,[136] Grenville took a leading part. At least, when the result of the vote was announced, he recorded in his "Diary" the "joy in the House of Commons was very great, all the country gentlemen coming around Mr. Grenville, shaking him by the hand, and testifying the greatest satisfaction."[137] As Horace Walpole wrote: "Grenville made a great figure on this unhappy question. . . .[138] It is not at all clear that Townshend fought hard to retain the four-shilling

---

[133] *Parliamentary History,* XVI, 369; *Journals of the House of Commons,* XXXI, 196–7.

[134] Secretary of State Conway, writing to George III the evening of February 27, did not intimate that there was any disposition on the part of the Ministry to resign: "I am very sorry to inform Your Majesty that the Question for 3s in the £ Land Tax has been carried in the Committee against the Motion & opinion of Your M's Chancellor of the Exchequer & Ministers.—It may be contested in the Report, but is a thing almost unknown in Par^t in such a case I think probably with no great prospect of Success" (*Correspondence of George III* [Fortescue], I, 453). Burke put the matter in its true light when he wrote: "But as things stand at present; it is matter rather of Laughter and surprise, than any ground to reason or act upon. . . . It is easy to overturn the ministry; far from easy to find one to succeed" (Burke to Charles O'Hara, February 28, 1767, *Correspondence of Edmund Burke* [ed.-in-chief, T. W. Copeland, 5 vols. +, Cambridge, Eng., and Chicago, 1958–65 +], I, *Correspondence, April 1744–June 1768* [ed. T. W. Copeland], p. 297).

[135] See the King to Conway, February 27, and the King to Grafton, February 27, 1767, *Correspondence of George III* (Fortescue), I, 454–5.

[136] For the list of speakers on the question of the reduction of the land tax as given by Conway see *ibid.,* I, 454.

[137] "Mr. Grenville's Diary," *Grenville Papers,* IV, 212. Horace Walpole (in a footnote to his *Memoirs of George III,* I, 452*n*) writes that according to Richard Rigby, a Bedford supporter, he and Alexander Wedderburn went to Grenville's country home to secure his support for a reduction of the land tax by two shillings in the pound. Grenville, however, would not hear of it but agreed to support a motion to reduce it by one shilling. This he did and "spoke ably" to that effect. But the Rockingham group under the leadership of Dowdeswell, it is clear, was chiefly responsible for the step that was taken in the House. Preliminary meetings were held in private and country members of the House were warned to be present. See correspondence between Charles Yorke and his brother, the Earl of Hardwicke, early in February, Hardwicke Papers, B.M., Add. Mss. 35362, folios 61–6; also for the same period the correspondence between Rockingham and Newcastle, Newcastle Papers, B.M., Add. Mss. 32980, folios 138–9, 144–6. The account of the episode as given by John Brooke: *op. cit.,* pp. 105–9, is especially commended to readers.

[138] *Memoirs of George III,* I, 453.

tax.[139] He had hoped to lighten it the following year if all worked out well and he already had plans that would, he was confident, largely make up the loss of almost £500,000 in revenue.

The Chancellor of the Exchequer was blamed by Chatham for the defeat of the government on this major taxation measure as well as for undermining his position on the question of the East India Company acquisitions. It was at this point that an attempt was made to displace Townshend, but, disliked as he was by many, he was equally respected and feared because of his brilliance and incisiveness as a speaker. In fact, so little did his defeat apparently affect his standing that early in March the press announced among the contemplated changes in the administration that he was to replace Grafton as First Lord of the Treasury, with Grafton and Gower to become the Secretaries of State; Charles Yorke, Lord High Chancellor; Lord Mansfield, Lord President of the Council; and the Marquess of Rockingham, Lord Chamberlain.[140] There was no truth in this nor was there any solid basis for the announcement by a correspondent to the *Pennsylvania Gazette* on March 7 that: "This day the Right Hon. Charles Townshend resigned his place of Chancellor of the Exchequer."[141] In fact, it is evident that instead of losing stature in the eyes of his fellow ministers, he had gained in prestige. For he was to dominate the scene as soon as it became clear that no acceptable person was available to assume the enormous responsibilities of his post. That this ascendancy of Townshend came to pass was simply due to the lack of leadership among the other members of the Cabinet Council.

The chief problems facing the ministers in 1767 were fiscal in nature. Grafton, who, as First Lord of the Treasury, should have taken initiative, looked in vain to Chatham for ideas; Shelburne, Secretary of State for the Southern Department, was intensely disliked by most of his fellow ministers and seems to have returned this dislike to the extent of even withdrawing in March from the meetings of the Cabinet Council; Conway, very unhappy in office, became increasingly detached from affairs that did not concern his post of Secretary of State for the Northern Department. Thus Burke, in his speech on American taxation in 1774, was to say of the decline of Chatham and the rise of Townshend: "For even . . . before this splendid orb was entirely set, and while the western horizon was in a blaze with his descending glory, on the opposite quarter of the

[139] For Walpole's account of the debate see *ibid.*, I, 451–5.
[140] London advices, March 3, *Pennsylvania Gazette,* May 14, 1767.
[141] *Ibid.*

heavens arose another luminary, and, for his hour, became lord of the ascendant."[142] Burke, one of the greatest public speakers that England or any other country has produced, sought further to explain why Townshend came to exercise so dominant a position in the House of Commons and in the affairs of state up until the time of his death in September 1767. In the same speech quoted above he declared that Townshend was in truth

> "the delight and ornament of this house, and the charm of every private society which he honoured with his presence.[143] Perhaps there never arose in this country, nor in any country, a man of more pointed and finished wit; and (where his passions were not concerned) of a more refined, exquisite, and penetrating judgment . . . He particularly excelled in a most luminous explanation, and display of his subject. His style or argument was neither trite and vulgar, nor subtle and abstruse."

Burke concluded with the significant statement: "He conformed exactly to the temper of the house; and he seemed to guide, because he was always sure to follow it."[144] Guided by this principle of action in expressing his views in the House of Commons on more than one occasion, Townshend made pronouncements of policy—often speaking ostensibly for the government, but without authorization from his colleagues and even in contravention of their views—that would have resulted in the retirement into private life of any man of meaner capacities.[145]

---

[142] *The Works of the Right Honourable Edmund Burke* (8 vols., London, 1803), II, 422.

[143] Townshend was during the spring of 1767 frequently the supper guest of the Marquess of Rockingham, who obviously sought to win him over. See John Brooke: *op. cit.*, p. 118.

[144] *Works of Burke,* II, 422–3.

[145] For example, in March 1763 a resolution of the whole House proposed that the duties imposed by the Molasses Act of 1733 be continued. Townshend, President of the Board of Trade, took it upon himself to move that the duty on foreign molasses imported into the British colonies should be reduced from sixpence to twopence a gallon. As this change was considered to be a matter of the highest importance that should depend on a decision of the Cabinet Council, it caused dismay in the government, although no one ventured to rebuke the speaker. Writing to Lord Bute soon after the incident, George III expressed this feeling: "Mr. Jenkinsons account has much hurt me with regard to the part every branch of government took of being silent on the proposal of Mr. Townshend for the American tax, not only the Treasury but Mr. Fox and Mr. Greenville [Grenville] ought to have spoke, this subject was new to none, having been thought of this whole winter; all ought to have declar'd that next session some tax will be laid before the House but that it requires much information before a proper one can be stated, and thus have thrown out this insidious proposal; I think Mr. Townshends conduct deserves the dismissing him or the least the making him explain his intentions" (*Letters from George III to Lord Bute, 1756–1766,* pp. 201–2). The Namier-Brooke *Charles Townshend* stresses this point; see pp. 91–2.

Townshend was, moreover, listened to with marked respect when he spoke on American matters. For years he had been identified with the Board of Trade—which dealt largely with colonial concerns—and for a brief period had been its President, or First Lord Commissioner. As a result, he had a knowledge of American affairs and held to a point of view about them that accorded with the attitude of the majority of the members of Parliament. As early as September 1754, he had assured the Duke of Newcastle that he would prepare a plan for the creation of an American fund, into "which all the [American] Provinces will, I am certain, approve and chearfuly pay."[146] But no further steps appear to have been taken at that time. When Grenville introduced his bill in the spring of 1765 for levying stamp duties, it was strongly supported by Townshend. That he voted in February 1766 to repeal this act did not affect his basic position that America should make a definite contribution to the support of the Empire, the nature of which should be determined by Parliament—a view that he had expressed in his above-mentioned communication to Newcastle. In voting for repeal it seems that he was influenced by the strong stand taken by the colonials—and openly expressed by Franklin in 1765 at the bar of the House of Commons—that there was a fundamental difference between paying internal taxes levied by Parliament and import duties levied by the same body.[147] Townshend doubtless reasoned: Why have a war to collect internal taxes when the same results may be secured peacefully by colonial customs? As he explained to the House in the spring of 1767, he "had been for repealing the Stamp Act to prevent mischief."[148]

Townshend's thinking was parallel to that of Grenville on American affairs. According to the Duke of Grafton, when on March 12, 1767, a Cabinet Council meeting was held to consider "the vote of supply for the American extraordinaries," Townshend declared that if the amount involved were not reduced "by drawing the troops nearer the great towns,[149] laying the Indian charges upon the prov-

[146] See Newcastle Papers (B.M., Add. Mss. 32736, folios 508–14) for the Townshend letter and remarks. What this plan was is not clear. Sir Lewis Namier surmised (*op. cit.*, p. 19) that it was the plan finally offered in the spring of 1767.

[147] See Volume X in this series, p. 385. For a view that the colonials made no distinction between internal and external taxation by Parliament, see E. S. and Helen M. Morgan: *The Stamp Act Crisis: Prologue to Revolution* (Chapel Hill, N.C., 1953), pp. 34–9, 113–15, 212–17, 273–6.

[148] See Horace Walpole's account of Townshend's address of May 13, 1767, in his *Memoirs of George III,* II, 26–8.

[149] Grafton to Chatham, March 13, 1767, *Pitt Correspondence,* III, 232. This proposal to withdraw from the frontier posts and concentrate the troops in the chief American towns had earlier been voiced by Grenville.

inces, and by laying a tax on the American ports, he would not remain chancellor of the exchequer."[150] Although Grafton complained to Chatham that Townshend's behaviour on the occasion "on the whole, was such as no cabinet will, I am confident, ever submit to,"[151] nothing was done. In fact the government had been drifting along without any "settled plan," ever waiting in vain for Chatham to chart the way.[152] Townshend now sought to lay down the course it must take in American affairs if he were to retain his post. In this connection it may be noted that, when these matters were to be settled in the House, the Chancellor of the Exchequer was accustomed to seek out Grenville in order to talk with him.[153] Doubtless Townshend felt that whatever definite proposals he would make must win the hearty concurrence of Grenville and his friends, since the members of the House committed to Chatham's earlier expressed views, such as Conway, could not be depended upon for support.

By the beginning of April the Chancellor of the Exchequer intimated to the House of Commons that he had arrived at a position "for asserting the Superiority of the Crown, and endeavouring to lay a foundation for such a taxation as might in time ease this country of a considerable burden;"[154] but it was not until the following

---

[150] *Ibid.* The Earl of Shelburne also wrote to Chatham on March 13, 1767, about the Cabinet Council meeting concerned with the funds needed for America and, of the position taken by Townshend, that it was necessary to settle upon a sum for that purpose, "which he said he neither could nor would move [as Chancellor of the Exchequer], unless the cabinet previously took the whole state of America into consideration, and enabled him to declare to the House the opinion of the administration as to the forts, the Indian trade, the disposition of the troops, in short the whole arrangements, considered with a view to a general reduction of expense, and a duty which he undertook should be laid to defray what remained: that he had promised this to the House, and upon the authority of what passed in the cabinet; and if he could not make it good, he should be obliged to consider the best means, by what he should say or by his conduct, to make it appear that it was not his fault, and against his opinion" (*ibid.*, III, 233). As to the promise that Townshend had made to the House that he would secure a revenue from America, this took place, it would appear, in the course of the debate on January 26, when, according to Grafton, he declared he "knew the mode by which a revenue might be drawn from America, *without offence.* Mr. Grenville fixed him down directly to pledge himself on the declaration, which was received with such welcome by the bulk of the House as dismayed Mr. Conway, who stood astonished at the unauthorized proceeding of his vain and imprudent colleague" (Grafton's *Autobiography*, p. 126).

[151] *Pitt Correspondence*, III, 232.

[152] *Ibid.*

[153] Under date of April 1 Grenville recorded in his "Diary": "Mr. Charles Townshend comes every day in the House to talk with Mr. Grenville, and to abuse Lord Chatham, and laugh at the Administration; and speaking in relation to what would be proper to be done in America, he said Mr. Conway was upon that subject below low-water mark" (*Grenville Papers*, IV, 222).

[154] For this see Newcastle Papers, B.M., Add. Mss. 32936, folio 321. D. A.

month that he was prepared to submit his proposals. Meanwhile, on May 8 he delivered one of his most brilliant and subtle speeches, in which, while bringing into view a variety of topics and personalities, he sought to undermine the standing of his two chief opponents within the Ministry who might seek to thwart his far-reaching designs. James West, a member of the House, wrote that the address was received "with the most universal applause I have ever heard"; he referred to it as "the greatest, wisest, wittiest speech . . . praying for a long and permanent administration of people of rank, ability and integrity, and experience, particularly of those who had formerly been in office, and that it might be speedy, and that youth and vanity might no longer make us the jest of our own country and the contempt of foreigners. . . ."[155] According to Sir George Colebrooke, who was also present, "It was a speech in which he treated with great levity, but with wonderful art, the characters of the Duke of Grafton and Lord Shelburne, whom, though his colleagues in office, he entertained a sovereign contempt for, and heartily wished to get rid of."[156]

With the reverberations of his great May 8 speech still resounding in his favour, Townshend at last presented his plan for an American revenue to the House, when it resolved itself into a committee of the whole to consider certain papers concerning the North American colonies on the 13th.[157] This time he made no at-

---

Winstanley in his *Lord Chatham and the Whig Opposition* (Cambridge, 1912), p. 142*n*, points out that this paper is wrongly endorsed April 3, 1762, instead of 1767.

[155] James West to Newcastle, May 8, 1767, Newcastle Papers, B.M., Add. Mss. 32981, folio 323. This was the famous so-called "champagne speech" of Townshend. It was supposed to be concerned with the motion made by Jeremiah Dyson for leave to bring in a bill for regulating the making of dividends of the East India Company. See Walpole: *Memoirs of George III,* II, 23.

[156] For the above extract from Colebrooke's unpublished "Memoirs" see *ibid.,* II, 24*n,* introduced by the editor, Sir Denis Le Marchant. Colebrooke, a member of the House who had dined that evening with Townshend and had been present when he spoke, denied that he was under the influence of wine. Nor was the speech a mere spontaneous outpouring, but one which Townshend "had meditated a great while upon" (*ibid.*). Writing to Horace Mann on May 12, Walpole called it "a wonderful speech . . . apropos to nothing, and yet about everything, about ministries past, present, and to come; himself in particular, whom I think rather past than to come. It was all wit and folly, satire and indiscretion—he was half drunk when he made it, and yet that did but serve to raise the idea of his abilities" (*Walpole-Mann Correspondence,* VI, 512). See also Walpole's version of the speech in his *Memoirs of George III,* II, 23–5.

[157] *Journals of the House of Commons,* XXXI, 358. Horace Walpole stated that it had been agreed, when General Conway declared in the Cabinet Council "against the intended plan for America, . . . that Charles Townshend should conduct it through the House, and the fifth of May was settled for his opening it: but his strange irresolution and versatility could not conceal itself, even on so public an occasion. That very morning he pretended to have fallen down stairs and cut his

tempt at brilliance. To the contrary, as Horace Walpole noted, the Chancellor spoke "fully, clearly, and with both authority and moderation. . . ."[158] The most circumstantial account of his remarks on that day is by Charles Garth, a member of the House, acting in his capacity of London agent for South Carolina.[159] According to Garth, Townshend declared that both during and immediately after the Stamp Act crisis the legally constituted government in the colonies had been found to be weak and ineffective; he therefore stressed the necessity of "improving the System of Government in the Colonies in order that the Authority of the executive Power might carry . . . the Weight and Respect essentially necessary. . . ." He then showed the extent of the provision made for officials of the civil administration in the colonies and suggested his readiness to propose that His Majesty should be enabled to provide salaries better suited to these officers—by means of current American duties or those to be imposed in the future—so that they would be "no longer dependent upon the pleasure of any Assembly." Toward this end Townshend now outlined certain steps for securing the desired revenue. To begin with, he pointed out the absolute necessity of establishing a central custom house in North America that would be so situated as to compel the customs officers there to discharge their duty, rather than "enriching themselves at the Expence of the Public by Conniving [a lawless practice]." Such an establishment would make it easy and inexpensive for people to refer complaints about the misbehaviour of subordinate officials. There was an equal necessity to increase the number of dutiable articles, such as raisins, oranges, lemons, oil, port wine, china-ware, glass, paper, together with red and white lead. He also mentioned that the Committee on Ways and Means had "in Contemplation" duties on tea and salt. As to providing duties on tea, this could await the outcome of negotiations with the East India Company. The question of duties on salt, he indicated, had been put aside on account of the "Difficulty of adjusting the Drawback to be allowed on the Exports of cured

eye dangerously. On this Lord North was deputed to execute the task, . . . when Rigby . . . moved, with affected compliments on Townshend's absence, to wait till he could appear, and it was agreed to" (*Memoirs of George III*, II, 22). In this statement Walpole hardly does justice to Townshend's astuteness. It would seem more logical to attribute his delay in presenting his plan for America to a strategy to wait until after he had found the occasion to deliver the speech, which he doubtless hoped would serve certain important and anticipated ends, although the speech itself was apparently not at all related to American matters.

[158] *Memoirs of George III*, II, 26.

[159] See Garth to the South Carolina committee of correspondence, May 17, 1767, *South Carolina Historical and Genealogical Magazine*, XXIX, 227–9.

Fish and Provisions, and of Salt to cure the same at the [Newfoundland] fisheries."[160]

In the course of his remarks Townshend also dealt with the question of providing all the colonies with a reliable paper currency—something Benjamin Franklin had been urging. He pointed out that to do this the paper-money act passed by Parliament in 1764 would have to be repealed. According to Garth, the colonies would, under the plan, receive permission to establish loan offices with a power of issuing paper currency that would be loaned at interest to those able to provide good security, and the money accruing from the interest would be appropriated to the King's service.[161] The South Carolina London agent made this statement, it would appear, only after George Grenville had stated that the proposed import duties would amount to but "trifles" and had declared, according to Franklin: "I will tell the honourable gentleman of a revenue, that will produce something valuable in America; make paper money for the colonies, issue it upon loan there, take the interest, and apply it as you think proper." To this suggestion Townshend replied that it was really his own proposal, which he had intended to make but which for the moment had slipped his mind; as proof, he assured the House that a bill was already prepared for that purpose and would be laid before the members.[162] This was never done. The concession made in connection with the New York currency act of 1770 (mentioned briefly in the preceding chapter) and the statute passed in 1773[163] will be discussed in a subsequent chapter.

The idea that Great Britain might secure a substantial revenue from an American paper currency issued by the government and loaned on interest to Americans was not original with either Grenville or Townshend. It is clear that early in 1765, before the bill for stamp duties was presented to the House of Commons, Franklin had urged Grenville, as a substitute to this bill, to turn his attention to the possibilities of an American revenue secured in this manner.[164] But by 1767 Franklin had completely changed his point of

[160] *Ibid.*, XXIX, 227–30.

[161] It was not clear to Garth whether this money raised by the loan offices in the respective colonies would be appropriated to the King's service by Parliament or by the individual assembly. See *ibid.*, XXIX, 228.

[162] Franklin to Joseph Galloway, June 13, 1767, *Writings of Benjamin Franklin* (ed. A. H. Smyth, 10 vols., New York, 1905–7), V, 25–30.

[163] For the act explaining and amending 4 Geo. III, c. 34, see 13 Geo. III, c. 57, "An Act to explain and amend an Act, made in the fourth Year of his present Majesty . . . ," which gave a limited legal-tender quality to colonial bills of credit.

[164] For the development of this point see V. W. Crane: "Benjamin Franklin and the Stamp Act," Colonial Society of Massachusetts *Transactions*, XXXII, 58. For

view. Writing to his friend Joseph Galloway on June 13, about his hopes of securing a repeal of the paper-money act of 1764, he had the following to say:

> "The ministry had agreed to the repeal, and the notion that had possessed them, that they might make a revenue from paper money in appropriating the interest by Parliament, was pretty well removed by my assuring them, that it was my opinion no colony would make money on those terms, and that the benefits arising to the commerce of this country in America from a plentiful currency would therefore be lost, and the repeal answer no end, if the Assemblies were not allowed to appropriate the interest themselves; . . . [for] they would never establish such funds as to make themselves unnecessary to government."[165]

It therefore becomes apparent why Townshend lost interest after May 13 in the American currency bill the Committee on Ways and Means had drafted, and why those who had prepared petitions for the modification of the Currency Act of 1764 no longer ventured to submit them.[166] Thus the government left in abeyance an issue that was prominent in the eyes of some colonial legislators.[167]

On June 1, 1767, the House of Commons by formal vote agreed to consider in committee of the whole "proper Methods for raising a Revenue, in the British Colonies and Plantations in America, for making a more certain and adequate Provision for the Charge of the

---

the interest of Thomas Pownall, former Governor of Massachusetts Bay, in evolving this 1765 plan for a general American paper currency to be established by the British government, see Thomas Pownall: *The Administration of the Colonies* (4th edn., 2 vols., London, 1768), pp. 186–90, 195–208, and *passim*. In this connection see also W. R. Riddell: "Benjamin Franklin and Colonial Money," *Pennsylvania Magazine of History and Biography*, LIV, 52–63.

[165] *Writings of Benjamin Franklin* (Smyth), V, 25–6. For Franklin's continued interest in securing a relaxation of the currency restraining act of 1764 see his long and able article entitled "Remarks and Facts Concerning American Paper Money," which was written on March 11 and appeared in the *Pennsylvania Chronicle*, June 1, 1767. This is to be found in the *Writings* (Smyth), V, 1–14.

[166] Charles Garth wrote to the South Carolina committee of correspondence on June 6: "But as to Paper Currency our Hands are tied up for this Sessions, . . . the intention of that part of the Ministry who sit in the House of Comm^{s}, being to Confine the Emission of Paper Money to be agreeable to the Directions of an intended Bill of Repeal whereby the Colony Legislatures are to issue upon Loan only, and for that Purpose to establish a Loan Office, but the Interest arising from such Loans to be by the British Act given to the Crown to be apply'd first to defray the Necessary Expenses of Emission and Establishment and Management of the Office, and then the Surplus towards defraying the Expence of defending protecting and securing the Colonies and Plantations; I presume you will think either Merchants or Agents would not be doing America any real service to proceed farther therein with such an Idea prevailing in the Minds of Men in Power and Authority" (*South Carolina Historical and Genealogical Magazine*, XXIX, 296–7).

[167] For a discussion of the subsequent steps to ease the currency shortage in the colonies, see Chap. 8 of this volume.

Administration of Justice, and the Support of Civil Government, in such Provinces where it shall be found necessary, and towards further defraying the necessary Charges of defending, protecting, and securing, the said Colonies and Plantations."[168] The following day some twenty resolutions involving the ways and means of raising the needed revenue were submitted and passed. The last nine of them were concerned with contemplated American import duty measures.[169] There was little delay after the approval of the resolutions, for predicated upon them were drafts of bills ready to be submitted. The first bill, presented on June 3, was "to enable His Majesty to put the Customs and other Duties, in the British Dominions in America, and the Execution of the Laws relating to Trade there, under the Management of Commissioners, to be appointed for that Purpose, and to be resident in the said Dominions."[170] This was followed by the legislation that the American Board of Commissioners was to implement and enforce—the two revenue bills which were to raise so many colonial objections. On the 10th came the American revenue bill "for granting certain Duties, in the British Colonies and Plantations in America . . ."; this provided import duties, payable in sterling, on various grades of glass, red and white lead, paint, certain types of paper, and all tea entering British colonial ports; it also designated that the funds so raised were to support the civil government, and specified that smuggling was to be more effectively prevented.[171] The second bill for raising a revenue, introduced on the 11th, was "for taking off the Inland Duty of one Shilling per Pound Weight upon all Black and Singlo Tea[172] consumed in Great Britain, and for granting a Drawback [of all duties paid in Great Britain] upon the Exportation of Tea to Ireland, and the British Dominions in America"—thus making possible the low import duty on tea of threepence a

[168] *Journals of the House of Commons,* XXXI, 392.

[169] *Parliamentary History,* XVI, 374–6.

[170] *Journals of the House of Commons,* XXXI, 396.

[171] *Ibid.,* XXXI, 398. The Act specified the duties; for example, on glass, depending on quality, the rates varied from four shillings eightpence to one shilling twopence per hundredweight; on lead and painters' colours it was two shillings for the same amount; on paper it varied greatly, from "Atlas Fine" at twelve shillings to "Small Ordinary Brown" at threepence per ream; and for tea it was, regardless of quality or brand, threepence. The funds so raised were to be expended in America, as the preamble of the Act stated, "for making a more certain and adequate Provision for . . . the Administration of Justice, and the Support of Civil Government, in such Provinces where it shall be found necessary; and toward further defraying the Expences of defending, protecting, and securing the said Dominions . . ." (7 Geo. III, c. 46, *Statutes at Large,* VIII, 38–42).

[172] That is, a tea secured from Ngan-hui in southern China on a mountain called Singlo.

pound in the colonies, but leaving the East India Company to provide specified indemnification.[173]

At no time—so far as can be gathered from the debates that took place—were the principles involved in the Townshend measures seriously questioned in Parliament. As has been noted in the preceding volume of this series, General Conway had attacked the enactment of the Stamp Act and later had taken the leading part in its repeal; nevertheless, as titular leader in the House of Commons, he reluctantly supported these bills designed to raise a revenue in America—once he had overcome his surprise at Townshend's unauthorized commitment of the government to this program. So, too, did Alderman William Beckford, who also had vehemently denied the right of Parliament to levy internal taxes on the colonies and who, of all members of the House of Commons, was considered to be the Earl of Chatham's mouthpiece and the chief spokesman for America. As for Chatham, was it true—in terms of the question posed by Horace Walpole—that "while the Ministers humbled the Colonies, his lordship [so conducted himself that he] might still be supposed favourable to them, [since] such a duplicity from his silence ran through the whole of that his second administration?"[174] Where, in the spring of 1767, was the Barré who in 1765 had denounced in the most eloquent terms Townshend's statement that the colonies were under obligation to support their mother country financially? Where was that great orator, Edmund Burke, who had declaimed against the Stamp Act in 1766 and in praise of Pitt, and who in 1774 delivered his great speech on American taxation calling for the repeal of the tax on tea? Where, when these revenue bills reached the House of Lords, over which he presided as Lord High Chancellor, was the Camden who, in the winter of 1766, had pressed for the repeal of the Stamp Act, declaring: "taxation and representation are inseparably united; God hath joined them, no British parliament can separate them . . . it is itself an eternal law of nature,"[175] and who later was to join with Burke in denouncing the attempt to raise a revenue in America?

That the bills passed through the two houses of Parliament with almost no opposition is clear.[176] The flank of the supposed opposition forces, made up largely of Chatham supporters, had been

[173] *Journals of the House of Commons,* XXXI, 401.

[174] *Memoirs of George III,* II, 29.

[175] *Parliamentary History,* XVI, 178.

[176] *Journals of the House of Commons,* XXXI, 399, 401, 403, 405, 407, 408, 410, 412, 413.

turned by a key man in the administration—Charles Townshend.

On June 29 the King, through a royal commission set up under the Great Seal, gave his assent to the bill for establishing an American Board of Customs Commissioners, as well as to the first American revenue bill; the second bill for raising a revenue he approved in person on July 2.[177]

It was upon this legislation, passed in defiance of the Earl of Chatham's stand on the taxation of America, that the strong man of the Cabinet Council, Charles Townshend, based his hopes of finally securing an American revenue that would cover much of the cost of administering that part of the Empire which lay in North America and would also guarantee the proper submission and good behaviour of the colonials.

By the time Parliament carried through this and other legislation and was ending its session, it was clear that the administration was in danger of falling to pieces. On June 25 the King with great concern wrote to Chatham: "Lieutenant General Conway has declared his intention of resigning as soon as the Parliament is prorogued; [also] the Lord President's health declines so visibly —that He cannot any longer go through the functions of his employment; Mr. Townshend says he is willing to remain provided stability can be obtained, but not if the Administration is *patched* as He terms it; the Duke of Grafton tho full of Zeal for my person, yet is unwilling to trace a plan for my Approbation. . . ."[178] All that Chatham would say in reply—secluded as he was in his London residence—was that "if The Duke of Grafton can be prevailed upon to remain at the head of the Treasury, with a Chancellor of the Exchequer agreeable to his Grace [,] Success to your Majesty['s] affairs in Parliament and in the Publick, wou'd be insured. . . ."[179] But the ailing Earl's reference to the displacement of Charles Townshend by some person who was "agreeable" to Grafton did not take into account the fact that the prestige of the Chancellor of the Exchequer was never higher in Parliament than at that very moment, despite his manifest faults of character. He had had his way not only on his bills for creating an American Board of Customs Commissioners and for levying American import duties, but also on the bill he had introduced to discipline the New York Assembly for its attitude toward the Barracks Act. His views on reaching an ac-

[177] *Ibid.*, XXXI, 414, 415, 418; see 7 Geo. III, c. 41; 7 Geo. III, c. 46; 7 Geo. III, c. 56, *Statutes at Large*, VIII, 24–5, 38–42, 48–50.

[178] *Correspondence of George III* (Fortescue), I, 492.

[179] Chatham to the King, June 25, 1767, *ibid.*, I, 493.

commodation with the United East India Company also formed the basis for the agreement embodied into law. It was for his services in this connection that he received the freedom of the city of London. With such an impressive record of accomplishment behind him, upon the ending of the session of Parliament on July 2, he appears to have turned his thoughts to the stabilization of the Ministry and to have "projected a new administration, of which he should be the leader."[180]

The news of the intended resignation of Conway and of the determination of Lord Northington to resign as Lord President on the grounds of his infirmities, together with the manifest incapacity of Chatham to continue even nominal leadership, revealed that there was a pressing need to reconstruct the Ministry. On July 2 Grafton joined Northington in an appeal to the King to ask Chatham "whether he can devize any Plan by which the immediate Execution of Government can be carried on. . . ."[181] That same day the King wrote to the Earl that within a period of ten days the present administration would be falling "into pieces" unless he could suggest proper persons to fill the anticipated vacancies, which also included the office of Chancellor of the Exchequer.[182] But all that Chatham could do was to beg the King's compassion "for the cruel situation which still deprives him of the Possibility of Activity. . . ."[183] Something manifestly had to be done. A correspondent, who seemed to be well informed (could it have been William Strahan, London printer and friend of Benjamin Franklin?), writing to Philadelphia from London on July 11, stated: "Many Conferences have been held, and various Proposals offered. C[harle]s T[ownshen]d hath been tendered the Secretaryship [to be vacated by Conway] but he wants to be First Lord of the Treasury [thus displacing Grafton], and for this End he is paying great Court to Lord B[ute]."[184] But so long as Grafton—as the minister most

---

[180] John Aldolphus: *The History of England from the Accession . . . of King George the Third*, I, 304. It should be pointed out that although both Townshend and Conway were opposed to the bill regulating the dividends of the East India Company, it passed "by a great majority." See *Historical Manuscripts Commission, Report on the Manuscripts of Mrs. Stopford-Sackville*, I, 124.

[181] *Correspondence of George III* (Fortescue), I, 495.

[182] *Ibid.*, I, 494.

[183] *Ibid.*, I, 495. This letter was in the handwriting of Lady Chatham.

[184] An extract of this letter is in the *Pennsylvania Gazette*, October 8, 1767. For the connection of Strahan with William Hall, sole owner of the *Pennsylvania Gazette* after Franklin's retirement in 1766, see J. E. Pomfret: "Some Further Letters of William Strahan, Printer," *Pennsylvania Magazine of History and Biography*, LX, 456. For Strahan see J. A. Cochrane: *Dr. Johnson's Printer: The Life of William Strahan* (Cambridge, Mass., 1965).

closely associated with Chatham—possessed the confidence of the King, there was no likelihood that Townshend's potential claims to political leadership would be given a moment's consideration. It is, nevertheless, not without some significance that two items appeared in the press under August date-lines. One, in the London *Gazetteer and New Daily Advertiser* of August 8, read: "The appointment of Lord Viscount Townshend, elder brother of the Right Hon. Charles Townshend, to the important post of Lord Lieutenant of Ireland, is not a temporary nomination . . ." The other said: "August 14. Yesterday Lady Dalkeith, Lady of the Right Hon. Charles Townshend, kissed his Majesty's hand, on being created a Peeress in her own right, by the title of Countess of Greenwich."[185] Then, on August 8, a London correspondent interested in rumoured plans for changes in the Ministry wrote that "the following Changes will soon take Place, viz. Lord Townshend, Lord Lieutenant of Ireland, in the Room of Lord Bristol; Mr. Conway, Master of the Ordnance, in the Room of Lord Townshend; Mr. Charles Townshend, Secretary of State, in the Room of Mr. Conway; Lord North, Chancellor of the Exchequer, in the Room of Mr. Townshend; and Lord Egmont, President of the Council, in the Room of Lord Northington, who retires on his pension."[186] In other words, Townshend's shadow—despite the views of hostile critics, such as Horace Walpole—certainly loomed much larger on the political horizon during the months of June, July, and August 1767 than at any other period.[187] Yet, nowhere among the leaders of the important Whig groups did his name appear as a prospective chief minister of the King. Rockingham was hoping to take his old place at the Treasury, [188] while Bedford favoured George Grenville's return to it. Grafton was gradually coming to the conclusion that—if Conway would

[185] *Pennsylvania Gazette,* October 15, 1767. Horace Walpole, who was closely in touch with developments, in his *Memoirs of George III* (II, 58) wrote that "Lord Townshend, to please his brother Charles, was destined to be Viceroy of Ireland in the room of Lord Bristol."

[186] *Pennsylvania Gazette,* October 15, 1767. The date of this letter is given as October 8, which undoubtedly is a misprint for August or September.

[187] On this point see John Brooke: *op. cit.,* p. 313.

[188] In view of the need to strengthen the Ministry, the King gave Grafton permission to sound out Rockingham on the possibility of entering it. Rockingham was hoping to be called by the King to create a new administration, but the latter, again using Grafton as the intermediary, insisted that Rockingham must first "specify the plan on which you and your friends would come into office," something that the Marquess, after conferring with the Bedford and Grenville groups, was unable to do because of the deep differences arising between them respecting the filling of places. For the negotiations see Grafton's *Autobiography,* pp. 138–53, especially p. 144; *Memoirs of the Marquis of Rockingham,* II, 46–59; *Correspondence of John, Fourth Duke of Bedford* (ed. Lord John Russell, 3 vols., London, 1842–6), III,

give up his plans to resign—he himself, in line with the desires of George III and Chatham, would remain entrenched as First Lord of the Treasury. But not a word about Townshend.[189] Indeed, Grafton, fully aware that he had been thwarted at every turn by the Chancellor of the Exchequer, was deeply "enraged at Charles Townshend, with whom, he declared, he would not sit in Council."[190] The necessity of doing so was, however, never put to the test. On September 4 Townshend passed away with a putrid fever at the age of forty-two. What his future would have been had he survived no one can say.[191]

365–89; *Grenville Papers,* IV, 227–31; Walpole's *Memoirs of George III,* II, 36–8, 46. Thomas Whately's letter to Lord George Sackville of July 2, 1767, is illuminating on the negotiations between Rockingham, Bedford, Grenville, and Temple; see *Report on the Manuscripts of Mrs. Stopford-Sackville,* I, 68–70.

[189] Referring to negotiations that took place over the reorganization of the Ministry, Horace Walpole notes that "the names of Lord Chatham and Charles Townshend were scarce mentioned, so insignificant had both rendered themselves to the nation and to every faction in it" (*Memoirs of George III,* II, 56). Yet Townshend's success in pushing his program through Parliament, in face of the hostility of certain of his colleagues in the Ministry, belies the fact that he had become at all "insignificant." It is also doubtless true that not one of the older leaders wanted him as chief minister.

[190] *Ibid.,* II, 40.

[191] Sir George Colebrooke, a contemporary who knew him intimately, and was a member of Parliament, has the following to say of him in his unpublished "Memoirs": "The ambition of Mr. Townshend would not have been gratified but by being Minister; and doubtless, had he lived to see the Duke of Grafton resign, he must have had the offer which was made to Lord North, who succeeded him as Chancellor of the Exchequer. But he never would have remained Premier as long as Lord North did. Though much his superior in eloquence and abilities, he wanted the nerve necessary to conduct business with steadiness; and instead of engaging in hostilities with America, he would have been the first to flinch from them, had he lived and been allowed to guide. So far, therefore, his death may be considered as a public loss. As a private man, his friends had used to say that they should not see his like again. . . . Vanity was his ruling passion, and he sacrificed, even before his wife and daughter all sense of decorum to a joke. . . . Where he was really a great man was in Parliament." For the above extract from Colebrooke's unpublished "Memoirs" see *ibid.,* II, 59–60*n.* Among the Germain Papers in the Clements Library is the following estimate of Townshend in the handwriting of Henry Fox, Lord Holland: "In these our days, a Genius hath arisen with such power of intellect that history affords no equal to him . . . and yet, with all these (deficient in constancy and firmness), he hath hitherto done as little good as mischief to his country. His heart is often penetrated with the love of virtue and possessed at times of the noblest feelings of patriotism; for, as he has studied everything, he cannot but perceive . . . the primary virtue of a social being is to promote the happiness of the community of which he is a member; and though this is a duty he frequently wishes to perform, it is always with a proviso that it does not interfere with his love of midnight roar, his propensity to joke, fun and laughable bagatelles of life, which governs all his actions and predominates in the minutest, as well as in the important, affairs." For Sir Lewis Namier's final estimate of Charles Townshend (as recorded by Lady Namier) see Namier and Brooke: *Charles Townshend,* pp. 184–6.

CHAPTER IV

The Implementation of the Townshend Acts

CHARLES TOWNSHEND, who, in the words of the Duke of Grafton, was "led to pledge himself . . . , contrary to the known decision of every member of the Cabinet, to draw a certain revenue from the colonies without offence to the Americans themselves,"[1] did not live to see to what extent this optimistic prophecy would be fulfilled. Having instituted and pressed through Parliament successive bills for setting up an American Board of Customs Commissioners, for providing duties on certain specified articles imported into the colonies, and for making an accommodation with the East India Company concerning disposal of its tea, he left behind him the unfinished business of implementing the measures for more effective enforcement of the trade and navigation acts—including his own additions to them—and for securing an American revenue.

The act for setting up the Board of American Customs Commissioners pointed out the inconveniences under which the customs collectors had been obliged to work as a result of having to apply to the Commissioners in England "upon every particular Doubt and Difficulty." It set forth the conveniences attendant upon having a separate customs system in America, and therefore enacted:

> "That the customs . . . be put under the Management and Direction of such Commissioners . . . as his Majesty . . . by . . . Commission or Commissions under the Great Seal . . . shall judge to be most for the Advantage of Trade and Security of the Revenue of the said British Colonies."

It further enacted that any three or more of the Commissioners so appointed should possess full powers to carry the trade laws into

[1] Grafton's *Autobiography*, p. 137.

execution.[2] Since normally only the royal Governors or the most important civil officers stationed in America were appointed under the Great Seal, the above provision indicated clearly enough the key role in the American revenue system the Commissioners of Customs were expected to play in this altered administrative system. Initially the government had contemplated extending the jurisdiction of the Board to the British West Indies; however, such strong objections were raised by merchants trading to these islands that the Treasury Board had concluded it would be best "to limit the extent of the intended Commission to the Continent of America [including Newfoundland] and the Islands of Bermuda and the Bahamas."[3] Nevertheless, the task of controlling the customs in the more limited area presented formidable problems for effective administration, since the new Board was to have the supervision of forty-two regular ports of entry, as well as nine lesser ports, the whole of which were scattered over an immense area from St. John's, Newfoundland, and the city of Quebec to Nassau in the Bahamas and Mobile in West Florida.[4]

As to the reasons for the selection of Boston by the Lords Commissioners of the Treasury as the American headquarters for the new Customs Board, rather than the more centrally located New York or Philadelphia, one can only speculate.[5] Since the greatest

[2] 7 Geo. III, c. 41, *Statutes at Large*, VIII, 24–5.

[3] Grey Cooper to the Commissioners of Customs, August 7, 1767, P.R.O., Treas. 11. 27:144. See also Professor O. M. Dickerson's article "England's Most Fateful Decision," *New England Quarterly*, XXII, 388–94, in which his position is summed up in the last two lines: "The areas not under the control of the American Commissioners remained loyal and are still a part of the British Empire. The whole course of British history was thus altered by what followed from the fateful decision in 1767."

[4] For the list of chief ports of entry and lesser ports see the scholarly article by Dora M. Clark: "The American Board of Customs, 1767–1783," *American Historical Review*, XLV, 777–806; these ports are listed on p. 793*n*.

[5] William Samuel Johnson, the Connecticut London agent, in a letter to Jared Ingersoll, dated November 12, 1767, wrote: "The Establishment of the Board at Boston rather than at N.Y. was owing to Mr. Paxton's Interest with Charles Townshend who conducted that whole affair" (William Samuel Johnson Papers, Vol. I, No. 23, Connecticut Historical Society Archives, Hartford, Conn.).

In writing to Lord Barrington, Secretary at War, on July 25, 1766, Governor Bernard of Massachusetts Bay commended to him Charles Paxton as "a Gentleman of Boston who has been in the Service of the Crown in the Custom House the best part of his Life with the highest Fidelity & Reputation" (*The Barrington-Bernard Correspondence . . . 1760–1770* [eds. Edward Channing and A. C. Coolidge, *Harvard Historical Studies*, XVII, Cambridge, Mass., 1912], p. 111). That Paxton became an intimate friend of Charles Townshend before returning to America is indicated by a letter written on November 6, 1769, to the latter's brother, Lord Townshend, serving as Lord Lieutenant of Ireland. In this letter Paxton said: "It is not possible for me to forget my Obligations to my Dear deceased Patron [Charles Townshend died in September 1767]. If he had lived, the office I owe to his favor would have been easy to me, his death has made it a most heavy burden . . ." ("Letters of Charles Paxton,"

violence had taken place there in the course of the resistance to the enforcement of the Stamp Act and since violations of the navigation and trade acts had been much more wide-spread in the more northern colonies than elsewhere, they may have felt that it would be wise to have the new watch-dogs of the Treasury established at this critical spot, which also had nearby the greatest concentration of naval forces.[6] It would seem to have been logical reasoning on the part of the framers of the bill that once the Massachusetts Bay merchants were brought into line by close supervision of their conduct, the even more flagrant violators of these laws in nearby Rhode Island could be controlled.

In the selection of personnel for the American Board of Customs Commissioners, the Treasury seems to have looked chiefly for men of experience in the customs service. Henry Hulton had acted as comptroller at the custom house at St. John's in Antigua, and had later served as an inspector in the London custom house; he therefore was well acquainted with problems of law-enforcement in the colonies.[7] John Temple, as has already been emphasized in this series, had had years of experience with the American customs as Surveyor General of the Northern District and was a native of Boston.[8] This was also true of Charles Paxton, who had been the surveyor of the customs at Boston for years and whose father had been a Boston ship captain. John Robinson, before his appointment to the Board, had long been in the English customs service and in 1763 received an appointment as collector in Rhode Island, in which capacity, incidentally, he had suffered great indignities and frustrations. Finally, William Burch was also an Englishman who, in view of the great responsibilities of his position, may be presumed to have had experience in the English customs service. Each member

---

Massachusetts Historical Society *Proceedings*, LVI, 349–51). For other details touching upon the relations of Townshend and Paxton see the article by Dr. Clark cited in the preceding footnote, particularly p. 778*n*. Whether Paxton played a leading role in the decision of the Treasury Board to locate the American Customs Board in Boston can only be conjectured.

[6] See O. M. Dickerson: *The Navigation Acts and the American Revolution* (Philadelphia, 1951), pp. 198–9, in which the author takes the view that the Treasury officials in England knew the relative amount of collections at the various American ports and that the Ministry chose Boston because it represented one-third of the colonial tax returns and not because of any overt acts of resistance on the part of its people.

[7] See C. M. Andrews: *Guide to Materials for American History . . . in the Public Record Office of Great Britain* (2 vols., Carnegie Institution of Washington *Publication* No. 90a, Washington, 1912), II, 61.

[8] For Temple's close association with the Boston radicals see John Cary's *Joseph Warren . . .* (Urbana, 1961), pp. 71–2.

of the Board was entitled to an annual salary of £500.[9] The newly appointed Commissioners, who held their first meeting in Boston two months after Townshend's death, were quickly made aware of two things: the vast number of unprosecuted cases of trade-law violation within the colonies, and the degree of colonial antagonism toward the authority of the Board now charged with controlling these incidents. How the American Customs Commissioners met the situation will be dealt with subsequently.

The final step Townshend had taken for rounding out his revenue program was to secure Parliament's seal of approval on the plan devised by the Treasury Board in 1765 to reorganize the American vice-admiralty courts. These courts, as a separate judiciary system, may be said to have had their rise as the result of the comprehensive Navigation Act of 1696.[10] This act (7 and 8 William III, c. 22, sec. 7) stated that penalties for violating an earlier trade law, "An Act for preventing Frauds, and regulating Abuses in His Majesty's Customs" (14 Charles II, c. 11), could be recovered in any of the courts at Westminster, "or in the Kingdom of Ireland, or in the Court of Admiralty held in His Majesty's Plantations respectively, where such Offence shall be committed, at the Pleasure of the Officer or Informer. . . ." In order to enforce the provisions of this statute a number of vice-admiralty districts were created the following year in America.[11] These districts were altered from time

[9] For the commission, dated September 14, 1767, appointing the specific Customs Commissioners mentioned above, see *Pennsylvania Gazette Postscript* of September 15, 1767, and *Boston Evening-Post,* September 26, 1767. In the former it fills two columns and a half; in the latter, the whole of the front page and more than a column on the second.

[10] It is true that in 1662 a vice-admiralty court was erected in Jamaica. Admiralty jurisdiction also seems to have been exercised at an early period in New York. In the words of E. A. Werner: "The Governor and Council acted in the time of the Dutch as the Judges of the Court. Subsequently, under the Duke of York, special commissions were issued by the Governor to determine such cases according as they occurred, until 1678, when authority was given to appoint a judge and other officers of the Court, which, at first, was established by warrant, or by virtue of the governor's commission; but eventually depended on the Lords of Admiralty in England" (*Civil List and Constitutional History of the Colony and State of New York* [Albany, 1855], p. 371). For reference to an early admiralty court in Connecticut see *Connecticut Colonial Records,* III, 132.

[11] For the beginnings of vice-admiralty jurisdiction in America see C. M. Andrews: *The Colonial Period of American History* (4 vols., New Haven, 1934–8), IV, 222–9, and his introduction, "Vice-Admiralty Courts in the Colonies," to *The Records of the Vice Admiralty Court of Rhode Island, 1716–1752* (ed. Dorothy S. Towle, Washington, 1936); see also Helen J. Crump: *Colonial Admiralty Jurisdiction in the Seventeenth Century* (London, 1931), and Carl Ubbelohde: *The Vice-Admiralty Courts and the American Revolution* (Chapel Hill, N.C., 1960).

to time, and—it is a matter of interest to note—by royal commission in 1701 William Attwood, chief justice of New York, and Sampson Shelton Broughton, attorney general of the same colony, were appointed respectively judge of the admiralty and advocate general in New York with their jurisdiction extended to comprehend New Hampshire, Massachusetts Bay, Rhode Island, Connecticut, and East and West New Jersey.[12] By the middle of the eighteenth century there were twelve vice-admiralty districts: Quebec; Nova Scotia; Newfoundland; New Hampshire and Massachusetts Bay; Rhode Island; Connecticut, New York, and New Jersey; Pennsylvania and the Lower Counties on the Delaware; Maryland; Virginia; North Carolina; South Carolina; and Georgia.

Since these vice-admiralty courts were civil courts, their organization and procedures differed markedly from common law courts. There was no jury. A single judge heard and determined all cases; he was aided by an advocate general, a register, and a marshal. He determined the time and place for holding court.[13] His decisions were, as a rule, made without much delay, for his pay depended upon bringing trials to a conclusion. Matters involving maritime activities—such as seamen's wages, ship salvage, and prize cases in time of war—as well as violations of the navigation and trade acts, might come before him.[14] In fact his court was preferred to the common law courts because of the speedy decisions obtained in it on such issues as disputes over wages. In salvage and prize cases he also performed a function of great importance to shippers and ship-masters.

Originally the vice-admiralty courts in America were expected to deal with seamen's wage disputes and salvage cases as well as to uphold the navigation and trade acts, but their duties were gradually extended. For example, in 1707 "An Act for ascertaining the Rates of foreign coins in her Majesty's Plantations in America" (6 Anne, c. 30) provided that those who violated its provisions might be sued by the injured party "in any of her Majesty's Courts

[12] *Acts of the Privy Council, Col. Ser., 1680–1720,* p. 363.

[13] For example, in 1752 Lewis Morris, both chief justice of New York and judge of the Court of Vice-Admiralty for Connecticut, New York, and New Jersey, held the vice-admiralty court in New London which heard the famous case of the Spanish ship *St. Joseph and St. Helena* and its cargo. See the author's *Jared Ingersoll: A Study of American Loyalism in Relation to British Colonial Government* (New Haven, 1920), p. 63.

[14] For a detailed discussion of the work of vice-admiralty courts before 1763 see C. M. Andrews: *op. cit.,* IV, 230–47.

of Justice within any of the said Plantations," thus not limiting such action to courts of record. The act of 1721 for the preservation of white pine trees (8 George I, c. 12, sec. 5)—unlike the earlier statutes concerning these trees (3 and 4 Anne, c. 10, sec. 6, and 9 Anne, c. 17) which had included provisions for enforcement by one or more justices of the peace in the place where the violation took place—stipulated that hearings should be "before a Judge of the Admiralty, or his Deputy. . ." of the vice-admiralty district in question.

The gradual expansion of power in the colonial vice-admiralty courts may be further illustrated. The Molasses Act of 1733 (20 George II, c. 13, sec. 3) provided for violations of this act to be prosecuted in any court of vice-admiralty or court of record in the colony where the offence was committed, at the election of the informer or prosecutor. In 1764 the Sugar Act (4 George III, c. 15, sec. 41) not only gave the same recourse for violations of its terms but went beyond the statute of 1733 by declaring that "Forfeitures and Penalties inflicted by this or any other Act or Acts of Parliament relating to the Trade and Revenues of the said British Colonies shall . . . be prosecuted . . . in any Court of Record, or in any Court of Admiralty, in the said Colonies . . . where such Offence shall be committed, or in any Court of Vice Admiralty which may . . . be appointed over all America. . . ." This law was designed to clear up uncertainties in early trade regulations that would seem to have confined action to a court of record.[15] The Stamp Act (5 George III, c. 12, sec. 57), it may be noted, although repealed in 1766, had sought to widen the range of powers of the colonial vice-admiralty court by offering the informer a choice between this court

[15] For example, there was "An Act for the Encouragement of Trade," passed in 1663 (15 Chas. II, c. 7), which provided that penalties for violations of it could be sued "in any of his Majesty's Courts in such . . . Colonies . . . where the Offense was committed, or in any Court of Record in England. . . ." Thomas Whately, a secretary of the Treasury, replying on February 16, 1765, to a query from Attorney General Charles Yorke on what cases could go to general courts of vice-admiralty, gave an extended account of the courts' jurisdiction, adding: "I have been informed that the construction of the words of 15th Charles 2nd, *any court* has often been litigated before the Council." He then referred to the cases: Kennedy vs. Forbes, decided February 1742, Ritchie vs. Newton, decided March 1759, and Major vs. Newton, decided March 1763; in all of these cases the Act was interpreted to mean that trial was to take place in a court of record; however, in the case of Laurence vs. Gaffer, a case arising in Newfoundland that was decided in December 1763, the jurisdiction of the court of vice-admiralty was applied and the former decisions questioned. See Hardwicke Papers relating to America, B.M., Add. Mss., 35911, folio 11

and a court of record,[16] with the court in either case having jurisdiction within the colony where the violation took place. As had been true of the Sugar Act, one of the clauses of the Stamp Act having to do with vice-admiralty jurisdiction (sec. 58) embraced any act of Parliament relating to trade or revenue. Under the terms of the statute of 1768 designed to enforce the Townshend Acts, there was now no mention of courts of record. All forfeitures and penalties for violating any act of Parliament relating to trade or revenue were to be recovered in the vice-admiralty court which had jurisdiction in the colony where the violation took place, "any Law, custom, or Usage, to the contrary notwithstanding."[17] This meant, provided its provisions were enforced, that the common law courts were no longer competent to hear such cases. It therefore also spelled the end of the practice in a number of colonies of having cases of trade law violations transferred from a court of vice-admiralty to a common law court by means of a writ of prohibition issued by a common law judge or even by a colonial Governor acting alone or with the Council[18]—with a consequent verdict of acquittal of the accused generally assured.

In contrast to the steady increase in the powers of the American vice-admiralty courts was the limited role of the Admiralty Court of Great Britain[19]—outside of such matters as seamen's wages and prize cases in time of war. As Blackstone pointed out, this court could try only maritime cases arising "on the high seas, out of the reach of our ordinary courts of justice . . . and not within the

[16] Writing of the Court of Admiralty in England, Sir William Blackstone has the following to say (*Commentaries on the Laws of England* [4 vols., 4th edn., Oxford, 1770], III, 69): "It is no court of record, any more than the spiritual courts." Earlier in his treatise he explained the difference between courts of record and those that were not (*ibid.*, III, 24): "A court of record is that where the acts and judicial proceedings are enrolled in parchment for a perpetual memorial and testimony: which rolls are called records of the court, and are of such high and super eminent authority, that their truth is not to be called in question."

[17] It may be noted that despite the terms of the Sugar Act, Grey Cooper, a secretary of the Treasury, strongly opposed to the extension of the jurisdiction of the vice-admiralty courts in America, took the position in writing to Secretary of State Conway in 1766, cited above, that under the terms of the Act for the Encouragement of Trade, passed in 1663 (15 Chas. II, c. 7), the recovery of penalties and forfeitures for violation of its provisions had been vested exclusively in the courts of common law in the colonies. See P.R.O., C.O. 5:67, pp. 239–40.

[18] For the use of writs of prohibition in the colonies see C. M. Andrews: *op. cit.*, IV, 261–3.

[19] In the *Pennsylvania Journal* of January 26, 1774, a letter by one signing himself "Russel" contrasts the limited powers of the Court of Admiralty in England with the powers conferred by commission on the judges of American vice-admiralty courts. The public letter was in reality addressed to Judge Jared Ingersoll of the vice-admiralty court at Philadelphia.

precincts of any county."[20] This limitation of activity came about by acts of Parliament—including that of 1389 in the reign of Richard II, which directed that "the admiral and his deputy shall not meddle with any thing, but only things done upon the sea," and the statute of 1391, also in the reign of Richard II, which declared that the court of the admiral "hath no matter of cognizance of any contract, or of any other thing, done within the body of any county, either by land or by water. . . ."[21] It was further circumscribed by writs of prohibition, issued by Sir Edward Coke, Chief Justice of the Court of Common Pleas and later of the King's Bench, and other judges of common law courts at Westminster, forbidding the Court of Admiralty to interfere in issues not concerned with the high seas.[22]

Before 1764, the jurisdiction of the admiralty courts had not been deemed a serious grievance by colonials. The hostility of Americans toward these courts appears to have been directed more against their objective of enforcing parliamentary measures for taxation than against the regulation of colonial trade or the actual competence of the courts. The situation, however, began to change in 1764, with the creation, under the Great Seal, of the Court of Vice-Admiralty over all America, with headquarters at Halifax.[23] The government had hoped that this court, with original jurisdiction involving cases of seizure, and presided over by Dr. William Spry, a judge deeply learned in the law, would have the effect of instilling vitality into the enforcement of imperial trade regulations. But it was soon realized that the new court—isolated as it was from the main stream of colonial commerce—could not prove effective.[24] Furthermore, reaction quickly set in in Massachusetts Bay, where in November the House of Representatives prepared a petition, in which the Council concurred, protesting that "the extension of the powers of the Courts of Vice Admiralty have, so far as the jurisdiction of the said Courts hath been extended, deprived the Colonies of

[20] Blackstone: *op. cit.*, III, 106.

[21] *Ibid.*

[22] Sir William Holdsworth: *A History of English Law* (13 vols.+, London, 1903+), XII, 697–8.

[23] See Volume X of this series, pp. 229–31; see also Carl Ubbelohde: *op. cit.*, pp. 3–4, 48–50, 53–6, 60–9, 72–3, 130–1.

[24] The only case tried successfully in Judge Spry's court was that of the *Polly*, seized at Newport and ultimately sold at auction after the case was brought before the court at Halifax. See Volume X in this series, pp. 243–4, and Carl Ubbelohde: *op. cit.*, pp. 67–9. For the cases which customs collectors sought unsuccessfully to prosecute at the Halifax court during the period of the Stamp Act crisis, and the continued trial of seizure cases in the local vice-admiralty courts during that period, see *ibid.*, pp. 84–8.

one of the most valuable of English liberties, trials by juries."[25] The petition, directed chiefly against the Sugar Act of 1764, named, as its first grievance against the Halifax Court of Vice-Admiralty constituted over all America, the hardship imposed by the court's distance from the scene of the seizure and the attendant possibility that "many persons, however legally their goods may have been imported, must lose their property, merely from an inability of following after it, and making that defence which they might do if the trial had been in the Colony where the goods were seized." Another major objection was that the officers "by this Act are indemnified in case of seizure whensoever the Judge of Admiralty shall certify that there was probable cause, and the claimant can neither have costs nor maintain an action against the person seizing, how much soever he may have expended in defence of his property."[26] An additional condemnation of Judge Spry's court was not well founded, since it rested on arguments concerning the payment of his salary out of a percentage received from the seizures confirmed in his court. Actually, the provincial vice-admiralty judges had always depended upon their share of condemnations for their salaries, whereas, in point of fact, the payment of Judge Spry's salary was guaranteed by the home government, whether the funds were available from seizures and forfeitures or not.[27]

It was evident that any effort on the part of American customs officials located south of Halifax to see that cases were brought before the new court led to serious protests from colonial merchants and ship-owners, who continued to claim the right of trials by jury for those accused of violating the trade and navigation laws. The officials of the Treasury had little sympathy with the demand for jury trials in cases involving smuggling, on the ground that there was no trusting "the Breach of Revenue Laws to a Jury . . . where the Offence is Committed, that they find even in England they never can obtain Verdicts in the Counties where Smuggling is practiced and therefore always bring the Causes up for trial to

[25] See *Journal of the House of Representatives* (Boston, 1764–5), pp. 129, 132, 133, 135. On the issue over the right of trial by jury see also G. A. Washburne: *Imperial Control of the Administration of Justice in the Thirteen American Colonies, 1684–1776* (Columbia University *Studies in History,* CV, No. 2 [238], New York, 1923), pp. 176–7. Blackstone himself (*Commentaries,* III, 379) declared that "trial by jury ever has been, and I trust ever will be, looked upon as the glory of the English law."

[26] For the petition see "Bowdoin-Temple Papers," Massachusetts Historical Society *Collections,* 6th ser., IX, 32–6.

[27] For Judge Spry's commission see Hardwicke Papers, B.M., Add. Mss. 35910, folio 225.

London."[28] They did feel, however, that there was reasonable ground for complaint against taking people for trial "from one End of America almost to the other"[29] and on July 4, 1765, in a representation to the King in Council, they proposed "that the Vice Admiralty Court at Halifax be transferred to Boston and that two other courts be established at Philadelphia and Charleston."[30] This recommendation was referred to Attorney General Charles Yorke and Solicitor General William de Grey for their opinion as to whether His Majesty could revoke the letters patent creating the Vice-Admiralty Court for all America in order to establish the three other courts proposed by the Treasury Board.[31] On December 21 they gave their opinion "that the Admiralty Court may be revoked by the Same Authority under which it was Established; and that in lieu thereof the three other courts mentioned in the Memorial of the late Lords Commissioners of his Majestys Treasury may be established by the Comissioners . . . ," but that the judges of these courts should "be directed by Express Words in their Commission to hold their Courts at a Place certain, within the Several Districts to be Marked out."[32]

The next step in the direction of reorganizing the vice-admiralty

[28] Jared Ingersoll to Governor Fitch, March 6, 1765, "Jared Ingersoll Papers," New Haven Colony Historical Society *Papers,* IX, 318–19.

[29] *Ibid.*

[30] *Acts of the Privy Council, Col. Ser., 1745–1766,* p. 664. This plan was formulated by Grenville. On June 6, 1765, a minute of the Treasury stated that to enforce the Stamp Act and other acts it recommended the removal of the Vice-Admiralty Court at Halifax to Boston and the establishment of courts at Philadelphia and Charleston. The following day its Secretary, Charles Jenkinson, wrote to the Board of Trade concerning the extent of the districts proper to be allowed to each of the proposed courts and the manner in which each district could best be marked out and described. See P.R.O., C.O. 5:323, pp. 281 and 285, and *Journal of the Commissioners for Trade and Plantations, 1764–1767,* pp. 185–6. This will be referred to hereafter as Board of Trade *Journal.* Under date of July 4, 1765, there is a paper entitled "A plan of Districts proper to be allotted to the Courts of Vice Admiralty to be appointed in America," which accompanied the representation of the Treasury Board of that date, attached to the "Memorandum Relative to the Appointment of Vice-Admiralty Courts in America" (1767). These are among the Plantations General papers, P.R.O., C.O. 5:67, pp. 277–94. That the matter had been under consideration for some time is indicated in the letter written by Jared Ingersoll early in March 1765 to Governor Fitch of Connecticut telling of the plan to have "three Judges . . . sent from England" to be placed at Boston, New York or Philadelphia, and Charleston, and who, with salaries of £800, would have both concurrent and appeal jurisdiction with relation to the other vice-admiralty courts established in America. See *Mr. Ingersoll's Letters Relating to the Stamp-Act* (New Haven, 1766), pp. 23–4.

[31] *Acts of the Privy Council, Col. Ser., 1745–1766,* p. 664.

[32] "Copy of the Report made by the Attorney & Sollr General in pursuance of the Committee Orders. December 21, 1765," Stowe Americana, Miscellaneous File, 1670–1813, Huntington Library. See also *Acts of the Privy Council, Col. Ser. Unbound Papers* p. 403.

court system took place on January 31, 1766, when, as a result of the address of the House of Commons to the King calling for the papers relating to the American Stamp Act crisis, Secretary of State Conway laid before the House the representation of the Treasury Board together with the law officers' report upon it.[33] On March 3, copies of fourteen other papers concerning the colonial situation were presented to the House. Among these were the memorial of the Treasury of October 4, 1763, that had led to the creation of the Court of Vice-Admiralty over all America and the plan of July 4, 1765, to supplement this court.[34] Other more pressing matters occupied the attention of both the Rockingham and Chatham administrations until the spring of 1767, but meanwhile Grey Cooper, a secretary of the Treasury, wrote on December 18, 1766, to Secretary of State Conway to offer certain proposals for reforming the American vice-admiralty jurisdiction. Cooper proposed to achieve this reformation by doing away with the Vice-Admiralty Court for all America and transferring the judge of this court, Dr. Spry, to the provincial New York–Connecticut–New Jersey vice-admiralty district as judge of this court "with a considerable Salary"; he also suggested appointing two other able civilians to be judges at the provincial courts of vice-admiralty at Boston and Charleston "or any other two Stations which shall be thought more convenient with such Salaries as may render the Offices respectable"; finally, he sought such other reforms as giving credit to the proceedings of these provincial courts, and regulating the fees which "depend in great measure upon the Condemnation of the Ship or the conviction of the Offender" so as to "reconcile the Americans to the decision of the Provincial Courts of Vice Admiralty."[35] In April 1767 Secretary of State Shelburne—in a communication to the Board of Trade requesting a detailed account of financial provisions made for the Governors and those officers in the colonies concerned with the administration of justice—complained of having "no Account of any of the Admiralty Courts in the Plantations" and asked for a statement on the establishment of these courts and the salaries of the judges and other officers.[36]

It is clear that Shelburne, along with others in the government,

---

[33] *Journals of the House of Commons*, XXX, 508.

[34] *Acts of the Privy Council, Col. Ser., 1745–1766*, pp. 664–5; see also C.O. 5:67, pp. 256–64.

[35] For this letter see P.R.O., C.O. 5:67, pp. 237–48. See also Carl Ubbelohde: *op. cit.*, pp. 91–2.

[36] Shelburne to the Board of Trade, April 9 and 28, 1767, Shelburne Papers, 53:55, 77–8, Clements Library.

saw a disturbing disparity between the small amount of revenue being derived from the continental colonies and the mounting cost of maintaining and defending them, as has been emphasized earlier in this volume. The following item among the Shelburne Papers illustrates the heavy expenses involved: "The sum voted by Parliament for America for the Service of the Year 1765 amounted to £363,582.15.9½, exclusive of the Naval Establishment."[37] But this figure apparently covered only a portion of the expense of maintaining America, as was made clear in the preceding chapter.

Whatever may have been the total expense of supporting civil government in North America, of maintaining an army there for security purposes and a patrol of royal navy ships off its shores as a check on smuggling activities, it is at least clear that the concentration of British regulars and naval strength in 1767 could not be construed as a threat against the refractory older continental colonies. In a "List of His Majesty's ships stationed or intended to be stationed at Newfoundland and in America," seven were given as stationed off Newfoundland, six in the Gulf of St. Lawrence down to Cape Sable, three about the Bay of Fundy, two from the Bay of Fundy to Sandy Hook, two from Sandy Hook to Cape Henlopen, two from Cape Henlopen to Cape Henry, two from Cape Henry to Cape Fear, two from Cape Fear to Cape Florida and the Bahama Islands, ten about Jamaica and the Gulf of Mexico, and seven at the Leeward Islands.[38] As for the British regular forces stationed in North America, presumably as of February 22, 1767, there were apparently 59 companies stationed in Canada, Nova Scotia, and Newfoundland; the rest were distributed as follows: 9 in the Great Lakes region, 12 in the Illinois country and the upper Ohio (Fort Pitt), 5 in New York, 6 in Philadelphia, 9 at Elizabeth and Perth Amboy, New Jersey, 3 on the frontier of South Carolina and Georgia, 18 in West Florida, 6 in East Florida, with 1 each in

[37] *Ibid,* 57:231. The item quoted above was apparently part of a memorandum from the Chancellor of the Exchequer prepared in 1767 (*ibid.,* 57:261), which throws additional light on the problem of the support of the Empire. See, for example, the following notation from it (the meaning of which is not entirely clear): "Memorandum from Mr. Townshend of Expense on account of America etc: Expense of Senegal £6,500. America without Extraordinaries £165,000. In General the Expense supposed to be within £800,000 of the Publick Income counting the Encrease of the Excise and Customs[,] not counting Indian Expences Ext[raordinar]y[,] Admiralty Expence etc." The figure of £800,000 as American expense must have included the cost of the naval patrol in the New World as well as of the army, along with the support of all civilian officials and the payment of subsidies to the weaker colonies.

[38] Shelburne Papers, 49:629–30.

Bermuda and Providence Island of the Bahamas.[39] But in a suggested disposition of the troops sent by Gage to Lord Barrington, Secretary at War, also on February 22, 1767, showing the distribution of 15 regular regiments and 10 companies of artillery, it was proposed to quarter one of the regiments either in Massachusetts Bay or in Connecticut.[40] In fact, the question of the desirability of concentrating all the armed forces in North America in the newer colonies—rather than in the older ones, as Grenville sought to require the government to do—was under discussion in the spring of 1767. Gage, not averse to the idea, recommended in his letter of April 3 to Shelburne that, if this were done, a fifth regiment should be stationed in the Province of Quebec, but he pointed out that a proper disposition of the remaining regiments in the new colonies would require the construction of additional barracks in each of them except Nova Scotia.[41] All this would, of course, require additional funds for constructing the barracks and for meeting additional costs of supplying and provisioning the troops so located.

In view of the great burden that rested on the shoulders of the people of Great Britain for maintaining the home government, for servicing the immense public debt, and for administering the Empire,[42] it can be understood why even the Chatham administration—before the passage of the Townshend Acts—studied what steps might be taken to check smuggling into the colonies. George Grenville calculated that as the result of the clandestine trade in America the Treasury lost more than £500,000 a year in revenue.[43] In writing to Thomas Gage, Commander-in-Chief of all His Majesty's Forces in North America, on December 11, 1766, Secretary of State

---

[39] "General Distribution of His Majesty's Forces in North America," February 22, 1767, *ibid.*, 49:646–7.

[40] *Gage Correspondence,* II, 408–10. Gage's proposed disposition of troops shows a variation from the number of companies and their location as given in the Shelburne Papers. Of the 15 regiments, 4 are shown for Quebec, 1 for the Great Lakes area, 2 for Nova Scotia and Newfoundland, 1 for West Florida, 2 for East Florida, Georgia, and South Carolina, 1 for the Illinois country and the upper Ohio (Fort Pitt), 1 for New York, 1 for Pennsylvania, 1 for New Jersey, and 1 for either Massachusetts Bay or Connecticut. The artillery company disposition (in figures which do not agree with the total given) shows 2 companies for Quebec, 2 for the posts on the Great Lakes, 2 for Nova Scotia and Newfoundland, 1 for West Florida, 1 for East Florida, 1 for Pennsylvania, and 2 for New York.

[41] Shelburne Papers, 51:78–83; see also *Gage Correspondence,* I, 124–8.

[42] See Volume X of this series, especially Chap. 9.

[43] Grenville to Lord Botetourt, November 3, 1765, Grenville Letter Books, Vol. 2, Stowe Collection, Huntington Library.

Shelburne stressed the point that the suppression of smuggling there was essential from the point of view of "the well-being of Commerce in general, and the Finances of this Country [Great Britain] in particular." He therefore called upon him to suggest "the best manner of attaining this very desirable end . . . ; and . . . spare no pains to be well informed of the several Species of Smuggling in the different Provinces. . . ."[44]

Replying to Shelburne's letter on April 28, 1767, Gage wrote:

> "The principal Articles Smuggled into North America, are several sorts of Dutch East-India Goods, particularly Teas in great Quantitys, Spices, Chintzes, etc. Dutch Gun-Powder, German Linnens, Hemp, Yarn, etc. from Holland, Hamburgh, Curosoa, Monte Christie, S[t] Eustatia [and] Likewise from our own Islands, where it is brought in from the foreign Islands. . . . The Merchant reckons the Duty . . . on foreign Sugars high, and consequently a great deal is smuggled. . . . The Act of the 6th of George the 3[d] [6 George III, c. 52, sec. 116], which grants Liberty of storing Sugars for twelve Months before the Duty is paid, or that it is exported, gives a great opening to Fraud. . . . The Trade to Holland becoming hazardous [in the New England provinces], . . . those heretofore concerned in Smuggling directly from Holland, have directed their Correspondents there, to deposit annually at the Island of S[t] Eustatia certain Quantitys of Teas and other Commodities . . . The Merchants send from the Provinces a Cargo to some of the British Islands, where they ship a small Quantity of Molasses, and other Commodities which they clear out legaly, and then proceed to S[t] Eustatia for Teas and other Dutch East India Goods."

As to the best manner of preventing this wholesale smuggling, Gage suggested that this might be accomplished "if armed cutters were properly impowered to visit vessels bound to North America which come from any foreign port, and if small detachments of troops were posted along the [North American] Coast to assist the Custom house Officers in the execution of their Duty."[45]

It was not until early in 1768, however, that any definitive steps were taken to implement the Treasury recommendations for strengthening the American vice-admiralty courts. In February the House of Commons was concerned with ways and means to meet deficits in expenditures in America beyond the sums granted. On the 22nd a resolution from the committee of the whole House

---

[44] *Gage Correspondence,* II, 50.

[45] "Abstracts from Gage's Dispatches, April 28, 1767," Shelburne Papers, 51:97–101. *Gage Correspondence,* I, 135–7.

recommended various means for "defraying the extraordinary Expences of His Majesty's Land Forces, and other Services, incurred to the 25th Day of December 1767, and not provided for by Parliament."[46] The resolution only served to highlight what was felt to be the unfair distribution of burdens for the support of the Empire. As a result, on the following day leave was given to bring in a bill "for the more easy and effectual Recovery of the Penalties and Forfeitures, inflicted by the Acts of Parliament relating to the Trade or Revenues of the British Colonies and Plantations in America. . . ."[47] On the 24th a bill was presented to that end by Lord North, as Chancellor of the Exchequer, a post he had taken over after some hesitation soon after the death of Townshend.[48] The bill passed through the various stages of enactment in both houses without debate and received the royal approval on March 8.[49]

The importance of the statute lies in the fact that it was aimed at curtailing American smuggling by providing for the prosecution of violations of all acts of Parliament relating to trade or revenues "in any Court of Vice-Admiralty appointed or to be appointed, . . . which shall have Jurisdiction within the Colony . . . where the Cause of such Prosecution . . . shall have arisen." It further provided that "either party who shall think himself aggrieved by such Determination may appeal, from such Determination, to any Court of Vice-Admiralty . . . which shall have Jurisdiction within such Colony . . . ; which Court of Vice-Admiralty is hereby authorized and required to proceed . . . and determine, all such Suits, Prosecutions, and Appeals; any Law, Custom, or Usage, to the contrary notwithstanding."[50] This law represents the culmination of the gradual growth in jurisdiction of the courts of vice-admiralty in the British colonies.

The Treasury Board did not begin to implement the above statute until July 2, 1768, when it sent a representation to the Privy Council. Recommending the revocation of the commission creating the Court over all America, it specified in lieu thereof the establishment of

[46] The deficit was apparently quite large as, among other recommendations, it was proposed that the sum of £106,358.17.8 be utilized out of the monies received for provisions delivered to the troops serving in North America. Additional recommendations included one that a certain sum be drawn "out of the Balance of the Twelve Pence in the Pound Deduction from the Pay of the Out Pensioners of Chelsea Hospital [for invalid soldiers]." *Journals of the House of Commons,* XXXI, 625–6.

[47] *Ibid.,* XXXI, 630.

[48] Grafton's *Autobiography,* pp. 166–7.

[49] *Journals of the House of Commons,* XXXI, 633, 649, 661.

[50] 8 Geo. III, c. 22, *Statutes at Large,* VIII, 60–1.

the following courts: (1) a district court at Halifax[51] with original jurisdiction in all cases arising within the limits of Quebec, Newfoundland, and Nova Scotia and also all cases involving the capture of ships to the northward of 43° 15′ north latitude, or of ships whose port of destination was within this district; (2) a district court at Boston, comprehending the colonies of New Hampshire, Massachusetts Bay, Rhode Island, and Connecticut, and the waters between 40° 30′ and 44° 30′ north latitude (3) a district court at Philadelphia, which would include New York, New Jersey, Pennsylvania, the Lower Counties on the Delaware, Maryland, and Virginia, with jurisdiction over ships captured between 41° and 36° 15′ north latitude; and (4) a district court at Charlestown comprehending the colonies of North Carolina, South Carolina, Georgia, East Florida, and West Florida, and including the North Atlantic waters to the southward of 36° 45′ north latitude.[52] An order in council was issued on July 6 covering these recommendations, which was followed on August 4 by letters patent under the Great Seal creating the four courts in place of the one.[53] On September 7 another order in council, following the precedent set in the establishment of the Vice-Admiralty Court for all America, provided that the judges should receive a stated salary of £600 in lieu of fees of office.[54] The commission appointing Spry was revoked on September 21, and warrants were then issued on September 22 for the preparation of letters patent under the seal of the High Court of Admiralty for each of the four judges, who were therein named.[55]

When the problem of the reorganization of the vice-admiralty jurisdiction in America had first been under serious consideration in 1765, it had been contemplated, following the example of the creation of the Vice-Admiralty Court for all America, to send over

---

[51] The Treasury Department's proposal in 1765 had been the substitution for the Halifax Vice-Admiralty Court over all America of only three courts, all situated in North American ports south of Nova Scotia. Doubtless, the fact that the heaviest concentrations of patrol ships off the coast of North America were in the waters of the Gulf of St. Lawrence and the Bay of Fundy area had determined the Treasury officials to plan for a fourth court with headquarters to remain at Halifax. There it would be handy for dealing with cases relating to violation of the trade acts in the vicinity of St. Pierre and Miquelon (so that these two small French Islands might not become great smuggling centres similar to the Dutch island of St. Eustatius in the West Indies), as well as in those areas comprehending the Province of Quebec and Newfoundland.

[52] *Acts of the Privy Council, Col. Ser., 1766–1783,* pp. 151–3.

[53] See P.R.O., Admiralty Papers, Secretary's Department, In-Letters, 3679.

[54] *Acts of the Privy Council, Col. Ser., 1766–1783,* p. 153.

[55] P.R.O., Admiralty 2:1057, pp. 402–9, 409–14. The warrants also contained a recital of the King's letters patent.

from England the judges for these new courts.[56] By 1768, however, it was determined to select colonials trained in the law who were deserving of consideration and would be disposed to help bring about the enforcement of the acts of Parliament relating to trade and revenue. The appointment for the Halifax District was Jonathan Sewall, attorney general of Massachusetts Bay and advocate general of the vice-admiralty court in that province. A graduate of Harvard College and an excellent lawyer, he long enjoyed the confidence of John Adams.[57] The appointment to the Boston District was given to the judge of the Court of Vice-Admiralty for Massachusetts and New Hampshire, Robert Auchmuty, who had served in that post since 1766. It may be noted that his father, also trained in the law, had held this position until 1741, when he went to England as a special London agent for Massachusetts Bay. It had then gone to Chambers Russell, who passed away in 1766.[58] For the Philadelphia District there was named as judge the eminent Connecticut lawyer Jared Ingersoll, a graduate of Yale, one-time London agent for his colony, and later stamp distributor for it.[59] Finally, as judge of the Charleston District the choice fell on Augus-

---

[56] Jared Ingersoll to Governor Fitch, London, July 4, 1765, *Mr. Ingersoll's Letters Relating to the Stamp-Act,* pp. 23–4. Spry, it may be noted, was commissioned Governor of Barbados, a post he held until his death in 1772. The imposing-sounding office of "Vice Admiral over all America," held in absentia by the Earl of Northumberland (P.R.O., Adm. 2:1057, p. 213), being but a paper commission, was not affected by the revocation of the single judge and single court.

[57] Adams wrote of Sewall in his "Diary" on November 21, 1772, that he was "the best Friend I had in the World. I loved him accordingly and corresponded with him many Years without Reserve." He then went on to state: "But the Scene is changed. At this Moment I look upon him [as] the most bitter, malicious, determined and implacable Enemy I have. God forgive him the Part he has acted, both in public and private Life! It is not impossible that he may make the same Prayer for me" (*Adams Papers,* 1st ser., *Diary and Autobiography of John Adams* [eds. L. H. Butterfield, *et al.,* 4 vols., Cambridge, Mass., 1961], II, 67).

[58] Robert Auchmuty, Sr., was a Scot and a student of law at the Middle Temple in London who won distinction as a Boston lawyer before his appointment in 1733 as judge of the local court of vice-admiralty. It was in his office that his son received his legal education.

[59] See L. H. Gipson: *Jared Ingersoll . . . ,* pp. 294–8. It may be noted that Lord North, soon after taking office as Chancellor of the Exchequer, got in touch with Ingersoll's friend Thomas Whately, who had been a secretary of the Treasury under Grenville, to learn if it would be agreeable to the late Connecticut stamp distributor to receive the appointment of judge of vice-admiralty "at Phila. Virg^{ia} or S^{o} Carolina," with a salary of £400 a year. Whately, after advising with the Connecticut London agent, William Samuel Johnson, indicated to North that he thought Ingersoll would accept a post at Philadelphia or in Virginia but not at South Carolina; "that seems too far South for a Northern Constitution . . ." (William Samuel Johnson to Jared Ingersoll, November 30, 1767, Johnson Papers, Vol. 1, No. 25, Connecticut Historical Society Archives, Hartford, Conn). This was a year before the actual appointments were made.

tus Johnston, who from 1757 to 1766 served as attorney general of Rhode Island, being re-elected each year, and who in 1765 had received the appointment of stamp distributor for his colony. Not only were these men well trained in the law but their loyalty to the government of Great Britain had been tested in an area where violations of the trade laws had been flagrant—New England.[60]

Commissioned under the seal of the Admiralty, the four new judges bore the title of "Judge Commissary Deputy and Surrogate of the Court of Vice Admiralty."[61] They were provided with liberal salaries, clearly designed to place them out of reach of the venal influences that had occasionally played upon the local courts of vice-admiralty, where compensation depended entirely upon the fees of office.[62] Furthermore, they enjoyed increased authority over the powers held by any of the local judges. The original jurisdiction of the new courts extended not only to all civil and maritime causes arising within their respective districts common to admiralty law, such as had been heard by the provincial admiralty courts, but also to all district cases concerned with breaches of the trade laws. Further, they had jurisdiction in appeals from the local courts, "but such Appeals not be final and saving always a Right . . . to appeal

---

[60] Both Lewis Morris, Jr., and Richard Morris, his son, who succeeded him in 1762, held the post of judge of the Court of Vice-Admiralty for New York, Connecticut, and New Jersey. For many years they were identified in the public mind as opponents of the royal Governor of New York and therefore they encountered very little popular opposition. This was also true of Judge Edward Shippen of the local Philadelphia Court of Vice-Admiralty, who, according to Governor Hamilton, connived at the Philadelphia merchants' "illegal and treasonable trade with the French West Indies" during the late war. The same thing may be said of Egerton Leigh of the local Charleston Court of Vice-Admiralty, who in 1761 refused to condemn vessels trading with the enemy though the evidence was clear on the point at issue. For the Morrises see *New York Colonial Documents,* VII, 455; VIII, 455; and the author's *Jared Ingersoll,* pp. 63–4, 83, 103. For Shippen see Andrew Hamilton to William Pitt, November 1, 1760, *Correspondence of William Pitt with the Colonial Governors* (ed. G. S. Kimball, 2 vols., New York, 1906), II, 352–3. For Leigh see Peter Blake to the Earl of Egremont, Charleston, November 27, 1762, C.O. 5:390. For the local American vice-admiralty courts in general see Carl Ubbelohde: *op. cit.,* especially pp. 5–36, and G. L. Beer: *British Colonial Policy, 1754–1765* (New York, 1907), 1922 edn., pp. 249–51. For the weakness of the Vice-Admiralty Court in Rhode Island see Volume X of this series, pp. 228–9.

[61] For the commissions and the scope of the powers of the American vice-admiralty courts see the recital of the royal letters patent of August 4, 1768, P.R.O., Admiralty 2:1057, pp. 409–14; see also the extended statement of Thomas Whately to Charles Yorke, February 16, 1765, listing the acts of Parliament that fell within the jurisdiction of these courts. This important document is among the Hardwicke Papers, B.M., Add. Mss., 35911.

[62] Adm. 2:1057, pp. 409–14, where it is specified that the salaries are "to be paid in the first place out of the Moiety of the Money arising from any Penalties and Forfeiture . . . and if this Fund shall not be sufficient out of the Money arising from the Sale of Old Naval Stores. . . ."

again, either to the King in Council, or to the High Court of Admiralty of England and from thence to his Majesty's High Court of Delegates," if such matters as wills were involved.[63]

Despite all these inducements, when the commissions were brought to America by Captain Roland early in 1769, the new judges, with one exception, did not move promptly to take over their new office and set up the new district courts.[64]

The moment for setting up the new courts could not have been less auspicious; for by January 1769 the local vice-admiralty courts as adjuncts to the customs service were already targets of bitter resentment on the part of colonial merchants, representing as they did additional evidence of government control. The efforts of those engaged in illegal commerce to circumvent the regulation of trade, by smuggling and by subverting customs officers, has already been mentioned earlier in this chapter and in the preceding volume of this series in connection with the Sugar Act of 1764 and the Stamp Act of 1765. The importance to imperial administrators of bringing illicit trade under control cannot easily be over-emphasized; for so much of the Townshend American plan hinged on tightening up the enforcement methods in order to collect the revenue.

---

[63] *Ibid.* See also J. H. Smith: *Appeals to the Privy Council from the American Plantations* (New York, 1950), pp. 191–2. The High Court of Delegates, a court of final appeals in ecclesiastical matters, arose out of an act of Parliament in the reign of Henry VIII (25 Henry VIII, c. 19). See William Blackstone's *Commentaries,* III, 66. Grey Cooper, a secretary of the Treasury, was strongly opposed to the idea of the new courts having appellate jurisdiction, as he thought it would be of "dangerous consequence to allow the final determination of cases relative to the duties of customs, etc. and the construction of British Acts of Parliament to be made and settled within the Pale of the Colonies"; for it was apparent that few would think of carrying an appeal to the High Court of Admiralty in England after a first appeal had failed locally. See Grey Cooper to Secretary of State Conway, December 18, 1766, P.R.O., C.O. 5:67, p. 243. In this same document Cooper proposed to "regulate and reform the fees of the Officers, which are at present settled with so little regard to Justice or Equality, that they depend in a great measure upon the Condemnation of the Ship or the Conviction of the Offender" (*ibid.*, pp. 237–49).

[64] See Boston advices, January 19, *New-York Gazette, and Weekly Mercury,* January 30, 1769. It would appear that the new court was set up without delay only at Boston, where Judge Auchmuty already had his place of residence. In April Judge Ingersoll left New Haven for Philadelphia to establish his court, appointing James Biddle as deputy judge, but not until the spring of 1771 did he himself take up his residence there and assume his duties. Judge Johnston went to Charleston in May; before returning to Newport in the summer he appointed a deputy and thereafter spent only the winter months in South Carolina. As for Judge Sewall, although he went to Halifax in June and set up his court, throughout the remainder of the period before the outbreak of the War for American Independence, he acted by deputy, in the person of Joseph Gerrish, who had also served as deputy for Judge Spry at the Court of Vice-Admiralty for all America when Spry had left Nova Scotia early in 1767 to take up his appointment as Governor of Barbados. For the setting up of the district vice-admiralty courts see Carl Ubbelohde: *op. cit.,* pp. 140–1, 148–58.

CHAPTER V

Massachusetts Bay and Resistance to the Townshend Program

WITH the setting up of the district vice-admiralty courts, the Townshend American program had been completed. In its entirety the plan, as has been seen in the two preceding chapters, provided for the payment of import duties on a number of specified articles; it set up an American Board of Customs Commissioners to watch over the custom houses and customs officers; and, finally, by the creation of the system of district vice-admiralty courts, it looked to the rigid enforcement of the trade and revenue acts passed by Parliament and, with this, toward the securing of an American fund sufficient "for defraying the Charge of the Administration of Justice, and the Support of Civil Government, in such Provinces where it shall be found necessary; and towards further defraying the Expenses of defending, protecting, and securing the said Dominions" in America.[1] As the system began functioning, it was envisioned that the fund thus created out of the customs duties would ultimately provide revenues not only to support security forces on the frontiers and in the newly conquered areas but also to pay adequate salaries to the law-enforcement agents and to those occupying administrative positions in the very colonies where defiance of imperial regulations had been most pronounced. These objectives seemed to be designed to bring to heel such a recalcitrant colony as Massachusetts Bay, clearly the leader in active opposition to the trade regulations. But this dynamic colony was not to be so easily leashed or led. Rather it was progressively to become the nerve centre of the revolutionary movement.

[1] See 7 Geo. III, c. 46, *Statutes at Large,* VIII, 38.

The economic and political activities of most of New England centred in Boston. It was therefore not surprising that this city should have been designated as the seat of the Vice-Admiralty Court for the New England district as well as of the headquarters of the American Board of Customs Commissioners. It is even less surprising that the Bay town should have chafed under the weight of the attention thereby focused upon it.

In 1767 Boston was still a great commercial metropolis. It was also the seat of government of a province that possessed more towns than any other British colony—towns whose inhabitants were among the most enlightened and literate in British North America. Massachusetts Bay's leadership in colonial affairs had been manifested both in peace and in war. No other colony had so greatly contributed, in men and money, to the successful outcome of the Great War for the Empire; nor had any other such a high standard of fiscal integrity in the 1760's and 1770's—one that other colonies, such as Virginia, could well have emulated. Although Massachusetts Bay had received a total of £328,000 sterling from the government of Great Britain as generous reimbursement for its war debt, a balance of £490,000 had remained to be liquidated by raising taxes or otherwise. This the colony did—aided by the sale of provincial lands. By 1771 only £40,000 remained and by 1773 the war debt was paid off.[2] Speaking of the province as a "Silver money colony," Governor Bernard wrote to the Secretary of State for the Colonies, Lord Hillsborough, on July 16, 1768, that it was so blessed with specie and enjoyed so high a credit rating in the money markets that the bills of exchange of its merchants were accepted at par without the usual two per cent discount to pay charges.[3]

Here then was a mature, flourishing, solvent colony, boasting a highly articulate and powerful middle class,[4] which expressed itself

---

[2] For the liquidation of the war debt of Massachusetts Bay see Volume X of this series, pp. 53–61. In his *History of the Colony and Province of Massachusetts-Bay* (ed. L. S. Mayo, 3 vols., Cambridge, Mass., 1936, III, 251), Thomas Hutchinson, referring to the period of the early 1770's, wrote: "From the surplusses of former funds, and from debts due to the government for lands which had been sold, there appeared a fund sufficient to raise money, not only for the service of the present year [that is, 1772] but of some years to come, so as to render any tax unnecessary."

[3] For this letter see the Shelburne Papers, 85:201–4, Clements Library.

[4] In this connection, the student should consult R. E. Brown: *Middle-Class Democracy and the Revolution in Massachusetts, 1691–1780* (Ithaca, N.Y., 1955), and with it the article examining this book by Dr. John Cary in the *William and Mary Quarterly*, 3rd ser., XX, 251–64, together with Dr. Brown's rebuttal, *ibid.*, XX, 265–76.

on political issues at times through violent mob action,[5] but more frequently in the town meetings or before the General Court. Among the chief agencies for forming public opinion, as expressed both from the pulpit and at these meetings, was the press—especially through the columns of the *Boston Weekly News-Letter* (called in 1767 the *Massachusetts Gazette and Boston News-Letter*), the *Boston-Gazette, and Country Journal,* the *Boston Post-Boy & Advertiser,* and the *Boston Evening-Post.*[6] Of these papers, the one that most consistently displays an attitude of considerable detach-

---

[5] See A. M. Schlesinger: "Political Mobs and the American Revolution, 1765–1776," American Philosophical Society *Proceedings,* XCIX, 244–50.

[6] The newspaper titles given above are as they appeared in 1767. It should be noted that the *Massachusetts Gazette* was established in 1768 as a semi-weekly addendum, appearing alternately on Mondays and Thursdays, to the *Boston Weekly News-Letter* and the *Boston Post-Boy* during its brief life from 1768 to 1769. In this connection see O. M. Dickerson: "British Control of American Newspapers on the Eve of the Revolution," *New England Quarterly,* XXIV, 453–68, which examines the so-called "kept press" (kept by the Board of Customs Commissioners) of the late 1760's and "subsidization" of a Tory press in the 1770's.

For the part of the propagandists in the revolutionary movement through the use of broadsides, pamphlets, and newspaper publications see C. A. Duniway: *Development of Freedom of the Press in Massachusetts* (*Harvard Historical Studies,* XII, Cambridge, Mass. and London, 1906), Philip Davidson: *Propaganda and the American Revolution, 1763–1783* (Chapel Hill, N.C., 1941), and A. M. Schlesinger: *Prelude to Independence, The Newspaper War on Great Britain, 1764–1776* (New York, 1958) as well as his "Propaganda and the Boston Newspaper Press, 1767–1770," Colonial Society of Massachusetts *Publications,* XXXII, *Transactions,* pp. 396–416, and his *Colonial Merchants and the American Revolution, 1763–1776* (Columbia University *Studies in History,* LXXVIII, No. 182, New York, 1918), to be cited hereafter as *Colonial Merchants;* see also B. I. Granger: *Political Satire in the American Revolution, 1763–1783* (Ithaca, N.Y., 1960), and L. W. Levy: *Legacy of Suppression. Freedom of Speech and Press in Early American History* (Cambridge, Mass., 1960).

The intellectual influences that motivated those who expressed themselves through press and pulpit—not to mention the pamphleteers, the polemicists, or the partisans on either side who resorted to the spoken word in town meeting, government council, and even in more informal gatherings—are not dealt with in this series. This subject had been announced—in an earlier plan of the author—as one to be treated in a separate final volume. Circumstances, however, intervened. In the past forty years, during which this writer has been completing his series, certain notable scholars have made this aspect of the history of the period their specialty. Therefore the student seeking enlightenment in depth in this field—as well as certain allied aspects of the cultural and social history of the period—should consult the works of C. L. Becker, Carl Bridenbaugh, Daniel Boorstin, Michael Kraus, J. C. Miller, Max Savelle, T. J. Wertenbaker, and L. B. Wright, to name but a few. Most recently, the first of four projected volumes on *Pamphlets of the American Revolution, 1750–1776,* has just appeared (Cambridge, Mass., 1965). Dealing with the pamphlets published in America from 1750 to 1765, it contains a useful introductory essay by the editor, Bernard Bailyn, which analyzes the sources of colonial ideas.

In this connection, the student should also consult Chapter 7 of the present volume, which deals with the political theorists on the British side in discussing the growing movement for political reform in England in the 1760's. Attention should likewise be called to the numerous private transatlantic exchanges of correspondence that served to foster the libertarian ideas evolving in Great Britain and the colonies.

ment during the 1760's and 1770's, in presenting the views of both those who supported and those who attacked the colonial policy of the government of Great Britain, was the *Boston Evening-Post*, printed by Thomas and John Fleet.[7] Therefore one may turn to it for a fairly balanced view of the reactions of the people of Massachusetts Bay during the period under review.

In the August 31, 1767, issue, the *Boston Evening-Post* published the resolution of the House of Commons of June 2 for raising a revenue on imports into the colonies and noted the presentation to the Commons on June 3 of a bill to provide for a Board of American Customs Commissioners. In the same issue, a letter from London dated June 15 told of a series of meetings of the London colonial agents with the ministers, who gave "strong Assurances that nothing should be neglected which can contribute to render them [the colonies] flourishing and happy, but that the C[our]t and P[arliamen]t were firmly resolved to support by all constitutional Means, their just Rights and Privileges, and to secure the Dependence of the said Colonies on Great Britain." A final item, an extract from a London letter dated June 13, asserted that "the Salaries for the Governor, Secretary, and Justices of the Superior Court [in the colonies] were settled; . . . and that the justices of the Inferior Courts . . . were also to have fix'd Salaries, the first justice £300 sterl, per ann' and the others £100 each." In the September 7 issue, a long article by "Libernatus" presented the view that the only expedient now left to the colonies to convince Great Britain "of her error and mutual dependence as well as our importance, is to put an immediate stop to the importation of any of her manufactures." The same issue printed a letter from London dated June 13 which gave "Lord Mansfield's Opinion, that the Authors of the Riots and seditious Pieces in America, should be sent . . . to England and there tried for Treason; particularly the Writer of the Pamphlet . . . published in Boston; . . . against which Author [James Otis, Jr., presumably] there is particular Evidence for his seditious and treasonable Speeches in an American Ass[embl]y."

In the September 14 issue of the *Boston Evening-Post*, "Sobrius" took a more advanced position than had "Libernatus." He concluded his letter to the publishers with the truly revolutionary statement: "The [English] bill of rights is our special security that we shall be

---

[7] For example, the *Boston Gazette*, published by Benjamin Edes and John Gill, was so committed to the radical cause that the news and contributions of letters printed in it give little indication of the earnestness with which the conservative view was being presented to the public.

governed by no law to which we do not consent in our own persons or representatives by us elected for that purpose, & never shall part with the goodly inheritance while we possess a drop of the blood derived from the heroes who committed to us the inestimable legacy." On the other hand, in the September 21 issue, "A True Patriot," writing from Swansea (Swanzey), blasts all those—such as "Libernatus" and "Sobrius"—who, under the name of patriotism, were stirring up the people against the government of Great Britain. However, this did not hinder "Britano Americus," in his appeal "To the Commons of Great Britain" in the issue of September 28, from denouncing, among other "unconstitutional innovations," the attempt to provide places for judges and other Crown officers at the expense of Americans. In this same article he wrote: "Now, Brethren, when we find . . . a generation of vipers, sons of tyranny and oppression, venality and corruption, who . . . would . . . plunge so many millions into inevitable destruction, how can we be silent?" This same issue contains a second letter from "A True Patriot" scoring such "vile incendiaries" as "Determinatus" and his article in the *Boston Gazette* as seeking to "alienate the minds of a truly loyal and affectionate people from their dependence on the Mother Country."

In an answer to "A True Patriot" in the October 5 issue of the *Boston Evening-Post,* "Conscius Recti" declared it to be no time for moderation and prudence in the face of "an open and daring attack upon the natural and constitutional rights of these people [the colonials] . . . when we are saluted by an A[ct] of P[arliament] . . . totally . . . subversive of the fundamentals of our constitution; add to this the large accession of place men and task-masters, leeches who rejoice to fleece these beasts of burthen, THE PEOPLE, over whom they . . . boast a proud independence. . . ." Continuing, "Conscius Recti" affirmed that "there is no POWER on earth so great or so dreadful that may dare . . . or hope to awe them [the colonials] into submission.." "Libermoriturus," in the same issue, also took "A True Patriot" to task: "Are you certain the entire abolition of the rights of the people and introduction of lawless power and arbitrary authority are greatly promising to the public welfare? . . . If you have such pleasing ideas of slavery, may you alone enjoy the monopoly unenvy'd and unpity'd."

Discussions of the proposal to cease all trade with Great Britain occupied the attention of the *Boston Evening-Post* in October. "A Trader" charges, in the issue of the 12th, that this was a plan of "new and strange politicians" who "consist chiefly of persons who have no property to lose, . . . and whose only hopes of living are founded on anarchy and confusion. . . ." They, the "Trader" asserts, propose that those who do not voluntarily come into this non-importation scheme "are to be compelled thereto by threats, and . . . mark'd out in the public papers, and thereby exposed in their persons and properties . . . to actual violence." Supporting this conservative position in the same issue, "a Gentleman in Providence" claims that, even assuming it to be true that Parliament was establishing a Board of Customs Commissioners in America and that Governors and judges are to be paid, he does "not see how our Rights are thereby so much as infringed upon, nor do any of the Writers pretend to prove they are." As to a certain "interogatory" by "Libermoriturus" of October 5, which the "Providence Gentleman" quotes, his comment is: "nothing is asserted, much less proved. . . . And not withstanding this author's obliquely charging the Parliament of G[reat] B[ritain] with tyranny, we cannot in this part of the country, barely on that, persuade ourselves that that respectable body is deserving of the censure."

In the following week's edition of the paper, "A True Patriot" replies to both "Libermoriturus" and "Conscius Recti" by affirming that

> "every man of sense must know, . . . the very essence of the British constitution is founded on liberty; . . . it is impossible to conceive . . . that Britons who (to a man) detest the name of slavery, should once think of governing their colonies by any other method than that of the full enjoyment of the same liberty [that they] themselves so highly prize. Away then, my countrymen, with those imaginary notions of chains and slavery, so extravagantly bandied about by those turbulent men! . . . Let us . . . examine what real cause those gentry have for such extravagant murmuring—there is no new internal taxation imposed on them, therefore it cannot come into dispute, and assuredly they cannot pretend to dispute the right of an external one; as that is a point that has been given up these many years, by all the colonies in America; particularly during the dispute over the stamp-act: Where then are all those chains, and this slavery so artfully turned and twisted by my very good friends?"

Also in the October 19 number, an article from the August 8 copy of the London *Craftsman* is reprinted. Signed by "A Briton," it expressed a point of view doubtless held by all those in Great Britain who opposed the repeal of the Stamp Act. In it the writer refers to

> ". . . that unaccountable & unjustifiable conduct of the colonies; a conduct which has been premeditated by them; but which never

dared to be put in execution till they received that sanction which was given them by the treacherous and pernicious language held here by *one* or *two* (then) *popular men* [Pitt and Camden], joined to the conduct and baneful measures pursued by *one* or *two leaders* then in power [Rockingham and Conway]; and who, so fatally for this country promoted a late *repeal,* which at once gave an alarming blow to the S[overeign]ty of these kingdoms over the colonies. . . . Let the pompous trumpeters of L[ord] C[hatham]'s fallacious declarations tell us—where is that submission of the colonies promised to this country for the repeal of the Stamp-act? Where is their just sense of that lenity shewn in the repeal of the Stamp-act? Where is their obedience to the legislative power of this country, which was immediately to manifest itself after the repeal of the Stamp-Act?"

In the issue of October 26 "Libermoriturus" answers the writer from Providence with the rhetorical question:

"What can we be *jealous* of when our property is once and again granted out of our hands without the least ceremony, to purposes we never intended? What check has the people on the crown if it may appoint what officers it pleases, pay them out of the people and never ask their advice in the matter? Where is the privilege of Britons, who not only grant but demand an account of the disposal of their monies, and can therefore withhold when they please if they do not approve?"

He then adds: "we do not complain of a slight *wound,* a scratch, but a mortal stab to the vitals; not a trifling mutilation, but an utter subversion of those well known, inherent, and unalienable *rights,* of being governed only by laws of our own making, and granting our own property"—in other words, Parliament had not power to legislate on matters involving the colonies. "Pastor Fido," in a supplement to this number, makes the point that surely an American could take it for granted that Parliament had no right to raise money in the colonies for revenue purposes, "especially as he has the authority of the Great Commoner to appeal to.—This being true, we have only to enquire what is meant by a revenue, and then I apprehend it will be easy to determine whether the late Acts of P[arliamen]t are of such consequence, and as big with mischief, as our fears seem to make them."

The above divergent views on the question of parliamentary powers over the colonies may well serve as a background for the decisions reached at the Boston town meeting held on October 28, 1767. With James Otis in the chair, a petition of "a number of inhabitants" was read. It called for some effectual measures to be agreed upon "to promote Industry Oeconomy & Manufactures; thereby to prevent the unnecessary Importation of European Commodities, which threaten the Country with Poverty and Ruin." Acting upon the petition, the meeting adopted resolutions to combat "the excessive use of foreign Superfluities . . . the chief Cause of the present distressed State of this Town . . . drained of its money; which Misfortune is likely to be increased by Means of the late additional Burthens and Impositions on the trade of the Province, which threatens the Country with . . . Ruin." Domestic manufactures should therefore be encouraged, the resolutions proposed, and the importation of certain articles, some fifty-four in all, should be suspended. Subscription papers were then presented by a committee appointed for securing the signatures of those who would agree not to purchase after December 31 any of the enumerated articles. Further, to make sure that Boston would not stand alone, the meeting directed the town selectmen to forward a copy of the vote to the selectmen of every other town in the province and to the principal officers of the chief towns in the several colonies on the continent.[8] It should be noted that none of the extreme revolutionary claims asserted by writers in the press was set forth in the October 28 resolutions; nor was there any denial of the right of Parliament to levy import duties. Instead, emphasis was placed upon the necessity of taking steps to avoid the impending ruin of one of the most prosperous towns in North America as a result of the excessive purchase of foreign superfluities and the consequent drainage of money, which admittedly was plentiful.[9] All of this pointed not only to a domestic manufactures and non-importation movement, but also to one for non-consumption of imported articles already in the colony, such as tea.[10]

Commenting on the resolutions of the town meeting in the November 2 issue of the *Boston Evening-Post,* "A True Patriot" referred to the plans for setting up domestic manufactures and cutting off the

[8] See *Reports of the Record Commissioners of the City of Boston* (38 vols., Boston, 1876–1908), XVI, 1758–1769, 220–5. A broadside covering the activities of this meeting was printed, apparently by Edes and Gill, for general distribution. Copies of it are to be found at the American Antiquarian Society headquarters and at the Boston Public Library; see also *Boston Evening-Post* of November 2, 1767.

[9] The profusion of advertisements in the Boston papers of this period detailing the importation of luxury articles by various business firms, indicates that the inhabitants must have been in a position to spend large sums of money as fancy directed. There was no such extensive display of importers' advertisements elsewhere in the colonial press, not even in the prosperous city of Philadelphia.

[10] See *Boston Post-Boy,* November 16, 1767. But the actual non-consumption resolutions did not come until late in February 1768, again first in Massachusetts Bay. See A. M. Schlesinger: *Colonial Merchants,* pp. 111–14

importation of certain British goods as "chimerical projects." Speaking of the heavy tax burdens due to an expanding Empire that people of England were obliged to shoulder, he asked:

> "What article, or what necessary have they free of taxation? . . . And surely none can deny, that a large share of the burdens those people now labour under, have arisen through the protection afforded us (in the late war in particular) to preserve us from being swallowed up by a merciless & ambitious enemy; who would inevitably have reduced us to the most abject slavery had we been but left to ourselves; but thank God, through the kind interposition of our parent country, we have lost sight of those melancholy apprehensions. . . . Sorry I am to find myself under the disagreeable necessity of rehearsing the rest; but to our immortal shame be it spoken, we soon, very soon forget our danger, and with it our obligations to the mother country; and have been endeavouring . . . to sow the seeds of distrust and jealousy . . . , and have but too well succeeded. . . ."

To counter such an attitude "Libermoriturus,"—quoting the definition of a slave in Samuel Johnson's Dictionary as "one mancipated, not a freeman, a *dependent*"—stated in the November 9 issue of the *Post:*

> ". . . free and natural subjects of the crown of Great Britain, . . . are governed only by laws of their own making, taxed only by their own consent, advise in the appointment of officers, demand an account of every farthing of their money, and are dependent on no power on earth in any one particular: And yet three millions of freemen, of perhaps above two hundred counties, are to be ruled and taxed by any power independent of them, and in no possible sense their deputies, delegates or representatives, . . ."

But "A True Patriot" answered "Libermoriturus" in the issue of December 21. As to the right of Parliament to levy taxes on the colonials, he wrote: "I am thoroughly convinced that the right lies in the British Parliament so to do, or they never would have avow'd it in the ample manner they have, nor did I ever meet with any arguments . . . that have given me the least reason to think to the contrary." In the same issue "Mostin" also paid tribute to the government of the British Empire by affirming that there never before was known to man a constitution "so happy" as that of the British Empire, and contrasted its provisions for freedom and security of the individual and its appeal as a refuge for foreigners to the situation in "Spain, Portugal, and those haunts of tyranny and slavery, . . . abject misery, horror & Dispair." He finally warned that "if any ruthless group of infernals" would conspire to dissolve the bonds that for over a century have made "one entire people, . . . zealous for the glory, happiness & security of every part," if they "set the sword of every man against his brother, his fellow and his friend—what indignation can be hot enough for such miscreants?"

It is quite clear that the preceding quotation from "Libermoriturus" presented the real aims of the more extreme radicals, who insisted that as free men the colonials had a right to be governed, as well as taxed, only by those who represented them and whom they could call to account—a position utterly incompatible in the 1760's with the British view of the long-established colonial dependence upon the government of Great Britain. It is equally clear that the American public was not prepared at that time to accept the profound implications of this position, but would have to be led, step by step, and conditioned by constant propaganda to be ready to make the necessary sacrifices to achieve it. On the other hand, the slogan of a sound economy, based on the encouragement of domestic manufactures and the eschewal of purchasing foreign luxury articles, could appeal better to the generality of people in 1767, since it represented a sensible measure of colonial thrift.

By the middle of January of the new year, twenty-four Massachusetts Bay towns in the eastern part of the province had agreed to the Boston non-importation program.[11] Doubtless their subscription to these agreements was encouraged by the news circulated in the press "that Rhode Island, Connecticut, York, Jerseys, etc, are steadily pursuing measures for lessening their foreign imports, by encouraging frugality and their own manufactures."[12] Early in December 1767 the Rhode Island town of Providence adopted a non-importation policy covering a wide variety of English commodities; it was to be enforced "in the most effectual but decent and lawful Manner."[13] Shortly afterwards Newport fell into line by approving an agreement,[14] and was soon followed by other Rhode Island towns. Norwich, located in the eastern part of Connecticut and under the influence of Boston, led the way in that colony by approving the

[11] For the list of towns see A. M. Schlesinger: *Colonial Merchants*, p. 110. All the towns in western Massachusetts Bay, except Pittsfield, ignored the letter of the selectmen of Boston to join in the non-importation agreement. A Pittsfield town meeting appointed a committee to consider the letter, but when the question was raised at a subsequent meeting no action was taken. See *Connecticut Courant*, December 14, 1767. For an illuminating discussion of the conservative position of the western towns at this period see R. J. Taylor: *Western Massachusetts in the Revolution* (Providence, 1954), pp. 56–7.

[12] *Boston Evening-Post*, November 9, 1767.

[13] *Providence Gazette; and Country Journal*, December 5, 1767.

[14] *Newport Mercury*, December 7, 1767.

Boston measures and appointing a committee on December 7 to study and report on them.[15] It was ultimately joined by all the other leading Connecticut towns, among them New London, Windham, and New Haven.[16]

The Boston non-importation project was, in fact, not actively promoted by the merchants. The Rev. Andrew Eliot of Boston, in a letter to Thomas Hollis in England on December 10, 1767, stated: "Few of the trading part have subscribed. . . . Some are of opinion that if, instead of this bluster, we had exerted ourselves to promote those manufactures which we are capable of introducing, it had been better."[17]

The New England radical program now received aid from an unexpected quarter. Emphasizing non-importation of British manufactures, a series of twelve "Letters" by "A Farmer in Pennsylvania" appeared in the press. The first one was published on December 2, 1767, in the *Pennsylvania Chronicle and Universal Advertiser* and appeared again in the *Pennsylvania Gazette* the next day. Subsequent instalments continued to come out in these weekly publications, the last appearing on February 18 in the *Gazette.* The "Letters" were also published serially in most of the other colonial newspapers, and appeared in pamphlet form. Their influence on the American public must have been very great. From New England to Georgia, town meetings commended the author, who was none other than the aristocratic landowner and lawyer John Dickinson.[18]

In these "Letters" Dickinson—in contrast to the position taken by his political opponent, Benjamin Franklin, before the House of Commons in 1766—denied that Parliament had authority to levy either internal or external taxes on the colonies. He called the Townshend revenue act "an innovation; and a most dangerous innovation"; he held it to be not only "unconstitutional" but "destructive to the

[15] *Boston Evening-Post,* Supplement, December 28, 1767.

[16] *Pennsylvania Gazette,* April 7, 1768; see also *Connecticut Journal,* December 18, 25, 1767, and *New London Gazette,* December 25, 1767.

[17] Massachusetts Historical Society *Collections,* 4th ser., IV, 418–19. For the relationship of Thomas Hollis with Eliot and other patriot leaders see his correspondence published in the Massachusetts Historical Society *Proceedings,* LXIX; see also Caroline Robbins: "The Strenuous Whig, Thomas Hollis of Lincoln's Inn," *William and Mary Quarterly,* 3rd ser., VII, 406–53, and *ibid.,* VIII, 478.

[18] John Dickinson, after studying at the Middle Temple in London, had returned to Philadelphia to become its foremost lawyer; he was also a leading figure in the Stamp Act Congress, and was deeply involved in political activities in both Pennsylvania and the Lower Counties on the Delaware. See C. J. Stillé; *Life and Times of John Dickinson,* Historical Society of Pennsylvania *Memoirs, XIII* (Philadelphia, 1891).

liberties of these colonies."[19] At the same time he admitted that Parliament had a right not only to regulate colonial commerce but also to prohibit the manufacture of any article in the colonies: "Great-Britain has prohibited the manufacturing iron and steel in these colonies, without any objection being made to her right of doing it. The like right she must have to prohibit any other manufacture among us," since the colonies were settled with the intention that she should manufacture for them and that they should supply her with materials.[20] Yet—rather inconsistently, in view of this admission, which would narrowly restrict colonial freedom of action in earning a livelihood—he asserted in his next letter that "heaven itself 'hath made us free.' "[21] To him, a revolution in the attitude of the mother country toward her dependents had taken place:

> "Moderation has been the rule of her conduct. But now, a generous humane people, that so often has protected the liberty of strangers, is enflamed into an attempt to tear a privilege from her own children, which, if executed, must, in their opinion, sink them into slaves: And for what? For a pernicious power, not necessary to her, . . . but horribly dreadful and detestable to them."[22]

As for the great debt accumulated by Great Britain in the late war, he continued, this war was not undertaken by the mother country to defend the interests of the colonies, but *"solely for her own benefit"*; in fact the territories acquired in North America as the result of it were "greatly injurious to these colonies," and the colonials therefore owed her nothing.[23]

Most political scientists of today would question the soundness of Dickinson's above-stated political doctrine and would be likely to agree with the criticism of it made by William Knox in his *The Controversy between Great Britain and her Colonies Reviewed.* To Knox the right conceded to Parliament by colonials to regulate and suppress at will their trade and industry, while they denied its right to levy upon them, was "of all absurdities, the most ridiculous that ever was contended for." The Molasses Act of 1733 was per-

---

[19] *The Writings of John Dickinson* (ed. P. L. Ford, Historical Society of Pennsylvania *Memoirs,* XIV, Philadelphia, 1895), 312–16.

[20] *Ibid.*, I, 319–20. Dickinson was in error about the prohibition of iron and steel manufactures. The law prohibited the setting up of any additional steel works and iron-fabricating works.

[21] *Ibid.*, I, 322.

[22] *Ibid.*, I, 342–3.

[23] *Ibid.*, I, 341–3.

fectly legal, yet the Sugar Act of 1764 was unconstitutional, according to Dickinson. Knox's analysis of this position stated:

> "The right of Parliament to charge foreign molasses with a duty of six-pence a gallon was unquestionable; but, for parliament to *reduce* the six-pence to three-pence, is a violent usurpation of unconstitutional authority, and an infringement of the rights and privileges of the people in the Colonies. . . . But (says Mr. Dickenson) the heavy tax would have operated as a prohibition, which is a *regulation of trade;* the light tax is intended to *be paid,* and is laid for the *purpose of revenue.*"[24]

Thus, Knox argued, Dickinson was conceding the greater right of Parliament through *regulation* to choke and even to destroy American commerce and industry by extending the principles embodied in the Molasses Act of 1733 and the Iron Act of 1750 whenever it saw fit, but was denying the lesser right of Parliament to reduce prohibitive regulatory imposts for the purpose of securing a revenue. Nevertheless, with all its manifest defects as a contribution to the theory and practice of government, *Letters from a Farmer* quickly became the political bible of the Americans, retaining that honoured place until it was displaced in 1776 by *Common Sense,* Thomas Paine's call for a declaration by the colonies of their independence from Great Britain.

It may be surprising to realize that the inhabitants of Pennsylvania, in the main, were not greatly stirred to action by their fellow citizen's "Letters." "A Freeborn American," writing in the *Pennsylvania Gazette* of February 18, 1768, felt impelled to upbraid Pennsylvanians for their lethargy at a time when "the judicious *Farmer* opens to view the terrible effects of a late act of parliament in all their native horrors. . . . Will the chains of *slavery,* rattling in your ears, excite your attention?"[25] For the most part, however, the Pennsylvania people remained passive during the first two months of 1768. They felt no chains; they were living in the midst of abundance and prosperity. The chief concern of the public and the Assembly was that the frontier be pacified to prevent a renewed Indian war, which threatened as the result of the lawless murder of some natives by scoff-law whites. Furthermore the conservative Quaker influence in the Assembly was still an effective rein on radical tendencies. The

[24] William Knox: *The Controversy between Great Britain and her Colonies Reviewed* (London, 1769), pp. 35–7. Knox had acted as a Crown official in Georgia and later as the London agent for that province and for East Florida.

[25] Although born in Ireland, the Presbyterian merchant and radical Whig leader Charles Thomson, later Secretary to the Continental Congress, was the writer who signed himself "A Freeborn American."

only important step taken during this period—possibly as the immediate result of the incitement of Thomson's "Freeborn American" article—was the Assembly's agreement on February 20 to a letter drafted by its committee of correspondence to the London agents of the province, calling upon them to unite with the other colonial agents to obtain a repeal of the act imposing import duties.[26]

In view of the tight hold over the Pennsylvania Assembly of its Speaker, Joseph Galloway,[27] it is not surprising that Dickinson should have foreseen the apathy in Pennsylvania and have taken the action he did in publishing his "Farmer" letters and in turning to Massachusetts Bay for leadership at this juncture. For, on December 5, 1767, Dickinson wrote to James Otis: "Whenever the Cause of American Freedom is to be vindicated, I look towards the Province of Massachusetts Bay. She must, as she had hitherto done, first kindle the Sacred Flame, that . . . must warm and illuminate the Continent."[28] He was not to be mistaken.

In an effort to arouse public opinion in all the colonies against the Townshend measures, the Massachusetts Bay House of Representatives drew up its famous circular letter on February 11, 1768.[29] It was framed with great care to take into consideration the sensibilities of those not yet prepared to accept the extreme radical point of view. For example, it conceded that the King's High Court of Parliament was "the supreme Legislative Power over the whole Empire," but qualified this by adding

> "that in all free States the Constitution is fixed . . . [and] that it is an essential, unalterable right, in nature, engrafted into the British

---

[26] *Pennsylvania Archives,* 8th ser., VII, 6168.

[27] Theodore Thayer: *Pennsylvania Politics and the Growth of Democracy, 1740–1776* (Harrisburg, 1953), pp. 135–7.

[28] See "Warren-Adams Letters, 1743–1777," Massachusetts Historical Society *Collections,* LXXII, 3–4.

[29] On January 22, 1768, the proposal was first advanced in the House of Representatives that a circular letter be sent to the other assemblies in North America to advise them of the importance of their joining with the House in petitioning the King. On the 26th the matter again came up for consideration but no decision was reached; however, on February 4 the House moved and approved that a committee be appointed for this purpose. The committee of seven subsequently designated included Speaker Thomas Cushing, James Otis, Samuel Adams, and Major Hawley, with Adams apparently carrying the chief responsibility for framing the letter. It was approved on February 11 and the Speaker was ordered to sign all copies. See *Journal of the House of Representatives* (Boston, 1767–8), pp. 129, 135, 148, 157. According to Bernard, writing to Lord Barrington on February 20, the friends of the administration during the early part of the year were able "to keep the factious Party of the House in awe" and, by a vote of two to one, to prevent the sending of such a letter, but they finally lost ground. See *The Barrington-Bernard Correspondence . . . 1760–1770* (eds. Edward Channing and A. C. Coolidge, Cambridge, Mass., 1912), pp. 145–6.

Constitution, as a fundamental Law . . . that what a Man has honestly acquired . . . cannot be taken from him without his Consent. . . . . It is, moreover, their [the House's] humble opinion, . . . that the acts made there, imposing duties on the people of this province with the sole and express purpose of raising a revenue, are Infringements of their natural and constitutional Rights; because . . . they are not represented in the British Parliament . . . this House think that a Taxation of their Constituents, even without their Consent, grievous as it is, would be preferable to any Representation that could be admitted for them there."

The letter then submitted for consideration the questions:

". . . whether any people can be said to enjoy any Degree of Freedom, if the Crown, in addition to its undoubted authority of constituting a Governor, should appoint him such a Stipend as it shall judge proper, without the Consent of the People and at their Expense; and whether . . . the Judges of the Land and other civil Officers . . . having Salaries appointed for them by the Crown, independent of the People, hath not a Tendency to . . . endanger the Happiness and Security of the Subject?"

The next paragraph of the circular letter made reference to the hardships imposed by the Mutiny Act and the act setting up an American Board of Customs Commissioners. Finally, it denied that the members of the House of Representatives were "factious, disloyal, and having a Disposition to make themselves independent of the Mother Country," and expressed the hope that the other assemblies would signify "any thing further which may be thought necessary."[30]

Signed by the Speaker of the Massachusetts Bay House of Representatives, Thomas Cushing, the letter was forwarded to the speaker of every other North American assembly. Its purpose was to induce the other colonies to follow the example of the Massachusetts Bay House, which, on January 20, purposely ignoring the High Court of Parliament, had petitioned the King to repeal the Townshend

[30] For the circular letter of February 11, 1768 see *Journal of the House of Representatives* (Boston, 1767–8), Appendix, pp. 20–3, where it carries the following information: "The Circular Letter to the Speakers of the Respective Houses of Representatives and Burgesses on this Continent; a copy of which was also sent to Dennis de Berdt, Esq., their Agent, by Order of the House, that he might make use of it, if necessary, to prevent any misrepresentation of it in England." The letter is also printed, among other places, in *Pennsylvania Archives*, 8th ser., VII, 6181–4, and in *Speeches of the Governors of Massachusetts Bay . . . and other State Papers* (ed. Alden Bradford, Boston, 1818), pp. 134–6.

legislation.[31] A copy of the circular letter was also presented to Governor Bernard, together with an address from the representatives requesting the Governor to turn over to them the exchange of letters of the previous fall between him and the Earl of Shelburne, the then incumbent Secretary of State for the Southern Department, concerning Shelburne's criticism of the Assembly.[32] Bernard agreed to send them a copy of the Shelburne letter, but as to his own letters, he simply stated that he had written none to the Secretary of State that would be of use to the House on this occasion.[33] Realizing the implications of the Assembly's circular letter, he immediately sent his copy to England. There it was turned over to the Earl of Hillsborough, who also on January 20 had become Secretary of State for the Colonies—a new office, the creation of which will be dealt with later in this volume.

On April 22, 1768, Hillsborough wrote to Governor Bernard expressing the concern of His Majesty that the Massachusetts Bay House should "resolve upon a measure of so inflammatory a Nature as that of writing to the other Colonies on the Subject of their intended Representation against some late Acts of Parliament." Such action, he pointed out, might tend "to create unwarrantable Combinations to excite an unjustifiable Opposition to the constitutional Authority of Parliament." In view of the earlier temperate proceedings of the House, he added, His Majesty could not but feel that this measure was "procured by Surprise." Therefore, it was the King's pleasure that, as soon as the General Court had reassembled, the Governor should call upon the House in His Majesty's name to rescind the resolution that gave birth to the circular letter and "to declare their Disapprobation of, and Dissent to, that rash & hasty Proceeding." If, however, the new House were to refuse to comply with His Majesty's "reasonable Expectation," the Governor should immedi-

---

[31] For the petition see *ibid.*, pp. 121–3; see also *Boston Evening-Post,* March 21, 1768, and the Appendix of the *Journal* cited in the preceding footnote, where the petition is followed by a series of letters addressed between January 15 and February 22 by the House to high government officials in London (Shelburne, Conway, Rockingham, Camden, Chatham, and the Lords Commissioners of the Treasury) and to London agent De Berdt.

[32] For a copy of the letter of the House of Representatives to the Governor, dated February 13, 1768, see *Boston Chronicle,* March 7, 1768, published by John Mein and John Fleming.

[33] For the full text of the Shelburne letter to Bernard, dated September 17, 1767, see *ibid.* The Shelburne letter was also published in 1768 by Green and Russell of Boston in a pamphlet containing the January 20 petition, together with copies of the various letters and other papers printed in the Appendix of the *Journal* cited above, of which it likewise formed the final item (p. 34). For the pamphlet see *Early American Imprints, 1639–1800* (ed. C. K. Shipton), Readex Microprint, Evans. No. 10970.

ately dissolve it and present an account of its proceedings to be laid before Parliament so as to prevent in the future "a conduct of so extraordinary & unconstitutional a nature."[34]

During the 1768 election—and even before Governor Bernard had received the Hillsborough directive—the situation began to deteriorate rapidly in the Bay province. In an effort to prevent the provincial Council from growing even more radical in its attitude toward public issues than it had become after 1766, the Governor rejected six of those nominated by the House of Representatives, among them James Otis, John Hancock, and Artemus Ward.[35] However, the representatives from Boston—Otis, Hancock, and Samuel Adams, as well as Thomas Cushing, in his capacity of Speaker of the House—continued to dominate the proceedings of the House of Representatives as well as those of the town, whether in town meeting or in action by the mob.

In view of the efforts of the radicals to stir up the people against the measures of the government of Great Britain, it is not surprising that a serious incident should have occurred late in the spring of 1768. On June 10, the customs officers seized the sloop *Liberty*, which belonged to Hancock, on the charge that it had come to the port loaded with Madeira wine and had been cleared by means of a false entry. When the vessel was put under the protection of the guns of H.M. *Romney*, a fifty-gun ship that had recently arrived in the harbour, the mob resorted to violence. Although the large crowd that gathered at the wharf—estimated by Hutchinson at between two and three thousand—could not rescue Hancock's vessel, it was able to vent its anger on the customs officers when these men

---

[34] See Shelburne Papers, 85:184–6, Clements Library.

[35] *Journal of the House of Representatives* (Boston, 1768), pp. 6–7; see also *Boston Chronicle*, June 6, 1768. It should be noted that Thomas Hutchinson still had a strong following in the House of Representatives. His election as chairman of the Massachusetts Bay commission to settle the boundary dispute with New York as well as the eminence of his other services to the province undoubtedly helped to maintain his prestige, despite the earlier rejection of him as an elected member of the Council. In the voting on May 25 he received 68 votes, just three short of election. Writing to former Governor Thomas Pownall on June 7, 1768, he has the following interesting comment on the sequel of the first balloting: "There being but 17 chose [within the limits of the earlier bounds of Massachusetts Bay, before the absorption of Plymouth and Maine, which were voted for separately], my friends then imagined that at the next trial [that is, ballot] they would carry it no body else standing so high on the list; but Otis like an enraged Damos ran about the House . . . crying Pension or no Pension and intimidated some who had voted for me before & made a majority for one [Artemus] Ward, a very sulky fellow . . ." (Hutchinson Correspondence, Massachusetts Archives, 25:262). While James Otis and John Hancock, together with Thomas Cushing, elected Speaker, and Samuel Adams, elected Clerk, represented Boston in the House, Ward represented Shrewsbury in Worcester County; later he was to serve briefly under Washington as a major general in the Continental Army.

came ashore. Pelting them with stones and breaking the windows of their houses, the rioters forced the officers to seek safety on board the *Romney*.[36]

Thoroughly aroused at this assault on what they considered to be American freedom of action, the Sons of Liberty on the 13th of June called a meeting at the Liberty Tree, but adjourned to meet in Fanueil Hall, where a legal town meeting could be held. Because of the size of the crowd, the gathering was again transferred, this time to South Church. As on other occasions, James Otis acted as moderator. The gathering adopted a petition to Governor Bernard appealing for the rights of Englishmen under the British constitution. That constitution, the petition claimed, had established the principle that

> "no man shall be governed by laws, nor taxed, but by himself or representative legally and fairly chosen, and to which he does give his own consent. In open violation of these fundamental rights of Britons, laws and taxes are enforced on us, to which we not only have not given our consent, but *against* which we have firmly remonstrated."

Here was a ringing declaration that, as Englishmen not represented in Parliament, that body had no right either to bind them by laws or to tax them. The petition also denounced the appointment of a Board of Customs Commissioners vested with such "enormous powers," and called upon the Governor to order the commander of

[36] The charge was that the cargo was landed at the dead of night and that the next morning the ship-master entered four or five hogsheads of wine and swore that this was the whole cargo. Early in April 1768 an effort had been made by the customs officers to make a search for dutiable articles on another vessel belonging to Hancock, the *Lydia*, but the tidewaiter was so terrified by the reception he got that he gave up the attempt. In the subsequent attempt of the Customs Board to prosecute Hancock for interfering with a customs officer in the discharge of his duty, the Massachusetts Bay attorney general, Jonathan Sewall, handed down an opinion denying that Hancock had tried to circumvent the law, a decision which was upheld by the Treasury Department in London. See O. M. Dickerson: "Opinion of Attorney General Jonathan Sewall . . . ," *William and Mary Quarterly*, 3rd ser., IV, 499–504; see also P.R.O., Treas. 1:465. In the case of the *Liberty*, the tidewaiter, Thomas Kirk, after boarding the vessel was, according to his testimony, forced below the deck and kept there some hours during the night while the cargo was removed. See *ibid.*, and the report from Boston, June 13, in the *Pennsylvania Gazette* for June 23 and 30, 1768; see also Hutchinson to Richard Jackson, June 16, 1768, Massachusetts Archives, 26:300–1. O. M. Dickerson's "John Hancock: Notorious Smuggler or Near Victim of British Revenue Racketeers?" *Mississippi Valley Historical Review*, XXXII, 517–40, presents a very dark picture of the designs of the customs officials. The other side of the picture is presented by the collector of the Port of Boston, Joseph Harrison (who numbered among his intimate acquaintances in England Lord Rockingham, Edmund Burke, and Sir George Savile), in his long letter of June 17, 1768, to Lord Rockingham. Edited by D. H. Watson, it is printed under the title "Joseph Harrison and the *Liberty* Incident," *William and Mary Quarterly*, 3rd ser., XX, 584–95.

the *Romney* to leave the harbour.[37] To make the proper impression on Bernard, who was then at Roxbury, the selectmen of the town and fourteen others were appointed to wait upon the Governor with the petition. This they did, going to the Governor's residence in a procession of eleven carriages.

Bernard's reply was necessarily tactful, considering the extreme delicacy of his position. In it he said: "My office and station make me a very incompetent judge of the rights you claim against Acts of Parliament." Declaring that he himself would not infringe any of their rights and privileges, he added: "I cannot pretend to enter into any dispute between you, and your parent-state. I desire to be a faithful servant in regard to both. . . ." He pointed out that by the instructions that bound him, and also by His Majesty's special orders, he was obliged "to protect . . . and assist the Commissioners of the Customs appointed under the Great Seal of Great Britain." As for the *Romney*, he made clear that he had no command over His Majesty's ships and therefore could not issue such orders as were desired.[38] Thus the *Romney* remained in Boston Harbour[39] and the case of the *Liberty* continued to stir up the people.

In the trial of Hancock and his alleged accomplices—which was to open in October 1768, but only after the testimony of the tide-waiter had been sent to London for the opinion of the Attorney General there as to whether it was valid grounds for prosecution[40]—John Adams, as counsel for the defence, raised issues of a constitutional nature which were to have wide repercussions. Attacking not only the legislative authority of Parliament—by questioning the validity of the Sugar Act itself, which Hancock was accused of violating—but also the jurisdiction of the vice-admiralty court, Adams successfully defended Hancock against the smuggling charge while constantly emphasizing his rights as a subject under the British constitution. The result was that Attorney General Sewall withdrew the case early in the spring of 1769, but not before the colonial presses had given it extensive publicity, with emphasis

[37] For the petition see *Boston Gazette, and Country Journal,* June 20, 1768. This newspaper will be cited hereafter as *Boston Gazette.*

[38] For this letter see *ibid.* It may be noted that an additional cause for objection against the presence of the *Romney* in Boston Harbour was that the commander had impressed a seaman for the royal service, although the sailor was later released. The *Boston Chronicle,* issue of June 20, here cited, carried the notice that no one else in the province would be pressed for service.

[39] See Thomas Hutchinson: *op. cit.,* III, 137–40, 144.

[40] For tidewaiter Kirk's testimony and Attorney General De Grey's report see P.R.O., Treas. 1:463 and 465.

upon the fundamental constitutional principles which Adams had highlighted so vigorously.[41]

But to return to the month of June 1768. Hard on the heels of the episode over the seizure of the *Liberty* came Bernard's message on June 21 to the House of Representatives giving an extract of the letter addressed to him on April 22 by the Secretary of State for the Colonies, in which Hillsborough called upon him to secure a repudiation of the circular letter issued by the House to the other colonial assemblies. The Governor took the position that the resolution to send it had been procured "by Surprise: . . . by a desperate Faction to disturb the public Tranquility," and requested that the House now repudiate the letter. A committee of nine, dominated by the most radical members of the House, including Speaker Thomas Cushing, James Otis, Samuel Adams, John Hancock, and Colonel James Otis, was appointed to answer the Governor.[42] Its work was suspended while the House sent a message to Bernard requesting him to lay before it the complete text of the Hillsborough letter together with copies of all pertinent letters sent by him as Governor. On the 24th Bernard forwarded the remainder of the Secretary of State's letter, namely that part which called upon him to dissolve the House if it refused to rescind the circular letter to the other colonial lower houses. He also took the opportunity to warn the

[41] For the most objective account of the case of the *Liberty* and the events leading up to the trial of Hancock see Carl Ubbelohde: *The Vice-Admiralty Courts . . .*, previously cited, pp. 121–7; for an earlier account see G. G. Wolkins: "The Seizure of John Hancock's Sloop *Liberty*," Massachusetts Historical Society *Proceedings*, LV, 251–61; see also W. T. Baxter: *The House of Hancock* (Cambridge, Mass., 1945), an interpretation of the *Liberty* incident from the point of view of a personal attack against Hancock; O. M. Dickerson: *The Navigation Acts . . .* (Philadelphia, 1951), pp. 236–45, which leans heavily on the charge that the customs officers were in effect customs "racketeers"; see further H. S. Allen: *John Hancock, Patriot in Purple* (New York, 1948), pp. 105–8; John Cary: *Joseph Warren . . .* (Urbana, Ill., 1961), pp. 74–9; finally D. S. Lovejoy: "Rights Imply Equality: The Case Against Admiralty Jurisdiction in America, 1764–1776," *William and Mary Quarterly*, 3rd ser., XVI, 478–82, which gives the fullest account of John Adams's defence of Hancock, for which the author relied not only upon Josiah Quincy's *Reports of Cases . . . in the Superior Court of Judicature of the Province of Massachusetts Bay between 1761 and 1772* (ed. S. M. Quincy, Boston, 1865) but upon John Adams's "Admiralty Notebook" (to be found among the Adams Family Papers, Miscellany, Legal Papers, Massachusetts Historical Society, Boston). Mention should also be made of "The Journal of the Times," which appeared in the *New-York Journal* and several other colonial newspapers and covered among other current news the course of the trial, and which may be found collected and edited by O. M. Dickerson: *Boston Under Military Rule, 1768–69 . . .* (Boston, 1936), as well as in John Adams's own record of his thoughts and memories of the trial, *Works of John Adams* (C. F. Adams, ed., 10 vols., Boston, 1850–6) II, 215–16, and III, 507–10.

[42] *Journal of the House of Representatives* (Boston, 1768), pp. 68–9, 70–1.

members of the consequences of a dissolution without a tax bill.[43] Not having heard from the House by the 29th, Bernard sent another message to say that he could not, with any sense of his duty, adjourn or prorogue the General Court until he had received an answer from the House. As a result, on the 30th, Otis, acting on orders, informed the Council that the House was "now entering on a Debate of Importance" and should not be interrupted. At this point a letter framed to the Secretary of State for the Colonies was read and accepted by a vote of 92 to 13.[44] Next, a motion was taken "whether this House will Rescind a Resolution of the last House which gave birth to the circular Letter to . . . the other Colonies on this Continent?" It was agreed that the vote should be recorded by individual yeas and nays. The vote was 17 in favour of rescinding as against 92 opposed. Of the 17 rescinders, it may be noted that five were from Essex County, whose only seaport and chief town, Salem, had refused to approve the Boston non-importation agreement; six were from the western counties of Berkshire and Hampshire, and the rest from the outlying counties of Worcester, Barnstable, Duke's, and York (the old province of Maine); of the members from Worcester County, only the conservative Brigadier Timothy Ruggles voted to rescind.[45]

This frank show of loyalty to the mother country by the "rescinders," it may be added, resulted in an open denunciation of them as enemies of their country and ultimate political oblivion. At the following year's election of representatives only five of the rescinders were re-elected and but two of these ventured to take up their duties.[46]

The day of the vote on the rescinding resolution, a special committee of five representatives laid before the House a petition to the King asking that Bernard be removed from his post on the basis of fourteen charges listed against him. Among the charges brought were: that he was identified with a party whose principles were repugnant to His Majesty's service; that he had treated the House

---

[43] *Ibid.*, pp. 72, 75.

[44] For the letter to Hillsborough, signed by the Speaker and dated June 30, see *ibid.*, Appendix, pp. 1–6. The letter took the position that the requisition of His Majesty, in calling upon the House to rescind its action, was unprecedented since the time of the Revolution of 1688; it emphasized the fact that not just a few people, but the most respectable and responsible on the continent, took the view that Parliament did not possess the power to raise a *revenue* in the colonies; finally, it stated that the House was fulfilling its duty under the charter that had been granted to it.

[45] *Ibid.*, pp. 89–90.

[46] See Bernard to Hillsborough, June 1, 1769, Bernard Papers, 3:27, Houghton Library, Harvard University.

of Representatives with contempt and had sought to be an absolute judge of the qualifications of its members; that he had also, presumably, attempted to persuade the ministers of His Majesty "that a Plan [was] settled, in this, and the rest of your Colonies, treasonably to withdraw themselves from all Connection with, and Dependence upon Great-Britain; and from their natural Allegiance to your Majesty's sacred Person and Government."[47] After the petition was debated it was recommitted so that the committee should bring in evidence "in Support of the divers Articles alleged." In the midst of this business, the House was called to the Council chamber, where the Governor, after approving bills already passed, abruptly adjourned the Assembly until the following August 3.[48] The very next day, however, a proclamation declared the House dissolved.

With the House of Representatives thus unable to complete its work of petitioning the King for the removal of Bernard, the Council was given leave to continue to sit "as a Privy Council" and to prepare a statement on the grievances of the people.[49] This the Governor forwarded to Hillsborough, requesting him to present it to His Majesty and adding in his covering letter: "I am not a Party to it; nor could I think it proper that I should be." Then, referring to the fact that he had been desired by the Council "to recommend the Prayer of the Petition," he went on to say:

> "I can readily recommend that Part of the Petition which prays Relief against such Acts as are made for the Purpose of drawing a Revenue from the Colonies. For they are so little able to bear the drawing Money from them, that they are unable at present to pay the whole Charges of their own Support & Protection."[50]

This letter was so framed that it could be shown to the provincial Council, but accompanying it was another which gave Bernard's true "Sentiments" upon the petition as one who, in the position of chief executive for the past eight years, had been closely in touch with Massachusetts Bay affairs.

As to the great and oppressive debt, which amounted to but £75,000 sterling, Bernard pointed out in his second letter, "untill within these two last years, it had been usual to raise half that Sum every year for a Sinking Fund." Therefore "a Debt could not

[47] *Journal of the House of Representatives* (Boston, 1768), pp. 95–6.
[48] *Ibid.*, pp. 97–8.
[49] For this petition, signed on July 7, 1768, see the Massachusetts Historical Society *Collections*, 6th ser., IX, 93–9.
[50] Bernard to Hillsborough, July 16, 1768, Letter No. 1, Shelburne Papers, 85: 201–4, Clements Library.

be called great which might easily be sunk in 2 years." On the subject of the discouragements on trade, he stated (as has been mentioned earlier in this chapter) that the "Ballance of Trade in the generality of the Colonies may be against them; but it can't be so in this Province; for Bills of Exchange of late have been done at Par; which rather shows the ballance to be in [our] favour. For if it was quite even, then [the Bills of Exchange] ought to be 2 per Cent above par to pay charges. . . ." Again, concerning the scarcity of specie, he asserted that this

> "Province is the only Colony that has a Currency of Specie, and therefore the Want of Specie is a more proper test here than in the other Colonies. . . . But there is no Want of Specie among those who do not Want property: I have heard it averred by a Gentleman well acquainted with Money that greater Inconveniencies arose to the Trade here from abundant of Specie than from want of it & he supported his Opinions with very plausible Reasons. It is certain that there is no Appearance of the want of money at present."

With regard to the burden of the import duties levied by Parliament, he maintained that it "cannot be pretended that the late Act of Parliament, which has been made a cause of this uneasiness, can embarras trade or be burthensome to the People. Upon the whole, it is rather an Act of Bounty than of Imposition; for the Drawback upon Tea more than pays the Duties upon other Articles. Nor is it easy, now the Duty upon Melasses is lowered, to shew any Act of Revenue which is really burthensome." Regarding the claim that the payment of duties was drawing money out of America, he pointed out the fallacy of saying this, "as it is known that they are not to be remitted to England" since the revenue thus obtained "shall be applied for the Supporting the Government and protecting the Country of the Colonies. . . ." What is more, he continued, there would be a deficiency of funds to accomplish this, which must be made up in Great Britain. In fact, Bernard held that although the petition of the Council sought to conceal it, the whole matter was really "a Dispute of Right & not a Complaint of Burthen. In the present case the Council have carefully avoided disputing the Right of the Parliament's imposing port Duties; and indeed 4 years ago no Man in America could have disputed it."[51]

The control of Boston by the mob, the flight of the customs officers to the protection of Castle William and to the British warship

[51] It may be pointed out that Bernard, before agreeing to submit the petition of the Council to the King, objected to several passages, "which were altered accordingly." Bernard to Hillsborough, July 16, 1768, Letter No. 2, Shelburne Papers, 85:201–4.

Romney now anchored nearby, and the utter helplessness of the provincial government to insure law and order, led the Board of Commissioners on June 15 to appeal for support from the Commander-in-Chief of all British Forces in North America, Major General Thomas Gage, then stationed at New York.[52] Upon receiving this appeal, Gage wrote to Governor Bernard on the 24th of that month and sent a copy of a letter he was forwarding to Lieutenant Colonel William Dalrymple at Halifax in which he directed him to be prepared to send to Boston all or any part of the King's forces under his command that the Governor should require.[53] In a letter to Hillsborough on the 28th, Gage explained that by this action "Time is Saved, if Governor Bernard thinks it proper to demand the Aid and Assistance of His Majesty's Troops. . . ."[54] But Bernard was reluctant to assume the responsibility for requesting troops. To the Secretary at War, Lord Barrington, he wrote on July 11:

> "Death has been denounced against those who are concerned in bringing Troops here: and yet I believe one Regiment at least is now ordered from Halifax. I have kept clear of being concerned in it by the Indulgence of Genl Gage who knows my Situation; but it will not follow that I shall not be charged with it. However I must take Care of myself as well as I can; and if I can't stand my Ground I must go to the Castle, which is now become a Place of Security, tho' in a Manner without a Garrison, having a 50 Gun Ship, two 16 Gun Sloops & two armed Cutters stationed about it."[55]

On July 11 Gage sent word to Bernard that he would not move troops "to quell Tumults and Riots" unless required by the civil power.[56] Thus Bernard was presented with a cruel dilemma. This he laid bare to Barrington later that month. If he had to request troops, he wrote;

> "I answer that then they [the troops] will never move: for I shall not make such a requisition without the Advice of Council; & I never expect to obtain that; neither their popular Constitution nor the present intimidation [of the Council by the mob] will permit it. . . .
>
> "Troops are not wanted here to quell a Riot or a Tumult, but to rescue the Government out of the hands of a trained mob . . . The sending Troops to Boston . . . ought to have been done two years & a half ago. If it had, there would have been no opposition to Parlia-

---

[52] Gage Papers, Clements Library.
[53] Gage to Dalrymple, June 25, 1768, *ibid.*
[54] *Gage Correspondence,* I, 182–3.
[55] *Barrington-Bernard Correspondence,* p. 165.
[56] Gage Papers, Clements Library.

ment now, & above all no such Combination as threatens (but I hope vainly) the Overthrow of the British Empire. . . .

"Regiments have been sent into Quarters at Philadelphia & New Jersey where the People are . . . in peace & Submission to civil Order; & Boston has been left under the uninterrupted Dominion of a Faction supported by a trained mob from Augst 14, 1765 to this present July 23, 1768. . . .

"To discharge myself as well as I can of being answerable for Consequences I have ordered a general Council to meet on Wednesday next . . . and require them to give me their Advice whether I shall or shall not send for the Troops . . . at Halifax."[57]

As the Governor had anticipated, the Council voted against sending for troops. In view of the unanimity of the Board's decision and the similarity of its sentiments to the popular view in the town, Governor Bernard was made to realize that he could no longer rely on the Council for support in upholding "the small Remains of royal & parliamentary Power now left" in the province[58]—that he stood isolated, as it were, in the midst of a sea of opposition.

In answer to Bernard's letters the Secretary at War was able to assure him that General Gage had received orders from home to send troops to Boston; that two regiments had sailed from Ireland for Boston on September 10, and that three regiments had been assembled at Halifax to support British authority in Massachusetts Bay.[59] In fact, Gage had written to the Governor on September 12, long before Hillsborough's letter could reach him, that by His Majesty's command he had ordered the 14th and 29th regiments to proceed as soon as possible from Halifax to Boston, where one of them would be quartered at Castle William and the other in the town.[60] With this information at hand Bernard summoned a meeting of the Council. The upshot was agreement between the Governor and Council that a committee of the Board should meet with the Boston selectmen and seek a solution to the problem of quartering the troops in the town proper with the least inconvenience to the inhabitants. In reporting the results of the conference to the Council, the committee reiterated the selectmen's view that the Quartering Act "indispensably requires" troops to be accommodated in barracks, and submitted that the facilities at Castle William were adequate.[61]

---

[57] Bernard to Barrington, July 20, 1768, *Barrington-Bernard Correspondence,* pp. 167–9.

[58] Bernard to Barrington, July 30, 1768, *ibid.,* pp. 169–70.

[59] Barrington to Bernard, October 3, 1768, *ibid.,* p. 171.

[60] "Proceedings of the Council," Massachusetts Historical Society *Collections,* 6th ser., IX, 100–1.

[61] *Ibid.,* pp. 101–3.

This position was confirmed also by the Council in reporting back to the Governor on September 26.[62]

When news spread of the expected arrival in Boston of some three regiments, rumours as to the purposes of their coming were rife. A report was circulated that Governor Bernard had told the Council "that he has three things in command from the ministry, more grievous to the people than any thing heretofor made known." On the basis of this report it was "conjectured" in the *Boston Gazette* of September 26 by a writer who signed himself as "A.B.C.":

> "1st. That the inhabitants of the province were to be disarmed. 2d. That the province was to be governed by martial law. 3rd. That a number of gentlemen, who have exerted [themselves] in the cause of their country, are to be seized and sent to Great Britain."[63]

It was undoubtedly previous rumours of this nature that had led to a town meeting on September 12 presided over by James Otis. Held to determine what steps could be taken to prevent the arrival of troops or the materialization of the other threats, the meeting appointed a committee of seven—including Cushing, Samuel Adams, Hancock, and Dr. Joseph Warren[64]—to wait upon the Governor and determine upon what grounds the soldiers were to be brought in, and to request that an Assembly be called. Bernard's response was that the only intimation he had of the arrival of troops was from private sources and that the matter of calling an Assembly was now before the King and could only await his command. The following day the committee of seven prepared a set of resolutions which were virtually a declaration of independence from Parliament, as the following preamble line to the first resolution indicates:

> "Whereas, it is the first Principle in Civil Society, founded in Nature and Reason, That no Law of the Society can be binding on any Individual, without his Consent, given by himself in Person, or by his Representative, of his own free Election. . . ."

This constituted a denial of the validity of the great mass of legislation enacted by Parliament relating to the internal and external

---

[62] *Ibid.*, pp. 105–8.

[63] It should be noted that the *Boston Evening-Post* of October 3, 1768, declared that its publishers had been authorized to inform the public that the report of the sayings of the Governor in the *Boston Gazette* was "an infamous Lye, invented for the wicked Purpose of . . . creating an unnatural Disaffection to his Majesty and his Government."

[64] For the leading role of Warren, who had by now emerged as an important leader in the radical faction, in the September 12 town meeting, see John Cary's *Joseph Warren*, pp. 80–1.

affairs of the colonies since the days of Charles II. The resolution then pledged the town to defend "the Rights, Liberties, Privileges, and Immunities" granted to them by "Royal Charter," and also "the Person, Family, Crown, and Dignity of . . . George the Third." In other words, the inhabitants of Boston upheld their allegiance to the King but repudiated the right of a Parliament in which they were not represented to interfere with their internal affairs. During the meetings, which lasted two days, it was also voted that—since, from the days of William and Mary, all subjects who were Protestants had a right to carry arms in their own defence, and since a wholesome law of the province provided that every householder should always be provided with a well-fixed flintlock, musket accoutrements, and ammunition, and, finally, since there was an apprehension of a new war with France—all inhabitants should be requested to observe the law for carrying arms at this time. What is more, the minutes of the meetings of September 12 and 13 were given the widest publicity in the newspapers.[65]

Manifestly Boston alone could not defy the agencies of the government of Great Britain seeking to enforce the laws of Parliament. The whole of the Bay province would have to support the movement, with the hope that other American colonies, too, would fall into line. Since the Governor had refused to summon an Assembly without the King's permission, a new outlet for action was needed. The Boston town meeting therefore resolved to choose a suitable number of persons "to Act for them as a Committee in Convention, with such as may be sent to join them from the several Towns in this Province, in Order that such Measures may be consulted and advised as his Majesty's Service, and the Peace and Safety of his Subjects in the Province may require." James Otis, Thomas Cushing, Samuel Adams, and John Hancock were appointed to represent Boston. By direction they wrote on September 14 to the selectmen of the several towns of the province "to propose that a Convention be held . . . at Faneuil Hall, . . . Thursday, the 22nd of September . . . at ten o'Clock Before-noon." Their letter referred to the unconstitutional taxes levied by Parliament on the Colony and the unconstitutional "Maintenance of a large Standing Army; not for the Defence of the newly acquired Territories, but for the old Colonies, and in a Time of Peace." The communication further emphasized that the loyal petitions from the House of Representatives had been ineffectual for the redress of "these heavy and very threatening Grievances"; instead, one or more

---

[65] See, for example, the minutes of the Boston town meeting as published in the *Boston Evening-Post,* September 19, 1768.

regiments were expected to arrive in the province for the purpose, it was apprehended, of "nothing short of Enforcing by military Power the Execution of Acts of Parliament. . . ."[66]

As a result of this alarming news, when the delegates convened on the scheduled day 66 towns were represented by upwards of 70 people, a number that increased later. The Convention drew up a petition to the Governor stressing the vital importance of calling an Assembly at this juncture. Bernard, however, could not officially receive the document since it emanated from an illegal assembly. In a letter to the gathering he made this clear, pointing out that he had received strict orders from the King to support his constitutional authority within the province and therefore could not "sit still and see so notorious a violation of it, as the calling an Assembly of the people by private persons only." He also expressed his belief that they "were not fully aware of the high nature of the offence they were committing" or "the penalties which they will incur if they should persist in continuing their session," and ended with the warning that the King "is determined to maintain his entire sovereignty over this Province, and whoever shall persist in usurping any of the rights of it, will repent of his rashness."[67]

A reply to the Governor's letter was framed and signed by the chairman of the Convention, Thomas Cushing. Among other things it requested the Governor to make clear the nature of the criminality of the gathering. When Bernard refused to receive this message, it, together with the petition and the Governor's letter, was given to the press. Before the committees of convention separated, however, "they appointed nine gentlemen of their number to consider and report the most effectual Measures consistent with the express Design of their Convening."[68] As a result, an address to the public appeared in the form of a statement of unanimous agreement arrived at by the chosen representatives of the 96 towns and eight districts met in convention on September 22; it ended with the assurance that "for the Recovering the Exercise of their just Rights and Liberties," the people of the province "may promise themselves Success. . . ."[69]

[66] *Ibid.*, see also J. C. Miller: "The Massachusetts Convention, 1768," *New England Quarterly*, VII, 445–74, especially 454–5.

[67] For the petition, the Governor's letter, and the message of the Convention see the Supplement to the *Boston Evening-Post*, September 26, 1768.

[68] *Ibid.*

[69] For this manifesto, see *ibid.*, October 3, 1768; it was first published as a broadside by the printers of the *Boston Gazette*, Edes and Gill. A copy of the broadside is preserved by the American Antiquarian Society. It may be noted that there is a discrepancy here on the number of towns represented (96) over the earlier report of 66 in the September 26 issue of the *Boston Evening-Post*.

On the morning of September 28, 1768, a flotilla of six warships and numerous transports appeared in Boston Harbour. The next day the warships ranged themselves in front of the town "as if intended for a formal siege." Then, on Friday the 30th, the 14th Regiment disembarked and—with drums beating, fifes playing, and colours flying—marched to the Town House, where later it was joined by the 29th Regiment. From there they marched to the Common. That evening the main body of the 14th Regiment was housed in an empty factory building, despite the initial refusal of the person in charge to obey the Governor's authorization orders. Those who could not be accommodated there were temporarily billeted in the Town House. With some thirteen ships of war facing the town and two regiments in the heart of it, the populace maintained an unnatural calm.[70] Calling attention to this, the Council argued on October 5 that it must be quite evident to the commander of the troops, Colonel Dalrymple, that the town was not manifesting the bad spirit that had been charged against it, but was, rather, "in a state perfectly peaceful and quiet." Thus, the Council reasoned, General Gage's orders had obviously been given under a misapprehension. Accordingly, the Board requested that the Governor send a special commissary to persuade the Commander-in-Chief to take all necessary steps for relieving the town and province of "anxiety and distress."[71] But once the regular soldiers had established themselves in Boston they were not to leave—except for the withdrawal to Castle William in 1770—until, in the midst of the War for American Independence, their position had become untenable.

This, then, was the position of Massachusetts Bay in the fall of 1768. Its Great and General Court had been dissolved because of the determination of its leaders to seek fundamental alteration of the constitution of the Empire through their own initiative. Its metropolis, the chief North American centre of disaffection to the government of Great Britain, had been turned into a garrison town where the Customs Commissioners, who had fled from the terror of the Boston mob, were able to carry on their duties only under the protection of the guns of Castle William. To Governor Bernard the situation represented a crisis of the highest magnitude in the relations of Great Britain and the North American colonies, for he saw the other colonies destined to follow the lead of Massachusetts Bay as they had done in 1765. But his own solution of the problem—rep-

[70] See *Boston Evening-Post*, October 3, 1768.

[71] "Proceedings of the Council," Massachusetts Historical Society *Collections*, 6th ser., IX, 108–11.

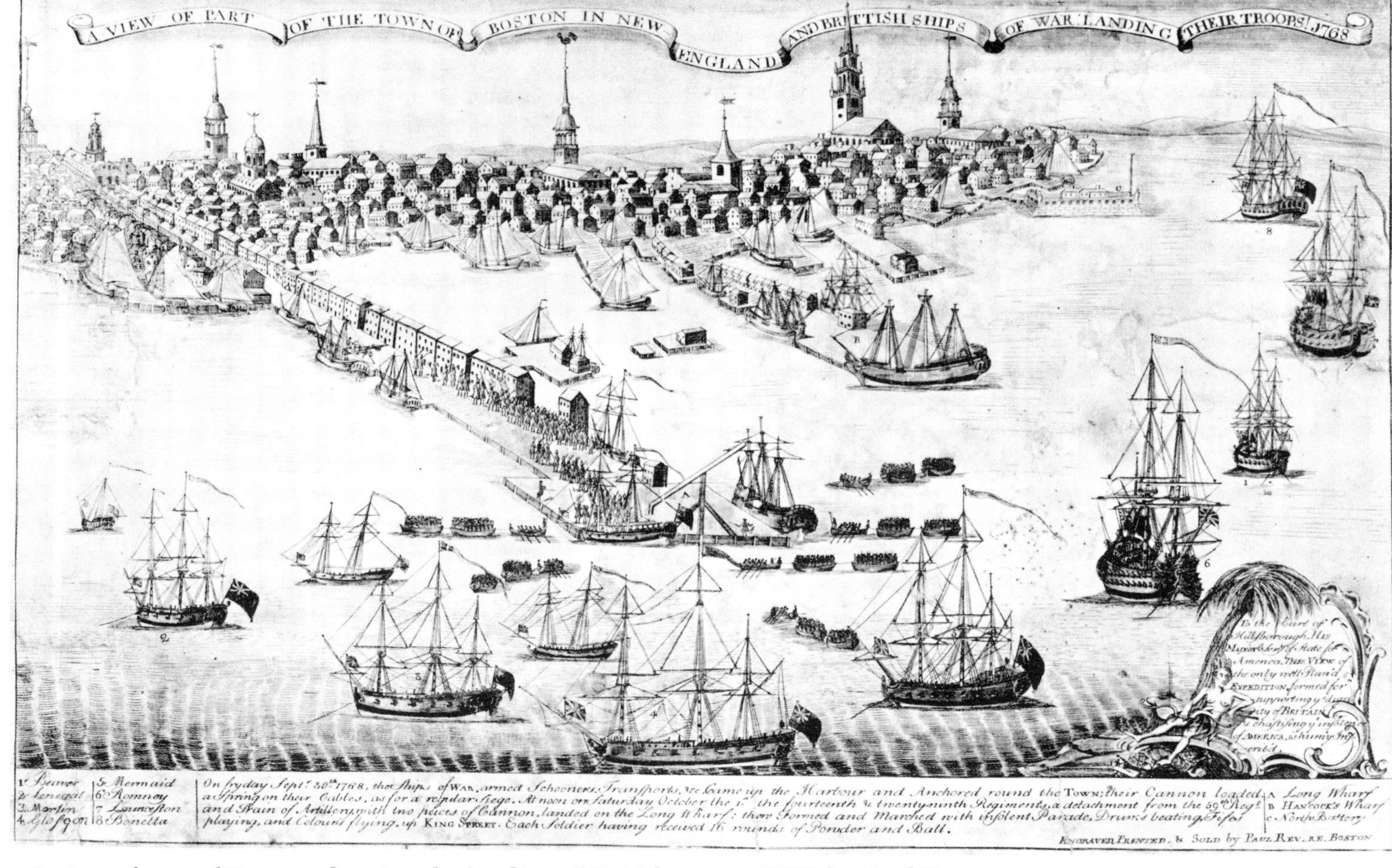

A view of part of Boston, showing the landing of British troops, 1768, by Paul Revere. (American Antiquarian Society)

"An attempt to land a Bishop in America."

(From the *Political Register*, Vol. V, 1769)

resentation in the House of Commons—was acceptable neither to the colonials nor apparently to the members of Parliament. When Lord Barrington informed him in the spring of 1768 "that there were not 10 Persons in either House that were favorable to an American Representation,"[72] Bernard replied "that this Measure is not only the most proper to remove the Causes of the present Dissentions; but that an incorporating Union is the *only* Provision which can prevent a Separation of the Colonies from Great Britain. If it is not done soon, it will be too late; & a Separation will take Place at no great Distance of Time."[73] Thus both the Governor of Massachusetts Bay and the leaders of the Assembly were in agreement on the necessity of a constitutional change to preserve the Empire, but their differences in point of view were fundamental. One looked to a closer union between the mother country and the colonies by giving the dependencies a voice in the deliberations of Parliament; the other was demanding virtual autonomy for the colonies, with the only binding tie to Great Britain resting in the recognition of the King as titular head of the Empire. The fact was that the presence of British regulars in Boston made the two factions irreconcilable.

[72] Barrington to Bernard, March 12, 1768, *Barrington-Bernard Correspondence*, p. 140.

[73] Bernard to Barrington, October 20, 1768, *ibid.*, p. 180.

CHAPTER VI

Other Colonies Follow the Lead of Massachusetts Bay

WHILE Massachusetts Bay was taking vigorous steps to protest parliamentary interference with the legislative authority of its Assembly, the other colonies were not idle. Individuals in several provinces were formulating ideas and plans to protest the Townshend Acts and other restrictive legislation and—as in the case of Dickinson's "Farmer Letters"—were making their voices heard through the press. Yet, the initiative throughout the 1760's remained primarily in the hands of the Boston radical leaders. By the early spring of 1768 the circular letter sent by the Massachusetts Bay House of Representatives on February 11 to the other colonial assemblies had begun to stimulate responses.

When news of this step on the part of the Bay colony reached London, the Secretary of State for the Colonies, Lord Hillsborough, on April 21, 1768, addressed a circular letter[1] to the Governor of every colony in North America whose assembly had received the Massachusetts Bay letter. His letter called upon each Governor to exert his "utmost Influences to defeat this flagitious Attempt to disturb the public Peace by prevailing upon the Assembly of Your Province to take no Notice of it, which will be treating it with the Contempt it deserves."[2] In the case of the royal and proprietary colonies there was added a final clause that "if, notwithstanding these Expectations . . . there should appear in the Assembly . . . a Disposition to . . . give any Countenance to this seditious Paper, it

[1] For Hillsborough's circular letter see John Almon: *A Collection of Interesting Authentic Papers . . . 1764–1775* (London, 1777), pp. 191–3; this collection is better known by its short title, *Prior Documents.*

[2] See, for example, *The Pitkin Papers . . . 1766–1769,* Connecticut Historical Society *Collections,* XIX, 120–1.

will be your Duty to prevent any Proceeding upon it by an immediate Prorogation or Dissolution."[3]

Despite the attempt by Hillsborough to scotch any trend toward colonial unanimity of action as an aftermath of the Massachusetts Bay circular letter, the other colonial assemblies took steps not only to evade the directive from the Secretary of State but also to reply to the Bay colony.[4] Their responses appear to have depended upon several factors: first, the extent to which they were individually affected by the parliamentary legislation in question (mainly the Townshend Acts, the Quartering Act, and the Legal Tender Act of 1764, which—in its continuing restrictions on the issuance of colonial paper money—was also an issue at stake); second, the speed of communications, determining when they received the Hillsborough letter; third, the circumstance of whether or not the particular provincial assembly was in session at the time; finally, the relationship of the respective colonial Governor with his legislature. As the steps taken by the various North American colonies during the developing crisis give a rather clear picture of the growing sense of power of most of the colonial assemblies and of an increasing tendency toward colonial solidarity, it may be well to examine their actions in some detail.

Although Virginia was not the first colony to receive the Massachusetts Bay circular letter, it was first to follow the lead of the northern province in seeking to bring all the North American colonies into a united front against the government of Great Britain. When the letter was read to the assembled House of Burgesses on April 2,

[3] See p. 491 of the *Correspondence of Governor Horatio Sharpe, 1761–1771* (ed. W. H. Browne, Baltimore, 1895), which forms Vol. XIV of the *Archives of Maryland.* It should also be noted that the *Archives of Maryland* (eds. W. H. Browne, C. C. Hall, B. C. Steiner, and J. H. Pleasants, 69 vols.+, Baltimore, 1883–1961+), published for the Maryland Historical Society, include, among other colonial records, the balance of Governor Sharpe's correspondence and addresses (Vols. VI, IX, and XXXI). The most valuable printed sources for North Carolina colonial history are to be found interspersed in the 30 volumes published by order of the North Carolina General Assembly; these are numbered consecutively Vols. I–X in the *Colonial Records of North Carolina* (ed. W. L. Saunders, Raleigh, 1886–90), and Vols. XI–XXVI in the *State Records of North Carolina* (ed. Walter Clark, Winston, Goldsboro, and Charlotte, 1895–1905); the key to these records is to be found in Vols. XXVII–XXX, which form the *Index to the Colonial and State Records of North Carolina* (ed. S. B. Weeks, Goldsboro, Charlotte, and Raleigh, 1909–14). For the above citation from the Hillsborough directive see also *North Carolina Colonial Records,* VII, 712–13.

[4] For the replies to the Massachusetts Bay circular letter from various colonies, as received by the Massachusetts Bay House through August 1768, see the Appendix of the *Journal of the House of Representatives* (Boston, 1767–8), pp. 6–14, in which appear the letters signed by the speakers of the lower houses of Virginia, New Jersey, Connecticut, Georgia, South Carolina, Rhode Island, and New Hampshire.

that body immediately resolved to consider it in a committee of the whole House. Also referred to the committee were petitions from "Sundry Freeholders" in four counties protesting the New York Restraining Act, the Townshend Acts, and other measures passed by Parliament affecting the interests of American colonials. The committee, under the able chairmanship of Richard Bland, whose *An Inquiry into the Rights of the British Colonies* had appeared in Williamsburg in 1766, continued to sit from time to time until on the 14th it finally agreed upon a petition to the King, a memorial to the House of Lords, and a remonstrance to the House of Commons. Thereupon, a conference with the Council "upon Matters of the highest importance to the Safety and well being of this colony was sought." This was granted and the Council fully concurred in the step taken by the lower house recommending that the two London agents, James Abercrombie for the Council and Edward Montague for the House of Burgesses, should act together in presenting the documents and in "endeavouring to obtain the ends thereof." With this accomplished the House of Burgesses authorized its Speaker to write not only to the Speaker of the Massachusetts Bay House of Representatives, applauding the attention that the body had given to "*American* Liberty," but also to the speakers of all other American assemblies to make known the steps taken by the Virginia Assembly and to urge them to similar action.[5]

The Virginia protests against taxation by Parliament—as well as against the New York Restraining Act, which involved the same principle—were very competently drawn and were moderate in tone. The remonstrance to the House of Commons, for example, expressed "Amazement" that the people of Virginia had been represented in Great Britain "as disloyal to their most gracious Sovereign and disaffected to his Government. . . ." "As members of the British Empire," it went on to state, Virginians did not claim other than "the common unquestionable Rights of British Subjects" not to be taxed without their consent. Let no one make the mistake, the remonstrance continued, of thinking the people were seeking "an Independency of Great Britain"; they "rather rejoice in that constitutional Connexion . . . essential to the Happiness of both." In proof of this, they had "acquiesced in the Authority of Parliament to make Laws for preserving a necessary Dependence, yet they cannot think it essential to this Purpose . . . that she [the "Parent Kingdom"] should raise

[5] *Journals of the House of Burgesses of Virginia, 1766–1769*, pp. 143, 145, 146, 149, 151, 152, 157–8, 161, 165–71, 172–4. *Legislative Journals of the Council of Colonial Virginia* (ed. H. R. McIlwaine, 3 vols., Richmond, 1918–19), III, 1383–4.

Money upon them without their Consent."[6] None of the documents, it may be noted, was in the language or temper of Patrick Henry; in general they reflected the more conservative, constructive approach of Bland.[7]

When, on April 16, the Speaker of the House of Burgesses delivered the petition, memorial, and remonstrance to the President of the Council, John Blair, for transmittal to the Secretary of State, Blair agreed to take this action. However, on that same day, as acting Governor, he prorogued the Assembly to the third Thursday in July, stating:

> "The great relief you have given to the distress of the country, in easing them of the land and poll taxes, gives me much pleasure; but as the session has trespassed so much on the General Court, by obstructing all business there for several days, I find it necessary to put an end to it. . . ."

By subsequent proclamations, the Assembly was further prorogued to the last Thursday in January 1769. However, upon his arrival in October 1768, the new Governor-in-Chief, Lord Botetourt, "for divers considerations regarding his Majesty's Service" and, one may add, in line with the Earl of Hillsborough's direction, dissolved the Assembly.[8]

Thus, by the time the other colonial assemblies were in a position to consider the Massachusetts Bay letter of February 11, many of them also had before them the precedent set by the Virginia burgesses as outlined in their letter of May 9, 1768.

Earliest to receive the Massachusetts Bay circular letter was the New Hampshire Assembly, whose Speaker presented it on February 19, 1768. But the only action taken by that body before Governor Wentworth dissolved the Assembly on March 24 was the approval of a reply, to be signed by the New Hampshire Speaker, expressing satisfaction with the proceedings of the Massachusetts Bay House.[9] When the new Assembly convened, it voted on June 1 that "a Committee . . . prepare in the Recess of the Court a Proper Address to

[6] *Journals of the House of Burgesses, 1766–1769*, pp. 168–71; see also *Virginia Gazette* (Rind), April 21, 1768.

[7] In this connection see Clinton Rossiter: *Seedtime of the Republic* (New York, 1953), Chap. 10, "Richard Bland," especially p. 262; see also R. D. Meade: *Patrick Henry, Patriot in the Making* (Philadelphia and New York, 1957), pp. 264–5, for Henry's indirect influence on the proceedings of the Assembly.

[8] *Journals of the House of Burgesses, 1766–1769*, pp. 177, 183–5.

[9] This letter, not found on file among the papers of the New Hampshire Assembly, is printed in the *Journal of the House of Representatives . . . of Massachusetts-Bay* [May 25–June 30, 1768] (Boston, 1768), Appendix, p. 14.

his Majesty's ministers Respecting the several things mentioned" in the Massachusetts Bay letter. However, between the time the Assembly was adjourned, on June 9, and the following August, no conclusive action was taken. On August 27, the New Hampshire House heard a petition to the King drawn up by the committee appointed for that purpose and immediately voted that it be signed by the Speaker and sent to the London agent to be presented to His Majesty. That same day the Assembly voted that a letter, heartily concurring in the sentiments expressed by the Virginia House of Burgesses, be sent to the Speaker of that House, and followed this action by requesting a recess, which the Governor then granted.[10]

The Rhode Island Assembly took up the Massachusetts Bay circular letter on February 29, 1768, and immediately voted that a committee be appointed "to draw up a suitable address to His Majesty; and also a letter to one of His Majesty's principal secretaries of state. . . ."[11] There the matter rested officially until the September session, although Speaker Metcalfe Bowles sent an acknowledgment to the Massachusetts Bay Speaker on August 3 saying that a committee was working on a reply.[12] Private individuals were also making their voices heard, especially in Providence, where, for example, at the dedication of the Liberty Tree on July 25, 1768, Silas Downer made a decidedly revolutionary speech, in the course of which he said: "I cannot be persuaded that the parliament of *Great Britain* have any lawful right to make *any laws whatsoever* to bind us. . . ."[13] On September 12 the special committee

[10] *Provincial Papers: Documents and Records Relating to the Province of New Hampshire* (7 vols., ed. N. Bouton, Concord, Manchester, and Nashua, 1867–73), VII, 152–3, 157, 165, 180, 187–90; these volumes form part of a continuing series of *Provincial and State Papers, 1623–1800,* cited hereafter as *New Hampshire Provincial Papers.* These records indicate that the petition to the King was not sent until April 14, 1770, at which time it was printed in the Journal of the House; see *ibid.,* VII, 248–9. It may also be noted that there is no record in the *Provincial Papers* of Governor Wentworth's having received the Hillsborough directive or of his having brought it to the attention of the New Hampshire Assembly. For the opinion of R. F. Upton—citing Governor Wentworth's manuscript letter to Hillsborough of June 25, 1768—that the Governor "brought great pressure to bear upon the Assembly to decline to take any action," see his *Revolutionary New Hampshire* (Hanover, 1936), p. 7.

[11] *Rhode Island Colonial Records* (10 vols., ed., J. R. Bartlett, Providence, 1856–65), VI, 534–7. The Massachusetts Bay letter of February 11, 1768, is here printed in full. Among the members appointed to consider it was the Governor himself.

[12] *Journal of the House of Representatives* (Boston, 1768), Appendix, p. 13.

[13] See *A Discourse Delivered in Providence . . . By a Son of Liberty* (Providence, 1768), p. 6. Previously the *Providence Gazette* had already taken up the cause, having among other items published on July 9 Roger Martyn's lengthy protest of the Hillsborough directive, in which he concluded by saying: "If our petitions are prevented from reaching the royal ear—if the most dutiful supplications are called unwarrantable combinations—and, in fine, if legislation in this country is suspended, because we decidedly declare our rights, and pray for a continuance of them, of what use are

reported to the Assembly "a draught of a humble, dutiful and loyal address to His Majesty; which being maturely considered" was approved. The Governor was thereupon requested to sign and transmit copies to Lord Hillsborough and to the colony's London agent.[14]

In the meantime, however, the Secretary of State's circular letter of April 21 had been received by Governor Josias Lyndon, who had acknowledged it on June 20 by stating simply that since it had not been received until the day before the closing of that session of the Rhode Island Assembly "they could not then give it the consideration its importance required. . . ."[15] In a second letter of acknowledgment, on September 17, Lyndon stood firmly with his Assembly in expressing "great surprise and concern, that an attempt to unite fellow subjects, laboring under the same hardships, in petitioning the throne in a constitutional, humble and loyal manner, for redress, should be termed a factious and unwarrantable combination."[16]

In Connecticut, as in Rhode Island, the Governor upheld the legislative body's official action, which was expedient but mild. When the General Assembly met on June 10, it resolved that Governor Pitkin "be desired and authorized to sign the . . . Petition of the Governor and Company of this Colony . . . to the King," as well as letters to the Earl of Hillsborough and to the colony's London agents, as prepared and approved by the Assembly. This was done forthwith.[17] A letter in reply to the Massachusetts Bay Speaker was sent

---

agents at the court of Great Britain? If I might advise in this matter, I would propose a general revocation of their powers, and a discontinuance of any further commerce or business with the inhabitants of a country, who, being only fellow-subjects, would tyrannize over us."

[14] *Rhode Island Colonial Records,* VI, 556–7.

[15] *Ibid.,* VI, 541, 548.

[16] For the letter to the King of September 16, signed by Governor Lyndon, the two September 17 letters, one to Hillsborough and the letter of transmittal to the London agent, see *ibid.,* VI, 559–64. (Governor Lyndon, who was described in the *Newport Mercury* [*ibid.,* VI, 550] as a Hopkins party man, amiable, inoffensive, and moderate in politics, held the place of Governor for only one year.) For the later replies of Hillsborough (November 15, 1768) and of the London agent, Joseph Sherwood (December 8, 1768), the former indicating that the sentiments "of both Houses of Parliament . . . do entirely concur with those of His Majesty"—who had expressed disapproval of the Rhode Island address—see *ibid.,* VI, 571–2.

[17] *Public Records of . . . Connecticut* (eds. J. H. Trumbull and C. J. Hoadly, 15 vols., Hartford, 1850–90), XIII, 76; see also *ibid.,* XIII, 84–9, for the petition to the King and the letters to London agents Richard Jackson and William Samuel Johnson. It may be noted that in Pitkin's letter of June 10, 1768, to Hillsborough, the Governor made no mention of having received his circular letter of April 21—which he acknowledged only in January 1769—and at no time did he explain his failure to carry out the orders contained therein to use his influence on the Assembly to persuade it to disregard the Massachusetts Bay letter. Nevertheless, Hillsborough apparently did not feel called upon to censure the Connecticut Governor as he had some of the other

the following day.[18] Although there was considerable support throughout the colony for these moves,[19] Connecticut remained on the conservative side for some time as the controversy developed.

From New York, where the Assembly had been restrained from meeting by a series of prorogations in 1767 and again in 1768,[20] Governor Moore reported to Hillsborough on May 12, 1768, that New Yorkers were not treating "inflammatory Publications in the printed newspapers" with "the contempt they really deserve." His reply on July 7 to the Hillsborough directive of April 21 simply stated that since the Assembly was not in session it could not take action on the Massachusetts Bay letter.[21] When it did meet again, the new legislature postponed consideration of the letter from the Speaker of the Virginia House until October 31. On November 8, however, it formed a committee to prepare representations to the King and to both Houses of Parliament "praying Relief from the Grievances his Majesty's Subjects within this Colony labour under, from the Act of Parliament . . . imposing Duties in the Colonies for the Purpose of raising a Revenue and of several other Acts. . . ." Replying on November 23 to Governor Moore's address concerning recent riots, the General Assembly stated: "tho' we feel in Common with the Rest of the Colonies, the Distresses occasioned by the new Duties imposed by the Parliament of Great-Britain, and the ill-policed State of the American Commerce; yet, we are far from conceiving that violent and tumultuous Proceedings, will have any Tendency to promote suitable Redress." At the same time the Assembly members announced that they were preparing representations to be sent to the appropriate authorities in England. Between November 24, when the Assembly resolved itself into a committee of the whole House to "draw up proper and constitutional Resolves, asserting the Rights of his Majesty's Subjects within this Colony," and December 31, when the final resolutions were read and approved, the special committee formed on November 8 was also at

---

colonial Governors. See *The Pitkin Papers, 1766–1769,* pp. 120, 132–9, 148, 153–4, 163–4, 166. For the Governor's letters to the London agents at this period, setting forth the position of the colony, and their replies, see *ibid.*, pp. 136, 146, 151, 152, 161–2; see also, for London agent William Samuel Johnson's reports on political affairs in England during the period April 29, 1768, to January 3, 1769, "Trumbull Papers," Massachusetts Historical Society *Collections*, 5th ser., IX, 264, 270, 289, 295, 300, 304.

[18] *Public Records of . . . Connecticut,* XIII, 90–1.

[19] For the action of the "moderate Whigs" see Oscar Zeichner: *Connecticut's Years of Controversy, 1750–1776* (Chapel Hill, N.C., 1949), pp. 83, 280–1.

[20] *Journal of the Legislative Council of New-York, 1743–1775,* pp. 1620–2, 1654–6.

[21] *New York Colonial Documents,* VIII, 58–9, 68–9, 80.

work. Thus, on December 17, the engrossed petition to the King, the memorial to the House of Lords, and the remonstrance to the House of Commons were ordered to be signed by the Speaker and transmitted to the Assembly's London agent, Robert Charles, with authorization for his expenses in engaging counsel to solicit "the Prayer of the said Petitions,"[22]

On the 31st of December even stronger resolutions were brought forward by the special committee. Four in number, they asserted on behalf of New York colonials, *nemine contradicente,* that no tax whatsoever ought to be placed upon them without their expressed consent; that they had the constitutional right to petition, and to "correspond and consult with any of the neighbouring colonies . . . whenever they conceive the rights, liberties, or privileges of this House or constituents to be affected"; and, most forcibly in the third resolution,

> "That it is the Opinion of this Committee, That this Colony lawfully and constitutionally has and enjoys an internal Legislature of its own, in which the Crown and the People of this Colony are constitutionally represented; and that the Power and Authority of the said Legislature cannot lawfully or constitutionally be suspended, abridged, abrogated or annulled by any Power, Authority or Prerogative whatever, the Prerogative of the Crown ordinarily exercised for Prorogations or dissolutions only excepted."[23]

Once the above resolutions had been read to the General Assembly, it was ordered that a committee of correspondence be appointed to comunicate with the London agent "during the recess of this

[22] For this Assembly action see *Journal of the Votes and Proceedings of the General Assembly of . . . New-York. Began the 27th of October, 1768; and ended by Dissolution, the 2d of January, 1769* (New York, 1769), pp. 8, 15, 30, 34, 40, 46, 48, 51, 53, 55, and *passim,* to be cited hereafter as *Votes and Proceedings of the New-York Assembly, 1768–1769.* Although the documents of the representations themselves are missing (because of the destruction by fire of much of the manuscript material in the New York State Library) the memorial to the House of Lords was reported as protesting that "their trade was languishing" and that "by British Act of Parliament they are to lose their legislative authority, and to have duties imposed on them for the express purpose of raising the revenue." See *Manuscripts of the Earl of Dartmouth, Vol. II, American Papers, Historical Manuscripts Commission, Fourteenth Report,* Appendix, Part X, 64. For the New York Assembly's special method of appointing its London agent, Robert Charles, which was questioned by Hillsborough in 1768, see Nicholas Varga: "Robert Charles: New York Agent, 1748–1770," *William and Mary Quarterly,* 3rd ser., XVIII, 211–35.

[23] For these resolutions see *Votes and Proceedings of the New-York Assembly, 1768–1769,* pp. 73–4, and *Boston Evening-Post,* January 9, 1769; see also, for the political background of New York at this period, *Memorial History of the City of New York . . .* (ed. J. G. Wilson, 5 vols., New York, 1822–3), II, 395–6, and C. L. Becker: *History of Political Parties in the Province of New York, 1760–1776* (Wisconsin, 1909, 1960 edn.), pp. 58–75.

House." At this point, Captain James de Lancey proposed that an addition be made to the third resolution to condemn the Restraining Act as "a high infringement of the Freedom of the Inhabitants of this Colony," but his motion was carried in the negative as being "already substantially, fully and clearly, contained in the said third Resolve." It was only after the resolutions had been approved that the Assembly turned to consideration of the letters from the Speakers of the Massachusetts and Virginia lower houses, ordering that replies be sent to both.[24] On the heel of these actions, Governor Moore on January 2, 1769, dissolved the Assembly, stating that "the extraordinary Nature of certain Resolves lately enter'd into your Journals . . . have put it out of my Power to continue this Assembly any longer. . . ."[25]

When the New Jersey Assembly met in April 1768 and took up the matter of the Massachusetts Bay circular letter, it agreed to draw up a petition to the King along the lines of that of Massachusetts Bay. This was accordingly done and duly signed by Speaker Cortland Skinner on May 6, 1768, without notifying the Governor of the proceedings.[26] In writing to Hillsborough on June 14. Governor William Franklin reported that "by Advice of the Council, I dissolv'd the Assembly," adding that he had never seen the address to the King until the minutes of the Assembly were printed. Again, on July 11, he wrote to the Secretary of State that he had no prior knowledge of the Massachusetts Bay circular letter until receiving the copy sent by Hillsborough, nor of the answer signed by the New Jersey Speaker on May 9, which had not been put in the minutes of the House, but a copy of which he enclosed therewith for Hillsborough, together with "a pamphlett publish'd in New York & reprinted at Philad.—the author unknown."[27] As the result of these letters Franklin was censured several times by Hillsborough

[24] *Votes and Proceedings of the New-York Assembly, 1768–1769,* p. 75. It will be recalled that during this period New York was perhaps not predisposed to act in close concert with Massachusetts Bay because of its continuing border dispute with that province, and, in this connection, the legislature was obviously anxious to put on a good front to the mother country at this critical juncture, following so soon after the passage of the Restraining Act. See Nicholas Varga: "The New York Restraining Act . . . 1766–1768," *New York History,* XXXVII, 233–55.

[25] *Votes and Proceedings of the New-York Assembly, 1768–1769,* pp. 79–80, and *Journal of the Legislative Council,* p. 1683; for Governor Moore's account of his dissolution of the Assembly, see *New York Colonial Documents,* VIII, 143–4.

[26] *Documents Relating to the Colonial History of the State of New Jersey* (36 vols., Newark, 1880–1941), 1st ser., X, 18–25. These *Documents* will be cited hereafter as *New Jersey Archives.* For the reply of the New Jersey House of Representatives, signed by Cortland Skinner, sent to the Massachusetts Bay Speaker on May 9, see *Journal of the House of Representatives* (Boston, 1768), Appendix, pp. 9–10.

[27] *New Jersey Archives,* 1st ser., X, 33, 36–7.

for his "entire Ignorance of what was passing in the Assembly . . . [which] betrays a very blameable Inattention to your Duty. . . ."[28] Franklin's very lengthy reply of November 23 to these censures gave a detailed account of the actions taken in both New York and Pennsylvania, in the course of which he stated:

> "My Motive in giving your Lordship so particular an account of the Transactions of the Assemblies of New York and Pennsylvania, is not to palliate or justify the Conduct of the Assembly of New Jersey, but merely to shew that they have not been singular on the occasion, and that even the Colonies which his Majesty thought had set them an Example to the contrary, had acted in a manner nearly similar. Indeed I think it my Duty to assure your Lordship, . . . that it is my firm Opinion, That there is scarce an Assembly man in America, but what either believes that the Parliament has not a Right to impose Taxes for the purpose of a Revenue in America, or thinks that it is contrary to Justice, Equity and Sound Policy to exercise that Right, under the present Circumstances of the Colonies, supposing it ever so unquestionable."[29]

As Governor Franklin had made clear in the letter just cited, Pennsylvania was not sitting idly by, despite the fact that when the Massachusetts Bay circular letter had been presented to its Assembly on May 10 by the unsympathetic Speaker, Joseph Galloway, that body had taken no action. For, as the Franklin account disclosed, "some of the leading Members of the Pennsylvania House, to obviate the Reflections which had been cast upon them by many of their Constituents for having too much slighted the Massachuset's Letter," published a special notice on July 25, 1768, claiming that the Pennsylvania Assembly had given consideration to the Townshend Acts as early as the previous February and had sent instructions to their London agents to unite with other colonial agents to press repeal of the acts.[30] Furthermore, on July 28 the following notice appeared in the *Pennsylvania Gazette*: "The Freemen of the City and County of Philadelphia are desired to attend at the State-House, on Saturday next, . . . to consider of proper Instructions to be given to our Representatives, on the present alarming and critical Situation of these Colonies," followed by the words: "Those who would give up *essential Liberty*, to purchase a little *temporary Safety*, Deserve neither *Liberty* nor *Safety*." Accordingly, when the meeting was

---

[28] *Ibid.*, X, 45–6 and 58–9.

[29] *Ibid.*, X, 64–95.

[30] *Ibid.*, X, 67–8; see also "Votes of Assembly," February 20, 1768, *Pennsylvania Archives*, 8th ser., VII, 6167–9.

held on July 30, the freemen heard an address in the strongest terms protesting the New York Restraining Act, the "levy of money upon us, without the intervention of provincial assemblies," the Declaratory Act, and "the enlargement of the powers of the admiralty court," as well as the Hillsborough directive, which was termed "the ministerial mandate, by which it seems we must bow our neck to the yoke, without uttering one groan. . . ."[31] Thus, when the Pennsylvania Assembly met again on September 16, 1768, the members resolved themselves into a committee of the whole House in a session which resulted in the signing by Speaker Galloway on September 22 of petitions to the King and to both Houses of Parliament. On that same date the Pennsylvania committee of correspondence addressed the London agents to transmit the petitions and took the opportunity to recall their earlier communication of February 20 of that year directing the agents to try to obtain repeal of the Townshend Act.[32]

Delaware was not far behind its neighbouring province to the north in action on the issue; for, on October 21, 1768, without reference to the Massachusetts Bay circular letter, the Assembly of the Three Lower Counties on the Delaware passed a resolution "That the House take into Consideration the State of the Government, and particularly how far the Inhabitants thereof are affected, by . . . some late Acts of . . . Parliament, for granting certain Duties in the British Colonies. . . ." Whereupon the Assembly, meeting as a committee of the whole, reported two resolutions on October 24 which resulted in the appointment of Cæsar Rodney, Thomas McKean, and George Read to draw up an address to the King.[33]

---

[31] *Pennsylvania Gazette,* August 4, 1768. In the following issue of the *Gazette,* that of August 11, the "Instructions to the Representatives of Philadelphia" were printed in full, calling upon them to exert themselves, "as soon as the House meets, that a Petition to His Majesty, a Memorial to the House of Lords, and a Remonstrance to the House of Commons be immediately drawn up, and transmitted Home."

[32] For the petitions and the letter to the London agents see *Pennsylvania Archives,* 8th ser., VII, 6270–80; these petitions were not printed in the *Pennsylvania Gazette* until February 2, 1769, when the paper also published the King's speech of November 8, 1768, to Parliament and the addresses of both Houses in reply. That both the rather neutral *Pennsylvania Gazette* and the partisan *Pennsylvania Chronicle* were instrumental in stirring up action in that province may be seen by a perusal of the files for this period, during which full accounts of developments in the other colonies, especially in Massachusetts Bay, were published in the form of the official documents.

[33] *Minutes of House of Representatives of . . . New Castle, Kent and Sussex, upon Delaware, 1765–1770* (Dover, 1931), pp. 156–8, 163–4. For the address to the King, signed by Speaker John Vining, and the resolutions for its transmittal to the London agent, named also by resolution on the same day to be Dennys De Berdt or, as an alternate, David Barclay, Jr., see *ibid.,* pp. 166–70. For the reading of the Virginia circular letter and the preparation of a reply to it see *ibid.,* pp. 159, 166.

To the south of Delaware, Maryland had already moved in a somewhat conservative but effective way. When the circular letter from Massachusetts Bay had been presented to the House of Delegates on May 26, it was tabled. However, after Governor Sharpe reluctantly sent a message on June 20 to the Assembly in conformity with the Hillsborough directive of April 21, the lower house replied at once with an address to him, signed by the Speaker, deploring these attempts to intimidate the colonies and to "suppress all Communication of Sentiments between" them. "What we shall do upon this Occasion," the Assembly went on to add, "or whether in Consequence of that Letter we shall do anything, it is not Our Present Business to Communicate to your Excellency. . . ." Upon receiving the address, the Governor, acting upon the advice of the Council, immediately prorogued the Assembly, which he continued to prorogue until his successor, Robert Eden, took over in July 1769. But the Assembly had already approved a petition to the King, had ordered it to be transmitted to London agent Garth for presentation, and had unanimously passed a series of eight resolves covering the rights and privileges of Marylanders. It had, furthermore, approved letters, to be signed by its Speaker, in reply to both the Massachusetts Bay and the Virginia circular letter.[34] That the power of the press was increasing in Maryland, as well as in other colonies, may be shown by the role of the *Maryland Gazette* in the controversy growing out of the new parliamentary legislation. On July 14 it printed the Hillsborough circular letter and again on July 28 it published the letter to the Massachusetts Bay Assembly Speaker, signed by the Maryland Speaker, in which the Maryland

[34] *Proceedings and Acts of the General Assembly . . . , 1766–1768, Archives of Maryland* (eds. W. H. Browne, *et. al.*, 65 vols., Baltimore, 1883–1952), LXI, 324, 334–5, 352, 360, 399, 405–9, 412–14, 415–17, 420; see also *Proceedings of the Council, 1761–1770, ibid.*, XXXII, 239–45. On June 24, 1768, Speaker Robert Lloyd wrote to Charles Garth, London agent for the House of Delegates, enclosing a petition to the King which had been framed before the House was prorogued. In this petition the royal charter given to Lord Baltimore by Charles I was cited as granting to those who would settle in Maryland "all Privileges, Franchises and Liberties of this our Kingdom of England" with the covenant that neither the King nor his successors would place "any Impositions, Customs or other Taxations, Quotas or Contributions whatsoever, in or upon the Residents or Inhabitants of the Province. . . ." See the *Maryland Historical Magazine*, XII, 377–81. For Governor Sharpe's rather apologetic reports on the issue to Hillsborough and to Lord Baltimore of June 22 and 23 in reply to the Hillsborough directive, see *Correspondence of Governor Sharpe, 1761–1771, ibid.*, XIV, 491, 506, 510–11, and, for Baltimore's notification of the appointment of his brother-in-law to succeed Sharpe as Lieutenant Governor, see *ibid.*, XIV, 523. Was this appointment the result of Sharpe's ineffectuality in preventing his Assembly's action? We do not know, but surely a certain apprehensive note may be detected in the Governor's letters to his superiors, when he takes pains to expatiate upon why he had prorogued rather than dissolved the Assembly.

assemblymen "acknowledge themselves . . . persuaded of the Necessity of harmonizing as much as possible, in proper Measures for Redress." Since it was dated June 24, or after the adjournment of the Assembly, it could not be included in the *Journal of the Lower House*.[35]

In North Carolina the letters from the Speakers of the Massachusetts Bay and Virginia assemblies were entered on the records, but as the Assembly was not in session—by successive prorogations from January 16 to November 7, 1768—no action could be taken on them. Meanwhile Governor Tryon—quite sick at the time and disturbed by the colony's internal problems over boundaries, Indian affairs, and the conflict with the Regulators (a problem to be dealt with later in this volume)—did not reply to Hillsborough's April directive until December 15. On that date he reported that "the moderation of that house with respect to the circular letter—made it unnecessary for me to prorogue the Assembly before the business of the session was ended." This was an obvious inconsistency,[36] for the Assembly had resolved on December 2 not only to appoint Henry Eustace McCulloh agent for the province, empowering and requiring him "to present our Address to his Majesty for the repeal of the several Acts of Parliament . . . imposing duties on Goods imported into America," but also to name members of a committee of correspondence to deal with the new agent on these and other matters.[37] Furthermore, on December 5, the lower house had resolved and read into the record an address to the King—clearly objecting to taxation without representation—in which the upper house at once concurred. It was then that the Governor prorogued the Assembly.[38]

Although the Commons House of Assembly was in recess when the circular letter from Cushing arrived in South Carolina, Speaker Peter Manigault replied on July 10 to the Massachusetts Bay House of Representatives that the message had just been received, and

[35] For the propagandist role which the *Maryland Gazette* continued to play in subsequent events see C. A. Barker: *Background of the Revolution in Maryland,* Yale Historical *Publications, Miscellany,* XXXVIII (New Haven, 1940), p. 319 *et seq.*

[36] *North Carolina Colonial Records,* VII, 881. It is true, however, that the lower house had taken no action on November 11, when the Massachusetts Bay and Virginia circular letters were read (*ibid.,* VII, 928–9).

[37] *Ibid.,* VII, 918, 974. It may be noted that in his circular letter of November 15 to all colonial Governors, enclosing copies of the King's speech to Parliament at its opening on November 8 and of the addresses to the King from both Houses, Hillsborough had added a final paragraph in the letter to Governor Tryon stating that the affairs of North Carolina were suffering from the lack of having an agent in London and therewith authorizing the appointment of such an agent (*ibid.,* VII, 867–8).

[38] *Ibid.,* VII, 980–2, 986.

that before the last adjournment of his Assembly on April 12, it had already been ordered that the committee of correspondence write to London agent Garth to seek repeal of several acts of Parliament, which letter had gone forward on April 14.[39] During the summer and fall of 1768, while the Governor, Lord Montagu, was in the north to recover his health, Lieutenant Governor William Bull was acting in his place. Thus it was Bull who was in temporary charge of the administration of South Carolina at the time the Earl of Hillsborough's letter arrived. On September 10 Bull wrote to the Secretary of State informing him that he had dissolved the Commons House of Assembly. Although uncertain of the temper of the House to be elected, he did not fail to mention the fact "that the circular Boston letter has been published in every Gazette on the Continent, as have the Answers from the respective Speakers."[40] There the matter rested until Governor Lord Montagu opened the new Assembly on November 17 with a speech invoking the Hillsborough directive. The South Carolina Commons House promptly took action by meeting as a committee of the whole. Out of the deliberations came a series of resolutions which led to conflict with the Governor, who then dissolved the Assembly, but not before the members had ordered all the documents "and other matters relating thereto to be printed and made public."[41]

At the time the Massachusetts Bay circular letter was received in Georgia—a colony still largely supported by annual parliamentary appropriation—the Assembly was not in session. Alexander Wylly,

---

[39] For this letter see *Journal of the House of Representatives* (Boston, 1768), Appendix, p. 12, and *Pennsylvania Gazette,* August 25, 1768. On July 26 Manigault also wrote to an unknown party quoting the committee of correspondence instructions to the agent of the House of Assembly to join with the other agents in obtaining a repeal of the late acts of Parliament laying duties in America and also directing him to take steps to see that the clause for billeting soldiers in America was not inserted in "the next Mutiny Act." A copy of this letter is among the Manigault Papers in the Carolinia Library, University of South Carolina.

[40] William Bull to Hillsborough, September 10, 1768, George Chalmers Manuscript Collection (25 vols.), "Papers Relating to Carolina, 1662–1795," New York Public Library. See also Bull's letter to Hillsborough of October 18, 1768 (South Carolina Archives), which stresses the influence of Boston on the members of the Assembly.

[41] For the proceedings of the Commons House of Assembly from November 17 to the date of its dissolution see the Journal of the Commons House of Assembly (mss.), 37, Part III: 6–22, South Carolina Archives Department, Columbia, S.C. An excellent, if brief, account of the reaction in the South Carolina Commons House of Assembly to the Massachusetts circular letter is to be found in W. R. Smith: *South Carolina as a Royal Province, 1719–1776* (New York, 1903), pp. 359–66; see also the files of the *South-Carolina Gazette* for the last quarter of 1768, when it began to reprint the "Boston Journal of Occurrences" and other pertinent articles. For the November 17, 1768, letter of the new committee of correspondence to London agent Garth, see *South Carolina Historical and Genealogical Magazine,* XXX, 224–5.

however, as Speaker of the last session of the Commons House of Assembly, acknowledged its receipt in a reply which expressed approval of the Massachusetts Bay action, pledged that the Assembly would deal with the letter when next it met, and disclosed that its London agent had been instructed to seek repeal of the Townshend Act.[42] When the newly elected House met on November 15 Governor Wright's address to it referred to the published letter of the late Speaker and clearly warned the members that if they gave any countenance to the Massachusetts Bay letter "it will be my Duty to prevent any proceedings thereupon by Immediately putting an End to your Sitting."[43] The House, in reply, assured the Governor "that no Letter of any Publick Nature has been laid before or presented to this House"[44] and proceeded directly to the consideration of various bills. With this business, including the tax bill, completed by the latter part of December and with the desired legislation approved by Wright, the Commons House on the 24th suddenly turned to a burst of activity relating to the Townshend legislation. It approved an address to the King (prepared in advance) "Imploring Relief from the Grievances and burden which by the late Acts of Parliament . . . this Province in Common with the other Colonies . . . labours under."[45] Replies to the Massachusetts Bay and Virginia circular letters (also prepared in advance) were likewise endorsed.[46] Finally, it was voted to publish in the *Georgia*

[42] For the resolution of the Commons House on April 11, 1768, appointing Benjamin Franklin as its London agent and directing the committee of correspondence to send these instructions to him, see *The Colonial Records of the State of Georgia* (ed. A. D. Candler, 26 vols., Atlanta, 1904–16) XIV, 584. Volumes 27–39 of the records are to be found in manuscript at the Georgia Department of Archives and History, Atlanta, and will be cited hereafter as Georgia Colonial Records (mss.). It may be noted that April 11 was the date on which the Assembly was dissolved. Wylly's letter was published on August 31 in the *Georgia Gazette,* which had been printing Dickinson's "Farmer Letters" from January 27 through April 27, 1768, together with favourable comment upon them.

[43] *Colonial Records of Georgia,* XVII, 454.

[44] For the reply see *ibid.,* XIV, 595–6.

[45] *Ibid.,* XIV, 643–5.

[46] *Ibid.,* XIV, 645–55. It is interesting to note that the circular letters were presented by Wylly only after the address to the King, which he helped to prepare, was approved. Was Wylly instrumental in stirring the Georgia Commons House to action? The records are not clear. We know that Governor Wright, who had been instructed by Hillsborough to disapprove him as Speaker, should he be elected (Colonial Records of Georgia, [mss.], 37, 332–3), had appointed Wylly to the committee that qualified members by having them take required oaths. We know also that Wylly by leave of absence did not take his seat until December 5. Also a matter of conjecture is the question whether the upper house was divided in loyalty to the Governor and to the common cause, as the record concerning its stand on the letter from the committee of correspondence to the London agent seeking repeal of the Townshend Acts would seem to indicate. The lower house had raised the point on December 8 that this

Gazette "the several Proceedings and Resolutions respecting the said Letters. . . ."[47] As the result of these actions, Wright dissolved the Commons House on December 24, 1768, but not before severely rebuking the members for their conduct, especially in view of the "Protection and Support" the colony had long enjoyed from the mother country.[48]

The response of the other North American colonies to the Massachusetts Bay circular letter is indicative of the extent to which their assemblies looked to that New England province for leadership. It also discloses the degree to which these bodies were asserting themselves in growing defiance to the directives of their Governors or, where a Governor and assembly were of one mind, to the higher authority of the Secretary of State and ultimately of the Crown. The part played by the colonial newspapers in keeping the issues before the public was also significant. Thus, the Townshend Acts were producing a reaction in America by 1768 that was adding fuel to the embers of the revolutionary fires kindled by the Stamp Act, which had by no means been extinguished. A new movement toward coordinated colonial resistance now rapidly mounted in intensity.

In John Dickinson's "Letters of a Pennsylvania Farmer" he had urged the use of the non-importation weapon that had seemed so effective in forcing the Stamp Act repeal. Steps in this direction, as an expression of protest rather than a matter of economy (such as had ostensibly influenced the movement for non-importation of luxury goods under the 1767 agreements), again got under way. As might have been anticipated, Boston led the march. On March 1, 1768, a large group of merchants and traders assembled at the British Coffee-House to consider measures for dealing with the "present distressed and embarrassed state of the trade." From subsequent meetings an agreement was reached on the 4th pledging the signers not to import any goods from England (except what was absolutely needed for the fisheries) for a period of twelve months—

letter "did not sufficiently instruct the Agent as the former House of Assembly required," owing to a refusal of some of the committee of correspondence from the upper house to concur in it. The upper house, however, replied "that the aforesaid Resolution is an Act of your House only, having Never been communicated to this House for Concurrence therein; (to which they might have had no Objection) And therefore the Members . . . could not . . . join in any instruction to the said Agent." See *Colonial Records of Georgia,* XIV, 586–7, 610, 613, 618–19, 621–2, and *ibid.,* XVII, 469–71.

[47] *Ibid.,* XIV, 655, and *Georgia Gazette,* December 28, 1768.

[48] *Colonial Records of Georgia,* XIV, 656–9; see also Kenneth Coleman: *The American Revolution in Georgia, 1763–1789* (Athens, 1958), pp. 28–9, and W. W. Abbot: *The Royal Governors of Georgia, 1754–1775* (Chapel Hill, N.C., 1959), pp. 148–9.

provided that the merchants of the "other Governments come into the same resolution."[49] Accordingly, on March 16 letters were sent to other colonial merchants as far south as Charleston. Of critical importance to the success of the plan was the cooperation of other colonial merchants, especially those of the other two great northern ports, New York and Philadelphia.

New York merchants and traders met as early as April 1768 to consider the Boston proposal. Although they reached a tentative agreement to receive no goods shipped from Great Britain to New York after October 1, their pledge was contingent upon the willingness of Philadelphia and Boston to join in their plan of boycott by the middle of June.[50] Boston quickly accepted the New York resolution on May 2. But Philadelphia was not prepared to act at that time.

A meeting of merchants had been held in the Pennsylvania metropolis on March 26, 1768, but no agreement had been reached; nor was a subsequent meeting on April 25, even though addressed by Dickinson, any more fruitful.[51] The chief cause for their hesitation doubtless stemmed from a desire not to disturb the increasing prosperity that was resulting from the rapid growth of frontier settlements. Again, many of the merchants of this thriving Quaker city were much more conservative in action than were those of Boston or New York. Moreover, there was a feeling among them that the Boston merchants sought to use them and others for their own purposes. "A Chester County Farmer," in the *Pennsylvania Gazette* of June 16, gave expression to this feeling when he wrote that Philadelphians probably "have discovered some secret Intentions in the New-England Scheme, that would be very disadvan-

---

[49] Thomas Cushing, Speaker of the House of Representatives, to Dennys De Berdt, London agent for the province, April 18, 1768, Massachusetts Historical Society *Collections*, 4th ser., IV, 350–1. The student in this connection should consult C. M. Andrews: "The Boston Merchants and the Non-Importation Movement," Colonial Society of Massachusetts *Publications*, XIX, 201–2, which prints the articles of agreement as passed.

[50] See *New-York Gazette; and the Weekly Mercury*, April 18, 1768, and *New-York Journal or, the General Advertiser*, April 21, 1768; see also A. M. Schlesinger: *The Colonial Merchants and the American Revolution, 1763–1776* (Columbia University *Studies in History, Economics, and Public Law*, LXXVIII, No. 182, New York, 1918), p. 115, to be cited hereafter as *Colonial Merchants;* and Virginia D. Harrington: *The New York Merchant on the Eve of the Revolution* (Columbia University *Studies in History* . . . , No. 404, New York, 1935), p. 335.

[51] See *Pennsylvania Gazette*, March 31 and April 21, 1768; see also for Dickinson's address, *Pennsylvania Journal*, April 28, 1768, and *The Writings of John Dickinson, 1764–1774* (ed. P. L. Ford, Philadelphia, 1895), Historical Society of Pennsylvania *Memoirs*, XIV, 407–17.

tageous to the Trade of this Province; and when we compare the flourishing and great increase in our Trade with the various accounts we have heard of their [Boston's] *long declining state,* it speaks . . . loudly, in Favour of your [the Philadelphia] merchants Oeconomy."[52]

Open resistance to the Townshend Act duties increased as a result of the Massachusetts Bay circular letter, but it became apparent that the generality of people in Pennsylvania were more receptive to persuasion than were the Philadelphia merchants. Even the July 30 State House meeting of the Philadelphia freemen—which resulted in the proposal that strong representations be made to the King and to both Houses of Parliament—failed to move the merchants to take the action desired by Boston and New York. Nor were they persuaded by the publication in the *Pennsylvania Gazette* on September 15 of the New York merchants' new agreement of August 27 not to import merchandise from Great Britain (with certain exceptions specified) after November 1 and to treat as an enemy of his country any person subscribing who might later violate the agreement. Even though the Assembly had adopted petitions to the King, the House of Lords, and the House of Commons asking for recognition of the rights of Englishmen on September 22, this action did not seem to influence the meeting of merchants and traders held the next day at the courthouse to consider letters of importance addressed to them; for they still took no action. "Philadelphus," in a letter published in the *Gazette*[53] on October 20, made clear that a majority of the leading merchants importing dry goods "had the concurrence of the members of both branches of the legislature," as well as "the general voice of the most sensible thinking people throughout the province" in their opposition to "a general non-importation" of British goods. It appeared that the Philadelphia merchants preferred to await the outcome of the Assembly petitions and of the memorial embodying their grievances sent to the merchants in England on November 1. The signers of this memorial agreed to join the non-importation movement in the spring if no

---

[52] The writer was Joseph Galloway, Speaker of the Assembly, according to P. L. Ford. See *ibid.*, XIV, 435.

[53] The *Pennsylvania Gazette* had been published before 1766 by Benjamin Franklin and David Hall. When Franklin withdrew, William Sellers took his place. The paper was conservative under the new publishers and, in its issue of September 22, had to defend itself in particular against the charge that it "suppressed Dr. Franklin's Pieces against the Stamp-act." The attacks were printed in the rival paper, the *Pennsylvania Chronicle.*

steps had been taken to grant them relief.[54] Only in February 1769 was the first definite action taken in the Quaker city, when some sixty merchants agreed not to import from Great Britain and a beginning was made to foster home manufactures.[55] Finally, by early March, more than three hundred merchants "cooly & with great unanimity resolved to decline ordering any more goods—until those acts of Parliament—are repealed."[56]

The progress of the American non-importation, non-consumption, and domestic manufactures movement was most pronounced in those colonies that possessed important commercial and industrial centres. It took a slightly different direction in the plantation colonies. While, by the spring of 1769, the merchants in each of the three commercial colonies had established agreements for the ports of Boston, New York, and Philadelphia, other colonies lagged behind. Nevertheless, Maryland soon joined them. The town of Baltimore made the first move in March by adopting an agreement in harmony with that of Philadelphia. By June 22 a general agreement had been reached covering "the Merchants, Traders, Freeholders, Mechanics and other Inhabitants of the Province of Maryland,"[57] which reflected the recent action in Virginia. In this province it was the great planter George Mason who, with the support of George Washington, early in the year drew up a plan of non-importation, one that ultimately was adopted in most of its features at Williamsburg on May 18 by members of the House of Burgesses meeting privately after the House had been dissolved by the Governor, Lord Botetourt, on the 16th.[58] Despite this move, the Virginia merchants had not acted, and were reluctant to do so. To secure their support it was necessary

---

[54] A. M. Schlesinger: *Colonial Merchants,* pp. 116–19, 126–8. For the earlier newspaper "warfare" see R. L. Brunhouse: "The Effect of the Townshend Acts in Pennsylvania," *Pennsylvania Magazine of History and Biography,* LIV, 362.

[55] *Pennsylvania Gazette,* February 2, 16, March 16, April 13, 1769.

[56] Thomas Clifford to Walter Franklin (New York merchant), March 11, 1769, Clifford Correspondence, Vol. 28, Pemberton Papers, Historical Society of Pennsylvania; see also A. M. Schlesinger: *Colonial Merchants,* 129–30, and Theodore Thayer: *Pennsylvania Politics and the Growth of Democracy, 1740–1776* (Harrisburg, 1953), p. 144. For the continued reluctance of the merchants and the threats of mob violence which finally impelled them to action, see R. L. Brunhouse: *op. cit.,* pp. 365–6.

[57] For this agreement see *Maryland Gazette,* June 29, 1769; it is also to be found in "The Case of the *Good Intent,*" published in 1770 and reprinted in the *Maryland Historical Magazine,* III, 144–9.

[58] For Washington's action in promoting a non-importation agreement in Virginia, see Washington to George Mason, April 5, 1769, *Writings of George Washington* (ed. J. C. Fitzpatrick, 39 vols., Washington, 1931–44), II, 500–4. The Virginia non-importation agreement is printed in the *Journals of the House of Burgesses, 1766–1769,* pp. xl–xlii.

to modify the plan. This was not effected until the following year at a joint meeting of traders and members of the Assembly on June 22, 1770.[59]

In South Carolina the picture was confused. The movement for non-importation centred at first among the Charleston mechanics, tradesmen, and artisans, who had been so vigorously active in opposition to the Stamp Act.[60] The planter group later joined in the movement, but the great Charleston merchants showed their indifference to it as early as September 1768, when they received the circular letter addressed to them by the Boston merchants.[61] However, Peter Timothy, the editor of the *South-Carolina Gazette,* published in his February 2, 1769, issue a form of non-importation which the public was urged to adopt. Moreover, Christopher Gadsden, influential both as merchant and as planter, threw his weight behind this plan and also that for promoting local manufactures. In the June 22 edition of the *Gazette* he appealed to planters, mechanics, and freeholders of the province to bring pressure to bear upon the Charleston merchants, "whose *private interest* is *glaringly* against us." Early in July there was a gathering of mechanics at the Liberty Tree in Charleston at which over two hundred of them signed a non-importation agreement.[62] On the 7th of that month the merchants also came forward with a plan for non-importation which ignored one of the chief planks made by the mechanics—the support of local manufactures.[63] With two rival agreements in circulation, there was great confusion until a compromise plan was approved on July 22. The reconciliation of the views of the mechanic-planter groups on the one hand and the merchant group on the other was largely due to the work of Gadsden.[64] A general committee of thirty-nine, consisting of thirteen merchants, thirteen planters, and thirteen mechanics, was appointed to carry out the unusually comprehensive provisions of the agreement. The plan prohibited, until the Townshend legislation should be repealed, imports from Great Britain of European and East India goods—with the exception of certain essential articles—as well as wines; further, no slaves were to be brought into the province from abroad during

[59] The agreement of June 22 is printed in the *Pennsylvania Gazette,* July 12, 1770.
[60] See Richard Walsh: *Charleston's Sons of Liberty. A Study of the Artisans, 1763–1789* (Columbia, S.C., 1959), pp. 44–7.
[61] See *South-Carolina and American General Gazette,* July 10, 1769.
[62] *South-Carolina Gazette,* July 6, 1769.
[63] *Ibid.,* July 13, 1769.
[64] *Ibid.,* July 27, 1769.

the year 1770. Those who refused to be bound by the agreement were to be treated "with the utmost contempt" and isolated.[65]

The merchants of Savannah, Georgia, displayed the same reluctance to come into a non-importation agreement as had those of Charleston, but the South Carolina example was too powerful to resist. On July 26 the *Georgia Gazette* published the substance of the various South Carolina resolutions, and on September 6 the same paper printed a most forthright letter addressed "To the Inhabitants of Georgia," which argued: "that since we are no longer to be allowed the rights of Britons; WE MUST be Americans; let us live within ourselves; our real wants which cannot be supplied without importations are but very few. . . . The two great points in view, therefore, are non-importation of European goods, and the encouragement of manufactures of our own. . . ." A meeting of "Merchants, Planters, Tradesmen and others" was then held, at which a committee was appointed to prepare resolutions; these, in turn, were considered and adopted the following week. They were, in the main, patterned after those of South Carolina.[66] Although, in the October 4 edition of the *Gazette,* "A Merchant" denied that half the merchants of Savannah had signed them, and although Governor Wright on October 31 in an address to the two houses of the Assembly warned that efforts to distress the mother country were a "two-edged Sword,"[67] the resolutions were considered to be binding on the people of the province. There was, nevertheless, great opposition to them and they were only partially successful.[68] It may be added that one of the chief promoters of non-importation was Jonathan Bryan, who had previously held many important provincial offices and at the time was a member of the Governor's Council. For this conduct he was dismissed from his post by the Governor.[69]

Just as Georgia followed the non-importation lead of South

---

[65] For the South Carolina resolutions of July 22, see C. M. Andrews: "The Boston Merchants and the Non-Importation Movement," *op. cit.*, XIX, 217–19; see also A. M. Schlesinger: *Colonial Merchants,* 140–7, and Richard Walsh: *op. cit.*, pp. 47–50.

[66] For these resolutions see *Georgia Gazette,* September 13 and 20, 1769; see also *Pennsylvania Gazette,* November 9, 1769, for the meeting of merchants on the 16th and the general meeting of inhabitants on the 19th.

[67] *Colonial Records of Georgia,* XVII, 489.

[68] Wright to the Earl of Hillsborough, September 20, 1769, *ibid.*, XXXVII, 417–18. For evidence that the shippers of slaves, when turned away from South Carolina, had recourse to ports in Georgia, see *South-Carolina Gazette* for May and June 1770.

[69] For the non-importation movement in Georgia see Kenneth Coleman: *op. cit.*, pp. 29–32, and W. W. Abbot: *op. cit.*, pp. 151–2. In 1775, although eighty years of age, Bryan participated actively in the revolution, first as a member of the Committee of Safety, two years later as a member of the Executive Council, and finally as commander-in-chief of the armed forces of Georgia.

Carolina, so North Carolina fell in behind Virginia. As Georgia had found a leader in Jonathan Bryan, so North Carolina found one in John Harvey, a native of the Albemarle Sound region, who first appeared in the Assembly in 1746 and in 1766 was elected Speaker, a position that he filled up to the outbreak of the American War for Independence with the exception of the period 1770 to 1773. A man of cultivation and deep conviction, he had taken a strong stand in opposition to the Townshend legislation. On November 11, 1768, the Assembly under his leadership adopted an address to the King against the Townshend Revenue Act, which, among other things, declared: "Free Men cannot legally be taxed but by themselves or their representatives, and that your Majesty's subjects within this province are represented in Parliament we cannot allow. . . ."[70] No further steps were taken, however, until in September 1769 the Sons of Liberty in the Cape Fear region adopted certain resolutions.[71] The next move was toward a general association when, in November 1769, again under the leadership of Harvey, the Assembly was presented with resolutions that paralleled those of Virginia. But before these could be acted upon Governor Tryon dismissed the Assembly on November 6.[72] Thereupon the members met in private and created an association to carry out the non-importation agreement.[73] But it must be stressed that, as had occurred in the other plantation colonies, the conflict between the merchants and the other inhabitants created a disunity that undermined the association. As Tryon wrote to Hillsborough on February 1, 1771:

> ". . . Notwithstanding the boasted associations of people who never were in trade, and the sham patriotism of a few merchants to the southward of the province, the several ports of this province have been open even since the repeal of the Stamp Act for every kind of British manufactures to the full extent of the credit of the country."[74]

The action taken in the remaining colonies was less forceful. Of the Three Lower Counties on the Delaware, only in New Castle County—which encompassed the ports of Wilmington and New Castle—did the freeholders and freemen take any boycott action. On August 28, 1769, they drew up and signed a compact to discontinue trade with Great Britain until those acts of Parliament

[70] For excerpts from this address see H. T. Lefler and A. R. Newsome: *The History of a Southern State, North Carolina* (Chapel Hill, N.C., 1954), pp. 185–6.

[71] *South-Carolina Gazette,* August 9, 1770.

[72] *North Carolina Colonial Records,* VIII, 105.

[73] *South-Carolina Gazette; And Country Journal,* December 8, 1769.

[74] *North Carolina Colonial Records,* VIII, 496. In this connection see R. D. W. Connor: *History of North Carolina* (6 vols., Chicago, 1919), I, 334–7.

were repealed that threatened "Calamity, Misery and Slavery" for all North America; they also declared that any man who would violate this agreement would be "deemed infamous, and an Enemy of his Country." The agreement—to take effect immediately—was signed by Samuel Patterson, foreman, in behalf of the grand jury of the county. It was ratified the following Saturday at a meeting of the principal freeholders held "at Christiana-Bridge," at which time it was said "that it will soon be signed by every Freeholder and Freeman in the County, and that the other Counties in that Government will immediately follow the Example."[75]

In New Jersey the House of Assembly on October 18 unanimously passed a formal vote of thanks to "the Merchants and Traders of this Colony, and of the Colonies of New-York and Pennsylvania, for their disinterested and public spirited conduct in withholding their Importations of British Merchandize, until certain Acts of Parliament, laying Restrictions on American Commerce, for the express Purpose of raising a Revenue in America, be repealed . . ."[76]—an action which shows that by this time the New Jersey importers were following the example of merchants in the two neighbouring colonies through whom they traditionally dealt.

The leading Connecticut towns, beginning with those in the eastern part of the colony, had adopted late in 1767 and early in 1768 non-consumption agreements against the use of certain "enumerated Articles, imported from abroad."[77] Yet a "Son of Liberty" was led to lament early in 1769: "all our Trading Seaport Towns are stored full as ever with British goods."[78] In fact, it was not until July that the New Haven merchants were persuaded to accept without much modification the New York non-importation resolutions.[79] The merchants of New London and Groton took similar action the following month,[80] with Wethersfield and Norwich later falling in line. On October 2, 1769, the farmer-dominated House of Representatives passed a resolution approving the non-importation stand of the merchants.[81] Finally, a general agreement among the merchants of the various towns was reached in February 1770.[82]

Rhode Island was also a laggard in coming to an understanding

[75] *Pennsylvania Gazette*, August 31, 1769.
[76] *New Jersey Archives*, 1st ser., XXVI, 546.
[77] See *Connecticut Journal*, February 12 and March 4, 1768.
[78] *Ibid.*, January 6, 1769.
[79] *Connecticut Courant*, November 6, 1769.
[80] *Boston Chronicle*, August 28, 1769.
[81] *Boston Evening-Post*, January 22 and February 5, 1770; see also *Colonial Records of Connecticut, 1768–1772*, p. 236.
[82] *Connecticut Courant*, February 26, 1770.

on non-importation. It is true that on December 2, 1767, inhabitants of the town of Providence had reached an agreement "similar to the one entered into about the same Time by the Town of Boston," but it had not been effectively put into practice. This was equally true of Newport. For example, in August 1768, some months after Boston had forbidden the importation of tea from Great Britain, a Bostonian wrote to his Newport correspondent that a hundred chests had been received, having come over "the Newport Turnpike."[83] Again, in the August 28, 1769, edition of the *Boston Chronicle,* it was charged that two British merchant ships which had not been permitted to land goods in Charleston, South Carolina, or New London, Connecticut, were allowed to dispose of their cargoes at Newport. This information was also given due publicity in New York.[84] In the face of this criticism, on October 24 the merchants and others, meeting in Providence, agreed to uphold strictly the resolutions of 1767. To that end, anticipating the arrival of a merchant ship with forbidden articles in it, they agreed to deliver up the merchandise to a committee which would see that it was stored until the Townshend Revenue Act was repealed. In addition, the public was warned not to purchase such items.[85] On October 30 Newport also came to an agreement not to purchase any British or East India goods—with certain specified exceptions—until Parliament repealed the act. Nothing, however, was said about European goods,[86] so that Rhode Island merchants and traders continued a lucrative trade. Only when the other colonial ports made clear their hostile attitude toward this evasiveness on the part of the Rhode Island ports, and threatened to boycott them, was the agreement broadened to conform to the agreements of Boston, New York, and Philadelphia, but this was not until early in the new year.[87]

Thus, by the end of 1769, New Hampshire was the only colony that did not have a non-importation covenant. There a peculiar situation existed in the political and trading centre, Portsmouth.

[83] John Powell to Christopher Champlin, August 23, 1768, *Commerce of Rhode Island, 1726–1800* (eds. C. F. Adams *et al.*, 2 vols., Boston, 1914), I, 246. This title forms Vols. IX and X of the Massachusetts Historical Society *Collections,* 7th ser.

[84] See *New-York Gazette: or, the Weekly Post-Boy,* August 28, 1769.

[85] See *Pennsylvania Gazette,* November 16, 1769, for details of the Providence meeting.

[86] For the Newport agreement, which was more detailed than that of Providence, see *ibid.* For an effective treatment of Rhode Island's failure to support non-importation see A. M. Schlesinger: *Colonial Merchants,* pp. 152–5.

[87] See *Boston Gazette,* January 27, 1770; see also D. S. Lovejoy: *Rhode Island Politics and the American Revolution, 1760–1776* (Brown University Studies, XXIII, Providence, R.I., 1958), pp. 142–4, and J. B. Hedges: *The Browns of Providence Plantations, Colonial Years* (Cambridge, Mass., 1952), pp. 203–5.

The growth in trade and prosperity of this town was closely identified with the activities of the Wentworth family and those connected to it by marriage, who virtually controlled its politics and commerce.[88] In 1767 John Wentworth took the place of his uncle Benning as Governor of the province, a post he retained until the outbreak of hostilities in 1775. As had been true during his uncle's administration, many of the new Governor's associates in government were also concerned with trade. Under the Wentworth influence they refused to fall in line with the Boston radicals,[89] just as the earlier Wentworth influence had been responsible for the refusal of the province to send delegates to the Stamp Act Congress.[90] Up to the spring of 1770 the Portsmouth merchants continued to show an unwillingness to cooperate with the other colonies in the campaign against the Townshend Acts.[91] Only after the incident in Boston known as the "Boston Massacre" were the New Hampshire towns at last stirred to action. Then, when a wealthy Scot, James McMasters, arrived in Portsmouth with a stock of goods which he had not been permitted to sell at Boston, the inhabitants of Portsmouth agreed on April 11, 1770, that anyone who should deal with him would be considered "unfriendly to the Interest of his Country."[92] But that was as far as the people would go in pledging a commercial embargo.

The outcome of the non-importation movement must be reserved for treatment later. Suffice it to say that by the early spring of 1770 it was still gathering momentum in some areas—at the very time that Parliament was in the process of repealing most of the Townshend Acts—and that some similarity of action was manifested in the three great metropolitan cities of the North in contrast to the reluctant participation in the plantation colonies of the South, South Carolina excepted. Thus, it may be said that by 1770 the colonies, led by Massachusetts Bay, were beginning to take a considerable degree of united action in the revolutionary movement.

---

[88] See Volume III, revised, pp. 51–3, of this series for a description of the power of the Wentworths.

[89] See L. S. Mayo: *John Wentworth, Governor of New Hampshire 1767–1775* (Cambridge, Mass., 1921), p. 125.

[90] See Volume X, of this series, p. 330, for New Hampshire's refusal to support the Stamp Act Congress.

[91] It should be recalled, however, that in 1768, in reply to the letter from the Virginia House of Burgesses, the New Hampshire House of Representatives expressed full accord with the Virginia position opposing a measure so "little different from the former oppressive STAMP ACT." See *Provincial Papers: . . . of New Hampshire* (7 vols., ed. N. Bouton, Concord, Manchester, and Nashua, 1867–1873), VII, 189–90.

[92] *Boston Gazette,* April 16, 1770; for New Hampshire and non-importation see R. F. Upton: *op. cit.,* pp. 8–10.

CHAPTER VII

The Discontented—"Wilkes and Liberty"

If in the 1760's there was resentment of the British government on the part of the colonies because of the Townshend revenue program, there was during the same period, no lack of discontent in England with the government, for a variety of reasons. The nation had had a long history. It had a background of remarkable successes in many fields of endeavour and equally remarkable failures, of movements that had taken deep root, of other movements that had not, despite much popular support.

Out of the collapse of the republican experiments during the so-called Interregnum of the seventeenth century had emerged the restored monarchy and a restored aristocratic social structure. Yet, firmly as these institutions were planted, a residue of opinion survived into the eighteenth century that seemed to look back with a certain nostalgia to the days of the Commonwealth and the Great Rebellion and forward with a passionate advocacy toward a new order of things based upon the assumption that certain principles of organized society were divinely ordained as man's natural heritage. Such, during the reign of George III, was the outlook of a group of "outright republicans" which included, among others, Thomas Hollis, wealthy book-collector and philanthropist;[1] Richard Baron, editor of seventeenth-century tracts; diarist Sylas Neville; historian Catherine Macaulay and her brother, John Sawbridge, who was successively sheriff, alderman, and Lord Mayor of London, as well as a member of the House of Commons and an early Wilkes sup-

[1] See Caroline Robbins: "The Strenuous Whig, Thomas Hollis of Lincoln's Inn," *William and Mary Quarterly*, 3rd ser., VII, 406–53, and her *Eighteenth-Century Commonwealth Man . . . English Liberal Thought from the Restoration of Charles II until the War with the Thirteen Colonies* (Cambridge, Mass., 1959), pp. 259–68 *et. seq.*, hereafter cited as *Commonwealth Man.*

porter.[2] Yet these strong individualists—although in close association with each other and with like-minded people—never attempted to organize a republican party. On the contrary, they accepted the Hanoverian monarchs as symbols of national unity, while seeking to revitalize what they considered to be the seventeenth-century doctrines of the "Real Whigs"[3] and aligning themselves alternately with one or another of the liberal, radical, or reform groups which proliferated during this period. For example, there was the group calling themselves the "Honest Whigs," which met fortnightly at the London Tavern near St. Paul's, frequented by Franklin along with men who crossed over professional and political divisions, such as lawyers John Lee and Theophilus Lindsey; Boswell, on the literary side; John Canton, member of the Royal Society; James Parsons, the philologist; William Rose, teacher and co-editor of the *Monthly Review;* and political theorist James Burgh. Among the outstanding clergymen who also forgathered with the Honest Whigs were the eminent dissenters Richard Price and Joseph Priestley and their biographer, Andrew Kippis, as well as the Anglican Bishop of St. Asaph, Jonathan Shipley, a staunch supporter of the American cause —perhaps through his close friendship with Franklin—as were most of the others of this circle.[4]

Then, in 1769, came the Society of the Supporters of the Bill of Rights, in the organization of which John Horne, who later took the name of John Horne Tooke, played a prominent role, if not the leading one—and with which the American brothers Arthur and William Lee were closely affiliated.[5] Originally this Society had been founded for the purpose of giving financial and political support to John Wilkes,[6] as will be developed later in this chapter, but in its

[2] *Ibid.*, pp. 335–46, 358–63.

[3] *Ibid.*, pp. 5, 323–4.

[4] *Ibid.*, pp. 329, 333, 336, 347.

[5] For the leading members of the Bill of Rights Society see Alexander Stephens: *Memoirs of John Horne Tooke* (2 vols., London, 1813), I, 163; S. Maccoby: *English Radicalism, 1762–1785: The Origins* (London, 1955), pp. 105–9; and I. R. Christie: *Wilkes, Wyvill and Reform: The Parliamentary Reform Movement in British Politics, 1760–1785* (London, 1962), pp. 33–4. See also George Rudé: *Wilkes and Liberty: A Social Study of 1763 to 1774* (Oxford, 1962), pp. 61–2, and Lucy Sutherland: *The City of London and the Opposition to Government, 1768–1774: A Study in the Rise of Metropolitan Radicalism* (1958 Creighton Lecture, London, 1959), pp. 19–21, which also lists (p. 19*n*) some of the other societies which were primarily political in purpose. For the part of the Virginia-born Lees see R. H. Lee: *Life of Arthur Lee* (2 vols., Boston, 1829), I, 22, 25–8. Arthur Lee also won the acquaintance and friendship of Shelburne and other liberals (whom he called "the constitutionalists") as the result of his "Junius Americanus" letters. See *ibid.*, I, 17, 195, 199.

[6] For the formation of the Bill of Rights Society on February 20, 1769, see *Annual Register, 1769*, p. 75, and *Gentleman's Magazine*, XXXIX, 108.

early days it also attracted some of the republicans, liberals, and reformers mentioned above. But the so-called Real Whigs and Honest Whigs, while concerned in theory with parliamentary government, were not the practical political Whigs, and were only indirectly and ineffectively aligned with the opposition. For it must be recalled that we are dealing with a period before the party system had evolved.

As Sir Lewis Namier has pointed out so brilliantly in his Romanes Lecture of 1952, there were by the late 1760's in Parliament only "three broad divisions, based on type and not on party": (1) the followers of the Court and the administration, or those dependent upon patronage and places, whom he calls the "ins"; (2) the independent country gentlemen, or permanent "outs," by their own choice, and certain urban counterparts; (3) finally, at the centre, "the political factions contending for power, the forerunners of parliamentary government based on a party-system."[7] In this third division among the chief contending political factions were, the aristocratic Whigs, who formed a divided opposition—the Rockingham group, supported by the great orator Burke, among others not of the aristocracy, and the Chatham-Shelburne group, supported by certain non-aristocratic liberals and republicans, including Colonel Barré and John Dunning and such urban independents as William Beckford, and later John Sawbridge, James Townsend, and Richard Oliver,[8] once the last three had broken with Wilkes and the Bill of Rights Society.[9] There were in addition the uncommitted groups surrounding the Bedfords and the Grenvilles[10] and a power-

[7] Sir Lewis Namier: *Monarchy and the Party System* (Romanes Lecture, Oxford, 1952), reprinted in both volumes of his collected essays: *Personalities and Powers* (London, 1955), Chap. 3, pp. 21–2, and *Crossroads of Power* (London, 1962), Chap. 20, p. 220. In this connection, see also Richard Pares: *King George III and the Politicians* (Oxford, 1953), Chap. 3, "George III and the Parties."

[8] For Sawbridge, Townsend, and Oliver see Sir Lewis Namier and John Brooke: *History of Parliament: The House of Commons, 1754–1790* (3 vols., London and New York, 1964), III, 224–5, 409–11, 537–8, cited hereafter as *House of Commons, 1754–1790.* For Shelburne as reformer and his connections with the London politicians see John Norris: *Shelburne and Reform* (London and New York, 1963), especially pp. 55–60.

[9] For the split in the ranks of the Bill of Rights Society beginning in 1770 and culminating in the spring of 1771, see Alexander Stephens: *op. cit.*, I, 179–319, and J. Horne Tooke: *Controversial Letters of Wilkes and Horne* (London, 1771); see also I. R. Christie: *op. cit.*, pp. 45–8.

[10] For an illuminating account of political activity in the late 1760's see John Brooke: *The Chatham Administration, 1766–1768* (London, 1956), especially the last four chapters and the Epilogue. For an earlier view see D. A. Winstanley: *Lord Chatham and the Whig Opposition* (Cambridge, 1912), *passim.* Chapter 8 in the present volume deals with the realignment of the factions after the resignation of Chatham in 1768 and of Grafton in 1769; Chapter 3 has already described the break-up of the Rockingham Ministry.

ful extra-parliamentary pressure group centred in the City of London and the surrounding metropolitan area.

In the City proper, the Court group and "monied interest" were firmly on the side of the government, some of the wealthier merchants and office-holders were traditionally independents, while the middle-class merchants, traders, and master craftsmen were on the side of the opposition.[11] It was from the last two groups that the urban radicals were to emerge. But, as Dr. Sutherland has so aptly put it: "It was only when the City began to some extent to disassociate itself from the politics of Opposition as well as those of Government . . . that it can begin to be considered a focus of Radicalism as distinct from a centre of traditional anti-ministerialism."[12] This point was fully reached by 1769, when the Middlesex freeholders on January 12, those of Westminster on January 25, and those of the City on February 10 decided to send instructions to their representatives in Parliament to protest the steps taken by the Commons against Wilkes.[13] The most important of the fourteen City instructions, which Beckford encouraged fully, called for protection of the Habeas Corpus Act, shorter Parliaments, a place and pension bill, no bribery at elections, and a review of any call for payment of the debts on the civil list—the fund allocated by Parliament for the support of the Crown establishment.[14] These demands were quickly adopted as a reform program by the London radicals and were later taken up by the Bill of Rights Society.[15] For example, at a meeting held at the Southwark town hall on March 1, 1769, the electors voted a series of twelve very similar instructions for the guidance of the two members of the House of Commons from that borough—Sir Joseph Mawbey, a leading member of the Bill of Rights Society, who strongly defended the propriety of the in-

---

[11] See Lucy Sutherland: "The City of London in Eighteenth-Century Politics," *Essays Presented to Sir Lewis Namier* (eds. Richard Pares and A. J. P. Taylor, London, 1956), pp. 49–74, especially p. 54.

[12] For the history of "corporate solidarity" in the political activity of London, before the crisis of 1768–9 over Wilkes and the Middlesex election, see Lucy Sutherland: *The City of London . . . 1756–7* (Oxford, 1960, reprinted from the British Academy *Proceedings*, XLVI, 147–93), which traces the growth of London radicalism with the early career of William Beckford, as does her *City of London and the Opposition to Government, 1768–1774,* previously cited in full, in which see p. 7 for the textual citation. See also George Rudé: *op. cit.*, pp. 149–52, and I. R. Christie: *op. cit.*, Chap. 1.

[13] *Annual Register, 1769,* pp. 66–7, 70, 73.

[14] *Gentleman's Magazine,* XXXIX, 73–4, 107.

[15] See Lucy Sutherland: *City of London, 1768–1774,* pp. 22–3, which also points out that Beckford spoke out on the subject of rotten boroughs throughout 1769.

structions, and Henry Thrale, who acquiesced in them.[16] The Southwark members of Parliament were called on to work to confirm the right of trial by jury, to guard that "great bulwark of our liberties" the Habeas Corpus Act, to preserve the right of electors and the privileges of the elected, to encourage application to the House for redress of grievances, to make secure all liberties derived from the constitution, to try to reconcile the differences between the mother country and the colonies, to enquire into abuses of the use of military power, to promote a standing committee on public accounts, to determine the causes of the rise of the civil list debt, to work toward getting bills to limit placemen in Parliament and for preventing peers from interfering in elections, to quiet the minds of the people by a bill dealing with "obsolete claims of the crown," and finally to secure a bill to shorten the duration of Parliament.[17] Like the City instructions, this attempt by urban radicals to bind the Southwark members of Parliament to a program of action more or less specific in nature is notable "as setting a high constitutional example,"[18] to the credit of a member of the Bill of Rights Society.

Among the reforms called for in a long and revealing essay that appeared in March 1768 in reformer John Almon's newly established *Political Register,* were the following: annual elections for seats in Parliament as something which would produce "effects of inconceivable importance to the state"; a widening of the franchise so as to include "every substantial *housekeeper*" throughout the country, with the voting to be by ballot as the means by which "corruption must soon become impracticable"; and a re-examination of borough representation in Parliament in order to eliminate such disparities as allowing the counties of Cornwall and Devon—contributors of but minor amounts of land tax and subsidies—to have seventy members in the House of Commons while Greater London, with its huge contribution to these levies, was permitted but eight members. Behind the demand for these reforms was the complaint of the

---

[16] *Gentleman's Magazine,* XXXIX, 161–2, and *Annual Register, 1769,* pp. 78–9. For Mawbey and Thrale see *House of Commons, 1754–1790,* III, 121–3, 527–9.

[17] *Annual Register, 1769,* pp. 78–9.

[18] S. Maccoby: *op. cit.,* p. 108. It should be made clear that the justification for drawing up the elaborate set of instructions for the Southwark members of Parliament, rather than resorting to petitions to Parliament or the King, was doubtless the argument that the right of political petitioning as set forth in 13 Chas. II, c. 5—a Restoration statute still in force—was limited to a county meeting called by the gentry or, in the case of London, to a meeting of the Common Council; see Peter Fraser: "Public Petitioning and Parliament before 1832," *History,* XLVI, 200–1. The breakdown of the binding power of this law came with the Middlesex County petition later in 1769.

reformers that as the constitution then stood "we have no check on the arbitrary power of our *grandees* [members of the House of Lords], who can . . . command the concurrence of the sovereign, if they be joined by a corrupt lower House; and by means of military force, can do with our liberties what they please."[19]

In addition to the dissatisfactions with political life in England expressed by the more literate section of society, even greater discontent was directed toward economic conditions by the artisan and labouring class, especially in the metropolitan area of Greater London, where the population was estimated at 676,750 in the middle of the eighteenth century and 900,000 by 1800.[20] For example, in 1768 a burst of violence broke out among the coal-heavers of the river-front slums in Wapping and Stepney. Among their grievances was the complaint that wages were often held back or were paid in liquor or inferior goods, and that while they and their families were starving, their employers were gaining fortunes. On April 21 a great riot took place, "attended with much blood shed, the rioters having met with opposition fought desperately, and several lives were lost." On June 6 another riot involving the coal-heavers and sailors resulted in many wounded on both sides. Upon this occasion one commentator reported: "The coal heavers are grown a terror to the whole neighbourhood of Stepney and Wapping, and commit the most shocking outrages." When two of their number were hanged for murder on July 11 at Tyburn, hundreds of their fellow-workers paraded through the streets armed with bludgeons, cutlasses, and other weapons, shouting: "*Five pounds for a Sailor's head, and twenty for a Master's; we'll cut the Lightermens throats, and murder all the Masters, burn their houses, and set fire to their ships.*"[21]

In another large area of London, which included Bethnal Green but went under the general name of Spitalfields, thousands of silk-weavers had congregated. This group of labourers was especially subject to periodic fluctuation of employment, which depended on the health of the silk trade. When it was depressed, as it frequently

[19] *Political Register*, II, 218–42. This article also is quoted at length by I. R. Christie: *op. cit.*, pp. 19–23. For a discussion of Almon's founding of the *Political Register* in 1767 as an organ of the Temple-Grenville faction, see R. R. Rea: *The English Press in Politics, 1760–1774* (Lincoln, Neb., 1963), pp. 134–5.

[20] M. Dorothy George: *London Life in the Eighteenth Century* (London, 1951), pp. 24 and 329. For the view that the industrial disputes as a movement "ran side by side" with the Wilkes movement, but merged "only in exceptional circumstances," see George Rudé: *op. cit.*, Chap. 6, especially p. 104.

[21] For the above incident see *Gentleman's Magazine*, XXXVIII, 197, 298, 347.

was, widespread unemployment followed and the workers were then usually obliged to plunge deeply into debt to provide the necessities of life for their families. In the 1760's wages were never high, even when work was plentiful, because of the over-supply of skilled journeymen and apprentices.[22]

But the weavers were helpless to improve their standard of living by lawful means, for united action was forbidden by statutes against combinations of workers. In 1725 a law had been passed by Parliament (12 George I, c. 34) making it unlawful for weavers engaged in the production of woolen goods to enter into a combination. This statute referred to the fact that such workers had lately formed "Clubs and Societies" in which, by means of "By-Laws and Orders . . . , they pretend to regulate the Trade and Prices of their Goods [that is, goods produced to the account of their employers], and advance their Wages unreasonably," and that in unlawful assembly they had committed "great Violences and Outrages upon many of his Majesty's good Subjects, and by Force protected themselves and their wicked Accomplices against Law and Justice." To prevent such activity in the future the law provided that those convicted of violating it were liable to imprisonment for three months; moreover, a weaver was also liable to this penalty should he quit his employer's service before the time for which he had agreed to serve had elapsed. What is more, should a worker in wool assault his employer or another worker for not complying with the by-laws or orders of such a club or society and inflict bodily harm upon him or should he write or send any threatening letter to a woollen manufacturer or verbally threaten to destroy any houses, trees, or cattle for not so complying with demands made upon him, such person upon conviction would be subject to sentence as a felon to transportation to the colonies for a period of seven years. In 1749 Parliament extended the scope of this statute to include all workers engaged in the manufacture of silk, fur, hemp, linen, cotton, fustian,

[22] Dr. Dorothy George gives a most revealing picture (*op. cit.*, Chap. 4) of conditions in Spitalfields and the silk industry, such as the employment of large numbers of women and even young children. In 1765 thousands of unemployed silk-weavers had gone in a body to Parliament to present a petition setting forth their plight while the market was being flooded with foreign-produced silks. By May of that year great riots of the weavers took place. As a result, Parliament was induced to pass two acts, one (5 Geo. III, c. 29) for reducing the import duty on raw silk and another (5 Geo. III, c. 48) prohibiting the importation of stockings, mitts, or gloves of silk. Nevertheless, the over-abundance of silk-weavers and apprentices kept wages depressed. In the London *Public Advertiser* of February 18, 1769, the large number of apprentices being trained by the master weavers was noted and the question raised: "How are all these to find employment when their time of apprenticeship is expired?"

iron, and leather (22 George II, c. 27). Thus the workers had a realistic basis for their discontent.

The fact that there had been much invective in the papers during the past year was stressed in the April 1768 number of *Gentleman's Magazine* in a letter to the editor signed by "Medius" which took the side of the rich. Some of his arguments would undoubtedly sound more than specious to an English worker in the latter part of the twentieth century. Nevertheless, he does make a valid point in his claim that, outside of England and the American colonies, there was no country in the world at that time which taxed the rich to keep the poor from beggary by laying a burden which, in some parts of the kingdom, amounted to from five to six shillings on the pound. He is also doubtless correct in asserting that no nation exceeded eighteenth-century England in private benevolence—such as the erection of schools and various types of hospitals "at an immense expense" and contributions to those who suffered loss by fire, storm, or flood or to others in need in times of scarcity. Likewise, he makes the point that the rich—who were chiefly instrumental in passing the laws placing high duties on the importation of certain choice foreign goods—taxed themselves in order to encourage domestic manufactures and thereby provide work for the poor. In dealing with the "malignant censure" of the rich by some writers who denounced "their luxury and expensive living, while the poor are starving," "Medius" justifies this inequality with the argument that in the final analysis "our labouring poor do in every year receive *the whole revenue of the nation*" in funds paid out for various things furnished to them. As to low wages, while granting that the worker should be better paid, he took the position that the cheapness of many articles was due to their plenty, "so the cheapness of labour is, in most cases, owing to the multitude of labourers, and to their underworking one another in order to obtain employment."[23]

In addition to the discontent of the working people already mentioned, there was also general unrest due to the depression that had followed the boom days of the Great War for the Empire and particular dissatisfaction with the increase in taxes and the prices of necessities. The common complaint was that wages had not kept pace with the rises in the cost of living.[24] Hand in hand with this

[23] *Gentleman's Magazine*, XXXVIII, 156–7.

[24] This point is stressed in two works that appeared during this period; one was by Thomas Mortimer: *The Elements of Commerce, Politics, and Finances* (London, 1772), and the other published anonymously under the title *Considerations on the Policy, Commerce, and Circumstances of the Kingdom* (London, 1771), in which, among other things, the writer stressed (p. 44) the unsympathetic attitude of the

went the criticism, noted in the beginning of this chapter, that the government was being run not for the benefit of all the people but for the enrichment of a favoured few. The working people were especially resentful of places and pensions awarded to those who already possessed wealth.[25] These resentments, along with blasts at

---

public toward the labouring classes in that "those unhappy, distressed, oppressed and useful people have become the objects of abuse throughout the kingdom." For a study relating to this problem see A. W. Coats: "Changing Attitudes to Labour in the Mid-Eighteenth Century," *Economic History Review*, 2nd ser., XI, 35–51. As to the rise in prices, the price of wheat, a basic necessity, rose from 27 shillings a quarter in 1761 to 60 shillings a quarter in 1767, according to a table presented by T. S. Ashton: *An Economic History of England: The Eighteenth Century* (London, 1955), Appendix, p. 239. Ashton's figures are based upon tables compiled by J. E. T. Rogers: *A History of Agriculture and Prices in England . . .* (7 vols., Oxford, 1866–1902), Vols. VI and VII.

On March 22, 1769, the day chosen to present an address to the King from the merchants and traders of the City of London, the populace caused such a disturbance, dispersing the carriages of the merchants, that the Riot Act was read at St. James's. In giving an account of this, with the comment that "excessive taxation may be adduced as one cause of the violence on the part of the people," Robert Huish, in his *The Public and Private Life of . . . George the Third . . .* (London, 1821, p. 329) appends the following note, purportedly written by "a foreigner": "In England the people are taxed in the morning for the soap that washes their hands; at nine for the coffee, the tea, and the sugar, they use for breakfast; at noon, for starch to powder their hair; at dinner, for the salt to savour their meat, and for the beer they drink; after dinner, for the wine they drink; in the evening, for the spirits to exhilirate; all day long, for the light that enters their windows; and at night, for the candles to light them to bed."

[25] *The North Briton*, September 16, 1769, referred to the number of "placemen" whom the writer, "Observator," called "horse-leeches." He asserted that for every placemen in the kingdom a century ago there are now fifty, if not a hundred. This was due not only to the creation of new places but to the splitting up of old ones. "Instead of a Lord Treasurer, we have five Lords of the Treasury; instead of a Lord Admiral, we have seven Lords of the Admiralty; we have seven Commissioners of the Customs; nine of the Excise, ten of the Navy-office, five of the Stamp Office, five of the Salt-office, sixteen Commissioners of Trade and Plantations, two of the Post-office, five for Hackney Coaches and Chairs, four for wine licences, seven for the Victualling-office, and multitudes of other Officers, which it were needless to enumerate." For an illuminating account of the problems facing a loyal supporter of the Crown who was both civil servant and member of Parliament and who basically did not wish to be a placeman, see I. R. Christie: "The Political Allegiance of John Robinson, 1770–1784," *Bulletin of the Institute of Historical Research*, XXIX, 109–22. For a picture of the British Isles in the middle of the eighteenth century see Volume I, Revised, of this series. That the social and economic situation in general and the condition of the poor in particular were the subjects of serious consideration in England in the second half of the century may be attested by the prominence given to the new publications or reprintings of the works of Bishop George Berkeley, James Burgh, Richard Burn, Nathaniel Forster, David Hume, Soame Jenyns, Sir William Mildmay, Malachy Postlethwayt, Richard Price, Joseph Priestley, Adam Smith, Sir James Steuart, Dean Josiah Tucker, and Arthur Young, to name only the more prominent of the writers and political theorists who dealt with political economy at this period. For a key to the large number of contemporary tracts and pamphlets on social and economic subjects published at this time see *A Guide to the Printed Materials for English Social and Economic History, 1750–1850* (ed. Judith Blow Williams, 2 vols., New York, 1926).

rotten boroughs, were freely voiced in Almon's *Political Register*.[26] Even the far more moderate *Gentleman's Magazine*, early in 1768, printed an appeal "To the Electors of Members of Parliament" to come to the rescue of the poor,

> "who in many places are now starving for want of provisions . . . in some measure, unavoidable through the many lucrative posts and p[ension]s held under, and paid by, the G[overnmen]t. . . . The poor of all denominations, from the necessitous tradesman to the meanest mechanick and common day labourer, pay them [places and pensions] in the taxes laid upon the necessaries of life. For numbers of families to be pinched with hunger, and have scarce wherewith to cover their nakedness, that others may abound in superfluities of food and rayment, be cloathed in fine linnen, and fare sumptuously every day, How hard, how partial, how unfeeling is this?"[27]

The feeling that government was being run for the enrichment of those who enjoyed the royal favour and that the King's revenue —derived largely from the civil list fund granted by Parliament annually to permit him to live as was fitting to one of his rank— was being improperly diverted, to his impoverishment and that of the British people, led the House of Commons early in 1769 to take the matter into serious consideration. The occasion was the King's request, presented to the House on February 28 by Lord North, to make good the arrears in the civil list since His Majesty's debts now exceeded, by over £500,000, the amount granted each year, which was £800,000.[28] What added to the feeling that the King was being ruthlessly exploited by those who surrounded him was that upon the death of George II there had actually been a surplus of £172,605 in the civil list which was applicable to meet the needs of George III, in addition to the rather large amount

[26] For the political connotations of the *Political Register* see R. R. Rea: *op. cit.*, pp. 134–9, as already mentioned above in note 19. Almon and others also published the *Royal Kalendar*, an unofficial almanac containing official national lists, including the court lists which give in detail the members of the King and Queen's household together with their salaries and other statistical information concerning the court. *The Royal Kalendar* was a rival to the *Court and City Kalendar: or, Gentleman's Register;* see, in this connection, Bernard Knollenberg: *Origin of the American Revolution, 1759–1766* (New York, 1960), Appendix to Chap. 16, "Private Enrichment from Public Funds," which reprints from the *Kalendar* for 1764 the offices of the royal household and discusses sinecures and pensions.

[27] *Gentleman's Magazine*, XXXVIII, 17–18; see also S. Maccoby: *op. cit.*, pp. 78–109. For a brief study of the poor laws at this period see A. W. Coats: "Economic Thought and Poor Law Policy in the Eighteenth Century," *Economic History Review*, 2nd ser., XIII, 39–51.

[28] See *Journals of the House of Commons*, XXXII, 255–6, for a list of the King's debts.

now annually made available to him.[29] William Beckford, in the debate on Lord North's motion that the royal request be referred to the committee of supply, pointed out that King William had received but £700,000 a year and that this sum in the latter part of his reign had been reduced to £600,000. In a cutting reference to those receiving pensions from the King, he said:

> "A pensioner is an alms-man. . . . An alms-man cannot vote; and why should a pensioner? . . . We have at present a frugal king: it is the ministers who take away the money from the Crown. I am always afraid of a change of administration. Gentlemen get round a table —'you shall go out,' they say to one 'but you shall have two thousand pounds a year'; to another, 'you shall have three thousand a year pension.' I want to see a list of the pensions paid by Lord Gage, paymaster of the band of pensioners."

He therewith proposed that an account be laid before the House that would include all monies paid out of the receipt of the exchequer on account of the privy purse, secret service, pensions, bounties, and contingencies from the beginning of the reign of George III to February 25, 1769.[30]

Far from opposing this, Lord North moved for a similar account that would cover the period from October 10, 1752, to October 10, 1760.[31] William Dowdeswell, who had been Chancellor of the Exchequer during the Rockingham administration, asserted that the "bulk of this debt was not contracted in our time."[32] Grenville, also speaking for the opposition, declared: "I am extremely sorry that it is become necessary to lay before the House, accounts so little for the honour and credit of government." He, moreover, objected to payment of the debts, as was the intention of the King's chief minister, until the accounts had been thoroughly examined.[33] North's

---

[29] To give the new King a more dependable revenue than his grandfather had enjoyed, Parliament agreed that, in place of the hereditary revenues and the excise duties that King George II had enjoyed but which were no longer dependable, a fixed sum of £800,000, to be paid out of the aggregate fund, should form the civil list. This list was designed to support the establishment of the Crown and embraced the salaries of all the civil offices and other expenses of government, including those considered necessary for the support of the honour and dignity of the court. See *Sir Henry Cavendish's Debates of the House of Commons, during the Thirteenth Parliament of Great Britain, commonly called The Unreported Parliament* . . . (ed. John Wright, 2 vols., London 1841, 1842), I, 267*n*, to be cited hereafter as *Cavendish's Debates.*

[30] *Ibid.*, I, 268; *Journals of the House of Commons,* XXXII, 256. In 1769, at the time of the debates on the civil list, Beckford was Lord Mayor of London.

[31] *Ibid.*, XXXII, 256; *Cavendish's Debates,* I, 268–9.

[32] *Ibid.*, I, 270.

[33] *Ibid.*, I, 270–1.

reply pointed out that time must necessarily elapse before accounts suitable to be laid before the House could be made available. Meanwhile, he contended, "His Majesty's honour should be secured, his debts should be paid; his creditors should not suffer." When these accounts were ready it would then be possible to assess the responsibility for the accumulated debt borne by the various Chancellors of the Exchequer who had served since the King's accession to the throne.[34] Edmund Burke, speaking out forcibly on the subject, contended:

> "the Crown of Great Britain cannot, in my opinion, be too magnificent. Let us see some great public works set on foot: let it never be said, that the Commons of Great Britain failed in what they owe to the first Crown in the world. Looking up to royalty, I do say, it is the oldest and one of the best parts of our constitution. . . . But if there is a suspicion that the revenues of the Crown have been employed for purposes of corruption, shall I not inquire into the misapplication?"[35]

To the great orator there were plenty of grounds for suspicion.

In fact, so firmly was Burke persuaded of the existence of a secret influence at court, which he believed to be so powerful as to have made the King a virtual prisoner, that he determined to appeal to the public against it. On the basis of this conviction, in the spring of the following year he published his notable pamphlet *Thoughts on the Cause of the Present Discontents,* which represented in a sense the combined thinking of the Rockingham group of Whigs.[36] In it the thesis was expounded that the "power of the Crown, almost dead and rotten as Prerogative, has grown up anew, with much more strength, and far less odium, under the name of Influence . . . which operated without noise and without violence; an influence which converted the very antagonist, into the instrument, of power. . . ." To Burke "disconnexion and confusion, in offices, in parties, in families, in parliament, in the nation, prevail beyond the disorders of any former time."[37] This he attributed to the fact that

---

[34] *Ibid.*, I, 271–2.

[35] *Ibid.*, I, 273–4.

[36] See Burke to Rockingham, [post November 6], November [24], and December 5, also Sir George Savile to Rockingham [prior to December 18, 1769], *Correspondence of Edmund Burke* (ed.-in-chief, T. W. Copeland, 5 vols.+, Cambridge and Chicago, 1958–65+; ed. Vol. I, T. W. Copeland, ed. Vol. II, Lucy S. Sutherland), II, 108–10, 112–16, 118–21, cited hereafter as *Correspondence.*

[37] *The Works of the Right Honourable Edmund Burke* (8 vols., London, 1792–1827), II, 220 and 229, cited hereafter as *Works.*

an inner group of the Ministry, a cabal, sought to control the financial and other policies of the government. To him it was a most insidious thing. However, to the student of today it is evident that this inner group, far from representing anything nefarious, was only the beginnings of what was to evolve into the modern British cabinet system, which, in close cooperation with the incumbent on the throne, still works, as it then did, in secrecy.

But the most important contribution of *Thoughts on the Cause of the Present Discontents*, in view of subsequent developments in the political alignment, was its powerful advocacy of the role that political conviction, or party, should play in government. This struck at the underlying thesis of Bolingbroke's *The Idea of a Patriot King* and Chatham's ideas of the basis upon which the King should choose his servants—that is, that the King should bring into office and power the best men obtainable, irrespective of their political philosophy or political practice. "Party," affirmed Burke, "is a body of men united, for promoting by their joint endeavours the national interest, upon some particular principle in which they are all agreed." Only an administration made up of men drawn together by adherence to certain common principles and having won the support of the country could fulfil the true purposes of government. He also asserted that the House of Commons should keep "its powers, and its privileges" as independent of the other branches of government as possible, in order to carry the proper weight and enjoy due influence. These convictions formed Burke's only claim to be considered a reformer at this period.

In the face of the parliamentary changes being demanded by the urban radicals, Burke declared: "I have no sort of reliance upon either a triennial parliament, or a place-bill." As to frequent elections, he asserted, "unless the influence of government in elections can be entirely taken away," more frequent elections will "harass private independence." On the subject of excluding all office-holders from Parliament, he pointed out that "a great official, a great professional, a great military and naval interest, all necessarily comprehending many people of the first weight, ability, wealth, and spirit, has been gradually formed in the kingdom . . . [and] must be let into a share of representation, else possibly they may be inclined to destroy those institutions of which they are not permitted to partake." Rather, turning back to the reign of George II, he pointed to the period of control of government by the great Whig families who, despite divisions, stood together in upholding the principles of the Glorious Revolution.[38]

To a reformer such as the republican Catherine Macaulay, the Burke pamphlet was a "pernicious work." While crying out against "the dangerous designs of a profligate junto of courtiers . . . against the liberties of the constitution," she contended, it sought at the same time to mislead the people as to the "no less dangerous, manœuvres of aristocratic faction and party, founded on and supported by the corrupt principles of self-interest, and to guard against . . . an effectual reformation in the vitiated parts of our constitution and government . . ."[39] Writing to a friend in Ireland after the publication of *Thoughts*, Burke commented that the party most displeased with his pamphlet was "a rotten subdivision of a Faction amongst ourselves, who have done us infinite mischief by the violence, rashness, and often wickedness of their measures, I mean the Bill of rights people. . . . Mrs. Macaulays performance was what I expected . . ."[40]

Burke's *Thoughts* further asserted that for the court to have "exceeded the sum given for the civil list, and to have incurred a debt without special authority of parliament, was, *prima facie*, a criminal act."[41] However, when the detailed reports of the royal expenditures covering the period from 1752 to February 1769 were finally presented to the House on January 11, 1770, no great scandal was uncovered, such as had been anticipated.[42] For the pattern of expenditures remained remarkably uniform throughout those years, including the gift of pensions. While it is true that in five years of the reign of George III the expenditures were somewhat over £800,000,

---

[38] For the entire pamphlet see *ibid.*, II, 215–345; for an analysis of it, especially that portion relating to the recognition of political parties as necessary to the health and proper running of government machinery, see C. B. Cone: *Burke and the Nature of Politics: The Age of the American Revolution* (Lexington, Ky., 1957), Chap. 7, "Apologist for Party."

[39] *Observations on Burke's pamphlet, On the Cause of the Present Discontents* (London, 1770), p. 7.

[40] Burke to Richard Shackleton, before August 15, 1770, *Correspondence*, II, 150.

[41] *Works*, II, 311. In 1780 Burke, in a weighty and lengthy speech, presented a "Plan for the better Security of the Independence of Parliament and the economical Reformation of the Court and other Establishments"; although it failed to secure approval at the time, the basic features of it were incorporated in the law (22 Geo. III, c. 82) enacted in 1782. This brought the civil list under control and abolished many sinecure offices. See *Parliamentary History*, XXI, 174, and XXII, 1412–16.

[42] See *Journals of the House of Commons*, XXXII, 465–603. The listing of the expenditure of the £172,605, left as surplus in the Exchequer on the death of George II, is given on pp. 466–7; the expenditures covering the period from October 10, 1752, to October 10, 1760, and the accession of George III are to be found on pp. 467–536, and the expenditures covering the reign of George III, including all pensions, bounties, and contingencies, are set forth on pp. 537–603.

in three other years they were under that amount; similarly, during five years of the reign of George II they had exceeded £800,000, but in three others had been slightly under that sum.[43] As to the use of money by officers of the Crown to influence elections to the House of Commons, at no time during the reign of George III was there a mechanism so expertly structured as that which had existed during either the administration of Sir Robert Walpole or that of the Duke of Newcastle.

Nevertheless, people felt that they were being exploited—doubtless largely as the result of the pinch of the economic depression and the influence of such letters in the press as those by "Junius." Many were persuaded that the nation was being ruined by the King's ministers. In the words of "Junius":

> "In one view, behold a nation overwhelmed with debt; her revenues wasted; her trade declining; the affections of her colonies alienated; the duty of the magistrate transferred to the soldiery; . . . and, in the last instance, the administration of justice become odious and suspected to the whole body of the people. This deplorable scene admits but of one addition—that we are governed by councils, from which a reasonable man can expect no remedy but poison, no relief but death.
>
> If, by the immediate interposition of Providence, it were possible for us to escape a crisis so full of terror and despair, posterity will not believe the history of the present times. . . ."[44]

But the remorseless and bitter criticism of the government by "Junius," who blasted away with sledge-hammer blows at certain members of the ministry, had but a temporary influence upon those

[43] For the tables summarizing the expenditures from 1752 to January 5, 1769, see *Journals of the House of Commons,* XXXII, 626–7.

[44] *The Letters of Junius* (ed. C. W. Everett, London, [1927]), p. 28. There has been no agreement on the identity of "Junius." Some fifty-three different persons have been given credit for the letters—among others, Lord Shelburne, General Charles Lee, Thomas Pownall, Lord George Sackville, Colonel Barré, Earl Temple, John Dunning, George Grenville, and Alexander Wedderburn. The *Dictionary of National Biography* (1889) and the 11th edition of the *Encyclopaedia Britannica* (1911) both favour as the author Sir Philip Francis, attached at the time to the war office and later a royal commissioner in India; present scholarly data seem to uphold the position, as does current scientific methodology. Using computers, Alvar Ellegård, in his *Who Was Junius? A Statistical Method for Determining Authorship: The Junius Letters, 1769–1772* (Stockholm, 1962), gives the verdict that Francis was "Junius." John Brooke, authoritative historian on this period, finds Ellegård's arguments "completely convincing" (*History,* XLIX, 82). Sixty-five of the "Junius" letters were brought together and published in various editions. The first letter, printed in the *Public Advertiser,* was that of January 21, 1769, and the last, an undated letter addressed to Lord Camden, was presumably written shortly after the very long and bitter letter addressed to Lord Mansfield on January 21, 1772.

ripe for scandal-mongering, whereas Burke's *Thoughts* provoked some long-term thinking on the part of those earnestly concerned with governmental reform and political theory, Mrs. Macaulay's attack notwithstanding. One important result of the differences of opinion between Burke and Mrs. Macaulay, however, was that the Rockinghamites—who had aligned themselves with the urban radicals as a political expedient—now broke this connection.[45] With this rift there began a new struggle for influence in the City, which was to culminate in victory for Wilkes later in the 1770's.

Here then is the setting for turning again to the career of that remarkable demagogue John Wilkes.[46] In view of the strong impact of his activities not only upon the government of Great Britain but also upon the attitude of American colonials toward it, his turbulent actions at the end of the 1760's call for something more than casual reference. Although Wilkes was the subject of attention in an earlier volume of this series, that account only took into consideration his public life up to the sentence of outlawry passed upon him on November 1, 1764, by the Court of King's Bench, when he himself was basking in the security of self-imposed exile on the Continent.[47] In 1766 and also in 1767 he revisited England quietly, hoping in vain to secure a reversal of the sentence through the efforts of the Duke of Grafton. At last he determined on a course of action that was to carry him to undreamed-of heights of popularity, at least with the populace of Greater London. For early in February 1768 he returned boldly to England.

It will be recalled that before his expulsion from Parliament Wilkes had sat for Aylesbury. He now set out to contest for one of the four City of London seats, despite the pains and penalties hanging over his head which had induced him to go to France late in 1763. Being a spendthrift and addicted to loose living, he had incurred so many debts in Paris by 1768 that his creditors virtually forced him to return home in order to escape from their clutches and

[45] See I. R. Christie: *op. cit.*, pp. 40–5.

[46] Back in 1765 Wilkes was characterized by one of his contemporaries, Charles Gore (in writing to Nathaniel Ryder, November 15, 1765, "General Correspondence of Nathaniel Ryder," Vol. VI, Ryder Papers, Harrowby Mss. Trust, Sandon Hall, Sandon), as "the most extraordinary man I was ever acquainted with. Has Firmness of Spirit to resist every severe stroke of Fortune and a Confidence to think he can get through all Difficulties." On the other hand Benjamin Franklin called him "an outlaw and an exile, of bad personal character, not worth a farthing" (*Writings of Benjamin Franklin* [ed. A. H. Smyth, 10 vols., New York, 1905–7], V, 121), while Edmund Burke described him as "a lively agreeable man, but of no prudence and no principles" (*Correspondence*, I, 352).

[47] See Volume IX of this series, Chap. 2.

"John Wilkes Esq., before the Court of King's Bench, 1768."

(From *Gentleman's Magazine*, 1768)

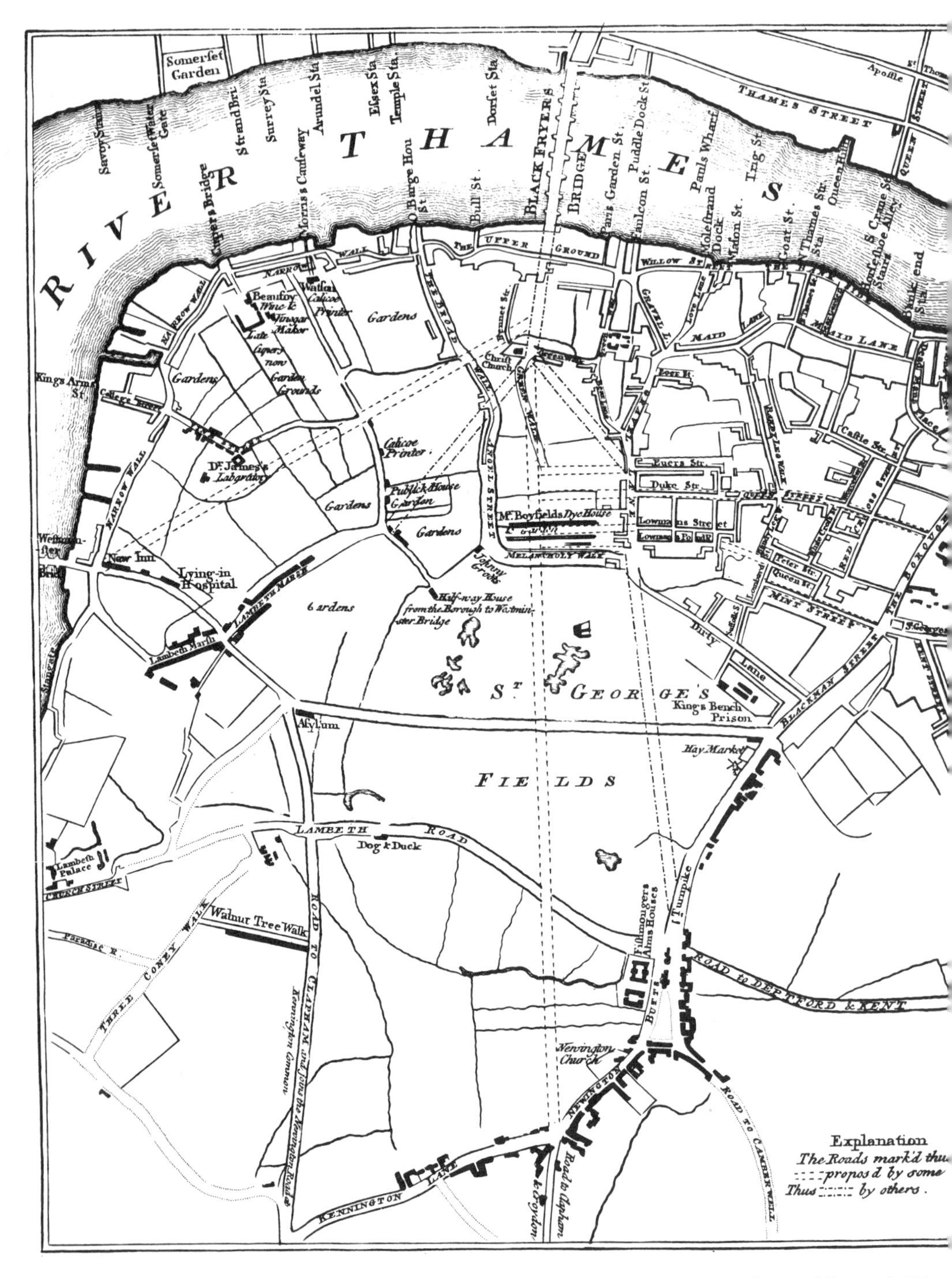

"A Map of the Surrey Side the Thames . . . ," showing St. George's Fields and Kin
Bench Prison.

(From *Gentleman's Magazine,* 17

the alternative of a French debtor's prison. Even so, his decision to attempt once more to seek a seat in Parliament—and thereby openly face a cloud of enemies at home and possible imprisonment—seemed to be either a display of bravado or part of a calculated risk of martyrdom.[48] Yet, the times were favourable for such action.

Well aware of the upheaval of discontent among those in humble circumstances, Wilkes entered the list of candidates for London when Parliament was dissolved on March 12, 1768, and a new election ordered. Given the freedom of the city by the Joiners' Company, he was also admitted "to the livery" and a fund was created among his admirers to defray the election expenses.[49] His address "To the Worthy Liverymen of the City of London" on March 10 is not without political acumen in its demagogic appeal to them as gentlemen whose chief merit was having "a sacred love of Liberty, and of those generous principles, which at first gave, and have since secured to this nation, the great Charter of Freedom. . . ." He then declared: "The two important questions of Public Liberty, respecting General Warrants and the Seizures of Papers, may perhaps place me among those who have deserved well of mankind, by an undaunted firmness, perseverance and probity: These are the Virtues which your Ancestors never failed to exert in the same national Cause of Liberty. . . ."[50]

---

[48] On February 7, 1768, Wilkes wrote to publisher John Almon to announce his arrival in London. See John Almon: *The Correspondence of the late John Wilkes . . . in which are Introduced Memoirs of his Life* (5 vols., London, 1805), III, 237; this will be referred to hereafter as *Memoirs of John Wilkes;* see also for this period *Letters to and from Mr. Wilkes* (London, 1768) and *A Collection of all Mr. Wilkes's Addresses to the Gentlemen, Clergy, and Freeholders of . . . Middlesex* (London, 1769). For the old standard biographies of Wilkes see Horace Bleackley: *Life of John Wilkes* (London, 1917), O. A. Sherrard: *A Life of John Wilkes* (London, 1930), and Raymond Postgate: *"That Devil Wilkes"* (London, 1930); see also, more recently C. C. Trench: *Portrait of a Patriot: A Biography of John Wilkes* (Edinburgh and London, 1962) and, most importantly, George Rudé's *Wilkes and Liberty* and I. R. Christie's *Wilkes, Wyvil and Reform,* both previously cited in full.

[49] John Almon: *Memoirs of John Wilkes,* III, 265–6. For the Joiners' Guild minutes see W. P. Treloar: *Wilkes and the City* (London, 1917), p. 63. *The Gazetteer and New Daily Advertiser* (London) for March 11, 1768, to be cited hereafter as the *Gazetteer,* carries the following item: "On Wednesday next at the general election for Members to represent this city in Parliament . . . John Wilkes, Esq., intends offering himself a candidate, having purchased his freedom of this city for that purpose, in the Worshipful Company of Musicians [Joiners], and paid his money, as customary, in the Chamber of London, in order to be admitted into the freedom of London next Tuesday, at a Court of Aldermen. . . . The gentlemen who have given one guinea for a hundred in case Mr. Wilkes is returned for the City of London, have now insured themselves . . . from paying that sum; so great is the expectation of his succeeding: and we hear that the amiable and respectable Ald[erme]n of the city are to support his interest."

[50] *Ibid.*

Meanwhile the presence of Wilkes in England was ignored by both the King and the ministers,[51] who doubtless were persuaded that to take any steps against this man of the people would only add to his popularity.[52] The London election took place on March 16 with the cry of "Wilkes and Liberty" ringing on the air. Although the mob appeared to be behind him and 1,247 liverymen voted for him, when the poll closed Wilkes was at the bottom of the list of seven candidates, while the Hon. Thomas Harley, Lord Mayor, topped the list with 3,729 votes, followed by former Lord Mayor Sir Robert Ladbroke, Alderman William Beckford, the wealthy West India planter, and Alderman Barlow Trecothick, the great merchant prince—the four chosen to sit in Parliament.[53]

Not to be daunted in his determination to return to Parliament, on the day following his defeat in the London election Wilkes announced his candidacy for one of the two seats of Middlesex County, for which polling would take place on March 28. The election was held not in London, the county seat, but at the market town of Brentford, or, more accurately, at Brentford Butts, in an open area where a temporary polling booth was erected with fifteen poll books, one for each division of the county. In addition to Wilkes, Sir William Beauchamp Procter and George Cooke, Esq., London marshal, both of whom had previously sat for Middlesex, were on the ballot. Wilkes, amply supported with funds, went from London to the polling place, a distance of seven miles, in a coach drawn by "six long tail horses, and was attended by an amazing number of people" in 250 coaches and other means of conveyance. It was also reputed that the "infatuation for Mr. Wilkes was so great, that every person was obliged to declare for him, and have blue cockades [the Wilkes emblem] before they were admitted to poll."[54]

Appealing to those opposed to "the encroachments of arbitrary

[51] On March 4 Wilkes addressed a letter to George III, begging for clemency, which he sent by a servant to His Majesty, who was then at the Queen's palace. This letter was ignored, and very properly so, as Wilkes's friend Almon pointed out, since all communications to the King were to be transmitted only by a minister or one in the royal confidence. For the letter see Almon: *Memoirs,* III, 263–5.

[52] Horace Walpole: *Memoirs of the Reign of George the Third,* (ed. Sir Denis Le Marchant, 2 vols., Philadelphia, 1845), II, 98.

[53] *Gazetteer,* March 17 and 18, 1768; see also London, March 24 advices, *Pennsylvania Gazette,* June 2, 1768. It may be noted that on March 16 the *Gazetteer* published an article giving two precedents for the election to Parliament of men under the sentence of outlawry; but the issue of the 17th prints an attack on this argument by one signing himself "Legum Amator." It also prints the address by Wilkes to the liverymen of the previous day, in which he appeals to them "as a private man, unconnected with the Great, and unsupported by any party," and adds, "I have no support but you: I wish no other support."

[54] *Ibid.,* March 29, 1768.

power, despising ministerial influence, and maintaining the rights and privileges of the freeborn subjects in a land of liberty,"[55] Wilkes carried the election, aided by his supporters, who, among other things, had distributed 40,000 handbills. Fortunately for candidate Cooke, he was absent because of illness. However, his son, present to look after his father's interests, was treated "in a very outrageous manner." He was knocked from his horse by the London mob at Hyde Park Corner; one of the carriages accompanying him, which carried a flag inscribed "No Blasphemer!" (meaning Wilkes), had its windows smashed, its harness cut, and its wheels taken off. Several other carriages belonging to the supporters of Cooke and Procter were also "greatly damaged." Nevertheless, at the insistence of Wilkes, the polling was orderly. At the end of the day the people's hero had received 1,292 votes, Cooke, 827, and Procter, 807, with the result that Wilkes and Cooke were declared elected. Wild with excitement, the returning mob went through the streets of London compelling people to wear the Wilkes cockade and to illuminate their windows. The darkened windows of the Mansion House were smashed, as were those in the London residences of Lords Bute and Egmont and other known friends of the court.[56]

Wilkes had notified the Solicitor of the Treasury on March 22 that he would present himself before the Court of King's Bench on the first day of its ensuing term, which was April 20. As promised, he duly appeared on that date to surrender himself and to plead his innocence as one acting "in support of the laws against the arbitrary acts of ministers."[57] Chief Justice Mansfield, however, refused to receive his surrender, as his appearance was neither by virtue of a *capias utlagatum*[58] nor by a surrender to the sheriff.[59] When the formality of a proper writ had been observed, Wilkes

[55] *Ibid.*, March 28, 1768. For the nature of Wilkes's supporters and opponents, and the political climate among the Middlesex freeholders, see George Rudé: "The Middlesex Electors of 1768–1769," *English Historical Review*, LXXV, 601–17. It should be added that the London *Gazetteer* throughout the month of March 1768 was generously filled with advertisements and accounts having to do with the elections.

[56] *Gazetteer*, March 30, 1768; see also London advices, March 29, *Pennsylvania Gazette*, June 2 and 9, 1768, especially the long, detailed letter dated London, March 29, in the June 9 edition. For Franklin's description of the riots see *Writings* (Smyth), V, 132–3 and 135.

[57] For Wilkes's letter of March 22 pledging his surrender to the court see the *Gazetteer* for March 28, 1768; for an account of the fulfillment of this promise see *ibid.*, April 22; for his speech before Judge Mansfield see *ibid.*, April 25, 1768, and *Pennsylvania Gazette*, June 16, 1768.

[58] A writ for the arrest of an outlaw.

[59] For Lord Mansfield's reply, as well as the comment of Mr. Justice Willes, see London advices, April 23, *Pennsylvania Gazette*, June 16, 1768.

appeared again in court on the 27th, with his counsel, Serjeant John Glynn.[60] In behalf of his client, Glynn had taken out three writs of error: one on the general proceedings against Wilkes, one on the outlawry charge, and one on the libel issue against him for *The North Briton,* No. 45 (dealt with in Volume IX of this series); he also offered to furnish bail to any amount. This was refused and Wilkes was committed to the King's Bench prison.[61] As the hackney coach carrying Wilkes and the marshal arrived at Westminster Bridge the people took the horses from the carriage and drew it through the city to a public house in Spitalfields, home of the weavers. Once he had entered the tavern, Wilkes donned a disguise, slipped out, and made his way to the King's Bench prison. After his incarceration at this gaol, vast numbers of people repeatedly gathered in the neighbourhood, especially in St. George's Fields. This inevitably led to trouble, and on May 10 the mob, spurred into action by the destruction of a Wilkes handbill, showered the Foot Guards with sticks and stones. The Riot Act was read, but the mob refused to disperse. Thereupon the troops fired, with the result—according to John Almon, who witnessed the scene from Wilkes's prison window—that several persons were killed and a number wounded. Among the dead were two non-participants in the mob action. The riot was finally broken up by the Horse Guards.[62]

Meanwhile, the Court of King's Bench took under consideration the three writs of error. In the final argument, which occurred on June 8, the Court agreed to sustain the writ of error respecting Wilkes's outlawry and to reverse the sentence, but it overruled the other two writs. On the 18th of the month the accused again appeared in court, to receive the sentence delivered by Justice Yates. For the re-publication of *The North Briton,* No. 45, and for the publishing of the "Essay on Woman" he was fined a total of £1,000 and was sentenced to imprisonment for a total of two years.[63]

---

[60] For the form of the writ *capias utlagatum* see *ibid.,* June 16, 1768. For Glynn see *House of Commons, 1754–1790,* II, 506–7.

[61] John Almon: *Memoirs of John Wilkes,* III, 269–70; see also the London *Gazetteer,* April 28, 29, and 30, 1768. See further George Nobbe: *The North Briton: A Study in Political Propaganda* (Columbia University *Studies in English . . . ,* No. 140, New York, 1939); this should be consulted in the light of the review by Sir Lewis Namier (*English Historical Review,* LVII, 274–5), which points out that while Nobbe's study possesses many virtues it lacks an understanding of the history of the period, among other lesser defects.

[62] *Gazetteer,* May 11, 1768, Almon's *Memoirs,* III, 273–9, and *Gentleman's Magazine,* XXXVIII, 242, 244.

[63] John Almon: *op. cit.,* III, 271–2; *Gentleman's Magazine,* XXXVIII, 299–300; and especially Thomas Howell: *State Trials* (28 vols., London, 1809–15), XIX, 1109–17.

From the prison Wilkes continued his fight. The new Parliament met on May 10 but transacted little business before it was adjourned on the 21st. By a series of adjournments and prorogations it did not settle down to work again until November 8. The claim of the prisoner to the Middlesex seat was not raised during the short session in May, but on November 14 his case, as set forth in a petition he himself had prepared, was presented to the House of Commons.[64] When this was read, the House ordered: "that the said Petition do lie upon the Table." On the 23rd the clerk of the King's Bench treasury appeared at the door of the House with the record of the proceedings in the Court, which was presented and embodied in the Journal. Wilkes's petition was read again and the House agreed to bring it up for consideration on December 2 together with the proceedings of the court.[65] On November 24 it was further agreed in the Commons that the prisoner, in the custody of the marshal of the prison, should be permitted to appear at the bar of the House to support his allegations; also ordered to attend were all those connected with the publication of *The North Briton*, No. 45, against whom charges of misconduct had been directed.[66] The hearing was delayed, however, until February 2 of the new year,[67] after a new factor appeared in the case. Wilkes, it seems, had secured a copy of a letter sent on April 17, 1768, by Lord Weymouth, Secretary of State, to Daniel Ponton, chairman of the quarter sessions for the county of Middlesex, calling upon the justices of the peace to fix upon some plan for securing the public tranquility and indicating that in view of "the recent alarming instances of riot," if need should arise, they would find a military force ready to march to their assistance. Wilkes succeeded in getting this letter published in the *St. James's Chronicle* on December 10, 1768, together with a foreword written by himself. In this foreword he asserted that "the horrid massacre in St. George's Fields" had long been planned, and called it "a hellish

[64] *Journals of the House of Commons*, XXXII, 33–4. In November, Lord North wrote to the King that when "Mr. Martin the banker" (apparently Joseph Martin, an alderman of London) proposed a motion to the Commons "That John Wilkes, Esq.: tho he is convicted of a seditious Libel is intitled to Priviledge," it was amended to read: 'That John Wilkes Esq.: tho he is convicted of a malignant, seditious & scandalous Libel, & of three other impious & obscene Libels, & stands committed to the King's Bench Prison by virtue of two judgements . . . is intitled, by Privilege of Parliament, to be discharged from this imprisonment for the said offences." The motion as amended was defeated by a vote of 165 to 71. See *The Correspondence of King George the Third* (ed. Sir John Fortescue, 6 vols., London, 1927–8), II, 61.

[65] *Journals of the House of Commons*, XXXII, 58–65. In these proceedings the basis for the reversal of the sentence of outlawry is set forth at large.

[66] *Ibid.*, XXXII, 68, 74, 79, 81–2.

[67] It had been set for January 27. See *Ibid.*, XXXII, 99, 157.

project . . . brooded over by some infernal spirits, without one moment's remorse."[68]

With the appearance of the letter in the press, Lord Weymouth complained to the House of Lords of a breach of privilege. As a result of a conference between the two houses of Parliament, Wilkes was brought to the bar of the House of Commons, where he coolly acknowledged his responsibility. In the session of the House on February 3, 1769, his action was denounced—in line with a pronouncement of the House of Lords—as "an insolent, scandalous, and seditious Libel, tending to inflame and stir up the Minds of His Majesty's Subjects to Sedition, and to a total Subversion of all good Order and legal Government." In view of this, as well as the fact that he had previously published "Three obscene and impious Libels," as a result of which he had been sentenced to twenty-two months' imprisonment, the members decided by a vote of 219 to 137 that he "be expelled this House." Following this action the Speaker was ordered to issue a warrant to the Clerk of the Crown for a new writ, to elect a member for the county of Middlesex in Wilkes's place.[69]

But Wilkes was not to be disposed of as easily as most members of Parliament had anticipated. In fact, his popularity was never higher among the artisans and members of the London livery. On January 2, 1769, he was elected to fill the vacancy caused by the death of one of the London aldermen. However, because of a mistake in the voting formalities, the election was declared void. Nevertheless, on the 27th of that month Wilkes was re-elected "unanimously." Only when the Court of Aldermen realized that a mandamus might be issued from the Court of King's Bench was a motion to notify Wilkes of his election rescinded.[70] Then, on February 14, the county

---

[68] See *Cavendish's Debates,* I, 106–7.

[69] *Journals of the House of Commons,* XXXII, 175, 178–9. It should be noted in this connection that George Grenville made what was undoubtedly the greatest speech in his career as a statesman against the expulsion of Wilkes. For this closely reasoned and lengthy address see *Cavendish's Debates,* I, 158–76. *The North Briton,* for April 15, 1769 (and later the *Gentleman's Magazine* for that year, XXXIX, 631–7), published the complete division lists on the motion in the House of Commons to expel John Wilkes. Since the list of those who voted for expulsion gave the posts in the government held by the respective members or by anyone connected with them, it was possible to conclude that only forty-three of those on the majority list had no connection with the government, and of this number many were members of Scottish boroughs or of small English boroughs under royal influence. For the principal parliamentary lists available for the period under consideration see Namier and Brooke's *House of Commons, 1754–1790,* I, Appendix 3.

[70] John Almon: *Memoirs of John Wilkes,* IV, 1–2.

of Middlesex freemen resolved to re-elect him, and on the 16th, with no other person venturing to contest the seat he was again re-chosen unanimously.[71] The following day, when the re-election of Wilkes was announced to the House, a motion was made and carried, by a vote of 235 to 89, "That John Wilkes, Esquire, having been, in this Session of Parliament, expelled this House, was, and is, incapable of being elected a Member to serve in this present Parliament." With the election thus invalidated, a new writ for the election of a member from the county was ordered.[72]

On February 22 the Middlesex freeholders met at Mile End and resolved to support Wilkes once again.[73] The election took place at Brentford on March 16. Charles Dingley, Esq., appeared to oppose the popular candidate, but "being very roughly handled by the populace, he was advised to retire," and did so when no person could be found "hardy enough" to propose him. Wilkes was chosen a third time, again without opposition.[74] After another serious debate on the implications of this denial of the right of the Middlesex electors to choose whomever they pleased to represent them, Wilkes's request to act in the House was finally denied by the House of Commons without a division.[75] A new election was thereupon ordered. When this took place at Brentford on April 13 a contest ensued. For on March 23 Lieutenant Colonel Henry Lawes Luttrell, who had sat for Bossiney in Cornwall but had vacated this seat in March, announced his candidacy. In addition, there were two other names on the list. At the time of the voting, John Sawbridge, an active supporter of Wilkes, addressed the assembled freeholders, claiming that the Bill of Rights was at stake and that the cause of

---

[71] See *Annual Register, 1769,* pp. 74–5, for an account of the re-election, also printed in *Cavendish's Debates,* I, 227–8. It may be noted that Wilkes was placed in nomination at Brentford by a Chatham supporter, James Townsend, a member of the House of Commons from West Looe, Cornwall; the nomination was seconded by another follower of Chatham, John Sawbridge, a member from Hythe, Kent, one of the Cinque Ports, and, as has already been noted, a brother of the famous feminist historian Catherine Macaulay. Both these men were prominent residents of London. For a characterization of them see Horace Walpole: *Memoirs of George III,* II, 142–3; see also W. P. Courtney: "James Townsend, M.P.," *Notes and Queries,* 11th ser., V, 2–4, which points out the close connection between Townsend and the Earl of Shelburne.

[72] *Journals of the House of Commons,* XXXII, 228–9.

[73] *Annual Register, 1769,* p. 75.

[74] *Ibid.,* p. 82. For the election see also a detailed account by John Smith, under-sheriff of Middlesex, in *Cavendish's Debates,* I, 354–5; for Dingley's own account to Lady Chatham see *Pitt Correspondence,* III, 352*n.*

[75] See *Cavendish's Debates,* I, 345–55; see also *Journals of the House of Commons,* XXXII, 324–5.

Wilkes was the cause of liberty. With the closing of the poll it was found that Wilkes had received 1,143 votes, Luttrell, 296, Serjeant William Whitaker, 5, and Captain David Roach, who withdrew his candidacy on the day of the election, none.[76]

For a fourth time the House of Commons was required to act on a Wilkes election. In the April debate Charles James Fox upheld the right of the House of Commons to judge the qualifications of its members and declared: "The sheriffs have, in my opinion, committed a great crime, by returning a man, in flagrant violation of our privileges." Again the following day he asserted that "the contest was between the House of Commons and the lowest scum of the people: and what can be lower, than the inhabitants of Billingsgate and Wapping?"[77] On the other hand, George Grenville took the position that no vote of the House of Commons could deprive the freeholders of Middlesex of a right of choice of candidates: "You have no such right: the right of electors is guaranteed to them by the law of the land. You have no right to put in any disqualification, that is not put in by the law of the land."[78] A final vote was taken on the motion that since, by the decision of the House, John Wilkes could not sit in the present Parliament, "Henry Lawes Luttrell Esquire, ought to have been returned a Knight of the Shire to serve in this present Parliament for the County of Middlesex." The vote was uncomfortably close for those upholding the privilege of the House, being 197 yeas to 143 noes.[79] Leave was therefore given to petition the House regarding the election of Luttrell. On May 8 a petition of the freeholders of Middlesex against his election was presented.

In the debate that followed, William Blackstone, author of the *Commentaries,* threw the weight of his authority in support of the claims of the House of Commons, while Alexander Wedderburn, a legal light of much learning, took the following position:

> "What you may vote, what you legally can do, is the very subject of our present deliberation. That vote cannot controul our deliberation. . . . You are now in a court of judicial proceedings: you are judges, not politicians: you are not to act upon principles of expedience, but upon the strict, narrow lines of justice. . . ."

---

[76] *Annual Register, 1769,* pp. 86, 89–90. See also George Rudé: *op. cit.,* Chap. 4.

[77] *Cavendish's Debates,* I, 361 and 378.

[78] *Ibid.,* I, 384.

[79] *Ibid.,* I, 386; *Journals of the House of Commons,* XXXII, 386–7. For the division lists on this vote see *Middlesex Journal,* May 4, 6, 9, 1769; *The North Briton,* May 6, 1769; and *London Magazine,* 1769, pp. 270–1.

Charles Cornwall[80] thereupon laid down the proposition that the House did not possess "a power *jus dare,* with regard to the rights of the electors, as well as the elected," and ended by declaring: "It is not right to alarm the passions, by vilifying the freeholders of the county of Middlesex." Sir Henry Cavendish, a member representing Lostwithiel in Cornwall, was even more emphatic in declaring: "I do from my soul abhor, detest, and abjure, as unconstitutional and illegal, that damnable doctrine and position, that a resolution of the House of Commons can make, alter, suspend, abrogate, or annihilate the law of the land."[81] Nevertheless, when the question was put, "That Henry Lawes Luttrell, Esquire, is duly elected a Knight of the Shire to serve in this present Parliament for the County of Middlesex," the vote was 221 in favour with 152 opposed.[82]

It was at the time Parliament was repudiating the election of Wilkes in the early part of 1769 that the Supporters of the Bill of

---

[80] Cornwall, a trained lawyer and brother-in-law of Charles Jenkinson, was representing Grampound at this time and acting with the Rockingham Whigs, a position he was shortly to desert to become a lord of the Treasury in the North administration and subsequently Speaker of the House of Commons (1780).

[81] For the debate on May 8 see *Cavendish's Debates,* I, 406–33; See also *Annual Register, 1769,* pp. 68–73. It may be noted that Cavendish, the speaker referred to above, was the compiler of the two volumes of debates. These may be considered to have a high degree of accuracy, for Cavendish the reporter had mastered shorthand. Thus, while his reports may be taken to be almost verbatim, the same thing cannot be said of all the other collections of parliamentary debates. See in this connection the important studies by P. D. G. Thomas: "The Beginning of Parliamentary Reporting in Newspapers, 1768–1774," *English Historical Review,* LXXIV, 623–36, especially p. 635, and *Sources for Debates of the House of Commons, 1768–1774,* Institute of Historical Research *Bulletin,* Special Supplement No. 4, pp. v–x; see also the earlier study by F. S. Siebert: *Freedom of the Press in England, 1476–1776* (Urbana, Ill., 1952), Chap. 17, "Reporting Parliament," and that by A. Aspinall: "The Reporting and Publishing of the House of Commons Debates, 1771–1834," *Essays Presented to Sir Lewis Namier* (London, 1956), pp. 227–57. Earlier, the standard work on the subject was Paul Mantoux's *Notes sur les Comptes-Rendus des Séance du Parlement Anglais au XVIIIe Siècle Conservée aux Archives du Ministère des Affaires Étrangères* (Paris, 1906). These works make clear, however, that while *Cavendish's Debates* are the most accurate and the collection in *Parliamentary History* is the most comprehensive, there are other reports that may be considered quite dependable. See Sir Lewis Namier and John Brooke: *History of Parliament: The House of Commons, 1754–1790,* I, Appendix II, pp. 522–3. It may further be noted that the use of shorthand was becoming increasingly common by the middle of the eighteenth century, and that a fairly extensive bibliography on the subject is available. See *Bibliography of British History: The Eighteenth Century* (eds. Stanley Pargellis and D. J. Medley, Oxford, 1951), pp. 378–9.

[82] *Journals of the House of Commons,* XXXII, 451. Luttrell was thereafter seated for Middlesex and held this place until 1774, when he resigned it to re-occupy the seat for Bossiney. For the division list on the motion to confirm Luttrell see *The North Briton,* May 27, 1769; an analysis of this list may be found in John Brooke's *Chatham Administration,* pp. 351–2, which also analyzes the problems of using eighteenth-century division lists.

Rights Society was founded and that the preparation of the instructions for members of the House of Commons from metropolitan boroughs, as inspired by the metropolitan radicals, was begun—events described earlier in this chapter. It was at this time also that political activity reached a new height in metropolitan London. For, with the seating of Luttrell, the electors of Middlesex County sent a petition to the King on May 24 not only protesting the action of Parliament but fully airing their grievances and raising certain political and constitutional issues: they also likened the American grievances to their own.[83] The City followed suit in a petition from the livery on June 24, but the substance of subsequent petitions from other parts of the metropolis and the nation at large was confined to protests against the Middlesex election.[84] The petition movement was not without political overtones. It appears that two days after the House had reached a decision to select Luttrell, seventy-five members of the minority group in the House met for a dinner at which twenty-one toasts were drunk, including pledges to the King and the Constitution, the Right of Electors, and the Law of the Land. Those present at this occasion may have appeared to be ill-associated, since among the company were Edmund Burke, Lord Clive, George Grenville, Alderman Beckford, Colonel Barré, Alexander Wedderburn, and Thomas Whately, with Lord George Sackville, later Lord Germain, and Earl Temple from the House of Lords.[85] But though this meeting produced a united opposition, and a joint plan of action was concerted between both the Rockingham and Shelburne factions and the metropolitan politicans, the campaign that resulted failed of its mark. The attempt to get a nation-wide expression of protest through petitions and other public activity was only partially successful and the movement gradually lost impetus, as did the attempts of the radicals to set up local Bill of Rights societies. For, meanwhile, addresses of loyalty to the King convinced the administration that it had nothing to fear.[86]

As a further step on the part of the opposition to pursue the constitutional aspects of the Wilkes issue, the Earl of Chatham

---

[83] For the Middlesex petition see *Annual Register*, 1769, pp. 197–200.

[84] For the City petition, those from Westminster, Surrey, Buckingham, and Yorkshire, as well as a list of other petitions "delivered or prepared within the year," see *ibid.*, pp. 200–6.

[85] See Earl Temple to Lady Chatham, May 10, 1769, *Pitt Correspondence*, III, 359–61.

[86] For the fullest account of the petition campaign see George Rudé: *op. cit.*, Chap. 7, "The Petitions of 1769." For an excellent analysis of the significance of the movement see Lucy Sutherland: *City of London, 1768–1774*, pp. 23–33. See also I. R. Christie: *op. cit.*, pp. 32–40.

came forward. On January 9, 1770, he sought to amend the address of thanks of the House of Lords—in reply to the King's speech on opening the third session of the present Parliament—by inserting the words:

> "we will, with all convenient speed, take into our most serious consideration, the causes of the discontent which prevail in so many parts of your Majesty's dominions, and particularly the late proceedings of the House of Commons, touching the incapacity of John Wilkes, esq., expelled by that house, . . . thereby refusing, by a resolution of one branch of the legislature only, to the subject his common right, and depriving the electors of Middlesex of their free choice of a representative."

Lord Camden supported the Chatham motion and stated that he considered the resolution of the House of Commons "a direct attack upon the first principles of the constitution." In turn, Lord Mansfield warned the Lords:

> "That a question, touching the seat of a member in the lower house, could only be determined by that House. . . . That there never was an instance of the Lords inquiring into the proceedings of the House of Commons with respect to their own members; much less of their taking upon them to censure such proceedings, or of their advising the Crown to take notice of them."

Chatham indulged in no reply to Mansfield save by pressing his amendment to the address, but it was rejected by 203 to 36.[87]

In the House of Commons an attempt, without mentioning Wilkes by name, was made, also on January 9, in line with the Chatham amendment, to amend the address of Commons to the King by assuring him of their desire to serve the country "by immediately enquiring into the Causes of the unhappy Discontents which at present prevail in every Part of His Majesty's Dominions. . . ." This amendment, too, lost by a vote of 254 to 138.[88] Next, on February 16, the committee of the whole House reported on a motion concerning elections with the following statement:

> "That this House, . . . in Matters of Election, is bound to judge according to the Law of the Land, . . . and Custom of Parliament, which is Part thereof; and that the Judgment of this House . . . 'That John Wilkes . . . was, and is, incapable of being elected a

[87] For the Chatham speeches and those of Camden and Mansfield see *Pitt Correspondence,* III, 369–87*n.* Among those who voted for the amendment, in addition to Chatham and Camden, were Temple and Rockingham, together with the latter's Whig supporters in the upper house.

[88] *Journals of the House of Commons,* XXXII, 456.

> Member to serve in this present Parliament,' was agreeable to the said Law of the Land, and fully authorized by the Law and Custom of Parliament."[89]

An objection—contending that the matter as stated in the report was a complex one—led to an extensive debate, continued on the 19th, in an effort to separate what were held by many to be two distinct questions. But a motion to divide the report accordingly was rejected by a vote of 243 to 174. A final motion to approve the report as given by the committee of the whole was carried by 237 to 159.[90]

As for John Wilkes, his term in prison was coming to an end. On March 13, 1770, the Society of Supporters of the Bill of Rights published a report showing that there had been paid "by voluntary subscriptions of this Society" to the Wilkes fund the following sums: £1,000 "for his support," £500 "for his first fine," £1,705 to cover "the expences of his three last elections for Middlesex," and £4,198 "to compromise £14,345.15.8 of his debts;" the report went on to show—in figures that do not balance—that although a balance of some £776 in cash remained in the treasurer's hands, there remained to be paid on debts and fines close to £6,000.[91] By April 17 his debts had been settled "by the committee of the supporters of the Bill of Rights" and in the evening of that day he was released from confinement. This was a national event. In the words of the *Annual Register:* "It has been remarked with astonishment, that there never was perhaps so general and voluntary illuminations and rejoicings on any occasion, as on the event of Mr. Wilkes's release; not in London only, but in every part of England. . . ."[92] Soon after, he was sworn in as a London alderman, as elected by the ward of Farringdon Without in 1769,[93] after which a great banquet was tendered in his honour at the Mansion House by Lord Mayor Beckford.[94] As a further honour, in 1771 the people of Middlesex elected Wilkes as their sheriff. Nor was this the end to the extraordinary

---

[89] *Ibid.*, XXXII, 707.

[90] *Ibid.*, XXXII, 710. For the debate covering February 16 and 19 on the report of the committee of the whole House see *Cavendish's Debates*, I, 458–75.

[91] *Annual Register, 1770*, p. 80. For the meeting of the Bill of Rights Society on February 7, 1770, under the chairmanship of Serjeant Glynn, at which it was announced that the South Carolina Assembly had contributed the equivalent of £ 1,500 sterling for the use of the society, see *ibid.*, p. 71, and *Gentleman's Magazine*, XL, 94.

[92] *Annual Register, 1770*, p. 94.

[93] For Wilkes's address to the inhabitants of the above ward see John Almon: *Memoirs of John Wilkes*, IV, 20n.

[94] Wilkes to his daughter, April 27, 1770, *ibid.*, IV, 25–6.

career of this extraordinary man, for ahead lay even greater offices.[95]

In 1771 Wilkes once again was involved, although somewhat indirectly, in a great contest in the House of Commons. This was over the right of newspapers to publish reports of parliamentary debates—such publication having been banned in 1660 by order of the House of Lords and in 1661 by a House of Commons resolution and formally restated, again by a Commons resolution, in 1723. While the *Gentleman's Magazine* and the *London Magazine* had continued to evade the prohibition by special kinds of reporting, the newspapers had restricted their information on Parliament to the most general kind of news.[96] When four newspapers published what purported to be a verbatim account of two speeches in the House of Commons in January 1760, they had been formally charged with contempt and breach of the privileges of the House, and their printers had been obliged not only to print public apologies but also to kneel at the bar in the Commons while being reprimanded by the Speaker and to pay fines.[97] Nevertheless, John Almon in 1768 had begun to give detailed accounts of proceedings in Parliament, and other daily and weekly papers had followed his lead. As a result, eight newspapers were prosecuted by the House of Commons during the early part of 1771. The issue became acute when printers John Wheble of the *Middlesex Journal* and Roger Thompson of the *Gazetteer* openly defied a House order for their arrest. The order had been issued as a result of a protest made in the House of Commons by Colonel George Onslow,[98] who objected to the printing—in the *Middlesex Journal* on February 7, 1771, and in the *Gazetteer* the next day—of an offensive report (attributed to

---

[95] In October 1774, with his popularity unabated, Wilkes became Lord Mayor of London; this was after having been returned to the top of the poll both in 1772 and in 1773 only to be rejected by the final choice of the Court of Aldermen in actions that resembled those of the House of Commons. Also in 1774, he was again returned to Parliament as member for Middlesex, taking his seat without opposition on December 2, a seat he was to hold until his voluntary retirement in 1790. Although he was chosen to the lucrative office of Chamberlain of London in 1779, it was only after four previous attempts had failed. But again his popularity held and he continued in that post for the rest of his life. By means of it he was at first able to pay off all his current debts, but when he passed away on December 26, 1797, he was, as might have been anticipated, a bankrupt. For the career of Wilkes in the 1770's see the previously cited biographies and especially the newer studies by Rudé and Christie.

[96] For the early steps to control parliamentary reporting see F. S. Siebert: *op. cit.*, pp. 279–88.

[97] For the House of Commons action against the printers in 1760 see R. L. Haig: *The Gazetteer, 1735–1797* (Carbondale, Ill., 1960), pp. 40–2.

[98] For a characterization of Colonel Onslow see Walpole's *Memoirs of George III*, II, 143.

Wilkes) of his motion in the House of Commons seeking an order against printing debates.[99] When Wheble was apprehended he was brought before John Wilkes, sitting as a magistrate in his capacity of alderman of the City of London. Wilkes promptly dismissed the printer. When Alderman Richard Oliver followed this precedent in dealing with Thompson, and Lord Mayor Brass Crosby upheld the decisions, by order of the House of Commons they were both committed to the Tower, since they were both members of the House and therefore within its jurisdiction. Wilkes, on the other hand, could not be so handled without acknowledging him as a member for Middlesex.[100] The issue aroused the populace to such a degree that popular demonstrations were made not only against Lord North but even against the King.[101] But the upshot of the matter was that the offending printers went unpunished and newspapers continued to print parliamentary debates.

Thus, although the old resolutions prohibiting parliamentary reporting were never officially rescinded, Parliament in 1771 permitted a constitutional amendment to come into being by not fully pressing the charges against the printers in the face of popular sentiment. In this way John Wilkes may be said to have furthered the cause of freedom of the press, although his actions at the time are considered by some scholars to have been less worthily motivated. Certainly his followers in the Bill of Rights Society had doubts about his motivation, for it was at this juncture that a breach developed in the ranks of the Supporters of the Bill of Rights Society, as was mentioned briefly earlier in this chapter. Horne-Tooke held the view that the Society should have a broader objective than the payment of the debts incurred by Wilkes, whereas Wilkes resented the diversion of some of the funds to help the cause of the printers. On this disagreement the most important members of the Society—Horne-Tooke, Sawbridge, Sir Robert Bernard, Townsend, Oliver, and their close followers—withdrew to form their own Constitutional Society.[102] However, within several months of this event the remaining members of the Bill of Rights Society undertook an important new reform measure, when on June 11, 1771, they resolved to recom-

---

[99] For the debates see *Journals of the House of Commons,* XXXIII, 142–284, *passim,* and *Parliamentary History,* XVII, 58–119.

[100] For the part of Wilkes in the crisis see P. D. G. Thomas: "John Wilkes and the Freedom of the Press (1771)," Institute of Historical Research *Bulletin,* XXXIII, 86–98, and his article in the *English Historical Review,* LXXIV, 623–36; see also F. S. Siebert: *op. cit.,* Chap. 17, R. L. Haig: *op. cit.,* pp. 89–92 and Chap. 6, and George Rudé: *op. cit.,* pp. 155–65

[101] *Gentleman's Magazine,* XLI, 141, and *Annual Register, 1771,* "Chronicle," pp. 84–5.

[102] See note 9 in this chapter.

mend that all candidates for Parliament throughout the Kingdom should be obliged to take election pledges to support a program to secure shorter Parliaments, reduce the number of placemen and pensioners in the Commons, and seek a more equal representation of the people[103]—in other words, Beckford's original reform program, as discussed in the early part of this chapter. Shortly after this, the Society produced an eleven-point program to be recommended to parliamentary candidates,[104] also reminiscent of the Beckford-sponsored City instructions of 1769. How much all this was a political manœuvre or a bid for the support of the London radicals is not clear, but that it was an innovation which was carried forward into the century to follow is certain.[105]

It may be said in the final analysis that the rise to power of John Wilkes after 1768 is highly indicative of the confused state of affairs in England at that time. What the opposition in the House of Commons called the "universal discontent" reflected the social and economic conditions of the poor, the urban radicalism of the "middling" population, especially in metropolitan London, and the unsteadiness of the government. The discontented poor sought refuge in riots as the result of the industrial unrest and mob action in response to the demagogic leadership of Wilkes. The discontented "middling" population, along with certain liberals among the independents and in the opposition, sought programs of parliamentary or constitutional reform, and many of them supported the American cause in varying degrees. As for the unsteadiness of the government, this will form the subject of the chapter to follow.

Many of the reforms advocated by such pressure groups as the Bill of Rights Society and the Constitutional Society were not to be effected until later in the eighteenth century or in the following one, but some of the issues raised by Wilkes in the course of his chequered career brought immediate and needed changes in the government and were embodied in constitutional law and custom. Among the most fruitful of Wilkes's actions were: his opposition to general warrants; his support of the principle laid down in the eighth article of the Bill of Rights, "That elections of members of Parliament ought to be free"; his demand that the House of Commons should have a more truly representative basis; finally, his stand for freedom of the press, not only to report the proceedings of Parliament but to criticize the government.

---

[103] *Public Advertiser,* June 13, 1771, reprinted in I. R. Christie *op. cit.,* p. 48.
[104] *Public Advertiser,* July 25, 1771.
[105] See I. R. Christie: *op. cit.,* pp. 48–9. See also George Rudé: *op. cit.,* pp. 194–5, and Lucy Sutherland: *The City of London, 1768–1774,* pp. 22–3.

Perhaps equally important to the domestic reforms resulting from Wilkes's rise to power was his influence on the attitude of Americans toward King George and the mother country.[106] While Franklin was impressed with the leadership qualities of Wilkes,[107] he did not see in him a strong ally of the American cause, as did other Americans living in London, who sent back to the colonies glowing reports of the actions taken by the Supporters of the Bill of Rights Society and by members of the Beckford and Shelburne factions.[108] But the cry of "Wilkes and Liberty" echoed loudly across the Atlantic Ocean as wide publicity was given to every step of Wilkes's public career in the colonial press—as indeed it was in the British press.[109] The reaction in America took on significant proportions. Colonials tended to identify their cause with that of Wilkes.[110] They saw him as a popular hero and a martyr to the struggle for liberty. They subscribed money for the fund being raised by the Society of Supporters of the Bill of Rights. They named towns, counties, and even children in his honour. Finally, colonial ceremonies commemorating the repeal of the Stamp Act held by the Sons of Liberty in Boston, New York, and elsewhere during the period 1768 to 1770, repeatedly raised the toast of "Wilkes and Liberty."[111]

[106] According to Stella Duff in "The Case Against the King: The *Virginia Gazettes* Indict George III," *William and Mary Quarterly,* 3rd ser., VI, 383–97—it was the attitude of the King toward Wilkes and the radical faction that crystallized the growing adverse feeling toward George III as a tyrant both in England and in the colonies.

[107] For Franklin's note in his diary of 1781 that "if George the Third had had a bad private character, and John Wilkes a good one, the latter might have turned the former out of his kingdom," see *Writings* (Smyth), X, 358.

[108] See *Life of Arthur Lee,* I, 22, 185–7, 189, 195–7.

[109] See, for example, *Boston Gazette,* July 4, and August 29, 1768, July 17, 1769, and April 23, 1770.

[110] See the important article by Pauline Maier: "John Wilkes and American Disillusionment with Britain," *William and Mary Quarterly,* 3rd ser., XX, 373–95.

[111] For reactions in the British press, and the part of South Carolina, Virginia, and Maryland in subscribing to the Wilkes fund, see Dora Mae Clark: *British Opinion and the American Revolution* (New Haven, 1930), pp. 154, 356–62, 372–3, 376–86; see also *ibid.,* p. 153, for the action taken in Boston. A detailed discussion of the constitutional issue raised in South Carolina over the appropriation of money for the Wilkes fund by its Commons House will be found in Chap. 15 of the present volume. Pertinent documents of the Boston Sons of Liberty are reprinted in "John Wilkes and Boston," Massachusetts Historical Society *Proceedings,* XLVII, 190–215. The article "John Wilkes and William Palfrey" (ed. G. M. Elsey, Colonial Society of Massachusetts *Transactions,* XXXIV, 411–28) reveals that even prominent colonials named their children after Wilkes. Georgia, for one, named a county after Wilkes, and Pennsylvania gave the name of Wilkes-Barré to a new settlement in 1769 to honour him and Colonel Barré. The pamphlet *Britannia's Intercession for the Deliverance of John Wilkes, Esq. . . .* (presumably the London sixth edition, reprinted in Boston, 1769) virtually apotheosized the man. See A. M. Schlesinger: *Prelude to Independence* (New York, 1958), pp. 113, 122, and Raymond Postgate: *op. cit.,* Chap. 10.

CHAPTER VIII

The British Ministry at Sea

WITH the passing of Charles Townshend, Chancellor of the Exchequer, from the London scene in September 1767, there disappeared also the bright promise of an effective plan for the administration of British North America. For, as has been discussed in the preceding chapters, not only had colonial opposition to Townshend's program gained such headway—especially through the non-importation movement—as to signal the failure of imperial regulation, but the Ministry's inadequacy in dealing with domestic political and social discontent also pointed to confusion within the government itself.

The lack of stability and direction in the Ministry now became increasingly apparent. Townshend's death, reported the Duke of Grafton, "distressed us much; as the filling properly up so great a chasm in our body was of the utmost importance."[1] Since the Earl of Chatham was inactive as titular head of the Ministry, the King commanded Grafton to approach Lord Frederick North with a renewal of the offer made in March, that he accept the office left vacant by Townshend's death.[2] At first North declined the offer

[1] *Autobiography . . . of Augustus Henry, Third Duke of Grafton* (ed. Sir William R. Anson, London, 1898, p. 166), cited hereafter as Grafton's *Autobiography*.

[2] As has been indicated earlier in this volume, Lord Chatham was indignant when Charles Townshend openly opposed his views on the proper way for the government to come to an accommodation with the United East India Company in regard to its landed possessions; he was even more provoked when the Chancellor of the Exchequer lost the vote in the House of Commons on his proposal to continue the land tax at the rate of four shillings on the pound. It was then that Chatham, acting through Grafton, had sought to persuade North to take over this office. See North to Grafton [March 4, 1767], Grafton's *Autobiography*, p. 123; Grafton to the King, March 5, 1767, *The Correspondence of King George the Third* (ed. Sir John Fortescue, 6 vols., London, 1927–8), I, 461–2, cited hereafter as *Correspondence of George III* (Fortescue). In connection with the changes in the Ministry see John Brooke: *The Chatham Administration, 1766–1768* (London, 1956) and D. A. Winstanley: *Lord Chatham and the Whig Opposition* (Cambridge, 1912).

because of the illness of his father, Lord Guilford, but on September 10 he declared himself "ready to obey any call from His Majesty."[3] As "a man of strict honor," and an able parliamentarian, gifted with an equable temper and a sense of humour, North was the choice not only of the Earl of Chatham but of other members of the Cabinet Council. It was under these circumstances that he left the relatively quiet office of Joint Paymaster-General to enter upon the active political life that later was to carry him into turbulent events as the King's chief minister.[4]

Other changes in the Ministry followed. In January 1768 Leveson-Gower, Earl of Gower, a Bedford Whig, succeeded the ailing Robert Henley, Earl of Northington, as President of the Council—thus opening a breach in the Rockingham-Bedford-Grenville *entente* directed against the Chatham administration. General Conway, still retaining his ties with former associates in the preceding Rockingham Ministry, now resigned the post of Secretary of State for the Northern Department,[5] which was assumed by another Bedford Whig, Thomas Thynne, Viscount Weymouth, a somewhat dissipated man but an able speaker. Other Bedfordites, such as John Montagu, Earl of Sandwich, and Richard Rigby, were given lesser places. Their inclusion as "party men" by Grafton, in the face of Chatham's opposition to the idea of party in administration, laid the foundation for the final break between the two.[6]

A change of equal, if not greater, importance to the public also took place in the Ministry at this time, when it was determined to divide the functions of the office of Secretary of State for the Southern Department by creating the post of Secretary of State for the

---

[3] North to Grafton, September 10, 1767, Grafton's *Autobiography*, p. 167.

[4] The post of Chancellor of the Exchequer was filled *ad interim* by Lord Mansfield.

[5] In August, Conway took over the post of Lieutenant General of Ordnance, while continuing to act as Secretary of State without pay.

[6] In his "Diary" entry of December 4, 1767, George Grenville records the plan to bring into the government certain of Bedford's friends, referred to in the text, and place them in important posts. He then wrote: "These posts were to be vacated by Lord Northington, Lord Shelburne, Mr. Barré, and Mr. Cooke, all of whom are the immediate friends of Lord Chatham; it therefore remains to be seen whether his power is sufficient to stop it, and to overrule the Duke of Grafton in this attempt" (*The Grenville Papers* . . . [ed. W. J. Smith, 4 vols., London, 1853], IV, 238–9). Thomas Whately, writing to Grenville on January 1, 1768, stated that "the Duke of Grafton settled the whole plan of arrangement with the Bedfords, without the participation of his brother Ministers. . . . The discontent among Lord Chatham's friends seems to be, as far as I can trace it, general. . . . The Duke of Grafton's distance from Lord Chatham is more marked since I wrote to you than it was then [December 25, 1767], and he enters with eagerness into the opinions of the Duke of Bedford concerning America . . ." (*ibid.*, IV, 240–9).

Colonies.[7] There had been periodic agitation for the creation of this new post during the eleven years since Pitt, in 1757, foiled an attempt by the Earl of Halifax, President of the Board of Trade, aided by the Duke of Newcastle, to create that office.[8] Again, during the Rockingham administration it had been proposed "to separate American from European business" by making the President of the Board, the Earl of Dartmouth, Colonial Secretary and the Board "a separate and independent department," but no action had been taken before the Marquess resigned.[9] That it was proper and desirable to separate the business of the colonies from that of the countries of southern Europe, India, and Ireland, as well as from domestic preoccupations—especially in view of the commanding importance of colonial affairs at this time—is clear. Benjamin Franklin gave the plan his blessing in the press by refuting the argument that it was a development dangerous to "the freedom and trade of England."[10] Wills Hill, the Earl of Hillsborough, who was President of the Board of Trade from the fall of 1763 to the summer of 1765, returned to this post the following year for a brief period, after the accession of Chatham to office, under the following conditions: that the Board "should be altered from a Board of Representation to a Board of Report upon Reference only; that the order to the Governors in America to correspond with the Board of Trade *only*, should be rescinded; . . . and that I should not be of the Cabinet (which was also offered to me)."[11] But when Hillsborough was appointed Secretary for the Colonies in 1768 he had been acting as a Joint Postmaster-General since December of 1766.

[7] For a history of the Secretary of State for the Colonies see Margaret M. Spector: *The American Department of the British Government, 1768–1782* (Columbia University *Studies in History* . . . , No. 466, New York, 1940) and A. H. Basye: "The Secretary of State for the Colonies, 1768–1782," *American Historical Review*, XXVIII, 13–23, in which the author stresses the legal question of the equality of the new third secretaryship with the two older offices, one for the Northern Department and the other for the Southern Department.

[8] *Ibid.*, XXVIII, 14.

[9] Lord Edmond Fitzmaurice: *Life of William, Earl of Shelburne* . . . (3 vols., London, 1875–6), II, 1–2, 69.

[10] See the London *Gazetteer and New Daily Advertiser* for January 21, 1768, for Franklin's defence of the new office, signed "Old England, in its senses," reprinted by V. W. Crane in his *Benjamin Franklin's Letters to the Press, 1758–1775* (Chapel Hill, N.C., 1950), pp. 108–10.

[11] Hillsborough to George Grenville, August 6, 1766, *Grenville Papers*, III, 294–6. In this letter the Earl explained to Grenville that it was "certainly most desirable for the public, that it [the Board of Trade] should be made an independent department upon an extensive plan," but since the opposition to this would be too great, he had come to the conclusion to "contract the plan so as that I might do the business in an easy manner to myself, and free from that very unpleasant, and in some measure unbecoming, attendance upon others. . . ."

Prior to the division of the office of Secretary of State for the Southern Department, the secretaryship had been held by William Petty, Earl of Shelburne. Although devoted to Chatham and his policies, Shelburne had little use for Grafton, who was equally devoted to the King's chief minister and was acting for him during his incapacity. Shelburne was, moreover, disliked by the King and by certain members of the Cabinet Council, whose leaders felt, perhaps with good reason, that "the great coldness" shown to them by Shelburne made him "a secret enemy."[12] In 1767, after the March 13 Cabinet Council meeting, the Earl had temporarily ceased to attend these important policy-making gatherings. This rather surprising conduct resulted from the unwillingness of his colleagues to respect his views on many American matters, almost all of which came within the scope of his department.[13] For he felt that "disastrous effect . . . could not fail to flow from their policy,"[14] and did not want to bear any responsibility for it.[15]

Although the division of the office of Secretary of State for the Southern Department had been under consideration by the Duke of Grafton since the summer of 1767, it was not until the Bedford Whigs came into the Ministry that the matter became pressing, since Bedford had made it a condition that the Earl of Shelburne should give up the management of colonial affairs.[16] According to the Earl, Grafton on the evening of December 11 of that year called him aside at the home of the Lord Northington, and for the first time opened up the question of the division of the department. As recorded by Shelburne, the discussion was cold and formal, but polite.[17] Referring to the office of Secretary of State for the Southern Department, Grafton declared:

> "I must say that it has ever been my opinion that it ought to be separated. I have declared it a hundred times to the Chancellor

[12] The King to Chatham, May 30, 1767, *Correspondence of William Pitt* (eds. W. S. Taylor and J. H. Pringle, 4 vols., London, 1838–40), III, 260, hereafter cited as *Pitt Correspondence.*

[13] Fitzmaurice: *op. cit.,* II, 58.

[14] *Ibid.*

[15] *Ibid.,* II, 67–8.

[16] For Shelburne's American policy see R. A. Humphreys: "Lord Shelburne and British Colonial Policy, 1766–1768," *English Historical Review,* L, 257–77. As this policy was largely concerned with the expansion of the frontiers, it will be given fuller emphasis in Chap. 12 of this volume.

[17] See among the Shelburne Papers a memorandum marked "Friday night, December 11th, 1767. At the Lord President's," Fitzmaurice: *op. cit.,* II, 68–72; see also Shelburne to Lady Chatham, December 13, 1767, *Pitt Correspondence,* III, 292–6.

[Lord Camden]; I told General Conway so expressly at the meeting we had about him last summer before [that is, in the presence of] Mr. Walpole and Lord Hertford."

With the reduction of functions of the Board of Trade, the business of the Secretary of State was now far too vast for any one man to handle, Grafton concluded. Shelburne's reply admitted that, since the Earl of Chatham's illness and his own absence from the Cabinet Council meetings, he had "not heard the least of what has been carrying on or projected, except the business that occurred necessarily in the course of my own office." After expressing his surprise at the plan now projected, he asked Grafton "whether any American event has given rise to this new opinion of your Grace's . . . ?" Grafton answered that the American business had been very ably managed, and added: "I should wish on that account your Lordship was to remain at that part, but it is my decided opinion that it [the Department] ought to be divided" and must be or the King must find another person to head the Treasury.

At a second interview between Grafton and Shelburne on the following day, Shelburne deplored the fact that it was impossible to get Chatham's views on the question, but announced that under the circumstances, since this division must take place, he would acquiesce. He then said: "Your Grace understands me however to mean my continuing in my present office, as I do not choose to take upon me the framing and modeling of this new office"—an arrangement that he felt did not conform to Grafton's expressed views that he (the Earl of Shelburne) "should take the American part, as the Bedfords cannot be trusted with it on account of different principles . . ."[18] Without going into the question of the inconsistency of Grafton's position—assuming that he had promised Bedford to remove Shelburne from colonial affairs—one may be permitted to reflect on the possible course of events if Shelburne had agreed to head the new office. Had his views on American policy been accepted by the Cabinet Council it might have made a great deal of difference. But they were not, as he had been made to realize. Moreover, had he taken the new office it might not have been considered to be of cabinet rank. It is clear that when Grafton in his *Autobiography* listed the "Cabinet" as constituted in 1768, he did not include the

[18] "Memorandum by Lord Shelburne of the conversation at the Queen's House," Fitzmaurice, *op. cit.*, II, 73; Shelburne to Lady Chatham, December 13, 1767, *Pitt Correspondence,* III, 296–8.

Secretary of State for the Colonies.[19] This would have meant that had Shelburne assumed the post, he would have been downgraded.

The first man to be appointed Secretary of State for the Colonies was, as indicated above, the Earl of Hillsborough, a natural choice in view of his record. As President of the Board of trade for two periods, he was well acquainted with colonial problems. Moreover, his views appeared to be in harmony with government policy on American affairs. This became clear when some assemblies of the colonies to the south of New England sought to overturn the Currency Act of 1764[20] so that their bills of credit would have a legal-tender quality—a status not permitted the New England local currency by the New England Restraining Act of 1751 (24 George II, c. 53). A legal-tender status for the currency of Southern colonies was held by the government of Great Britain to be not only unnecessary but highly undesirable in view of the confiscatory nature of attempts by the Virginia Assembly to liquidate planter debts owed to merchants resident in the colony as well as in Great Britain.[21] The new Secretary of State fully agreed with the position taken by the government that the Currency Act was based upon "sound principles" and that a colonial legal-tender currency had been found to be "big with Frauds, and full of Mischief to the Colonies, and to Commerce in general. . . ."[22] He also was in general agreement with most of the other ministers about American policy in general, as he showed soon after taking office by his actions in dealing with the Massachusetts Bay circular letter of February 11.[23]

With Hillsborough installed as Secretary of State for the Colonies on January 20, 1768, the reorganization of the Ministry seemed to be complete. However, its titular head, the Earl of Chatham, was so incapacitated that he was unable to perfom even the *pro forma*

---

[19] The Cabinet included only the following: Lord Camden as Lord Chancellor, Earl Gower as Lord President, the Earl of Chatham as Lord Privy Seal, Lord Shelburne and Lord Weymouth as Secretaries of State, the Duke of Grafton as First Commissioner of the Treasury, Lord North as Chancellor of the Exchequer, Lord Granby as Commander-in-Chief, General Conway as Lieutenant General of Ordnance, and Sir Edward Hawke, as First Commissioner of the Admiralty. See Grafton's *Autobiography,* p. 183. Later in the year, however, Hillsborough, as Secretary of State for the Colonies, was taken into the Council; on July 24 it met in his home. See *Pitt Correspondence,* III, 335*n.*

[20] 4 Geo. III, c. 34, "An Act to prevent Paper Bills of Credit, hereafter to be issued in any of his Majesty's Colonies . . . from being declared a legal Tender in Payments of Money . . ." (*Statutes at Large,* VII, 483–4).

[21] A fuller discussion of the currency problem in the colonies is presented at the end of this chapter.

[22] Hillsborough to Governor Tryon, April 16, 1768, *Colonial Records of North Carolina,* VII, 709.

[23] See Chap. 6 of this volume.

duties of Lord Privy Seal. The King therefore felt it necessary to issue a commission under the Great Seal on February 2, 1768, authorizing three individuals or any two of them to execute this office for a prescribed limited period.[24] Although on March 21 the Earl once again took possession of the seals of office,[25] throughout the balance of that year and the following year he remained at Hayes unable to fulfill his public responsibilities. The Duke of Grafton continued to turn to him to make the difficult decisions, but Chatham was unwilling to do so. To Grafton, in consequence, accrued the odium of having directed the measures against Wilkes, considered in the preceding chapter, which so rankled the public that had rallied behind the demagogue. This was so despite the fact that the Duke had shown considerable sympathy for Wilkes on the occasion of his first imprisonment in 1763 and again upon his return to London in the fall of 1766, and that at the beginning of 1768 he was still indisposed to act against the outlaw so long as he remained quiet.[26] Even after Wilkes was elected to Parliament from Middlesex it was not Grafton's plan to expel him from the House—provided that he first serve out his short term in prison and did not petition the King for protection against what he charged were the unfair methods used to convict him,[27] What undoubtedly influenced the other ministers was the lawless actions of the London mobs and the fear that if

---

[24] *Pitt Correspondence,* III, 319*n.* The occasion for putting the Privy Seal in commission is of interest to students of American colonial history as it involved Lord Botetourt, later in the year to be appointed Governor of Virginia. It seems that Botetourt had invested most of his fortune in a manufacturing company. However, a *caveat* was entered in the Privy Seal Office against the scheme and apparently against incorporating the company. Since the Lord Privy Seal, Chatham, was unable to act in the case, nothing was done, a situation which Botetourt claimed was threatening him with ruin. He therefore was determined to publicize Chatham's incapacity to act, even in the House of Lords if necessary. See Botetourt to Grafton and Grafton's reply, both of January 19, 1768, Grafton's *Autobiography,* pp. 185–6. In the face of this threat, Grafton, by written recommendation to Chatham, secured his agreement that the seal of his office be placed in commission for the specific purpose in question. See Grafton to Chatham, January 21, and Lady Chatham to Grafton, January 22, 1768, *ibid.,* pp. 186–7. With this business completed the seal was returned to Chatham by Lord Camden in the presence of members of the Privy Council, all of whom went to the Earl's country seat, Hayes, for the simple yet important ceremony.

[25] *Pitt Correspondence,* III, 323–5.

[26] For correspondence relating to Grafton and Wilkes see Grafton's *Autobiography,* pp. 191–4.

[27] John Almon, in his *Correspondence of the late John Wilkes . . .* (5 vols., London, 1805), III, 293–300, gives evidence of how hard Grafton tried to prevail upon Wilkes not to reopen the issues that had led to his outlawry by promising that if he acceded he would not face expulsion from his seat. Grafton in his *Autobiography* (pp. 194–203) goes into great detail on how carefully the whole matter of Wilkes's expulsion was considered and presents Lord Camden's views against this step.

Wilkes were permitted to take his seat, the mob leaders would feel that their methods of violence had been vindicated.

But the Ministry was not a united body on any issue in 1768. Shelburne alone in the Cabinet Council opposed the expulsion of Wilkes.[28] Likewise, when, as Secretary of State for the Southern Department, he sought to name a minister resident at the capital of the Kingdom of Sardinia, the King refused to accept his nomination and ordered Grafton to inform the Secretary that another person had been selected for the place.[29] Shelburne's differences with his colleagues on American affairs became evident when news arrived of the violent action taken by the Boston mob in June, at the time Hancock's sloop *Liberty* had been seized by the customs officers. Upon receiving word of the incident, the Bedford party in the Ministry demanded the use of force. Shelburne's position, however, was "that it would be absurd to wish to send to America a single additional soldier or vessel of war to reduce colonies which would return to the mother-country of themselves from affection and from interest, when once the form of their contributions should be agreed upon"[30] —a view rejected by other ministers as chimerical.

In view of the lack of unity in the Cabinet Council, an effort was made in July to find a successor for Shelburne, but without result.[31] Toward the end of September, Grafton consulted Camden on the need to replace Shelburne. The Lord Chancellor replied: "It is unlucky." He then went on to state: "The Administration, since L[d] Chatham's illness, is almost entirely altered, without being changed," and added that he now found himself surrounded by people with whom he had no connection and was tired of his employment.[32] Yet, in a later letter to Grafton dealing with Shelburne's opposition in the Cabinet Council, he admitted that "it does behove his lordship, either to be cordially reconciled, or to resign: for it is neither just nor honorable to confound, much less to betray an Administration, while he remains a member of it."[33] This was also the opinion of the King, who informed Grafton that because of the Earl of Shelburne's "continual attempt to thwart the measures of Administration, & in particular

---

[28] Whately to George Grenville, October 11, 1768, *Grenville Papers,* IV, 371.

[29] George III to the Duke of Grafton, September 22, 1768, *Correspondence of George III* (Fortescue), II, 46–7. Gerard Hamilton to John Calcraft, July 20, 1768, *Pitt Correspondence,* III, 333*n.*

[30] Fitzmaurice: *op. cit.,* II, 160–1. It may be noted that Fitzmaurice incorrectly calls the *Liberty* the *Romney.*

[31] Gerard Hamilton to Calcraft, July 24, 1768, *Pitt Correspondence,* III, 334*n.*

[32] Camden to Grafton, September 29, 1768, Grafton's *Autobiography,* p. 214.

[33] Camden to Grafton, October 4, 1768, *ibid.,* pp. 215–17.

whatever springs from You . . . most of the Members of my Administration separately . . . mention to Me the impossibility of his longer continuing in Office. . . ."[34]

It now seemed absolutely necessary for Grafton to get Chatham's views on this contemplated step. He therefore wrote to Lady Chatham at Hayes, asking for an appointment. Her reply disclosed that it would be impossible for him to speak with the Earl, but that she herself would be pleased to see him. In the interview, when the matter of the dismissal of Shelburne came up, Lady Chatham stated: "I am able to tell your Grace from my Lord himself . . . . that it will never have his consent nor concurrence, as thinking it quite contrary to the King's service."[35]

Another matter arose at this juncture to influence Chatham's subsequent course of action—the removal of Sir Jeffrey Amherst from the post of Governor of Virginia. Sir Jeffrey had held this appointment since September 1759 but had been acting through his deputy. Virginians themselves, according to Grafton, had complained "that their salary to a Governor was perverted to a *sinecure* place." The growing unrest in America made it clear to the Cabinet Council that the time had come to put an end "to this unjustifiable abuse" of the office. Amherst was therefore informed that the King, upon advice of his ministers, had decided to send over a resident Governor. Although offered ample compensation in the way of a pension, Sir Jeffrey could not be reconciled to the loss of his post; he therefore resigned in anger from all his offices and commands.[36] Chatham, who had secured both of Amherst's appointments—to command in North America and to be Governor of Virginia—took deep offence at his removal, despite the many sound reasons advanced to justify it. This step, combined with the plan to deprive his loyal and able follower Shelburne of one of the most important state offices within the gift of the King, determined the Earl to request the King's permission to resign the seals of office. Before concluding his letter to Grafton seeking the resignation, he stated: "I cannot enough lament the removal of Sir Jeffrey Amherst and that of Lord Shelburne."[37] Both the King and Grafton did their utmost to persuade Chatham to remain in the administration, even in an inactive capacity, but to no

[34] The King to Grafton, October 5, 1768, *Correspondence of George III* (Fortescue), II, 49–50.

[35] *Pitt Correspondence* III, 337.

[36] Grafton's *Autobiography,* pp. 212–13. For a detailed account of the relieving of Amherst from his post see Thomas Whately to George Grenville, August 24, 1768, *Grenville Papers,* IV, 348–52.

[37] *Pitt Correspondence,* III, 338.

avail.[38] In later years Grafton, in his *Autobiography*, affirmed the conviction that the illness of Chatham and his subsequent resignation constituted "the most unhappy event that could have befallen our political state." He also stated that, had this not occurred, "I would think that the separation from America might have been avoided." This would appear to corroborate the impression that his letters imploring Chatham not to take the step expressed his true feelings at the time.

Without the moral support of Chatham in the Cabinet Council, the Earl of Shelburne did not wait for dismissal. On October 19 he obtained an audience with the King and, upon coming out of the royal closet, told Lord Northington that he had just resigned the seals of office and that the ministers would be so informed.[39] Manifestly the Chatham Ministry was disintegrating. Northington had resigned in favour of Lord Gower; General Conway had resigned as Secretary of State to make way for Lord Weymouth; Lord Hillsborough, whose views respecting America differed decidedly from those of Chatham, had become Secretary of State for the Colonies. Upon Shelburne's resignation, Lord Weymouth took over his post of Secretary of State for the Southern Department, while Lord Rochford, who had been Ambassador to the Court of Louis XV of France, was promoted to Weymouth's late office of Secretary of State for the Northern Department.

None of these new ministers had any affiliation with Chatham. Yet the great potential power of the Earl, should he recover from his illness, was not overlooked by either the King or the Duke of Grafton, who now became the acknowledge first minister. Therefore, Lord Camden—who, as Chatham's devoted follower, had been anxious to follow him into retirement—was prevailed upon to remain as Lord High Chancellor. Further, to fill the post of Lord Privy Seal, George William Hervey, Lord Bristol, was chosen, according to Horace Walpole, "as a particular compliment to Lord Chatham."[40]

---

[38] For Grafton's answer of October 12, 1768, Chatham's reply to this letter of October 13, Grafton's acknowledgment of October 14, together with the exchange of letters between the King and Chatham on the same day, see *ibid.*, III, 339–44; to these letters should be added those that passed between the King and Grafton covering October 10–14, to be found in the *Correspondence of George III* (Fortescue), II, 51–8.

[39] Fitzmaurice: *op. cit.*, II, 163; Whately to George Grenville, October 27, 1768, *Grenville Papers*, IV, 390.

[40] Horace Walpole: *Memoirs of the Reign of George the Third* (ed. Sir Denis Le Marchant, 2 vols., Philadelphia, 1845), II, 126, hereafter cited as Walpole's *Memoirs of George III*. Bristol had been sent to Spain by Chatham (then William Pitt) in 1758 to take the place of Sir Benjamin Keene, British Ambassador at Madrid,

Nevertheless, the men who now molded policy in the Cabinet Council no longer reflected Chatham's views. Far from it. "We are shifted, by I know not what fatality, upon Mr. Grenville's ground," complained Camden in writing to Grafton on October 4, 1768.[41] That this was true of American affairs cannot be doubted. For among those who viewed colonial developments as Grenville did must be counted the new members of the Cabinet Council, in particular the Earl of Hillsborough and the followers of the Duke of Bedford. Grafton, a well-meaning man, anxious to reconcile the colonies with the mother country, was temporarily carried along with the tide.[42]

The Bedford party favoured strong measures in dealing with the recalcitrant colonies. Therefore, as has been developed in an earlier chapter of this volume, by September 1768 regular troops had been sent to garrison Boston by decision of the British Ministry. The issue between the British government and the continental colonies involved not only the question of the fairness of the Townshend Acts but, even more crucially, the *right* of Parliament to raise a revenue from America. As Lord Camden pointed out to Grafton, the government was so

> "pressed on the one hand by the Declaratory Law [of 1766, asserting the authority of Parliament to legislate on all matters whatsoever relating to the colonies], and on the other by the colony's [that is, Massachusetts Bay's] resolute denial of Parliamentary authority, that the issue is now joined upon the right, which in my apprehension, is the most untoward ground of dispute that could have been started: fatal to Great Britain, if she miscarries: unprofitable if she succeeds. For it is (as I believe your Grace thinks with me, it is) inexpedient to tax the colonies, as we maintained, when the Stamp Act was repealed."

Yet Camden could not condone the conduct of Massachusetts Bay, especially since it exerted such a powerful influence over the other colonies as "the ringleading province"; therefore, in his opinion, "if any country [colony] is to be chastised, the punishment ought to be levelled there." As a method of accomplishing this, he suggested

---

and had conducted his delicate mission there with great ability. See Volume VIII of this series, pp. 243–53. When he returned home in 1762, Chatham appointed him Lord Lieutenant of Ireland.

[41] Grafton's *Autobiography*, p. 216.

[42] In the words of D. A. Winstanley (*Lord Chatham and the Whig Opposition*, p. 195): "With the entry of the Bedfords into the government, the party system came into its own once more, Grafton, in order to avoid shipwreck, having thrown himself into the arms of one of the political factions which Chatham had set out to destroy."

that if the Townshend Duties Act was repealed in all the other provinces, but "executed with proper vigour [in Massachusetts Bay], . . . such a measure might not be unsuccessful" in bringing this colony back to its duty. The idea of repeal as a concession measure, he admitted, would scarcely receive any support "as almost every body else [in the government] holds the Declaratory Law to be a sacred fundamental, never to be departed from."[43]

The position of Secretary of State Lord Hillsborough on the grave issue presented by the conduct of Massachusetts Bay was made clear on December 15, 1768, in the House of Lords, when he presented and moved the adoption of eight resolutions directed severally at: the unconstitutional behaviour of the province's House of Representatives, the laxness of the Council and the magistrates, and the illegality of the proceedings of the Boston town meeting, as well as the unconstitutional assembling of the committee of convention of the province in September.[44] His resolutions were adopted after only the most perfunctory opposition to them had been expressed by Earl Temple, the Duke of Richmond, and the Earl of Shelburne.[45] Furthermore, the Lords therewith approved an address to the King, offered by the Duke of Bedford, supporting the measures already taken by the government to hold Massachusetts Bay in obedience to the Crown and strongly recommending that those "wicked and designing men, . . . chief authors and instigators of the late disorders," who by their acts were deluding His Majesty's subjects in that province, should be brought "to condign punishment." This could be done, the address pointed out, by directing the Governor to procure the fullest information

> "touching all treasons, or misprision of treason, committed within this government since the 30th day of December last, and to transmit the same . . . to one of your Majesty's principal secretaries of state, in order that your Majesty may issue the special commission for enquiring of, hearing, and determining, the said offences within this realm, pursuant to the provisions of the statute of the 35th year of the reign of King Henry the eighth, in case your Majesty shall . . . see sufficient ground for such a proceeding."[46]

[43] Lord Camden to Grafton, October 4, 1768, Grafton's *Autobiography,* pp. 216–17.

[44] For these resolutions see *Parliamentary History,* XVI, 476–80. They were sent to the American press by correspondents and appear, for example, in the *Pennsylvania Gazette* of March 23, 1769.

[45] *Parliamentary History,* XVI, 476*n*.

[46] *Ibid.,* XVI, 479–80. The Bedford address was seconded by Holderness. As the Earl of Hardwicke's minute on the debate over the address pointed out, "Nobody much objected, but the duke of Richmond, and he was not very clear. . . . he

The Lords then agreed that the resolutions and the address should be sent down to the House of Commons for concurrence.

The House of Commons was already engaged in considering the ominous developments in Massachusetts Bay. For on November 28, 1768, Lord North at the King's command had presented to the House copies of sixty pertinent Massachusetts Bay papers—including correspondence, votes of the Assembly, minutes of the Council, and proceedings of Boston town meetings, together with those of the convention of Massachusetts Bay towns held in September. Again by royal command, on December 7 North presented another body of papers relating to the movement of regular troops to Boston for the purpose of establishing the royal authority there.[47] The House of Commons therefore decided that, until these materials had been examined, no action should be taken on the resolutions and address sent down on December 16 by the House of Lords. Further, on January 20, 1769, additional papers bearing upon the Massachusetts Bay situation were laid on the table.[48]

It is manifest that what was taking place in Massachusetts Bay was regarded in the most serious light in the House of Commons. On January 25 Alderman Beckford of London presented a petition from most of the members of the Council of Massachusetts Bay, but the House ruled that it might be read only if it were held to be not from the Council but from individual councilmen. The document stressed not so much the question of the right of Parliament to levy upon the colony as the burden that the new import taxes placed upon the colonists, who, it was claimed, were paying taxes as high as those in Great Britain.[49] When the question whether the petition should be referred to the consideration of the committee of the whole House

---

was answered by lord Weymouth. . . . Lord Shelburne seemed to dislike the Address, and thought the administration negligent. . . . He and Lord Hillsborough had some sparring about the conduct of governor Barnard. The duke of Grafton spoke as a minister for maintaining the right of parliament, and that he desired every body to understand that by these Resolutions and Address parliament had precluded itself from respecting [repealing?] any of the acts for laying duties in the colonies for this session. Lord Hillsborough had before declared, that for commercial reasons he should be for repealing one of them, when the point of right was no longer in dispute. Lord Lyttelton and lord Mansfield were not there: the Lord Chancellor [Lord Camden] was silent" (*ibid.*, XVI, 477*n*).

[47] *Journals of the House of Commons*, XXXII, 74–6, 91–2.

[48] *Ibid.*, XXXII, 107–8, 123–4.

[49] *Ibid.*, XXXII, 136–7. For the debate over the question of receiving the petition see *Sir Henry Cavendish's Debates of the House of Commons* . . . (ed. John Wright, 2 vols., London, 1841), I, 185–7, hereafter cited as *Cavendish's Debates.* George Grenville's remarks pointed out that "the petitioners desire that all the acts of parliament made for the purpose of raising a revenue in America may be repealed." He also queried: "Would you receive a petition from any man in this kingdom, desiring all the taxes to be repealed?" (*ibid.*)

was put before the Commons, the vote was lost by a count of 133 to 70. The following day Sir George Savile, an influential but politically independent Yorkshire gentleman, sought to present a petition from William Bollan, London agent for the Massachussets Bay Council,[50] praying that "the Concurrence of the Commons, in the Resolutions and Address communicated by the Lords at a Conference, may not take place."[51] Its main burden was that the law of Henry VIII having to do with treasons and misprision of treason "committed out of the King's Dominions" (35 Henry VIII, c. 2) did not extend to America. After some argument, the House voted 136 to 105 not to receive the petition. With this out of the way and faced by the great mass of papers relating to the disturbance in Massachusetts Bay, Lord North now stated that he would read the resolutions that had come from the House of Lords. This was done, along with the address to the King.[52]

In the debate that followed, Attorney General William de Grey presented evidence that under the statute of Henry VIII concerned with treasons "out of the King's Dominions," those accused of treasons committed on the Isle of Man, at Calais (when under the dominion of the Crown), and in Ireland had been brought to trial in England. "Why then," he argued, "should it not extend to our colonies; and why should they complain of it as a matter of hardship? They [the Americans] carried with them the 25th of Edward the Third,[53] and shall they not carry with them the 35th of Henry the Eighth?" In reply, Grenville asked:

> "Why have the Lords named in their address the act of Henry the Eighth, an act which has a very odd meaning?—an act 'concerning the trials of treasons committed out of his Majesty's dominions?' Will not the Americans say, 'we, then, are out of his Majesty's dominions?' . . . In truth, you do not mean to send for any body, and this resolution is so much waste paper."

The problem, he went on to observe, was to establish Great Britain's "jurisdiction and power of every kind, within the words of the act of parliament, over the colonies." As to the attitude of the Americans, he continued:

---

[50] Bollan had been dismissed in 1762 as London agent for the House of Representatives, but continued to represent the Council in London.

[51] *Journals of the House of Commons,* XXXII, 151.

[52] *Cavendish's Debates,* I, 190–3.

[53] The act was 25 Edw. III, stat. 5, c. 2: "A Declaration which Offenses shall be adjudged Treason"; the act was confirmed by 1 Henry IV, c. 10, 1 Edw. VI, c. 12, and 13 Chas. II, stat. 1, c. 1; it bound all courts in the colonies.

> "Those who have deluded them [as to their freedom from taxation by Parliament] are in this country. . . . If they [the Americans] think you have no authority to tax them, not being represented, they must think you have no power to make laws for them. . . . Many have come to the essential part, and say, the navigation acts are a grievance, we want to have them repealed."

Indeed, the conduct of government in the face of this issue raised by Americans, he concluded, "is not only odious and contemptible, but destructive."

Brushing aside Grenville's criticism of the government, Lord North moved in favour of adopting the resolutions of the House of Lords and the address. Referring to the fact that the riots in Boston had been "great and dangerous," he declared:

> "If any overt act of treason had been actually proved, I should not agree to this address; for, in that case, we should have sent over for the individuals who were guilty. The meeting of [the convention of the towns] of the 12th of September, the voting a standing army to be contrary to the bill of rights, the calling upon the inhabitants to arm on the report of a French war, and the intention to seize Castle William were all acts approaching . . . treason. . . . I partake in the sorrow that has been expressed at the fact, that there is no jury in America which can be trusted. . . . I adopt the measure of the House of Lords, because I think it a good measure, not a futile one. . . . I hope we shall abide by the declaratory law, and neither to-day nor at any future period, repeal an act of parliament in consequence of any resistance the Americans may give to it. . . . Let us never give up an iota of the authority of Great Britain."

The debate was long. It was resumed on February 8, when Edmund Burke, Alderman Trecothick, Colonel Barré, as well as Thomas Pownall and George Johnstone—both of whom had served as Governors in North America—and others voiced strong objections to the resolutions and the address.[54] This position was also taken by a

---

[54] For the most detailed account of the debate on the Lords' resolutions and address in the House of Commons see *Cavendish's Debates,* I, 194–227. The most balanced summary of it that has come to the attention of the author of this series was prepared by Charles Garth, a member from Devizes and also London agent for South Carolina and Maryland. This is embodied in his letter to the South Carolina committee of correspondence dated February 9, 1769, which is printed in *South Carolina Historical and Genealogical Magazine,* XXXI, 46–52. Another excellent account of the debate, but not quite as detailed, is contained in the long letter written by the London agent for Connecticut, William Samuel Johnson, to Governor William Pitkin on February 9, 1769, which is printed in the Massachusetts Historical Society *Collections,* 5th ser., IX, 312–21; reference must also be made to the summarization of the debate in the *Annual Register,* 1769, pp. 52–61. Writing of the

majority of the speakers. Nevertheless, on the vote, the resolution of the Lords, with minor amendments, and the address were supported by 169 to 65.[55]

On February 13 the address to the King relating to the disturbances in Massachusetts Bay was presented by both Houses. Replying to it, the King declared:

> "The sincere Satisfaction you express in the Measures which I have already taken, and the strong Assurances you give of supporting Me in those which may be still necessary to maintain the just Legislative Authority, and the due Execution of the Laws, in My Province of Massachusetts Bay, give Me great Pleasure.
>
> I shall not fail to give those Orders, which you recommend as the most effectual Method of bringing the Authors of the late unhappy Disorders in that Province to condign Punishment."[56]

Yet, one thing was clear. The ministers had no intention at that time of bringing those who had fomented the disturbances in Boston to England for trial. Grey Cooper, a secretary of the Treasury and a member of the House, assured Parliament that "it was not meant to put the act [of Henry VIII] in execution, but only to shew to America, what government could do if pushed to it."[57]

It would, however, be a mistake to think that a threat of future

---

debate to Hutchinson, Thomas Whately indicated that the friends of Lord Rockingham and Lord Shelburne "objected to the whole of the resolutions" (Letter of February 11, 1769, Hutchinson Correspondence, Massachusetts Archives, 25:298–301).

[55] *Journals of the House of Commons,* XXXII, 185–6. The amendments were agreed to in conference.

[56] *Ibid.,* XXXII, 207.

[57] *Parliamentary History,* XVI, 507. While Cooper was correct in his statement, a rumour was spread in the American press that James Otis, Samuel Adams, and Thomas Cushing, regarded as ringleaders of the opposition to effective British control in Massachusetts Bay, were to be arrested, transported to England, tried for treason, and hanged. See *Pennsylvania Gazette,* March 9, 23, and 30, and April 13, 1769. Thomas Pownall, a former Governor of Massachusetts Bay, writing on February 13, 1769, to the eloquent and radical Dr. Samuel Cooper, pastor of Brattle Church in Boston, gave his judgment that the act of 35 Henry VIII "is not meant to be or ever will be carried into execution," yet it deserved "serious consideration to guard agst the ill-use that might be made of it . . ." (King's Manuscripts, No. 202, British Museum). In another letter to Cooper on February 25, Pownall, who was sympathetic with the colonial position on the issue thus presented, raised the question whether the rights and privileges guaranteed by the Petition of Right of 1628, as well as by the act abolishing the Star Chamber, the Habeas Corpus Act, and the Bill of Rights, extended to the colonies. He then went on to say that, if the King by royal charter or by royal assent to provincial laws could not extend the benefit of these measures to the colonies, it could be done by act of Parliament and he had in mind bringing in a bill to extend these rights to the King's dominions in America. Yet he admitted that such an attempt at present could be attended with "many difficulties" *(ibid.).*

action was all that the Secretary of State for the Colonies had in mind for dealing with refractory Massachusetts Bay. On the very day that the address of the two Houses was presented to the King, Hillsborough submitted to the Cabinet Council a series of proposals that would, he felt, place proper restraints upon that colony. The first was for the alteration of its government by means of an act of Parliament, whereby the Council instead of being elected should be appointed by the Crown, "in the same manner and under the same Regulations as in the Royal Governments." In the proposal he also recommended that a clause should be embodied in this statute to the effect that the entering in the journal of the Massachusetts Bay House of Representatives of any vote or resolution whereby the authority of Parliament to make laws of sufficient force to bind the colony "in all cases whatsoever" should be called into question, would constitute grounds for the forfeiture of the province's charter. His second proposal was that the King should make Governor Bernard a baronet as a mark of approval of his conduct and should direct him to avail himself of his current leave of absence to return to England for a limited period, so that he might report in person to His Majesty on the state of the province, which during his absence could be administered by Lieutenant Governor Hutchinson. His third was that the instruction to the Governor—concerning the holding of the next Assembly at either Salem or Cambridge—should be so construed that he could use his discretion, based upon the situation in Boston at the time. His fourth was to permit a certain latitude to General Gage, so that if he were of the opinion that it was unnecessary to maintain so large a body of regular troops in the province, he could return them to their base in Nova Scotia. In other words, the Secretary clearly was thinking in terms of withdrawal of the troops from Boston and a return to the normal disposition of British forces in America.[58]

In the program submitted to the Cabinet Council Hillsborough did not restrict his considerations to Massachusetts Bay. He also recommended the removal of the four members of the New York Council who had voted on January 2, 1769, against dissolving the Assembly for passing resolves that Governor Moore considered incompatible with the Declaratory Act.[59] Further, he proposed that the

[58] Hillsborough to the King, February 15, 1769, *Correspondence of George III* (Fortescue), II, 81–3.

[59] See Governor Moore to Hillsborough, January 4, 1769, *New York Colonial Documents*, VIII, 143–4. For the resolutions of the New York Assembly denying the right of Parliament to tax them, which came before the House of Commons on March 14, 1769, see *Parliamentary History*, XVI, 603–5.

papers received from the Governor concerning these resolves should be placed before Parliament and that an address should be moved calling on Moore to require, in His Majesty's name, that the offensive resolutions be erased from the minutes of the Assembly or, if this were refused, that a bill should be brought into Parliament whereby the movers of the resolves, together with the Speaker of the House, the Clerk, and any other person so acting in defiance of the Declaratory Act, should be given a *praemunire,* and thus incur a disability to serve in any public office.

As to the Townshend Revenue Act, Hillsborough favoured amending it so as to exclude Virginia and the British West Indies, since these colonies already had made permanent provision for maintenance of the civil establishment. He likewise proposed that as soon as any other colony had made similar permanent provision for civil administration, the statute should no longer be applicable to it. Finally, with respect to the American Mutiny or Billeting Act, he advised that it be amended so that, unless a colony were to build barracks or rent adequate housing in suitable locations, the troops should be placed in public houses and furnished with the same necessaries and rates as prevailed in England, or should the public houses not be sufficient, troops might then be billeted in private houses. Such an amended Mutiny Act, he urged, should also provide that civil officers refusing to assist in billeting troops be liable to penalties and that the Governor of the colony in question be required to appoint billeting commissioners in their stead. In this connection he recommended that whenever a colony should pass a proper quartering act that could be approved by the King in Council the new statute would not apply.[60]

Here we have the Hillsborough program for bringing order out of the confusion that reigned in the public affairs of the colonies. It is clear that in presenting it the Secretary of State for the Colonies was seeking to take over in 1769 the leadership in the field of colonial policy that Charles Townshend had exercised in 1767 in the Cabinet Council. He was, however, to meet with less success. Writing to the King, he indicated that his proposals were approved by most of the Council members with the exception of Lord High Chancellor Camden, General Conway, and the Duke of Grafton, who were, incidentally, three key men. However, the more drastic of his recommendations met with little royal encouragement. While the King

[60] For the Hillsborough proposals see *Correspondence of George III* (Fortescue), II, 83–4.

admitted that a situation could arise which might necessitate a change in the method of selecting members of the Massachusetts Bay Council, his position was, simply stated, that "the altering of Charters is at all times an odious measure"; nor was he any more willing to support Hillsborough's drastic proposal for dealing with the Massachusetts Bay House of Representatives. Moreover, "the conduct of the Virginians was so offensive the last Spring" to the King that he was opposed to altering the Revenue Act in their favour at this time. Nevertheless, he agreed that a hint might be dropped to the effect that colonies submitting to this statute and making proper permanent provision for the support of their civil establishment might look forward to exemption from all other provisions of the Act "except the Tea Duty."[61]

One thing was clear: the expectation that the Townshend Revenue Act would produce significant income from the colonies for the support of the American military and civil establishments had vanished by the beginning of 1769. The cost of maintaining the regular troops in America, Africa, Gibraltar, and Minorca for that year was estimated at £397,835. Most of this was to be devoted to the security of the British possessions in the New World, although not a penny of it was budgeted upon the assumption that any part of the sum would be derived from America import duties.[62] In a statement prepared by the American Board of Customs Commissioners covering the gross revenues secured from import duties between September 8, 1767, and January 5, 1769, on all articles, including those provided for in the Townshend Revenue Act as well as by earlier acts, the fact was disclosed that the total sum collected was only £28,904.17.83/4.[63] The cost of collection was placed at £16,430.7.1—leaving a net sum of but £12,474.10.73/4. In other words, the cost of collection amounted to more than the net revenue secured. Of the total receipts, £11,135.17.2 came from

---

[61] "Memorandum by the King," *ibid.*, II, 84–5.

[62] "Supplies granted for the Year 1769," *Parliamentary History*, XVI, 621–2; see also *Journals of the House of Commons*, XXXII, 40.

[63] The financial statement presented to the House of Commons on April 4, 1769, gave the gross produce of duties collected "towards the Expences of defending, protecting, and securing, the British Colonies and Plantations in America," as £5,787.17.8 then available in the Exchequer, as against £70,000 given by Parliament to cover the anticipated collection for the year 1768. The gross collection of all American duties, including the above sum of £5,787.17.8 for the year in question, is given as £27,528.4.7½, or somewhat less than the amount mentioned above in the text, leaving a deficit of £41,471.15.4½ against the £70,000. See *ibid.*, XXXII, 356.

duties provided for by the Townshend Revenue Act.[64] This puny sum, moreover, was secured at the price of further alienating the colonies from the mother country, not to mention the loss of much trade.

At this juncture Benjamin Franklin (writing under the *nom de plume* "Another London Manufacturer") sent a letter to the London *Public Advertiser* (January 17, 1769) that could only serve to reinforce the realization that the policy adopted toward America—just and proper as it seemed to be to most people of understanding in Great Britain—was not only leading the Kingdom toward bankruptcy but was also dangerous for the continued unity of the Empire. In the letter Franklin asserted that the loss to the British public as the result of the policy was £7,250,000 and that a continuance of it would inevitably lead to a revolt of "the whole fifteen colonies," containing 3,000,000 inhabitants. To subdue them, he warned, would take at least ten years of effort by an army of a minimum of 25,000 men supported by the navy and at a cost of £100,000,000, without taking into account the loss of life involved in such a war or the aftermath of hatred which would follow its termination.[65]

Undoubtedly the growing awareness of the validity of Franklin's view of the American situation—confirmed as it was by reports of the highly combustible state of the colonies and in conjunction with some manifestations of a decline in British trade to America[66]—finally led the British Ministry and Parliament to reconsider colonial policy. For they could not fail to realize that the Townshend Revenue Act, far from fulfilling its objective of restoring an orderly system of administration in the colonies, was having an opposite and adverse effect. Accordingly, on April 19, 1769, Thomas Pownall proposed that the Act be referred to the committee of the whole

---

[64] The cost of collecting the American import duties was £2,965.5.5 between September 8, 1767, and January 5, 1768; it was £9,826.19.3 between January 5, 1768, and January 5, 1769, with incidental charges amounting to £2,693.14.6¾, not including a loss by exchange of £944.7.10¼. This statement was prepared by the American Board of Customs Commissioners and forwarded to the British Treasury. John Temple, a member of the Board, submitted a copy of it to George Grenville in writing to him on April 15, 1769. See John Temple Correspondence, Box 102, Stowe Americana, Huntington Library.

[65] For the reprinting of this letter see, for example, *Pennsylvania Gazette*, April 13, 1769; Franklin's authorship of it is discussed by Professor V. W. Crane in the Bibliographical Society of America *Papers*, XXVIII, Part I, p. 24, *n.* 53.

[66] For the relatively low state of the British export trade to America at this period see T. S. Ashton: *Economic Fluctuations in England, 1700–1800* (Oxford, 1959), p. 61.

House of Commons for the purpose of bringing about its repeal.[67] In doing so, he delivered a vigorous speech strongly upholding the idea of the "sovereignty and supremacy" of Parliament throughout the Empire as embodied in the Declaratory Act. However, his chief plea was to put aside theoretical positions and return "to that old safe ground of administration on which the American affairs were conducted until within the last few years of experiment." The Townshend Act, he declared, was "unjust, inefficient, and directly contrary to all the principles of commerce" and the true interests of Great Britain. It was particularly unjust, he asserted, to Barbados, Jamaica, and Virginia, colonies that already, before the passage of the Act, had provided permanent revenues to cover civil administration. Moreover, in Virginia in the past year more than £27,500 had been raised in permanent revenues as against but £360 raised there by the Act. As to the import duties on painters' colours, glass, and paper, he continued, their only effect had been to encourage the colonies to prove that they were capable of producing their own supplies. On the subject of tea, he disclosed that never was more of this article imported from Holland or the Dutch West Indies than during the past year. Pownall's motion was seconded by Alderman Barlow Trecothick.[68] Lord North, however, took the position that repeal of the act would be a measure neither of credit nor of reconciliation:

> ". . . if you lose your credit with your colonies you never can be reconciled with them. We will not consent to go into the question [of repeal], on account of the combinations going on in America

[67] *Journals of the House of Commons,* XXXII, 421. For the full text of Pownall's speech of April 19, 1769, see B.M., King's Mss., 202, also found in the transcripts of the letters of Thomas Pownall to Samuel Cooper, Samuel Adams Papers, New York Public Library. It would seem that Pownall was more successful in influencing the colonial leaders with whom he was in private correspondence—such as the Rev. Samuel Cooper—than he was in gaining acceptance for his ideas among members of the administration or of Parliament. See in this connection the above-mentioned letters of Pownall to Cooper, some of which are published in Frederick Griffin: *Junius Discovered* (Boston, 1854), and "Letters of Samuel Cooper to Thomas Pownall, 1768–1777," *American Historical Review,* VIII, 301–30. This correspondence is an interesting example of the interplay of ideas resulting from the exchange of letters between various people in positions of influence in Great Britain and in the colonies.

[68] For an excellent brief account of the Pownall speech see the letter from William Samuel Johnson, London agent for Connecticut, to Governor William Pitkin, April 26, 1769, Massachusetts Historical Society *Collections,* 5th ser., IX, 334–6, and *Parliamentary History,* XVI, 610–22. For Barlow Trecothick's career as merchant, alderman, and Lord Mayor of London, as well as his position on Wilkes and his importance as a political figure in London among the merchants, see the article by T. D. Jervey in *South Carolina Historical and Genealogical Magazine,* XXXII, 157–69.

> against the mother-country . . . I see nothing uncommercial in making the Americans pay a duty upon tea. I give no opinion, one way or the other, what it may be right to do in a future session; provided America shall have behaved with duty and proper respect, and take no undue steps to enforce the repeal of this act."

So saying, he moved that the order of the day be read. After some other members had spoken, the House accepted his motion.[69]

At the time Parliament was prorogued on May 9, 1769, the most salient issues being deliberated were those aroused by the disputed Wilkes elections, the arrears in the King's civil list, and American grievances over the Townshend Act. Concurrently, a ministerial crisis was at hand. In his prorogation speech, the King referred to the disturbances in North America, declaring: "Nothing in My Opinion could be more likely to . . . defeat the Designs of the *Factious* and *Seditious,* than the hearty Concurrence of every Branch of the Legislature in the Resolution of maintaining the Execution of the Laws in every Part of My Dominions; and there is nothing I more ardently wish for, than to see it produce that good Effect."[70] Yet, even before the prorogation had taken place, the American Revenue Act had come under consideration in the Cabinet Council and "the Administration agreed to do that by their own authority which they would not permit Parliament to do; viz. to declare that the late revenue act shall next winter be repealed, and no new taxes imposed upon America, provided the Colonies continue quiet, and no new provocations are given."[71] As a result the Secretary of State for the Colonies was empowered by the Council on May 1 to write a circular letter to the American Governors. The letter, dated May 13, stressed the point that

> "the whole Legislature concur in the opinion adopted by His Majesty's Servants, that no Measure ought to be taken which can any way derogate from the Legislative Authority of Great Britain over the Colonies; but I can take it upon me to assure you, notwithstanding Insinuations to the contrary from men with factious and seditious views, that His Majesty's present Administration have [at] no time

[69] For the debate in general, following Pownall's address, see Massachusetts Historical Society *Collections,* 5th ser., IX, 336–14; see also *Cavendish's Debates,* I, 391–401.

[70] *Journals of the House of Commons,* XXXII, 453.

[71] William Samuel Johnson to Governor Pitkin, May 25, 1769 *op. cit.,* IX, 346. On May 19 De Berdt waited upon Lord Dartmouth, who confirmed "that the ministry gave out that the ['obnoxious'] Acts would be repeal'd the first thing next Sessions . . . I also waited on Mr. Burke who gave me the same account . . ." (De Berdt, London agent for Massachusetts Bay, to Speaker Thomas Cushing, May 20, 1769, Colonial Society of Massachusetts *Transactions,* XIII, 373).

> entertained a Design to propose to Parliament to lay any further Taxes upon America for the purpose of raising a Revenue, and that it is at present their Intention to propose in the next Session of Parliament to take off the Duties upon Glass, Paper & Colours, upon consideration of such Duties having been laid contrary to the true principles of Commerce."[72]

This communication, upon review by members of the Council, was regarded by Grafton and Camden—and doubtless also by Conway and Granby—as most unfortunate, containing as it did what might have been interpreted to be aspersions on American leaders who were in opposition to British policy. Hillsborough was charged by some of his ministerial colleagues with departing from the spirit of the minute which the ministers had framed on May 1,[73] and of referring to the Americans without using certain expressions "as kind and lenient as could be proposed by some of us . . . which were too evidently displeasing to his lordship."[74] Moreover, Grafton, Camden, Conway, and Granby favoured the inclusion of the duty on tea in the proposed repeal act, but were voted down.[75]

The episode just related has important bearing upon reaching an understanding of the Grafton administration's attitude toward American affairs. After Grafton succeeded to the post of the King's chief

---

[72] Earl of Hillsborough to the Governors in America, May 13, 1769, *New York Colonial Documents*, VIII, 164–5.

[73] The minute of the Council of May 1, in its fair draught after amendment, reads: "It is the unanimous opinion of the lords present to submit to His Majesty as their advice that no measure should be taken which can any way derogate from the legislative authority of Great Britain over the colonies. But the Secretary of State in his correspondence and conversation be permitted to state it as the opinion of the king's servants that it is by no means the intention of Administration nor do they think it expedient or for the interest of Great Britain or America to propose or consent to the laying any further taxes in America for the purpose of raising a revenue, and that it is at present their intention to propose in the next session of Parliament to take off the duties upon paper, glass, and colours, imported into America, upon consideration of such duties having been laid contrary to the true principles of commerce" (Grafton's *Autobiography*, p. 232).

[74] For this censure by Grafton see *ibid.*, p. 230. See also the correspondence between Camden and Hillsborough with reference to the letter on June 9, 1769, *ibid.*, pp. 231–2. As Grafton wrote years later in his *Autobiography*: "This unfortunate and unwarrantable letter, (to give it no harsher epithet) of Lord Hillsborough to the governors . . . was many years after the subject of discourse between Lord Camden and myself. This circular was calculated to do all mischief, when our real minute might have paved the way to some good. Besides many other objectionable points, how could Lord Hillsborough venture to assert in the first lines of this letter the word *unanimous?* For he could not have so soon forgotten that there was but one single voice for the measure more than was the number of those who were against it" (*ibid.*, pp. 233–4).

[75] *Ibid.*, pp. 229–30. Against these four were the Earl of Hillsborough, Lord North, Lord Rochford, Lord Gower, and Lord Weymouth. Sir Edward Hawke, also of the Council, was not present due to illness.

minister, he gradually lost favour in the eyes of George III, who not only disapproved of his private life[76] but began to feel that the Duke was not properly fulfilling his great responsibilities to the nation as head of the Ministry. It is not without significance that Hillsborough's circular letter of May 13 employed the same wording used by the King in proroguing Parliament on May 9—when referring to the "Factious and Seditious" views of certain men—phrasing deeply resented by Grafton and Camden because it seemed to indicate that they were not consulted in the preparation of the King's speech whereas the Hillsborough group probably was. Of equal significance is the fact that Grafton no longer had the confidence of a majority of the Cabinet Council, and was out-voted on an issue of national importance when he sought on May 1 to secure a complete repeal of all items in the Townshend Revenue Act. It will be recalled that the King, as early as February of that year, had decided that tea must remain as a dutiable article in any repeal act—a decision which would suggest that by that date he no longer was disposed to accept Grafton's advice, at least on American matters.[77]

Grafton, now isolated by the King, had also lost the support of Chatham, who deeply resented the inclusion of members of the Duke of Bedford group in the Ministry, as has been indicated. What made this hostility especially ominous for Grafton's future as a statesman was that by the summer of 1769 Chatham—who had recovered his mental balance and much of his physical strength—began to appear in public and openly manifested a "cold politeness" toward the man who had supported him so devotedly during most of the period of his incapacity.[78] Nor was this all. Grafton was attacked with almost unparalleled ferocity by the press. In the widely read and comment-provoking letters by "Junius" or "Philo Junius" that began to appear in the London *Public Advertiser* in January 1769, he was held up to bitter scorn.[79] *The North Briton*, even more savage in its attacks, is illustrative of the unbridled vindictiveness of the less responsible press at this period. In its number for September 30, 1769, a writer signing himself "G.D." asks rhetorically:

[76] Grafton became enamoured of a Mrs. Horton. In March 1769 he was divorced from the first Duchess of Grafton and about that time also broke with Mrs. Horton, but only to marry still another lady in June of that year. See *ibid.*, p. 235.

[77] "Memorandum by the King [February, 1769]," *Correspondence of George III* (Fortescue), II, 85.

[78] Grafton's *Autobiography*, p. 236.

[79] See especially "Junius'" letters addressed to the Duke of Grafton starting with Letter No. 8 of March 18, 1769, and continued by Letters No. 9, 11, 12, and 15, *The Letters of Junius* (ed. C. W. Everett, London, 1927), pp. 46–51, 53–63, 68–73. The problem of the identity of "Junius" has been considered in the preceding chapter.

> "Has not the Duke of Grafton, that compound of pride, peevishness, and obstinacy—the supposed [illegitimate] descendant of King Charles the Second, but probably the real descendant of some lacquey or chairman, as it is not likely that all King Charles's mistresses were true to his bed—whose ministry has been marked with more various, and more atrocious crimes, than any ministry . . . since the Revolution [of 1688]; who . . . I believe . . . has committed . . . such great enormities, that, if he escape the block, the national justice must certainly be defeated, and the hangman defrauded of his due—has not this nobleman, I say, so profligate . . . and so odious, been . . . lately dignified with the Order of the Garter?"[80]

The writer might also have added that upon the death of the Duke of Newcastle in 1768, Grafton had succeeded him as Chancellor of Cambridge University. But to call attention to this marked honour could not have served his purpose, since the article was an oblique attack upon the King for showing marked favour to the very man who had incurred "the public hatred."

It should be pointed out that, after his defeat in the Cabinet Council on May 1, 1769, Grafton (according to his *Autobiography*) resolved to withdraw from office "at the first favourable opportunity that offered." He was, however, particularly reluctant to resign at that time, when the populace was aroused over the seating of Luttrell as the member for Middlesex in the place of Wilkes and agitation in protest was rife, especially in the form of a campaign to flood the King and Parliament with petitions.[81] He felt that an offer to do so, "while the spirit of petitioning was so violent in many counties, would have been highly blameable . . . for the petitions were directed against the Administration and the Parliament which had supported us."[82] In fact these petitions, as well as the attacks upon him in the press, had the effect of strengthening his position at court, at least temporarily.

At this juncture the King had come to the conclusion that Lord Camden—on whom he had already turned his back after the latter's dispute with Lord Hillsborough over the circular letter of May 13

---

[80] In 1769 Grafton was made a Knight of the Garter. See *Correspondence of George III* (Fortescue), II, 117, and Grafton's *Autobiography*, pp. 241–2.

[81] See Chap. 7 for a fuller discussion of the petitions; see also George Rudé: *Wilkes and Liberty* . . . (Oxford, 1962), Chap. 7, "The Petitions of 1769," and Lucy Sutherland: *The City of London and the Opposition to Government, 1768–1774* (London, 1959), pp. 24–30.

[82] Grafton's *Autobiography*, pp. 234–5. The petitions called for a dissolution of Parliament and a general election, some of them claiming that the seating of Luttrell in the House, rather than Wilkes, invalidated all its business. See *Parliamentary History*, XVI, 630–41.

and who continued to hold views so contrary to those of most of his colleagues and of the Court—was a serious liability to the administration in the office of Lord Chancellor. Even before the meeting of Parliament early in the New Year, His Majesty conveyed to Grafton his desire that the incumbent be relieved of his high office, for he felt that "the Government would be too much lowered by the Great Seal appearing in opposition."[83] But Grafton, although unwilling to argue with the King against taking this step, begged that he "might be in no way instrumental in dismissing Lord Camden"—an understandable attitude in view of the fact that for years the two men, had been linked together as Chatham supporters.[84] George III had already made up his mind that Charles Yorke was the man whom he desired to displace Camden as Chancellor.

Yorke, the son of Philip Yorke, Earl of Hardwicke (one of the greatest Lord High Chancellors England ever had), was trained in the law and had made a great reputation in private practice and as member of the House of Commons. When the Marquess of Rockingham had formed his administration in 1765, the King had pressed Yorke to accept the chancellorship. Although desiring the honour, Yorke declined it under the conviction that Rockingham would not long remain in power; nevertheless, he had agreed reluctantly to become the Attorney General. When that administration did indeed fall the following year, Chatham's choice of Camden as Chancellor, rather than himself, had led the disappointed Yorke to resign the office he held and return to private life.[85]

After a series of prorogations, Parliament resumed its business on January 9, 1770. The King, on this occasion, delivered the speech from the throne in person. While the reply to the King was under consideration in the House of Lords, Chatham denounced the measures of the Ministry—both those relating to the treatment of Wilkes and those relating to the colonies.[86] He was supported by his faithful follower Lord Camden, who reportedly declared

> "that he had accepted the seals at first without any conditions; that he meant not, therefore, to be *trammelled* by his Majesty, I beg

[83] Grafton's *Autobiography*, pp. 245–6.

[84] *Ibid.*

[85] In the summer of 1767, when a move was made to restore Rockingham to power, the choice of Rockingham and his friends for the post of Chancellor was Yorke. For example, Newcastle, writing to the Duke on July 8, 1767, referred to the plan of "giving the Seals, as you always intended, to Mr. Charles Yorke . . ." (*A Narrative of the Changes in the Ministry, 1765–1767, told by the Duke of Newcastle in a Series of Letters to John White, M.P.* [ed. Mary Bateson, Royal Historical Society, London and New York, 1898], Camden Second Series, LIX, 113).

[86] *Parliamentary History*, XVI, 644*n*. and 647–53.

pardon, said he, by his ministers: that he had suffered himself to be so too long; that, for some time, he had beheld, with silent indignation, the arbitrary measures which were pursuing by the ministry; . . . that, however, he would do so no longer, but would openly and boldly speak his sentiments. That, as to the incapacitating vote [against Wilkes] . . . he considered it as a direct attack upon the first principles of the constitution . . . In a word, he accused the ministry . . . of having formed a conspiracy against the liberties of their country."[87]

Nevertheless, at the end of the debate on the reply to the King's speech, only 36 peers were prepared to vote against the minister who had framed it, while 203 supported the reply as framed.[88] As for Camden, he had burned his bridges behind him. After the debate he informed Grafton "that he was sensible that the Seal must be taken from him, though he had no intention to resign it"—thus challenging the King and the Ministry to dismiss a popular figure.[89] It was at once decided at St. James's to demand the return of the Great Seal to the King. However, before doing this it was necessary to secure a successor. The King commanded Grafton to approach Yorke, who at first appeared to be receptive, but who, after a day's reflection, refused the offer from Grafton and later from the King. Yet George had set his heart upon Yorke and, following a levee held shortly thereafter, called him into the royal closet and persuaded him to assume the great responsibility.[90] However Yorke was destined never to administer the Great Seal. It would appear that he could face neither the reproaches of Rockingham nor those of his own brother, the 2nd Earl of Hardwicke, to whom, according to Walpole, he had given his solemn promise not to accept the office.[91] On January 20, he died in great "agitation."[92]

---

[87] *Ibid.*, XVI, 644*n*.

[88] *Ibid.*, XVI, 665–6.

[89] Grafton's *Autobiography*, p. 246.

[90] *Ibid.*, pp. 247–8.

[91] Walpole says of Charles Yorke: "He had been with the King over night . . . and had again declined; but being pressed to reconsider, and returning in the morning, the King had so overwhelmed him with flatteries, entreaties, prayers, and at last with commands and threats, of never giving him the post if not accepted now, that the poor man sunk under the importunity, though he had given a solemn promise to his brother, Lord Hardwicke and Lord Rockingham, that he would not yield" *(Walpole: Memoirs of George III*, II, 218). See also *Parliamentary History*, XVI, 665, for the opprobrium both Temple and Shelburne were ready to attach to any successor to Camden.

[92] See Walpole, *op. cit.*, II, 219, and Grafton's *Autobiography*, 248–9, which indicates the belief that Yorke committed suicide. In this connection see Basil Williams: "The Eclipse of the Yorkes," Royal Historical Society *Transactions*, 3rd ser., II, 146–51.

The sudden demise of Yorke, who under the title of Baron Morden was to have held the Great Seal and presided in the House of Lords, was a heavy blow to Grafton. The Duke now tried in vain to persuade Attorney General William de Grey to accept the office. With the Ministry thus disorganized, not only by the dismissal of Camden but also by the resignation of Lord Granby,[93] Grafton determined that he could no longer carry on. He therefore begged the King to relieve him of his heavy responsibilities. His resignation was accepted on January 27, 1770.[94] In evaluating Grafton's role as the King's first minister, one must, while acknowledging his shortcomings, not fail to recognize what Sir William Anson called "the honesty of purpose and sense of public duty with which [he] was inspired."[95]

Even before the chief minister's resignation, George III had tended to lean heavily on Lord North, who had been showing a surprising capacity to lead the House of Commons in support of the royal views—on the problems created by John Wilkes as well as a number of other domestic issues—and who, in addition, stood for a policy of firmness toward the colonies. Now the King turned to North—the man destined to be his chief support during the next twelve years. On the 22nd of January, knowing full well that Grafton was about to retire, the King commissioned Lords Weymouth and Gower to wait upon the Chancellor of the Exchequer and press him "in the strongest Manner to accept the Office of the first Commissioner of the Treasury."[96] Writing to North the following morning,

---

[93] John Manners, Marquis of Granby, won high reputation in the war in Germany. At the time of his resignation he was a master general of Ordnance as well as a lieutenant general in the Army. In the Cabinet Council he had been inclined to vote with Camden as a follower of Chatham. The *Pitt Correspondence* (III, 384–97), covering the period January 7 to 17, 1770, shows the pressure brought upon Granby by the King to retain his post and, by the Chatham group, to quit it.

[94] Grafton's *Autobiography*, p. 250; Walpole (*op. cit.*, II, 221–5) goes into detail in dealing with the immediate background of Grafton's resignation.

[95] See the introduction to Grafton's *Autobiography*, p. xxxix.

[96] The King to North, January 23, 1770, *Correspondence of George III* (Fortescue), II, 126. It appears that Grafton himself had come to the conclusion that it was best for the King's service to have his chief minister in the House of Commons. At least, it was reported that the Duke two days after surrendering his office had "told a Great Personage, that 'as he found the great strength of the increasing Minority was in the Lower House, he thought it most natural, as well as advisable, to nominate a Premier there, in the scene of action; as he found by daily experience, that that was the fittest place for a Prime Minister, . . . as in the cases of Walpole, Pelham and Pitt; and that he saw it was impracticable to stem the tide of opposition from above. He assured the Great Personage at the same time that he would continue to support the measures of administration with all his interest, tho' he should decline taking the lead any longer, for the reason above mentioned'" (London advices, *Pennsylvania Gazette*, April 26, 1770).

George III presented his dilemma: "You must easily see that if You do not accept, I have no Peer at present in my Service that I would consent to place in the Duke of Grafton's employment. . . ."[97] As a result, two days after Grafton's resignation on January 27, North accepted the office of First Lord of the Treasury and with it the post of first minister to the King.

Son of the Earl of Guilford, whose title he was to inherit, Frederick North was a man of cultivation and a minister skilled in the field of public finance—doubtless as the result of the years spent at the Treasury in a minor position before he became Chancellor of the Exchequer and ultimately First Lord of the Treasury. As the King's first minister, he proved to be a loyal servant. Although he was an easy-going procrastinator, who sought to avoid conflict, he could, when called upon, ably defend whatever policy the government favoured and could do so without creating fresh antagonisms. In fact, in the years to follow, his capacity to win over certain members of the opposition gave the North administration a degree of stability that had been lacking in all the earlier administrations of the reign of George III. For example, Sir Fletcher Norton, an extremely capable lawyer—who had previously been successively Solicitor General and Attorney General and had been elected Speaker in the House of Commons upon the death of Sir John Cust on January 22, 1770—was to prove a source of strength to the chief minister. Moreover, early in the year following the death of Grenville in November 1770, the chief member of his party, the Earl of Suffolk, was appointed to the office of Lord Privy Seal, and later in the year to that of Secretary of State for the Southern Department. Also in 1771, Edward Thurlow, as Attorney General, and Alexander Wedderburn, as Solicitor General—both of them effective and hard-hitting in debate—joined the Ministry.

Along with the work of stabilizing the Ministry, there took place in the House of Commons in the early part of 1770 a series of heated debates over the continuing domestic issues of the King's civil list expenses and the unwillingness of the majority of members to recognize the right of Wilkes to a seat in the Commons, as has been discussed in the preceding chapter. On February 5 came the debate when Henry Herbert sought leave to bring in a bill to regulate the consequences of the expulsion of members, which was granted; the bill was subsequently presented on March 5. On February 16, the resolution on the state of the nation declaring that the expulsion

---

[97] *Correspondence of George III* (Fortescue), II, 126.

of John Wilkes was agreeable to the law of the land and authorized by the law and custom of Parliament was debated; it was so moved on the 19th. On March 7, George Grenville asked leave to bring in a bill for regulating the trials of controverted electors. Finally, on the 15th of the month, Sir Thomas Clavering introduced his motion respecting the remonstrance of the City of London and the petition to the King calling for the dissolution of Parliament and "the removal of Evil Ministers."[98] In these prolonged debates the ministerial majority held fast.

Concurrently, American affairs were also occupying the attention of Parliament, the paramount question being what action to take with respect to the Townshend Revenue Act. It was recognized by all that the decision reached, whatever it might be, would have vital bearing upon the maintenance of the integrity of the Empire. The Cabinet Council, by vote on May 1 of the preceding year, had committed itself to the repeal of most of the Townshend Act duties. With the stage now carefully set, the time had come for action. The first step was apparently to resort to a device which had successfully contributed to the repeal of the Stamp Act—the stirring up of English merchants and traders to petition for "the immediate Interposition of Parliament."[99]

The merchants and traders of London trading with North America had presented a petition to the House of Commons on February 6 asserting the distressed situation of their trade, "at present in an alarming state of suspension," and seeking "such Relief as to the House shall meet."[100] The petition was brought up for consideration

[98] See *Cavendish's Debates,* I, 435–75, 505–45, and *Journals of the House of Commons,* XXXII, 658, 707–8, 710 For the bill introduced on March 5, 1770, see *ibid.,* XXXII, 749.

[99] For the part played by Rockingham and Barlow Trecothick in securing petitions from the various towns in 1765–6, see Volume X of this series, pp. 382–3. For the debates on the repeal of the Stamp Act—based upon the assertion that "the Continuance of the said Act would be attended with many Inconveniences . . . greatly detrimental to the commercial Interests of these Kingdoms" (6 Geo. III, c. 11) and upon the fear of a colonial war involving the Bourbon powers—see Volume X, Chap. 17.

[100] *Journals of the House of Commons,* XXXII, 664–5. That the London merchants were not the promoters of the petition may be inferred from a letter that Franklin wrote to an unnamed correspondent on March 18, 1770, in which he said: "The merchants here were at length prevailed on to present a petition, but they moved slowly, and some of them, I thought, reluctantly . . . The Manufacturing towns absolutely refused to move at all; some pretending to be offended with our [that is, the colonials] attempting to manufacture for ourselves; others saying, that they had employment enough, and that our trade was of little importance to them, whether we continued or refused it" (*Writings of Benjamin Franklin* [ed. A. H. Smyth, 10 vols., New York, 1905–7], V, 253).

It should be noted that, also on March 5, William Bollan, as agent for Mason March 5, and immediately after its reading Lord North rose and commended the merits of its appeal to the favourable consideration of the House.

The chief minister's lengthy speech stressed, among other points, that most of the duties provided for in the Townshend Revenue Act were

> ". . . really founded upon such anti-commercial principles, that every member [of the House] will be of the same opinion this year that he was in the last; he will wish they had never been passed . . . I refer, Sir, to those duties which bear upon the manufactures of this country . . . We must, therefore, consider the taxes in this act of parliament . . . upon a ground properly British, properly commercial: paying no regard to the combinations [entered into by the Americans against paying the duties] . . . When the stamp act was first proposed, I saw nothing unjust, nothing uncommercial, nothing unreasonable in it—nothing but what Great Britain might fairly demand of her colonies. America took flame; America united against it. I still think, that if there had been a permanence of ministers—if there had been a union of Englishmen in the cause of England, that act would at this moment have been a subsisting act. . . ."

The Townshend duty upon tea, the speaker emphasized,

> "operated as a bounty to the Americans. . . . [Yet] America, not conceiving much dislike to the duty itself, but a great dislike to the preamble of this act, has laid it down as a rule, that England has no right to tax her, for the purpose of raising a revenue. . . . If the House will admit of that distinction, . . . the Americans will call all duties for the purpose of [raising] a revenue; we shall call them for the purpose of trade. . . . The next [American] associations will be against the acts of the fourth and the sixth of the King.[101] . . . In the course of the present year, many of the associations have declared that they will hold this language, until all these revenue acts are repealed. Therefore, Sir, upon my word, if we are to run after America in search of reconciliation, in this way, I do not know a single act of parliament that will remain. . . . [As to the evidence that] the exportation [from Great Britain to America] has been

sachusetts Bay, asked to be heard on behalf of that province's grievances against the Townshend measures as listed in a petition which he presented therewith, but which was tabled. See *Journals of the House of Commons*, XXXII, 745–6. For Bollan's account of the debates over the petition, together with a copy of it, see *The Bowdoin and Temple Papers*, Massachusetts Historical Society Collections, 6th ser., IX, 121–7.

[101] 4 Geo. III, c. 15, the so-called Sugar Act, and 6 Geo. III, C. 52, "An Act for repealing certain Duties . . . and for granting other Duties instead thereof," which, for example, reduced the duty on molasses from threepence to a penny a gallon.

much less than in the former year . . . it is certain that the exports to America, between Christmas 1767 and Christmas 1768, were £2,378,978; and that they only amounted, from 1768 to 1769, to £1,634,760. . . ."

But, Lord North contended, "the year before exceeded any of the three former years." Observing that "the duty upon tea fell still more short," he deduced that the Americans laid in a greater stock in 1769 "with a view to these combinations," but that it was likely that the combinations directed against the commerce of Great Britain would, in fact, be a burden upon the colonies. Citing the bad effects felt in Boston, where "the prices of some articles have risen eighty per cent; tea one hundred," he went on to say:

> "I am informed, that many ships are gone full freighted from England to America; and there is every reason to expect, that these associations will not long continue. . . . But we will not be driven to repeal, by any threats held out to us. I will trouble the House no longer; but move, Sir, 'That leave be given to bring in a bill to repeal so much of the said act as lays duties upon glass, red lead, white lead, painters' colours, paper, pasteboards, millboards, and scaleboards, of the produce or manufacture of Great Britain, imported into any of his Majesty's colonies in America.' "[102]

In the debate that followed—begun by Alderman Beckford, who declared himself "for a total repeal of the act"—the principal reply to North's speech was made by Thomas Pownall, former Governor of Massachusetts Bay. Presenting the point of view of the people of America toward the preamble of the Townshend Revenue Act, with its stated "purpose of raising a revenue for the support of civil government in that country," he declared: "The grievance is this—that by raising a revenue for the support of the civil government, you destroy the utility of their assemblies." Pownall also pointed out the American position, which held that British merchants had set the highest possible rate upon goods exported to America which they could get, to which British legislators had added a tax. Upholding the American view, he added: "I will call a price superadded to the highest price an arbitrary one." He therefore moved, as an amendment to North's motion, "that after the words 'Great Britain,' and before the word 'imported,' the words 'and upon tea' be inserted"—thus calling for virtual repeal of the entire act.[103]

Colonel Alexander Mackay then spoke. His remarks were en-

[102] *Cavendish's Debates,* I, 483–9.
[103] *Cavendish's Debates,* I, 489–92; see also *Parliamentary History,* XVI, 852–74.

lightening, as he had recently returned from Boston. Able, therefore, to report what he "saw and heard from men of the best understanding," he said:

> "I am fully persuaded, that if the right honourable gentleman who proposed the first duty had been aware of the true state of America, he never would have proposed the stamp act. . . . It is the sober conviction of the Americans, that you have no right to tax them. . . . They . . . adduce the authority of the first man of the law [Lord Camden], and the first man of the state [Lord Chatham]. . . . I have read letters from England, advising them to persevere [in their opposition], and they would be sure to obtain their ends. . . . The mischief has come all of a heap; particularly from our getting [the] better of the French, who were a tie upon them, and held them more to you than has been the case since."[104]

George Grenville, very naturally, felt called upon to challenge Mackay's statement about the passing of the Stamp Act. After the visitors' gallery had been cleared, he defended the Act, saying that before he proposed it he had sought the advice of

> "men of the first respectability, of the first trust. . . . Far from thinking the tax impracticable, some of the assemblies applied to me, by their agents, to collect this very tax. . . . Many, almost all, of those persons have since been active against it. Did they not, Sir, at the time, think the tax could be levied? Did they [not] apply to me to appoint their relations, their sons, their best friends, and afterwards desire to tear them in pieces? . . . Why, Sir, that opposition I own I did not foresee. If I had imagined, that great bodies of people would, in the space of a few months, have changed their opinions, I would not have proposed it. . . ."

Nevertheless, he added: "Nothing could ever induce me to tax America again, but the united consent of King, Lords, and Commons, supported by the united voice of the people of England. His Majesty's American subjects should be treated as mildly as the rest of his subjects." And, before ending his speech, Grenville stressed the point that it had become a favourite doctrine among those seeking to extend the power of the Crown to say: "Leave America to the Crown; do not let parliament intermeddle." For his part, he affirmed that to have the powers of the Crown extended beyond its true bounds was a dangerous doctrine, for "the parliament of England is, in all cases, supreme: I know no other law; I know no other rule."[105]

---

[104] *Cavendish's Debates,* I., 492–3.
[105] *Ibid.*, I. 494–6.

Clearly, uppermost in the minds of Grenville and other speakers was the fact that Great Britain no longer had an effective plan for "establishing a government in the colonies." Even Lord North admitted "that such a plan is wanted. . . . The want of a strong government is obvious; but to effect that, it requires great abilities, great experience, great knowledge."[106]

After other speakers had expressed themselves,[107] Governor Pownall's amendment to North's motion, in favour of including tea among the articles to be relieved of American import duties, was rejected by a vote of 204 to 142. Thereupon, leave was granted to bring in a bill for the repeal of certain portions of the Townshend Revenue Act as proposed by the King's first minister.[108] The bill was presented by North on March 9; on April 8, after its third reading, it was passed without debate and sent to the Lords, whose concurrence was secured by the 11th. On the following day it received the royal assent. The ostensible reason for the repeal, as stated in the act itself, was that "the said Duties, in so far as they affect the Produce and Manufacture of Great Britain, do in their Nature tend to the Prejudice and Discouragement thereof, and are therefore contrary to the true Principles of Commerce." But the true motive was as hidden in this repeal act as it had been in the statute repealing the Stamp Act.[109]

With the repeal of the specified duties in the Townshend Revenue Act disappeared one of the final hopes of ever securing from the colonies some definite contribution—over and beyond the indirect one they made in the way of trade—for the support of British imperial interests in North America. Thus ended the high hopes Charles Townshend had held in 1767 that by means of British-imposed port duties, to which the colonies long had been accustomed, a revenue

---

[106] *Ibid.*, I, 496.

[107] For views of Alderman Trecothick, General Conway, Welbore Ellis, Alexander Wedderburn, Lord Barrington, Rose Fuller, Sir William Meredith, and Colonel Barré see *ibid.*, I, 497–500.

[108] *Journals of the House of Commons*, XXXII, 751.

[109] *Ibid.*, XXXII, 769, 870, 890. The act is 10 Geo. III, c. 17. On April 7, 1770, William Strahan, the London printer and publisher, wrote to David Hall, publisher of the *Pennsylvania Gazette*, "that tho' the exports to Boston, New York, and Philadelphia have been considerably diminished during this Contest, those to Rhode Island, Quebec, and other Places, have proportionably increased, and that Goods there imported find their Way to the other Provinces by the Back Settlements, or by some Means or other." As evidence of this he also added: "The *Silence* of *all* our Manufacturers, is *Demonstration itself*" that they were suffering no great hardship. On July 7 of that year he wrote again to Hall that "the Stagnation of our Trade to the Colonies makes no sensible Difference to the British Manufacturers. They either find other Markets for their Goods, from whence they are transmitted to you; or else they are smuggled in upon you. . . ." For these letters see the *Pennsylvania Magazine of History and Biography*, LX, 477, 483.

could be secured without serious American protest whereby the colonial system of government could be made more efficient within the existing framework of the larger imperial system. It is true that the preamble of the Revenue Act of 1767 remained, as did the duty on tea. But these were in reality little more than symbols of what had once had been in the eyes of the government the bright promise of an effective plan for the administration of British North America.

Before turning to consider the situation in America after the repeal of most of the Townshend Act duties, it is important to take notice of another concession made to colonial demands—in this instance the demand for paper money to relieve the shortage of currency due to the drain of specie from many of the colonies. Ever since the parliamentary legislation of 1751 and 1764 prohibiting the colonies from issuing paper money as legal tender, the question of an adequate currency had been raised repeatedly in the colonial assemblies, especially in connection with funds to satisfy the demands of the Quartering Act.[110] In 1769 the London agents had become interested in this problem—which Benjamin Franklin had earlier had so much at heart—now under the leadership of Charles Garth, agent for South Carolina and member of Parliament. In fact, by March 1769 Garth had apparently induced the agents of all the colonies except New Hampshire and North Carolina to consider petitioning the House of Commons for the repeal of the Townshend Revenue Act "among other Reasons" on the ground that "in most of the Colonies the Current proportion of Silver Money is so exceeding small . . . that the Collecting the Silver in duties . . . disturbs and obstructs the common Course of Commerce. . . ." This petition, however, was never presented to the Commons, perhaps due to the influence of Benjamin Franklin, who as this juncture was advising against seeking repeal of the Currency Act of 1764.[111] Nevertheless, many of the colonial legislatures were anxious to see an end to the restrictions imposed upon them by this statute.

While the Currency Act of 1764 (4 George III, c. 34) was aimed particularly at the legal-tender currencies of Virginia and North Carolina, it was made to apply to all the colonies south of New Eng-

[110] See the brief treatment of this problem in connection with New York in Chapter 2 of this volume and in Chapter 3.

[111] For the petition see Garth Correspondence, March 12, 1769, *South Carolina Historical and Genealogical Magazine,* XXXI, 52–5. Franklin's argument was that the scarcity of money would add an additional incentive for maintaining the non-importation association and for inducing an effective domestic manufactures movement in colonies. See Franklin to Lord Kames, January 1, 1769, *Writings of Benjamin Franklin* (Smyth), V, 189.

land. But New England was already under currency regulation. In a measure aimed chiefly at preventing the Rhode Island Assembly from further depreciating the currency of that colony—as it had been doing by repeated issues of bills of credit without taking proper steps to redeem them—Parliament in 1751 had passed an act (24 George II, c. 53) to regulate and restrain paper bills of credit from becoming legal tender in Rhode Island, Connecticut, Massachusetts Bay, and New Hampshire.[112]

The law of 1764 was designed to place all the colonies on an equal basis with respect to their issues of legal tender. This did not mean that bills of credit could not be emitted. For example, after the passage of the New England Restraining Act, the four colonies continued to issue paper money in large quantities. But these new emissions were not designated as legal tender, were kept upon a "lawful money" basis, were redeemed as such, and were called in and sunk according to the provisions of the Act of 1751 and of the colonial law authorizing each issue of money.[113] That the colonies did not suffer from this restriction, but rather benefited, is indicated by the fact that specie, in the form of Spanish and Portuguese coins, was plentiful in 1768 in Massachusetts Bay, a "silver money colony." In fact, as was cited in Chapter V, Governor Bernard wrote to the Earl of Hillsborough from Boston in 1768 that he had it on good authority that the trade in that town found the abundance of specie an inconvenience.[114] According to Benjamin Franklin, Hillsborough told him that, when a rumour had spread that a movement was on foot to take off this restraint, New Englanders had petitioned to continued it.[115] Where specie was notably scarce in a colony with important commercial

---

[112] For the background of the New England Restraining Act see Volume III revised, in this series, pp. 68–73. A brief discussion of the Currency Act of 1764 is given in Volume X of this series, pp 174–6; for a full and illuminating account see J. P. Greene and R. J. Jellison: "The Currency Act of 1764 in Imperial-Colonial Relations, 1764–1776," *William and Mary Quarterly*, 3rd ser., XVIII, 485–518, and the recent, balanced and important study by J. A. Ernst: "Genesis of the Currency Act of 1764," *ibid.*, 3rd ser., XXII, 33–74; see also E. J. Ferguson: "Currency Finance: An Interpretation of Colonial Monetary Practices," *ibid.*, 3rd ser., X, 153–80, especially pp. 177–80. For the currency problem in the Southern Colonies see J. P. Greene: *The Quest for Power: The Lower Houses of Assembly in the Southern Royal Colonies, 1689–1776* (Chapel Hill, N.C., 1963), pp. 387–98.

[113] For a study of New England public finance covering the years from 1754 to 1775 see Volume X of this series, Chap. 3, "The Liquidation of Colonial War Debts: The New England Colonies." By lawful money is meant paper currency that could be exchanged for a Spanish milled dollar or piece of eight at the rate of six shillings of the bills for a dollar, in accordance with Queen Anne's proclamation.

[114] Bernard to Hillsborough, July 16, 1768, Shelburne Papers, 85:201–4.

[115] Franklin to Joseph Galloway, February 17, 1768, *Writings of Benjamin Franklin* (Smyth), V, 98.

interests, it may be inferred that Gresham's Law was operating, in other words, money of low exchange value drove out of circulation the money of high exchange value.

After the passing of the Currency Act of 1764 the only colony to persist in an attempt to continue to issue currency which would be expressly denominated a legal tender was North Carolina. In 1754 it had issued £40,000 in legal-tender bills; likewise, in 1760 and 1761 two further legal-tender issues were put into circulation. Although in 1764 £25,286 of these bills had been called in and burnt, £68,003 still remained in circulation despite the liquidation provisions in the Acts authorizing them.[116] In 1771 the amount of these bills of credit outstanding was £61,350. Although £60,000 in so-called debenture notes were emitted in that year to replace them, nevertheless, according to Governor Martin, in 1774 "a vast sum" of the legal-tender emission of 1754 was yet in circulation—but he thought these bills of "no value," since the Currency Act of 1764 the prop that had in a manner supported them had been removed.[117] As to the £60,000 in debenture bills referred to above, to improve their standing in 1774 the Assembly fruitlessly appointed a committee to petition the King that these bills might be permitted to be used as "a legal Tender in all payments. . . ."[118] There is no denying that no other colony so badly needed a currency adequate to support its credit and thereby to attract specie into the colony. What had added to the disrepute of the North Carolina legal-tender bills was that by 1771 "a great quantity of Counterfeit money," according to the Governor, "has entered into circulation, with the various [currency] emissions."[119] In 1769 the Earl of Hillsborough pointed the way to North Carolina's financial salvation. This was to follow the good example of the New England colonies and of the Province of Maryland in "Establishing a Paper Currency upon a just foundation of Credit without making it a legal Tender. . . ."[120]

Of all the colonies to the south of New England none had a more stable financial system than Maryland. This was largely due to the fact that the province had failed to participate in the Great War for

[116] For the report of the two joint treasurers of that year see C.O. 323:19, pp. 113–7.

[117] Governor Martin to the Earl of Dartmouth, April 2, 1774, *North Carolina Colonial Records,* IX, 960–1. See also Volume X of this series, p. 104.

[118] Journal of the Assembly, March 23, 1774, *North Carolina Colonial Records,* IX, 937.

[119] Governor Martin to the Earl of Hillsborough, August 15, 1771, *ibid.,* IX, 18. See also, for counterfeiting in general, Kenneth Scott: *Counterfeiting in Colonial America* (New York 1957).

[120] Hillsborough to Governor Tryon, March 1, 1769, *North Carolina Colonial Records,* VIII, 18.

the Empire, except by way of purely defensive measures, and thus had accumulated only an inconsequential war debt; also its currency had long been supported by a fund invested in Bank of England stock. By 1765 almost all its £90,000 issue of 1733 and £60,000 reissue of 1749 of bills of credit had been called in and sunk. Its circulating medium from that time on, although not technically a legal tender, served that purpose as it was based upon the ability of the London fund to maintain it on a steady lawful-money basis.[121] The four Middle colonies, New York, New Jersey, Pennsylvania, and the Three Lower Counties, likewise had consistently maintained the soundness of their bills of credit.[122] Yet, in the eyes of the Board of Trade and the Privy Council strict interpretation of the Currency Act of 1764 stood in the way of any colonial issue of currency that might violate the legal-tender provision of this statute. In 1769 the South Carolina Assembly passed "An Act for stamping and issuing the sum of one hundred and six thousand and five hundred pounds, . . . and for calling in and changing the paper Bills of Credit now outstanding, which are a legal tender by law in all payments"; another Act was passed in 1770 issuing £70,000 which could be used in payment of all duties and taxes. Both were disallowed. So likewise were two New York bills, one passed in 1769 and the other, an explanatory act, passed in 1770, both designated to set up a loan office by emitting £120,000 in bills of credit.[123]

Nevertheless, the feeling had grown that the New York colony should be allowed to pass such legislation as it had at heart for the proper expansion of its currency to meet the needs of the business community. This was doubtless the result of a petition from the New York Assembly, the strong representations of Governor Moore[124]

---

[121] For Maryland public finance for 1733 to 1765 see Volume X of this series, pp. 91–4. Massachusetts Bay, Connecticut, and New Hampshire also maintained the integrity of their respective currency by investment in England of reimbursement funds voted by Parliament.

[122] For the public finance of the four Middle colonies covering the period from 1754 to 1775 see Volume X of this series, Chap. 4. The highly creditable history of the bills of credit of New York, New Jersey, and Pennsylvania led the Earl of Hillsborough in 1768 to indicate that he himself would not oppose giving their bills of credit a legal-tender designation. See Benjamin Franklin to Joseph Galloway, February 17, 1768, *Writings of Benjamin Franklin* (Smyth), V, 98.

[123] See *Acts of the Privy Council, Col. Ser., 1766–1783,* pp. 215–16, 319–20, and the Board of Trade *Journal, 1768–1775,* pp. 167, 173, 211; see also the Earl of Hillsborough to Lieutenant Governor Colden, December 9, 1769, the same to the same, January 18, 1770, the same to the same February 17, 1770, *Cadwallader Colden Papers,* IX, 217, 219, 220–2.

[124] For Governor Moore's letter to Hillsborough of August 18, 1768, complaining of "the scarcity, not only of Silver but of every other Currency even paper . . . for some few Years past," see P.R.O., Treas. 1, Bundle 488, 191–2.

and Lieutenant Governor Colden supporting the New York currency acts, as well as the fact that New York bills of credit had never depreciated. Writing to Colden on February 17, 1770, the Earl of Hillsborough severely rebuked the Lieutenant Governor for giving his assent to the Act of 1769 and asserted that all His Majesty's servants felt it was against the true interests of the colony to have a currency "attended with any degree of legal Tender"; yet he added that he had reason to believe Parliament would enable the New York Assembly to carry into execution such an act as its members had in mind.[125] He was correct. On April 24, 1770 a petition from the London agent for New York, Robert Charles, was presented to the House of Commons that the Assembly be permitted to give a limited legal-tender character to a special emission of bills of credit which would be legal tender only at the provincial loan office or treasury in payment of duties laid by the colony, and the interest on which would help support the local government. A motion was passed that leave be given to bring in the necessary bill, and Jeremiah Dyson and Richard Jackson were given the task of drafting it.[126] Two days later a bill was presented by Dyson "to explain and amend" the Currency Act of 1764 so as to enable the government of New York to pass the appropriate legislation for "issuing upon Loan, Paper Bills of Credit" redeemable "as a legal Tender at the Loan Offices and Treasury of the said Colony." On May 8 the bill had its third reading and was sent up to the House of Lords for concurrence. It was returned to the Commons on May 16 without change and on the 19th received the King's approval.[127]

Had New Jersey and Pennsylvania also pressed for a concession similar to that made in favour of New York in 1770, it would undoubtedly have been granted, especially in view of their consistent record of financial responsibility. This was not done.[128] Yet Parlia-

---

[125] *Colden Papers,* IX, 220–2.

[126] Jackson, as a lawyer of high repute and legal advisor to the Board of Trade, had been obliged to advise the Lords Commissioners against permitting any violation of the Currency Act of 1764; at the same time he had long been a strong supporter of an expanded but stable colonial currency. For Jackson's proposals in 1754 for setting up a Pennsylvania "Provincial Bank," with power to issue notes payable "at sight," see his expanded views enclosed in a letter to Franklin under date of March 17, 1754, in *Letters and Papers of Benjamin Franklin and Richard Jackson, 1753–1785* (ed. Carl Van Doren, Philadelphia, 1947), pp. 42–54.

[127] See *Journals of the House of Commons,* XXXII, 895–6, 899, 908, 913, 919, 962, 979, 982. The statute is cited as 10 Geo. III, c. 35.

[128] Charles Garth, London agent for the South Carolina Commons House of Assembly, in writing to its committee of correspondence on May 14, 1770, stated: "I prepared a Clause for a general Amendment and Explanation of the Act [that is, a clause that would embrace all the colonies rather than simply New York] but which

ment manifestly had recognized the validity of the appeal of one colony that, at least for limited purposes, its colonial currency should have a legal-tender quality. The extension of this privilege to the rest of the colonies south of New England came three years later. Parliament may have delayed in taking this step in order to determine whether the New York act had been a proper one or whether exceptions could be made in the case of any one colony. The Ministry, apparently satisfied that the original step to relieve the colonies of a currency shortage was a sound one, initiated proceedings on April 28, 1773, to amend the Currency act of 1764. The amendment bill secured the royal approval on June 18.[129] Cited as 13 George III, c. 57, it carries the title "An Act to explain and amend an Act, made in the fourth Year of his present Majesty, intituled. An Act to prevent Paper Bills of Credit, hereafter to be issued in and of his Majesty's Colonies or Plantations in America from being declared to be a legal Tender in Payments of Money, and to prevent the legal Tender of such Bills as are now subsisting from being prolonged beyond the Periods limited for calling in and sinking the same." It provided that after September 1, 1773, all certificates, notes, bills, or debentures which should be voluntarily accepted by creditors of the public within any of the colonies of America, might be made a legal tender to the public treasurers in the colonies for the discharge of duties or taxes, but "in no other Case whatsoever," and ended with the proviso that nothing in the Act should alter the New England Currency Act passed in 1751.[130]

The importance of the statute of 1773 lies in its attempt to pave the way for the expansion of currency in the colonies most in need

---

was not permitted to be made part of the Bill: the Objection thereto was, that nothing was before the House to shew that other Colonies wished such a Power . . . and therefore before such a general Amendment was come into, it was fit to try the Effect and Operation of this particular Departure . . ." (*South Carolina Historical and Genealogical Magazine,* XXXI, 285–6). It should, however, be pointed out that in 1768 New Jersey passed an act to establish a land bank with the issue of £100,000 in bills of credit, but this legislation failed to win the approval of the Privy Council because the clause that the bills "should pass current" implied that they would be "a legal Tender in payments of Money" (*Acts of the Privy Council, Col. Ser., 1766–1783,* pp. 196–7). Then in November 1769 the Assembly passed a new act to issue £100,000 that would be accepted for the next twenty years at the loan office in payment of all debts. This also was rejected by the Privy Council, on June 6, 1770, as being in substance identical with a New York act disallowed on February 14 of that year. See *ibid.*

[129] For the motion to bring in the Currency Act of 1764 for amendment, the appointment of Bamber Gascoyne and Richard Jackson to frame an amendment bill, and the passage of the bill through both houses during May and June 1773, see the *Journals of the House of Commons,* XXXIV, 288, 302, 312, 325, 332, 342, 346, 348, 359, 373, 384.

[130] See *Statutes at Large,* VIII, p. 240.

of legal tender, while guarding against any efforts to liquidate with depreciated bills the private debts incurred in sterling or proclamation money. In this respect it, at least partially, met the colonial grievances against a lack of currency.[131] However, there is no means of determining what conciliatory effect this concession might have had, coming as late as it did in the mounting crisis.

---

[131] For the most recent study on colonial currency see J. M. Sosin: "Imperial Regulation of Colonial Paper Money, 1764–1773," *Pennsylvania Magazine*, LXXXVIII, 174–98.

More than one attempt was made in the course of the eighteenth century to provide the American colonies with an adequate and staple economy. A single currency for all the colonies would have been of great advantage in a variety of ways. But, as Professor C. M. Andrews has stressed (*Colonial Period of American History* [4 vols., New Haven, 1934–8], IV, 350–1), the government of England or later of Great Britain never took any steps in that direction. This may be considered one of its serious failures in statesmanship.

Henry McCulloh, with great experience in the Southern colonies as a collector of royal quit-rents, in 1765 submitted a document to the Rockingham Ministry which, while very critical of certain features of the Stamp Act, embodied a proposal to supply the needs of the American colonies with a currency in the form of orders on the British Exchequer to be placed in circulation to cover payment of the troops in America and other public expenses. These orders were to be received in payment of customs duties, stamp duties, quit-rents, and other obligations. McCulloh also advocated a "New Coinage for America" that would have a lawful or proclaimed money value. See J. P. Greene: "'A Dress of Horror'; Henry McCulloh's Objections to the Stamp Act," *Huntington Library Quarterly*, XXVI, 253–62, especially p. 259. That same year Benjamin Franklin submitted his plan for an American loan office. This was to involve the printing of some millions of bills of credit in England and the erection in each colony of a loan office that would issue these bills in proper security of double the value of the loan, which would run for ten years with interest of six per cent, with a provision that one-tenth of the total be paid back each year. These bills were to be a legal tender for all payments and counterfeiting them was to be made a felony carrying the death penalty. To maintain their lawful money value the loan offices would have a credit with the Bank of England and would therefore always be prepared to exchange these bills for sterling at the rate of £133.6.8 currency for £100 sterling. This wise plan, however, met with indifference on the part of the Ministry and the active hostility of colonials in that it would have put a large fund at the disposal of the government of Great Britain to support its American policy. For the plan see V. W. Crane: *Benjamin Franklin's Letters to the Press, 1758–1775*, pp. 25–30; for Thomas Pownall's incorporation of this proposal in his own plan see his *Administration of the Colonies* (4th edn., London, 1768), pp. 240–53.

CHAPTER IX

"The Universal Discontent and the Inflamed State of America"*

THE discontent on both sides of the Atlantic was not to be easily dissipated. Although the repeal of most of the Townshend program was to bring about the collapse of the non-importation movement and an apparent calm descended on the American scene, this was but a temporary lull before the storm. Actually, minor crises abounded during this period. One incident in particular loomed menacingly at the time—the so-called Boston Massacre. Another issue provoked many repercussions—the revival of fears over the possibility of an Anglican episcopate being established in the colonies. Thus there was ample indication that many colonials would remain adamant in their bitter opposition to policies

* This quotation is from a letter written by Dennys De Berdt, London agent for the Massachusetts Bay House of Representatives (1765–1770), concerning proposed steps to re-establish good relations between the American colonies and the mother country; see "Extract of a Letter, London, 1770," Colonial Society of Massachusetts *Transactions,* XIII, 455–61, especially p. 456. De Berdt was undoubtedly echoing the keynote opposition speech on the state of the nation made by Rockingham before the House of Lords on January 22, 1770, in which he spoke of "the present unhappy condition of affairs, and the universal discontent of the people," that "had grown upon us by degrees, from the moment of his Majesty's accession to the throne." Rockingham's thesis was that the new administration "had introduced a total change in the old system of English government" and "had adopted a maxim . . . 'That the royal prerogative alone was sufficient to support government, to whatever hands the administration should be committed.' " He further attacked the method by which the Peace of 1763 had been secured, the Cider Act, the debt on the King's Civil List, conditions in Ireland, American policy, and international relations, especially the approach to foreign affairs that had permitted the acquisition of Corsica by France, not to mention the "great invasion of the constitution" perpetrated by the administration. In short, Rockingham saw the country as injured "in all its relations and dependencies, foreign, provincial, and domestic." See *Parliamentary History,* XVI, 741–5.

of the home government and would not hesitate to use their influence to persuade others to share their discontent.

The Collapse of the Non-Importation Movement

The preceding chapter described the steps taken to enact a new law to repeal those parts of the Townshend Revenue Act which provided import duties on glass, paints, and paper. The bill which received the royal assent on April 12 retained the original enacting clause, so offensive to Americans, as well as the duty on tea.[1] News of its passage reached America early in May 1770.

The probable action of Parliament for amending Townshend's American Revenue Act had been accurately forecast in January and February of 1770 by London correspondents writing to their associates in the colonies.[2] The question now arose: what would be the effect of the partial repeal of the Act on the promoters of the non-importation agreements at the various American seaports? For, up to this point, the efficacy of the associations in cutting off imports from England had differed from colony to colony, depending upon several factors—especially the local enforcement measures.[3]

[1] O. M. Dickerson in his "Use Made of the Revenue from the Tax on Tea," *New England Quarterly*, XXXI, 232–43, paints in very dark colours the purposes that animated the British Ministry in providing for the collection in the colonies of duties on tea. After reviewing the payments made out of the American revenue, he concludes (p. 242) that "the total receipts from the tax on tea were used by Lord North and his associates for plain political patronage. No other reasonable explanation can be given for the selection of recipients of royal payments out of the American revenue, except they were 'friends of Administration' and could be used." Without attaching the sinister aims that Professor Dickerson attributes to Lord North and his fellow ministers, it is doubtless a fact that in the face of the American crisis they sought to give support to those they thought were "friends of Administration" who might help check the revolutionary tide.

[2] A correspondent, writing from London on February 7, 1770, referred to a meeting of the London merchants held on the 1st, which formed a committee that, on the 2nd, framed a petition to Parliament praying for redress and, on the 6th, presented it. The writer went on to state that on the 5th he "and four others were deputed to wait upon Lord Hillsborough and Lord North. . . . Lord North was not at home, but Lord Hillsborough answered for himself and Lord North, that they would both oppose the Repeal of Tea, to the utmost of their Interest" (*Pennsylvania Gazette*, April 26, 1770). For other letters from London having to do with the American Revenue Act covering the period January 18 to February 22, 1770, see *ibid.*

[3] For an excellent account of "the force of this newly erected power beyond that of the established powers of government"—that is, of the enforcement committees—particularly in Massachusetts Bay, see Thomas Hutchinson's *History of the Colony and Province of Massachusetts-Bay* (ed. L. S. Mayo, 3 vols., Cambridge, Mass., 1936), III, 184–8 and 191–4, especially the asterisk footnote on p. 188. In the trend toward a "uniformity of measures" the weapons of enforcement were those of boycott and publicizing violators in the press. In the case of John Mein, the Boston bookseller

A speculative estimate of the comparative effectiveness of the non-importation agreements may be gained from a survey of the custom-house books for 1767 to 1769 at the various English ports. The chart gives the following picture of the value of British exports to the respective North American colonies:

TO:	*From 1767 to 1768*	*From 1768 to 1769*
Canada	£ 110,000	£ 174,000
Carolina	289,000	306,000
Florida	32,000	29,000
Georgia	56,000	58,000
Hudson Bay	5,000	4,000
New-England	419,000	207,000
Newfoundland	46,000	64,000
New-Providence	6,000	6,000
New-York	482,000	74,000
Nova-Scotia	19,000	19,000
Pennsylvania	432,000	199,000
Virginia and Maryland	475,000	488,000
	£2,371,000	£1,628,000[4]

To the extent that this picture is accurate, it would appear that Canada, South Carolina, Georgia, Newfoundland, and the two great tobacco colonies, Virginia and Maryland, actually increased their imports in 1769; on the other hand, those of East and West Florida, Hudson Bay, New England, New York, and Pennsylvania decreased, either slightly or drastically, as in the cases of New York, New England, and Pennsylvania. But it is doubtful whether such conclusions are valid, since the associations did not preclude the landing of cargoes that had been ordered prior to the effective dates of the agreements.[5]

who dared to oppose non-importation, however, he was virtually run out of town. See *ibid.*, III, 186–7. For the similar case of William Henry Drayton in Charleston, see A. M. Schlesinger's *Colonial Merchants and the American Revolution, 1763–1776* (New York, 1918), pp. 202–6.

[4] *Pennsylvania Gazette,* May 24, 1770. For other tables giving import-export figures for this period see David Macpherson: *Annals of Commerce* (Edinburgh, 1805); see also U. S. Bureau of Census: *Historical Statistics of the United States* (Washington, D.C., 1960), pp. 757–61.

[5] The most extended account of the effort to support the local non-importation agreement that has come to the attention of the writer has to do with the case of *The Good Intent,* which arrived in Annapolis, Maryland, early in 1770 with goods ordered by a number of Maryland merchants, so it was claimed, before the association was formed. As a result of the findings of the committee on enforcement, the vessel returned to England toward the latter part of the month without delivering any of its cargo. The case was presented to the public in a pamphlet which appeared in Annapolis that same year entitled *The Proceedings of the Committee Appointed to*

With at least partial repeal a foregone conclusion by the beginning of 1770, many English merchants who had loaded their ships sent them to the intended destinations. One, writing from London on March 26, 1770, to a New York friend, declared that "large Quantities of Goods have been lately shipped, and are now daily shipping to Virginia, Maryland, Rhode-Island, Boston, Montreal, which will doubtless circulate all through the Colonies. . . ."[6] The reception of these ships varied from colony to colony according to the stand taken by colonials on upholding the non-importation agreements. Except for Boston, the trading ports faced with mixed feelings the problem of accepting partial repeal as a signal to resume free trade; for pressures were mounting both for and against such a move as long as duties remained on tea and other imports not listed in the Townshend Revenue Act. For example, after the news of the repeal had reached America, the *Cambridge* arrived at Baltimore, Maryland, on the 24th of May with a cargo from Liverpool. A committee of inspectors for the non-importation association was willing to permit the landing of goods not forbidden by the Maryland agreement, but decided that the remainder of the cargo must be returned to England. As a result, the owner of the cargo, a Mr. James Ward of Liverpool, determined to land nothing and sailed for home.[7] On the other hand, early that same month at Newport, Rhode Island, a number of merchants—or so it was charged by the local committee—began importing English and East India goods in defiance of the agreement entered into the preceding October.[8]

The defection in Rhode Island was denounced at a meeting on May 23 of Philadelphia tradesmen and artisans, who expressed an "abhorrence" of the conduct of the Newport merchants and unanimously resolved to have "no Dealings, traffick or commerce with them."[9] This action was followed on May 28 by a similar denunciation on the part of Boston merchants and other townsmen.[10] On the 31st, at a meeting held in New York City, the Newport merchants were declared to be "enemies to the liberties of North-America" who were to be treated as such unless they "returned to their duty."[11]

examine into the Importation of Goods, [by] the Brigantine GOOD INTENT, Capt. Errington, from London, in February 1770. This is reprinted in the *Maryland Historical Magazine,* III, 141–57, 240–56, 342–63.

[6] *Pennsylvania Gazette,* May 24, 1770.

[7] *Providence Gazette,* June 9–16, 1770.

[8] *Boston Evening-Post,* May 28, 1770.

[9] *Pennsylvania Chronicle,* May 28, 1770; see also the *Pennsylvania Gazette,* May 24, 1770.

[10] *Boston Evening-Post,* May 28, 1770.

[11] *Providence Gazette,* June 9–16, 1770, and *New-York Gazette: or, the Weekly Post-Boy,* June 4, 1770.

It should be added that many other trading towns followed the example of these three leading ports. with Charleston taking a particularly strong stand. as had its general committee as early as April in a circular letter calling for strict adherence to non-importation.[12]

In the midst of these recriminations the New York merchants proposed that a congress be held at Norwalk, Connecticut, to consider the whole question of non-importation. Their letter was read at a meeting of the Boston associators on June 7. The merchants, after considering the proposal, passed a "unanimous" vote to adhere to their non-importation agreement and refused to participate in the congress.[13] This, too, was the decision of the Philadelphia merchants.[14] Since the Providence merchants had agreed to attend the congress only under condition that Boston would be represented, on June 11 they decided to adhere to their earlier agreement and likewise refrain from supporting the Norwalk meeting.[15] The Connecticut merchants followed suit.[16] As a result of these decisions plans for the congress were dropped.

Nevertheless, by the summer of 1770 it was apparent that the non-importation movement was breaking down. By then Georgia merchants were freely importing all manner of commodities from Great Britain—exclusive of tea—much to the anger of the Charleston Sons of Liberty.[17] The merchants of Portsmouth, New Hampshire, who had never entered into a non-importation agreement, also began importing freely. This led the Boston trade on June 7 to vote to put Portsmouth in the same category with Newport and to cease dealing with its merchants.[18] But the great break came from New York City after the plan for a congress on non-importation had failed. Its inhabitants, meeting on June 11, decided to query the signatories to the agreement on whether they would agree to the importation of all articles except tea or preferred to continue the earlier rigid combination. The votes of a majority appeared to favour modification.[19] When the accuracy of this poll was challenged by the New York Sons of Liberty, a second vote was taken on July 7; this again showed that a majority supported importation, except for tea. Upon

[12] Supplement to the *Pennsylvania Gazette,* May 24, 1770.
[13] *Boston Evening-Post,* June 11, 1770.
[14] *Pennsylvania Gazette,* June 7, 1770.
[15] *Providence Gazette,* June 9–16, 1770.
[16] *Boston Gazette,* July 2, 1770, and *Connecticut Journal,* August 3, 1770.
[17] *South-Carolina Gazette,* June 28, 1770.
[18] *Boston Evening-Post,* May 28 and June 11, 1770.
[19] *New-York Gazette; and the Weekly Mercury,* June 18, 1770.

the basis of this vote orders were sent to England for the goods.[20] This was done despite the stand taken by the leader of the radicals, Isaac Sears, that any man who would import before the other colonies had agreed to do so "would lose his life in the attempt."[21] The New York action was denounced and the conduct of the merchants was stigmatized in bitter terms by most of the trading towns along the Atlantic seaboard.[22] For example, in a meeting held at the Charleston Liberty Tree on August 22, the South Carolina Sons of Liberty voted—"the Common Cause of America having been most basely and traitorously deserted by a Number of Merchants, Traders and others of the City of New-York"—to break off all relations with New York as a mark of "our Detestation of the late abominable Measure."[23] Nevertheless, the New York action proved to be a fatal blow to non-importation. In "A Letter from a Merchant in London," published in the June 14 issue of the *Pennsylvania Gazette,* the Boston merchants were accused of having imported from England since the preceding Christmas goods to the value of £150,000. The feeling grew among Philadelphia merchants that they were being duped by those of other towns who were quietly violating their commitments.[24] As a result a number of importers in the Quaker

---

[20] One of the most circumstantial accounts of the repudiation of the earlier agreement is found in a letter written by Alexander Colden to Anthony Todd of London, July 11, 1770, *New York Colonial Documents,* VIII, 218–20.

[21] *Ibid.*

[22] In this connection the student should consult the detailed account of the changing attitude toward non-importation by the people of the trading towns, in the north and the south, by C. M. Andrews in his "The Boston Merchants and the Non-Importation Movement," Colonial Society of Massachusetts *Publications,* XIX, 245–59; see also A. M. Schlesinger: *Colonial Merchants,* pp. 209–36, and R. L. Brunhouse: "The Effect of the Townshend Acts in Pennsylvania," *Pennsylvania Magazine of History and Biography,* LIV, 355–73.

[23] *Boston Evening-Post,* October 8, 1770.

[24] A report in the *Boston Gazette* of July 9, 1770, under a Philadelphia June 28 date-line, stated that a pamphlet had appeared in that city entitled "An Account of the late importations etc. into the Port of Boston" which, the newspapers charged, was plainly the work of "the detestable Board of [Customs] Commissioners . . . ; it is printed by Mein & Fleming, printers in Boston, and is filled with a number of the most gross lies and contradictions, evidently calculated to blacken the character of the people of Boston." What was referred to, undoubtedly, was John Mein's pamphlet *A State of Importations from Great-Britain into the Port of Boston* . . . (Boston, 1769, reprinted in 1770 to bring the list up to January 1770 and again to June 1770), which disclosed that John Hancock and other merchants of Boston and Salem were themselves evading the non-importation agreements. For Mein's influence on the collapse of the non-importation movement as the result of this pamphlet and of the newspaper war carried on in the *Boston Chronicle,* which he published with John Fleming, see C. M. Andrews: "Boston Merchants . . . ," Colonial Society of Massachusetts *Transactions,* XIX, 227–30, A. M. Schlesinger: "Propaganda and the Boston Press, 1767–1770," *ibid.,* XXXII, 411–16, J. E. Alden: "John Mein,

City decided to withdraw from the agreement. In line with this, at a meeting called in September they voted to modify their agreement to conform to the decision of the New York group; they also agreed that there was no necessity to consult the other colonies in taking this action. Nevertheless, the Philadelphia committee sent a circular letter to the committees of other ports to relate the circumstances of the breach.[25] By the end of 1770 goods from England, except those carrying a duty, were flowing freely into the port of Philadelphia.

In the light of the attitude of New York and Philadelphia, the Boston merchants were now squarely faced with a serious choice. They—who, a year earlier, on October 17, 1769, had voted to adhere to the agreement, but had been forced to retract a subsequent compromise to import only on a conditional basis[26]—were made to realize that they could not hold out for a continuation of non-importation. A notice was therefore sent out calling the merchants and other inhabitants to attend a meeting to be held on September 13. Some 2,000 people reportedly were present on that date, among them "a great number of the principal and most wealthy merchants." They there agreed to write a letter to the Philadelphia merchants proposing a meeting of committees from the neighbouring colonies "to consider the most effectual way to strengthen and confirm the happy union that now subsists"; they also agreed to abide by the non-importation agreement until the committees could meet and report

---

Scourge of Patriots," *ibid.*, XXXIV, 571–99, and Schlesinger's *Prelude to Independence, The Newspaper War on Great Britain, 1764–1776* (New York, 1958), pp. 104–8.

The feeling that Boston was not playing fair with the other ports was also expressed in a letter written from London to New York in which the writer declared: "It is amazing to me that the Gentlemen of New York should be so imposed upon by the Bostonians." For, he alleged, "it is true that goods to the value of about £15,000 were returned, but it is equally true, that £100,000 and more were sent out," and, he further stated, when the packages sent back were opened at the custom house, some contained "a ham or two, others straw, old mats, stones, &." See *Boston Evening-Post*, October 1, 1770.

It must be noted also that confused reports were circulated intermittently concerning smuggling of dutiable imports and trade in them. It seems logical to assume that the well-established smuggling trade in New England, especially in Rhode Island and Massachusetts Bay, did not cease with the non-importation agreements. Nor, under the terms of those agreements signed by the Maryland and Albany merchants, were certain importations hindered from coming in for use in the Indian trade. See Schlesinger's *Colonial Merchants*, Chaps. 4 and 5, especially pp. 187–196, 207, 209.

[25] For the above letter see *Pennsylvania Gazette*, October 4, 1770.

[26] For the resolutions of October 17 endorsed by a majority of the Boston merchants see *Boston Evening-Post*, November 20. It may be noted that those few who refused to continue the association had their names published in the press; for this list of violators see *ibid.*, December 11, 1769. For the news of the action of the New York and Philadelphia merchants in sending orders for conditional shipment of goods, which persuaded the Boston merchants to do the same, see *ibid.*, November 20, 1769.

what alterations might be deemed necessary.[27] But the plan for this meeting collapsed, as had the New York merchants' plan for a congress. As a result, on October 12, Boston decided to follow New York and Philadelphia.[28] Goods from storage began to be offered for sale on the Boston market and new imports also began to appear.[29] Non-importation was at an end in New England and the Middle colonies.

The Southern colonies—which had been slower to act—revoked their agreements. At a gathering in Baltimore on October 5 the merchants proposed that a general meeting of the trade be held in Annapolis on the 25th to consider the question of continuing the association, with the proviso that if such a meeting did not take place the merchants could look upon the agreement as dissolved and could resume the general importation of goods, with the exception of tea. Although the meeting was duly held and resolutions were passed in favour of upholding the earlier covenant, the Baltimore merchants informed the gathering that "they were determined to depart from the Non-importation Agreement" and to import from Great Britain any article that did not carry a duty. Nor were they later deterred by the threat of boycott issued at the Annapolis gathering.[30] At Charleston, where the influence of the Sons of Liberty had been extremely powerful, Henry Laurens presided over a meeting held on December 13 at the Liberty Tree. It was there agreed to follow the example of the northern towns by permitting free importation of all commodities but tea. Soon afterwards imported goods that had been stored were released for sale in Charleston.[31]

The collapse of the colonial non-importation movement was not surprising. Those who favoured continuance of the agreements were, by and large, political idealists who had determined to force the Parliament of Great Britain to a total repeal of the Townshend Revenue Act together with all other parliamentary acts laying duties on American imports. On their side, too, were the Sons of Liberty and certain members of the non-mercantile and non-propertied populace

---

[27] *Boston Gazette,* September 17, 1770.

[28] *Massachusetts Gazette and Post-Boy,* October 13, 1770.

[29] The *Boston Evening-Post* of November 26, 1770, ran an advertisement for J. Russell offering "a great variety of English goods"; in the December 3 issue Joseph Peirce gave notice that he could supply not only English but East India fabrics, while Colborn Barrell offered the public painter's colours. In the January 7, 1771, issue Gilbert Deblois announced the receipt of a fresh and large assortment of merchandise "just imported from London." Among items advertised were Bohea tea and choice Souchong and Hyson teas.

[30] See *Pennsylvania Gazette,* October 18 and November 8, 1770.

[31] *South-Carolina Gazette,* December 13 and 27, 1770; see also Richard Walsh: *Charleston's Sons of Liberty . . .* (Columbia, S.C., 1959), pp. 49–55.

who had been stirred up by these zealots. Arrayed against them, however, were the powerful merchant groups whose living depended upon importing. With the repeal of most of the import duties levied by the Act, these commercial men, feeling that a major concession had been won, were convinced that America could live and prosper without using tea—or, as a last resort, could pay the duty on this item. They also were determined to mend their decaying business affairs and recoup their fortunes. According to a London report dated January 18, orders from America for goods amounting to £1,500,000 sterling were being held in that port, with the stipulation that the articles were not to be shipped until the duties, including those on tea, were taken off.[32] But, as has been stressed above, with the news of partial repeal, waves, which ultimately became a flood, of merchandise began moving toward the colonial seaports to help weaken the wavering resolves of the merchants.

The resumption of normal trade with the mother country brought the earlier trend toward unified colonial action to a state of suspended animation as certain colonies began to voice mutual recriminations for failure to maintain the agreements.[33] Each group that had entered into combinations had been influenced, very naturally, by specific local needs and desires as well as by the degree of success with which those who had no stake in trade and commerce had been able to stir up their communities and impose their will upon the merchants. The movement, therefore, only partly achieved its objective. As the late Charles M. Andrews pointed out, while acknowledging that non-importation had helped to bring about the partial repeal of the Townshend Act:

> "It failed to effect the repeal of the acts of 1764, 1765, and 1766 and the removal of the duty on tea, and it accomplished nothing whatever in the effort to obtain British recognition of the constitutional claims of the colonies. . . . The . . . movement began as a merchant's device wherewith to obtain a redress of trade grievances; it ended as an instrument in the hands of political agitators and radicals for the enforcement of their claims of constitutional liberty and freedom."[34]

Yet the results of the North American agitation against the payment of duties for revenue must be regarded as a victory for the

[32] *Boston Gazette,* April 16, 1770.

[33] *Boston Gazette,* July 30, 1770; *New-York Gazette; and the Weekly Mercury,* August 27 and October 1, 1770. For Hutchinson's report of the anger of Bostonians against New Yorkers, see Hutchinson Correspondence, Massachusetts Archives 26:523.

[34] See C. M. Andrews: "Boston Merchants and the Non-Importation Movement," *op. cit.,* XIX, 256–9; see also A. M. Schlesinger: *Colonial Merchants,* pp. 236–9.

colonials. It is true that the duty on tea remained and that this beverage was a favourite among colonials; nevertheless, Americans were ready to demonstrate that it was not essential to their well-being. For many who did not choose to smuggle, or to encourage smuggling, took steps to stop the use of tea. Furthermore, colonial leaders learned from this, as well as the Stamp Act experience, that non-importation could be an effective weapon for bringing pressure to bear upon the government in London, especially if means could be found to form a solidly united association among all the colonies.

What was becoming clear in 1770 was the growing evidence that Americans were suffering much more severely from non-importation than was the British public. Markets elsewhere had opened up for British manufacturers, but the colonial effort to supply domestic manufactures could not begin to meet American demands for certain commodities long directly imported or trans-shipped from the British Isles. Doubtless even the radical agitator in the colonies was by no means infatuated with paying scarcity prices for items of merchandise needed by him and his family. With British goods once again appearing for sale, however, he could pick up his crusade against regulation by the government of Great Britain, as manifested by the customs service, the presence of regular troops in Boston, and the many restrictions under which colonials laboured—for example, those on issuing bills of credit. In addition, he could focus public attention upon such an issue as the desire of many supporters of the Church of England to have a bishop in America.

There can be no doubt that the incitement of crowds by popular leaders was breeding an ineradicable hatred of the British government among the common people. Equally demonstrable is the part of the newspapers in 1770 in fostering this sentiment by opening their columns to anonymous letters to the editor, by reprinting from the British press such diatribes as those signed by "Junius," and by publishing innumerable letters to American correspondents, written by enemies of the government in England, calling upon the colonials to resist to the end what were held to be the despotic designs of the Ministry.[35] Especially susceptible to these influences were the inhabitants of the leading commercial cities. To them, the ministerial

[35] For an earlier mention of the "Junius" letters see Chap. 7 of this volume; for the propaganda influence of the press see A. M. Schlesinger's *Prelude to Independence;* see also Philip Davidson: *Propaganda and the American Revolution, 1763–1783* (Chapel Hill, N.C., 1941), B. I. Granger: *Political Satire in the American Revolution, 1763–1783* (Ithaca, N.Y., 1960), and C. A. Duniway: *The Development of Freedom of the Press in Massachusetts* (Cambridge, Mass., 1906), Harvard Historical *Studies,* XII.

majority in Parliament were men who had become pliant tools of those in power in the mother country and who were now seeking to enslave the colonials; to them, the King was a prisoner of these powerful men as they pursued their nefarious designs. It does not matter, in the light of what developed, whether these views were true or false. What is important to bear in mind is that the people believed they were true and acted according to these beliefs. Nowhere was this attitude more pronounced than in the town of Boston.

The "Boston Massacre"

Boston had been the site of the greatest violence against British authority during the Stamp Act crisis. Again, in 1768, tragedy had been narrowly averted there in the *Liberty* affair (as was described in Chapter V). The metropolis continued to be the nerve centre of the revolutionary movement down to the outbreak of open hostilities. There were such incidents as the attack upon John Mein, the Loyalist publisher, after the Pope's Day parade of 1769, which resulted in calling troops to arms.[36] Then came the affair centring on a signed advertisement that James Otis had inserted in the *Boston Gazette* of September 4, 1769. In it he denounced four of the Customs Commissioners for having represented North Americans "as *traitors* and *rebels*, and in a general combination to revolt from Great Britain," and called upon all leading British officials concerned in American affairs to pay no regard to such abusive representations, as being no more worthy of credit than those reports sent to them by Governor Bernard. The next evening Otis went to the British Coffee House, where British army, navy, and revenue officers were accustomed to gather. What his purpose was in going there is not clear. But in the heated altercation that ensued between him and Customs Commissioner John Robinson, blows were exchanged with canes. Others took sides. After the scuffle was over, Otis, wounded in the head and bleeding, was helped home.[37] The account of the

---

[36] See Thomas Hutchinson: *History of Massachusetts-Bay* (3 vols., Cambridge, Mass., 1936), III, 186.

[37] See the account in the *Boston Evening-Post*, September 11, 1769. William Tudor, in his *Life of James Otis of Massachusetts* (Boston, 1823), gives an extended account of the incident and its background (pp. 359–66) in which he treats fairly the charges that the blow on the head received by Otis at this time was responsible for his later insanity. Tudor points out that his "disposition was so ardent, and his mind so excitable, that its natural tendency, under aggravating circumstances, was to insanity." See also John Cary: *Joseph Warren . . .* (Urbana, Ill., 1961), p. 90.

fight as printed in the newspapers[38] did little to eradicate hostility against British officials, already unwelcome guests of the town.

Early in 1770 another incident occurred in Boston which showed the temper of its people and the susceptibility of the mob to action. On February 22 a band of young boys set up on a pole "a large wooden hand, with a Board . . . on which were painted the figures of four importers who had violated the merchants' agreement." This took place in front of the home of Theophilus Lillie, who was held to be one of the violators. A near neighbour, one Ebenezer Richardson, sought in vain to get some carters to knock down the sign. This action diverted upon him the attention of the crowd which had forgathered. With their encouragement the boys followed Richardson, accusing him of being an informer for the customs service and pelting his house with various handy objects. When they succeeded in breaking the windows, Richardson fired into the crowd, fatally wounding an eleven-year-old boy, Christopher Snider. Someone rang the bell of the nearby church and an even larger crowd assembled. The door of the house was forced and Richardson and a companion, George Wilmot, were seized and carried to Faneuil Hall. There, in the presence of a thousand people, a tragedy was narrowly averted when, after taking testimony, a justice of the peace committed the captives to gaol. The funeral of the child some days later became a demonstration out of all proportion to the boy's station in life, and was attended by a vast concourse of people eager to show their sympathy.[39]

The inhabitants of Boston had an intense aversion not only to custom-house informers but especially to the two regiments of regular soldiers cantoned in their midst since 1768. Although the troops were under the strictest orders to be on their good conduct and were unarmed when off duty, they were, as might have been anticipated under the circumstances, constantly subjected to harassment, particularly, it so happened, from the men who manned the rope-walks where ship tackle was made.[40] The soldiers, there

[38] See, for example, *Boston Evening-Post,* September 11, 1769, or John Gridley's report in the *Boston Chronicle,* September 14–18, 1769.

[39] *Boston Evening-Post*, February 26, 1770; see also Thomas Hutchinson: *History of Massachusetts Bay* (Mayo edn.), III, 193–4, and A. M. Schlesinger: *Colonial Merchants,* pp. 179–80.

[40] "On Saturday, the 3rd of March, lieutenant-colonel Carr, the commanding officer of the 29th regiment, made complaint in a letter to the lieutenant-governor of the frequent abuses offered to his men, and of the very insolent, provoking language given to some of them on that day, by certain journeymen ropemakers, which had brought on a fray, in which one of the soldiers was very dangerously wounded"

is no doubt, had come to return their dislike in full measure.[41]

On the evening of March 5 the townsmen and the troops met in a clash that has gone down in history as the Boston Massacre. It began—if the account of March 12, 1770, a very circumstantial version in the *Boston Evening-Post,* is correct—with a scuffle between a soldier and some young men of the town in an alley leading off of Cornhill Street to Murray's barracks. Other soldiers gathered and moved on to King Street, where a detachment of regulars under the command of Captain Thomas Preston had arrived to support the guard posted in front of the Custom House. When the troops attempted to push back the crowd that had assembled there and was milling about, threatening the sentry, things got out of hand. The newspapers asserted that Preston ordered the troops to fire.[42]

(Thomas Hutchinson: *op. cit.*, III, 195). Councilman James Bowdoin wrote to William Bollan on March 27 concerning past abuses by the soldiers, and spoke of the quarrel between the men of the 29th regiment and the ropemakers: "In the contest the soldiers were worsted, and this reflecting, as they thought, on [the] honor of the regiment, there was a gen[l] combination among them to take vengeance on the town indiscriminately" (Massachusetts Historical Society *Collections,* 6th ser., IX, 167–8).

[41] The most detailed accounts of the growing animosity between the citizens of Boston and the British regular soldiers is contained in the so-called "Journal of the Times," sometimes headed "Journal of Occurrences," which, first printed in the *New-York Journal* from communications sent from Boston, was reprinted in other papers, such as the *Boston Evening-Post,* the last of which appeared in this paper on December 18, 1769. These contributions have been gathered together and edited by O. M. Dickerson in his *Boston Under Military Rule, 1768–69 . . .* (Boston, 1936). For comment upon these despatches as part of a propaganda offensive, see A. M. Schlesinger: *Prelude to Independence,* pp. 100–3. As the Rev. Andrew Eliot wrote to Thomas Hollis in England on June 28, 1770, on the tragedy of March 5: "There had been such an animosity between the inhabitants and the soldiery some time before this tragedy, that I greatly feared the event" (Massachusetts Historical Society *Collections,* 4th ser., IV, 451).

[42] *Boston Gazette, and Country Journal,* March 12, 1770. This was also asserted in *A Short Narrative of The horrid Massacre in Boston, Perpetrated In the Evening of the Fifth Day of March, 1770, By Soldiers of the XXIXth Regiment; which with The XIVth Regiment Were then Quartered there: with some Observations on the State of Things prior to that Catastrophe* (Boston, 1770), p. 28. The pamphlet was the result of the findings of a Boston committee composed of James Bowdoin, Joseph Warren, and Samuel Pemberton, and was published by order of the town of Boston; its appendix prints ninety-six depositions, all except two unfavourable to the soldiers. For the part played by Bowdoin in preparing the pamphlet, see Philip Davidson: *op. cit.*, pp. 214–15, and, by F. G. Walett, "James Bowdoin, Patriot Propagandist," *New England Quarterly,* XXIII, 329–30, and "James Bowdoin, Massachusetts Patriot and Statesman," Bostonian Society *Proceedings* (Boston, 1950), pp. 32–3. For the part played by Warren and Pemberton, and the high importance of this pamphlet, see John Cary: *op. cit.*, 95–6. On the other side there appeared in London *A fair Account of the late Unhappy Disturbance At Boston in New England; extracted From Depositions that have been made concerning it by Persons of all Parties. With an Appendix, containing Some Affidavits and other Evidences relating to the Affair, not mentioned in the Narrative of it that has been published at Boston* (London, 1770). A copy of this rare pamphlet is in the Harvard Library. It presents twenty-six affidavits which place the blame on the people of Boston.

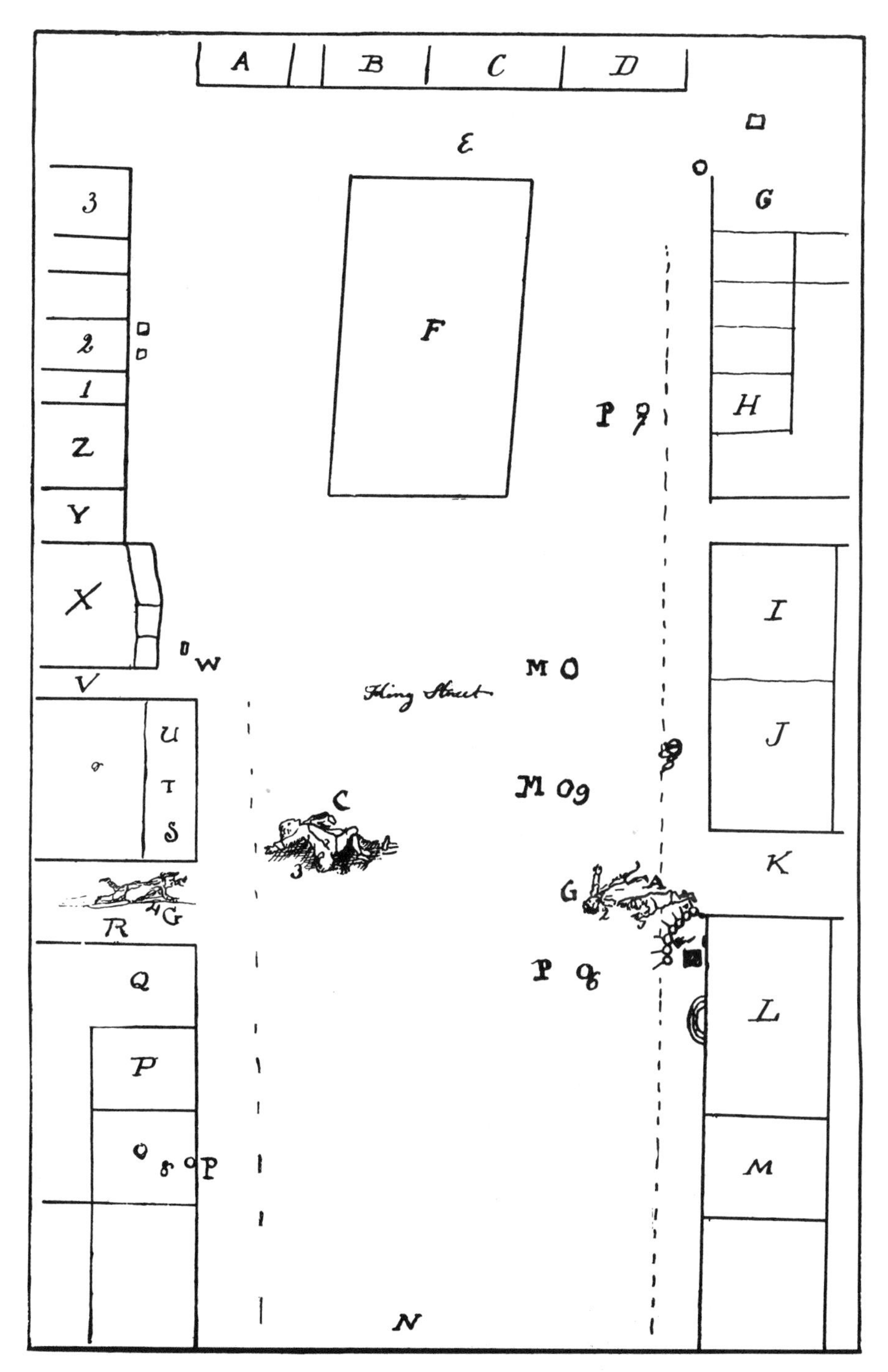

"Plan of King Street and Vicinity" at the time of the Boston Massacre, 1770, by Paul Revere. (From the Boston Public Library)

"The Bloody Massacre perpetrated in King Street, Boston, on March 5th, 1770," by Paul Revere.
(Massachusetts Historical Society)

The captain—who, according to the Rev. Andrew Eliot, pastor of Boston's New North Congregational Church, "had the character of a benevolent, humane man"[43]—presented a different account of the event. According to his version, in his attempt to quell the rioters, who seemed bent on wrecking the Custom House and plundering the "King's Money" lodged there, he placed himself between the soldiers and the rioters, and pleaded with the latter to retire peaceably. Instead—still according to Captain Preston's statement—the mob, not satisfied with throwing lumps of ice and snowballs at the troops, advanced to the very point of the bayonets of the soldiers and, using the most abusive language, struck some of them, daring them to fire. Preston was still out in front of the half circle formed by the troops when one of his men, upon being clubbed, slipped aside and fired. Turning to rebuke the soldier, the captain himself was hit with a club. Then, without orders, the other soldiers began to fire upon the steadily advancing mob.[44] Three people were instantly killed and two fatally wounded; still others were hit by the shots, but less seriously.[45]

---

[43] Eliot to Thomas Hollis, June 28, 1770, previously cited.

[44] Writing to General Gage on March 19 from the Boston gaol, Preston reported the following: "As the strongest ties of humanity & the tenderest regards for my fellow Creatures, together with a strict attention to my duty, are the causes of my present distress, I cann't suppose but they will merit your attention, who possess them in so eminent a degree. I went to the fatal place purely from that motive, to passefy the Mob if possible, to support the Sentry in his material trust, & restrain the Soldiers by my presence, from committing the mischiefs that happened; but the Mob were violent & the Soldiers insulted & struck were stimulated to execute the tragical scene that happened to my surprise and astonishment."

This may be found in one of seventy-seven letters relating to the incident that the late R. G. Adams of the Clements Library brought together in his article "New Light on the Boston Massacre," American Antiquarian Society *Proceedings*, new ser., XLVII, 259–354; for the Preston letter see pp. 290–1. See also Preston's long account of the incident, signed on March 13, 1770, sent to General Gage, which is among the Board of Trade Papers, C.O. 5:759; Professor Merrill Jensen has printed it in his *English Historical Documents, American Colonial Documents to 1776* (New York, 1955), pp. 750–3; see also *The Correspondence of General Thomas Gage . . . 1763–1775* (ed. C. E. Carter, 2 vols., New Haven, 1931, 1933), I, 249, and "Documents Relating to Captain Thomas Preston and the Boston Massacre" (ed. Albert Matthews), Colonial Society of Massachusetts *Publications*, VII, 7–8. A colorful but scholarly account of the incident is to be found in Esther Forbes's *Paul Revere & The World He Lived In* (Boston, 1942), Chap. 5; this account is illustrated (following p. 146) by a pen-and-ink diagram "which is said to have been prepared by Paul Revere for the trial of the soldiers" as well as by Revere's famous print of the Massacre which was so clearly drawn for propaganda purposes.

[45] In his letter to Gage of March 18 Hutchinson has the following to say about the fatalities of the incident: "The killing and wounding so many people either passengers in the streets or meer spectators, for I have heard but of one of them who was an assailant, had the effect which some of our people who are called Patriots have long wished for and I find more people, the first night, had actually taken to their Arms than I imagined in the time of it" (American Antiquarian Society *Proceedings*, new ser., XLVII, 286–7). According to depositions taken between March 13 and 22, some

Lieutenant Governor Hutchinson, when alerted to the seriousness of the incident, rushed from his home a half mile away. Facing the enraged people, who were converging on the Town House, many of them armed, he turned them away with the promise that he would order "a full and impartial inquiry" so that justice should be done.[46] Without delay the town magistrates assembled in the Council chamber and, with Hutchinson present, spent most of the night examining witnesses. Meanwhile Preston and his detail surrendered themselves and were committed to gaol.[47]

The next morning selectmen and justices of the peace among others appeared before the Lieutenant Governor and the Council to demand the removal of the troops from the town and to warn that otherwise the inhabitants of Boston and neighbouring towns would force them out. "I told them," wrote the Lieutenant Governor to Gage, "that an attack upon the Kings Troops would be High Treason & every man concerned would forfeit his life and Estate."[48] Hutchinson insisted he had no authority to bring about the removal of the troops. Nevertheless, the Council supported unanimously the position of the town authorities that, to prevent a rebellion, the soldiers must be removed to Castle William in the harbour. In view of this attitude on the part of the civil authorities the commanding officers of the two regiments, Lieutenant Colonels Dalrymple and Carr, finally agreed to take this step.[49]

As to the imprisoned soldiers, they were most fortunate to have for counsel Robert Auchmuty, John Adams, and Josiah Quincy, Jr., the latter two, as Hutchinson pointed out, "strongly attached to the cause of liberty."[50] The Crown, as prosecutor, was represented by

---

of the firing took place from a window in the Custom House. See *A Short Narrative of The horrid Massacre . . .* , pp. 12–13; see also O. M. Dickerson: "The Commissioners of Customs and the 'Boston Massacre,'" *New England Quarterly,* XXVII, 307–25, and Richard Frothingham: *Life and Times of Joseph Warren* (Boston, 1865), Chap. 6. For a challenge to this contention see John Cary: *op. cit.,* p. 94 *n.*

[46] See Thomas Hutchinson: *op. cit.,* III, 196.

[47] *Ibid.,* III, 196–7. For a contemporary account of the massacre, as sent to Thomas Pownall in London by the Rev. Samuel Cooper, see Dr. Cooper's letters from Boston of March 26 and July 2, 1770, *American Historical Review,* VIII, 316–20. For two additional contrasting letters on the subject, see that of William Palfrey to John Wilkes of March 13, 1770, and the one from Thomas Hutchinson to Lord Hillsborough, dated simply "Boston, March, 1770," both of which are to be found in the Massachusetts Historical Society *Proceedings,* VI, 480–7. An early standard account is Frederick Kidder's *History of the Boston Massacre* (Albany, 1870).

[48] Hutchinson to Gage, March 6, 1770, American Antiquarian Society *Proceedings,* new ser., XLVII, 270–2.

[49] Minutes of the Council, March 6; Carr to Gage, March 7, Dalrymple to Gage, March 7, Dalrymple to Gage, March 8, 1770, *ibid.,* XLVII, 273–81.

[50] Thomas Hutchinson: *op. cit.,* III, 235–6. See also *Adams Papers,* 1st ser., *The Diary and Autobiography of John Adams* (eds. L. H. Butterfield *et al.,* 4 vols.,

the Solicitor General of the province, Samuel Quincy, the elder brother of Josiah, and Robert Treat Paine, a later signer of the Declaration of Independence. The judges wisely adjourned the time of the hearing until the October session of the court.[51] The trial of Captain Preston took place between the 24th and 30th of that month. It resulted in acquittal.[52]

Then came the trial of the soldiers on November 27.[53] In the indictment they were described not as soldiers but as "labourers," who had been "seduced by the instigation of the devil and their own wicked hearts." When the jury panel was presented, twenty of the jurors were challenged. None of those finally selected was from Boston; they came, rather, from nearby villages.[54] The trial opened with Samuel Quincy's charge that the prosecution would prove the defandants guilty of "the wilful premeditated murder of five different persons."[55] After five days of examining the witnesses, Quincy

Cambridge, Mass., 1961), III, 292–3, and Josiah Quincy: *Memoirs of the Life of Josiah Quincy, Jr. . . .* (Boston, 1825), pp. 32–3. For two colorful accounts of John Adams's role in the defence of Captain Preston see Catherine Drinker Bowen: *John Adams and the American Revolution* (Boston, 1950), Chaps. 20 and 21, and Page Smith: *John Adams* (2 vols., New York, 1962), I, 121–6.

[51] For the resistance of the judges to the demand by John Hancock and Samuel Adams that a trial of the soldiers take place while the minds of the people of Boston were inflamed, see the statement by one of the judges in *Peter Oliver's Origin & Progress of the American Rebellion: A Tory View* (eds. Douglass Adair and J. A. Schutz, San Marino, Calif., 1961), pp. 87–8, to be cited hereafter as *Peter Oliver's Origin of the Rebellion.* For the role of Adams in the events surrounding the massacre see J. C. Miller: *Sam Adams* (Boston, 1936), Chap. 7, "The Boston Massacre."

[52] For brief notices of the trial of Preston see *Boston Evening-Post,* October 29 and November 5, 1770. It will be noted that the court took the precaution of preventing the jury from separating during Preston's trial, although this was not done at the later trial of the soldiers. Little information respecting the trial of Preston seems to have survived. However, it is clear that the chief point in the acquittal was the lack of solid evidence to show that he had ordered the troops to fire; conversely, testimony indicated that he tried to restrain them. Judge Oliver, who was on the bench, wrote later that the problem of the identity of the man who called on the soldiers to fire was not cleared up until many months after the trial, "when the Soldier who gave the Word of Command . . . solved the Doubt" (*Peter Oliver's Origin of the Rebellion,* pp. 89–90).

[53] The trial of the common soldiers is set forth in great detail. It was taken down in shorthand by John Hodgson and published in 1770 at Boston by permission of the court. The pamphlet appears under title *The Trial of William Wemms, James Hartegan, William M'Cauley, Hugh White, Matthew Killroy, William Warren, John Carrol, and Hugh Montgomery . . . for the Murder of Crispus Attucks, Samuel Gray, Samuel Maverick, James Caldwell, and Patrick Carr . . . at the Superior Court of Judicature, Court of Assize, and General Gaol Delivery, held at Boston. The 27th Day of November . . . ,* and covers 217 pages.

[54] *Ibid.,* pp. 3 and 7–8. During the trial of Preston, the jury was made up of inhabitants from both the town and the countryside; see *Boston Evening-Post,* October 29, 1770.

[55] *The Trial of William Wemms . . . ,* p. 9.

presented the evidence upholding the contention of the prosecution. His brother replied,[56] followed by John Adams.[57] Thereupon Justice Trowbridge summarized the evidence to the jury.[58] Next came the address of Justice Oliver.[59] The other justices also addressed the jury, but the transcript of the trial does not record their words. The jury then retired and returned a verdict after deliberating for two and a half hours. Six of the soldiers were found not guilty; discharged, they returned to Castle William to join their regiment. Two, Killroy and Montgomery, were found guilty of manslaughter; having sought benefit of clergy, they each received the penalty of "burning in the hand" in open court, after which they were discharged and likewise returned to the 29th Regiment.[60]

Next came the trial of William Warren and four others accused of murdering Crispus Attucks[61] by firing upon him from the windows of the Custom House. The witnesses were found to be so unreliable and contradictory in their statements that—after hearing them and after the charge by the bench—the jury, without leaving their seats, acquitted the prisoners.[62]

Certain observations may be made on this famous trial. First of all, the Crown prosecutor, Samuel Quincy, went beyond the indictment of the grand jury in charging the defendants with "premeditated murder"—a charge that he must have realized would be most difficult to prove. This raises the question whether he really sought to convict the soldiers. While his address to the jury was not included in the transcript of the trial, those of his brother and John Adams in serving the defendants have been preserved. They are in the best tradition of English criminal trials, and would have done credit to any English barrister of that period. The commendable and able summarizing of the case by Justices Trowbridge and Oliver, with careful citation of pertinent precedents, is also indicative of the care given to both cases by the counsel for the defence. The uppermost thought in their minds was, clearly, that there should be no miscarriage of justice. A study of the testimony of witnesses and of the cross-examinations demonstrates that all the pertinent facts on which to make a decision in harmony with this objective were placed before

[56] The remarks of Josiah Quincy are given in full; for these see *ibid.*, pp. 134–48.

[57] For Adams's address to the jury see *ibid.*, pp. 148–78.

[58] *Ibid.*, pp. 178–97.

[59] *Ibid.*, pp. 197–207.

[60] *Ibid.*, pp. 208–9. Killroy is also spelled Kilroy and Kilroi.

[61] Attucks was apparently a mulatto who had been active in the attack on the soldiers, according to *Hutchinson's History* . . . , III, 196.

[62] *The Trial of William Wemms* . . . , pp. 212–17.

the jurors. Thus, the jury was compelled to brush aside the charge against the soldiers of "the wilful premeditated murder of five different persons." One factor that appears to have influenced them, as well as the judges, was the evidence that the crowd milling about the Custom House was there for no lawful or useful purpose and that it used the most blatant provocations to incite the soldiers to fire.

The publication of the highlights of the trial, so soon after its termination, by express leave of the court, would seem to indicate that the bench as well as the defending lawyers felt this would serve the useful purpose of putting the whole March 5 incident in proper prospective. Moreover, it would appear that Trowbridge, Oliver, Adams, and Josiah Quincy cooperated in preparing the case for publication.[63] Nevertheless, if any of the protagonists thought the appearance of the highlights of the trial in print would quiet the minds of the people, they were to be disappointed. Even Josiah Quincy, Jr., in the *Boston Gazette* of February 11, 1771, writing under the *nom de plume* of "Mentor," lamented "hearing so little discourse relative to a decent, manly, and instructive commemoration of the melancholy tragedy of the 5th of March, 1770," in order that there might be an annual observance of the "fatal effects of the policy of standing armies, and . . . quartering troops in populous cities in time of peace."[64] As Thomas Hutchinson wrote later of the trial: ". . . a great part of the people were induced to believe the acquittals unjust, and contrary to evidence; and the killing of the men was declared to be a horrid massacre, with the same freedom as if the jury had found those concerned in it guilty of murder."[65] March 5, 1771, therefore became a day of mourning and commemoration in Boston; the bells of the Congregational meeting houses tolled for an hour at noon and from nine to ten o'clock in the evening. Thousands of people flocked to an "exhibition" at a private home to view, in one window, a display of young Snider trying to stop the blood flowing from his wound and, in another, a picture, captioned "Foul-Play," showing the soldiers firing on the people. At the "Factory-Hall," which the troops had abandoned, Dr. Thomas Young spoke that evening to a mass meeting. The orator's subject

[63] One need only peruse the citation of cases by the two lawyers and the two judges (*ibid.*, footnotes) to observe that it is highly unlikely that anyone, however skilled in shorthand, could have taken them down.

[64] See also Josiah Quincy: *op. cit.*, pp. 66–7.

[65] Thomas Hutchinson: *op. cit.*, III, 237. For the view that "The result of the trial reflected great honour on . . . the council for the prisoners, and on the integrity of the jury," see Abiel Holmes: *American Annals* . . . (2 vols., Cambridge, Mass., 1805), II, 295.

was the "Imputation of Treason and Rebellion with which the Tools of Power endeavoured to brand the Inhabitants."[66]

Apparently, a feeling persisted that Young had not been sufficiently vigorous in setting forth the rights of the colony.[67] Consequently, it was arranged that James Lovell, a graduate of Harvard and an usher in the South Grammar School, should give an additional address to keep alive the memory of "the bloody Tragedy." Lovell (who later was arrested by the British for spying, carried to Halifax, released on exchange, and soon after sent to Philadelphia as a delegate to the Continental Congress) appeared before a great crowd duly assembled on April 2 at Old South Church and there delivered a speech that was fairly temperate on the subject of the Massacre, but full of the sort of political doctrine that men such as Samuel Adams were seeking to implant in the minds of the people. At one point in his oration, equating Parliament with foreign governments, he asked:

> "Who are a free people? Not those who do not suffer actual oppression; but those who have a *constitutional check upon the power* to oppress. We are slaves or freemen; if, as we are called, the last, where is our check upon the following powers, France, Spain, the States of Holland, or the British Parliament? . . . Make the bloody 5th of March the Area of the resurrection of your birthrights, which have been murdered by the very strength that nursed them in their infancy. I had an eye solely to parliamentary supremacy; and I hope you will think every other view beneath your notice in our present most alarming situation."

After paying his respects to Chatham, Camden, and others, whom he called "gods among men," he turned his eyes critically upon the position held by them that constitutionally "England has right to exercise every power over us, but that of taking money out of our pockets without our consent." Continuing in the same vein, he added: "Tho' it seems almost too bold therefore in us to say 'we doubt in every single instance her *legal* right over this province,' yet *we must assert it*." The legal independence of the province from the Parliament of Great Britain was stated even more clearly when, after referring to George III, Lovell declared that "the claim of the

[66] *Boston Evening-Post,* March 11, 1771.

[67] It may be noted, however, that in 1774 Dr. Young's name was among those who were accused of being authors of "rebellion" in the province. See Hezekiah Niles: *Principles and Acts of the Revolution in America* . . . (Baltimore, 1822), p. 374.

British Parliament over us is not only ILLEGAL IN ITSELF, but A DOWN-RIGHT USURPATION OF HIS PREROGATIVE as KING OF AMERICA."[68]

The result of Lovell's pronouncement was that the people held a town meeting immediately after the oration and voted unanimously that Thomas Cushing, the meeting's moderator, together with John Hancock, Samuel Adams, Dr. Benjamin Church, and three others constitute "a committee to return the Thanks . . . for the Oration . . . in Commemoration of the horrid Massacre. . . ."[69] A copy of Lovell's oration was requested for release to the press, and the town meeting agreed to take measures "to perpetuate the Memory of that wanton and bloody Massacre to all Generations."[70]

True to this commitment, Joseph Warren was chosen to deliver the oration on March 5, 1772. Old South Church was again selected for this occasion and the people so jammed into it at midday that only with difficulty could Warren make his way to the black-draped pulpit. Denouncing "the ruinous consequences of standing armies to free communities," and the British Parliament's claim to the right to levy upon the people of the colonies, he declaimed:

> "The voice of your fathers' blood cries to you from the ground, MY SONS SCORN TO BE SLAVES! . . . If you, with united zeal and fortitude, oppose the torrent of oppression; . . . if you, from your souls, despise the most gaudy dress that slavery can wear, . . . you may have the fullest assurance that tyranny, with her whole accursed train, will hide their hideous heads. . . ."[71]

That same night—to dramatize the picture painted by Warren of the people of Boston under the heel of a tyrannical government—a number of "Friends of Liberty" met at Mrs. Clapham's in King Street, near the scene of the fatal shooting on March 5, 1770, and placing a magic lantern on the balcony, exhibited to the crowd gathered in the street transparencies depicting "the bloody Massacre." Also, to the accompaniment of tolling church bells, a monument to the victims "barbarously Murdered by a Party of the 29th Regiment" was unveiled.[72]

On March 5 of the following year, Dr. Benjamin Church (who, in the fall of 1775, was to be court-martialed at a trial presided over by Washington for "holding criminal correspondence with the

[68] *An Oration delivered April 2d, 1771, at the Request of the Inhabitants of the Town of Boston; to Commemorate the bloody Tragedy of the Fifth of March, 1770. By James Lovell, A.M.* (Boston, 1771), especially pp. 11–16.

[69] *Ibid.*, p. 4.

[70] *Boston Evening-Post*, April 8, 1771.

[71] Hezekiah Niles: *op. cit.*, pp. 4–9; see also John Cary: *op. cit.*, pp. 106–10.

[72] *Boston Evening-Post*, March 9, 1772.

enemy") delivered the memorial oration. Among other things he charged:

> "Breach of trust in a governor, or attempting to enlarge a limited power, effectually absolves subjects from every bond of covenant and peace; the crimes acted by a king against the people, are the highest treason *against the highest law among men.* . . . Numberless have been the attacks made upon our free constitution; numberless the grievances we now resent; but the *Hydra* mischief, is the violation of my right, as a *BRITISH AMERICAN* freeholder, in not being consulted in framing these statutes I am required to obey."[73]

Nor was John Hancock in his oration in 1774, any less successful than had been his predecessors in inspiring the people with a hatred of the system of government to which they were subjected. This government he denounced in the following terms:

> "The town of Boston . . . has been invested by a British fleet: the troops of George III have crossed the wide Atlantic, not to engage an enemy, but to assist a band of *TRAITORS* in trampling on the rights and liberties of his most loyal subjects in America. . . . Let all America join in one common prayer to heaven, that the inhuman, unprovoked murders of the fifth of March, 1770, planned by Hillsborough, and a knot of treacherous knaves in Boston, and executed by the cruel hand of Preston and his sanguinary coadjutors, may ever stand in history without a parallel."[74]

So the anniversary of this tragic event continued to be celebrated as a focal point for rebellion even after the outbreak of open hostilities.[75]

The emphasis placed on the events surrounding the so-called Boston Massacre during the period 1770 to 1775 serves to demonstrate that the repeal of most of the Townshend duties, although attended by the collapse of the non-importation movement, in no way reconciled the popular leaders of Massachusetts Bay to the type of control being exercised over them by the mother country. If these leaders were not then demanding independence, they were at least bent upon securing recognition of the autonomous position of the province. What they wanted was a colony free from the presence of British ships of war and regular troops, free of any obligation to contribute financially to the support of the Empire, beyond what the General Assembly might voluntarily offer, and, finally, free to make the laws that alone would be binding on the inhabitants.

---

[73] Hezekiah Niles: *op. cit.,* pp. 8–12.
[74] *Ibid.,* pp. 12–17.
[75] *Ibid.,* pp. 17–59.

Such an extreme position was not compatible with the doctrine of the sovereignty of King, Lords, and Commons throughout the Empire, as promulgated by Parliament in 1696 and solemnly reaffirmed in the Declaratory Act of 1766. Therefore, the leaders of the colony were supporting a movement that, to British statesmen, was distinctively revolutionary in nature. In the forefront of the ranks of the radical movement must be counted some of the clergy.

The Clergy and the Revolutionary Movement

No account of the rising spirit of disaffection of the people of Massachusetts Bay toward the government of Great Britain should fail to mention the attitude of the clergy of the established Congregational Church. Judge Peter Oliver (who in 1771 became chief justice of the superior court and in 1776 went into exile as a Loyalist), in describing the events connected with the incident of March 5, 1770, in his clearly partisan but valuable *Origin & Progress of the American Rebellion,* wrote:

> "The [Congregational] Clergy, both before & after the Trials . . . were by no means guilty of doing their Work negligently. *Before* the Trials, the Pulpits rung their Chimes upon blood Guiltiness, in Order to incite the People, some of whom were to be Jurors, to Revenge . . . ; but happily . . . they could do little more than cry aloud . . . in blowing up the Coals of Sedition."[76]

The Rev. John Lathrop, pastor of the Boston Second Church, preached a sermon at the Custom House the day after the tragedy. Taking as his text Genesis 4:10—"The voice of thy brother's blood crieth unto me from the ground"—he referred to the "unparalleled barbarity of those . . . guilty of murdering a number of our innocent fellow-citizens . . . victims to the merciless rage of wicked men . . . the worst of murderers." Assuring his audience that the "cry of innocent blood cannot be allayed, but by the death of the guilty!" he went on to exhort: "There is no evading this law . . . God, the supreme legislator, has given the magistrate no authority to alter or dispense with his law, or mitigate the punishment in any manner or degree. *He shall surely be put to death!*"[77] Lathrop was not alone

[76] *Peter Oliver's Origin of the Rebellion,* p. 91.

[77] John Lathrop: *Innocent Blood Crying to God . . . A Sermon Occasioned by the Horrid Murder of . . . the Fifth of March, 1770* (London, 1770, reprinted in Boston, 1771), pp. 5, 6, 12. It may be noted that Lathrop gave the chapter and verse of his text as Genesis 3:10, but cited the text as given.

among the Boston ministers in demanding that the soldiers be put to death. According to Oliver, the Rev. Charles Chauncy, the eminent pastor of First Church, when referring to the coming trial of Captain Preston, asserted: "if I was to be one of the Jury upon his Trial, I would bring him in guilty, *evidence or no* evidence."[78]

Lathrop, Chauncy, and most of their fellow clergymen, although often praising the English constitution, were quite alienated from the government of Great Britain by 1770. That they used their great talents to implant in their congregations their own spirit of hostility cannot be doubted. One can easily understand their point of view. Their ancestors had left England to be free of control by the Anglican Church Establishment, and had in turn created the Congregational Church Establishment. It was a church without bishops and without regular ecclesiastical courts, which is not to say that a Roger Williams or an Anne Hutchinson could not be tried for heresy by the ministers in a special court and cast out of the church. Nevertheless, in the eighteenth century, as Alice M. Baldwin has made clear in her study on the New England clergy, they were firm believers in "the doctrines of natural right, the social contract, and the right of resistance," especially when government was thought to have transcended its authority by acting in violation of the very constitution that bound it.[79] A typical expression of this view was the sermon of the Rev. Jonathan Mayhew, pastor of the West Church in Boston, delivered early in 1750 and printed by request—*A Discourse Concerning Unlimited Submission and Non-Resistance to the Higher Powers: With some Reflections on the Resistance made to King Charles I. And on the Anniversary of his Death: in which the Mysterious Doctrine of that Prince's Saintship and Martyrdom is Unriddled.*[80] In it Mayhew referred to the bad use that clergymen of the Church of England had made of the anniversary of the death of Charles; at the same time he expressed confidence "that it will prove a standing memento that Britons will not be slaves, and a warning to all corrupt counsellors and ministers not to go too far in advising to arbitrary, despotic measures."[81]

When the news of the repeal of the Stamp Act had reached Massa-

---

[78] *Peter Oliver's Origin of the Rebellion*, pp. 91–2.

[79] Alice M. Baldwin: *The New England Clergy and the American Revolution* (Durham, N.C., 1928), p. xii.

[80] For this sermon see J. W. Thornton: *The Pulpit of the American Revolution* (Boston, 1860), pp. 39–104. For an excellent brief study of Mayhew see Clinton Rossiter: *Seedtime of the Republic: The Origin of the American Tradition of Political Liberty* (New York, 1953), Chap. 9.

[81] *Ibid.*, p. 104.

chusetts Bay, it was at the desire of both the House of Representatives and the Council that the Rev. Mr. Chauncy, on July 24, 1766, delivered his *Discourse On "the good News from a far Country."* In it he combated the idea that the people of the colony were lacking in "love or subjection to the British throne." It was to William Pitt, however, that he paid the greatest tribute, speaking of him "as the saviour, under God, . . . both of the nation and these colonies, not only from the power of France, but from that which is much worse, a state of slavery. . . ."[82]

The attitude of the New England Congregational ministers toward the issues that arose between Great Britain and the colonies between 1763 and 1775 reflected the views of the clergy in most of the colonies. Yet, individually, they were often more influenced by factors which might affect their position in the communities they served.

Since the days of Archbishop William Laud, intermittent efforts had been made to appoint a bishop to supervise the Anglican churches in the colonies.[83] It was hoped that a bishop resident in America would solve the vast difficulties confronting the Bishop of London in performing his supervisory function over the colonial church—a function which, according to tradition, had been exercised by him from the days of Laud, if not before.[84] As a result, beginning

---

[82] *Ibid.*, pp. 105–46. Even earlier, on May 23, 1766, the Rev. Mayhew had delivered a Stamp Act repeal Thanksgiving sermon based upon the text "Our Soul is escaped as a bird from the snare of the fowlers; the snare is broken, and we are escaped" (Psalms 124:7). When printed it was dedicated to Pitt, "who hath . . . been a principal Instrument in the hand of GOD . . . by exerting Himself to prevent a fatal rupture between BRITAIN and her Colonies." In it Mayhew made the point that the colonials, unlike slaves, were free-born and so had a natural right to their own property, a right secured them as British subjects by Magna Charta; further, whereas the "snarers" were using every dishonest means to enslave the King, Parliament, and the good people of America, their plan was undoubtedly concerned only as a service to "the Houses of Bourbon and the Pretenders," by fostering an open rupture between the colonies and the mother country. See *The Snare Broken. A Thanksgiving Discourse . . . occasioned by the Repeal of the Stamp Act* (Boston, 1766).

[83] In dealing with the above point the student should consult the previously cited work by Alice M. Baldwin: *The New England Clergy and the American Revolution*, A. L. Cross: *The Anglican Episcopate and the American Colonies* (*Harvard Historical Studies*, IX, New York, 1902), and, especially, the recent important study by Carl Bridenbaugh: *Mitre and Sceptre: Transatlantic Facts, Ideas, Personalities and Politics, 1689–1775* (New York, 1962). Professor Bridenbaugh has provided the reader with a detailed study of the methods employed by American dissenting clergymen, supported by leading British dissenters, to meet what they felt to be the menace of Anglicanism to them and their congregations.

[84] For the history of the relations of the Bishop of London to the Anglican churches in America, see the Right Rev. Dr. Sherlock, Bishop of London, to the King in Council on "Some considerations humbly offered . . . relating to the Ecclesiastical Government in His Majestys Dominions in America," *New York Colonial Documents*, VII, 360–9. This was presented to the Privy Council, February 19, 1759.

in 1638 efforts were made to meet the need for a proper clergyman to supervise the colonial churches. Among other duties, he would confirm applicants for church membership, ordain colonial divinity students aspiring to become Anglican ministers, and supervise the disciplining of clergymen. In order to meet the need, at least partially, the office of Commissary had been created in 1689. The chief functions of this official—in addition to acting as liaison to the Bishop of London—were to visit and exhort the Anglican churches in his district and, where feasible, to supervise and administer them. But the new office, from the point of view of most Anglican clergymen serving in America, was ineffectual. Moreover, by the period under consideration a Commissary was no longer appointed to look after the spiritual interests of Anglicans living in the more northern colonies.[85]

With the founding, by royal charter, in 1701 of the Society for the Propagation of the Gospel in Foreign Parts, an active Anglican missionary movement was created. The growth of the S.P.G., as it was familiarly called, led the missionaries, especially those labouring in the New England and Middle colonies, to set up a demand for one or more American bishops. Queen Anne was finally won over to the idea, but a bill, although drafted and ready to be submitted to Parliament, was forgotten when she died.[86] Yet pleas continued to go forward for an American bishop. As a result, the Rev. Dr. Sherlock, Bishop of London, attempted in 1759 to persuade the government to make the requested appointments where desired. His lengthy report provided that there should be no ecclesiastical courts with coercive powers, but that bishops should simply be received "as an *Order* of the Christian Church, to inspect the conduct and behaviour of the [Anglican] Clergy and to perform the duties of their Office in examining and ordaining ministers for the services of the Church."[87] But the Pitt Ministry, with a great war on its hands, was not anxious to run the risk of diminishing the war effort by antagonizing the large segment of the colonial population opposed to such a move.

Undoubtedly, one of the reasons for the bitter opposition of the American Congregational and Presbyterian clergy to the idea of

[85] A. L. Cross: *op. cit.*, p. 247.

[86] *Ibid.*, pp. 88–112; see also Part II of H. P. Thompson's *Into All Lands: The History of the Society for the Propagation of the Gospel in Foreign Parts, 1701–1950* (London, 1951).

[87] *New York Colonial Documents,* VII, 368.

having an Anglican bishop in America was the fear of losing leading members of their own churches to the Anglican communion; for the missionaries of the Society for the Propagation of the Gospel had been active in the work of proselyting, especially in Connecticut. It was in this colony, in 1722, that the Rev Timothy Cutler, Rector of Yale College, the Rev. Samuel Johnson, pastor of the West Haven Congregational Church and later President of King's College in New York. and other Congregational clergymen had espoused the doctrines of the Anglican church—with the result that from a single church of this denomination at Stratford in that year, the number in Connecticut grew to 35 by the beginning of 1763 and to over 80 by 1775.[88] It can therefore readily be understood why the clergy of the Congregational establishment in Connecticut, as well as in Massachusetts Bay, should have been deeply concerned with this trend.

Typical of the concern of the dissenting clergy was the argument of the Rev. Noah Hobart of Stamford, Connecticut, who in 1748 published in Boston *A Serious Address to the Members of the Episcopal Separation in New England etc.* In it he raised certain questions: whether it was the duty of colonials "to conform to the Prelatic Church, by Law established in the South part of Great Britain," whether it was prudent for those settled in New England churches to go over to that communion, and, finally, whether "it be LAWFUL for particular members of New-England Churches to separate from them and join in Communion with the Episcopal Assemblies. . . ." This *Address* started a lively controversy in the press, which shifted to Boston by 1763 when the Rev. Jonathan Mayhew delivered a heavy attack upon both the charter and the

---

[88] See E. E. Beardsley: *The History of the Episcopal Church in Connecticut* (2 vols., New York, 1868), I, Chaps. 17–22; see also W. W. Manross: *A History of the American Episcopal Church* (New York and Milwaukee, 1935), pp. 102–3; L. C. Jarvis: *Sketches of Church Life in Colonial Connecticut* (New Haven, 1902), pp. 26, 53, 183–4; Glenn Weaver: "Anglican-Congregationalist Tensions in Pre-Revolutionary Connecticut," *Historical Magazine of the Protestant Episcopal Church*, XXVI, 269–85; Maud O'Neil: "A Struggle for Religious Liberty: An Analysis of the Work of the S.P.G. in Connecticut," *ibid.*, XX, 173–89; and L. L. Tucker: *Puritan Protagonist: President Thomas Clap of Yale College* (Chapel Hill, N.C., 1962). For the Rev. Ezra Stiles's constant concern over Anglican affairs in the colonies, especially the plans for an episcopate, see his *Literary Diary . . .* (ed. F. B. Dexter, 3 vols., New York, 1901), I, 103–4, 116, 138, 221, 238, 317, and II, 45–7; see also E. S. Morgan: *The Gentle Puritan: A Life of Ezra Stiles, 1729–1795* (New Haven and London, 1962), p. 110, and, for Stiles's suspicions of Anglican intrigue, *ibid.*, pp. 215–19, and especially Carl Bridenbaugh: *op. cit.*, pp. 1–20, *et seq.*

conduct of the Society for the Propagation of the Gospel[89] in which he charged that its design was the destruction of Presbyterian and other churches in America to be followed by the establishment in the colonies of the Anglican Church and its bishops.[90] This was in reply to a pamphlet, entitled *Considerations on the Institution and Conduct of the Society for the Propagation of the Gospel in Foreign Parts,* issued that same year by the Rev. East Apthorp. A missionary of the Society, he had been educated at Cambridge University, but was then serving the Anglican congregation at Cambridge, Massachusetts.

The Mayhew pamphlet led to rebuttals and replies, the most noteworthy of which came from the pen of Archbishop Thomas Secker in London. Reprinted anonymously in Boston the following year, it sought to calm the fears of Congregationalists and Presbyterians by its conciliatory tone. In it the Archbishop stressed that:

> "The Church of *England* is, in its Constitution episcopal. It is, in some of the Plantations, confessedly the established Church; in the rest are many Congregations adhering to it . . . All Members of every Church are, according to the Principles of Liberty intitled to every Part of what they conceive to be the Benefits of it . . . ; yet the Members of our Church in *America* do not thus enjoy its Benefits, having no Protestant Bishop within 3000 Miles of them; a Case, which never had its Parallel before in the Christian World."

He also emphasized the point that there was no desire whatsoever for the bishops that might be appointed to serve in America to hold courts or to infringe upon the privileges of the laity, even those within the Anglican communion; their mission would be simply to ordain ministers, confirm children, and to generally oversee the Episcopal clergy.[91] But nothing that the Archbishop of Canterbury wrote could mitigate the hostility of Congregational and Presbyterian clergy and congregations toward the activities of the S.P.G. and the stated desire of its missionaries to have a bishop. In the face

[89] *Observations on the Charter and Conduct of the Society for the Propagation of the Gospel in Foreign Parts* . . . (Boston, 1763). For the concern of dissenting clergy in 1763 over "the affair of American Bishops," see Bernhard Knollenberg: *Origin of the American Revolution: 1759–1766* (New York, 1960), Chap. 5, "The Disturbing Activities of Archbishop Secker."

[90] See Mayhew's *Observations,* particularly "Section XIV, "That the Society have long had a formal design to root out Presbyterianism, &c., and to establishing both Episcopacy and Bishops in the colonies . . ." (pp. 103–8); in this connection see also Carl Bridenbaugh: *op. cit.,* pp. 224–9.

[91] [Thomas Secker]: *An Answer to Dr. Mayhew's Observations on the Charter and Conduct of the Society for the Propagation of the Gospel in Foreign Parts* (London and Boston, 1764), pp. 50–1.

of the Stamp Act crisis—which arose soon after Secker had issued his pamphlet and which threatened to wreck the Old British Empire before the Act was repealed—the government of Great Britain had little desire to stir up the great mass of colonials identified with churches outside the Anglican communion.

From the point of view of the British Ministry, the question of appointing bishops for America was dead after 1765. Nevertheless, Episcopalian clergymen in the colonies continued to agitate toward that end. In 1767 the Rev. Dr. Thomas Bradbury Chandler—Yale graduate, Doctor of Divinity of Oxford, and pastor of the Anglican church in Elizabethtown, New Jersey—issued his *Appeal to the Public in behalf of the Church of England in America,* published in New York as the result of conventions held during the preceding years of clergymen from New York and New Jersey "assisted by some of their Brethren from the neighbouring Provinces."[92] In it he asserted that "the Church of England is the only religious body in America not fully tolerated." Quoting a sermon delivered the preceding February by the Rev. Dr. John Ewer, then Bishop of Llandaff, before the Society for the Propagation of the Gospel, Dr. Chandler related how the Bishop lamented the lack of bishops in America, the more since even "the Romish superstition, within a province lately added to the British dominions, is completely allowed in all points; it hath Bishops. . . . Thus stands the case of all churches in our colonies, except only the church here by law established; that alone is not tolerated in the whole, it exists only . . . in a maimed state. . . ."[93]

[92] For the Anglican activities in New Jersey see N. R. Burr: *The Anglican Church in New Jersey* (Philadelphia, 1954), especially Chap. 15; for Chandler's career see S. G. McCulloch: "Thomas Bradbury Chandler: Anglican Humanitarian in Colonial New Jersey," which forms Chap. 6 of *British Humanitarianism,* a collection of essays edited by Dr. McCulloch in honor of Frank J. Klingberg (*Church Historical Society Publications,* No. 32, Philadelphia, 1950). See in this connection W. S. Perry: *The History of the American Episcopal Church, 1587–1883* (2 vols., Boston, 1885), I, 415; for the minutes of conventions held in 1766–7, see *Historical Magazine of the Protestant Episcopal Church,* X, 124–62.

[93] *An Appeal to the Public,* pp. x and xi. The Bishop did not stop here in his sermon; for he painted a very dark picture indeed of the condition of many colonials, who in forsaking their mother country had likewise turned their back on their native manners and religion, "living without remembrance or knowledge of God, without any divine worship, in dissolute wickedness, and the most brutal profligacy of manners" (*A Sermon Preached before the Incorporated Society for the Propagation of the Gospel in Foreign Parts; . . . On Friday February 20, 1767* [London, 1768; reprinted New York, 1768], p. 5). Although this was highly unfair to most of the colonials, it is true that the Rev. Charles Woodmason, going into the backcountry of South Carolina in 1766, found the people there to be "of abandon'd Morals, and profligate Principles—Rude—Ignorant—Void of Manners, Education or Good Breeding" (*The Carolina Backcountry on the Eve of the Revolution: The Journal and Other Writings of Charles Woodmason* [ed. R. J. Hooker, Chapel Hill, N.C., 1953], p. 6).

Chandler presented the case for American bishops broadly and effectively and apparently with utmost frankness.[94] His pamphlet was to provoke a veritable war of words in the form of newspaper articles and pamphleteering. Most important of the pamphlet answers was the one by the redoubtable Charles Chauncy in 1768. In his extended *Appeal to the Public Answered: In Behalf of the Non-Episcopal Churches in America . . .*, he denied that there was a real need for Anglican bishops and stated that only the clergy in the Episcopal communion were really interested in the plan.[95] Then came Chandler's reply, published in New York in 1769, *The Appeal Defended: or The Proposed American Episcopate Vindicated,* with its renewed assurances that the dissenting churches had nothing to fear from the presence of Anglican bishops in America.[96] In 1771 he also published in New York his *The Appeal Farther defended; in Answer to the Farther Misrepresentations of Dr. Chauncy.*[97]

Nothing that Chandler and other defenders of episcopacy could affirm in their writings, however, had any effect upon the great body of clergy and laymen of the dissenting churches in America. These groups by and large saw in the Anglican clergy a group of men in whom loyalty to the Crown and to their church transcended American rights and who therefore were increasingly suspected of

[94] Nevertheless, in a letter to the Bishop of London, written October 21, 1767, about the book, Chandler admits that there were "some other Facts . . . which could not be prudently mentioned in a Work of this nature, as the least Intimation of them would be of ill Consequence in this irritable Age and Country. . . ." For this letter see A. L. Cross: *op. cit.*, Appendix A, pp. 345–6. What were these other facts? G. M. Brydon (*Virginia's Mother Church and The Political Conditions Under Which It Grew* [2 vols., Richmond, 1947; Philadelphia, 1952], II, 345–7) makes clear some of them. One was the hostility aroused against the mother country in 1765 by the attempt to introduce stamp taxes and further regulate the affairs of the colonies. Another was that the King, as temporal head of the Church of England, alone had power to establish dioceses in America and lay down the conditions whereby a bishop might officiate there, and he alone could select him. Thus, whoever was appointed would inevitably represent the interest of the Crown and would use his influence to uphold the laws of Parliament as against colonial laws. Then, too, while Parliament could enact laws limiting the temporal power of a bishop, neither this body nor the King could dictate the use of the spiritual powers a bishop held according to the constitution and canons of the Church of England. His authority, once he was appointed, could therefore not be easily restrained.

[95] For the effect of Michaijah Towgood's comments in the *London Chronicle* in provoking Chandler's *Appeal Defended,* see Carl Bridenbaugh, *op. cit.,* pp. 308–9; for other views as to which answer caused Chandler to defend his position see also A. L. Cross, *op. cit.,* Chaps. 7 and 8, "The Chandler-Chauncy Controversy, 1767–1771" and "The Newspaper Controversy, 1768–1769," and G. W. Pilcher: "The Pamphlet War on the Proposed Virginia Anglican Episcopate, 1767–1775," *Historical Magazine of the Protestant Episcopal Church,* XXX, 266–79, especially pp. 268–71.

[96] *The Appeal Answered* (Boston, 1768), pp. 135–6.

[97] This was in reply to Chauncy's *A Reply to Dr. Chandler's Appeal Defended,* published early in 1770.

being disloyal to their own communities as the crisis grew with the revolutionary movement.

In New York in 1768 the Presbyterian layman, political liberal, lawyer, and wealthy landholder William Livingston published a biting tract.[98] In it he referred to a sermon that Bishop Llandaff had preached in 1767 before the S.P.G., and added: "I question whether there be a pamphlet in the nation, that in proportion to the length of the sermon, contains so great a number of aberrations from the truth." To the charge that the settlers in the New World failed to provide for the support of the Christian religion, Livingston replied that in New England alone there were no less than 550 congregations supplied with an educated ministry, some of them Presbyterian but most of them Congregationalist, and all men of irreproachable lives. With respect to the depravity into which, according to the Bishop, the people had fallen, Livingston retorted that the only people to whom this accusation might be applied were "some of the episcopal clergy in the province of Maryland, and the West India Islands." He also suggested that if the Bishop had been misinformed about the true state of religion in America, this was doubtless due to the reports of the Society's missionaries, who "for many years past, made it a practice to misrepresent facts."[99]

In addition to the William Livingston pamphlet directed against the Anglicans, articles by "The American Whig" began appearing in the *New-York Gazette: or, the Weekly Post-Boy* beginning with the issue of March 14, 1768. Attacking the Episcopalians for seeking to establish their system of worship amidst "the poverty and distress of the colonies," he asked: "Is this a time to think of episcopal palaces, of pontifical revenues, of spiritual courts, and all the pomp, grandeur, luxury, and regalia of an American Lambeth?"[100] A reply to this and other articles by "The American Whig" appeared in the April 4 edition of Hugh Gaines's *New-York Gazette; and the Weekly Mercury;* entitled "A Whip for the American Whig," they were signed "Timothy Tickle." Once started, the paper war flamed high

[98] *Letter to the Right Reverend Father in God, John, Bishop of Llandaff, occasioned by his Sermon . . . in which the American Colonies are loaded with Reproach* (New York, 1768; reprinted in Boston and London, also in 1768).

[99] *Ibid.*, pp. 3, 6, 9, 11.

[100] The attack by "The American Whig" was also engendered by the appearance in New York of Chandler's 1767 pamphlet, *Appeal to the Public in behalf of the Church of England in America.* Livingston with others of his group were responsible for "The American Whig" articles. See Dorothy R. Dillon: *The New York Triumvirate. A Study of the Legal and Political Careers of William Livingston, John Morin Scott, William Smith, Jr.* (*Columbia University Studies in History, Economics and Public Law,* No. 548, New York, 1949), p. 44.

during 1768 and 1769.[101] Doubtless one reason for the depth of feeling against the Anglicans on the part of the New York Presbyterians was their failure to obtain a charter after they had repeatedly sought to incorporate the New York Synod.[102] They had carried their appeal to the King in Council in 1767, but the Bishop of London had appeared in person to oppose them. This naturally embittered the Presbyterians. That the New York Anglicans rejoiced over their repulse by the Privy Council seems to be equally true.[103]

The controversy between the two religious factions had already spread from New England, New York, and New Jersey into Pennsylvania. The Rev. Dr. Francis Alison, Vice-Provost of the College of Philadelphia, on March 24, 1768, inserted the first of his "Centinel" articles into the *Pennsylvania Journal.* His broad thesis was stated in the following terms: "Every attempt upon American liberty has always been accompanied with endeavours to settle bishops among us."[104] The reply to the "Centinel" series—undertaken by Alison's Anglican colleague the Rev. Dr. William Smith, Provost of the College—was finally extended to a series of nineteen articles published in the rival Philadelphia paper, the *Pennsylvania Gazette,* under the title "The Anatomist."[105] At the heart of "The Anatomist" was the implication that the Presbyterians and Independents looked upon New England as their exclusive domain in the matter of religion:

> "Possessed with this notion (namely, that God and nature designed New-England as the sole property and inheritance of the *Saints*) they have always considered those among them, who said their prayers in a different manner from themselves 'as spies' . . . or as intruders into their new Canaan . . . and for above half a century have pursued, with the grossest calumny and abuse, a venerable society, for having only sent a few missionaries to preach the gospel of *Christ,* according to the mode of the Church of England,

[101] See *ibid.,* pp. 44–49, and A. L. Cross: *op. cit.,* pp. 195–201.

[102] For early attempts of the New York Presbyterians to incorporate, and the opposition they met, see Carl Bridenbaugh: *op. cit.,* pp. 127–8, 181.

[103] See the broadside published in New York in 1768, *Plain Truths in a few words. To Freeholders and Freemen,* in which the Presbyterians were accused of having in their application for a charter aims other than those stated in their petition; they were also charged with using "every Artifice" to prevent the appointment of an American bishop.

[104] See *Pennsylvania Journal,* July 7, 1768.

[105] These articles began with the *Gazette* issue of September 8, 1768, and concluded on January 12, 1769, with a personal appeal to "Centinel" that, in the face of the clouds gathering over America, "it might be better for you, and for me, to cultivate *domestic harmony* for the present. . . ."

to such members of that Church as should be found within their limits."[106]

To the south of Pennsylvania the Anglican clergy were comparatively inactive on the project for promoting an American episcopate.[107] In fact, the consensus of the New York and New Jersey Anglican ministers, who met at a convention in 1767, was that, in order to stir up interest to the southward, two of their number should be sent to Maryland and Virginia.[108] As a result, the Rev. Dr. Myles Cooper, President of King's College, and the Rev. Robert McKean of Perth Amboy, New Jersey, ultimately travelled to these colonies. Perhaps under their influence, a group of nine Maryland clergymen, meeting at Annapolis in the autumn of 1770, decided to petition the Crown for a bishop, giving among other reasons the need to reform the "Profligacies" of some of their members.[109] They also addressed letters to their Anglican Governor, Robert Eden, and to Proprietor Frederick Calvert, Lord Baltimore, as well as to the Archbishop of Canterbury and the Bishop of London, appealing for support of the plan.[110] The design was that the Governor should approve the letter to Lord Baltimore and send it on; he was also furnished copies of the petition to the King and of the two letters which presumably had gone direct to the Archbishop of Canterbury and the Bishop of London.[111] Eden, apparently sceptical as to whether this action represented "unanimous Opinion" of all the Maryland clergy, addressed a letter to the nine clergymen to inform them that he was

---

[106] *Pennsylvania Gazette,* September 15, 1768. In the above connection "The Anatomist" cites appeals made in 1734 by a group of New England dissenting ministers to Dr. Edmund Gibson, Bishop of London, on the grounds that "the missionaries are neither necessary or profitable, but as to many instances injurious to the interest of the kingdom of *Christ,* and the good of his Majesty's subjects."

[107] "The American Whig" in an article in the *New-York Gazette: or, the Weekly Post-Boy* for June 6, 1768, has the following to say about the appointment of an American bishop: "From the best information I have been able to obtain, the clergy of Maryland, Virginia, North Carolina, South Carolina, Georgia, and the West Indies had no concern in the late petition transmitted on this subject. . . ."

[108] W. S. Perry: *op. cit.,* I, 415–16. For the episcopal conventions see A. L. Cross: *op. cit.* Chap. 9; see also E. L. Pennington: "Colonial Clergy Conventions," *Historical Magazine of the Protestant Episcopal Church,* VIII, 178–218, and, for the minutes of the annual convention held in May 1767, as kept by the Rev. Samuel Seabury, *ibid.,* X, 155–62.

[109] *Virginia Gazette* (Purdie and Dixon), March 28, 1771; G. M. Brydon: *op. cit.,* II, 347–8; see also *Literary Diary of Ezra Stiles,* I, 91. For a defence of the generality of the Maryland clergy, as against the charges of scandalous living proven against only seven clergymen, see N. W. Rightmyer: "The Character of the Anglican Clergy of Colonial Maryland," *Maryland Historical Magazine,* XLIV, 229–50.

[110] For the above-mentioned documents see *Proceedings of the Council of Maryland, Archives of Maryland,* XXXII, 379–84.

[111] *Ibid.,* XXXII, 380.

referring their proposal, together with the papers, to the General Assembly.[112] The clergymen replied promptly to the Governor's letter, to the effect that their proposal had not been drafted for any eyes but the Governor's and was so framed.[113] There the matter seems to have come to a standstill; for it was clear that the Governor was acting in line with the Proprietor's view that a bishopric in Maryland would run counter to the charter of 1632.[114]

But in Virginia the issue led to an extensive series of articles in the press. This development came about after a meeting of the clergy was called for June 4, 1771, by Commissary James Horrocks to consider "the Expediency of an Application to proper Authority for an American Episcopate."[115] Either interest in the matter was lacking or there was some hostility to it, at least among most of the Virginia clergy, for only a dozen out of the hundred clergymen in the Old Dominion put in an appearance.[116] When eight of those present sought to establish themselves as a majority competent to conduct a valid convention, they were opposed by the remaining four. What is more, two of the minority, the Rev. Thomas Gwatkin, Professor of Mathematics and Natural Philosophy, and the Rev. Samuel Henley, Professor of Moral Philosophy, both of the College of William and Mary, united in publishing a protest in the next number of Purdie and Dixon's *Virginia Gazette.* This was later embodied by Gwatkin in his *A Letter to the Clergy of New York and New Jersey, occasioned by An Address to the Episcopalians in Virginia,* printed at Williamsburg in 1772, and was the most serious and able criticism of the whole project for an Anglican episcopacy in America.[117] The

[112] *Ibid.,* XXXII, 384–5.

[113] In this letter to Governor Eden of September 17, 1770, signed by H. Addison, B. Allen, and J. Boucher, the clergymen sought to clarify their position before the General Assembly. *Ibid.,* XXXII, 386–7. For a study of the problems of the clergy in Maryland see Spencer Ervin: "The Established Church of Colonial Maryland," *Historical Magazine of the Protestant Episcopal Church,* XXIV, 262–7.

[114] See C. A. Barker: *The Background of the Revolution in Maryland* (Yale Historical Publications, *Miscellany,* XXXVIII, New Haven, 1940), p. 359.

[115] See *Virginia Gazette* (Purdie and Dixon), May 9, 1771. A meeting of the clergy had been held on May 4, but since the question of the appointment of a bishop had not been mentioned in the newspaper advertisement announcing the meeting, it was agreed that this subject should be listed in the call for the June meeting (*ibid.*). See also Jonathan Boucher: *Causes and Consequences of the American Revolution . . .* (London, 1797), pp. 94–6.

[116] *Literary Diary of Ezra Stiles,* I, 116.

[117] It appears that when Gwatkin and Henley were unable to persuade the majority of the clergymen at the convention to submit the whole matter to the Virginia General Assembly, they decided to make public their protest. See Gwatkin's *Letter to the Clergy,* p. 5. The reason that the convention was opposed to placing the question before the Assembly was that the Rev. Mr. Camm, a leader in the movement to secure a bishop, "*was certain it would not succeed*" (*ibid.*). Camm at this

protest stressed the following seven points: That the views of the Virginia clergy as a body were not known in this important matter; that the resolution to address the King went contrary to a previous decision of the same body not to do so; that the move to create an "American Episcopate" would extend the jurisdiction of the bishop over other colonies, which would "materially affect the natural Rights and fundamental Laws of the said Colonies, without their Consent and Approbation"; that the attempt to establish the American episcopate, would, in view of the recent disputes, also tend to raise fresh disturbances such "as may endanger the very Existence of the British Empire in America"; that the framing of such an application by the clergy without the concurrence of the government of Virginia was not only "indecent" but "an Usurpation directly repugnant to the Rights of Mankind"; that applying to the King before waiting for the opinion of the Bishop of London was, moreover, "an ill Return for his past Labours, and contrary to our Oath of canonical Obedience"; and lastly, that the manner of getting the sense of the clergy of Virginia, by *"the Hands of the Majority"* was contrary to the universal practice of the Christian Church which required the clergy "to sign all Acts of an ecclesiastical Nature in publick Convention."[118]

The attitude of the House of Burgesses toward the Anglican proposal was not slow in being manifested. When they met in July for the opening session of 1771, the Burgesses on the 12th resolved unanimously "that the Thanks of this House be given to the Reverend Mr. Henley, the Reverend Mr. Gwatkin, the Reverend Mr. Hewitt, and the Reverend Mr. Bland, for the wise and well timed Opposition they have made to the pernicious project of a few mistaken Clergymen, for introducing an *American* Bishop. . . ."[119] Although

---

period, by reason of his activities against the Twopenny Acts, was very unpopular with the leaders of the House of Burgesses. Although he had been dismissed from his post as Professor of Divinity at William and Mary because of his opposition to those acts, he was, nevertheless, appointed in 1771 President of the College, Rector of Bruton Parish, Commissary of the Bishop of London, and a member of the Virginia Council.

[118] *Ibid.*, pp. 6–8.

[119] *Journals of the House of Burgesses, 1770–1772*, p. 122. It may be noted that Richard Henry Lee and Richard Bland were appointed a committee to acquaint the four clergymen of the thanks of the House (*ibid.*). Bland, who—as was indicated in the preceding volume of this series (see Volume X in this series, p. 153)—had taken a leading part in opposing the clergy over the issue of the Twopenny Acts, wrote on August 1, 1771, to Thomas Adams in England affirming that "if this Scheme had been effected, it would have overturned all our Acts of Assembly relative to *ecclesiastical* Jurisdiction, most of which acts have received the Royal assent, and have existed, amongst us, almost from the First establishment of the Colony" (*Virginia Magazine of History and Biography,* VI, 130). As for Lee, his attitude toward an

the matter continued to be aired in the press, the issue was dead in Virginia after the emphatic stand taken by the House of Burgesses.[120]

The potential intimate connection between the proposals for American Anglican bishops and for the alteration of the civil government of the colonies is brought out clearly in an interesting document entitled "A Plan . . . for the better Government of the British Colonies" which appeared in the *Boston Evening-Post* of December 31, 1770. The "Plan," it was asserted, was taken "from a late London Paper." Whether it was the brain child of some member of the Established Church of England who sought to see the colonies reorganized, or whether it was simply a shrewd way of creating American antagonism to the idea of permitting any political or ecclesiastical change in the New World, is not clear. In any case, it could only have served to arouse resentment.

Under some thirty-seven headings the "Plan" presented the changes required to secure better methods of governing the colonies. All trade and navigation statutes were to be scrapped in favour of one comprehensive act which would permit the colonies as free a trade "as is considered consistent with the interests of Great Britain." Then followed an outline for reorganizing colonial governments which Parliament would empower the King to bring to pass. This included the power to appoint and remove all colonial Governors, with an added proviso that no Governor was to hold office more than five years in any province. As a necessary step in this direction, all corporate and proprietorial governments were to lose their charters and were to be held directly from the Crown. Further, North America and the adjacent islands were to be erected into a kingdom inalienably annexed to Great Britain, with the King's title to be "King of North America and the Isles." As the King's representative, there should be appointed to oversee the new kingdom a Lord Lieutenant with the rank and authority of the Lord Lieutenant of Ireland. He was to be a peer of Great Britain holding a three-year term of office. In carrying out his duties the Lord Lieutenant was

---

American bishop was made clear in a letter to his brother William on June 19, 1771. Referring to the published protest of Henley and Gwatkin against the step taken by the eight clergymen, he wrote: "For peace sake let us [have no?] Bishop. Neither Tythes nor Ecclesiastical courts will do in America . . ." (*Letters of Richard Henry Lee* [ed. J. C. Ballagh, 2 vols., New York, 1911–14], I, 59). A part of the letter, shown in brackets above, was torn, but the meaning is clear.

[120] For the issue of an episcopacy in Virginia in the early 1770's see G. M. Brydon: *op. cit.*, II, 43–59, A. L. Cross: *op. cit.*, pp. 230–40, and G. W. Pilcher: "Virginia Newspapers and the Dispute Over the Proposed Colonial Episcopate, 1771–1772," *The Historian*, XXIII, 98–133.

to be aided by a Chancellor and other officers appointed to an administrative set-up corresponding to that of Ireland. Also, as in Ireland, the new kingdom was to have a parliament consisting of two houses: the upper one was to be drawn from members of the councils of the several provinces and islands who were to be nominated by the Crown to hold office for life; the lower one was to be selected by the popular assemblies of the various provinces from those Protestant members who held the necessary property qualifications. This parliament was to gather in October of every third year and the sessions were not to extend over three months. No parliament was to last over nine years without a dissolution and general election. Proper provisions for the new kingdom were to include a parliament house, a chapel, and a fortified palace for the Lieutenant Governor, to be erected "at or near Boston, as soon as possible."

As to ecclesiastical reorganization, according to the "Plan" the colonies were to be grouped into three bishoprics. The most northerly was to be the "Boston Bishopric" and should include all of New England, the provinces of Quebec and Nova Scotia, and the crown colony of Newfoundland, together with other islands to the east of Boston. The "Pennsylvania Bishopric" was to comprehend all the colonies south of New England as far down as North Carolina, plus the Bermudas; while the "Carolina Bishopric" would include the remainder of the continental colonies and the British islands of the West Indies. The American bishops were to be appointed by the King, and, if he judged it proper, the Bishop of Boston was to be made the Metropolitan. Each diocese was to erect a cathedral with a proper number of persons appointed to carry out the duties attached to it, as in England; for their maintenance they were to receive grants of lands, private donations, and, if need be, funds derived from colonial quit-rents and the sale of Crown lands. The eldest bishop or the one who was the Metropolitan was to rank next to the Lord Lieutenant, and the other bishops were to rank according to seniority with members of the upper house of the parliament, where they were to have seats but neither vote nor right of speech, except in matters of religion.

One can imagine the reaction of the New England Congregational clergy to the proposal to make the incorporated city of Boston not only the capital of the Kingdom of North America and the Isles—where, as Lord Lieutenant, a great peer would dwell in a fortified palace—but also the site of the palace and cathedral of the Anglican Metropolitan! That a reply should have appeared in the next edition of the paper which had presented the "Plan"[121] is not at all surprising.

Doubtless expressing the views of most Americans, the writer of the "Answer" freely admitted that no one could object to a plan for the better government of the American colonies "if such a one can be found"; he also agreed that colonials were quite willing to see all anti-commercial laws repealed and such as were pro-commercial enacted; nor did he object to the idea that His Majesty be empowered to form a new plan for the government of America, provided that it be submitted to and accepted by the colonies—"But not otherwise." As to the voiding of the charters held by some of the colonies, the author declared the willingness of Americans to see this done "when we have violated the conditions on which they were given and by which we hold them: But not 'till then." With respect to the idea that America should be placed under a Lord Lieutenant, he agreed that colonials would submit to it "when conquered by force of arms, as Ireland was: But not 'till then." With regard to an American parliament, this would be proper "when our General Assemblies fail to answer the Designs of Government, and are finally dissolv'd—But not sooner." In the field of religion and church government the writer declared: "we are willing Bishoprics, Metropolitans, Dioceses, etc. be appointed, when our Lord, . . . instead of saying 'Ye are all Brethren' in the ministry, shall say 'Some of you shall be Lords, Metropolitans, etc., other Officials, Underlings, and the like'—But not 'till then." Finally, concerning the "Articles etc." of the Church of England, the colonials were pictured as being quite ready to see them "revised, and reduced to the sacred Canon, before any Plan of Ecclesiastical Government be proposed for North-America: and 'till this is done . . . we must treat the Plan prepared, as injurious to the Laws of Christ, contrary to good and sound Policy; and even an high affront to reason, and common Sense."

That the opposition to an American episcopate was chiefly the result of fear on the part of the non-Anglican colonial clergy of a potential threat to their churches becomes increasingly clear, as is the fact that the Anglicans had a good case for desiring a bishop.[122]

---

[121] *Boston Evening-Post,* January 7, 1771.

[122] In Benjamin Franklin's pamphlet *Cool Thoughts on the Present Situation of our Public Affairs* (1764), in which he advocated a royal government for Pennsylvania, he also anticipated the objections that a royal government would mean a bishop and indicated that this should be no cause for alarm because of "the apparent Necessity of the Thing" and the limited role a bishop could play in the life of the colonies. See *Writings of Benjamin Franklin* . . . (ed. A. H. Smyth, 10 vols., New York, 1905–7), IV, 237.

Nevertheless, the political implications of such a step were so dangerous, in view of the growing American dissatisfaction with the home government, that no minister of the King was willing to add what would have been abundant fuel to the fires of American resentment toward British colonial policy. This was especially true after the crisis over the repeal of the Stamp Act. Thus no practical steps to send over a bishop were ever pursued by the British government. The Duke of Newcastle, when requested as early as 1749 by Bishop Sherlock to use his influence to secure the appointment of American bishops, replied that this was "a great, and national consideration; [something that] had long been under the Deliberation of great, and wise men, heretofore and was, by them laid aside."[123] Neither was Pitt, during his two ministries, nor Grenville,[124] Rockingham, Grafton (with his Unitarian leanings), or North prepared to give the least countenance to the scheme, so far as available evidence would show.

William Samuel Johnson, an Anglican who was the London agent for Connecticut at the time, wrote from London to Governor Jonathan Trumbull on February 26, 1770: "It is not intended, at present, to send any bishop into the American Colonies; . . . and should it be done at all, you may be assured, it will be in such a manner as in no degree to prejudice, nor, if possible, even to give the least offence, to any denomination of Protestants. It has, indeed, been merely a religious, in no respects a political design."[125] Yet

---

[123] See Norman Sykes: *Edmund Gibson, Bishop of London, 1669–1748* . . . (Oxford, 1926), p. 872. The attitude of the government in 1750 toward the appointment of American bishops was also made very clear in a long letter that Horatio Walpole, who was close to Newcastle, addressed to Sherlock on May 29, in which he pointed out that such a step would raise a storm against the government not only in America but among the dissenters at home who were then well affected toward the Ministry. See A. L. Cross: *op. cit.*, pp. 324–30.

[124] It is true that in 1763 the Earl of Halifax, serving under Grenville as Secretary of State for the Southern Department, appeared to favour the idea of appointing American bishops. At least Dr. Secker, Archbishop of Canterbury, writing on September 16, 1763, to the Rev. Jacob Duché of Philadelphia, declared that Halifax "is a friend to it. But as matters are at present amongst us I doubt whether he hath zeal enough to undertake what will certainly meet with opposition, and the more for Dr. Mayhew's late Pamphlet [*Observations on the Charter and Conduct of the Society for the Propagation of the Gospel in Foreign Parts* . . .] which I presume you have seen" (*Historical Collections Relating to the American Colonial Church, Vol. II, Pennsylvania* [ed. W. S. Perry, Hartford, Conn., 1871], p. 390). Grenville, as is well known, was at the time shaping his colonial financial policy and the last thing in the world that he desired was to stir up a hornets' nest in America over the issue of bishops.

[125] Trumbull Papers, Massachusetts Historical Society *Collections*, 5th ser., IX, 412–13.

colonials could not be persuaded that Anglican bishops would fit into the American scene or that a plot was not underfoot to bring about such a system in North America. Nor was the British Ministry unaware of these colonial feelings.

In fact, both press and pulpit in America echoed with antagonistic statements against religious absolutism, whether of the Church of England or of Rome,[126] as well as against what was considered to be the absolutism of parliamentary interference with the natural rights of colonials. The effectiveness of the press as a propaganda medium has been discussed elsewhere. It was, obviously, used in many ways to make religious issues serve the ends of colonial resistance. As for the pulpit, it too was a prime agency for the dissemination of propaganda, and was so used, especially in New England, where practically everyone went to church and where the sermon—an integral part of public events, such as elections and special celebrations—was often published, to become as widely, if not more widely read than the local newspaper. Much of the propaganda so disseminated, when not based on the religious fears and prejudices just mentioned, reflected the transition from the Puritan doctrine of divine law to the eighteenth-century doctrine of natural law as manifested, for example, in the writings of John Wise.[127] Thus, in the two decades preceding the outbreak of the War for American Independence, the exhortations from the non-Anglican pulpit and the outpourings of the press helped to create a climate of opinion ready not only to accept exploitation of religious issues to further the cause of American freedom, but also to predicate action on political and philosophical ideas. For example, one of the arguments used against the establishment of an Anglican episcopacy in America was that with an episcopal hierarchy would come the setting

[126] See especially Jonathan Mayhew: *Popish Idolatry: A Discourse Delivered in the Chapel of Harvard-College, . . . May 8, 1765* (Boston, 1765). This was one of the Dudleian annual lectures, founded to attack popery every fourth year, as was Samuel Cooper's *The Man of Sin* (Boston, 1774), a work equal to Mayhew's in invective against popery. For the most recent analysis of the anti-Catholic movement of the 1760's and 1770's, which persisted until 1776, when it became expedient to win over the Catholic colonials, see Father C. M. Metzger's excellent book, *Catholics and the American Revolution: A Study in Religious Climate* (Chicago, 1962), Chaps. 1 and 2.

[127] It is significant that the year 1772 saw the reprinting in Boston of two separate and heavily subscribed editions of John Wise's *A Vindication of the Government of New-England Churches . . .* , a work that leaned heavily upon Baron Samuel Pufendorf and made a distinction between the natural and the civil being of man. See, in this connection, G. A. Cook: *John Wise: Early American Democrat* (New York, 1952), Chap. 10, "Wise's 'Small Treatise'"; see also Clinton Rossiter: *Seedtime of the Republic*, pp. 212–26, and Max Savelle: *Seeds of Liberty . . .* (New York, 1948), pp. 319–23.

up in North America of ecclesiastical law.[128] Similarly, playing upon the hostile sentiments of New Englanders towards Catholicism, John Adams in 1765 published anonymously his observations "On Canon and Feudal Law" in four issues of the *Boston Gazette.*[129] Both John and Samuel Adams[130]—inconsistently enough—were past masters at cloaking the evils of "a Government of the Church" in praises of the founding fathers and at appealing to Puritan prejudices in order to pursue the patriot argument. It is therefore not surprising to find that a violent reaction—against what were called attempts on the part of the British government to establish popery in North America—should have followed on the heels of the passage of the Quebec Act in 1774 (a subject to be discussed in a later volume of this series). Yet freedom of faith was an issue, even among those who, strangely enough, denied it to others, as was the case in the disabilities suffered, as the result of the lack of toleration, by the Catholics or in the persecution by Connecticut "Saybrook Platform" Congregationalists of the "Separatists," even as late as 1777.[131]

In conclusion, it should be affirmed that the part played by the non-Anglican clergy[132] in furthering the revolutionary movement cannot be questioned and should not be minimized. Actually, when the lines were finally drawn, numbers of Anglicans, especially the

---

[128] For the continued use of the threat of episcopal bishops as a weapon to foment anti-British sentiment, see "Writings of the Rev. William Tennent, 1740–1777" (ed. N. B. Jones), *South Carolina Historical Magazine,* LXI, 129–45, especially for his letter which appeared in the *South-Carolina Gazette; And Country Journal,* August 16, 1774.

[129] See *Boston Gazette,* August 12, 19, September 30, and October 21, 1765; see also *Adams Papers* (Butterfield), 1st ser., I, 255–8, and *Adams Works* (C. F. Adams), III, 447–53.

[130] For the Samuel Adams articles, published in 1768–9 under such pseudonyms as "Vindex," "A Layman," "A Puritan," "Populus," etc., and in 1770–1 as "Candidus," "Valerius Popicola," "Determinatus," etc., see *Boston Gazette* (*passim*) for those years.

[131] For the persecution of the Saybrook Separatists see Volume III, revised, of this series, p. 80.

[132] By the non-Anglican clergy we mean, more specifically, the Congregationalists and Presbyterians. For the changing situation in Massachusetts Bay and Connecticut with respect to the Congregational Establishment, as viewed in the middle of the eighteenth century when the New Light Congregationalists and the Baptists were gathering strength, see Volume III, revised, of this series, pp. 21–6, 79–81. For the drift away from Calvinism and other aspects of the religious picture by the 1760's, see Volume X, pp. 21–4. For the leadership of Isaac Backus in the Baptist Church and his argument that if Samuel Adams saw oppression in taxation without representation, then he must realize that the taxes laid by the British Parliament on the American colonies represented no greater an oppression than the ministerial tax imposed by Massachusetts Bay upon the Baptists, see Isaac Backus: *A Church History of New England* . . . (3 vols., Boston and Providence, 1777–96), II, 303–5; see also G. E. Horr: "The Baptists," *The Religious History of New England* (Cambridge, Mass., 1917), 135–76, especially p. 160.

clergy, were strongly Loyalist—but with many notable exceptions, for they were divided among themselves—whereas the Presbyterians, for example, were ultra-patriotic, as were the Congregationalists. The majority of members of other churches, both Catholic and Protestant—outside the pacifistic sects—also apparently supported the American cause.[133] In the final analysis it is clear that the idea of local control of worship was more deeply rooted in the minds of the American people than was the Loyalist appeal for "Church and King."[134]

---

[133] For the best studies of the influence of religious factors on the revolutionary movement see C. H. Van Tyne: "The Influence of the Clergy, and of Religious and Sectarian Forces, on the American Revolution," *American Historical* Review, XIX, 44–64, J. W. Thornton: *op. cit.*, and A. M. Baldwin: *op. cit.*, as well as the standard works bearing on the individual sects in colonial times.

[134] In Chap. 2, "The Church and the American Revolution," of his *Story of American Protestantism* (Boston, 1951), A. L. Drummond states (p. 138) that "upwards of 80,000 'church and King' Loyalists migrated to Canada and the West Indies. These were mostly property-holders . . . ; poor Churchmen were more inclined to be American patriots."

CHAPTER X

Intercolonial Conflicts: New York and Its Rivals

THE early manifestations of colonial unity of action which, under the leadership of Massachusetts Bay, had been evident in 1768—in reaction to Lord Hillsborough's attempt to restrict the freedom of action of their assemblies and a little later in the movement for non-importation in protest against the Townshend Revenue Act—were but temporary expedients.

It is true that other colonies reacted strongly to the so-called Massacre that had taken place in the principal city of Massachusetts Bay; for it was played up prominently by the colonial press as a means of raising the issue of the right of Great Britain to maintain a standing army in the colonies in peacetime. Yet, neither this event nor the widely publicized objections to the establishment of an American episcopacy was sufficiently important to become a rallying point for binding the colonies together in united action. Something more was needed, especially in view of the diversity of interests[1] and bitter rivalry that persisted between many of the colonies over issues involving lands and boundaries.

Boundary conflicts between most of the colonies were inevitable in view of the nature of the original land grants made by the Crown and of the charters setting up the colonies, with their sea-to-sea claims. Most of these grants were made in the seventeenth century, at a time when no land surveys had been completed and an accurate knowledge of the geography of North America was lacking.[2] Further-

[1] See Volume X, of this series, Chap. 1.

[2] The degree of accuracy achieved by the government patent offices is notable considering the unparalleled conditions of the time: the lack of surveying instruments and the shortage of surveying personnel to cover such vast areas as needed to be covered on the North American continent. Furthermore the Crown was not always prepared to assume the enormous expense involved in laying down accurate boundaries, nor were the individual patent holders any more willing to do so, for both were

more, the terms of subsequent grants could not, in many cases, be easily reconciled with the terms of the original grant. Nor was there any consistent land policy on the part of the British government until the 1770's, as will be discussed in a subsequent chapter of this volume.

Beyond these factors lay the very nature of colonial Americans. They were, by and large, enterprising, resourceful, and aggressive. The display of such qualities had made it possible for them to achieve so much in the conquest of the wilderness by 1763 and to have become by that year a generally powerful, prosperous, and dynamic people. They fought stubbornly to attain their objectives, and did not hesitate to magnify their own rights against those who opposed them, whether they were confronting the government of Great Britain or each other. As a consequence, in most of the colonies the courts were loaded down with litigation, and packets plying the Atlantic carried a stream of appeals and petitions to the Board of Trade and the King in Council.

Thus, between the welter of conflicting evidence on boundaries—as found in early charters, grants, defective maps and surveys—and the eager pursuit of personal advantage on the part of speculators and settlers, the foundations were laid for a series of sharp intercolonial conflicts. This subject, however, would provide material for a large book in itself. Therefore, in order to throw some light upon it within the limitations of this series, we will confine our examination to the issues that arose between the provinces of New York and Pennsylvania and their respective neighbours, for these involved all the seaboard colonies from Quebec to Virginia, with the exception of Rhode Island.[3]

---

aware, as were colonial Governors and others in authority, that no one yet had the key to the topography of the land. For the problems of surveying and map-making in the eighteenth century see L. A. Brown: *The Story of Maps* (Boston, 1949), Erwin Raisz: *General Cartography* (New York, 1948), and Walter Thiele: *Official Map Publications* (Chicago, 1938).

[3] The only comparable situation in the south was that of South Carolina and its neighbours. The dispute between South Carolina and North Carolina continued from 1713 until 1815, despite a temporary settlement in 1772 based on surveys supervised by commissioners from both colonies in 1735, 1737, and 1772, and as the result of which South Carolina gained the "New Acquisition" area close to the Cherokee line. See M. L. Skaggs: *North Carolina Boundary Disputes Involving her Southern Line* (Chapel Hill, N.C., 1941). In 1761 Governor James Glen stated that the dispute resulted from "the dishonest Intentions of many lawless People, settled in those parts without legal Titles, and not to any Want of Attention in Government, . . . but those People, by keeping up a Dispute about the Boundaries between North and South Carolina, evade paying Quit-rents for their Lands, &c. and so long as they can enjoy the protection of Government without contributing their Quotas towards the Expence of it, they will be for keeping up the Dispute about Boundaries" (*A*

New York and Canadian Land Claimants

By the Proclamation of 1763 the boundary line between the provinces of New York and Quebec was laid down to be the forty-fifth degree of north latitude, thus leaving Lake Champlain to the south of that line.[4] But what about the rights of French Canadians who claimed patents to seigneuries to the south of that line in the region of Lake George and Lake Champlain?[5] Could these lands be granted to others and, more particularly, to American officers who had served in the late war and who had made application as early as 1762 for land grants in the area of Lake Champlain?[6] When

---

Description of South Carolina . . . [London, 1761], p. 3). In this same work Glen remarked: "It is evident that a considerable Part of the Territory of South Carolina lies to the southward of Georgia" (*ibid.*). This remark referred to the territory west and south of the Altamaha.

The problem between South Carolina and Georgia revolved around the interpretation of charter claims, the Georgia charter of 1732 having given to that newly created colony all land between the Savannah and the Altamaha rivers west to the Pacific. The issue centered on an interpretation of what was the head of the Savannah, with South Carolina holding that the river began at the junction of the Keowee and the Tugaloo. (The question of the Savannah as a line of demarcation, despite an agreement reached in 1787, was not finally settled until 1922.) Furthermore, after the Proclamation of 1763, which resulted in Georgia's annexation of lands lying between the Altamaha and St. Mary's rivers, the colony claimed that the lands so acquired extended west to the Mississippi, but South Carolina denied this, contending that Georgia had no right to attempt by regulation to monopolize the Indian trade with the Creeks within its borders. The Board of Trade sustained this contention to the extent of stating that in so far as the Indians were independent nations, trade with them was open to all colonials. See, in this connection, *Colonial Records of Georgia,* IX, 215–16; see also in this series Volume IV, 43–5, and IX, 182, 203, 220–1, especially for the involvement of East and West Florida in these disputes; D. D. Wallace: *South Carolina* . . . (Chapel Hill, N.C., 1951), Chaps. 20 and 21; and Kenneth Coleman: *The American Revolution in Georgia* (Athens, Ga., 1958), p. 258. For the aspects of these land disputes involving the Indian tribes see J. R. Alden: *John Stuart and the Southern Frontier,* and, for the final "Breakdown of the Royal Management of Lands in the Southern Provinces, 1773–1775," see St. George L. Sioussat's article under that title in *Agricultural History,* III, 67–98.

[4] For the Proclamation of 1763 see *British Royal Proclamations Relating to America, 1603–1783* (ed. C. S. Brigham in the *Transactions of the American Antiquarian Society,* 1911, XII, 212–18). For the background of the boundary decision separating the provinces of Quebec and New York see Max Savelle: *The Diplomatic History of the Canadian Boundary, 1749–1763* (New Haven, 1940).

[5] For reference to the memorial of the Marquis Michel Chartier de Lotbinière to the King for confirmation of two large concessions of land in the form of seigneuries lying both east and west of Lake Champlain and also in the Lake George country, see the Board of Trade to Lieutenant Governor Colden, July 13, 1764, *New York Colonial Documents,* VII, 642; see also *Documentary History of the State of New York* (ed. E. B. O'Callaghan, 4 vols., Albany, 1849–51), I, 347–9, to be cited hereafter as *Documentary History of New York.*

[6] Sir Jeffrey Amherst to Mr. Sharpe, October 20, 1762, *New York Colonial Documents,* VII, 508–10.

Governor Moore and Governor Carleton in 1766, acting for the provinces of New York and Quebec, personally designated the point on the Sorel River that was to be the dividing line, a number of Frenchmen came from Quebec to request confirmation of their claims to lands south of the line, "some of which consisted of Tracts containing 100,000 acres and others of 150,000 acres." Informed by Moore that if their grants were confirmed they would be expected to pay to the Crown a quit-rent of two shillings sixpence for each 100 acres, they replied that they were not prepared to do so, and requested that no land in the region of Lake Champlain be granted until their claims were laid before His Majesty.[7] However, some grants in this area had been made in 1765 by Lieutenant Governor Colden, and others were subsequently made by Governor Moore, without express permission of the Crown both before and after the meeting with the French claimants.[8] The sticky question of early French-Canadian rights to Lake Champlain lands was allowed to rest until 1768, when a decision was reached by the King in Council "not to allow any claims made upon the ground of ancient grants from the Government of Canada to Lands which were never acknowledged to belong of right to the Crown of France." At the same time, the Governor of New York was instructed that French claimants to lands which they had actually settled and improved were not to be disturbed but were to be permitted to maintain peaceable possession of them—"provided they consent to establish their Title by Grants under the seal of the Province of New York, upon the usual Conditions of Quit Rent and Improvement."[9] This was followed in 1769 by an additional instruction to Governor Moore which noted that "sundry persons, proprietors under titles derived from the Crown of France" of lands in the Lake Champlain area, had represented that several parts of the lands they claimed had been granted to other persons under the seal of the Province of New York, a move so prejudicial to their rights that they prayed the royal disapproval of those grants. The Governor was therefore

---

[7] Sir Henry Moore to the Board of Trade, November 7, 1766, *ibid.*, VII, 873–5, and Moore to the Earl of Shelburne, November 8, 1766, *ibid.*, VII, 875–7.

[8] For a list of grants made by the government of New York between 1765 and 1767 in the Lake Champlain area see *ibid.*, VII, 902–5. For a map of the British and French land grants about Lake Champlain see *Documentary History of New York*, I, opposite page 368.

[9] The Earl of Hillsborough to Governor Moore, February 25, 1768, *New York Colonial Documents*, VIII, 12; for the order in Council see *Acts of the Privy Council, Col. Ser., 1766–1783*, pp. 143–4.

directed to make no grants of these lands without prior approval by the Crown of the basic petitions.[10]

But the French claims to Lake Champlain lands continued to be "a consideration of great difficulty and delicacy, and by no means of a nature to admit of an hasty decision," according to the Earl of Dartmouth writing in 1772 to Governor Tryon, who had taken over the administration of New York.[11] In fact two petitions from French claimants were then before the government of Great Britain; one of these was by the Chevalier de Lotbinière for a confirmation of his rights and the other by several individuals. They based their rights to Lake Champlain lands and other lands south of the boundary upon five points: (1) that the lands in question were within the ancient boundaries of Canada; (2) that by the 37th article of the capitulation of New France, signed by General Amherst and the Marquis de Vaudreuil on September 8, 1760, the "Lords of Manors, . . . the Canadians as well in the towns as in the country, the French, settled, or trading in the whole extent of the Colony of Canada . . . shall preserve the entire . . . property and possession of the goods, . . . movable and immovable . . . ; they shall not be touched, nor the least damage done to them, on any pretence whatsoever," and by the Treaty of Peace, the British Crown agreed "That the French inhabitants of Canada . . . may sell their Estates, provided it be to the subjects of his Britannick Majesty . . ." ; (3) that the petitioners or their grantors had made actual improvements on the lands and were in possession of them; (4) that they had established their right by having paid the *quint* or fifth part of the purchase price to the Governor of New France; (5) that they had suffered a hardship by being dispossessed by titles granted by the government of New York.[12]

---

[10] For this instruction, dated July 5, 1769, see *New York Colonial Documents,* VIII, 175; see also Hillsborough to Lieutenant Governor Colden, December 9, 1769, *ibid.,* VIII, 193. Among other claimants of Lake Champlain lands under French title was Major General James Murray, who had been Governor of the Province of Quebec and who had purchased from a M. François Faucault his fief and seigneurie, which joined, on the eastern border of that lake, the seigneurie of M. de Noyan. Part of the Murray seigneurie was in New York and part in the Province of Quebec. Murray prayed His Majesty that the whole of his seigneurie might be preserved intact and confirmed to him. *Acts of the Privy Council, Col. Ser., 1766–1783,* pp. 144–5. Other Englishmen, such as Lieutenant Colonel Christie and Captain Robert Stobo, had also purchased seigneuries south of the boundary line and were in much the same position as Murray; Stobo had, it appears, purchased the seigneurie of Aux Loutres on Lake Champlain and Otter Creek. *Ibid.,* pp. 145–7.

[11] Dartmouth to Tryon, November 4, 1772, *New York Colonial Documents,* VIII, 317.

[12] The contents of the two petitions are summarized in a pamphlet authorized by

On May 25, 1775, the Board of Trade finally recommended the rejection of the claims of one of the French patentees, Chevalier de Lotbinière. But the Lords of the Committee of the Privy Council felt that the Frenchman deserved compensation and, on March 15, 1776, recommended that he be given 150,000 acres of land in another part of New York as recompense for the loss of his seigneuries.[13] It was now too late, however, for in July of that year New York and the other twelve older British North American colonies declared their independence of Great Britain. Thus collapsed the Lotbinière claims together with those of British officers to lands in the Lake Champlain area.

New York and the New Hampshire Land Patents

The issue between New York and New Hampshire over land was vastly more important in its final solution than that involving the Province of Quebec and therefore demands much fuller consideration.[14]

The southern boundary of New Hampshire, as recommended by a boundary commission, was fixed by an order in council in 1741. This order laid down that it should run from a point due north of Pawtucket Falls on the Merrimac River and then by "a strait line drawn from thence due west cross s[d] river till it meets with his Majesties other Governments."[15] What did this mean with respect to the western extension of the line? Governor Benning Wentworth of New Hampshire took the position that his province now extended as far to the west as did Massachusetts Bay and Connecticut and affirmed in a letter to the Governor of New York that "New Hampshire had an equal right to claim the Same extent of Western bound-

---

the New York Assembly, [James Duane]: *A State of the Right of the Colony of New-York, with respect To it's Eastern Boundary on Connecticut River, So far as concerns the late Encroachments under The Government of New-Hampshire, And also a State of the Rights of the Colony . . . So far as concerns the Grants formerly made by the French Government of Canada, of Lands on Lake-Champlain, And at and to the Southward of Crown-Point* (New York, 1773), p. 26. There follows (pp. 26–8) an exposition of the claims of New York as against the French pretensions.

[13] *Acts of the Privy Council, Col. Ser., 1766–1783*, pp. 147–9, and *New York Colonial Documents*, VIII, 577–9.

[14] See M. B. Jones: *Vermont in the Making, 1750–1777* (Cambridge, Mass., 1939), especially Chap. 2 for the speculative aspects of Governor Wentworth's activities. In consulting this work the student should also refer to John Clement: "Vermont in the Making, A Review," Vermont Historical Society *Proceedings*, new ser., VII, 178–84.

[15] *Acts of the Privy Council, Col Ser., 1720–1745*, pp. 594–600. See also instructions to Governor Wentworth respecting the boundary line in *Provincial Papers . . . of New Hamsphire*, V, 595–6 (this title is first cited in full in Chap. 6, note 10).

ary's with those Charter Governments. . . ."[16] What is more, since he had secured in 1748 a special commission from the Crown to make grants of land upon a quit-rent basis of a shilling proclamation money or ninepence sterling per hundred acres,[17] he proceeded to make grants of clusters of townships, each township six miles square, extending sixty miles both east and west of the Connecticut River. By 1765 at least 130 grants had been made.[18] The attitude of New York toward the New Hampshire claims was expressed by Governor George Clinton on June 6, 1750, when, with the advice of the New York Council, he replied to the Wentworth letter that the terms of a royal patent given by Charles II to the Duke of York had granted "all the lands from the West side of Connecticut River, to the East side of Delaware Bay."[19] In turn, Wentworth asked, if this were the case, by what right did Massachusetts Bay and Connecticut claim land far west of the Connecticut? He also stated that before receiving the New York letter he had made a grant of a township that extended as far west as a point twenty-four miles to the east of Albany.[20]

The position of New York, as outlined by Attorney General Richard Bradley in 1751, was that the western boundary of Connecticut, which was within twenty miles of the Hudson, was based upon an agreement going back to the year 1684 and had been marked out by commissioners in 1725. As for the claim of Massachusetts Bay to extend as far west as Connecticut, he asserted that that colony had simply "Intruded upon and taken possession of the Lands . . . without pretence of right . . ." and that all lands west of the Connecticut River belonged to New York.[21] The observations on this report made by the New York surveyor general later that same year pointed out that several tracts of land in the area now claimed by New Hampshire had been granted by New York to some of

---

[16] Wentworth to Governor George Clinton of New York, April 25, 1750, *Documentary History of New York*, IV, 332.

[17] For Wentworth's instruction of 1748 see P.R.O., C.O. 5:941, pp. 207–45; see also B. W. Bond, Jr.,: *The Quit-Rent System in the American Colonies* (New Haven and London, 1919), p. 60.

[18] For the list of Wentworth's grants up to 1765 see *New Hampshire Provincial Papers*, X, 204–7; see also *Vermont State Papers; Being a Collection of Records and Documents* . . . (ed. William Slade, Middlebury, 1823), pp. 13–16 (this single-volume collection should not be confused with the series of *State Papers of Vermont* to be cited subsequently), and maps facing pp. 46–7, Volume III, revised, in this series.

For the Boston land speculators, including such men as Boston town clerk William Cooper and Samuel Adams, who held grants from Wentworth, see G. P. Anderson's paper in the Colonial Society of Massachusetts *Transactions*, XXV, 33–8.

[19] *New York Colonial Documents*, VII, 595.

[20] *Ibid.*, VII, 595, and *Documentary History of New York*, IV, 333.

[21] For the Bradley opinion see *ibid.*, IV, 334–9.

its inhabitants.[22] It was argued by both governments that the matter should be submitted to the King in Council for final determination. But the decision was long delayed and Wentworth continued to make land grants. As a result, on December 28, 1763, Lieutenant Governor Cadwallader Colden issued a proclamation warning all people not to accept grants from the Governor of New Hampshire to lands west of the Connecticut River.[23] In a counter-proclamation issued on March 13, 1764, Governor Wentworth assured those who had taken out patents under his authority not to doubt that "All Grants made by New Hampshire that are fulfilled by the Grantees will be confirmed to them if it should be His Majestys pleasure to alter the Jurisdiction." To that end he urged all who had such claims "to be industrious in clearing and cultivating their Lands. . . ."[24]

Not until July 20, 1764, did the Privy Council finally act; its decision being based upon a representation of the Board of Trade made earlier in that month, which was itself grounded largely upon a long report covering the controversy written by Lieutenant Governor Colden on January 20.[25] According to the order in council the New Hampshire–New York boundary was fixed at "the Western Banks of the River Connecticut, from where it enters the Province of the Massachusetts Bay, as far North as the forty fifth Degree of Northern Latitude. . . ."[26]

The decision of the Privy Council might have settled the matter

---

[22] For Cadwallader Colden's observations see *ibid.*, IV, 339–40.

[23] For the Colden proclamation see *ibid.*, IV, 346–7.

[24] For the Wentworth proclamation see *ibid.*, IV, 353–4; see also *Vermont State Papers*, pp. 17–18.

[25] Representation of the Board of Trade, July 10, 1764, P.R.O., C.O. 5:942, ff. 284–301, which may be found printed in M. B. Jones: *op. cit.*, Appendix A. For the Colden letter see *New York Colonial Documents*, VII, 595–8. For the contest between the New Yorkers and those holding grants of land from New Hampshire see Irving Mark: *Agrarian Conflicts in Colonial New York, 1711–1775 (Columbia University Studies in History, Economics and Public Law*, No. 469, New York, 1940), Chap. 6, "Yorkers v. Yankees." For the position of New Yorkers see E. P. Alexander: *A Revolutionary Conservative: James Duane of New York* (New York, 1938), Chap. 5, "The New Hampshire Grants." Duane was appointed one of the agents and commissioners for New York in the later proceedings, when in 1784 a federal court was instituted to hear out the controversy between New York and Massachusetts. Although the trial never took place—the matter being settled amicably—Duane had prepared a brief on the "State of the Evidence . . . In support of the Territorial Rights and Jurisdiction of New York against . . . New Hampshire . . . and . . . Massachusetts," which contains the essence of the New York claims. This document is published in New-York Historical Society *Collections for 1870*, Section 1.

[26] *Documentary History of New York*, IV, 355, and *Acts of the Privy Council, Col. Ser., 1745–1766*, pp. 673–4; see also the Board of Trade to Lieutenant Governor Colden, July 13, 1764, *New York Colonial Documents*, VII, 642–3.

harmoniously, so far as the grantees of lands were concerned, had not the conditions under which lands in the disputed area were allotted varied for each side. Among other differences was the fact that under terms of the instructions given to the Governor of New York the quit-rent was fixed at two shillings and sixpence per hundred acres, whereas for the same acreage the government of New Hampshire charged but a shilling. Likewise, other conditions were more favourable to New Hampshire grantees.[27]

With New York now free to make land grants up to the Connecticut, and New Hampshire forbidden to interfere in matters west of that river, over a hundred New York grants were made between May 21, 1765, and January 12, 1776.[28] Some of these covered grants already made by New Hampshire. This again led to bitter complaints on the part of those affected. The Privy Council felt obliged to take these protests into consideration, along with a memorial sent by settlers holding New Hampshire patents who, faced with ejection from their property for not accepting the terms offered by New York, asked that they be confirmed in their property under the terms set forth by the "charter of incorporation passed in New Hampshire. . . ."[29]

On June 6, 1766, a New York ordinance was passed for setting up courts in the disputed area, and on July 3 the county of Cumberland was erected by act of the Assembly to embrace most of this region.[30] Although the act setting up the county was disallowed by the Privy Council on June 26, 1767, a new act, passed on March 19, 1768, was permitted to stand. Thus, with some minor alterations in its boundary lines the county continued to exist until the period of the War for American Independence.[31] It should, however, be

[27] For conditions other than the payment of quit-rents for land grants in New York or New Hampshire see *New York Land Patents, 1688–1786, Covering Lands now Included in the State of Vermont* (ed. Mary G. Nye), *State Papers of Vermont,* VII, 7–8.

[28] *Ibid.*, VII, 6. For a list of lands granted by New York in the disputed area between October 31, 1765, and February 13, 1767, see *New York Colonial Documents,* VII, 902–5.

[29] *Acts of the Privy Council, Col. Ser., 1745–1766,* pp. 673–4. The Privy Council, seeking enlightenment as to the situation in the disputed area, on October 15, 1765, directed the Board of Trade to write to the Governors of the two provinces "for particulars of the grants made by them respectively. . . ."

[30] "An Act for erecting certain Lands lying on the west side of Connecticut River within this Colony into a separate County, to be called . . . the County of Cumberland and for enabling the Freeholders and Inhabitants thereof to . . . build a Court House and Gaol in the said County." *Journal of the Legislative Council of New York, 1743–1775* (Albany, 1861), pp. 1594–6.

[31] For a detailed account of the creation of Cumberland County and the shifting of its bounds, see B. H. Hall: *History of Eastern Vermont . . . to the Close of the Eighteenth Century* (New York, 1858), pp. 1–3, 136–7.

added that in 1772 the huge county was divided into eighteen districts, each of which was permitted to elect local officers to deal with local functions.[32]

But, to return to the year 1766. On June 6 the New York Governor and Council issued an order that all land claimants with New Hampshire grants should bring their deeds and appear in person or by attorney before the New York Council within the space of three months to have their patents re-confirmed or forfeit all claims.[33] Upon receiving this news, the New Hampshire patentees from more than a hundred townships prepared a petition to the King. In it they pointed out that they had been led to believe that the lands they had acquired at considerable expense were a part of New Hampshire and, furthermore, that some settlers had actually taken up the lands as early as the restoration of peace, before the decision of His Majesty in Council had been made. This decision, they further stated, was followed by a proclamation requiring them to obtain new titles from the government of New York. Yet, when they had applied to that Governor to have their New Hampshire patents confirmed, to their "utter Astonishment" they were told that they must pay the New York fees of office amounting to £25 New York money (or £14 sterling) for each 1,000 acres of land or a sum of £330 sterling for the confirmation of each township, "which will amount in the Whole to about £33,000 Sterling, besides a Quit-Rent of Two Shillings and Six Pence Sterling, for every Hundred Acres of said Lands. . . ." They also asserted that the conditions thus attached to these lands would prevent any proper settlement of them, since it would eliminate all the poorer people anxious to establish themselves in this area. Therefore they begged His Majesty's intercession in their behalf.[34]

The petition of the New Hampshire claimants, signed by more than a thousand New Hampshire grantees, was presented in person to the King in Council by Samuel Robinson of Bennington "praying for a redress in several Great Grievances" and begging that their New Hampshire titles might be confirmed and that the region in dispute be made either "a separate colony or annexed to New Hampshire." The Privy Council also received at this time a petition

[32] *Ibid.*, pp. 743–4.

[33] For the New York order of June 6, 1766, see *Documentary History of New York*, IV, 363.

[34] See *A Petition to His Majesty King George the Third* . . . (Hartford, 1766); it is also printed in Hiland Hall: *The History of Vermont . . . to its Admission into the Union in 1791* (Albany, 1868), pp. 86–7.

from the Society for the Propagation of the Gospel in Foreign Parts relative to "lands reserved for pious uses in the townships granted by the Governor of New Hampshire to the west of the Connecticut River." These petitions impelled the Earl of Shelburne, Secretary of State for the Southern Department, in the spring of 1767 to inform Governor Moore of New York that, under the King's command and until further orders were forthcoming, no new grants of the lands in question should be made nor should any person be molested in the quiet possession of his grant who could produce good and valid deeds for such grant under the seal of the Province of New Hampshire. Later in the year, on July 24, the Privy Council passed a formal order to this effect.[35]

In a lengthy reply to Shelburne's letter, Sir Henry Moore stoutly defended the steps that had been taken by the New York government to deal justly with all claimants holding New Hampshire grants. He stressed the points that most of these petitioners had taken no steps to settle on or develop their properties, but continued to live in New Hampshire, Massachusetts Bay, or Connecticut, also that only a few had taken advantage of his offer to confirm their New Hampshire patents;[36] "on the contrary, they have made a merit of their Stubbornness."[37] For a period no land grants were made by New York. Nevertheless, when Lieutenant Governor Colden brought the order in council of 1767 before the New York Council on October 20, 1769, this body came to the conclusion that the order governed only the lands formerly claimed by New Hampshire and that other lands east of the Hudson and Lake Champlain were open to exploita-

[35] Shelburne to Moore, April 11, 1767, *New York Colonial Documents,* VII, 917–18, *Documentary History of New York,* IV, 365; *Acts of the Privy Council, Col. Ser., 1766–1783,* pp. 88–9, and Board of Trade *Journal, 1754–1767,* pp. 392–3.

[36] The grantees of the township of Brattleboro made their peace at this period with New York. The town was built on the site of old Fort Dummer on the west bank of the Connecticut. The first patent from New Hampshire covering it was received in 1753 and a renewal of the patent was granted both in 1760 and in 1761; on July 22, 1766, this patent was confirmed by New York. See *State Papers of Vermont,* Vol. I, *Index to the Papers of the Surveyors-General* (Rutland, Vt., 1918), p. 40. It may be noted that an order in council issued on September 6, 1744, recited that Fort Dummer, built about twenty years before by Massachusetts Bay, "is since fallen within the limits of the Province of New Hampshire by the Settlement of the Boundary Line between the two Provinces." The Province of New Hampshire was thereupon called upon to see that the fort did not fall into the hands of the French and Indians. See *Acts of the Privy Council, Col. Ser., 1720–1745,* pp. 787–9, and the full order addressed to Governor Wentworth as printed by Hiland Hall: *op. cit.,* Appendix 3, pp. 477–8.

[37] Moore to Shelburne, June 9, 1768, *Documentary History of New York,* IV, 365–73; see also Moore's defence of his policy toward the Society for the Propagation of the Gospel in his letter to Shelburne of June 10, 1767, *ibid.,* IV, 373–5.

tion.[38] It would appear, however, that Colden felt bound by the order, at least for the time being.[39] He even reported that people who had received grants under the seal of New Hampshire were quite willing to seek confirmation from New York under the terms he was offering, which were: ". . . to pay me such proportion of my fees as they could conveniently do, and that I would use my influence with the other officers of Govern^{t} to lower their fees in these cases." Although several townships accepted this offer, he was obliged to admit failure in the end. For, when Sir Henry Moore arrived in the colony in November 1765, he demanded that his full fees be paid. Thus Colden could not keep his promise to place the provincial seal on any of the New Hampshire patents. From that time on the New Hampshire grantees felt they could no longer depend upon justice from New York.[40] They were further alienated when Moore proceeded to make grants. Their complaints caused an additional instruction to Moore to be issued in 1770, reminding him of the binding power of the order in council of 1767 and warning him not to make any grant to the west of the Connecticut, "until our further pleasure shall be known . . . upon pain of our highest displeasure. . . ."[41] The instruction only added to the determination of those claiming land based upon New Hampshire grants not to submit to New York, especially in those cases in which there were overlapping land claims.

The first open and armed resistance seems to have occurred on October 19, 1769, in the township of Bennington, when an attempt was made by New York land commissioners and surveyors to lay down the division lines of the undivided patent of the Wallumschaack (Walloomsac, Walloomscoik) tract, granted to James de Lancey and others on July 15, 1739, but heretofore never developed. This survey was stopped when a body of armed men assembled about the home of a James Breckenridge, through whose farm the surveyors sought to pass. Writs of ejectment were issued. These led to trials before the circuit court of Albany, in June 1770, of the cases involving title to the disputed lands—among them, those claimed by Breckenridge. The verdicts brought in were favourable to the New York

[38] See minute of the Council of New York of October 20, 1769, in *ibid.*, IV, 375–6; see also *Historical Memoirs . . . 1763–1776 of William Smith* (ed. W. H. W. Sabine, New York, 1956), p. 56.

[39] See Colden to Hillsborough, January 4, 1770, *Documentary History of New York*, IV, 382–2.

[40] *Ibid.*

[41] For this instruction see *Royal Instructions to British Colonial Governors, 1670–1776* (ed. L. W. Labaree, 2 vols., New York and London, 1935), II, 607.

claimants, and the judges upheld the opinion that the New Hampshire patents for lands west of the Connecticut were valueless. The Wallumschaack patentees now appealed for partitionment of the patent. However, when the appointed commissioners attempted to carry out their task, they again were opposed by the Bennington township people, who continued to claim the land by New Hampshire title. This resistance led Governor Dunmore on November 1, 1770, to issue a proclamation ordering the sheriff of Albany County to take into custody the four leaders of the rioters, designating them by name.[42]

Let is not be understood that all the people settled in the disputed area favoured reunion with New Hampshire. On the contrary, the very day that Dunmore issued his proclamation against the rioters, 433 people of Cumberland County and of still newer Gloucester County, which lay directly to the north,[43] signed a petition to the King begging him to give them relief from the lawless activities of the New Hampshire men and to permit them to remain under the jurisdiction of the government of New York.[44] Two days later, that is on December 3, 1770, 411 New Hampshire grantees petitioned Governor Dunmore to have their grants confirmed with moderate fees, "under the Provisoes, limitations and restrictions prescribed in His Majestys instructions to your Lordship," and also begged that certain unoccupied western lands be granted under similar terms.[45] In this connection it may be noted that, by the spring of 1772, some fifteen townships having patents from the government of New Hampshire had had their lands confirmed by New York; confirmation of twelve other New Hampshire patents, although not as yet issued, had "long since [been] advised to be granted"; and, finally, the claims of twenty-one other townships, upon petition of the inhabitants praying confirmation of their lands, were ready to be acted upon favourably "whenever his Majesty's Instructions will permit Grants to be made of said Townships."[46] In writing on October 7, 1772, to Lord Hillsborough, Secretary for the Colonies, Governor Tryon sought the King's permission "to admit as many of the Townships of New Hampshire to take confirmations under this Gover^{nt},

[42] For the proclamation, which also gives the background of the dispute, see *Documentary History of New York*, IV, 405–6.

[43] As has been indicated, Cumberland County was created in 1768 to include all the lands west of the Connecticut River up to the point where Albany County lay. On March 16, 1770, Gloucester County was created to embrace the lands between the Connecticut and the Green Mountains.

[44] For this petition with the signatures see *ibid.*, IV, 406–9.

[45] These petitions with signatures are to be found in *ibid.*, IV, 409–11.

[46] For the list of towns in each of the above categories see *ibid.*, IV, 477–8.

on half fees, or such other Terms, as His Maj^{ty} shall prescribe . . . as every such confirmation is securing the inhabitants of that Township in the interest of, and obedience to this Govern^{t}."[47]

The sentiments of the people settled on the disputed lands were also sharply divided with regard to the government of New York. For example, late in January 1771, a petition to the King was signed by the inhabitants of Westminster and Rockingham, the townships just west of the Connecticut, stating that their only hope of relief "from the immediate poverty distress and ruin" was to have their lands reannexed to New Hampshire.[48] However, in the case of Westminster, which became the county seat of Cumberland County in 1772, it sought and received the confirmation by New York of its New Hampshire patent on March 26 of that year.[49]

The period of violence now approached, during which the settlers claiming rights under New Hampshire grants began to dislodge settlers holding lands under New York patents. If, by 1772, some towns, such as Brattleborough (Brattleboro) and Westminster on the west bank of the Connecticut were content to be a part of New York, others, such as Windsor—although one of the towns that had had its 1761 New Hampshire grant confirmed by New York—were strongly opposed to accepting the jurisdiction of that province and became the chief centres of dissatisfaction in the region along the Connecticut.[50]

Yet the scenes of greatest violence, accompanied by the burning of homes, the destruction of farm crops, and the overawing of New York sheriffs and their posses, were in the area to the east of Lake Champlain and to the west of the Green Mountains as well as in Bennington township. To oppose the New York authorities, a paramilitary organization known as the "Green Mountain Boys," headed by Ethan Allen, who bore the title "colonel commandant," was set up in 1770.[51] It was Allen who led the group that went to Albany in that year to support their township claims; it was he who secured

[47] *Ibid.*, IV, 484–5.

[48] *Ibid.*, IV, 412–13.

[49] *State Papers of Vermont*, I, 159.

[50] B. H. Hall: *History of Eastern Vermont*, pp. 290–8. It may be added that it was at Windsor that a convention was held, in 1777 in the midst of war, for the creation of the new state of Vermont.

[51] For the origin of this military group see Ira Allen: *The Natural and Political History of the State of Vermont* (London, 1798), pp. 26–7: This work is reprinted in Vermont Historical Society *Collections* (2 vols., Montpelier, 1870) I, 319–499; see especially pp. 345–6. For the early career of Ethan Allen up to the outbreak of the War for American Independence see John Pell: *Ethan Allen* (Boston and New York, 1929), pp. 1–73.

the services of the eminent Connecticut lawyer, the conservative Jared Ingersoll, in behalf of the New Hampshire patentees; when that means of protection failed, it was he who inspired the determination of the New Hampshire grants settlers to protect their rights by force if need be. His lieutenants were his cousins, Seth Warner and Remember Baker, together with Robert Cochran and Gideon Warren. These men, along with their supporters, became known as the "Green Mountain Boys," and it was they who drove off the New York people who were trying to take up lands in the disputed area, and later beat and otherwise harried the New York magistrates when they attempted to restore order.[52]

The confused and dangerous situation was brought before the attention of the government of Great Britain in the repeated representations made by the government of New York and in petitions from certain officers and soldiers who, having obtained patents from New York for lands to which they were entitled under terms of the Proclamation of 1763, had been prevented from occupying them by New Hampshire claimants. The Board of Trade was asked to make recommendations for a peaceful solution of the highly complex problem of the overlapping grants. Its representation of June 6, 1771, recommended giving priority consideration to two or three grants made by New York "antecedent to any pretence set up by the Government of New Hampshire" to lands west of the Connecticut—a clause favourable to the original New York proprietors. The second recommendation was in favour of those New Hampshire grantees who had made "actual Settlements and Improvements of any Lands not comprehended within the possessions above stated"; such settlers, it was urged, ought to be left in entire possession of the lands they had cultivated and improved, subject to no other condition "either of Quit Rent or otherwise than what is contained in the Grants under which they claim." The third set of claims "to merit particular indulgence" were those of "the reduced Officers and Soldiers" who had secured warrants from New York for lands and who had been obstructed in obtaining possession of them; in the eyes of the Board, no time should be lost in carrying into effect their grants, provided that these did not comprehend lands "actually & bona fide settled and improved by persons claiming under Grants from the Governor

[52] *Ibid.*, pp. 34–62. For the sworn testimony of witnesses to the conduct of the New Hampshire grants men before Chief Justice Daniel Horsmanden in 1771, as well as other affidavits sworn before other court officials, see *Documentary History of New York*, IV, 416–31, 446–52. For the proceedings in the New York Council in 1771 and 1772 dealing with the New Hampshire grants, see *Historical Memoirs . . . of William Smith*, pp. 110–16 *et seq.*

of New Hampshire antecedent to such warrants of Survey"; in such cases the officer or soldier should receive compensation in some other part of the district. It will be noted that in this representation the Lords Commissioners provided protection only to those New Hampshire grantees who had actually settled and improved the lands; as for those who were simply speculators in these lands as the result of "the exorbitant Grants from the Governor of New Hampshire," the Board of Trade felt that little consideration should be given to their pretensions. One final recommendation made by the Board, based on the claims of the Society for the Propagation of the Gospel to 500 acres in each of the New Hampshire township grants, was that, to encourage the Society to carry on its laudable and pious activities, a shilling proclamation money be levied annually on all lands within the disputed area, over and above the quit-rents payable to His Majesty.[53] Although the Board of Trade representation had many merits—except for the quite unrealistic plan for obtaining a revenue for the Society for the Propagation of the Gospel—the Privy Council failed to approve it.

On July 7, 1771, William Tryon landed in New York from New Bern to take over the office of Governor in place of Lord Dunmore, who had been commissioned Governor of Virginia. It well may be that had Tryon realized the frustrations that would face him in dealing with the claimants under the New Hampshire patents, he might have been willing—in so far as exerting his influence on the King could have effected it—to go along with Dunmore's desire to remain in New York while turning over the governorship of Virginia to him. One must hasten to add that Tryon, in addition to being a far abler Governor than Dunmore, was also less self-seeking.[54] Yet, he was forced to realize that the settlement of the vexing land disputes was beyond the power of his government acting

[53] For the above representation of the Board of Trade see *New York Colonial Documents*, VIII, 272–7.

[54] Such, at least was the opinion of the home government; although the evidence shows that Tryon, like his predecessor—despite the royal instructions he brought with him expressly reaffirming the earlier order of July 24, 1767, forbidding the granting of lands in the New Hampshire grant area until a Crown decision should be reached—continued to issue patents to a total that exceeded those granted by Dunmore. See, in this connection, Vermont Historical Society *Collections* (2 vols., Montpelier, 1870) I, 151–8. It should be pointed out, however, that approximately one half of the grants patented by Tryon were in confirmation of previous New Hampshire grants and that he himself advocated that such confirmation be upon an abatement basis of half the usual fees (as will be developed later in this chapter), so that his personal gain would have been considerably less than Dunmore's. Yet, it should also be noted that the so-called Norbury Grant of 32,000 acres in the name of Edmund Fanning and others was reputedly for himself. See *ibid.*

in its civil capacity. Writing to the Earl of Hillsborough on September 1, 1772, he remarked:

> "Your Lord^p is sensible, no Act of Govern^t will prevent individuals from settling and improving those large Tracts, which are already granted to them under this Govern^t. Proclamations have often issued to prevent the Grantees under New Hampshire and others from making any settlements in those parts, all of which have been treated with more or less neglect or contempt. I am under the firmest persuasion, no effectual measures at present, less than Military Force, can prevent the Eastern Colonies pouring in their Inhabitants between the [Connecticut] River and the Lake [Champlain]. . . ."[55]

On October 7 of the same year he stressed to the Secretary for the Colonies how important it was to be given permission to allow as many as possible of the New Hampshire townships to take out confirmations of their grant "on half fees"—a step that many grantees were prepared to take and were "very importunate" about; if refused this alternative, they would seek the support of "the Bennington people," daily increasing in strength, and reject all offers of the government.[56]

But there were delays. In fact, the letter was addressed to the Earl of Hillsborough, but in August 1772 his place as Secretary for the Colonies had been given to the Earl of Dartmouth. Thus, not until December 3 did Dartmouth and members of the Board of Trade sign a long representation to His Majesty in Council. This differed in some important respects from the one made by Secretary of State Hillsborough and the Board on June 6, 1771. First of all, it considered the "propriety or impropriety of reannexing to New Hampshire the Lands west of Connecticut River which the Govr and Council of that Province represent to be a measure of essential importance to its intents and of great Publick Advantage."[57] While

[55] *Ibid.*, VIII, 310–11.

[56] *Ibid.*, VIII, 312–13.

[57] *Ibid.*, VIII, 332. On August 10 (or 20), 1771, Governor John Wentworth wrote to Hillsborough enclosing a report of the New Hampshire Council "upon the state of private property and jurisdiction of land west of Connecticut River." See *Acts of the Privy Council, Col. Ser., 1766–1783*, p. 266. In the above connection refer-erence was made to the petition of "James Breckenridge in behalf of the Inhabitants of sundry Townships on the West side of Connecticut River, formerly under the Jurisdiction of this Province [New Hampshire], but now annexed to the Prov^e of New York Praying that the General Assembly would address his Majesty intreating that he would be pleased to reannex them to this Province etc." This petition was read in the New Hampshire Council on May 20, 1772, and sent down to the Assembly. See *New Hampshire Provincial Papers*, VII, 298. One thing that certainly con-solidated the position of New York with respect to its eastern boundary was the favourable reception by the King of the petition of inhabitants of Cumberland

admitting that proprietors of these townships had suffered both injury and oppression by the action of the Governor and Council of New York in granting warrants for the survey of lands already settled and improved, the report advised against making any alteration in the boundary of New Hampshire as laid down in 1764. In most other respects the representation adhered to that made by the Board the preceding year. Again it recommended that the New Hampshire townships should be confirmed by New York under the conditions specified in the original grant—but this provision applied only to lands under *actual* settlement and improvement. With respect to warrants for survey of lands granted to reduced officers and soldiers, it was recommended these should be honoured, except where they included lands actually settled and improved under some prior grant either by the Governor of New York or by the Governor of New Hampshire, in which case equivalent acreage should be given in some other part of the area. But all lands that had not been settled or improved in the New Hampshire townships or elsewhere in the disputed area—including early New York grants where no settlement or improvement had taken place—should be open for allotment by the government of New York, with certain provisos. For example, in every township granted either by New Hampshire or by New York some 500 acres should be set aside as a glebe for a Protestant minister and some 250 acres for a schoolmaster; further, in addition to paying the usual quit-rent collected by New York, the grantee should pay £5 sterling for every hundred acres as the purchase price.[58] It may be noted that the changes from the representation of June 6, 1771, provided improved methods for dealing equitably with actual settlers; but the provision placing the New York and New Hampshire land speculators outside the category of settlers, could not fail to arouse the antagonism of this powerful group, which operated on the basis of making profits on the sale or lease of unimproved lands. Similarly, the provision for the Anglican clergy was better conceived than that of 1771.

It was this report, accepted by the Privy Council on March 5, 1773, that became the basis of a policy for dealing with the disputed lands.[59] The position of the Privy Council remained unaltered when

---

and Gloucester counties "to be continued within the jurisdiction of the Government of New York. . . ." Informing Governor Tryon of this on April 10, 1773, Dartmouth, went on to state "there is not at present any intention of making any alteration in the boundary line on the side of the Connecticut River" (*New York Colonial Documents*, VIII, 358).

[58] *Acts of the Privy Council, Col. Ser., 1766–1783*, pp. 267–76.

[59] *Ibid.*, p. 267.

on October 16 of that year it received a long petition addressed to the King drawn up by "deputies from towns west of the Connecticut river to be re-annexed to New Hampshire." In this document the grievances of the inhabitants holding New Hampshire patents were set forth. Among other things it declared: "Your Majestys unhappy petitioners experience every day fresh proofs of its being impossible for them to remain in possession of their property, or in peace, under the government of New York." A counter-petition from those asking to be retained within the jurisdiction of New York was only secured, the petitioners asserted, by "promises, falsehoods, and force . . . even armed bodies have been sent down to terrify them [the inhabitants] into compliance." What had turned distress to "absolute dispair," the petitioners further affirmed, was that "your royal instructions not to molest us cannot control or arrest the proceedings at law . . . where, by refusing to admit the only possible evidence we can give of our titles, your Majesty's grants from the Governor of New Hampshire, . . . totally incapacitate us" to reply to the claims set up by new patentees for the same lands.[60]

But the solution of the harassing problem of the disputed lands presented by the Board of Trade and adopted by the Privy Council could not be implemented in New York. As Governor Tryon wrote in a letter to Lord Dartmouth on July 1, 1773, the measures recommended required the favourable action of the New York Assembly, which would be impossible to secure, the Governor felt, as they were "so repugnant to the claims of persons who from their numbers and connections have a very powerful influence in the Colony." What he had in mind, of course, was the Privy Council's policy, mentioned above, that the only claims to lands in the disputed region (held by either New Hampshire or New York patents and warrants to survey) which should be confirmed were those where *actual* settlement and improvement had taken place. Pointing out that New York patents alone contained "many hundred thousand acres" which "now belong to an infinity of persons," Tryon asked: How would it be possible to frame a law that would be just to the present claimants who had purchased from the original proprietors? What prospect was there that such a number of persons could be induced to diminish the estates they held under royal grants? Indeed, Tryon was persuaded that no measure would raise a more

---

[60] *Ibid., Unbound Papers,* pp. 543–7. This petition originated in Bennington township. Paul Wentworth, who submitted the petition, was not only London agent for New Hampshire but also acted for the petitioners; see *New Hampshire Provincial Papers,* VII, 350.

general discontent in the colony than a law to vacate patents for non-settlement. He reminded Dartmouth of how formidable a problem would arise in attempting to carry out the plan "by Inquests in so extensive Woodland Country." In this connection he observed that, in addition to the grants of the 15 New Hampshire townships which were now confirmed, there were 114 unconfirmed townships, and further that to certain officers and soldiers the New York government had allotted more than 600,000 acres in grants, many of them overlapping New Hampshire patents. Indeed, the problem of reconciling conflicting claims was so overwhelming to Tryon that he recommended all grants by New Hampshire patents within the boundaries of New York be declared void, but that "all occupants under New Hampshire Grants not covered by New York Patents, may have confirmations of their Possessions . . . upon such terms as His Majesty shall prescribe," and that "all occupants under New Hampshire Titles, within New York Patents, have such liberal equivalents out of the waste lands and such other indulgencies . . . as his Maj^ty shall think equitable. . . ."[61]

How much the Governor's report and recommendations were motivated by self-interest or a realistic appraisal of the situation is not clear. It is clear, however, that the land speculators—Wentworth in New Hampshire, the New York Governors, as well as prominent and wealthy landowners of that province, such as James Duane, together with the Allens and their relatives—were all equally self-seeking or, from their own points of view, equally far-

[61] *New York Colonial Documents*, VIII, 380–7. Two interesting and important pamphlets on this subject were published in New York in 1773, both apparently the work of the wealthy lawyer, landowner, and speculator James Duane (a conservative who, however, supported the Revolution): *A State of the Right of the Colony of New-York . . . So far as concerns the late Encroachments . . . of New-Hampshire* . . . (previously cited), supplemented by, *A Narrative of the Proceedings Subsequent to the Royal Adjudication; concerning the Lands To the Westward of Connecticut River, lately usurped by New-Hampshire, with Remarks on the Claim, Behaviour, and Misrepresentations, of the Intruders under that Government: Intended as an Appendix to the General Assembly's State of the Right of the Colony of New-York (with Respect to its Eastern Boundary . . .)* (New York, 1773). The following year these pamphlets were answered by Ethan Allen in a book of over 200 pages entitled *A Brief Narrative of the Proceedings of the Government of New-York relative to their obtaining the jurisdiction of that Large District of Land, to the westward from Connecticut River, Which, antecedent thereto had been patented by his Majesty's Governor and Council of the Government of New-Hampshire. And also, Of the monopolizing Conduct of the government of New-York, in their subsequently patenting Part of the same Land; and Oppressing the Grantees and Settlers under New-Hampshire* . . . (Hartford, [1774]). For the student of today it is extremely difficult to balance with fairness the charges and counter-charges contained in these three publications; nor do the partisan accounts left by the early historians of the state of Vermont dispel the mists. However, for an illuminating discussion of the problem see E. P. Alexander: *op. cit.*, Chap. 5.

sighted. For example, in 1772 there had been a lull in the dispute between New York and the Bennington group when, after being made aware that it was impossible to enforce his proclamations, Governor Tryon attempted to effect a compromise. At his invitation, two duly appointed agents—Stephen Fay and his son Jonas—came from the New Hampshire grant area in June to meet with him and iron out the difficulties, and it appeared by July that an agreement had been reached.[62]

But while the Fays were meeting with Tryon, the Allens were making inroads upon the settlers at Otter Creek—presumably repossessing land taken over by New Yorkers—and ousting surveyor Kockburn from an area nearby which fell within the sphere of interest of their so-called Onion River Land Company.[63] Thus, by August, a convention of the committees of the towns of Bennington and ten others met at Manchester to take into consideration a letter from Governor Tryon, protesting the action at Otter Creek, and to reply to it, and by October, at another convention held on the 21st, two agents were appointed to represent their grievances to the King.[64] As for Governor Tryon, by September 1773, in the face of the depradations of the "Green Mountain Boys," he came to the conclusion that he must have the aid of regular British soldiers stationed in the province. Accordingly, he appealed to Major General Haldimand, who was exercising the office of Commander-in-Chief of British Forces in North America during Gage's absence. But Haldimand, wary of the request, replied that "in the present circumstances of affairs in America, it appears to me of a dangerous tendency to employ Regular troops, where . . . the Civil Magistrate can at any time call upon its trained Inhabitants to aid and assist them—in the performance of their office, and the execution of the laws . . . against Rioters. . . ." He added that an admission by the New York government of inability to deal with "a few lawless Vagabonds" without calling for the aid of regular troops would undoubtedly render the authority of the "Civil Magistrate" contemptible in the eyes of the inhabitants. Haldimand concluded, however, by saying that if the Governor persisted in his request

---

[62] Vermont Historical Society *Collections*, I, 6–7; *Documentary History of New York*, IV, 778, 787, 792–3.

[63] *Ibid.*, IV, 720, 842–54; Slade's *State Papers*, pp. 29–33. For a brief account of Ira Allen's chief interest in the Onion River land speculation, which was to prove his ruin, see William Brewster: *The Fourteenth Commonwealths: Vermont and the States That Failed* (Philadelphia, 1960), Chap. 3, "Onion River Land Jobbing."

[64] Vermont Historical Society *Collections*, I, 7; see also *Documentary History of New York*, IV, 800–2, and Hiland's Hall's *History*, pp. 104 and 147.

he would like to know when and how many troops would be required and to be assured that their expenses would be provided.[65] To Tryon's added discomfort, the King, too, was reluctant to approve the use of regulars to quiet the disturbances east of Lake Champlain and the Hudson.[66] Nevertheless, by the latter part of the year the New York Governor was obliged to admit that "a Civil War [was] growing apace in the District of Bennington, and the adjacent Townships, . . . which I fear, will be found out of the reach of the Civil Authority to stop, even after the Declaration of the Royal Will is made known concerning the Controversies in Question."[67]

It may seem surprising that Tryon, who had led the militia companies against the rebellious Regulators in North Carolina and crushed their resistance to the civil authority, was unable as Governor of New York to act effectively against the "Green Mountain Boys" and their supporters. The truth seems to lie in the fact that almost all the New York militiamen were of the tenant class, with little or no direct interest in the struggle taking place in the area east of the Hudson River and Lake Champlain and were therefore not prepared to risk their lives to protect the holdings of wealthy New York land speculators. On the contrary, their sympathies were with the people of the New Hampshire grants. This was demonstrated by the behavior of the posses that the sheriffs of Albany and Charlotte counties sought to lead against the Bennington and Otter Creek rioters. Yet, the Governor was obliged to do something to deal with the anarchic situation. Supported fully by his Assembly, and acting upon the advice of the Council, on March 9, 1774, he issued a proclamation against "the Bennington Mob" for its "many atrocious Acts of Cruelty and oppressions"; it offered a reward of £100 for the apprehension of Ethan Allen and Remember Baker, and £50 for that of six other persons, including Seth Warner and James Breckenridge, and called upon the civil officers of Albany and Charlotte counties to perform their duty.[68] That very day Tryon also signed "An Act for preventing tumultuous and riotous Assemblies." This act, after reciting the various deeds of violence perpetrated by the New Hampshire men and their setting up of courts and military commands, stated that any one who should hurt an official publishing the proclamation would be adjudged to have committed a felony without benefit of clergy and would suffer death; the same

[65] For Tryon's request for troops on September 1, 1773, and Haldimand's reply of the same day see *New York Colonial Documents*, VIII, 394–5.

[66] See Dartmouth to Tryon, October 14, 1773, *ibid.*, VIII, 398–9.

[67] Tryon to Dartmouth, December 1, 1773, *ibid.*, VIII, 403.

[68] For the proclamation see *Documentary History of New York*, IV, 526–7.

penalty was declared for anyone who, without authorization, assumed judicial power or destroyed property. It further provided indemnification for anyone who might happen to kill an individual forming part of a group that disobeyed an order to disperse. Finally, the ringleaders of the "Green Mountain Boys" were called upon by name to surrender or suffer possible death as felons.[69] The proclamation and act of Assembly proved to be idle gestures.[70]

Early in April 1774, Tryon, having earlier been given a leave of absence, sailed for England, and once again Lieutenant Governor Colden was left in temporary charge of the New York administration. During the course of this critical year the conflict between settlers accepting the authority of the government of New York and those still looking for reannexation to New Hampshire was chiefly centred in the region just east of Lake Champlain in the newly formed Charlotte County, where, according to the depositions of a number of New York people, the "Green Mountain Boys" had erected "two Fortresses . . . , one at Onion River [now the Winooski River] and the other at Otter Creek, and openly threatened the Lives and Properties of all those who . . . are Friends to this Government. . . ." The New York Council, after reviewing the situation, advised the Lieutenant Governor to request General Gage, now in Boston, to support the government's efforts to keep peace in the county by sending 200 of his regulars.[71] But Gage was no more inclined than Haldimand had been to respond favourably, especially since the King in Council had upheld Haldimand's position.[72] Colden also wrote in vain to the Secretary for the Colonies, pointing out that "Fugitives from all the neighbouring Governments resort thither, so that they are now become a numerous and dangerous Body of Banditti," who "assume all power to themselves, choose Magistrates, erect Courts and inflict punishment &c."[73] Dartmouth,

---

[69] *New York Session Laws, 1774* (New York, 1774), III, 33–8.

[70] At two conventions held early in 1774, it was determined on March 1 by the committees of several townships on the west side of the Green Mountains to adopt a public declaration of their intention to hold their possessions and protect the individuals proscribed by the New York resolution; again, on April 11 and 12, "further defensive measures against New York were resolved upon" in defiance of the March 9 act of outlawry. Also among these proceedings was "a resolution forbidding anyone to hold an officer's commission from the New York government. See Vermont Historical Society *Collections*, I. 7–8.

[71] For the Council minute for September 1, 1774, see *Documentary History of New York*, IV, 534.

[72] Gage to Colden, September 19, 1774, *ibid.*, IV, 534.

[73] Colden to Dartmouth, October 4, 1774, *ibid.*, IV, 535. For the outrages committed by "the Bennington Mob" in the Lake Champlain region, see the petition of the Rev. Benjamin Hough of March 5, 1775, together with affidavits, *ibid.*, IV, 537–44.

however, was not convinced that the disorders had reached a point that demanded the use of regular troops, especially in view of the "very alarming situation of the King's affairs [elsewhere] in North America. . . ."[74]

Doubtless encouraged by the success of the "Green Mountain Boys" in defying the New York government, the rioters extended their activities into Cumberland County. When an attempt was made on March 13, 1775, to hold a court of law at Westminster, the county seat, rioters—many of them from nearby Rockingham, Fulham (now Dummerston), and Putney, later supported by a contingent from New Hampshire—took possession of the court house. They were finally dislodged only when the sheriff, supported by citizens of Westminster itself and those of such other loyal towns as Brattleborough (Brattleboro), forced his way into the building. In the course of the melee that followed some of the rioters were wounded, two of them mortally. But the following day their sympathizers gathered in force and with the help of recruits from New Hampshire and Massachusetts Bay took prisoner the magistrates and others, and held them in the county gaol for some days before carrying them into Massachusetts Bay for confinement.[75] Thus, when Lieutenant Governor Colden wrote to Lord Dartmouth on April 5, 1775, he was obliged to admit that "the authority of Government" was entirely lost in the region dominated by the Bennington rioters, and that the Assembly had failed him by granting a trifling sum of but £1,000 to enable him to restore order in the Cumberland County area.[76]

Colden's letter to Dartmouth of June 7, 1775, is the last that need concern us. It reported the capture of Forts Ticonderoga and Crown Point by the "Bennington Mob," aided by parties from Connecticut and Massachusetts Bay, and the taking prisoner of the garrisons of regular soldiers.[77] This action, of course, was an early phase of the War for America Independence, and helped lead to the emergence of the new state of Vermont and its final admission into the Union in 1791.

---

[74] Dartmouth to Colden, December 10, 1774, *ibid.*, IV, 537.

[75] For affidavits regarding the Westminster riot see *ibid.*, IV, 544–50. As these are all favourable to the conduct of the judges and the sheriff, the student is recommended to consult B. H. Hall: *op. cit.*, Chap. 9, "The 'Westminster Massacre,'" which rightly stresses the fact that the movement against holding court at Westminster was a phase of the American Revolution.

[76] *Documentary History of New York*, IV, 550–1.

[77] *Ibid.*, IV, 553. Ethan Allen and Benedict Arnold, holding a Massachusetts Bay commission, led the expedition against Ticonderoga on May 10, while Seth Warner the following day captured Crown Point.

To comprehend fully the rebellious nature of the stand taken by the inhabitants of the New Hampshire grants area against submission to the authority of the New York government, it is important to emphasize certain steps taken by these people toward achieving an autonomous status. Beginning in 1765, the settlers of several towns on the west side of the Green Mountains appointed agents to solicit the New York Governor's protection against New York grantees to the same lands;[78] the appeal was unsuccessful, as has been shown. These same settlers then appointed agents to represent their claims to the King in Council—without recourse to the governments of either New Hampshire or New York. Nor did they stop there in protecting their rights. By the close of 1770 committees of safety had been appointed by the several towns "to attend to their defence and security against the New York claimants." These committees met in general convention from time to time throughout the intervening years until the declaration of independence of the territory and the announcement of its status as a state (at first called New Connecticut). The proceedings of the conventions, in turn, embodied resolutions which became the basis of authority for the various actions taken by the settlers of the New Hampshire grants, whether those of force, to insure "their common protection," or of petition and demand for arbitration.[79] Although there are records of some ten conventions held between 1771 and 1775, there were undoubtedly many more such meetings of which no records are preserved.[80] The tenth recorded convention, that of April 11, 1775, held at Westminster, was the one at which a resolution was passed to petition the King to be either annexed to some other government or formed into a new one. Thereafter, all appeals to the King ceased, in view of the resolution of the Continental Con-

[78] For a full account of the "Conventions of the Inhabitants of the New Hampshire Grants in Opposition to the Claims of New York, 1765 to 1777," see Vermont Historical Society *Collections*, I, 1–54; Vol. I of these *Collections* also includes Hiland Hall's "New York Land Grants in Vermont," which gives a tabulation of New York patents in Vermont during the ten years 1765–75, together with a reprinting of the 1798 London edition of Ira Allen's *Natural and Political History of . . . Vermont*.

[79] See, for example, the resolution passed at the first recorded 1771 convention stating that "no officer from New York be allowed to carry out of the district of the New Hampshire Grants any person, without permission of the committee of safety, or of the military commanders. Surveyors of land, under New York, were forbid to run any lines within the Grants; transgressors in this point were to be punished according to the judgment of a court formed among the elders of the people or military commanders" (*ibid.*, I, 5). This account also states: "The convention met again and passed a decree forbidding all persons taking grants, or confirmation of grants, under the governor of New York."

[80] *Ibid.*, I, 5–9.

gress on June 23, 1775, recommending the employment in its army of "those called Green Mountain Boys under such officers as they should choose." With the inclusion of their forces in the Continental Congress, meetings of the committees of the several townships on the New Hampshire grants west of the Green Mountain range proceeded to complete the plans for statehood. The convention of January 15, 1777, declared their independence; the declaration and petition were submitted to the Continental Congress on April 8; finally, on June 4, at a convention held at Windsor, the name Vermont was announced for the new state.[81]

New York and Massachusetts Bay Charter Claims to a Western Boundary

The issue that arose over the western boundary of Massachusetts Bay came to a head in the early 1750's[82] when the settlers on the

[81] *Ibid.*, I, 9–54; see also *Connecticut Courant* for March 17 and June 30, 1777, and Slade's *Vermont State Papers*, pp. 68–73. It may be noted that the *Connecticut Courant* was consistently the propaganda mouthpiece of Ethan Allen and his faction during the dispute.

[82] See report of the New York Council on February 28, 1753 (*Documentary History of New York*, III, 439–41), and the report of the Council on March 2, 1753, in William Smith [Jr.,]: *The History of the late Province of New-York . . . to . . . 1762* (New-York Historical Society *Collections* IV–V, 2 vols., New York, 1829), Appendix, IV, 251. For an excellent study of the issue between New York and Massachusetts Bay over lands and boundary, down to 1767, see Oscar Handlin: "The Eastern Frontier of New York," *New York History*, XVIII, 50–75; see also the older study by F. L. Pope: *The Western Boundary of Massachusetts* (privately printed, probably for the Berkshire Historical and Scientific Society, Pittsfield, Mass., 1886), especially for the excellent map of the disputed area and the seventeenth-century background of the claims.

In 1722 the General Court of Massachusetts Bay, on petition, granted two townships in the county of Hampshire called the Upper and Lower Housatonic townships. Lying along the northwest boundary of Connecticut, they were seven miles square, embraced the upper waters of the Housatonic River, and included the lands of the present towns of Housatonic, Stockbridge, Alford, Great Barrington, and Egremont. See *Journal of the House of Representatives* (Boston, 1722–3), pp. 56–7. Apparently the first signs of friction between the Housatonic settlers and the inhabitants of New York developed in 1726 over titles to the land. In that year Governor William Burnett of that province sent Lieutenant Governor William Dummer a copy of a memorial by "divers Inhabitants" complaining of settlements by Massachusetts Bay people on their lands; see *ibid.*, (Boston, 1726–7), pp. 115, 117, 197. Although for the moment the Housatonic settlers were held in check by their government, they soon proceeded with the expansion of these settlements despite the New York protest; see Rev. Chester Dewey *et al.: A History of the County of Berkshire . . .* (Philadelphia, 1829), p. 203. In 1733 the Lower Housatonic township was given the name Sheffield and thereupon authorized to hold town meetings; see *Journal of the House of Representatives* (Boston, 1732–4), pp. 255, 305. The people of Sheffield seem to have been the most active in pressing into the region claimed by New York during this period.

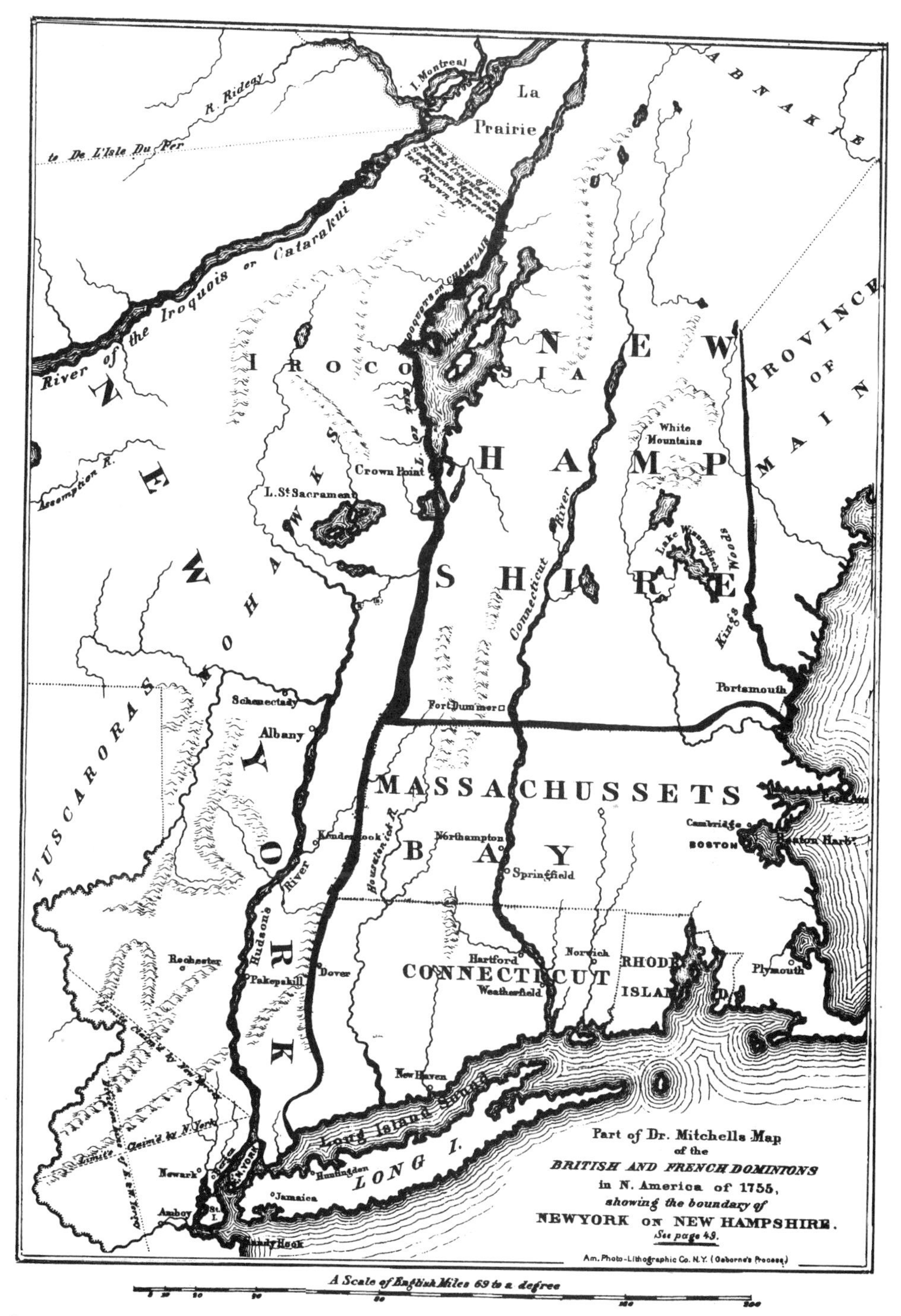

"Part of Dr. Mitchells Map," 1755, showing the boundary of New York and New Hampshire.

(From Hiland Hall's *History of Vermont*, 1868)

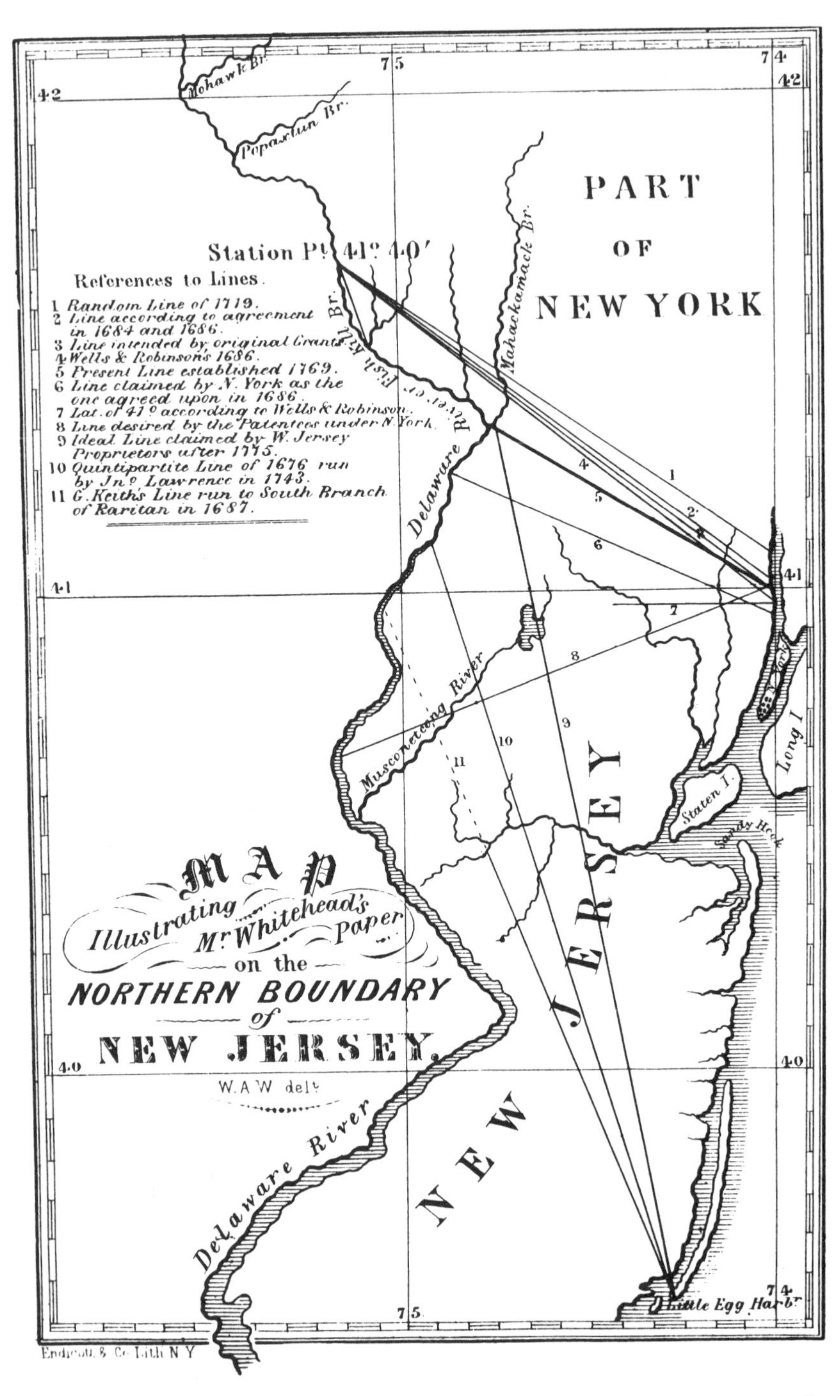

A map showing the various boundary lines between New York and New Jersey.

(From the New Jersey Historical Society *Proceedings,* Vol. VIII)

"tract of land called Westenhook"[83]—held to be a part of the county of Hampshire but also claimed by New York—began pushing even farther westward into an area long claimed as a part of the New York manor of Livingston.[84] Each of the rivals for the disputed lands was supported by his government. What made the contest so acute was that here was a clash between two fundamentally different land-holding systems—one based upon the practice of tenantry and payment of quit-rents, the other upon individual ownership of land in fee simple and its direct exploitation by the owner without the payment of these rents.

As has been established, the government of New York, early in its dispute with New Hampshire, had taken the position that it claimed all lands east of the Hudson River, west of the Connecticut River, and north of the Connecticut boundary line. As the result of what were considered to be the intrusions of the Westenhook settlers, petitions of protest were sent to the New York Council in 1752.[85] Governor George Clinton, after due consideration, wrote to Governor Shirley on March 6, 1753, on the subject of the "new Claims and Encroachments by the Inhabitants of Massachusetts Bay on the Province of New-York," and asked "by what Warrant they Claim or Exercise any right . . . west of Connecticut river. . . ."[86] When this letter[87] was laid before the Massachusetts Bay House of Representatives, it viewed the matter as "an extraordinary Title . . . set up in Favour of *New York,* to a valuable Part of this Province," and thereupon recommended that commissioners be appointed by the two colonies for settling the boundary between them "to the End that good Understanding may be preserved, which ought [to]

[83] See *New York Colonial Documents*, VII, 950–1.

[84] In this connection the student is again referred to Oscar Handlin's important article previously cited, which stresses (pp. 53–4) the fraudulent nature of Robert Livingston's dealings with the Wappinger Indians.

[85] See the petition of Robert Livingston to Governor Clinton, April 16, 1752, *Documentary History of New York*, III, 435–7.

[86] Ibid., III, 454. The lord of Livingston Manor, Robert Livingston, Jr., on March 26, 1753, wrote a letter—it would appear by internal evidence to be to William Smith the younger, whose father was on the Council—asking aid in persuading the New York government to take some steps to protect his manor. He was greatly alarmed by a meeting of his tenants at this time, since they, under the influence of men from Massachusetts Bay, were supporting the claims of that colony to the lands they had leased from Livingston. Unless something were done, he contended, "the Infection will very Soon be general and then no man that has an Estate in this Province or perhaps in North America, will be Safe or able to Call it his own" (William Alexander-Stirling Papers, Vol. I, p. 25, New-York Historical Society). Volume III of the *Documentary History of New York* contains a large number of Livingston letters and petitions.

[87] Report of the committee of the House of Representatives, April 12, 1753, *Journal of the House of Representatives* (Boston, 1752–3), pp. 164–5.

subsist between Fellow Subjects & neighbouring Provinces."[88] This offer was transmitted to the government of New York but was rejected. The issue was now joined.

The Massachusetts Bay General Court took the position that the right to the disputed territory went as far back as the year 1620 and that for over a hundred years the province had possessed and improved a considerable part of the lands westward of the Connecticut. In view of this contention, the Court maintained that it was incumbent upon the government to continue to exercise jurisdiction over these lands and to go on settling them and governing their inhabitants "according to the Right given them by Charter."[89] To New Yorkers there was also much at stake. The Lord of Livingston Manor felt that the issue was a "grand Governmential affair, and if finally determined in our favour, will be an adition to this Government of near Double to what it now is."[90]

During this impasse between the two governments violence broke out in the disputed area and arrests followed.[91] The upshot was that early in 1754 the New York government agreed to the appointment of commissioners. At the Albany Congress of that year the joint commissioners met, but nothing was accomplished—so far apart were the representatives of the two governments in their stands on the proper line of division. Each government continued to seek to administer the disputed region and to levy taxes upon the settlers.[92] As a result of the unsolved problem of jurisdiction, further riots broke out west of the Connecticut. When addressing the General Court on February 24, 1755, Governor Shirley felt obliged to point out that the new outbreak "is now become a very serious Affair between the two Governments, and happens at a very importunate Time

[88] *Ibid.*; see also Robert Livingston's long petition to Governor Clinton of May 31, 1753, *Documentary History of New York*, III, 442–7.

[89] Minute of June 12, 1753, *Journal of the House of Representatives* (Boston, 1753–4), p. 37. It appears that many Massachusetts Bay people "without any Grant or Liberty" had settled on lands across the Connecticut lying west of Sheffield and Stockbridge. It was therefore agreed by the General Court on June 19, 1753, that a committee be appointed with powers to dispose not only of the lands that were being squatted upon—either to those who had made improvements upon them or to others—but also "of the Province Lands lying West of said Township, which are not taken up by any Persons" (*ibid.*, p. 53).

[90] Robert Livingston, Jr., to [William Smith, Jr.], March 26, 1753, *loc. cit.*

[91] For a report on the disorders to the west of the Connecticut by the Massachusetts Bay General Court of September 11, 1753, see *Journal of the House of Representatives* (Boston, 1753–4) pp. 78–9. For a detailed account of clashes between Massachusetts Bay squatters and other settlers as well as New York tenants see Irving Mark: *op. cit.*, pp. 116–30; see also *New York History*, XVIII, 54–64.

[92] See the memorial of Daniel Kellogg, *Journals of the House of Representatives* (Boston, 1754–5), p. 41.

for their mutual Welfare."[93] At the same time the Governor realized that some of the Massachusetts Bay people had gone much too far into the settled part of Livingston Manor in claiming lands. For example, after a Massachusetts man named Benjamin Franklin, supported by others, had forcibly dispossessed a Robert Vandersen (Van Deusen) of his home, Shirley addressed a letter to him on November 16, calling upon him to vacate the property he had seized and warning him that if he were apprehended by the New York authorities, he need not expect any protection from Massachusetts Bay.[94] Franklin's position was that he and his son had bought the land, that it did not belong to Livingston, and that it was not in New York.[95]

In order to settle the controversy the Massachusetts General Court in 1756 encouraged Governor Shirley to address the Governor of New York, again with a proposal that commissioners be appointed, this time clothed with power "to settle the Boundary Line of the two Provinces," which determination should then be laid before the King for approval. But the government of New York would not agree,[96] despite the continued infiltration of Massachusetts Bay people and "further outrages." For these settlers kept on moving in not only upon lands claimed by Robert Livingston but also upon those claimed by John Van Rensselaer—lands included in manors which, according to Governor Charles Hardy of New York, had been handed down by ancestors "from old Times." What is more, the New York Governor reported, the intruders were discharging the Livingston and Van Rensselaer tenants from the obligation of holding their farms under these patroons and were giving them title to the lands they had been renting.[97] The sheriffs of both Albany County of New York and Hampshire County of Massachusetts Bay

[93] For Shirley's message see *ibid.*, p. 251.

[94] This letter is among the manuscripts of the Johnston Redmond Collection (formerly housed in the New-York Historical Society, now to be found at the Franklin Delano Roosevelt Library, Hyde Park, or on microfilm at Columbia University, Special Collections), an important collection for Livingston family material.

[95] For a deposition sworn on November 21, 1755, as to Franklin's reply when advised to vacate the property, see the Redmond Collection; see also *New York History*, XVIII, 61–3.

[96] Shirley to the General Court, August 20, 1756, *Journal of the House of Representatives* (Boston, 1756), p. 128.

[97] Governor Hardy to the Board of Trade, December 26, 1756, *New York Colonial Documents*, VII, 206. Writing to Governor Hardy on November 9, 1755, and also on the 23rd of that month, Livingston set forth in great detail the riotous action of large numbers of Masschusetts Bay men who had penetrated into his manor to a distance of but sixteen miles from the Hudson River, had carried off some of his tenants and employees at his iron works, and had lodged them in gaol at Springfield. See *Documentary History of New York*, III, 486–9.

entered into the conflict, arresting men and conducting them to the Albany and Springfield gaols respectively. In June 1757 Lieutenant Governor James de Lancey issued a proclamation against the Massachusetts Bay men who had forced their way into lands not more than eighteen miles from the Hudson, calling for their arrest.[98]

When news of these developments had reached Great Britain, the Board of Trade, after due deliberation, made a representation to the King in Council on May 25, 1757. Setting forth the history of the dispute, the representation pointed out the failure in June 1754 of the commissioners meeting at Albany to depart from "the descriptive words in the respective grant or Charter" of each colony and come to a meeting of minds. The Lords Commissioners therefore recommended the interposition of His Majesty's authority to settle a line of partition that would be just and equitable. In this connection they pointed out that such ancient papers as were in the Board's office seemed to indicate "that the Province of the Massachusetts Bay had in those times been understood to extend within 20 miles of Hudson's River, and that many settlements had at different times been made so far to the Westward by the people of that province." Since this evidence coincided with the general agreement between New York and Connecticut arrived at and confirmed by the Crown in 1683, it was recommended that it should be the basis for the line of division between New York and Massachusetts Bay.[99]

The "Riot and Bloodshed" that persisted in the area of dispute emphasized the great urgency for a settlement to be reached. During the outbreaks of violence in the spring of 1757 both a Massachusetts Bay man and a New York man were killed. This so impressed Lieutenant Governor James de Lancey of New York with the need for an immediate agreement that he wrote to the Board of Trade, declaring he would be pleased were the line fixed to accord with the boundary decided upon between Connecticut and New York—provided this should be "without prejudice to private property."

---

[98] For the de Lancey proclamation see *ibid.*, III, 490–1.

[99] For the Board of Trade representation see Board of Trade *Journal 1754–1758*, pp. 310–11, 320–1, 322. Royal commissioners, appointed in 1664 to visit Massachusetts Bay relative to its proper boundaries, reported in 1665 that its northern and southern boundary lines extended westward "till they come within twenty miles of Hudson's River, for that River is already planted & given to His Royal Highness [the Duke of York]" (see an extract from this report in "The Chalmers Papers: New York," Vol. 1, fol. 86, New York Public Library). There are other papers in the same collection, filed with the report of the commission in 1665, bearing upon the boundary dispute.

As a final settlement would require much time, he pleaded that His Majesty by "an Injunction" should fix a temporary line, until a permanent one could be established.[100]

With the Great War for the Empire so fully occupying the attention of Americans for a period of years, it was not until 1762 that the problem of fixing a boundary between the two provinces again loomed seriously.[101] In that year some Massachusetts Bay people appeared, according to Robert Livingston, with a deed for Livingston Manor lands which they had lately purchased "of some Stragling Indians," demanding that the lands in question be turned over to them. These "rioters," Livingston informed the Governor, in a plea for a proclamation to restrain them, were even receiving support from some of the New York tenants.[102] Accordingly, on March 31, 1762, Lieutenant Governor Colden issued a proclamation calling upon the sheriffs of Albany and Dutchess counties to apprehend all those who should unlawfully assemble together to foster "violent and unjust proceedings."[103] But this did not deter the government of Massachusetts Bay from granting in the disputed area nine townships, each six miles square.[104]

The following year, five members of the New York Council in a petition to the Governor, now General Robert Monckton, argued that an equitable boundary would be an extension northward of the line laying down the western limits of Connecticut. Lieutenant Governor Colden, however, strongly disagreed with them. Holding that the Connecticut River was the true eastern limit of New York north of the colony of Connecticut, he emphasized the benefits to the inhabitants in the disputed region that would result by fixing the lines at this natural barrier and cited in this connection the grant made to the Duke of York in 1664.[105] But the Board of Trade was firm in its position that a satisfactory solution of the inflammable issue could be achieved only by a boundary commission, to be

---

[100] James de Lancey to the Board of Trade, July 30, 1757, *New York Colonial Documents*, VII, 273–4.

[101] Referring to the Massachusetts Bay intruders, Robert Livingston wrote to Peter Livingston and James Duane on March 22, 1762: "These Rioters have given me no trouble Since the Proclamation Issued in 1757 & now they Intend to make their Last bold push, which I think will be prevented by another Proclamation comeing out in time" (*Documentary History of New York*, III, 493).

[102] *Ibid.* It may be noted that Livingston even offered to pay the printer's expenses for this proclamation.

[103] *Ibid.*, III, 494–5.

[104] *New York History*, XVIII, 65.

[105] Lieutenant Governor Colden to the Board of Trade, September 26, 1763, *New York Colonial Documents*, VII, 562–5; New-York Historical Society *Collections* for 1876, *Colden Letter Books*, I, 232–7.

appointed by the Crown, similar to that instituted for settlement of the New York–New Jersey line.[106] Colden, despite his own views, felt impelled to go along with the decision of the Board and was able to report before the close of 1764 that, upon his recommendation, the Assembly had passed an act incorporating the Board's plan.[107] However, Massachusetts Bay failed to pass a similar act and the New York statute therefore became inoperative.[108] It seems that other events, including the Stamp Act crisis, the New Jersey boundary dispute, and the problem presented by the New Hampshire grants west of the Connecticut, temporarily distracted the attention of the New York authorities from the situation along their borders facing Massachusetts Bay. Nevertheless, people from the Bay colony, joined by some from Connecticut, persisted in pressing westward upon lands long claimed by New York. In addition to the establishment of Sheffield and the Indian town of Stockbridge, by 1765 there had sprung up, well to the west of the Housatonic River, such settlements as Alford, Williamstown, Richmond, Taghconic (Taconick, later called Mount Washington), Egremont, and Nobletown.[109]

---

[106] Board of Trade to Colden, July 13, 1764, *New York Colonial Documents*, VII, 642–3. The New York-New Jersey issue is dealt with in detail later in this chapter.

[107] Colden to the Board of Trade, November 7, 1764, *ibid.*, VII, 676; *Colden Letter Books*, I, 394. The statute, entitled "An Act for facilitating the Settlement of the Partition Line between the Colony of New-York and the Province of the Massachusetts-Bay," was passed on October 19, 1764. It stipulated that all lands claimed by subjects of His Majesty in New York that might be affected were to be made subject to such method of decision as the Crown might think proper; further, it agreed that New York should pay one-half the joint expenses involved in laying down a partition line; finally, it designated a list of seven agents, headed by Robert R. Livingston, to act on behalf of New York in carrying out this assignment. *Laws of New-York from the year 1691 to 1773 inclusive* (2 vols., ed. Peter Van Schaack, New York, 1774), II, 446–8. To expedite the passing of the bill, on September 24, 1764, Lieutenant Governor Colden had sent a letter to the Assembly pointing out that the King had approved laws passed by New York and New Jersey for settling a common boundary and indicating that the same desirable results might be obtained were New York and Massachusetts Bay to agree upon like procedure. The original bill contained a clause which expressed the agreement of the New York patent holders of lands in dispute with New Jersey to pay all expenses above £1,500 involved in settling the New York–New Jersey boundary and stated that this principle should be applied to the cost of the New York–Massachusetts Bay boundary settlement; however, this clause was not included in the act that ultimately received the Lieutenant Governor's approval on October 20, 1764. *Ibid.*, and *Journal of the Votes and Proceedings of the General Assembly of the Colony of New-York, Vol. II, 1743–1765* (publ. Hugh Gaine, New York, 1766), pp. 756 and 780–1.

[108] See the pamphlet *A Conference between the Commissaries of Massachusetts-Bay, and the Commissaries of New-York; at New-Haven in the Colony of Connecticut, 1767* (Boston, 1768).

[109] Nobletown, lying to the west of Egremont township, was within the Van Rensselaer patent, and was destined to be included within the New York town of

By 1766 settlers claiming Massachusetts Bay titles to land as far west as Claverack, not far from the Hudson River and on the Van Rensselaer estate, were openly resisting the New York authorities. Two men were killed in a fight when, in June, an attempt was made by the sheriff of Albany County and his posse to place under arrest a Robert Noble. Whereupon Governor Moore early in July issued a proclamation offering a reward of £100 for apprehension of the wanted man.[110] When an effort was made to implement the proclamation and capture Noble and his associates, the men fled into Massachusetts Bay and Connecticut, where, according to Moore, they were protected by the magistrates.[111] In this connection the point should be stressed that these land disorders were closely connected with the great tenant riots which occurred in the spring of 1766, at first largely confined to Dutchess and Westchester counties but finally spreading into Albany County. The rioters threatened not only to march on New York City to rescue their comrades who had been gaoled there but also, according to Governor Moore, "to set the City on Fire in several different Places at the same Time."[112] Although the presence of the regular troops stationed at Fort George together with a proclamation issued by the Governor deterred them from this attempt to carry the conflict to the port city, the disturbances in Dutchess County reached such a point that by July it seemed beyond the ability of the civil authorities to deal with them. Therefore an appeal was made to Major General Thomas Gage, who immediately ordered the 28th Regiment to help restore order. This was accomplished.[113] When the tenant rioting spread to Albany County, regular troops also came to the support of the civil authorities in the area east of the Hudson.[114] In this effort to restore order, the most western of the Massachusetts Bay settlements, Nobletown, was apparently pretty well destroyed. Its inhabi-

---

Hillsdale. For these settlements west of the Housatonic River see J. G. Holland: *History of Western Massachusetts* (2 vols., Springfield, 1855), II, 470–1, 485–9, 491, 529–31, 561–9, 581–97, 608–15. For the leasing of lands claimed as part of the Philipse Manor by the Mohican Indians living at Stockbridge see *New York History*, XVIII, 68–70.

[110] *Documentary History of New York*, III, 496–7.

[111] Moore to the Board of Trade, August 12, 1766, *New York Colonial Documents,* VII, 849–51; see also Irving Mark: *op. cit.,* Chap. 5, "The Great Rebellion of 1766."

[112] Moore to Secretary of State Conway, April 30, 1766, *New York Colonial Documents,* VII, 825–6.

[113] Moore to Conway, July 14, 1766, *ibid.,* VII, 845; Gage to Conway, July 15, 1766, *The Correspondence of General Thomas Gage . . . 1763–1775* (ed. C. E. Carter, 2 vols., New Haven, 1931, 1933), I, 99, cited hereafter as *Gage Correspondence.*

[114] See Irving Mark: *op. cit.,* pp. 144–5.

tants were forced to flee eastward and were pursued to the town of Egremont, which also suffered damage.[115] According to Governor Bernard, there was real danger of an undeclared war between the people of the provinces, so enraged were the inhabitants of the western frontier towns of the Bay colony.[116] Writing to Governor Moore concerning the damage done by the New York people at Egremont "within the Massachusetts Line," Bernard referred to the attitude among the people in general as one of being "ready to rise against a common Enemy" and expressed fear that this feeling might lead to "a formal Rupture between the Borderers of the Two Provinces."[117]

A question that cannot fail to arise in the mind of the student at this point in the narration is: Why did not the Crown determine in a summary fashion the bounds that separated New York and Massachusetts Bay, as it had done in 1763 when laying down the boundary of the Province of Quebec and in 1764 in settling the dispute between New York and New Hampshire? The answer undoubtedly lies in the confirmed practice of the British government of encouraging the colonies to settle their territorial differences by means of commissions of their own appointment. Further, the Massachusetts Bay claim to lands west of the Connecticut River rested on a quite different basis from that of New Hampshire, in view of the fact that under the sea-to-sea terms of the colony's first patent—and before

[115] Governor Moore to the Board of Trade, August 12, 1766, *New York Colonial Documents*, VII, 849; Governor Bernard to the Board of Trade, August 16, 1766, Shelburne Papers, 51:459–63, Clements Library. Bernard, in writing to the Lords Commissioners for Trade and Plantations, enclosed a minute of the Massachusetts Bay Council asking him to pray Governor Moore that the inhabitants of Massachusetts Bay dwelling "to the westward of the Line reported by the Lords of Trade to be a divisional Line between the Two Provinces may not be disturbed or molested by the Sheriff of Albany, or any Troops acting under his orders 'till such Line shall be further considered & settled by His Majesty" (*ibid.*, 51:360). See also General Gage's report of this situation to Secretary of State Richmond on August 26, 1766, *Gage Correspondence*, I, 102–3.

[116] Bernard to the Board of Trade, August 21, 1766, Shelburne Papers, 51:461. In this letter Bernard mentions the fact that he had written to Colonel Williams of Pittsfield, at the head of the Berkshire militia, to try to keep things quiet and do nothing in a military way except as far as the law would justify him in assisting the civil magistrates.

[117] Shelburne Papers, 51:462. In writing to Shelburne on February 22, 1767, the New York Governor presented the other side of the picture, describing the Massachusetts Bay people as invaders of the lands of John Van Rensselaer, who had offered them leases on the same terms as his other tenants, and recounting how they, however, had refused to accept the New York leases on the grounds that they did not recognize Van Rensselaer's title to the lands. Moore complained that "it never was the intention of these People to submit their Title to a legal examinatn"—instead, they assembled in a great armed body, attacked the sheriff and his posse, and brought about a conflict that resulted in loss of life on both sides. *New York Colonial Documents*, VII, 911.

the issuing of the second patent—a temporary settlement had been made to the west of the Connecticut River. As early as 1636 the founder of Springfield, William Pynchon, had located on the west bank of the Connecticut and had moved to the east bank only when made to realize that the ground originally selected was subject to flooding. Then, with respect to the New Hampshire pretensions, there was manifestly a feeling in the Privy Council that Governor Benning Wentworth had acted in a most irresponsible way when handing out, in a manner that could only be described as precipitate, the scores of townships to the west of the Connecticut River. The peremptory action of the Crown in settling the New Hampshire western boundary may therefore be understood as a stinging rebuke to the Governor of New Hampshire.

When the Earl of Shelburne, Secretary of State for the Southern Department, received word of what was taking place on the borders of the two provinces, he wrote to both Moore and Bernard stating that these disturbances were "of a nature not to be suffered." He called upon them to appoint commissioners to settle the boundary differences amicably. Before closing his letter to Moore, he directed him to see that those people settled on lands lying westward of the line reported by the Board of Trade "as the Boundary of the two Provinces" should not be molested.[118] In line with the Shelburne directive, early in the spring of 1767 Massachusetts Bay chose three commissioners by vote of the General Court; a similar action was taken by the New York Assembly in June.[119]

---

[118] Shelburne to Moore, December 11, 1766, *ibid.*, VII, 879.

[119] By vote of the Massachusetts Bay General Court in March 1767, it was agreed that a commission of three be chosen by joint ballot of the two houses to act with the New York commissioners to settle the boundary. On the first ballot but two were chosen: William Brattle and Edward Sheaffe. James Otis and Thomas Hutchinson were thereupon placed on the ballot for the third commissioner. Although the House of Representatives, as already indicated in this volume, was bitterly opposed to Hutchinson's having a seat in the Council, this same House on March 13 voted by a majority that he should be on the boundary commission. This vote was ratified by the Council on the 17th. See *Journal of the House of Representatives* (Boston, 1766–7), pp. 379, 385, 408. Not only was Hutchinson made a commissioner but he was also placed at the head of the commission, "as no one in the province is so well acquainted with these matters as he is," wrote Bernard to the Earl of Shelburne on March 23, 1767. See Shelburne Papers, 51:561–2.

It was not until June that the New York Assembly passed an act to empower three commissioners to join those of Massachusetts Bay to settle the line of jurisdiction. The act referred to the bloodshed that had already attended the conflicts between the two colonies, "which are likely to be productive of the most mischievous Consequences," and to the necessity of coming to a settlement on a line of jurisdiction; it also appointed the Speaker of the General Assembly, William Nicoll, Robert R. Livingston, and William Smith, [Jr.], to act as the New York commissioners with full power to agree to a line. See *Laws of New-York from 1691 to 1773*, II, 495.

The joint commissioners did not, however, hold their first formal meeting until October 1. The following day they discussed the powers granted to the Massachusetts Bay commissioners, which were not stated in the definite and clear terms of the New York commission, and did not include full power to conclude an agreement.[120] After assurance was given that the General Court of Massachusetts Bay would ratify any "treaty" arrived at by its representatives, the next step was to agree on procedures. The New York commissioners insisted that all negotiations be carried on in writing, a requirement which brought objections from the Massachusetts Bay men, but was finally accepted. In the array of the opposing camps were the two leading authorities on the early history of New York and Massachusetts Bay, respectively, in the persons of William Smith, [Jr.],[121] author of *The History of the Province of New-York, from the First Discovery to the Year M.DCC.XXXII* (published in London in 1757), and Thomas Hutchinson, whose first volume of the *History of the Colony of Massachusetts-Bay* had appeared in 1764. In dealing with the conflicting territorial claims, each side relied heavily upon early patents granted by the Crown together with other seventeenth-century documents. Massachusetts Bay again set forth its right to a sea-to-sea territorial claim, while accepting the fact that this claim had been abridged when Charles II gave his brother a patent to lands lying along the Hudson River that the Dutch had "usurped"; similarly, New York insisted on the legality of its claim to all lands west of the Connecticut River and north of the colony of Connecticut. Yet both sides

[120] On March 17, 1767, the Massachusetts Bay House of Representatives passed the following resolution: "Upon a motion made and seconded, ordered, that the commissaries appointed to settle the boundary line, between this Province and *New-York*, be restricted to make report to the General Court, before they consent to a final determination thereon . . ." (*A Conference between the Commissaries of Massachusetts-Bay and New-York, 1767*, p. 2). This restriction was, however, not accepted by the Council and was not embodied in the instructions. Nevertheless, it raised a doubt in the minds of the New York commissioners.

[121] For a recent article on Smith see R. A. Wines: "William Smith, The Historian of New York," *New York History*, XL, 3–17. It may not be out of place to clarify the identity of some of the many William Smiths who appear in eighteenth-century colonial history, beginning with Judge William Smith, born in England (1697–1769), the jurist who came to New York and was the father of the historian and jurist William Smith (1728–93) mentioned above (denoted as "Jr." until his father's death). The latter became the last chief justice of New York under the Crown, and was in turn the father of the Canadian historian William Smith (1769–1847), born the same year his grandfather died. Not to be confused with them are Dr. William Smith (1727–1803), who was the first Provost of the College of Philadelphia, and the Rev. William Smith (1754–1821), the Scottish clergyman whose activities were centred in Rhode Island and Connecticut.

were disposed to make concessions for the sake of peace along their frontiers. By October 3 the commissioners of Massachusetts Bay offered to settle the boundary by a line drawn west from the Connecticut–Massachusetts Bay boundary line to a point twelve miles from the Hudson, to be connected by a straight line with another line drawn west from the Massachusetts Bay–New Hampshire boundary line until it reached a point twelve miles from the Hudson.[122] Two days later the New York commissioners offered a boundary line that would lie thirty miles east of the Hudson, although, they insisted, such a line would be "much short of the right of the Province."[123]

In this conciliatory atmosphere, on October 7 New York made its final proposals. Retreating from its earlier offer, it now signified a willingness to accept a line of demarcation that would begin on the south "at the northwest corner of the Oblong, fixed by New-York and Connecticut, to be twenty miles from Hudson's River"[124] and run north to a point twenty miles east of the Hudson, where an extension of the Massachusetts Bay–New Hampshire boundary would meet it. This was not acceptable to Hutchinson and his associates, who insisted that, in accordance with the 1757 recommendation contained in the Board of Trade representation to the Privy Council, a straight line be drawn northerly from a point actually twenty miles distant from the Hudson along the southern boundary of Massachusetts Bay to another point twenty miles from that river to connect with the northern boundary of that province. The difference between the two proposals lay in the breadth of the so-called Oblong. But behind this difference, which today may appear trivial, was the desire of the Massachusetts commissioners to protect the interests of "several hundred families in the townships of Noble-Town, Spencer-Town, and Taconick, who have been long in the regular possession of their estates, and who derive their title from

[122] *A Conference between the Commissaries of Massachusetts-Bay and New-York, 1767*, p. 3.

[123] *Ibid.*, pp. 9–11.

[124] *Ibid.*, pp. 24–5. On maps of New York of the period under consideration there is a long rectangular strip of land along the border of Connecticut designated "the Oblong." On November 23, 1683, New York and Connecticut had come to an agreement on a common boundary twenty miles distant from the Hudson. However, in an agreement with New York, arrived at in 1726, there had been an alteration in the boundary whereby, to retain certain settlements to the west of this line on Long Island Sound, Connecticut conceded to New York unsettled land north of the settlements on the Sound. The alteration in the common boundary between the two colonies will be considered later in this chapter.

the original proprietors with the consent and approbation of the Massachusetts Government."[125] As neither side would make further concessions, the Massachusetts commissioners indicated to their opponents on October 8 that "with great grief" they were obliged to return home, leaving the controversy between the two governments unsettled.[126] In the words of Lieutenant Governor Hutchinson, the dispute over a country fifty or sixty miles square was reduced to "an inconsiderable strip of land" and, for the sake of peace, Massachusetts Bay "conceded greatly."[127] What is more, the Massachusetts Bay General Court was so convinced of the strength of the position taken by its commissioners throughout the exchange of papers that it voted not only to express the thanks of the two houses to them but also to publish the text of the negotiations and place a copy in the hands of all members of the General Assembly as well as to send one to each town in the province.[128]

The truth is that what particularly disturbed the New York commissioners was the firm stand taken by Massachusetts Bay on the claim to lands as far west as the South Sea, a claim which would manifestly limit the indefinite western boundary of New York.

In view of the failure of the negotiations of 1767, the New York Assembly early in 1768 passed an act to expedite the settlement of the boundary. The act referred to the Earl of Shelburne's letter of December 11, 1766, which had requested that if the issue could not be settled by commissioners a full account of the facts and progress of the differences should be transmitted to His Majesty; it then stated that, since no amicable agreement had been reached, a history of the case should be prepared by William Smith, John Morin Scott, and James Duane.[129] But it is not clear that they did anything effective toward preparing a narrative of the dispute.[130]

[125] *Ibid.*, p. 26; this work is a journal of the proceedings of the commissioners of the two provinces, signed by the Massachusetts Bay commissioners on October 21, 1767.

[126] *Ibid.*, pp. 25–6.

[127] Hutchinson to Richard Jackson, October 20, 1767, Massachusetts Archives, 25:205–8. Addressing the General Assembly of New York on November 18, Governor Moore lamented the fact that "a negotiation of so much Consequence to both Provinces, . . . had not been attended with the wish'd for success." Nevertheless, he indicated the commissioners' "near approach to an Agreement" and expressed the hope that the legislators would concur on any measure that would bring the matter to "a desirable Issue" (*Journal of the Legislative Council of New York, 1743–1775*, p. 1623).

[128] For the resolution see *A Conference between the Commissaries of Massachusetts-Bay and New-York, 1767*, following p. 26.

[129] *Laws of New-York from 1691 to 1773*, II, 508–9.

[130] No mention is made in Smith's *Historical Memoirs . . . 1763–1776* of the preparation of such a narrative.

What counted heavily against New York and in favour of the Massachusetts Bay pretensions was that the Bay colony's position corresponded to the conclusions arrived at by the Board of Trade in 1757 and still held by this body. What is more, the disputed area continued to fill up with people who looked to Massachusetts Bay to support their rights.[131] Time was manifestly running out for New York. Yet, it would appear that there was no serious effort on the part of that province to reach a settlement until early in 1772, when William Tryon, who had become Governor in July of the preceding year, apparently made a new proposal.[132] Thomas Hutchinson, now Governor of Massachusetts Bay, was also extremely anxious to put an end to the controversy and was therefore pleased to find that the General Court, which took up Tryon's suggestion with alacrity, also appointed a joint committee to determine whether Hutchinson, in his new role as Governor, would be willing to take part in another attempt to terminate the controversy. When he signified his desire to aid the province in any way possible, a law was quickly passed appointing boundary commissioners and containing a special clause that made the presence of the Governors of both provinces mandatory during the deliberations between the commissions. It also, most significantly, provided that when an agreement had been reached and accepted by the two Governors it should be sent directly to the King for confirmation.[133] By the act William Brattle, Joseph Hawley, and John Hancock were appointed commissioners; of them, only Brattle had participated in the negotiations in 1767.[134] Even more important was the fact that Hutchinson, with his unrivalled knowledge of Massachusetts Bay history, would be present to guard the interests of the province.

Despite Tryon's overtures of the preceding year, it was not until the spring of 1773 that the New York General Assembly was prepared to act. On March 8 the Governor signed a law closely pat-

---

[131] In *A State of the Right of the Colony of New-York . . . So far as concerns the late Encroachments . . . of New-Hampshire . . .* (New York, 1773, pp. 12–13) the point was admitted that the lands in dispute between New York and Massachusetts Bay were "fully occupied"—a fact that had not applied to the area of the New Hampshire grants.

[132] The only direct evidence concerning Tryon's proposal found by this author is in Thomas Hutchinson to the Earl of Hillsborough, April 27, 1773, Massachusetts Archives, 27:320.

[133] *Ibid.* In his letter to the Secretary of State for the Colonies, Hutchinson could not forbear to mention this indirect tribute to his integrity and ability by the two houses and to add: "After all the illiberal treatment I have received for so many years together, this is a greater mark of real confidence than I have known any Assembly to place in a Governor" (*ibid.*).

[134] *Acts and Laws of Massachusetts-Bay, 1771–1772* (Boston, 1772), p. 601.

terned after that passed by Massachusetts Bay.[135] Both groups of commissioners, who began their negotiations on May 12 at Hartford, manifested a spirit of compromise. No longer did the New York commissioners insist that the New York eastern boundary line extend directly northward from the northeast corner of the "oblong" granted by Connecticut; they were willing to accept the northwest corner.[136] In turn, when the New York commissioners urged "as one of the indispensable articles" that Massachusetts Bay relinquish all claim to lands west of New York, the Massachusetts Bay commissioners were at first "disposed to a compliance." Later, after consulting with Hutchinson, they followed his advice "to refuse to concede to the demand," and the New York commissioners no longer pressed the point.[137] As a result, the agreement reached on the 18th of the month was promptly signed by all the commissioners as well as by Hutchinson and Tryon.[138] Hutchinson's decisive influence in securing this settlement of the highly inflammable issue in a manner

---

[135] By it John Watts, William Smith, Robert R. Livingston, and William Nicoll were named commissioners. It will be noted that the last three on the list had been commissioners in 1767. See *Laws of New York from 1691 to 1773*, II, 756–7.

[136] The boundary agreement read: "A Line beginning at a Place fixed by the Governments of New York and Connecticut in . . . 1731, for the North West Corner of a Tract of Land commonly called the Oblong or Equivalent Land, and running from Said Corner North Twenty one degrees ten minutes & thirty Seconds East, as the Magnetic Needle now points, to the North Line of the Massachusetts Bay, shall at all Times hereafter be the Line of Jurisdiction between the said province of the Massachusetts Bay and the said province of New York, in all and every Part and Place, where the said Province of New York on its Eastern Boundary shall adjoin the said Province of the Massachusetts Bay" (*Boston Evening-Post*, May 24, 1773).

[137] Thomas Hutchinson: *The History of the Colony and Province of Massachusetts-Bay*, III, 281*n*.

[138] Tryon to the Earl of Dartmouth, May 31, 1773, *New York Colonial Documents*, VIII, 371–2. In this letter Tryon noted that he had laid the agreement before the New York Council on May 26 and that it had been unanimously approved by that body. He also paid the following tribute to Hutchinson: "It is a matter of astonishment to me, that a Gentleman of such genuine worth, probity and decency of manners, should be made so unhappy in his Govern^{t}."

It is of interest to note that William Smith, one of the boundary commissioners and a member of the New York Council, kept a journal of the proceedings of the commissioners at Hartford. When Tryon asked him whether or not the journal should be sent to London along with the agreement, Smith advised against this step, on the grounds that the Massachusetts Bay claim of a western extent to the South Sea—that is, the Pacific—might be made "a Ground for suspending the Royal Assent, till Massachusetts waved her Exorbitant Claims, & so the East Limit should remain unsettled." In fact Smith felt that the proceedings of the commissioners in 1767 and of May 1773, gave "fair Ground for the Supposition that the Agreem^{t} of 18 May is conclusive to Massach^{s} on the West as well as to us on the East" (*Historical Memoirs . . . 1763–1776*, p. 148). It may be added that the New York–Massachusetts dispute over lands west of the settled part of New York was not brought to a conclusion until December 16, 1786, when an agreement was reached at Hartford; this was also favourable to Massachusetts. See George Dangerfield: *Chancellor Robert R. Livingston of New York, 1746–1813* (New York, 1960), pp. 204–7.

so favourable to Massachusetts Bay, was apparently acknowledged by the commissioners themselves.[139] When the agreement came before the Privy Council it was confirmed on February 2, 1774, after having been reported upon favourably by the law officers of the Crown.[140] It may be added that not until 1787—after an appeal to the Continental Congress had resulted in a compromise settlement with Massachusetts of New York's western boundary[141]—was the line actually run which set up a clear division of the disputed land.

But even before this, as a "residuary legatee" of all lands not clearly within the bounds of bordering colonies, New York had begun its expansion westward toward Lakes Ontario and Erie.[142]

New York and New Jersey's Northern Boundary

As the boundary line between New York and Connecticut had already been permanently settled before the period under consideration here, no intercolonial rivalry existed between the two colonies. Therefore only the question of the southern boundary of New York remains to be brought under review. In his *History of the late Province of New-York . . . to 1762* William Smith has the following to say about the southern and western boundaries of the colony:

> "On the west side of Hudson's River, from the sea, to the latitude of 41° lies New Jersey. The line of partition between that province and this, from that latitude to the other station on the Delaware is unsettled. From thence, wheresoever it may be fixed, we claim all the lands, on the east side of Delaware, to the north line of Pennsylvania; and all the territory, on both sides of the Mohawks' river, and westward to the isthmus at Niagara: in a word, all the country belonging to the crown of Great Britain, not already granted; for we are to consider New-York among her sister colonies, to borrow a law phrase, as a residuary legatee."[143]

The early history of the New York–New Jersey dispute[144] goes back to March 12, 1664, when King Charles II, gave a patent to his brother James, Duke of York, of the lands that later became the two provinces of New York and New Jersey, together with certain

---

[139] Thomas Hutchinson: *op cit.*, III, 281.

[140] *Acts of the Privy Council, Col. Ser., 1766–1783*, pp. 375–6.

[141] *Journals of the Continental Congress, 1774–1789*, XXVII, 547–50.

[142] See Ruth L. Higgins: *Expansion in New York . . . the Eighteenth Century* (Columbus, Ohio, 1931), Chap. 8, "Expansion, 1763–1783."

[143] Smith: *op. cit.*, I, Appendix, 251–4.

[144] See, in this connection, Volume III, revised, of this series, pp. 142–5.

lands in New England.[145] On June 23 of that year the Duke gave a one-year lease to John, Lord Berkeley, and Sir George Carteret for a tract of land "bounded on the East part by the Maine Sea and part by Hudsons River and hath Upon the West Delaware Bay or River [and] extendeth Southward to the Maine Ocean as farre as Cape May at the mouth of Delaware Bay or River of Delaware which is in fourty one degrees and fourty minutes of Lattitude and Crosseth over thence in a Straight Line to Hudsons River in Fourty one degrees of Lattitude which said Tract of Land is hereafter to be called by the name or names or New Cesarea or New Jersey. . . ." The following day James signed a formal release of the above territory to the two men to be held by them and their heirs forever in free and common soccage, with the proviso that every year they should render to His Majesty and heirs forty beaver skins whenever these should be demanded.[146] Although definite enough in most respects, the Duke of York deeds were confusing with respect, at least, to the northern line of demarcation of the new province from New York, and carried the seeds of future conflict. A decade later came the division of New Jersey, with the consignment in 1674 by the Duke of the northeastern part of the colony to Carteret,[147] and the remainder to two Quakers, John Fenwicke and Edward Byllynge. Other members of the Society of Friends became associated with the West New Jersey government at this time.[148] In 1682 (following Carteret's death in 1680) East New Jersey likewise passed into the hands of a group of proprietors. Both parts of New Jersey were administered separately until the two government were consolidated by the Crown in 1702, but the rights to the soil were reserved to the two groups of proprietors.[149]

The need of laying down the line, nevertheless, had long been felt to be a matter of great importance. At first it did not seem to present any great difficulties. For example, in 1686 the newly appointed Governor of New York, Thomas Dongan, at a meeting of the Council of that province held on June 30, reported that the Deputy Governor of East New Jersey, Gawen Lawrie, and the Deputy Governor of West New Jersey, John Skene, in the presence of

[145] For a copy of the patent to the Duke of York see *Documents relating to the Colonial History of the State of New Jersey,* cited as *New Jersey Archives,* 1st ser., I, 3–8.

[146] For the lease granted by the Duke see *ibid.*, I, 8–10; for the Duke's release of the territory see *ibid.*, I, 10–14.

[147] For the lease and release of 1674 see *ibid.*, I, 161–7.

[148] *Ibid.*, I, 205–19.

[149] *Ibid.*, II, 452–61.

other Jersey gentlemen, had informed him of their intention to run the lines between their two provinces and also between them and New York—a project to which he gave his consent. In so doing he proposed to them that the position of the most northerly branch of the Delaware River should first be agreed upon and fixed according to the patent; he also suggested that the surveyors meet on September 1 at the "Falls of Delaware River, & that which is the most Northerly Branch of Delaware River (if any Controversie arise about it,) be determined by Vote of two of these three Surveyor[s], George Keith, Andrew Robinson [Robison] & Phillip Wells; that what is concluded, by two of the said Surveyors, to be the Limits and bounds of the 3 Governm^{ts}, be so deemed and reported; & the Surveyor[s] to give in their Reports under their hands. All which was agreed upon, & concluded [by the Council]."[150] On September 1 the New York Council with the Governor present instructed Wells, the surveyor general for the province, to run an exact line between "this Province and that of East New Jersey beginning in the Latitude of 41 d: and forty m. upon Delaware River" and, in co-operation with the other two surveyors appointed, to report the findings as soon as possible to the provincial secretary.[151] As the laying down of a permanent line between East New Jersey and West New Jersey seemed to present many difficulties, it was determined on September 11 by representatives of the two provinces to submit the exact nature of the line to arbitration.[152] The only remaining problem to confront the three surveyors was that of laying down the line of division between New York and East New Jersey. On November 11 Wells and Robinson recorded that on September 11 and 28 observations "of the Sunns Meridionall Altitude" by them and Keith disclosed "that the fourtieth and one degree of Northern latitude upon Hudsons River is one minute and twenty five Seconds to the Northwards of Younckers [Yonkers] Milne and so falls upon the high Clifts of the Point of Tapaan on the West side of said River."[153] It would also appear that "the Respective Surveyors went out and affixed a Station on Delaware Diver in 41°: 40′ Latitude . . . , but tho' the Stations were fixed, yett the Lines were not drawn."[154]

Among the factors that seem to have caused the delay in marking

[150] For a certified copy of the minutes of the New York Council held on June 30, 1686, see *New Jersey Archives*, 1st ser., I, 517–18.

[151] A certified copy of this instruction is in *ibid.*, I, 518.

[152] For the agreement see *ibid.*, I, 519–20.

[153] For the certified copy of this recording see *ibid.*, I, 520–1.

[154] Deputy Governor Andrew Hamilton to Governor Benjamin Fletcher and the New York Council, February 13, 1693/4, *ibid.*, II, 105.

off the New York–East New Jersey boundary was the emerging conviction on the part of Governor Dongan that it was necessary to bring about the annexation to New York not only of Connecticut but of East New Jersey as well.[155] That others in New York either shared this view or at least sought to delay action on fixing a line is indicated by the failure of the Council of New York, while Benjamin Fletcher was Governor, to respond to the urging of Deputy Governor Andrew Hamilton of East New Jersey that surveyors be appointed for the purpose of marking out at least "the Line from the Said Station on Hudson's River as far as there are any plantations."[156] Again, in 1709, after the governments of East New Jersey and West New Jersey had been united, the receiver general of New Jersey wrote to the Governor of New York, Lord Cornbury—who was also commissioned Governor of New Jersey—showing how necessary it was for the northern limits of New Jersey to be ascertained.[157] Still no response came from the New York Council. However, by the spring of 1718 Governor Robert Hunter, also Joint Governor of the two provinces, was able to inform the New Jersey Assembly that the New York Assembly had empowered him to appoint the proper persons "for running its Division Line . . . to prevent future Disputes & Disquiet. . . ."[158] Following this step Hunter appointed two New York commissioners and a surveyor, Allane Jarratt (who soon became surveyor general of that province), to act in conjunction with commissioners and a surveyor to be appointed by New Jersey to determine once again where on the Delaware or its branches lay the north latitude of 41° 40′ and also where on the west bank of the Hudson was the point of 41° north latitude.[159] Responding to this move, the New Jersey Assembly also passed an act for ascertaining the division line,[160] and commissioners and a surveyor representing the proprietors of East New Jersey and West New Jersey were appointed. On July 25, 1719, after the commissioners of both provinces had made various observations as to the location of 41° 40′

---

155 Dongan to the Lords of Trade, n.d. but undoubtedly in 1687, *New York Colonial Documents,* III, 391–2.

156 Hamilton to Fletcher and the New York Council, February 13, 1693/4, and minute of the New York Council of February 22, 1693/4, *New Jersey Archives,* 1st ser., II, 105–6.

157 Peter Fauconnier to Lord Cornbury, April 2, 1709, *ibid.,* 1st ser., III, 388–9.

158 Hunter to the New Jersey Assembly, April 19, 1718, *ibid.,* 1st ser., IV, 365.

159 For the commission to the New York commissioners and the surveyor see *ibid.,* 1st ser., IV, 382–5.

160 *Acts of the General Assembly of the Province of New Jersey, . . . 1702–1776* (ed. Samuel Allinson, Burlington, 1776), p. 61, hereafter cited as *Acts of the New Jersey Assembly, 1702–1766.*

on the most northern branch of the Delaware River, they signed a tripartite indenture to that effect.[161] Everything at last seemed favourable for completing the essential task. The commissioners and the two surveyors[162] then went to the Hudson and on August 13 made their observations for the 41° northern latitude, but Jarratt left for New York City before confirming and ratifying them. Upon his return he avowed that the instrument used was defective. In September he petitioned the Council of New York, despite the agreement embodied in the tripartite indenture, to set aside the findings until a larger surveying instrument could be obtained and also until "able and skillfull Mathematiciants from Great Britain" could certify the findings, since these affected the town of Taphen (Tappan) "and Sundry other Gentlemens Estates." The Council approved the petition and accordingly directed that all further proceedings be halted.[163] In vain the Proprietors of both East New Jersey and West New Jersey submitted a long memorial to Lewis Morris, President of the New Jersey Council, for transmission to the Board of Trade, accusing Jarratt of giving "the Lye to himselfe."[164] Although both this and the New York memorial came before the Board of Trade early in 1720/1, no action was taken in that body.[165]

That no very serious clashes occurred between the inhabitants of the two provinces over the ownership of lands before the 1740's may be attributed to two factors. First, between 1702 and 1738 the two provinces were governed by a single man, who was able to harmonize their interests to a certain extent. Secondly, before the 1740's the movement of people into the area that eventually would be the scene of conflict was slow and gradual. It is true that the government of New York created Orange County in 1683 and that the town of Orange was settled by people coming directly from Holland in 1686; also, within the county, the Chesecock (Chesekook) Patent was granted in 1702, the Wawayanda Patent in 1703, and the great Minisink Patent in 1704.[166] Moreover, to the west of

---

[161] For this indenture see *New Jersey Archives,* 1st ser., IV, 394–9.

[162] Allane Jarratt (Jarrett) for New York and James Alexander for New Jersey.

[163] For Jarratt's petition and the action of the New York Council see *New Jersey Archives,* 1st ser., IV, 403–8; see also Philip Schuyler to the Board of Trade, October 31, 1719, *New York Colonial Documents,* V, 532.

[164] *New Jersey Archives,* 1st ser., IV, 408–31.

[165] See Board of Trade *Journal, 1718–1722,* pp. 243–4; among the papers placed before the Board was a petition by twenty-four inhabitants of New York stating their apprehensions concerning the running of the line. See *Calendar of State Papers, America and West Indies, 1719–1720* (ed. Cecil Headlam, London, 1933), p. 269.

[166] E. M. Ruttenber: *History of the County of Orange . . . with a History of the Town and City of Newburgh* (Newburgh, 1875), pp. 22, 26, 28.

Orange, in the area of what is now Delaware County, New York, lay much of the huge Hardenburgh Patent, issued in 1708.[167] But most of this vast holding was not even surveyed until 1749.[168] A census of the inhabitants of Orange County in 1702 revealed but 54 men, 40 women, 57 boys, and 84 girls among the whites, together with 33 Negro slaves; in 1712 there was a population of 439; in 1737 it was 2,840; in 1749 it had risen to 3,874; and in 1756 it was placed at 4,446.[169] What has been said of the slow development of Orange County may also be said of the New Jersey county bordering on it. Created in 1683 and named Bergen County, it was laid out to include all settlements between the Hudson and Hackensack rivers and extended from a point called "Constables-Hook . . . to the uppermost bounds of the Province Northward between the said Rivers."[170] In 1738, according to a census taken in that year, there were some 4,000 inhabitants in the county, many of them living in the disputed area.[171]

By the beginning of the 1740's, therefore, the situation was becoming serious. A joint committee of all the New Jersey Proprietors on September 2, 1741, represented in a memorial to Lewis Morris, who was now Governor, that it was necessary to redress "the many Grievances and Injurys" suffered by the Jersey inhabitants at the hands of their New York neighbours.[172] This was followed by an address to Morris from the East New Jersey Proprietors on June 28, 1742, complaining that writs of ejectment were being granted by the Orange County inferior court of New York against New Jersey settlers who were living almost seven miles south of what the Proprietors claimed to be the true line of demarcation.[173] In the fall of 1743 the New Jersey Governor wrote to Governor Clinton of New York emphasizing the potential dangers inherent in a situation that

---

167 J. H. French: *Gazetteer of the State of New York . . .* (Syracuse, 1860), p. 258. John Bradstreet, who in 1771 was anxious to secure a part of the Hardenburgh grant, claimed he had discovered that the patent was issued in 1706. See Governor Dunmore to Hillsborough, April 2, 1771, *New York Colonial Documents,* VIII, 268.

168 J. H. French: *op. cit.,* p. 258*n.*

169 For population tables see *Documentary History of New York,* I, 239, 471–3.

170 At the same time Essex, Middlesex, and Monmouth counties in New Jersey were brought into existence. See Aaron Leaming and Jacob Spicer: *Grants, Concessions, and Original Constitutions of the Province of New Jersey [before 1702]* (Philadelphia, [1752]; reprinted, Somerville, N.J., 1881), p. 229. See also W. W. Clayton: *History of Bergen and Passaic Counties, New Jersey . . .* (Philadelphia, 1882).

171 *New Jersey Archives,* 1st ser., VI, 244.

172 For this memorial see *New Jersey Archives,* 1st ser., VI, 138–40.

173 See *Ibid.,* VI, 144–9, which includes the affidavit of James Alexander, surveyor general of New Jersey.

found New Jersey settlers being taxed by New York authorities although long settled well outside that province's jurisdiction.[174] When Chief Justice Robert Morris carried these papers to New York to meet with Chief Justice de Lancey and others for discussions about the boundary, he came to the conclusion that the New York people were "against running the Line at all."[175] By the fall of 1744, with their patience exhausted, the East New Jersey Proprietors sent a memorial to Governor Morris begging him to recommend that the New Jersey Assembly "pass an Act for running the Said Line ex parte: and . . . to Recommend it for his Majesties Royall Aprobation."[176] However, it was not until February 17, 1747/8, that such an act was passed.[177]

Meanwhile there is every good reason to assume that the dispute over its southern boundary was one of the chief reasons for the appointment of a London agent by New York early in 1748, after a period of almost eighteen years without official individual representation. On April 9, 1748, the day Robert Charles was nominated, Speaker Jones of the New York Assembly wrote to the new agent directing him, among other things, "to endeavor to prevent its [the New Jersey Boundary Act] receiving the royal assent, until this colony can have an opportunity of making their objections, and of being heard against the said act."[178] The London agent was apparently able to delay action for two years, as it was March 1750 before he informed Speaker Jones that the Board of Trade was in

[174] Morris to Clinton, October 22, 1743, including the petition of New Jersey settlers, *ibid.*, VI, 162–8.

[175] *Ibid.*, VI, 168–71.

[176] *Ibid.*, VI, 216–19.

[177] "An Act for running and ascertaining the Line of Partition and Division betwixt this Province of New-Jersey and the Province of New-York," *Acts of the New Jersey Assembly, 1702–1776*, p. 172. By its provisions the act was not to go in force until receiving royal approval and the commissioners therein appointed for running the line according to the act of 1718 were to proceed only with the consent of the government of New York. See E. J. Fisher: *New Jersey as a Royal Province, 1738–1776* (New York, 1911), p. 214.

[178] *Journal of the General Assembly of New-York, Vol. II, 1743–1765* (Gaine), pp. 238, 393–5; see also William Smith: *History . . . of New-York*, II 118–19, 119–20*n.* For the internecine dealings between the respective New York political factions, as involved in the boundary dispute, see *ibid.*, II, 129–30, 130–1*n.*; see also Nicholas Varga: "Robert Charles: New York Agent, 1748–1770," *William and Mary Quarterly*, 3rd ser., XVIII, 216, 218, 221–4. That the East New Jersey Proprietors were likewise utilizing their London agent, Ferdinand John Paris, to further their cause may be seen in a letter addressed to him by James Alexander on April 16, 1748, informing him of the action of the New York Assembly in appointing an agent and advising him that Governor Belcher had promised to recommend the act. See *New Jersey Archives*, VII, 119–21.

the process of preparing a representation to submit to the Privy Council on the subject of the New Jersey act.[179] Speaker Jones, in what appears to be a reply to this letter, indicated that the Assembly was opposed to the appointment of a royal commission to settle the boundary and preferred to "rely on the merits of our cause." However, he suggested that if the agents for New Jersey would agree "that the head of Delaware Bay, which is at Reedy Island, is their north bounds on Delaware, . . . and [would consent to] run a line from thence to the latitude of 41 degrees on Hudson's river," the New York Assembly would then approve the appointment of a commission to run the line.[180] Thus, at this point in the controversy, the New York Assembly decided to emphasize the Delaware Bay rather than the river itself. Several years were to pass before the Board of Trade took final action. Then, in June 1753, came their carefully framed representation to the Privy Council upon the act.[181] Its conclusions made the points that the Province of New Jersey, in its distinct and separate capacity, could neither make nor establish boundaries involving another province,[182] and that the *legal* method of proceeding must be by authority derived from the Crown as signified by a commission under the Great Seal. The representation therefore recommended that the act should not receive the royal approbation.[183]

During the period that followed, hundreds of New Jersey families were pressing into the disputed region. To provide a government for them and also undoubtedly to strengthen their claims to the region, the New Jersey Assembly passed an act on June 6, 1753, for erecting the county of Sussex out of the northern portion of Morris County.[184] By the following year a committee of the New York Council drew up reports which detailed in numerous affidavits that "enormous Riots have been committed by the people of New-Jersey within the Jurisdiction of this Province." These disturbances involved especially the

---

[179] Board of Trade *Journal, 1742–1749,* p. 440; see also Nicholas Varga: *op. cit.,* p. 222.

[180] William Smith (*op. cit.,* II, 133–4) quotes from the Jones letter to Charles in dealing with the events of 1750. Reedy Island is approximately in latitude 39° 5′.

[181] For a detailed statement of the cause for delay see E. J. Fisher: *op. cit.,* pp. 214–21.

[182] The act itself favoured the tentative boundary of 1719.

[183] Board of Trade *Journal, 1749–1753,* pp. 432–6; *Acts of the Privy Council, Col. Ser., 1745–1766,* p. 214.

[184] For the act see *Acts of the New Jersey Assembly, 1702–1776,* pp. 194–6. It should be pointed out that on March 11, 1713/14 the northern part of Burlington County had been erected into Hunterdon County and that subsequently, on March 15, 1738/9, the northern part of Hunterdon was made into Morris County. See *ibid.,* pp. 25 and 109.

lands claimed by the proprietors of the Minisink and Wawayanda patents in Orange County, and provoked the arrest and imprisonment of Orange County authorities by those of Bergen and Essex counties.[185] Faced with this situation, the New York Assembly—no longer committed to the idea that the line of separation must be drawn from Delaware Bay to the Hudson and realizing that the disputed region was fast filling up with New Jersey people—passed on December 7, 1754, "An Act for submitting the Controversy between the Colonies of New-York and New-Jersey . . . to the final Determination of his Majesty."[186] When the Board of Trade turned to study this act, its members found serious objections to it as a very improper piece of legislation. In their representation to the Lords Justices on June 12, 1755, they pointed out that the method proposed by the law for determining the boundary, whereby private property would be affected, was contrary to accepted practice, which was by utilization of a royal commission; further, they held that the law was improper in declaring that "certain Patentees therein mentioned, shall not extend their claim beyond a Limit therein described"; and, finally, they objected to its ineffectualness in view of the fact that Proprietors of New Jersey had not consented to the method of decision outlined in it. For these reasons their recommendation to the Lords Justices that the act be repealed was carried out by the Privy Council.[187] Thereafter an additional instruction was sent to the Governor of New York, Sir Charles Hardy, calling upon him to recommend, in the King's name, that the Assembly agree to the appointment of a royal commission to settle the issue. The conditions setting up the royal commission were to provide a right of appeal to His Majesty's Privy Council for all parties which might feel aggrieved by the decision and to make provision for defraying half the expenses involved in the commission, since the New Jersey Proprietors had engaged themselves to pay the other half.[188]

---

[185] See *Two reports of a committee of his Majesty's Council for the Province of New-York . . .* (New York, 1754), especially pp. 4, 11–22. As was indicated in Volume III, revised, of this series, pp. 138–42, New Jersey was also the scene of the most serious riots against the East New Jersey Proprietors. For an extended account of these riots see E. J. Fisher: "Colonial Land Conflicts in New Jersey," Historical Society of Hudson County *Papers,* No. 6 (1909).

[186] *Laws of New-York, from The Year 1691, to 1773 inclusive* (2 vols., New York, 1774), I, 345; cited hereafter as *Laws of New-York, 1691–1773.*

[187] Board of Trade *Journal, 1754–1758,* pp. 119–20, 156; *Acts of the Privy Council, Col. Ser., 1745–1766,* pp. 301–2.

[188] For the additional instruction to Hardy, signed August 12, 1755, see *New York Colonial Documents,* VI, 960.

During the war years 1755 to 1762, affairs on the border remained comparatively quiet—except for some writs of ejectment issued by the New Jersey Supreme Court against certain New Yorkers who claimed that their lands lay not in New Jersey but partly in Orange County and partly in Ulster County, New York. These cases became the subject of correspondence and complaint on the part of the New York authorities.[189] In view of the growing dominance of New Jersey in the area, the New York Assembly finally decided to follow the recommendation contained in the royal instruction sent to Governor Hardy seven years earlier, and, accordingly, in December 1762, passed "An Act for submitting the Property of Lands which are held or claimed by Grant under the Great Seal of this Colony, and are affected by the Controversy about the Boundary . . . between this Colony and the Colony of New-Jersey, to such a method of Decision as His most Gracious Majesty shall think proper by his Royal Commission or otherwise to appoint; and for defraying the expenses to accrue on the Part of this Colony on the final settlement of this said Line."[190] When in the following year, the Assembly of New Jersey passed similar legislation, it failed to receive royal approval.[191] However, early in 1764, a revised act was passed free of objection.[192] On July 20 of this year the Crown approved both the New York and the New Jersey act, and the Board of Trade was thereupon instructed to propose suitable commissioners.[193] Accordingly, on December 19 a list of fifteen commissioners submitted to the Privy Council was approved.[194] As questions arose concerning some of these appoint-

[189] For the cases of Philip Swartwout and others see *New Jersey Archives,* 1st ser., IX, 178–82, 250–6.

[190] *Colonial Laws of New York,* IV, 640. New Jersey passed an act, on December 6, 1769, for advancing money to the agents engaged in setting the line. *Acts of the New Jersey General Assembly, 1702–1776,* p. 335.

[191] The act provided for agents to assume the responsibility (in cooperation with agents also provided for by the New York law) for settling the line, and one of those so designated was William Alexander, whose assumed title of the Earl of Stirling was mentioned in the act itself. The Board of Trade on November 22, 1763, pointed out that, since the House of Lords had not approved Alexander's claim to this title, it did not seem advisable to lay the act before His Majesty in Council. See Board of Trade *Journal, 1759–1763,* p. 409. Alexander's claim to the earldom—a title that had become extinct in 1739 with the death of the 5th Earl of Stirling—was rejected by the committee of privileges of the House of Lords on March 10, 1762. See Charles Rogers: *Memorials of the Earl of Stirling* (2 vols., Edinburgh, 1877), I, 282–3. Despite this decision, Alexander continued to use the title, as is well known.

[192] For the acts of 1763 and 1764 see *Acts of the New Jersey Assembly, 1702–1776,* pp. 254, 263–4. The wording of the New Jersey act of 1764 was all but identical with the New York act of 1762, except for necessary changes.

[193] *Acts of the Privy Council, Col. Ser., 1745–1766,* pp. 686–7.

[194] *Ibid.* The initial choice of commissioners very properly was left to be concerted, in the main, between the two governments. On June 27, 1763, Governor

ments, it was not until June 26, 1767, that an order in council finally appointed thirteen commissioners, any five of whom meeting together would constitute a quorum. All were incumbents in, or had previously held, offices by direct Crown appointment, including such men as Benjamin Franklin of Pennsylvania, joint deputy postmaster-general for North America, and Jared Ingersoll, formerly the appointed stamp master for Connecticut and later to be named judge of the Court of Vice-Admiralty for the Middle District of North America.[195] The final order in council, it may be mentioned, contained no statement that would bind the commissioners to settle upon any specific degree of latitude or any designated branch of the Delaware River. They were entirely free to make a decision.

Neither of the two colonies involved in the boundary dispute was represented on the royal commission, but agents of each were active in presenting their claims and in supervising the physical work of the surveys used by both sides to support their claims and to construct a common map for the commissioners. To help determine the latitude with accuracy, the services of David Rittenhouse, the Philadelphia mathematician and astronomer, were obtained by the agents of both sides. He brought with him the sextant and time-piece belonging to and employed for the Pennsylvania Proprietors in their land surveys. Rittenhouse was aided by the military engineer Captain John Montresor.[196]

The commission, which did not hold its first meeting to hear testimony until July 1769, continued to sit while the surveys were being made. Each colony took the opportunity to present its case fully.[197]

William Franklin of New Jersey informed the Board of Trade that the "Managers of the Controversy on both Sides have mutually agreed upon a Number of Gentlemen whom they have desired Governor Monckton [of New York] and myself to recommend to your Lordships in order to be nominated to His Majesty as Commissioners . . ." (*New Jersey Archives*, 1st. ser., IX, 388–91). The list of names agreed upon in 1763 was limited to seven, all of them "Gentlemen of Character & Fortune, who hold Offices under the Crown," living at a distance from the area in dispute—three from Virginia, three from Massachusetts Bay, including Thomas Hutchinson, whose name did not appear in the final list, and one from New Hampshire. Subsequently the Board was asked by the representatives of the two governments to have two more commissioners appointed so that at least five members should always be present at their meetings.

[195] For a copy of the order in council establishing the royal commission see *ibid.*, IX, 630–6; see also *Acts of the Privy Council, Col. Ser., 1766–1783*, pp. 44–5.

[196] See W. A. Whitehead: "The Circumstances Leading to the Establishment, in 1769, of the Northern Boundary Line between New Jersey and New York," New Jersey Historical Society *Proceedings*, VIII, 157–86, especially p. 178 and the frontispiece map.

[197] For the proceedings of the commission see the "New York–New Jersey Boundary Papers," Vol. 2, New-York Historical Society; see also *A Brief of the Claim on the Part of New-Jersey, . . . offered . . . before the Commissioners Appointed by*

On October 7, 1769, the commissioners arrived at the decision that the intent of the Duke of York in making his grant to Carteret and Berkeley was that it should begin on the Delaware River, not at 41° 40′ north latitude, but at the junction of the Mahackamack and Delaware Rivers, a fork at 41° 21′ 37″ north latitude, and that the location at 41° north latitude was on the west bank of the Hudson at a prominent rock duly marked by the surveyors. This opinion was signed by four of the commissioners.[198] Acting upon the provisions permitting the right of appeal to the Privy Council, both sides took preliminary steps to appeal against the decision, and a December 8 date was set for a hearing in Hartford.[199] When this day arrived, only two commissioners appeared; nor was there a quorum present for the next few days, so that the meeting was adjourned until July 4 of the following year.[200] Upon receiving a report of this reason for the failure of the commission to convene, the King in Council directed in 1770 that the order in council be altered to permit "a ma-

---

his Majesty, for settling the Boundary Line, between the said Province of New-Jersey and the Province of New-York [New York, 1769], a brief of forty-four pages, and "A Plain and full state of Demands & Pretentions of his Majestys Colony of New-York against the proprietary Colony of New Caesaria or New Jersey . . . ," [1769], *New Jersey Archives*, 1st ser., X, 119–30.

It is interesting to note that there was a spirit of determination as well as compromise brought to the settlement of the dispute on the part of the colonies involved. For example, on February 6, 1768, the New York Assembly passed a clarifying law entitled "An Act to remove Doubts and Scruples, concerning an Act, entitled, An Act for submitting the Property of the Lands, which are held or claimed by Grants under the Great Seal of this Colony, and are affected by the Controversy about the Boundary . . . between this Colony, and the Colony of New-Jersey, to such a Method of Decision, as his most gracious Majesty shall think proper . . ." (*Laws of New York, 1691–1773,* II, 512).

198 For the text of the decision of the boundary commission, together with the dissenting opinion of two commissioners, see W. A. Whitehead: *op. cit.*, pp. 180–2. Mr. Whitehead in this article wrote of the ruling (*ibid.*, pp. 174–80): ". . . I cannot conceive how the Commissioners could have arrived at the . . . decision. . . . It seems to be based upon no principle save that of accomodation to the claims of New York." E. J. Fisher in his *New Jersey as a Royal Province* points out (p. 235) that the Delaware River location for the starting of the line was a compromise between the Delaware location of 1719 favoured by New Jersey and that of 1686 favoured by New York.

199 The basis of the petition against the boundary decision on the part of New York was "that the interests of the Crown as well as those of the Province of New York had been injured." This is embodied in the letter of Edmund Burke, London agent of New York, to the committee of correspondence, August 6, 1771. See R. J. S. Hoffman: *Edmund Burke, New York Agent . . .* (Philadelphia, 1956), p. 199. The basis of the New Jersey appeal, contained in a letter to Benjamin Franklin, notifying him of his appointment as London agent by New Jersey, was that the line of 1719 had been constantly deemed the line of division and as a consequence great numbers of New Jersey people had settled up to that point and north of the line now laid down. See the New Jersey committee of correspondence to Benjamin Franklin, December 7, 1769, *New Jersey Archives*, 1st ser., X, 138.

200 *Ibid.*, XXVI, 586–7, and XXVII, 199.

jority of the commissioners present" to be effective in any future proceedings.[201] It was not necessary to put this ruling into action, however, as both parties had by this time "signified their Willingness to settle the Controversy in an Amicable manner." After several conferences the agents agreed to abide by the October 7 decision of the commission for final settlement of the line—doubtless to the great relief of the royal commissioners.[202]

The survey of the New York–New Jersey line now proceeded. Since the surveys between the location points on the Delaware and the Hudson were to be carried on in what the New York government considered to be a part of Orange County, Lieutenant Governor Colden's commission to the New York surveyors—who were to act in cooperation with New Jersey surveyors—embodied a directive to the local magistrates to suppress all threats of tumult and riot. Other instructions to the surveyors for both sides specified that they lay down stone monuments every mile between the location points, which was done.[203] Meanwhile, New Jersey passed an act in October 1770 confirming the agreement between the two governments; this was subsequently re-enacted on September 26, 1772, in order to put it into language almost identical to that of the law passed by the New York Assembly on February 16, 1771.[204] When the Privy Council approved these acts on September 1, 1773, the appeals of both colonies from the decision of the commissioners were referred to with the comment that the acts of the two assemblies "appear to be a disavowal of the appeals interposed by the agents."[205] Thus, with

---

[201] *Acts of the Privy Council, Col. Ser., 1766–1783,* p. 45.

[202] *New Jersey Archives,* 1st ser., X, 194. For an account of the actions of the commission and the agents see W. A. Whitehead: *op. cit.,* pp. 174–85, and E. J. Fisher: *op. cit.,* pp. 231–5. See also "New York–New Jersey Boundary Papers," Vol. 2, *loc. cit.*

[203] For Colden's commission to the New York surveyors, dated May 16, 1770, embodying the general terms of agreement see *New Jersey Archives,* 1st ser., X, 194–6, 501–2.

[204] For the act of 1771 see *Laws of New York, 1691–1773,* II, 602. The New Jersey acts may be found in *Acts of the New-Jersey Assembly, 1702–1776,* pp. 342, 368–73. It may be noted that this gesture of compromise was at the recommendation of Governor Franklin, but that the second act passed the Assembly by only a small majority (see E. J. Fisher: *op. cit.,* p. 234).

[205] *Acts of the Privy Council, Col. Ser., 1766—1783,* pp. 45–6. In the *Historical Memoirs . . . 1763–1776 of William Smith* (p. 79), under the date of March 10, 1770, Smith, a leading member of the New York Council, makes the point that both groups of landowners in the disputed area were deeply concerned about the costs involved in the appeal. In this connection he wrote: "The Jersey Proprietors have Reason to fear, that the Issue of the Appeal will not be favorable to their Interests & the Costs of prosecuting it . . . heavy. They have therefore lately proposed to our Managers an Agreem^{t} to supersede the Necessity of proceeding further with the Causes." As for the agents who had been acting for New York, Smith points out that although they

the final seal of approval of the King given to the implementing legislation—108 years after the original grant of New Jersey by the Duke of York—the boundary between New York and New Jersey was permanently fixed.[206]

In summarizing the intercolonial rivalries over lands and boundaries between New York and its neighboring colonies which came to a head in the 1760's and 1770's, it may be said that most of the disputes were bitter and some involved bloodshed among the settlers themselves. Here were groups of land-hungry men, some tenants, some freeholders, some landowners—including the officers and soldiers who had received grants for their service in the Great War for the Empire—all of them eager to retain their holdings. Caught in a speculator war, they were basically on the side of whichever government would protect their interests. In this connection, it is germane to recall that land was the soundest investment and the most important source of income in the colonial period, and constituted as well the basis of franchise privileges and the property qualifications for office-holding. It is also noteworthy that the landed gentry—who were the most powerful and privileged element of the population, especially in New York—had evolved no clear land system for their tenants and, in many instances, gave short shrift to those who were disgruntled or to squatters who, in their eyes, were merely trespassing upon their estates.[207] Therefore it is not surprising that settlers were pleased to have grants from whatever government would confirm them in their lands or that they should go by the rule of thumb that possession was nine-tenths of the law. Such, of course, were the sentiments of the Allen family—themselves speculators and land jobbers—who not only encouraged the New Hampshire land patentees to remain on their holdings but made common cause with them and defended them by force of arms in a lawless effort to avoid all governmental influence but one that

---

were in need of funds to press the New York appeal, the Council not only refused to give them the sum they needed but demanded a proper audit of the money already spent.

[206] *New Jersey Archives,* X, 416. For a scholarly account of the settlement of the New York–New Jersey boundary dispute, see J. H. Smith: *Appeals to the Privy Council from the American Plantations* (New York, 1950), pp. 453–63. As has been indicated in the text, no appeal was made to the Privy Council during this dispute.

[207] For the inequities of the land system in New York and the land speculation activities in that province, see Volume III, revised, in this series, Chap. 5, "In the Region of the Old Patronships"; see also Mark Irving's *Agrarian Conflicts in Colonial New York, passim,* E. P. Alexander's book on James Duane, *passim,* George Dangerfield: *Chancellor Robert R. Livingston . . . ,* pp. 16–20 and *passim,* and Dorothy Rita Dillon: *The New York Triumvirate . . .* (New York, 1949), Chap. 9, "Land—Goal of Tenant and Speculator."

resulted finally in the creation of the new government of the state of Vermont.

In the final settlements at the provincial government level, however, the government of New York succeeded in sustaining a fair margin of its claims. This was due in part to the fact that the most active New York land speculators in the disputed areas included such well-placed and privileged men as the successive Governors, Supreme Court Justice Robert R. Livingston, Attorney General John Taber (Tabor) Kempe, the influential triumvirate of eminent lawyers: William Livingston, John Morin Scott, and Councilor William Smith—not to mention lawyer James Duane, the largest speculator of them all. These wealthy absentee landholders did not hesitate to use their privilege and influence for the benefit of the claims of the provincial government as well as to protect their own vested interests.[208] But, in the main, the legal rights of the Province of New York were on a firmer footing than those of the rival governments. In this connection, it is interesting to note that when the question of the New York boundary was raised as recently as 1932, the United States Supreme Court decided that the royal order in council of 1764 confirmed but did not change the boundary of New York as fixed by the original grant given by Charles II to the Duke of York in 1664, and that therefore New Hampshire had never had any jurisdiction in the area west of the Connecticut River.[209]

Finally, it should be noted that in attempting to mediate the pretensions of New York and its rivals in connection with disputed lands, the government of Great Britain, acting through the Privy Council and Board of Trade, showed a spirit of impartiality and —following the pattern set for reimbursement of the colonial war debts after the Great War for the Empire[210]—wisely insisted that in so far as was possible differences should be settled between the contending parties themselves, rather than through exertion of

---

[208] See in this connection Lieutenant Governor Colden's complaints to the Lords of Trade against the courts and the judges, and especially his letter of February 22, 1765, to Lord Halifax: "The Proprietors of the great Tracts of land in this Province have united strongly with the Lawyers as the surest support of their enormous & iniquitous Claims, & thereby this faction is become the more formidable and dangerous to good Government." See *Colden Letter Books*, I, 455, 458, 470, and *passim* (New-York Historical Society *Collections, 1876*). Despite Colden's known animosities, his knowledge of the land system was extensive and he was in a position to observe the operations of the legal fraternity; see George Dangerfield, *op. cit.*, pp. 32–3; see also Irving Mark: *op. cit.*, Chap. 3, "Political Power and Landlord Dominance."

[209] See M. B. Jones: *Vermont in the Making*, pp. ix–x.

[210] See Volume X of this series, Chap. 2, "Parliament Reimburses the Colonies, 1756–1765."

Crown authority. The only serious exception to this policy was in the case of the dispute over the New Hampshire patents in the area west of the Connecticut River, which resulted in the decisive action taken by the Privy Council that produced the order in council of 1764. This action—as discussed earlier in the chapter—doubtless came as the result of what its members considered to be the irresponsible conduct of Governor Benning Wentworth in his land speculation activities, as well as in his hasty granting of a multitude of townships in the disputed area, some of them close to the Hudson River.[211]

It has been seen that New York's boundary problems with its neighbours were solved by different methods. For instance, in settling the line separating New York and Massachusetts Bay, the commissioners were chosen by their respective governments from residents of these two colonies, and their decision was ratified by both Governors. Whereas the commissioners who resolved the New York–New Jersey dispute were all residents of other colonies and were, moreover, appointed under the Great Seal, while their decision was subject to appeal to the Privy Council by either or both of the colonies. But the solutions were reached by mutual consent, and in each instance produced settlements that, all in all, seem to have been just and fair.

---

[211] For Wentworth's grants from 1749 to 1764 to some 6,000 individuals, and for the 130 township grants, see *New Hampshire State Papers* (33 vols., Concord, 1874–1915), XXVI, and M. B. Jones: *op. cit.*, Appendix G; for a discussion of the grantees, with emphasis on the Bostonians both Loyalist and patriot, see G. P. Anderson's paper on this subject, Colonial Society of Massachusetts *Publications*, XXV, 33–8 (Transactions, 1922–4).

CHAPTER XI

Intercolonial Conflicts: Pennsylvania and Its Rivals

THE Province of New York was not alone in its preoccupation with disputes over lands and boundaries during the 1760's and early 1770's. The proprietary of Pennsylvania was confronted with similar conflicts.[1] Some of these arose during its beginnings as a colony in the seventeenth century, others developed in the course of the eighteenth century, but all were based upon the apparently irreconcilable claims embodied in royal patents. The dispute with the proprietary of Maryland that began in 1681 and was not really terminated until the completion in 1767 of the well-known Mason and Dixon survey, was perhaps the most famous boundary dispute in American colonial history. Of another nature was the struggle over possession of the Wyoming Valley between the proprietary of Pennsylvania and the Connecticut settlers of the Susquehanna Company backed by the colony of Connecticut; this came to a climax in the years preceding the Revolution, but was not concluded until the following century. Both of these conflicts are of importance to an understanding of the local rivalries that complicated the development of the British Empire in North America before the War for American Independence. Therefore a somewhat detailed account of them is necessary to illustrate the background of intercolonial relations during the period under consideration.

The Rivalry between the Penns and the Baltimores

Since Cecil Calvert, 2nd Lord Baltimore, received a charter for the Province of Maryland in June 1632, almost a half century before

[1] For a general survey of the problems of both colonies see William Brewster: *The Pennsylvania and New York Frontier . . .* (Philadelphia, 1954).

William Penn secured his grant to Pennsylvania, it is well to examine the wording of the documents bearing on the common boundary between the two colonies. The royal letters patent to Baltimore, in describing the various limits of the grant, stated that the northern boundary of Maryland should be in that portion of what had been previously a part of Virginia "which lieth under the Fortieth Degree of North Latitude . . . , where New England is terminated", ". . . *que subjacet quadragesimo gradui latitudinis septentrionalis ab equinoctiali ubi terminatur nova Anglia* . . ."). The western extent of the province was to be a straight line along the northern boundary up to the point of the meridian of "the first Fountain of the River of Pottowmack," then south on this meridian to the fountain; its southern bounds from that point were to be the "further Bank of the said River," until it emptied into Chesapeake Bay.[2] Thus, by charter, Maryland was to extend from the south bank of the Potomac River northward to the point where New England terminated. During November 1620 the so-called Council for New England was granted under the Great Seal "all that Circuit, Continent, Precincts, and Limitts in America, lying and being in Breadth from Forty Degrees of Northerly Latitude, from the Equinoctiall Line, to Forty-eight Degrees of the said Northerly Latitude, and in Length . . . from Sea to Sea. . . ."[3] In view of these statements—that the territory of the Council for New England extended from 40° to 48° north latitude and that the Maryland grant extended to the beginning of this earlier grant—it would seem by all logical rules of interpretation that the expression in Baltimore's patent "which lieth under the Fortieth Degree of North Latitude" would mean all lands within the prescribed bounds that lay south of 40°. The charter of the Council for New England, it may be noted, was still valid at the time of the Baltimore grant, for it was not surrendered until 1635. Then, too, the intent of the grant to Baltimore may be indicated by the statement that he should possess all lands under 40° "in a right Line by the Degree aforesaid, unto the true Meridian" of "the First Fountain" of the Potomac. At

[2] For the Maryland charter, printed in both Latin and English, see *Laws of Maryland at Large* . . . (ed. Thomas Bacon, Annapolis, 1765); the Latin text appears in P.R.O., Patent Roll, 8 Chas. I, Part 3, No. 2594, and is reprinted in *Archives of Maryland*, III, 3–12, together with a collation provided by the editor, W. H. Browne, of the variant Latin readings; see Preface, pp. xi–xii.

[3] For the text of the patent granted to the Council for New England by James I, see Ebenezer Hazard: *Historical Collections . . . of State Papers* . . . (2 vols., Philadelphia, 1792, 1794), I, 103–18, see also William MacDonald: *Select Charters and other Documents illustrative of American History, 1606–1775* (New York, 1906), pp. 23–33.

that point the line would run "South" to the "further Bank of the said River."[4]

William Penn's charter for Pennsylvania, received at the hands of Charles II in March 1680/1, was to

> "all that Tract or Part of Land in *America*, . . . bounded on the East by Delaware River, from Twelve Miles Distance Northwards of New-Castle Town unto the Three and Fortieth Degree of Northern Latitude, if the said River doth extend so far Northward; but if the said River shall not extend so far Northwards, then by the said River so far as it doth extend; and from the Head of the said River the Eastern Bounds are to be determined by a Meridian Line, to be drawn from the Head of the said River unto the said Three and Fortieth Degree. The said Land to extend Westward five Degrees in Longitude, to be computed from the said Eastern Bounds; and the said Lands to be bounded on the North by the Beginning of the Three and Fortieth Degree of Northern Latitude, and on the South by a Circle drawn at twelve Miles Distance from *New Castle* Northward and Westward, unto the Beginning of the Fortieth Degree of Northern Latitude, and then by a straight Line Westward to the Limits of Longtitude abovementioned."[5]

During the year of the grant, Penn sent commissioners to the new province to take preliminary steps for developing the colony and particularly to lay out the town that would be the centre of government for the new province. His agents were directed to select a site on a part of the Delaware River that would be navigable for ships and yet be high, dry, and healthy. Their choice fell upon the lands enclosed by the junction of the Schuylkill and the Delaware, and there the foundations of the "great Towne" of Philadelphia were laid. When the discovery was made that Philadelphia lay to the south of 40° north latitude is not clear, but this realization caused perhaps the most embarrassing situation ever faced by the great and good founder of Pennsylvania—a situation that was at the core of the problem that still faced his descendents in the eighteenth century.

When, on June 14, 1680, the Lords of the Committee of the Privy Council for Trade and Plantations had considered William Penn's

---

[4] See *Laws of Maryland at Large . . .* (1765).

[5] For Penn's patent see *The Acts of Assembly of the Province of Pennsylvania . . .* (Philadelphia, 1775), pp. iii–vii; see also *Charter to William Penn and Laws of the Province of Pennsylvania . . .* (eds. George Staughton *et al.*, Harrisburg, 1879), pp. 81–90, and S. K. Stevens: *Pennsylvania, The Keystone State* (2 vols., New York, 1956), II, 7–17.

petition for a grant of land, they had felt it an incumbent duty to write to Sir John Werden, the agent of James, Duke of York, in order to ascertain that such a grant would not conflict with that made by Charles II to his brother in 1663/4; they also wrote to Richard Burk, agent for Charles Calvert, 3rd Lord Baltimore, as Proprietor of the Province of Maryland. On June 23 Burk replied: "It is desired, that if the Grant pass unto Mr. Penn, of the Land Petitioned for, by him in America, That it may be expressed to be land that shall lye North of Susquahana Fort, and North of all Lands upon a direct Line westward from the said Fort, for that Fort is ye Boundary of Maryland northward."[6] On June 25 the Lords of the Committee again turned to the petition and, after reading the letters from Werden and Burk, called in Penn. He was forthwith made aware that part of the land he desired was held by the Duke of York, and "Mr. Penn being also acquainted with the matter of the letter from the Lord Baltemore's Agents he does agree that Susquahannough Fort shall be the [northern] Bounds of the Lord Baltemore's Province."[7] The palisaded fort, it should be pointed out, was a well-known landmark, especially before the subduing of the Susquehanna Indians in the eighteenth century, and was located some two miles south of the present city of Columbia in Lancaster County, Pennsylvania,[8] close to 40° north latitude. According to Sir John Werden's account of a conversation with Penn over the bounds of his grant, the Proprietor announced his willingness "that 12 English Miles North of Newcastle be his Boundary and believes that that Distance will fall under the beginning of the 40th Degree of Lati-

---

[6] For copies of the replies of Werden and Burk, both dated June 23, 1680, see Penn Manuscripts, 11: 3, 5, 7, Historical Society of Pennsylvania.

[7] This minute, taken from the P.R.O. Colonial Entry Book, No. 106, p. 178, is printed in the *Archives of Maryland,* V, 272.

[8] The fort is clearly indicated on a 1740 map of Maryland, Delaware, and Pennsylvania which can be found in *Pennsylvania Archives,* 2nd ser., XVI, facing "The Breviate." See also H. F. Eshleman: *Lancaster County Indians. Arrivals of the Susquehannocks . . .* (Lancaster, Penn., 1908), p. 100. Under date of August 6, 1676, the Maryland Council wrote to the Governor of Virginia "that the Susquehanough Indians have resided at their Old Fort about sixty miles above Palmers Island [at the mouth of the Susquehanna River] for so many months that they have now Corne fit to roast" (*Archives of Maryland,* XV, 122). T. C. Holm in his *Short Description of the Province of New Sweden, now Called Pennsylvania* (Historical Society of Pennsylvania *Memoirs,* III, *Philadelphia,* 1834, p. 157) described the centre of the Susquehanna tribe as a mountain "very steep and difficult to climb; there they have a fort or square building, surrounded with palisades, in which they reside," which was some fifty-four English miles from the Swedish settlements. See also, for the Susquehanna Indians, F. W. Hodge: *Handbook of American Indians* (2 vols. or "Parts," Washington, 1910), II, 653–9.

tude."[9] Chief Justice Sir Francis North so fixed the bounds of the Penn patent at the desire of the Lords of the Committee.[10]

In 1681 an attempt was made by Charles Calvert, 3rd Lord Baltimore, to challenge the Pennsylvania-Maryland boundary. As a result, when William Markham, Penn's cousin, was sent over as Deputy Governor, he arrived in Pennsylvania in July bearing a royal command for speedy settlement of the boundary. The neighbouring Proprietor, who was living near St. Mary's in Maryland at this period, immediately sought to terminate the business. But Markham, while professing an equal avidity to settle the matter, found reasons of illness and other pressing business to justify a delay. His reluctance to act prevented any authorized person from being present to cooperate with Baltimore's commissaries to lay down the line.[11] By June 1682 the Maryland commissaries, after waiting in vain for any Pennsylvania people to appear, made certain observations in the neighbourhood of New Castle which helped to confirm Baltimore's views that the line of 40° north latitude fell well to the north of Philadelphia.[12] In September, Markham announced to Baltimore that he would not cooperate in laying down any line that could affect Penn's rights on the Delaware River, although he was well prepared to find one in the area of Chesapeake Bay. The basis of his refusal was expressed in the following terms:

> "My Lord, this is my reason, that as I received all that part of the river Delaware beginning twelve miles above New Castle Towne and soe upwards from the Government of New York which is according to the express words of His Majesty's Letters Pattents to our Proprietory Mr. Wm Penn Esqre I most humbly conceive that I am not to be accomptable to any other person [than] His Majesty or [his] royall Highness [the Duke of York] for any part of this Province laying upon Delaware river & soe bounded."[13]

---

[9] Werden to William Blaythwayt (Blathwait, Blathwaite), Clerk of the Lords of the Committee, November 23, 1680, Penn Manuscripts, 11:19.

[10] "Mr. Penn's Boundaries settled by My L. C. J. North [December 16, 1680]," *ibid.*, 11:25.

[11] Baltimore to William Blaythwayt, March 11, 1681/2, *Archives of Maryland*, V, 348–51, and "A narrative of the whole Proceedings betwixt the Lord Baltemore and Captain William Markham Deputy Governor under William Pen Esqre . . . ," *ibid.*, V, 374–9.

[12] The Maryland Boundary Commission to Baltimore, June 17, 1682, *ibid.*, V, 369–70.

[13] Markham to Baltimore, September 25, 1682, *ibid.*, V, 372; for Markham's sworn statement of March 17, 1684/5, of the details surrounding his meeting with Lord Baltimore on September 25, 1682, and the subsequent events that prolonged their disagreement, see *ibid.*, V, 430–3.

In October 1682 William Penn arrived in Pennsylvania from England, and on December 13 he met Baltimore at an Ann Arundel County plantation in Maryland.[14] According to Baltimore, Penn opened the initial private conference by saying that

> "he was sensible that without the Lord Baltemore's . . . kindness to him, a great part of that Countrey soe given him, would prove but a dead lump of earth, for without an Inlett the same would be useless, and therefore he requested the Lord Baltemore to be soe good and kind a neighbour as to afford him but a back door for the improvement of that which otherwise . . . would signify nothing to him; Adding this, that what was but the hundredth part of the Lord Baltemore's interest, would be ninety nine parts of the hundred of William Pen's."[15]

At the subsequent public conference Penn produced a letter from the King to Baltimore which seemed designed to favour Penn's desire for an outlet to the sea by its mention of "an admeasurement of two degrees according to the usuall computation of sixty miles to a degree to be the best, and certaine method of setting forth and ascertaining the boundaries between Maryland and Pensilvania." But Baltimore, who stood to see the northern extent of Maryland limited by two degrees, took the position that the King had received "some misinformation" and, producing the patent for Maryland and a copy of Pen's patent, declared that they must be governed by both, "I having for my northern Bounds the fortieth degree of northern latitude which by your Pattent is your Southern bounds as Watkins point is mine."[16] Without denying this contention, Penn proposed "as a more equall way for him, and the Lord Baltemore, [to measure the boundary] to take their comencement from the Capes," a point of latitude which for a long time had been considered by mariners to be 37° 5′ north. Baltimore rejected this accepted latitude of the Capes as being but an observation made with a small sea quadrant held by hand—thus always in motion, especially if the holder were on board a ship—and insisted that the only proper way to measure accurately the point of 40° north latitude was to use a sextant some six to ten feet in diameter placed in a

---

[14] Penn's version of the meeting, under date of August 14, 1683, is to be found in Penn Manuscripts, 11: 8–10. Baltimore's account is embodied in a narrative of his interviews with Markham and Penn, *Archives of Maryland*, V, 374–82; this is supplemented by a shorthand account of the conference taken down by the Clerk of the Maryland Assembly; for this see *ibid.*, V, 382–90.

[15] *Ibid.*, V, 379–81.

[16] From the shorthand notes, *ibid.*, V, 381 and 383.

frame on firm ground.[17] With each man remaining adamant about how to determine properly the line of 40° latitude, the conference adjourned—Penn urging to the last that he and Lord Baltimore "discourse the business in private" as the best means of coming to a fair accommodation.[18] In his own account, Penn stressed the vital importance to Pennsylvania of "harbourage," which Baltimore "had to excess."[19]

The next conference between the two Proprietors occurred on May 29, 1683, at New Castle. In this private meeting, according to Lord Baltimore, Penn insisted that in finding the 40° north latitude line the initial observation should be Watkins Point, the most southern point of Maryland and

> "from thence there should be an Admeasurement to the degree of forty saying that out of every degree he did not doubt but to gaine six or seaven miles and by that means to gett water at the head of Chesapeake Bay and that this was the Mistery which he was plaine to tell the Lord Baltemore and did assure me that he would procure it from his Maj^{tie} to which I [Baltimore] answered that if he [Penn] Could impose his dictates upon the King and Council it would be in vaine for me to hope to have Justice don me but I was not (as I told him) of opinion that he could impose in that kind. . . . He then proposed this that if I would lett him have Susquehanna River for an Inlett and Land Enough on Each Side the Said River Sufficient of his Occasions and that I would let him know certainly under my hand what price or value I would Sett upon the same he would then willingly joine with me to bring an observation to find the degree of forty Northerly Latitude and with such instruments as we had then propper for that purpose. To this I [Baltimore] answered . . . how he [Penn] would expect I was able to give him anything certaine under my hand afore I knew Certainly how far North up Susquehanno River the fortieth degree Northern Lattitude (my North bounds) could reach."

Penn then asked Baltimore in what degree of latitude Captain James Conaway had found Palmer's Island at the mouth of the Susque-

[17] From Baltimore's narrative *ibid.*, V, 381. Baltimore attempts at this point to explain Penn's dilemma in the following terms: That "having been misinformed as to the degree of forty northerly latitude (which he was assured would fall lower than Saxafras [Sassafras] river in the Bay of Chesapeake as by their false mapps appeare, and having assured his friends, and particularly those of his late Society for Trade, that all the head of the said Bay would fall within Pensilvania) is now unwilling to have the truth discovered" (*ibid.*, V, 381–2). A map produced in England in 1681, following Penn's conception of the location of 40° north latitude to the south of the Sassafras River, was one of those that Baltimore called "false mapps."

[18] *Ibid.*, V, 388–90.

[19] Penn Manuscripts, 11: 8–10.

hanna. When Baltimore replied that it was sixteen miles south of 40°, Penn requested him to suggest what he would demand for the land running up to this degree, "if sixteen miles how much for 16 miles and that after I had given him this Certaine under my hand he would then be willing to go with me to the heads of the Rivers [the Delaware and the Susquehanna] and joine with me in the taking observations as I had all along insisted on." But, as Penn insisted that his offer was to be accepted or rejected by the next day and as Baltimore apparently became suspicious and thought it "a very Strange way of proceeding" when Penn requested that the survey be made with only a few persons present, the conference broke up without results.[20]

What becomes clear from the account of the second conference is that Penn attached such importance to gaining a port of entry for his future fair province that he was willing to purchase all land to the south of 40° north latitude stretching northward from the mouth of the Susquehanna River, but not at the cost of sacrificing his rights in the Three Lower Counties on the Delaware. This he made clear in his written answer on October 31, 1683, to Lord Baltimore's demand that he turn over all the land on the west side of the Schuylkill River.[21] Although the Baltimore-Penn dispute extended to the area which is now the state of Delaware, this aspect of the quarrel—which was given extended treatment in an earlier volume of this

---

[20] The above report of the conference, dated May 31, 1683, was attached to a letter from Baltimore to William Blaythwayt, *Archives of Maryland,* V, 397–400. Penn's account of the conference of May 29, 1683, does not dwell upon the very important points raised in the Baltimore account, but emphasizes the means used by Baltimore to attract people to settle in the New Castle area on Maryland's terms. As to the location of 40° north latitude along the Atlantic seaboard, Penn wrote: "I have common fame on my side . . . y^{t} ye fortieth degree of north Latitude lyeth about Pool's Isle," which is in Chesapeake Bay to the south of the mouth of the Sassafras River. His argument was that if this were an error then the Baltimore grant was made upon the basis of this error and therefore Baltimore should not be allowed to take advantage of it. Penn Manuscripts, 11: 8–10.

[21] See Penn's answer to Colonel George Talbot, agent for Baltimore. In this letter Penn refers to the meeting with Baltimore held on May 29, 1683, at New Castle at which he offered to waive the advantage given him by the King's letter and to meet Baltimore at the head of Chesapeake Bay "and there try to find the 40th degree of North Latitude, provided he [Baltimore] would first please to sett me a Gentleman's price, soe much a mile, in case I should have noe part of the Bay by Lattitude, that soe I might have a back port to this Province. . . . To sell he refused, but started to [offer] an Exchange of part of that Bay for the lower Counties on the bay of Delaware. This I presume he knew I could not doe, for his Royall Highnesse [James, Duke of York] had the one halfe, and I did not prize the thing I desired [that is, access to the Susquehanna River] at such a rate" (Calvert Papers, Maryland Historical Society, printed in the *Archives of Maryland,* XVII, 146–50).

series[22]—will be dealt with briefly and only in so far as it is germane to the basic Pennsylvania-Maryland dispute. But it is necessary to call attention to the fact that both Penn and Baltimore tried to defend their respective claims to an interest in the colony of "Newcastle," as the Maryland Proprietor called it. Thus, when the Pennsylvania Proprietor decided to return to England after his failure to achieve a satisfactory agreement, it was for the purpose of securing his goal of a port of entry—a legitimate goal in the eyes of the government, but one which involved subsequent disputes with Lord Baltimore over both Philadelphia and "Newcastle."

It was not until August 1684 that William Penn set sail to present his case to the home government. By this time Baltimore had also gone home with the same purpose in mind. Thereafter the contest between them centred in the Privy Council, where it was heard by the Lords of the Committee for Trade and Plantations. Lord Baltimore stated his case in 1684 in the following summary terms:

> "That New Castle has been justly claimed by the present Lord Baltemore & his father [Cecilius]. That Mr. Pen had been assured that the degree of 40. N. Lat: would fall lower than Sassafras River in Chesopeak Bay. That the Lords of the Council were assured that New Castle Bay lay 7. 8. or 10. miles to the Northward of the 40th degr. but that the Chief of the Quakers [Penn] have since owned that New Castle lies some miles to the Southward of the 40th degree."[23]

Penn's case, as stated in the preceding year, was that under his patent his grant began "twelve miles above New Castle upon the west side of Delaware River, and soe to run to the 43th Degree of North Lattitude upon the said River. . . ."[24] Thus Penn, in order to gain his objective, seemed inclined to ignore the question of the extension of Baltimore's patent to the real position of 40° north latitude.

The numerous hearings of the Penn-Baltimore case before the Lords of the Committee, both before and after the appearance in London of the rival Proprietors—revolved almost entirely around the ownership of the Lower Counties on the Delaware.[25] Baltimore

---

[22] See Chap. 8, "A Nondescript Colony on the Delaware," in Volume III, revised, of this series.

[23] *Archives of Maryland,* V, 456.

[24] *Ibid.,* XVII, 147.

[25] For the details of the progress of the Penn-Baltimore controversy in England see the *Calendar of State Papers, Col. Ser., America and the West Indies* in the volumes covering the years 1681–5 and 1685–8. However, for a convenient summary of the activities of the Lords of the Committee for Trade and Plantations relating to this issue

was doubly handicapped during this period, because Penn's friend, the Duke of York, became James II and was therefore in a position to influence the decision of the Privy Council. He was also on the defensive because charges were brought by local customs officials that the government of Maryland was permitting violations of the trade and navigation acts, with a concomitant loss of the King's revenue, and because the collector of customs had been murdered by a member of the Council there, which led to the issuance of a writ of *quo warranto* against the province.[26]

On November 13, 1685, the King in Council issued an order which was destined to have a profound influence on the whole dispute. This order in council denied that Baltimore had any claim to the Lower Counties on the Delaware and then, in line with a recommendation made by the Lords of the Committee in its report on November 7, ordered that the land between Delaware Bay and the sea on the east and Chesapeake Bay on the west "be divided into two equal parts by a line from the latitude of Cape Henlopen to the fortieth degree of Northern latitude, and that one half towards Delaware Bay and the Eastern Sea be adjudged to belong to the King, and the other to Lord Baltimore."[27] This meant that Philadelphia, together with its access to the sea by way of the Delaware River and Bay, was protected from any interference by Baltimore so long as the order stood; it also meant that Penn could exercise what interest and authority in the Lower Counties he possessed under the grant to him by the King when still Duke of York.[28] In fact, the controversy now slept for many years.

In 1688 came the so-called "Glorious Revolution" which deprived

---

see E. B. Mathews: "History of the Boundary Dispute between the Baltimores and Penns resulting in the Original Mason and Dixon Line," *Report on the Resurvey of the Maryland-Pennsylvania Boundary, Part of the Mason and Dixon Line* (Harrisburg, 1909), pp. 140–51. This study was written in a spirit of great impartiality; although without supporting footnote references, it is buttressed with an exhaustive bibliography and is recommended to the student. In contrast to the Mathews study are the following works: G. W. Archer: *The Dismemberment of Maryland . . .* (Baltimore, 1890), which presents the controversy from the point of view of the Baltimore family, and C. C. Tansill: *The Pennsylvania-Maryland Boundary Controversy* (Washington, D.C., 1915), which is unwarrantedly critical of Penn and has other weaknesses as a study.

[26] See *Acts of the Privy Council, Col. Ser., 1680–1720,* pp. 28–31, 88. For the charges and counter-charges made in 1681 by Lord Baltimore and Christopher Rousby, the collector of customs in Maryland, see *Calendar of State Papers, Col. Ser., America and West Indies, 1681–1685,* pp. 78–80, 160–6; for the murder of Rousby in 1684 by Colonel George Talbot, a member of the Maryland Council and Baltimore's personal agent, see *ibid.,* pp. 731, 734–7.

[27] *Ibid., 1685–1688,* pp. 116–17.

[28] For the defective nature of Penn's claim to the Lower Counties on the Delaware, see Volume III, revised, of this series, pp. 184–93.

James II of his throne. By 1691 William and Mary had taken over the government of both Maryland and Pennsylvania. The land rights of Baltimore and Penn were of course not affected. Penn's full powers were returned by royal patent in 1694, but it was not until 1715 that the right was restored to the Baltimore family—now headed by the Protestant 5th Lord Baltimore, grandson of Charles Calvert—to name a Governor, subject to Crown approval.

Early in 1709, during the reign of Queen Anne, an attempt was made by Baltimore to overturn the order in council of 1685 "dividing the isthmus between Delaware Bay and Chesapeake Bay, thus endeavouring to deprive the petitioner of his inheritance. . . ." Penn's counter-petition begged that, after twenty-three years' quiet possession and improvement of the land assigned to him by this order of Charles II, the Queen "will not countenance an attempt so injurious to property and the rights of her subjects. . . ." Again Penn scored a victory, for on June 23 of that year the Baltimore petition was dismissed.[29] This may be said to mark the last serious attempt to incorporate into Maryland all the land extending to 40° north latitude that the patents to Cecilius Calvert seemed to entitle the Baltimore family to enjoy and hold.

However, as no boundary line had been laid down between Pennsylvania and Maryland after the order in council of 1685, and as the Proprietor of each province continued to make grants of land within the disputed area, the need for establishing a permanent boundary was becoming ever more apparent. This matter was soon to come to a head. Penn in 1701 had made grants of the so-called Nottingham and Welsh tracts as part of Pennsylvania; at the same time Baltimore was having lands surveyed in the vicinity of Conestoga as a part of Maryland.[30] The Nottingham settlement, however, was claimed as part of Cecil County in Maryland, yet Pennsylvania magistrates had been appointed to regulate it as a town located in Chester County. This jurisdictional dispute led to the conference of October 28, 1718, between Governor Willam Keith of Pennsylvania and Governor John Hart of Maryland, which also involved the settlement of Pennsylvania in New Munster, adjoining Nottingham, since the lands there "were held by Rights from Maryland." The conference resulted in agreement that people established in the boundary area should not be molested "until by a proper authority the Division

[29] *Acts of the Privy Council, Col. Ser., Unbound Papers,* pp. 84–6; Board of Trade *Journal, 1708–1715,* p. 51.

[30] E. B. Mathews: "History of the Boundary Dispute," *op. cit.,* pp. 155–6. The Welsh tract in dispute at this time lay near the present borders of Delaware, Maryland, and Pennsylvania. See *ibid.,* p. 158*n.*

Line between the two Governments Can be Run."[31] But in this unresolved situation it was impossible to collect taxes from those living on the disputed lands, even by using armed force. Furthermore, within four years after the agreement a Chester County surveyor was arrested by the Cecil County authorities for making surveys to the north of Nottingham.[32] As this potentially dangerous situation had been reported to the Crown,[33] Charles, 5th Lord Baltimore, and Hannah, the widow of William Penn, attempted to avoid contentions between the inhabitants of Maryland and Pennsylvania. To this end they entered into an agreement on February 17, 1723/4, specifying that for a period of eighteen months no person should be molested in his possessions nor should any lands be surveyed "near the boundaries which have been Claimed or Pretended on either Side"—during which time, it was hoped, the vexing matter would be settled.[34]

But—largely, it would seem, as the result of the confusion that arose with the death of Hannah Penn in 1726 and the financial entanglements and other complications in which John, Thomas, and Richard Penn, heirs to Pennsylvania, were involved[35]—nothing was done to establish the boundaries, so that after the lapse of the 1723/4 agreement, the officials of both Pennsylvania and Maryland again hastened to stake out their rival claims. Then on May 10, 1732, with family matters at last clarified and settled, the Penns reached an understanding with Lord Baltimore that commissioners should be appointed by each province to lay down the boundary and make provisions for the security and ease of those whose possessions might be affected. By this pact it was stipulated that the Maryland Proprietors would give up all pretensions to the Three Lower Counties, that a twelve-mile circle should be drawn around New Castle, and that the Pennsylvania Proprietors should be en-

[31] For Keith's report on the conference see *Minutes of the Provincial Council of Pennsylvania* (16 vols., Philadelphia, 1852–3, and General Index, 1860), III, 60–1, to be cited hereafter as *Pennsylvania Colonial Records.*

[32] *Ibid.*, III, 212–14.

[33] For example, in June 1722 Governor Keith—acting upon the report that the Marylanders were planning to survey lands on the Susquehanna—informed the Council of Pennsylvania that with its consent he would proceed to run "the old Auchteraroe [Ouchteraroe and Octararoe] Line [from the Susquehanna] as far West as the Branches of the Potowmack," as the only way to preserve the peace. The Council wisely opposed this unilateral step. See Keith to the Council June 18, 1722, and the Council to Keith, June 20, 1722, *ibid.*, III, 178–9.

[34] For the agreement see *ibid.*, III, 231–2.

[35] For the disputes between the branches of the Penn family over the inheritance see Thomas Penn to the Pennsylvania Boundary Commissioners, May 14, 1734, *Pennsylvania Archives,* 2nd ser., VII, 303–6.

titled to all land (outside of the circle) fifteen miles south of Philadelphia, but should give up all pretensions to any land to the south of this line.[36] This projected happy termination of the dispute did not take place.[37] On the contrary, Lord Baltimore on August 8, 1734, petitioned the King in Council to overturn the order in council of November 7, 1685, and by a further patent "confirm unto him and his Heirs and Assigns the whole of such Part of the said Peninsula as is contained within the Limits of said Charter [of 1632]. . . ."[38] In turn John, Thomas, and Richard Penn filed a bill in Chancery in June 1735 to compel Baltimore to carry out the articles of agreement.[39] However, the decision of the High Court of Chancery to reject the Baltimore claims was not destined to come until 1750.[40]

Meanwhile more violence burst out in the disputed area. For instance, in 1736 the sheriff of Lancaster County and his deputies burned the house of Marylander Captain Thomas Cresap, killing and wounding some who attempted to escape from it. This occurred after Cresap had made preparations to carry out a threat to drive from their homes in the midst of winter about three-score Pennsylvania families who had declined to accept the jurisdiction of Maryland. Further, to effect the capture of Cresap, the Pennsylvania sheriff penetrated well into territory that was alleged by Baltimore agents to be indisputably a part of Maryland.[41] The Marylanders, for their part, were accused of acting with great violence against

[36] "The Breviate in the Boundary Dispute between Pennsylvania and Maryland," *ibid.*, 2nd ser., XVI, 449–60. This *breviate* was filed in the High Court of Chancery in June 1735; see also *Acts of the Privy Council, Col. Ser., 1766–1783,* pp. 101–5. For an excellent recent account of the Penn-Baltimore agreement of 1732 see N. B. Wainwright: "Tale of a Runaway Cape . . . ," *Pennsylvania Magazine of History and Biography,* LXXXVII, 251–93.

[37] The Maryland boundary commissioners sought to run the circle not twelve miles from New Castle but two miles, declaring they understood that the periphery of the circle was only twelve miles and the diameter would therefore be less than four miles. *Pennsylvania Archives,* 2nd ser., XVI, 488.

[38] *Ibid.,* XVI, 483–5; *Acts of the Privy Council, Col. Ser., Unbound Papers,* pp. 233–4.

[39] For the bill filed in Chancery on June 21, 1735, by the Pennsylvania Proprietors see *Pennsylvania Archives,* 2nd ser., VII, 338–71; for the answer filed by Lord Baltimore see *ibid.*, VII, 371–93.

[40] For the decree of the High Court in 1750 see Francis Vesey: *Cases Argued and Determined in the High Court of Chancery . . . 1746/7 . . . 1755* (2 vols., 3rd edn., London, 1788), I, 452–5. It should be pointed out that before the dispute—involving mainly the Lower Counties on the Delaware—was transferred to the High Court of Chancery, the Board of Trade early in 1735 reported to the Privy Council that there was no doubt "that the disputed lands were included in Baltimore's patent in 1632" (*Acts of the Privy Council, Col. Ser., Unbound Papers,* p. 236).

[41] For a careful summarization of the charges and counter-charges exchanged in letters between the Pennsylvania and Maryland authorities, as prepared for the enlightenment of the Privy Council, see *ibid.*, pp. 239–44.

Pennsylvanians, of forcing them to travel over a hundred miles to the Annapolis gaol without proper food or clothing during wintry weather, and of breaking open the Lancaster gaol to free offenders charged with "high and grievous offenses."[42]

When the intolerable situation was brought before the Privy Council early in 1738, this body sought the King's approval to the following propositions agreed to by the Proprietors: (1) that the Governors of the respective provinces were to be responsible for preventing riots and disorders on the borders; (2) that all other lands in contest—except the Lower Counties on the Delaware, which were involved in a separate case then pending in Chancery—were to "remain in Possession as they now are," with the Proprietors continuing to hold jurisdiction over them; (3) that Pennsylvania should have temporary jurisdiction over "all Vacant Lands in Contest between the Proprietors not lying within either of the three Lower Countys and . . . East . . . of the River Susquehannah down so far South as fifteen Miles and one Quarter of a Mile South of the Latitude of the most Southern part of the City of Philadelphia And on the West side of the Said River . . . down so far South as Fourteen Miles and Three Quarters of a Mile South of Latitude of the most Southern part of the City of Philadelphia," with Maryland authorities exercising jurisdiction south of this line "without prejudice to either Proprietor"; (4) that the Proprietors of Pennsylvania and Maryland should be free to make grants on their respective sides, but that they should be accountable to each other for any profits derived therefrom; (5) that all prisoners taken as a result of the disturbances should be released on a reasonable bail, subject to trial by order of the Crown. These recommendations, which concluded with the proviso that the clauses were to be declared part of a provisional order to continue without prejudice to either party until the boundaries should be finally settled, were approved by His Majesty in Council on May 25, 1738, whereupon orders were so issued.[43]

In the light of the order in council, the Governors of the two provinces issued the appropriate proclamations. Late in 1738 steps were taken by commissioners of the two provinces to begin laying down the line by determining the position of the most southern point of Philadelphia and then extending the line some two miles,

---

[42] *Ibid.*, pp. 247–8.

[43] For the terms of agreement between the Proprietors and the order in council see *Acts of the Privy Council, Col. Ser., 1720–1745*, pp. 340–2; see also *Archives of Maryland*, XXVIII, 145–9.

but bad weather forced them to postpone the effort. They took up the work the following spring and, by the first week in May, had surveyed west to the Susquehanna River. After marking out on its west bank the offset from the line previously laid down, the Maryland commissioners were obliged to discontinue operations on account of the family problems of one of their number; however, the Pennsylvania commissioners continued westward with the *ex parte* survey until they came to the mountain country.[44] The accomplishment of these surveys seemed to signify that the great problem of drawing a line between the two provinces was nearing a solution.

The Chancery decision of 1750 clarified another disputed point: the location of Cape Henlopen. Since the position of the Cape on the so-called Visscher map had been accepted—in connection with the 1732 agreement between Lord Baltimore and the Penns—as indicating the southern line of the Lower Counties on the Delaware, this boundary point was made permanent, although Cape Henlopen is actually considerably to the north.[45]

When, on April 23, 1751, Charles, Lord Baltimore, passed away, he was succeeded by his son Frederick, who, although not of age, argued through the executor of the estate, his uncle Cecilius Calvert, that he was bound neither by the articles of agreement of 1732 nor by the decree in Chancery of 1750, by reason of certain other settlements executed by his family between 1698 and 1730.[46] This new case was brought before the High Court of Chancery; however, while it was still pending, the terms of the 1732 agreement and the Chancery decree of 1750 were accepted as binding by Baltimore and the Penns in an agreement which was finally signed on July 4, 1760.[47] This settlement signifies the final acceptance by the Baltimore

[44] See E. B. Mathews: *op. cit.*, pp. 161–3; for a map of the 1738–9 survey see *ibid.*, opposite p. 166.

[45] Actually, the point of departure for the survey of the southern bounds of the Three Lower Counties on the Delaware was Fenwick's Island. In surveying westward to Chesapeake Bay, in order to arrive at the middle distance between the Atlantic Ocean and Chesapeake Bay, the Baltimore commissioners wished to stop at Slaughter's Creek, but the Penn commissioners insisted that the line must reach the Bay itself and not a tributary, thus gaining additional land for the Lower Counties. See *Pennsylvania Archives*, 1st ser., IV, 18; see also N. B. Wainwright: "Tale of a Runaway Cape . . . ," *op. cit.*, LXXXVII, 251–93, and L. C. Wroth: "Joshua Fisher's 'Chart of Delaware Bay and River,'" *Pennsylvania Magazine*, LXXIV, 90–109, especially pp. 101–3; see further J. W. Jordan: "Penn versus Baltimore: Journal of John Watson, Assistant Surveyor to the Commissioners of the Province of Pennsylvania, 1750," *ibid.*, XXXVIII, 385–406.

[46] For the steps taken by the Penns to bring about the enforcement of the agreement and decree and the counter-measures taken by Baltimore in the High Court of Chancery see *ibid.*, 1st ser., IV, 19–22; see also E. B. Mathews: *op. cit.*, pp. 175–9.

[47] For the Indenture of Agreement of July 4, 1760, see *Pennsylvania Archives*, 1st ser., IV 1–36. The actual terms of agreement are to be found on pp. 23–36. It

family of the pretensions of the Penn family with respect to the Lower Counties on the Delaware and to a boundary between Maryland and Pennsylvania that would guarantee the position of Philadelphia as the chief commercial and shipping centre and colonial capital of Pennsylvania.

Little more need be said about the termination of the controversy beyond the fact that both sides now cooperated in good faith in laying down and marking the boundary lines separating Maryland from the Lower Counties on the Delaware and from the Province of Pennsylvania. This was not a simple task with the instruments then available, and some of the lines had to be run more than once in order to attain the proper degree of accuracy. To facilitate the task, the Proprietors of the two provinces in 1763 agreed to bring over and employ two Englishmen, the astronomer Charles Mason and the surveyor Jeremiah Dixon. Arriving in the fall of that year, these men worked until 1768, when they returned to England. Their survey along the Pennsylvania-Maryland border and beyond stretched over 233 miles from the starting point to a spot just above Dunkard Creek, west of the Monongahela River, where they were stopped by the Indians.[48] Lest any question be raised therafter, the Proprietors jointly asked that the line be confirmed by the King in Council. This was done by an order issued on January 11, 1769.[49]

It should be added that when the problem arose in 1779 of extending the Mason Dixon line so as to mark the boundary between Pennsylvania and Virginia beyond "the first fountain of the Potomac," difficulties were encountered. As will be made clear in the next chapter of this volume, which is concerned with trans-

---

may be noted that Lewis Evans, the Pennsylvania cartographer, having become convinced that the Proprietors of the province were not only ungrateful but untrustworthy, put his services at the disposal of Governor Horatio Sharpe of Maryland in 1753 and in October of that year presented him with a brief upholding the charter claims of the Baltimore family. Later he went to New York to collect additional proof among the Dutch manuscripts there. But the Proprietor of Maryland felt that the Evans evidence did not aid his cause. See the author's *Lewis Evans . . .* (Philadelphia, 1939), Chap. 3, "Pennsylvania Boundary Disputes."

[48] For a detailed account of the running of the boundary lines see E. B. Mathews: *op. cit.*, pp. 179–90. For the map of the survey—which stops at 33° west of the New Castle tangent—see *ibid.*, endpapers. See also the newest account of the surveyors' activities in H. M. Cummings: *The Mason and Dixon Line . . .* (Harrisburg, 1962). For the part of Benjamin Chew—head of the Pennsylvania commissioners and attorney general until 1765, when he became register general—in the laying of the boundary line from 1761 to November 9, 1768, when the final report of the commissioners was made, see B. A. Konkle: *Benjamin Chew, 1722–1810* (Philadelphia, 1932), pp. 120–2. See also "Mason and Dixon's Line," *Maryland Historical Magazine,* II, 315–18, for the surveyors' letter of January 29, 1768, to Hugh Hammersley concerning the final work of completing the west line.

[49] *Acts of the Privy Council, Unbound Papers,* pp. 469 and 539.

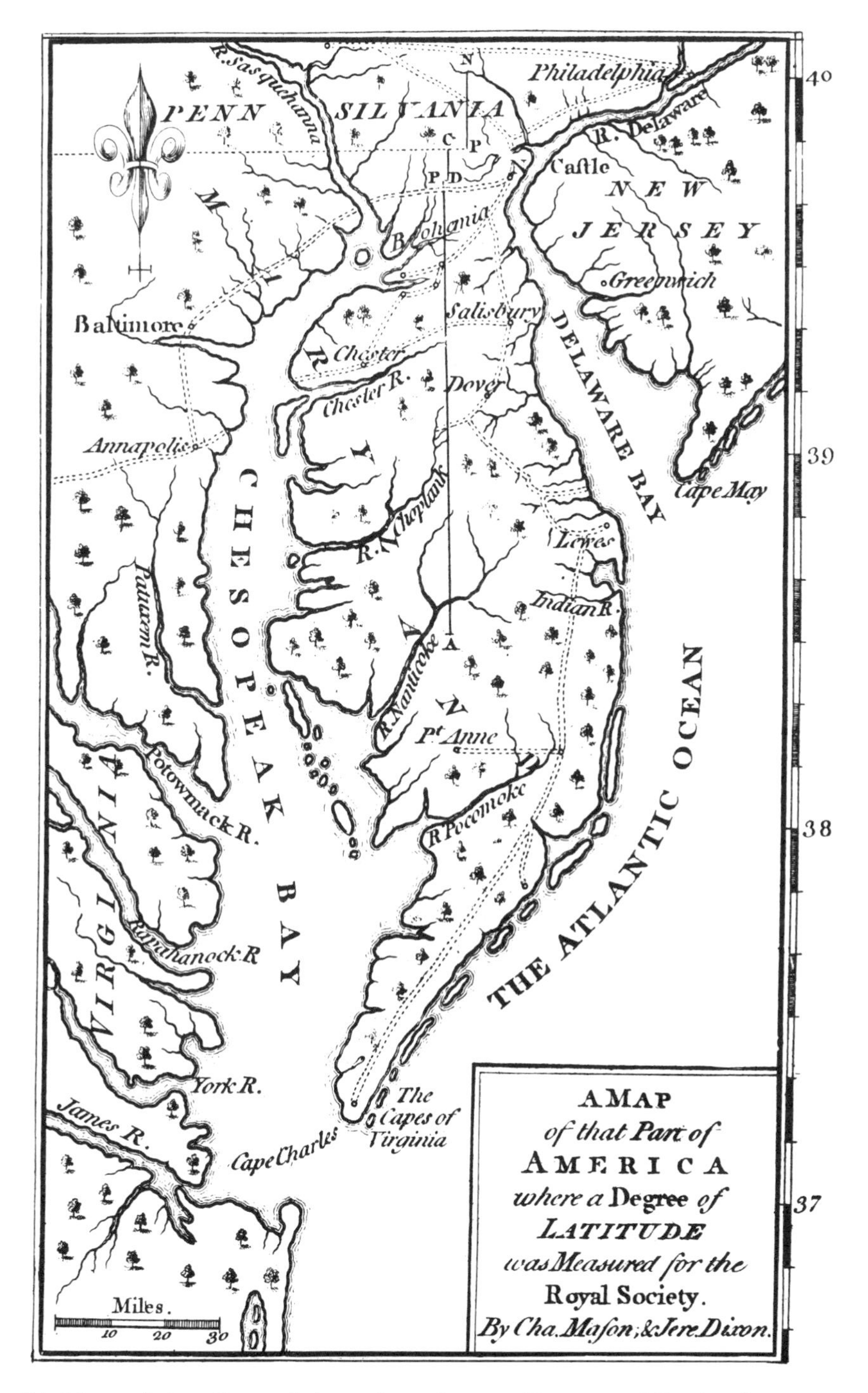

"A Map of that Part of America where a Degree of Latitude was Measured for the Royal Society" by Charles Mason and Jeremiah Dixon.

(From *Gentleman's Magazine*, 1769)

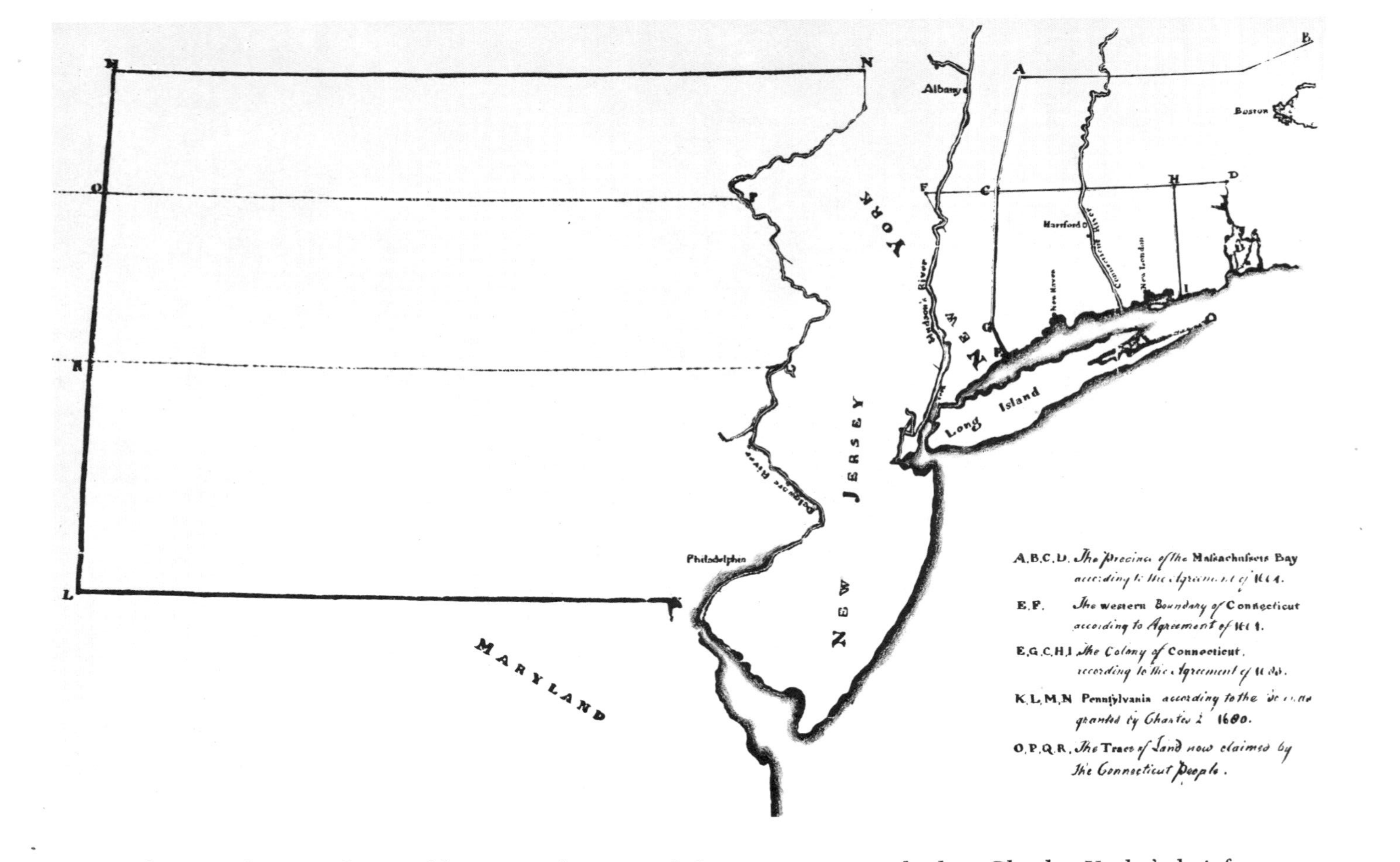

A map showing the area disputed by Pennsylvania and Connecticut, attached to Charles Yorke's brief, March 30, 1763.

(From the Penn Manuscripts, Historical Society of Pennsylvania)

Appalachian developments, Virginia laid insistent claims to the lands about the forks of the Ohio, basing its title upon the provisions of the royal charter of 1609, which granted to the London Company of Virginia all the lands within a four-hundred-mile strip running from sea to sea. However, as a result of the vigorous assertion by the government of Pennsylvania of its rights to the Pittsburgh area under terms of the charter granted to Penn, the government of Virginia was persuaded to abate its claims. The outcome, stated briefly, was that during the course of the War for American Independence the Old Dominion began to seek an amicable settlement. The two states finally agreed to appoint commissioners, who met at Baltimore in 1779. At the start of the negotiations the Pennsylvania commissioners contended that the southern boundary of their state beyond the western limits of Maryland should be the beginning of the 40th degree of north latitude, that is, at 39 degrees. The Virginia commissioners opposed this stand, taking the position that the Mason and Dixon line should be continued. Those representing Pennsylvania countered that they would consent to this, provided that Virginia would be willing to see the western bounds of Pennsylvania extended so as to compensate for the loss of territory. However, the final terms agreed upon were that the Mason and Dixon line should be extended five degrees of longitude westward from the Delaware and that a meridian at that point should be regarded as the western limits of Pennsylvania. Because of the war, the work of the survey was not taken up until June 1784; it was completed in September of the following year.[50]

Pennsylvania and the Susquehannah Company of Connecticut

At the very time that a settlement was being reached on the claims of the Penn family to a southern boundary that would safeguard Philadelphia, another serious threat to Pennsylvania territory arose. This was the organization in the colony of Connecticut of the Susquehannah Land Company—a company designed to occupy and settle the Wyoming Valley on the upper waters of the Susquehanna River.[51] Like the dispute between the Penns and the Balti-

[50] See E. B. Mathews: *op. cit.*, pp. 190–5, and especially J. E. Potter: "The Pennsylvania and Virginia Boundary Controversy," *Pennsylvania Magazine of History and Biography*, XXXVIII, 407–26.

[51] The greatest collection of sources having to do with the Susquehannah Company are in *The Susquehannah Company Papers*. Edited with care by Julian P. Boyd and

mores, the controversy which resulted involved charter rights; but unlike the other rivalry—which was largely restricted to the arguments of the respective Proprietors—this new threat saw the people of the two colonies arrayed against each other. Furthermore, the Pennsylvania-Connecticut conflict was important in the constitutional development of each of the colonies involved. Therefore it seems necessary to treat it in somewhat greater detail than the other intercolonial conflicts and to carry the account forward to the final outcome.

In the royal patent granted to the Governor and Company of the Colony of Connecticut in 1662 by Charles II the following terms were used to indicate the limits of the colony's bounds:

> "That Wee . . . Doe give, Graunt and Confirme unto the said Governor and Company and their Successors, All that parte of our Dominions in Newe England in America bounded on the East by Norrogancett River, commonly called Norrogancett Bay, where the said River falleth into the Sea, and on the North by the lyne of the Massachusetts Plantation, and on the South by the Sea, and in longitude as the lyne of the Massachusetts Colony, runinge from East to West, (that is to say) from the said Narrogancett Bay on the East to the South Sea on the West parte, with the Islands thereunto adioyneinge. . . ."[52]

What did this mean? Did it imply, as one writer stated in 1774, that the charter entitled the colony to claim "a very fine Tract of Land, comprehending the present inhabited Part of Connecticut, a great Part of the Province of New York, the whole of the Province of East

covering the period from 1750 to 1772, these documents originally appeared between 1930 and 1933 in four volumes under the imprint of the Wyoming Historical and Geological Society, and were reissued in 1963 by Cornell University Press, which has scheduled two more for future publication. Dr. Boyd has provided each published volume with an illuminating introduction. Materials for additional volumes have been collected by the Wyoming Historical and Geological Society, Wilkes-Barre, Pa., but must await the finding of an editor and funds before seeing the light of publication. For a brief summary of the Company's story beyond 1772 (the closing date of Vol. IV of the *Papers*) see J. H. Boyd: *Susquehannah Company: Connecticut's Experiment in Expansion* (Connecticut Tercentenary Commission *Publication*, XXXIV, New Haven, 1933), pp. 32–48. In this connection, see also Edith A. Bailey: *Influences toward Radicalism in Connecticut 1754–1775* (Smith College *Studies in History*, V, No. 4), Oscar Zeichner: *Connecticut's Years of Controversy 1750–1776* (Williamsburg 1949), Chap. 8, "The Susquehannah Issue and the Election of 1774," and *passim*, and H. B. Plumb: *History of Hanover Township . . . and . . . Wyoming Valley* (Wilkes-Barre, 1885).

[52] For a copy of the Connecticut charter see the *Public Records of the Colony of Connecticut, from 1636 to 1776* (eds. J. H. Trumbull and C. J. Hoadly, 15 vols., Hartford, 1850–90), II, 3–11, subsequently referred to as *Connecticut Colonial Records.*

and West Jersies; the greater part of the Province of Pennsylvania"?[53] In 1683, when giving the Governor's instructions to Major Robert Trent—who was to go to New York and treat with Governor Thomas Dongan over the boundary between New York and Connecticut—the General Court pointed out that Trent should not exceed Dongan's "demands of twenty miles eastward from Hudson's River, but get him to take up with as little [land] as may be."[54] In other words, far from setting forth such a vast claim, the General Court felt that the Governor in negotiating with Dongan should hold a western boundary of twenty miles east of the Hudson River, if he could not do any better. Trent succeeded in securing an agreement on precisely this boundary. The following year part of the line was surveyed.

In the course of time, however, a new factor entered into the boundary problem with the establishment of Connecticut settlements along Long Island Sound extending within ten miles of the river. As a result, in 1724 the Connecticut Assembly authorized a commission to negotiate a readjusted boundary; the following year New York created a similar commission. Later in 1725 the two entered into an agreement, which was approved by New York that same year and by the Connecticut Assembly in 1730. By it, Connecticut was permitted to retain possession of the lands its people had occupied on the Sound, but in return for this concession the colony agreed to surrender to New York some 62,000 acres north of the Sound, which now placed its boundary twenty-two miles east of the Hudson. A partial survey made in 1726 became a completed one in 1731. The Connecticut cession of land was known as "the oblong" and is so shown on early maps of New York.[55]

In reply to queries sent to the Connecticut government by the Board of Trade in 1729, one of which had to do with the "reputed boundaries" of the colony, a committee of the Assembly replied in 1730 as follows:

> "The reputed and known boundaries are: the Massachusetts on the north, Rhode Island Colony on the east, Long Island Sound on the south, and New York Province on the west. No points thereof are

[53] See the article signed B. Schemer in the *Connecticut Gazette,* April 13, 1774; see also my *Jared Ingersoll,* Chap. 11.

[54] *Connecticut Colonial Records,* III, 135.

[55] For the agreement of November 23, 1683, and the subsequent adjustment of the boundary in conformity with the agreement of 1725, see *New York Colonial Documents,* IV, 628–30; V, 953; VII, 564 (this title is cited in full in the preceding chapter); see also *Connecticut Colonial Records,* VII, 45, 294–6.

disputed, but all settled and ascertained, excepting some part of the dividing line betwixt, this Colony and New York. . . ."[56]

In a 1749 answer to similar queries, a committee of the Assembly stated the boundaries of the colony as follows:

"The Colony is bounded southerly on the sea or sound, easterly on Rhode Island, westerly on New York, north on the line of the Massachusetts Colony."[57]

Similar replies were again sent to the Board of Trade in 1756 and 1762,[58] but in 1774, the following answer was given:

"The Boundaries are expressed in our Charter,—viz. 'All that Part of His Majesty's Dominion in *New-England,* in *America,* bounden on the East by *Narraganset*-River . . . where the River falleth into the Sea; and on the North by the Line of the *Massachusetts*-Plantation; and on the South by the Sea; and in Longitide as the Line of the *Massachusetts* Colony, running from East to West, that is to say, from the said *Narraganset*-Bay on the East, to the South-Sea on the West Part, with the Islands thereunto adjoining.'

"A Number of the Inhabitants of this Colony, called the *Susquehannah,* and *Delaware* Companies, in the Year 1754, for great and valuable Considerations, in Money, paid and satisfied to the Indians of the Six Nations, purchased of them, as early as they, the Aboriginal Proprietors, were willing to grant and convey their Title to a large Tract of Land, within the Bounds and Limits of this Colony lying West of the River *Delaware,* and from thence spreading over the East and West branches of the *Susquehannah* River. Since such Purchases a great Number of our Inhabitants have made Settlements thereon."[59]

To reiterate: By the terms of his royal letters patent William Penn received in 1680/1 a tract of land running five degrees of longitude westward from the Delaware River and extending from a point twelve miles north of the town of New Castle, in the Three Lower Counties, northward to the 43rd parallel of northern latitude. At the time there was no indication that the government of Connecticut considered the lands in the Penn grant a part of its own domain. On the contrary, the Connecticut replies to the Board of

[56] *Ibid.,* VII, 582. There follows a statement that New York had unjustly refused to finish the line, which was struck out, presumably upon the basis of the new agreement reached in 1730, whereby the line was completed the following year.

[57] *Ibid.,* IX, 595.

[58] *Ibid.,* X, 622; XI, 628–9.

[59] *Ibid.,* XIV, 495–6.

Trade from 1730 up to 1774 only served to bolster the opinion that Connecticut's western extent was determined by New York's eastern boundary. The circumstances that led to the fundamental alteration in point of view found in the 1774 statement to the Board of Trade must therefore be given careful consideration.

One of the most striking characteristics of the British colonization of North America in both the seventeenth and the eighteenth century was the constant drive of settlers to search out new lands, to open up new frontiers, to expand ever westward from the Atlantic seaboard into the wilderness. Among the colonies in general, Connecticut was one of the most fruitful in population increase. Between 1732 and 1756 the number of its inhabitants doubled. By the latter year there were more than 127,000 whites and Negroes living within the narrow recognized bounds of the colony.[60] As a result, many of the sons of landholders were looking for lands that could be settled according to the traditional seventeenth-century pattern. But after 1737 there were no more ungranted lands available within the colony for those groups desiring to establish new communities. For in that year the remaining unappropriated lands lying in the northwestern corner of the colony had been disposed of by the establishment of seven townships in which the ownership of property was vested in the settlers.[61] It is not surprising therefore that, when the land hunger of the people could not be satisfied within the colony, they began searching elsewhere for homesites. This also helps to explain why Connecticut men were some of the most active and aggressive leaders among the New Hampshire grantees who resisted the claims of New York to the great disputed area that lay almost vacant in the 1740's—that is, the area to the west of the Connecticut River and to the north of the Massachusetts Bay line, stretching westward almost to the Hudson River and Lake Champlain. It also helps to explain why in the 1750's Connecticut people cast their eyes in the direction of another unsettled area west and south of New York and within the limits of Pennsylvania. They and their families could have gone peacefully into the Wyoming Valley—had they come to terms with the Pennsylvania Proprietors and had the latter reached a settlement with the Indians for the lands—but they

[60] *Ibid.*, X, 617–8, 623.

[61] *Ibid.*, VIII, 134–7; see also William Douglass: *A Summary, Historical and Political . . . and the Present State of the British Settlements in North-America* (2 vols., Boston, 1749–51), I, 244*n*, and Dorothy Denning: *The Settlement of Litchfield County* (New Haven, 1933) and *Settlement of Connecticut Towns* (New Haven, 1933).

had no interest in such a procedure. What was wanted were lands that could be secured and retained as freeholds without the payment of annual quit-rents to the Pennsylvania Proprietors. The only way open for the Connecticut men to attain their objective in the Wyoming Valley was to bring about a partial nullification of the Pennsylvania charter by reviving the Connecticut sea-to-sea charter claim, which had remained dormant for over ninety years, at least in so far as it extended to lands beyond New York.

In May 1750 a petition was presented to the Connecticut Assembly from a group living in Simsbury Township, located in north-central Connecticut. The petitioners, ten in number, pointed out that there was "a Large Tract of Land Lying within the bounds of this Colony as described in the Royal Charter Lying west of Hudsons River which is not Included in any of the Charters to any of the neighbouring Governments. . . ." They therefore requested a grant of a township of ten miles square in this region to be located "where we shall think proter [proper] to procure the same," upon which to settle sixty families. The petition was rejected by both houses.[62] In May of the following year a Norwalk attorney and land speculator, James Brown, presented a memorial, to the General Assembly indicating that a group of New Yorkers, who were involved in the land dispute with the Proprietors of East New Jersey, were ready to pay the Connecticut government a reasonable sum of money to secure a grant to the lands in question. The report of the committee appointed to consider the memorial disclosed that

> ". . . altho by ye Royal Charter ye Lands granted to this Colony do extend West to ye Sea Yet by ye Agreement between ye Commissioners of this Colony of those of ye Province of New York . . . ye Western Extent of this Colony is now fixed at about 20 miles East of Hudson's River. Therefore are of Opinion yt there is not ye Least Probability of this Colonys ever recovering ye Possession of any Lands Westward of sd Line setled and fixed as aforesd. Yet possably what claim we may be considered to have may be of some advantage to ye Tenants in Possession and upon Conferring with ye sd Mr. Brown find he is willing to pay into ye Treasury of this Colony; seven hundred and Sixty Spanish Dollars upon Condition that this Assembly will make and Execute to him a deed of Release under ye Seal of this Colony of all the Right this colony now hath to all ye Lands within ye following abutments viz bounded East on Hudsons River North on ye Massachusetts Line West on ye Extent of

[62] Although this petition is not mentioned in the printed *Connecticut Colonial Records,* it is found in Vol. 8 of "Towns and Lands" (mss.), Connecticut State Library, and is printed in *Susquehannah Company Papers* (Boyd), I, 1–2.

five degrees of Longitude west of Delaware River & and we are of Opinion y[t] it is adviseable for this Assembly to make s[d] Deed. . . ."[63]

The upper house of the General Assembly agreed to this offer, provided that the grant should extend only so far west as the west branch of the Delaware River; the Assembly, however, applied its negative.[64]

But this was not an end to the applications for western lands. In October 1751 the Simsbury promoters produced another memorial, signed by some sixty people, which referred to the sea-to-sea grant and asserted that there was "a vast Tract of Land West of the Province of New-York and North of the Western Governments of Jersys etc: not Included in any of the pattents to the Said Governments nor to any particular persons the Settlement & purchasing of which Lands of the native owners of Right belongs to this Colony. . . ." It went on to state that since the lands in Connecticut were almost all settled, the memorialists desired the grant of a township within this western area on the same general terms embodied in their request of 1750.[65] Apparently no action was taken on this application. However, a memorial signed by 424 people living in various parts of Connecticut, which was presented at the May 1752 session of the Assembly, was given more serious consideration and then referred to the session to be held in May 1753. It sought a grant of at least four townships "Lying at or Near y[e] place Called Delaware River" with liberty to purchase the same from the natives.[66] This was followed in 1753 by six more memorials concerning grants of western lands, all of which were referred to the October session for consideration.[67] Among them was one from Windham and four other towns signed by about 150 people. This requested a grant of land sixteen miles square lying on both sides of "a River Calld Suscohannah . . . at a Place Calld Quiwomock (Wyoming)."[68] It was the signers of this memorial who formed the nucleus of the so-called Susquehannah Company. On July 18, 1753, these subscribers met at Windham and drew up articles of agreement. According to the document, each subscriber was to pay two Spanish-milled dollars to meet the expenses of a committee authorized to purchase from the Indians land not less than twenty miles

[63] *Ibid.*, I, 4–5.
[64] *Ibid.*, I, 5–6.
[65] *Ibid.*, I, 6–9.
[66] *Ibid.*, I, 9–15.
[67] *Ibid.*, I, 16–28.
[68] *Ibid.*, I, 16–18.

in extent and ten in breadth, lying about an island called Chiwaumuck in the Susquehanna River; for the purchase the committee was authorized to pay not more than £1,000 lawful money.[69]

The Susquehannah Company now became active in seeking to attain its objective. According to the Pennsylvania provincial secretary, Richard Peters, the Company committee, when visiting the Wyoming Valley after the meeting in July, "made great disturbance among the People of Northampton County, alledging that the Connecticut Grant was prior to the Pennsylvania Grant and . . . those Lands are within the Latitude of their Province, & that they will come in the Spring with a Thousand Men and settle those lands."[70] In addition, they increased the number of subscribers to 500 and absorbed a potential rival, the Colchester Company, which had also been organized in eastern Connecticut.[71] Early in 1754 Governor Roger Wolcott gave the enterprise his blessing. The project now embraced not merely the idea of settling a township but the creation of "a New plantation or plantation[s]," that is, a new colony or new colonies."[72] Even before this the Company had attracted the support of such leading people of eastern Connecticut as Eliphalet Dyer,[73] who served as moderator at its meeting on January 9, 1754. Other provincial members were Colonel Elisha Williams, Roger Wolcott, Jr., son of the Governor, and Lieutenant Governor William Pitkin. They were the men sent as commissioners to the Albany Congress that was called in 1754 to treat with the Indians.[74] Working through the Rev. Timothy Woodbridge, a missionary to the Indians and now, by gift of a share, a member of the Company, and John Henry Lydius, the Indian trader, a purchase of some 5,000,000 acres of land was negotiated very secretly with the

[69] "Minutes of a Meeting of the Susquehannah Company," *ibid.*, I, 28–39; see also, for the minutes of this meeting, *Documents Relating to the Connecticut Settlement in the Wyoming Valley, Pennsylvania Archives,* 2nd ser., XVIII, 3–12. While the Susquehanna River is spelled with an "h" in the Boyd edition of the Susquehannah Company Papers, which is taken from the "Minute Book" of the Company at the Connecticut Historical Society, Hartford, W. H. Egle, editor of the *Documents* just cited, spells it without the "h," which seems to indicate that he either used a different copy of the minutes than the one used by Boyd or modernized the spelling.

[70] Peters to the Pennsylvania Proprietors, November 27, 1753, Penn Manuscripts, Official Correspondence, 6:141. Northampton County was created in 1752 and included all land to the north of Bucks County in northeastern Pennsylvania; today six counties, in addition to Northampton, are to be found in this area.

[71] *Pennsylvania Archives,* 2nd ser., XVIII, 12–22.

[72] *Wolcott Papers,* Connecticut Historical Society *Collections,* XVI, 428–9.

[73] See G. C. Groce, Jr.: "Eliphalet Dyer: Connecticut Revolutionist," *The Era of the American Revolution* . . . (ed. R. B. Morris, New York, 1939), pp. 290–304.

[74] *Connecticut Colonial Records,* X, 268.

Six Nations on July 11, after the formal closing of the Congress.[75] This land is described in the deed as lying between 41° and 43° north latitude "within the Limits and bounds of The Charter and Grant . . . To the Colony of Connecticut." As a consideration, £2,000 York money was paid to the Indians.[76] But previously, at an open conference on July 6, much of this land had already been deeded by the same Indians to the Pennsylvania Proprietors.[77]

With the purchase of the Wyoming lands completed, the next important step took place at a meeting of the Company on November 20, 1754, when a committee was empowered "to Prepare the Case of the Susquehannah Purchase Lately made of the Indians . . . in Order to Lay the Same before His Majestie for his Grant and Confirmation . . . and for the Incorporating the S[d] Company & forming a Government. . . ."[78] Thus, according to the plan, another colony, to be created by royal authority under the Great Seal, would arise in the Wyoming Valley portion of the lands granted to William Penn.

When the news reached the senior Pennsylvania Proprietor, Thomas Penn, that Connecticut men had come into the province with designs for appropriating part of the land there, he wrote from London to Secretary Richard Peters on February 1, 1754: "I am sorry to hear the People of Connecticut should have made such an attempt on our property, I do not fear the Success they will meet with here, but they may give us some uneasiness by instilling doubts into the People of our right to the Country. . . ." He also recommended to Governor James Hamilton that he not only write to Governor Wolcott of Connecticut about the matter but also issue a proclamation against the activities of the intruders.[79] When carrying out this assignment on March 4, 1754, Hamilton wrote to Wolcott that inhabitants of Connecticut coming into Pennsylvania had declared that "they had your Authority to come and settle them

[75] The report to Lieutenant Governor James Hamilton from John Penn and Richard Peters, two of the Pennsylvania commissioners to the Albany Congress, characterized the land purchase proceedings of the Connecticut people as "this dark Affair." See *Pennsylvania Colonial Records,* VI, 111–12 and 128–9.

[76] For the deed executed by the Indians in favour of the Company see the *Susquehannah Company Papers,* I, 101–21.

[77] By the payment to the Six Nations of £400 York money all the land lying southward of 41° 31′ north latitude and between the west bank of the Susquehanna River and the western boundary of the province was released to the Pennsylvania Proprietors. For the negotiations of the Pennsylvania commissioners with the Indians and the deed of cession see *Pennsylvania Colonial Records,* VI, 118–28.

[78] See *Susquehannah Company Papers,* I, 167.

[79] Penn Letter Books, 3:301–2, Historical Society of Pennsylvania.

[the lands], being included within the Boundaries of the Connecticut Charter." He further stated that these people were depending on an Indian title to the lands without paying any regard to "the Rights of our Proprietaries" and without applying to "this Government for their Leave and Authority." In addition, he warned Wolcott that if the enterprise were carried out, it would not fail "to exasperate the Indians, raise a Civil War in the Province and distract the Government" seeking "to preserve the Colonies from falling a Prey to our Enemies."[80] In his reply, the Connecticut Governor was less than frank. He wrote that inhabitants of Connecticut interested in the lands on the Susquehanna thought these lands lay "North of the Grant made to Mr. Pen" and therefore planned to purchase them from the Indians and then apply to the Crown for a grant, ostensibly in order "to promote His Majesties interest and render the Countrey more Defencible." Wolcott then explained that after being informed by Mr. John Armstrong (who had carried Hamilton's letter to the Connecticut Governor) that the land in question was entirely within the grant made to Penn, he did not suppose "our people had any purpose to quarrell with Pensilvania[.] Indeed I . . . never heard our leading men express themselves so inclined[.]"[81]

But the facts were entirely different from the information given by Wolcott. By the fall of 1754 the agents of the Susquehannah Company operating in the Wyoming Valley were having great success—according to Daniel Brodhead, a justice of the peace in Northampton County—in "seducing" Pennsylvanians settled to the south of this area to join the Company. Some thirty of them, Brodhead reported, had done so, including a constable who, when called upon to arrest and imprison one of the leaders of the Pennsylvanians involved in the plan, went off to Hartford to attend a Company meeting.[82] By the spring of 1755 the members of the Company, counting those living in Massachusetts and Rhode Island as well as the men from Connecticut and Pennsylvania, numbered 850. On May 7, in a memorial to the Connecticut Assembly, the Company asked for support of its plan to seek royal approval of their purchase from the Indians of Susquehanna River lands extending some sixty or seventy miles from north to south and including all lands from a point ten miles east of the river to two degrees westward, in

---

[80] *Susquehannah Company Papers,* I, 55–8.

[81] Wolcott to Hamilton, March 13, 1754, Connecticut Historical Society *Collections,* XVI, 435–7.

[82] Daniel Brodhead to Richard Peters, November 13, 1754, *Pennsylvania Colonial Records,* VI, 253–4.

order "to erect and settle a colony . . ." This approval, given forthwith, made no reference to any rights of the Pennsylvania Proprietors.[83]

With the Great War for the Empire now raging in North America and with the activities of the Indians in the service of the French increasing along the Pennsylvania frontiers,[84] the time was not ripe for planting new settlements in an area as exposed to enemy incursions as the Wyoming Valley. Nevertheless, the May 1755 meeting of the Susquehannah Company voted to lay out a township in the proposed "new Colony," to admit settlers within it, and also to erect "a Sufficient fortification," together with a grist mill and sawmill.[85] In June of that year two men, one of them a surveyor, were sent to the Wyoming Valley to observe conditions and locate sites; they found its latitude to be 41° 16′.[86] But that was the full extent of the Company's efforts during the war years—years in which the government of Pennsylvania had assumed full responsibility for protecting its frontier settlements and had erected a chain of blockhouses. However, with the collapse of French resistance in Canada and the gradual withdrawal of hostile Indians from the area after 1760, the way seemed open once again for Connecticut men to carry out their colonization enterprises within the borders of Pennsylvania.

The first new move was made by the so-called Delaware Company, which in November 1755 had purchased from the Delaware Indians a large body of land stretching from the Delaware River westward to a point "at or near the East bounds of the Lands on Susquehannah River Lately Purchased by New England Planters and Inhabitants."[87] In 1760 the Company made a settlement on the west bank of the Delaware at a place called Cushietunk (Cushitunk, Cashietan) in the northeastern part of Northhampton County.[88] A party of Pennsylvania officials, consisting of the sheriff of Northampton County and three justices of the peace, visited the place in the fall of the year. They found that mills and cabins had been

---

[83] For the above petition, and the Assembly's approval of it, see *Connecticut Colonial Records*, X, 378.

[84] For the ravishing of the Pennsylvania frontier see Volume VI of this series, pp. 127, 132, 189.

[85] Minutes of the May 1755 meeting of the Susquehannah Company, *Susquehannah Company Papers*, I, 283–4.

[86] *Ibid.*, I, 284–5.

[87] For the Indian land deed to the Delaware Company signed in Ulster County, New York, on November 11, 1755, see *ibid.*, I, 308–14.

[88] See Richard Peters to Lewis Gordon, September 15, 1760, *Pennsylvania Archives*, 1st ser., III, 754.

constructed or were being built by some twenty settlers; they also were informed that the Company, consisting of between 800 and 900 proprietors, was planning to send out 100 more people in the spring of 1761 and that the excursion into Pennsylvania had the support of all members of the upper house and of a majority of those composing the lower house of the Connecticut Assembly.[89] Although this report was rendered to the Governor in October 1760, it was not until late in February of the following year and after hearing from the Pennsylvania Proprietors in England, that Hamilton saw fit to issue a proclamation in which he voiced the anger of those Delaware Indians not involved in the secret sale of these Delaware Valley lands and the determination of the Pennsylvania Proprietors to prevent intrusion on their property by outsiders endeavouring to take illegal possession.[90] He also wrote to Thomas Fitch, now Governor of Connecticut, reminding him that both he (while Lieutenant Governor of Connecticut) and Governor Wolcott—in the exchange of letters on the subject in 1754—had given assurances to the Governor of Pennsylvania that the Connecticut government "knew nothing of it," and would use their endeavours to prevent any further progress of what was "justly termed so wild a Scheme." He therefore requested Fitch to use his influence with the promoters of the settlement to get them to remove themselves and their families before running the risk of being "cut off" by the enraged Indians.[91]

The Connecticut Governor's reply recited the steps taken by the Susquehannah Company in 1755 to gain the approval of the Assembly for its plan to erect a colony within the bounds of the Connecticut charter grant, and stressed the point that this assent was premised upon subsequent royal endorsement of the project. He added: ". . . whether the Assembly at that time had any apprehension those Lands were in the Limits of the Charter of Pennsylvania or not, I am not able to say. . . ." With respect to the Delaware Company, he stated that he knew little about it; however, he assured Hamilton that he would use what influences he had to prevent ill consequences, while pointing out that the chief responsibility for maintaining quiet in the area lay with the government of Pennsylvania.[92]

---

[89] Report of the sheriff and justices of the peace of Northampton County to Governor Hamilton, October 15, 1760, *Pennsylvania Colonial Records,* VIII, 564–6.

[90] For the proclamation of February 20, 1761, see *ibid.,* VIII, 566–7.

[91] Hamilton to Fitch, February 10, 1761, *ibid.,* VIII, 568–70. For Fitch's letter to Governor Hamilton, March 13, 1754, see *Pennsylvania Archives,* 1st ser., II, 125–6.

[92] Fitch to Hamilton, May 7, 1761, *Pennsylvania Colonial Records,* VIII, 626–7, and *Fitch Papers* (2 vols., Connecticut Historical Society *Collections,* XVII, XVIII), II, 124–6.

As for the Pennsylvania Proprietors, by the end of 1760 they had become so thoroughly alarmed at these developments that they drew up a statement of their territorial claims as against the pretensions of Connecticut to any portion of the same territory.[93] Although the Privy Council did not choose to hear the issue, it referred the ably penned case—largely the work of Henry Wilmot, Thomas Penn's attorney—to Attorney General Charles Pratt (soon to become Lord Camden) and Solicitor General Charles Yorke.[94] Pratt was very clear that the agreement between New York and Connecticut as to the western limits of the latter colony "conclusively precluded Connecticut from advancing one foot beyond these Limits."[95] Yorke, equally emphatic "that the People of Connecticut have no Colour of Right to Claim the Tract of Land in Question," used much the same line of reasoning.[96]

Meanwhile, both the Susquehannah and the Delaware Company continued to be active, apparently working in unison.[97] On April 9, 1761, the Susquehannah Company voted to send Eliphalet Dyer to London as a joint agent to memorialize the Crown that the lands purchased by the two companies might be consolidated for political purposes "into one Civil Government."[98] However, circumstances delayed Dyer's departure. Among other things, there was need to conciliate the Indians living in the area, who (under Teedyuscung, so-called King of the Delawares) were bitterly opposed to the Connecticut enterprise, as were many of the Iroquoian Six Nations.[99] In fact, by the spring of 1762 so dangerous to the peace of the colonies had the Susquehannah enterprise become that Governor Fitch of Connecticut deemed it wise to issue a proclamation warning all the inhabitants of the colony "to forbear making Entrance on the said Lands, lest they thereby occasion new Disturbances . . . and Subject themselves to the Royal Displeasure. . . ."[100]

The next step taken by the Susquehannah Company was to seek the cooperation of the Superintendent of the Northern Indians, Sir

---

[93] J. P. Boyd: "Introduction," *Susquehannah Company Papers,* II, xix.

[94] For the case of the Pennsylvania Proprietors see *ibid.,* II, 44–53.

[95] For Pratt's opinion see *Pennsylvania Colonial Records,* VIII, 620–1.

[96] For Yorke's opinion see *Susquehannah Company Papers,* II, 67–9.

[97] A meeting of each of the companies was called in February 1761, to meet at the same time and at the same place in Windham. See *ibid.,* II, 53, 72.

[98] For the Company minutes of April 9, 1761, see *ibid.,* II, 72–6; for the Delaware Company meeting on May 24, 1763, in which it is made clear that this group had decided to act in conjunction with the Susquehannah Company and the "Second Delaware Company," see *ibid.,* II, 233–4.

[99] See A. F. C. Wallace: *King of the Delawares, Teedyuscung, 1700–1763* (Philadelphia, 1949), pp. 237, 255–8.

[100] For this proclamation, which is not included in the *Fitch Papers,* see the *Sir William Johnson Papers,* III, 756–7.

William Johnson, to avoid a conflict with the Indians. Dyer, one of a committee of two appointed for that purpose, visited him at Johnson Hall later in 1762. But their efforts to secure Sir William's approval either of their pretensions to the land or of their plan of settlement were in vain. Writing later to Sir Jeffrey Amherst concerning the meeting, Johnson said that he made so clear to the gentlemen "not only the illegality of the purchase, but the ill consequences attending that Settlement . . . as entirely convinced them of its impropriety."[101] The Superintendent to the Indians, however, was mistaken. At the very time this meeting was being held, members of the Company, ignoring the anger of the Indians, began to cut a road through to the Wyoming Valley. According to the report brought back to Philadelphia by Governor Hamilton's agent—sent to check on any intrusive actions of the Connecticut people in the region—over 70 armed men, in an encampment, were occupied in building three blockhouses. On being questioned about the Connecticut Governor's proclamation, the report continued, these men had asserted that they could prove it "false and absurd," especially as Fitch and his two sons "were privy to their Undertaking, and were concerned with them"; they added that 1,000 more men would come into the Valley the following spring.[102] Nevertheless, it would appear that by November of 1762 all the Susquehannah men who had been in the Wyoming Valley had "thought it prudent to withdraw for a Season."[103] In that month it was decided that it would be well to be strongly represented at the Indian Congress Johnson was to hold in March 1763, so as to be in a position to satisfy those Indians who were opposed to the settlement of the lands purchased in 1754.[104] Provided with some £400 in money and a supply of presents, Dyer and the Rev. Timothy Woodbridge arrived at Johnson's home while he was in conference with the Mohawks. Again Dyer sought to win over Johnson, this time by offering to make him "a Partner in ye Land." But the Superintendent of the Indians refused the offer with the "slight it deserved" and reiterated his opinion of the unhappy consequences that would ensue should the Company "force a Settlement in them parts."[105] The Susquehannah representatives then asserted, according to Johnson, that the Company had

[101] Johnson to Amherst, September 24, 1762, *ibid.*, III, 884–6.

[102] For Daniel Brodhead's report to Governor Hamilton, submitted on September 29, 1762, see the *Susquehannah Company Papers,* II, 166–70.

[103] Minutes of the Susquehannah Company, November 16, 1762, *ibid.*, II, 177–80.

[104] *Ibid.*

[105] Memorandum of March 23, 1763, *Sir William Johnson Papers,* IV, 65–6.

been concerned for a long while with the enterprise, had expended much money on it, and was therefore determined to settle 1,000 families on the land—a sufficient force to defend their claims against any opposition.[106]

That the Susquehannah Company continued to grow in number of proprietors[107] and in the Connecticut public esteem is indicated by the fact that its shares, which at the time of its organization in 1753 had been placed at two Spanish pieces of eight (that is, twelve shillings proclamation money), had risen in value to £8 before the meeting held at Windham in April 1763, when these shares were now advanced to £15.[108] At this gathering—despite the previous disapproval of Johnson and the Indians—it was voted to lay out eight five-mile-square townships along the river in the Wyoming Valley and to send between 200 and 300 people into these townships the following month. An additional vote directed that the committee appointed to prepare the memorial of the Susquehannah Company complete it immediately and put the papers in the hands of Eliphalet Dyer, who should proceed to London without delay in order to lay the case before the King.[109]

But Dyer was to be delayed again, this time by events that had been happening concurrently in the mother country. The Earl of Egremont, who had succeeded William Pitt as Secretary of State for the Southern Department, wrote to Governor Fitch at the com-

---

[106] Johnson to Sir Jeffrey Amherst, March 30, 1763, *ibid.*, IV, 70–2.

[107] By 1763 the number of proprietors of shares in the Susquehannah and Delaware companies had risen to 2,000. See Eliphalet Dyer's petition to the King in Council, *Susquehannah Company Papers*, II, 293–6. The two companies were acting as one in 1763. See Dyer to the Susquehannah and Delaware Companies, May 25, 1764, *ibid.*, II, 291–3.

[108] The question may be asked whether the advance of the price of Company shares was influenced at all by knowledge of the existence of coal beds in the Wyoming Valley. In the minutes of the Company, covering the Windham meeting in April 1763, reference was made, in connection with plans for laying out townships there, that there should be a reservation of "all Beds of mine, iron ore and Cole That may be within The Town ordered for Settlement" (*ibid.*, II, 204). The more probable cause for the rise in the value of shares was a heightened expectation of profits from the enterprise, accompanied by a need of funds for carrying it forward to a successful conclusion.

[109] Minutes of April 7, 1763, *ibid.*, II, 204–9. As is well known, Benjamin Franklin was by this time bitterly opposed to the Pennsylvania Proprietors. It appears that Dyer before leaving for London talked with him and won his approval of the Connecticut settlement. Yet when Joseph Chew of New London, by now a leading opponent of the Susquehannah Company, sought out Franklin, the latter referred to the Connecticut claims as "Idle and Ridiculous" in that "no Person could pretend to think it consistent wth. common sense to have a Governm^{t} 60 miles wide & 3000 miles long . . ." (Joseph Chew to Jared Ingersoll, August 10, 1763, "Jared Ingersoll Papers," New Haven Colony Historical Society *Papers*, IX, 286–7).

mand of the King early in 1763, to express His Majesty's surprise and displeasure that, upon the basis of "pretended Purchases" from the Indians, certain inhabitants of Connecticut were attempting to settle lands on the Delaware and Susquehanna rivers, which would in all probability bring on "all the Horrors and Calamities of an Indian War." Egremont therefore notified Fitch that the King desired the Governor to use all legal authority to prevent the prosecution of plans for any such settlement until the state of the case could be laid before His Majesty.[110] Furthermore, when the matter came before the Lords of the Committee of the Privy Council, they decided to seek the recommendations of the Board of Trade. In due time the Board suggested that, to put a stop to the Connecticut settlement, the method be used that had been employed in 1758 against the lawless people who had attempted to settle south of the Altamaha River in Georgia.[111] At that time the governments of Georgia and South Carolina, at the request of the Privy Council, had cooperated fully in stopping the illegal enterprise. In line with the Board's representation citing this precedent, the governments of Pennsylvania and Connecticut were similarly called upon to work the matter out together by an order in council issued on May 11, 1763.[112]

When Egremont's letter of January 27, 1763, to Governor Fitch arrived, the Company, meeting on May 18, decided that none of its members should make any further settlement on any of the disputed lands until the case had been laid before the King and his further pleasure made known.[113] What is more, a delegation of Indians had come to Hartford in May to protest the appropriation of their lands on the upper Susquehanna River and had been given assurances by Governor Fitch that the government of Connecticut had had no part in it.[114] Following this, his government agreed to cooperate with that of Pennsylvania in accordance with the recommendations of the Privy Council and each appointed a commissioner to supervise the removal of all white settlers from the Wyoming

[110] Egremont to Fitch, January 27, 1763, *Fitch Papers,* II, 224–5; see also *Acts of the Privy Council, Col. Ser., 1745–1766,* pp. 555–6.

[111] Board of Trade *Journal, 1759–1763,* p. 350. For the attempt of Edmund Gray and others to settle on lands to the south of the Altamaha see Volume IV of this series, pp. 45–7.

[112] For a copy of the order see *Fitch Papers,* II, 237–8.

[113] Minutes of May 18, 1763, *Susquehannah Company Papers,* II, 219; for the Delaware Company's similar decision to withdraw settlers, reached at a meeting on May 24 at Norwich, see *ibid.,* II, 233–40.

[114] For the Hartford Indian conference of May 28 and 30, 1763, see *ibid.,* II 236–241, 266; see also *Sir William Johnson Papers,* IV, 123–9.

Valley,[115] a step highly necessary in the face of the great uprising of the northern Indians which had begun in May of that year. Unhappily, before the commissioners could act, the Indians fell upon the settlement, killing or capturing most of the settlers.[116] Dyer, who had meanwhile been dispatched to London to further the case of the Susquehannah Company, did not find any prospects there for favourable action by the British Ministry.[117] His petition,[118] which did not come before the King in Council until July 1764, brought no results. Referred by the Council to the Board of Trade, it was there quietly pigeon-holed.[119] Doubtless realizing the futility of remaining in London, Dyer returned to Connecticut in the fall of 1764. He reported the failure of his mission to a meeting of the Susquehannah Company held early in 1765.[120]

The Company, feeling that it was still bound by the order in council not to take any steps until the claims had been considered by the Privy Council, remained relatively inactive. Nevertheless, it seemed necessary to John Penn, who was now Lieutenant Governor of Pennsylvania, to issue a proclamation in 1766 directed against "many ill-disposed Persons" who, in express disobedience to royal instructions and the rights of Pennsylvania Proprietors, had seated themselves on lands within the province not yet purchased from the Indians; these intruders were commanded by Penn to remove from the lands or remain at their peril.[121] Further, to prevent any new incursions of the Connecticut people in the area of the upper waters of the Susquehanna River, Thomas Penn, the chief Proprietor, had

---

[115] See Fitch to the Board of Trade, September 14, 1763, *Fitch Papers,* II, 251–2; see also Colonel James Burd, the Pennsylvania commissioner, to Governor Hamilton, October 27, 1763, *Pennsylvania Archives,* 1st ser., IV, 128–9. The person selected as the Connecticut commissioner was Major David Baldwin; see *Susquehannah Company Papers,* II, 280, 302–3.

[116] Fitch to the Board of Trade, November 10, 1763, *Fitch Papers,* II, 258–9; James Burd to Governor Hamilton, November 4, 1763, *Pennsylvania Archives,* 1st ser., IV, 130–1.

[117] Dyer to the committee of the Susquehannah Company, October 18, 1763, *Sir William Johnson Papers,* IV, 217–19.

[118] For Dyer's petition of July 11, 1764, see *Susquehannah Company Papers,* II, 293–6.

[119] *Acts of the Privy Council, Col. Ser., 1745–1766,* pp. 680–1.

[120] Minutes of the Susquehannah Company, January 16, 1765, *Susquehannah Company Papers,* II, 307–8. For the subsequent career of Colonel Dyer as a delegate to the Stamp Act Congress and later to the First Continental Congress, and as a judge of the superior court of Connecticut, see O. J. Harvey: *A History of Wilkes-Barré* (6 vols., Wilkes-Barre, 1909–30) I, 393–4*n*; see also G. C. Groce, Jr., "Eliphalet Dyer: Connecticut Revolutionist," previously cited.

[121] For Penn's proclamation of September 23, 1766, see *Susquehannah Company Papers,* II, 316–17; see also *Early American Imprints,* Readex Microprint, Evans No. 10444, for the broadside as printed in Philadelphia.

reached the decision by 1766 to act favourably on a petition submitted by certain officers who had served in the late war, and now agreed to survey large tracts of land for them in the area of Fort Augusta and Wyoming as soon as relations with the Indians permitted.[122]

The famous Treaty of Fort Stanwix, which was concluded by Sir William Johnson and others with the Six Nations in November 1768, was of enormous importance to the problem of white settlement of western lands. It will be examined in detail in the next chapter of this volume, but its importance here is that as a result of the preliminary conferences a formal deed was signed by the Indians and by two representatives of the Pennsylvania Proprietors, Richard Peters, secretary of the province, and James Tilghman of the Land Office. In this document the Indians released to the Proprietors all lands in eastern Pennsylvania claimed by them, including those which the Susquehannah Company had planned to settle—thus repudiating their earlier negotiations with the Susquehannah and Delaware Company agents of 1754 and 1755.[123] Moreover, during the talks leading up to the treaty, the Indians stated their position respecting the illegality of the claims of the Company in the following clear language: "And as we know that Lydius of Albany did in the name of several persons lay claim to Lands in Pennsylvania, which we know to be unjust, and that the Deeds he pretends a right to were invalid, We expect that no regard will be paid to them or any such claims now or hereafter, as we have fairly sold them to the proprietors of Pennsylvania . . . and we shall now give them a Deed for that & other Lands there."[124]

For the release of the lands in northeastern Pennsylvania the Indians were duly and satisfactorily paid by the Pennsylvania Proprietors through their agents,[125] thus clearing the way for the land

[122] See Thomas Penn to Richard Hockley, Pennsylvania receiver general, April 2, 1766, *Susquehannah Company Papers*, II, 313.

[123] For the part played by Richard Peters, secretary of the Province of Pennsylvania, in securing the purchase of the Wyoming Valley lands in 1754 at the Albany Congress and again in 1768 at Fort Stanwix, see Hubertis Cummings: *Richard Peters, Provincial Secretary and Cleric, 1704–1776* (Philadelphia, 1944), pp. 165, 282–5, 297–9, 300–2; see also *Sir William Johnson Papers,* VI, 472, 478, 492, 517, 529–30. For the 1768 grant and map see *New York Colonial Documents,* VIII, 121.

[124] *New York Colonial Documents,* VIII, 128.

[125] It appears that the Pennsylvania Proprietors paid out 10,000 Spanish-milled dollars in order to consummate the purchase of the land. See James Tilghman to William Johnson, January 22, 1769, *Sir William Johnson Papers,* VI, 595–7. Governor John Penn had indicated to Thomas Penn that the purchase price would be more, or between £4,000 and £5,000. See Thomas Penn to John Penn, August 8, 1768, Penn Letter Books, 9:289–92.

to be parcelled out, especially the area in dispute with the Susquehannah Company. This seemed to demand speed, since it had been reported to Governor Penn by Attorney General Benjamin Chew that "the Connecticut people will seize upon it as soon as it is purchased of the Indians," and that Colonel Dyer with 4,000 men would be prepared to move into the Wyoming Valley for this purpose.[126] Even before the conclusion of the Indian treaty Governor Penn began to issue warrants for the survey of tracts of lands in the Valley. With this step completed, leases were granted to certain persons, such as Captain Amos Ogden, John Jennings, and Charles Stewart, all three local Northampton County officials who became key figures in the events to follow.[127]

Attorney General Chew had not been mistaken about the determination of the Susquehannah Company to act promptly. At a meeting held at Hartford on December 28, 1768, the members determined that forty selected people should proceed to take possession, by February 1 of the new year, of the Wyoming lands released by the Indians for settlement and that 200 more should follow as early in the spring as possible. For the encouragement of these vanguards, it was agreed that financial support should be provided, that five townships should be laid out, and that, should any of them be prosecuted by the Pennsylvania authorities, the Company would protect them and bear the costs of any suits.[128]

Bolstered by the Company's promises of support, the first group of new settlers appeared in the Wyoming Valley in February 1769. When their presence was noted, Stewart and Jennings sent warnings to Governor Penn and others that the intruders were cutting down trees and building cabins. By the middle of March warrants for the arrest of the Connecticut men were issued from the Northampton County court at Easton, after a presentment had been made by the grand jury. Those who could be brought to Easton were thereupon bound over to stand trial at the June session of the court.[129] When news reached Connecticut of the action at Easton, Eliphalet Dyer and two other leaders of the Susquehannah Company were ap-

[126] Governor John Penn to Thomas Penn, November 6, 1768, Penn Papers, Official Correspondence, 10:180, Historical Society of Pennsylvania.

[127] Ogden and Stewart were appointed justices of the peace and Jennings became sheriff of Northampton County; see Minutes of the Pennsylvania Council for February 13, 1769, *Pennsylvania Colonial Records,* IX, 569 and 575.

[128] See *Susquehannah Company Papers,* III, 43–7; see also *Pennsylvania Colonial Records,* IX, 569–72.

[129] For the warrant for the arrest of the Connecticut settlers on March 15 and the presentment of the grand jury two days earlier, see *Susquehannah Company Papers,* III, 91–3.

pointed to make their way to Easton "to Defend our Cause . . . in the Prosecution commenced against Sundry of our first 40 . . ."; the Company also voted to increase the number who were to settle at Wyoming to 540, including those awaiting trial as well as others already there. Realizing that the Pennsylvanians who were now established in the Valley shared the hostility of their government, the Susquehannah Company men also voted that during the emergency all their settlers should be grouped compactly in a fortified place under the direction of a committee appointed to take charge of communal activities.[130] Pursuant to these votes, between 200 and 300 more people, under the leadership of Major John Durkee, moved into the Wyoming Valley and proceeded to settle on the lands.[131] They were disposed neither to disperse, when Governor John Penn issued a proclamation on May 16 warning them to depart "on Pain of being prosecuted with the utmost Rigour of the Law,"[132] nor to heed a proclamation by Governor Pitkin of Connecticut advising the people of his colony not to participate in the attempt to settle in Pennsylvania.[133]

When Dyer and his colleagues arrived at Easton late in June to defend those indicted earlier in the year, they found that some 120 newly arrived Connecticut people had also been arrested and released only on high bail. Apparently now convinced that it was useless to contest the ground with the Pennsylvania authorities, the Company representatives, while at Easton, reportedly "agreed to remove immediately from the Susquehannah Lands and give the [Pennsylvania] Government no more trouble about their Claims, unless they shall be able to obtain a Determination in their favor in England. . . ."[134] Yet it seems clear that these representatives were never authorized to enter into such an agreement but had been appointed solely for the legal defence of the Connecticut settlers released on bail.

After Dyer returned to Connecticut, he acted as moderator at a meeting of the Company held on July 26, 1769. The first item of business was to determine whether the people who had settled on

---

[130] Minutes of April 12, 1769, of the Company, *ibid.*, III, 96–8.

[131] Dyer to William Samuel Johnson, August 8, 1769, *ibid.*, III, 159–60.

[132] For the proclamation see *Pennsylvania Gazette*, June 1, 1769; this proclamation was also issued as a broadside for public display. For the deposition of Sheriff Jennings concerning his reading of the proclamation to the settlers see *Pennsylvania Archives*, 1st ser., IV, 342–4.

[133] See *Connecticut Courant*, June 12, July 10, September 11, and November 8, 1769.

[134] Edward Shippen, Jr., to James Burd, June 25, 1769, and Dyer to William Samuel Johnson, August 8, 1769, *Susquehannah Company Papers*, III, 139–40, 159–60.

lands claimed by the Pennsylvania Proprietors should be recalled. This was voted in the negative.[135] The Company, as Dyer later explained to the London agent for Connecticut, did not seek to wage war with the government of Pennsylvania by its determination to support the enterprise, but rather to bring on a civil suit that would ultimately go to the King in Council. It was impossible to institute such a suit in the courts of Pennsylvania, Dyer wrote, without, by inference, recognizing the claim of the Proprietors of Pennsylvania to the Wyoming Valley. Moreover, his argument ran, to appeal from the criminal suits instituted at Easton against members of the Company would not settle the great question as to the charter rights of Connecticut to the western lands.[136]

During the summer and fall of 1769 the Connecticut settlers in the Wyoming Valley, released on bail, continued to clear the land, to sow crops, and to build. The opposition to their presence by the Proprietors and their deputy, Governor John Penn, was by this time receiving little support from the generality of Pennsylvania inhabitants. Yet the chief settlement—now known as Wilkes-Barre (in honour of two leading Englishmen who supported American claims against the mother country)[137]—and other townships that had by then been surveyed were without law and the people continued under a para-military regime. To remedy this situation and to clear the way for the formal assumption of Connecticut rights to the region, 169 of the male settlers signed a petition to the Connecticut General Assembly that the area of the Indian purchase of 1754 be erected into a Connecticut county and that officers be appointed and commissioned.[138] Although the Connecticut Assembly was unwilling to consider the memorial favourably, it did, in the October 1769 session, go so far as to approve a committee headed by Jonathan Trumbull to make a diligent search in the colony and in England for the titles to lands conveyed under the royal charter.[139]

With their appeal to the Connecticut Assembly for protection denied, the Wyoming Valley settlers were again subjected to harassment by the Pennsylvania authorities of Northampton County. In September 1769 not only was the produce of their fields seized but the trial of the 120 who had been released on bail took place and each person involved was found guilty of riot and fined £10 with

[135] Minutes of the meeting of July 26, 1769, *ibid.*, III, 155.

[136] Dyer to William Samuel Johnson, August 8, 1769, *ibid.*, III, 160–1.

[137] For the naming of Wilkes-Barre, then spelled Wilkes-Barré, see O. J. Harvey: *op. cit.*, I, 515.

[138] For this petition, dated August 29, 1769, see O. J. Harvey: *op. cit.*, I, 508–10.

[139] *Connecticut Colonial Records,* XIII, 247.

costs. Then, in November, Captain Amos Ogden, Northampton County sheriff John Jennings, and Charles Stewart, with a posse of some 200 men armed with a cannon, converged on the main settlement and, according to Dyer's account, threatened the destruction of the houses unless the occupants would surrender.[140] This threat led to a formal agreement on November 14 between the Pennsylvania authorities and representatives of the Susquehannah Company whereby the Company settlers were to surrender their fort and buildings, with the understanding that fourteen men be permitted to remain with their families "until his Majestys Decree or Royal Order be Issued, and publickly made known in America." Other provisions of the agreement limited the number of visitors the Connecticut claimants could receive, required them to furnish an inventory of their livestock, permitted them to harvest the crops in the ground, to have free access to their fields and to cut firewood, but forbade them to cut timber or build houses; finally, it was agreed that all houses within the fort, except those allocated to the party of fourteen, would be occupied by Pennsylvania settlers and that harmony should prevail among all of them.[141] However, the fourteen men left at the settlement departed soon afterwards, charging that the Pennsylvanians had broken the agreement by plundering the property left by the other Connecticut people. By the end of 1769 the province was free of the Susquehannah Company intruders and it now doubtless seemed that the issue was settled,[142] since there seemed to be no prospect that the government of Great Britain was prepared to countenance extravagant Connecticut claims to lands extending beyond New York and New Jersey to the Pacific Coast. Actually, it was at this juncture that the struggle for the Wyoming Valley entered a new phase, the so-called Pennamite-Yankee War, which must now be considered.

The whole area of Pennsylvania bordering the lower Susquehanna River was isolated from the eastern counties owing to poor means of communication. Baltimore rather than Philadelphia was the chief

---

[140] See *Pennsylvania Archives,* 1st ser., IV, 401–8, for a long letter from Colonel Dyer and others to Governor Jonathan Trumbull, March 27, 1771, which narrates in considerable detail the events of 1769 and 1770 in the Wyoming Valley from the Connecticut point of view; this letter as printed includes marginal comments obviously by someone supporting the Pennsylvania position. For the Pennsylvania version of the above events see *Pennsylvania Gazette,* December 21, 1769.

[141] For the agreement of November 14, 1769, see *Pennsylvania Archives,* 1st ser., IV, 352–4.

[142] For an account of developments toward the close of 1769 see O. J. Harvey: *op. cit.,* II, 629–34; see also Charles Miner: *History of Wyoming . . .* (Philadelphia, 1845), pp. 112–13.

trading centre for the section. Little relief from these handicaps appeared in sight, since the existing unequal representation had put the Assembly as well as the executive branch of the government in the hands of eastern Pennsylvania men.[143] Moreover, a group of Ulster Scots settled in this area had no patience with the land policy of the Proprietors as it affected them.[144] When coming to the western Pennsylvania frontier in 1730, they had squatted upon lands within the Conestoga Manor.[145] As frontiersmen they had been alienated from the provincial government because of what they felt was its indifference to the needs of the frontier section. When adequate protection had not been given them at the time of the great Indian uprising in 1763, in their fury they had massacred two groups of peaceful Christian Indians at Carlisle and Lancaster, and had even marched on Philadelphia, threatening to destroy the band of Christian Indians sent there for protection by the Moravians.[146] It was this group of hard-fighting, Indian-hating Ulster Scots from Lancaster County, Pennsylvania, known as the "Paxton (Paxtang) Boys," which now, under the leadership of Lazarus Stewart, unexpectedly came to the aid of the Susquehannah Company. In return for the promise of a land grant—a township six miles square in the Wyoming Valley—they agreed to send fifty of their men to settle there and abide by the regulations laid down for the Connecticut settlers.[147]

Early in 1770 two members of the Susquehannah Company, Ebenezer Backus and Captain Zebulon Butler, went from Connecticut to Lancaster County, where they were joined by forty of the Paxton Boys led by Stewart. This body of men, proceeding up the Susquehanna, broke into the blockhouse at Mill-Creek and took possession of a store of ammunition and the four-pounder cannon used by Captain Ogden the previous November to threaten the Company settlers. Moving on to Fort Durkee, they overwhelmed the ten-man garrison posted there by Captain Ogden, and installed

[143] See C. H. Lincoln: *The Revolutionary Movement in Pennsylvania, 1760–1776* (University of Pennsylvania *Publications*, Series in History, No. 1, Philadelphia, 1901), pp. 45–9. Also, by the same author, "Representation in the Pennsylvania Assembly Prior to the Revolution," *Pennsylvania Magazine of History and Biography*, XXIII, 23–34; and J. P. Boyd: "The Introduction," *Susquehannah Company Papers*, IV, i–xxv.

[144] See C. H. Lincoln: *Revolutionary Movement in Pennsylvania*, pp. 99–100.

[145] W. R. Shepherd: *History of Proprietary Government in Pennsylvania* (New York, 1876), p. 547.

[146] See Volume IX of this series, p. 114; see also Brooke Hindle: "The March of the Paxton Boys," *William and Mary Quarterly*, 3rd ser., III, 461–86.

[147] See the letter from the executive committee of the Company to John Montgomery and Lazarus Young, January 15, 1770, *Susquehannah Company Papers*, IV, 5–6.

themselves with the captured cannon.[148] In March, Butler, now in general command of the Company's affairs, was joined by Major Durkee with a contingent of Connecticut men. A period of confusion ensued, during which Ogden held a blockhouse with the help of a group of men owning Pennsylvania land grants.[149] But, by late April, the support that came from dissatisfied settlers also holding land grants from the Proprietors, tipped the scales so strongly in favour of the Connecticut people that Governor Penn was forced to inform his uncle, Thomas, that four-fifths of the people in the Wyoming Valley were supporting the intruders, so that it looked as though this region would become "a Receptacle for all the Murderers & Robbers in this part of America."[150] At this time the executive committee of the Company notified the committee of the Connecticut settlers that 240 more people would soon join them and that additional townships would have to be surveyed.[151] However, in this seesaw struggle the Pennsylvanians were on top once more by the spring of 1771, despite the killing of deputy sheriff Nathan Ogden by Lazarus Stewart.[152]

The violence in the Wyoming Valley finally shook the Pennsylvania Assembly out of its attitude of apparent indifference to what was taking place on the frontier lands of the Proprietors. In a message to Governor Penn, it called upon him to issue a proclamation offering a reward of £300 for the apprehension of Stewart and a lesser amount for the arrest of his chief supporters, and at the same time the Assembly promised all aid within its power to restore public tranquility within the province.[153] With this encouragement at hand, the Governor issued the requested proclamation. Stewart and his accomplices, however, had meanwhile sought and received asylum in Connecticut.[154] The Assembly, for its part, now proceeded to pass

---

[148] See O. J. Harvey: *op. cit.*, II, 640–5, especially Captain Ogden's deposition of May 25, 1770.

[149] Dr. Hugh Williamson to Governor Penn, March 24, 1770, *Pennsylvania Archives*, 1st ser., IV, 366–7.

[150] Governor Penn to Thomas Penn, April 24, 1770, Penn Manuscripts, Private Correspondence, 5:121, Historical Society of Pennsylvania.

[151] *Susquehannah Company Papers*, IV, 59.

[152] For a detailed description of events in the Wyoming Valley for the year 1770 see O. H. Harvey: *op. cit.*, II, 644–76.

[153] For the message of the Assembly of February 8, 1771, see *Pennsylvania Colonial Records*, IX, 715–16.

[154] For the proclamation of February 9, 1771, see *ibid.*, IX, 716–17; see also *Early American Imprints*, Evans No. 12178, for the broadside as published in Philadelphia in 1771. When Penn learned that Stewart and his close associates had gone to Connecticut he called upon Governor Trumbull on March 7, 1771, to apprehend the "daring Offenders so that they might be brought to justice" (*Susquehannah Company Papers*, IV, 175–6). Instead of acting so that Stewart might be extradited

"An Act for preventing Tumults and Riotious Assemblies, and for the more Speedy and effectual punishing the Rioters," to which the Governor gave a speedy assent.[155]

The Pennsylvania act, which was directed toward stemming Connecticut settlers' defiance of the authority of the Pennsylvania government, produced an opposite reaction in the Connecticut Assembly. In the May 1771 session the Assembly members were at last prevailed upon to give some backing to the Susquehannah Company, at least to the extent of stating that they, "having taken under their consideration the extent of their [that is, the members of the Susquehannah Company] title to the lands granted to the Governor and Company of this Colony, are of opinion that the lands west of Delaware River and in the latitude of that part of this Colony eastward of the Province of New York are well contained within the boundaries and descriptions of the Charter granted by King Charles 2d." Further, they again appointed a committee, headed by Governor Trumbull, to collect all possible evidence in support of the colony's title to those western lands and transmit it to the colony's London agents, who were to secure legal opinion as to the validity of this grant as well as of "the pretended title of the proprietaries of Pennsylvania to said land. . . ."[156]

Early in the spring of 1770 the petition of Thomas and William Penn to the King asking that "the inhabitants of Connecticut be removed from their forcible possession of a certain tract of land within the petitioners' charter, and that the Governor and Company of Connecticut set forth their claim for his Majesty's determination, and in the meantime forbear making further encroachments," was referred by the Lords of the Committee of the Privy Council to the Board of Trade. The Board took the position that the government of Connecticut should be ordered to set forth its claim to the lands in dispute. On July 10 it asked the London agents for Connecticut,

to Pennsylvania, Trumbull sent the Penn letter to Dyer, who, with other members of the executive committee of the Company, replied on March 27, in the long letter giving a history of the dispute which was previously cited. Trumbull enclosed this in a letter of his own to Penn, in which he ignored the request. For these letters see *Pennsylvania Archives,* 1st ser., IV, 394, 401–9. Dr. Boyd, who edited the *Susquehannah Company Papers,* presents evidence in the introduction to Vol. III (pp. xvi–xvii) that Trumbull himself wrote the reply that Dyer and the committee presumably sent him to be forwarded to Governor Penn.

[155] *Pennsylvania Colonial Records,* IX, 717; see *Statutes at Large of Pennsylvania from 1682 to 1801* (eds. J. T. Mitchell and Henry Flanders, 17 vols., Harrisburg, 1896–1915), VIII, 5–9. The statute provided that those who defied the law should be judged felons and should suffer the death penalty without benefit of clergy.

[156] *Connecticut Colonial Records,* XIII, 427. As was previously indicated, Trumbull had been appointed in 1769 to head a similar committee.

William Samuel Johnson[157] and Thomas Life, whether they had received any instructions to support the Connecticut settlement, as complained of in the petition, or to put forward any claim their colony might have to the lands in question, and was informed that the agents had received no such instructions.[158] The Lords Commissioners thereupon framed a report, which came before the Privy Council on June 7, 1771, and was ordered to be accepted. In substance it maintained that as Connecticut had set forth no claims to counter the petition of the Penns and had not recognized the proceedings of the Connecticut settlers in Pennsylvania, it was quite unnecessary for His Majesty to interpose his authority since, in the words of the order, "there is not the least Colour of a plea, that the Charter of the province of Pennsylvania does not Contain the powers necessary to the decision of any Suits . . . where the Title to the Lands may be in question nor . . . the means to support the Execution of the Laws to preserve the publick peace. . . ."[159] By this action the Privy Council ruled that Connecticut was not a party to the dispute, that the troubles lay simply between individuals within the charter limits of Pennsylvania, and that the government of the province possessed adequate powers to deal with disputes over lands within its limits and to enforce order.

Still the Susquehannah Company persisted in its endeavours to hold the country which it coveted. Even without its leaders—Zebulon Butler and John Durkee, who were in gaol in Philadelphia—toward the end of 1770, the Company settlers temporarily regained possession of Fort Durkee, but only to lose it again.[160] By the spring of 1771 the Pennsylvanians were in complete control of the Wyoming Valley, and Governor Penn determined to fill it with settlers by offering proprietary lands there on advantageous terms. As a

[157] It may be noted that Johnson, who was appointed London agent for Connecticut in 1767, gave up his post in 1771 and returned to Connecticut, where he became a member of the Council and a judge of the superior court. For Johnson's activities concerning the Susquehannah Company see G. C. Groce, Jr.: *William Samuel Johnson: A Maker of the Constitution* (New York, 1937), pp. 87–8, and Chap. 7, *passim;* see also E. E. Beardsley: *Life and Times of William Samuel Johnson* (2nd edn., New York, 1886).

[158] *Acts of the Privy Council, Col. Ser., 1766–1783,* p. 238, and Board of Trade *Journal, 1768–1775,* pp. 192, 195–8. For the petition see *Susquehannah Company Papers,* IV, 12–25, especially 22*n.*

[159] *Acts of the Privy Council, Col. Ser., 1776–1783,* pp. 238–9.

[160] For the loss of Fort Durkee and the minutes of the Susquehannah Company meeting of January 9, 1771, see O. J. Harvey: *op. cit.,* II, 669–71, 676–7; see also the *Connecticut Courant,* March 5, 1771.

result, the new surveys crossed the lines of the lands surveyed by the Connecticut people.[161]

Just when it seemed as though the issue over the Wyoming Valley had been settled, at a meeting held in Windham, Connecticut, on June 12, 1771, the Susquehannah Company voted to send forward immediately 540 settlers to repossess the lost territory. Once again Zebulon Butler led the expedition, and once again it was joined by Lazarus Stewart with a group of his Paxton Boys. Moving on Fort Wyoming, where 40 men and 150 women and children were sheltered by stockade defences, the combined forces threw up four redoubts around the post during the latter part of July. When by the middle of August the force available to the Northampton County authorities proved insufficient to relieve them, the besieged people in the fort were obliged to capitulate.[162] Once more the Valley passed under the control of the Susquehannah Company people. In a letter to Governor Trumbull, James Hamilton, President of the Council (who had taken over the administration of Pennsylvania with the departure for England of Lieutenant Governor John Penn upon the death of his father), accused the Connecticut invaders who had forced the surrender of the fort of having done so "Expressly on behalf of the [Connecticut] Government."[163] To this accusation Trumbull retorted: "Persons concerned in these Transactions have no Order and direction from me, or from the General Assembly of this Colony." He then countered that the members of the Susquehannah Company so charged had complained that they were first attacked and ill treated by the people of Pennsylvania while they were merely seeking possession of lands claimed by titles which they desired to have vindicated by due course of law. Trumbull then concluded: "Which have been most in fault it is not my part to determine."[164]

Thus, by the beginning of 1772 the Susquehannah Company settlers were again well established in the Wyoming Valley. Despite this and the manifest evidence that their numbers were constantly increasing, the Assembly of Pennsylvania in March of that year created the new county of Northumberland out of portions of Lan-

[161] See the map showing the criss-crossing of the Connecticut and Pennsylvania surveys, *Pennsylvania Archives*, 2nd ser., XVIII, 432.

[162] For depositions respecting the assault on Fort Wyoming and for the articles of capitulation of the fort on August 15, 1771, see *Pennsylvania Colonial Records*, IX, 767–71.

[163] James Hamilton to Jonathan Trumbull, October 4, 1771, *ibid.*, IX, 777.

[164] Trumbull to Hamilton, October 14, 1771, *ibid.*, X, 3–4.

caster, Cumberland, Berks, Bedford, and Northampton counties. This new county comprehended all the territory claimed by the Company as purchased from the Indians in 1754 and much more besides. The Assembly also made provisions for a full complement of county officers.[165] Sunbury, protected by Fort Augusta at the forks of the Susquehanna River, was designated as the county seat. By this time, however, the New Englanders had established five townships in the area about Fort Wyoming—Wilkes-Barre, Hanover, Kingston, Plymouth, and Pittston[166]—which were being rapidly settled by newcomers. With a feeling of confidence in the future and "Sensible of the Equity & Justice of their Claims to the Susquehannah Country," the Company at this juncture voted to send to Philadelphia Captain Joseph Trumbull, son of the Governor of Connecticut, with the mission of persuading the government of Pennsylvania and the Proprietors of the province to come to an agreement by civil action rather than by violence in order to determine the respective rights to the lands in dispute. It also voted that an application be made to the Connecticut Assembly to establish a civil government in that area by erecting it into a county.[167] But nothing came from these resolutions. Nor did an attempt made in the late spring of 1772 to plant a settlement of Company men in the region of the west branch of the Susquehanna River have any better success, since the party that set out was overwhelmed by the Northumberland County authorities.[168] Yet, the Connecticut people were at least firmly entrenched on both sides of the east branch of that river and on the west bank of the Delaware River. So much did they feel secure that they were not especially disturbed when Lieutenant Governor Richard Penn issued a proclamation on June 22, 1772, commanding them to depart from the lands at Wyoming and at two of the creeks emptying into the Delaware, the Shohola and the Lackawaxen.[169] In fact, at a gathering held at Wilkes-Barre on

[165] For the creation of Northumberland County on March 21, 1772, see *Statutes at Large of Pennsylvania,* VIII, 143–9. The act was referred to the Privy Council on January 15, 1773, and in the absence of any objection became a law. For the scope of Northumberland County see Reading Howell's "Map of the State of Pennsylvania" issued in 1792, which also depicts the new Luzerne County created in 1786 out of the northeastern part of Northumberland embracing the Wyoming Valley (*Pennsylvania Archives,* 3rd ser., Maps, Appendix I–X, and *American State Papers,* I, 830).

[166] See O. J. Harvey: *op. cit.,* I, 515. The first four of these townships are indicated on Howell's map. Pittston by 1792 had been absorbed into Lackawanock (Lackawanna) Township.

[167] Minutes of the Company, April 1, 1772, *Susquehannah Company Papers,* IV, 314–16; O. J. Harvey: *op. cit.,* II, 731–2.

[168] *Ibid.,* II, 736–7.

[169] For this proclamation see *Pennsylvania Archives,* 1st ser., IV, 453–4.

April 3, 1773, they adopted a petition to the Connecticut Assembly which asserted that there were "about 2,500 persons, who are at this time under the greatest difficulty . . . imaginable, *for want of being incorporated,* and officers civil and military appointed among us—not only for our defence . . . *against the vile encroachment of our neighbours the Pennsylvanians,* but to keep up good order and regularity among ourselves."[170] This petition, endorsed by the Company at a meeting held in Hartford on April 22, was presented to the May session of the Connecticut Assembly. Although no action was taken at that time, sentiment throughout the colony became so active in support of the Company's enterprise that at the October session the following resolution was passed: "That this Assembly . . . assert their claim . . . to those lands contained within the limits and boundaries of the charter of this Colony, which are westward of the Province of New York." A committee of eight was also appointed to assist Governor Trumbull in taking proper steps "to pursue the claim of this Colony to said Western Lands."[171] Members of this committee were authorized to go to Philadelphia in order to treat with Lieutenant Governor John Penn[172] for "an amicable agreement . . . concerning the boundaries of this Colony and the province of Pennsylvania."[173] Three of the committee—Eliphalet Dyer, William Samuel Johnson, and Jedidiah [Jedediah] Strong—were now commissioned to negotiate with Penn. They arrived in Philadelphia in the middle of December 1773.[174]

---

[170] For this petition, which bore the names of 315 men, see O. J. Harvey: *op. cit.,* II, 760.

[171] *Connecticut Colonial Records,* XIV, 161–2. For the argument as it appeared in print see *The Right of the Governor and Company, of the Colony of Connecticut, to Claim and Hold the Lands Within the Limits of their Charter, lying West of the Province of New-York, Stated and Considered: In a Letter to J. H. Esquire, to which is added, An Account of the Purchase from the Indians, of Part of Those Lands, by the Susquehannah and Delaware Companies, and their Proceedings thereon* (Hartford, 1773); this is available in Readex Microprint, *Early American Imprints, 1639–1800,* Evans No. 12978.

[172] From 1763 to 1776 John Penn was Lieutenant Governor of Pennsylvania, with the exception of the years 1771–2, when his brother, Richard, held that office.

[173] The Connecticut Assembly was undoubtedly influenced when the case for the colony, which had been drawn up largely by Governor Trumbull in 1771, then sent to England and there revised by the eminent lawyer Richard Jackson, had been returned in August 1773 "with opinion of counsel favourable to the claims of the Colony" (*Connecticut Colonial Records,* XIII, 427; XIV, 161*n*). *The Susquehannah Case,* printed as a pamphlet of twenty-four pages in 1774, is incorporated in the *Connecticut Colonial Records* (XIV, 445–60), together with the combined answers of Edward Thurlow, Alexander Wedderburn, Richard Jackson, and John Dunning to questions relating to the effect of the establishment of the common boundary between New York and Connecticut on the claim of the latter colony to lands west of New York.

[174] *Ibid.,* XIV, 465.

The Connecticut commissioners were courteously received by the Lieutenant Governor and the Council. They immediately proceeded to request definite answers from Penn to three questions: (1) whether he would enter into negotiations to settle the territorial limits respectively of Connecticut and of the grant made to the Pennsylvania Proprietors; (2) in case of refusal to negotiate, whether he would join with Connecticut in applying to His Majesty to appoint commissioners to decide the matter; and (3) whether he would agree on measures to preserve peace and good order in the contested area during the period of the dispute. The commissioners, upon request, then set forth the western claims of Connecticut. In reply, the Pennsylvania Lieutenant Governor stated that the western boundary of Connecticut had been settled prior to the grant of Pennsylvania to William Penn; he further observed that if the government of Connecticut felt it had a just claim to lands within the charter limits of Pennsylvania, it should petition the Crown so that the matter might be speedily settled, but assured the Connecticut commissioners the Proprietors of Pennsylvania would appear to defend their own claims. Before concluding, Penn referred to "the repeated Outrages . . . committed by a Number of lawless People from your Colony, who, without any Warrant or Authority from the Governor of Connecticut, have . . . in a hostile Manner, dispossessed the Tenants . . . settled on Lands under Warrants . . . of the Proprietors of Pennsylvania." The conference continued until December 25 with the Lieutenant Governor holding to his position. The Connecticut commissioners, realizing how fruitless the exchange of views was, took their departure.[175]

When the Connecticut Assembly met at Hartford on January 12, 1774, the commissioners made their report, which led to several acts and resolutions. The first resolution was for the appointment of a committee of eight to assist Governor Trumbull in preparing exhibits necessary to prosecute the Connecticut title to lands lying west of the Delaware River. The second desired the Governor to transmit these papers to the London agent of the colony and to give him instructions for his conduct in any cause that might be instituted in Great Britain touching the disputed lands. Then—taking into account the petition of the people settled in the Wyoming country

[175] The deliberations between the Connecticut commissioners and the Governor and Council of Pennsylvania took place in writing. The texts of these communications were published in Norwich, Connecticut, in 1774 under title *Report of the Commissioners Appointed by the General Assembly of this Colony, To treat with the Proprietaries of Pennsylvania, Respecting the Boundaries of this Colony and that Province,* which is reprinted in *Connecticut Colonial Records,* XIV, 461–82.

seeking the protection of the government of Connecticut—the Assembly enacted that "the inhabitants dwelling within the bounds of this Colony on the west side of the river Delaware," within the area bounded by the Delaware on the east and on the north and south by the north and south lines of Connecticut and on the west by a line drawn fifteen miles west of the place called Wyoming, be constituted a distinct town named Westmoreland and that it be annexed to the county of Litchfield, with the proviso that the new town should be isolated with regard to any civil actions. This was followed by another resolution, which provided for the employment of suitable persons to ascertain the latitudes and longitudes of the north and south lines of the colony at various points in the area west of the Delaware. Next, an act authorized the Governor to issue a proclamation forbidding any person to settle any lands included in the charter of the colony without first obtaining liberty to do so from the General Assembly. Two more resolutions provided respectively for a committee of three to adjust claims to lands and quiet the title to lands of all those settled within the limits of Connecticut to the west of the Delaware, and for the London agent, Thomas Life, to appear and defend the colony in all causes relative to its western land claims.[176]

With the above action of the Connecticut Assembly, the town of Westmoreland—a town almost as extensive as the original colony of Connecticut—was duly organized. Two justices of the peace were appointed and given authorization to issue a warrant for calling a town meeting to select officers and to transact whatever other business seemed proper.[177] A summons to a town meeting to assemble at Wilkes-Barre on March 1 was thereupon issued to the adult male members of the Susquehannah and Delaware companies settled within the bounds of the immense township. Gathering at the appointed time, the people organized and chose a moderator and a town clerk. The following day the town was by vote divided into eight districts, each with prescribed limits.[178] Then followed, after the New England manner, the election of a full complement of town officers: selectmen, a town treasurer, constable, collectors of

[176] See *ibid.*, XIV, 217–20.

[177] The Connecticut Assembly appointed two prominent residents of the Wyoming Valley as justices of the peace for Litchfield County: the redoubtable Captain Zebulon Butler and Nathan Denison. See *ibid.*, XIV, 220.

[178] The extent of Westmoreland town, as provided by act of the Connecticut Assembly, and its subsequent division into districts, including those on or near the Delaware River, indicates that by 1774 the Delaware Company had fused with the Susquehannah Company. For the identification of the Delaware Company with the Susquehannah Company see *Susquehannah Company Papers,* I, lxxxviii–lxxxix.

rates, surveyors of highways, fence viewers, listers, leather sealers, grand jurors, tithing men, sealers of weights and measures, and key-keepers.[179] What doubtless gave the people an added sense of security was that they, as part of Litchfield County, were now under the laws of Connecticut. Further, Governor Trumbull, as authorized, had issued a proclamation on January 27, 1774, directed against anyone who, without the express consent of the Connecticut Assembly, should attempt to settle any of the lands within Westmoreland or any other western lands claimed by the colony under its charter.[180]

On February 22 Governor Penn countered the Connecticut's Governor's proclamation with one of his own based on some resolutions passed by the Pennsylvania Assembly on January 13 in response to a petition for protection from the inhabitants of Northumberland County.[181] This proclamation warned all people living in the area of dispute not to yield obedience to anyone claiming to act by authority of the colony of Connecticut.[182] In this connection it should be mentioned that on January 31 Governor Trumbull wrote to Lieutenant Governor Penn to inform him of the Connecticut Assembly's decision to erect the town of Westmoreland as an appendage of Litchfield County. Penn's reply, dated February 24, pointed out that the jurisdiction of the Province of Pennsylvania had long been extended over the area occupied by this town and that a great part of the land had been granted to Pennsylvania applicants "long before your Colony ever determined to set up their Claim." Penn also told the Connecticut Governor that the best way to secure peace and good order in the disputed region was for the government of his colony to desist from trying to exercise any authority in the Wyoming Valley "until your new Claim had been heard and adjudged to have any real Foundation by His Majesty in Council, before whom you say you are preparing to lay your Case."[183]

The Pennsylvania Proprietors were not the only active opponents of the Susquehannah Company enterprise. Even in Connecticut it had its enemies. In the February 22, 1774, issue of the *Connecticut*

---

[179] For the minutes of the Westmoreland town meeting of March 1 and 2, see O. J. Harvey: *op. cit.*, II, 793–5.

[180] For the proclamation see the *Connecticut Courant* of January 27, 1774.

[181] For the petition, denouncing the attempts of Connecticut intruders to dispossess Northumberland County residents settled in the area of the west branch of the Susquehanna River, see *Pennsylvania Archives*, 8th ser., VIII, 7042–3; for the resolutions of the Pennsylvania Assembly see *ibid.*, VIII, 7066.

[182] For the proclamation see *Pennsylvania Colonial Records*, X, 153–5; for its appearance in the newspapers see, for example, the *Pennsylvania Gazette* of March 2, 1774.

[183] For the Trumbull and Penn letters see *Pennsylvania Colonial Records*, X, 151–2.

Courant an article appeared over the signature of "Many," deploring the influence that the Company had come to exercise in the government of Connecticut. The writer took the position that in assuming the responsibility of defending the Company's claims, the colony was opening the door to endless expense which would have to be borne by the Connecticut taxpayers, most of whom would derive no benefit from the expenditure. He concluded by calling upon the towns to elect two or more people to attend a meeting in Middletown late in the following month. In answer to this appeal, twenty-three Connecticut towns were represented at the Middletown convention that opened on March 30. Their delegates drew up a remonstrance addressed to the General Assembly against extending the jurisdiction of the colony over western lands as a step which, they felt, not only set a dangerous precedent but might have fatal consequences for the people of Connecticut. The remonstrance also called upon the members of the Assembly "to exclude the proprietors of The Susquehannah Company from a voice on these matters, and reconsider the . . . votes and doings of the Assembly in October and January last. . . ."[184] In Philadelphia, meanwhile, there had issued from the press anonymously in January of that year *An Examination of the Connecticut Claim to Lands in Pennsylvania . . .*[185] This was from the pen of the Rev. William Smith, Provost of the College of Philadelphia, but was based largely on data supplied by the distinguished Connecticut lawyer Jared Ingersoll, judge of the Middle District Court of Vice-Admiralty, whose headquarters were in Philadelphia.[186] The Smith pamphlet was answered by the Rev. Benjamin Trumbull in a series of articles which first appeared in the *Connecticut Journal* published in New Haven and soon afterward were brought together and issued there under the title *A Plea, in Vindication of the Connecticut Title to the Contested Lands, Lying West of the Province of New York.*[187] In turn Smith retorted, again anonymously, in the *Pennsylvania Gazette* with a series of six articles under the general heading of "The Examiner."[188]

Although the representatives from the town of Westmoreland

---

[184] For the resolutions of the Middletown convention see O. J. Harvey: *op. cit.*, II, 801.

[185] The pamphlet, issued anonymously, was 124 pages in length, about one-half of them given over to an appendix consisting of documents. One of the most able publications that appeared during this period in opposition to the claims of Connecticut, it may be found in the *Pennsylvania Archives*, 2nd ser., XVIII, 125–214.

[186] See the author's *Jared Ingersoll . . .*, pp. 323–4.

[187] Benjamin Trumbull was also the author of *A Complete History of Connecticut from 1630 till 1764* (New Haven, 1797, and 2nd edn., 2 vols., 1818).

[188] The Smith articles appeared in the *Pennsylvania Gazette* from April 27 to June 8, 1774.

were not permitted seats in the Connecticut Assembly that met at Hartford in May 1774—and therefore could not protest the petition of the Middletown convention against the activities of the Susquehannah Company—the petition received little consideration. While this session of the Assembly was drawing to a close the Company was holding the last meeting it was to have before the outbreak of the American Revolution, so far as the records show. It was destined not to meet again until the closing months of 1782.[189] Nevertheless, by 1774 the Susquehannah and Delaware Company settlers were firmly entrenched in the eight districts set up within the town of Westmoreland, even to the extent of having a military company organized in each district for defence. Moreover, the tide in favour of the Company ran so strongly within Connecticut that, in the October session of the Assembly, representatives of the town of Westmoreland were admitted as equal members of that body and continued to sit and act.[190] In December of the following year, at a special session for raising a body of "minute-men" for the revolutionary cause, Westmoreland was exempted from providing such troops, in view of the nature of its own defence needs, and a special law was passed re-defining the boundaries of the town of Westmoreland.[191] The next step in the Yankee colony was not to come until after the Declaration of Independence when, at the October 1776 session of the Connecticut General Assembly, it was voted that the town of Westmoreland be created a county of the same name.[192]

But the developments within the Wyoming Valley itself were of another nature. There the Pennamite War continued in its own small-scale fashion. In the summer of 1775, with the War for American Independence in progress, plans were laid by the Susquehannah Company settlers, who were now in firm control of the east branch of the Susquehanna River, to occupy the west branch by force, despite the large numbers of people settled in that area under grants from the Pennsylvania Proprietors.[193] In the latter part of September

---

[189] See O. J. Harvey: *op. cit.*, II, 809–11. It should be noted that one Westmoreland representative did attend the special session of the Assembly held April 26 to May 6 at Hartford, when by agreement of both houses the western boundary of Westmoreland was extended to meet the "Stanwix Line"—which was not properly understood by the Connecticut legislators—and both a court of probate and a military organization were established. See *ibid.*, II, 823.

[190] See *Connecticut Colonial Records,* XIV, 327, 391, 415.

[191] *Ibid.*, XV, 197.

[192] See "An Act making the Town of Westmoreland in this Colony a distinct County," *Public Records of the State of Connecticut, 1776–1796* (eds. C. J. Hoadly and L. W. Labaree, 8 vols., Hartford, 1894–1951), I, 7; see also an addition to this act passed in May 1777, *ibid.*, I, 229.

[193] See Zebulon Butler to Ellis Hughes, August 21 and 24, 1775, *American Archives,* 4th ser., III, 222, 259.

some 300 armed Connecticut men, under Colonel Zebulon Butler, moved across the country to a small stream called Warrior's Run, a mere thirteen miles above Sunbury, the county seat of Northumberland County. To counter this intrusion, about 500 Pennsylvanians were recruited and, under command of Colonel Thomas Plunket, marched against the Yankees. During a brief engagement—in which one life was lost, several Connecticut men wounded, and a number of prisoners taken—Plunket broke up the encampment.[194] On the heels of this initial success against the Susquehannah Company people, the settlers of Northumberland County, joined by those of Northampton County, decided to consolidate their gains. During the fall session of the Pennsylvania Assembly they presented a long memorial concerned with the invasion of their counties by the New England people and prayed for assistance.[195] On October 27, in a series of resolutions, the Assembly justified the repelling of the Susquehannah Company aggression and affirmed: "That those Connecticut intruders having, in a forcible and hostile Manner obtained . . . Possessions in this Province, ought . . . to surrender up those Possessions, and wait for a proper and legal Decision of their Claim." However, since the issue between the two colonies was now before the Continental Congress, the Assembly further resolved to acquiesce in any plan recommended by the Congress—even to permitting "the Intruders" to occupy their present settlement until the issue had been determined—provided that no more of these people should settle on controverted lands.[196] Nevertheless, they expressed themselves as firmly opposed to a resolution offered by the Connecticut delegates to the Congress that "a Temporary Line of Jurisdiction" be fixed whereby the town of Westmoreland should remain under the jurisdiction of the government of Connecticut until there should be "a *legal* Settlement of said Controversy. . . ."[197]

The next move on the part of the Pennsylvania authorities was an attempt late in 1775 to overwhelm the Connecticut settlements on the east branch of the Susquehanna. With warrants for the arrest of a number of persons residing there—some of them charged with "the greatest crimes"—Sheriff William Scull of Northumberland County, escorted by a posse of some 600 or 700 men under the command of Colonel Plunket, moved up the east branch toward

[194] See *ibid.*, III, 807; *Pennsylvania Archives,* 8th ser., VIII, 7260 and 7290; O. J. Harvey: *op. cit.*, II, 842–3.

[195] For the memorial see *Pennsylvania Archives,* 8th ser., VIII, 7314–23.

[196] For the resolutions see *ibid.*, VIII, 7330–2.

[197] For the Connecticut resolution placed before the Continental Congress see *ibid.*, VIII, 7320–1.

Fort Wyoming, or Wilkes-Barre. This force was opposed by Colonel Butler with 400 men of his regiment entrenched behind rock formations at the narrows of the river. Although this position was impregnable to frontal attack, Plunket assaulted it on December 21, but he was repulsed and retreated to count his dead and wounded. Two days later, under cover of night, an attempt was made by the Pennsylvanians to secure a landing on the east bank of the river. But Lazarus Stewart of Paxton Boys fame had a force waiting in ambush and again the attempt to break through failed, and more men were killed. In the face of the bitter winter's cold and the ice-clogged river, the Pennsylvania expeditionary force retreated down the river to Sunbury.[198] This so-called battle of "Rampart Rocks" on December 25 marked the end of the first Pennamite War—the last attempt on the part of the authorities of Pennsylvania to settle the issue of the disputed lands by force until after the War for American Independence.

Meanwhile, as early as July 1775 the dispute had come before the Continental Congress through petitions presented by the Assemblies of the two colonies.[199] On November 4, 1775, the Congressional body, acting on a report brought in by a special committee appointed to deal with the dispute, called upon both Connecticut and Pennsylvania to avoid all hostilities in the Wyoming Valley in view of the importance at this critical juncture of maintaining "the most perfect Union."

To further this laudable end the Continental Congress appointed Thomas McKean of Delaware and Silas Deane of Connecticut to carry the resolution to the Pennsylvania Assembly.[200] By November 27 the Congress had re-committed the committee's report, with instructions that this committee should hear "evidence on the possession and jurisdiction of the lands in dispute."[201] On December 20 the Congress again called upon the contending parties to refrain from the use of force until the issue could be peacefully terminated.[202] But, as has been mentioned, at this very moment Pennsylvania forces were moving in upon the Yankees. Three days later

---

[198] See "Extract of a letter from a Gentleman at Westmoreland [obviously Zebulon Butler] to his Friend in Hartford," December 27, 1775, *American Archives,* 4th ser., IV, 470, and Sheriff Scull, Colonel Plunket, and others to Governor Penn, December 30, 1775, *ibid.*, IV, 1473; see also O. J. Harvey: *op. cit.*, II, 859–63.

[199] *Journals of the Continental Congress, 1774–1789* (eds. W. C. Ford *et al.*, 34 vols., Washington, 1904–37), II, 235, 238; III, 268, 283, 287, 295, 297.

[200] *Ibid.*, III, 321 and 335.

[201] *Ibid.*, III, 349, 352, 377.

[202] *Ibid.*, III, 435 and 439–40.

the Congress resolved to recommend to Connecticut not to permit any further passage of its inhabitants into the area until the jurisdiction of the lands should be established.[203] By this time, however, the Connecticut Assembly was solidly behind the Westmoreland settlers. In April 1776 the Congress appealed once more to the rival groups in the area of the Susquehanna River not to injure the American union "by mutual acts of violence or oppression,"[204] and in August of that year, in a gesture of impartiality, it resolved to embody in the Continental Army six companies from Pennsylvania to be stationed along the frontiers of Northumberland and Northampton counties, and two companies to be raised in Westmoreland (County), for the defence of "said town and parts adjacent."[205]

The forces left behind were not sufficient to protect the Westmoreland area; thus the Connecticut settlers were not destined to remain unmolested on their farms and in their settlements. Many of the men enlisted in the Continental Army; others, realizing that the area was exposed to attack either by the Indians or by the enemy forces concentrated at such places as Fort Niagara, turned to the construction of new fortifications. They also appealed to the Continental Congress, through the Board of War, for reinforcements. Nevertheless, Loyalist forces overran the area in 1777 seeking recruits and supplies, and the final blow fell in the spring and summer of 1778. It was then that, with Major John Butler in command, the Tory Rangers and their Indian allies defeated the outnumbered settlers rallying under Colonel Zebulon Butler. The Battle of Wyoming in July 1778 was a rout of the worst order, only to be followed by the tragic massacre of those taken prisoner. The surviving settlers fled from the Wyoming Valley, and their deserted homes were wantonly destroyed by marauding Indians. Although General Washington detailed a special force, under the command of Major General John Sullivan, to clear the area of Indians and Loyalists alike, the settlers who returned after Sullivan's clean-up operations in August 1779 were still subjected to harassment by the Indians.[206]

---

[203] *Ibid.*, III, 452–3.

[204] *Ibid.*, IV, 283.

[205] *Ibid.*, V, 699.

[206] For the military activities of the Loyalists in 1777 see O. H. Harvey: *op. cit.*, II, 939–40; for their subsequent activities, along with the steps taken by the settlers to appeal to the Board of War and the action taken by the Continental Congress on June 23, detaching two of the already depleted Westmoreland Independent Companies from the main army for the defence of the frontier, together with details of the tragic outcome, see *ibid.*, II, 971–1048.

Although the Pennsylvania and Connecticut settlers joined forces in mutual defence against the British enemy during the Revolution, as the War for American Independence drew to a close the old dispute was revived. In November 1781 the Pennsylvania Supreme Executive Council petitioned Congress for a formal hearing of the controversy. Acting upon this appeal, the Continental Congress prepared a notice calling the attention of the government of Connecticut to the petition and requesting its appearance on a date set for the hearing,[207] as provided for by Article IX of the newly adopted Articles of Confederation.[208] With the appointment of five commissioners sworn to hear and determine the case "to the best of their judgment, without favor, affection, or hope of reward," the hearings took place in Trenton, New Jersey, lasting from November 19 to December 30, 1782. The government of Pennsylvania was ably represented by Attorney General William Bradford, Jr., together with Joseph Reed, Jonathan Dickinson Sergeant, and Henry Osborne, while Connecticut was equally well represented by Eliphalet Dyer, William Samuel Johnson, and Jesse Root.[209] At the conclusion of the hearings the court pronounced the following decree:

> "We are unanimously of opinion, that the State of Connecticut has no right to the lands in controversy.
>
> "We are also unanimously of opinion, that the jurisdiction and pre-emption of all territory lying within the charter boundary of Pennsylvania, and now claimed by the State of Connecticut, do of right belong to the State of Pennsylvania."[210]

Before handing down this decree, the commissioners had agreed among themselves never to give the reasons for their decision, which was to be made unanimous by the minority conceding to the majority.[211] Thus there is no record of a minority opinion. However, the day after handing down their decree, the commissioners as a body addressed President Dickinson in a letter pointing out that although, under the terms of their appointment, they could not

---

[207] *Journals of the Continental Congress*, XXI, 1092, 1115–16.

[208] For the Articles see *ibid.*, XIX, 214–23.

[209] The evidence used by the Connecticut representatives in presenting their case is to be found under the heading "Connecticut Records as Examined by the State of Pennsylvania," in the *Pennsylvania Archives*, 2nd ser., XVIII, 215–75. The documents as presented were all certified as true copies by George Wyllys, Connecticut secretary of state.

[210] For the proceedings of the commissioners, including their decree, see *Journals of the Continental Congress*, XXIV, 6–32.

[211] See Judge Cyrus Griffin to John Dickinson, January 1, 1783, *Pennsylvania Archives*, 2nd ser., XVIII, 631–2.

permit individual claims to come before them, they urged the government of Pennsylvania to take proper steps to adjust the question of private rights.[212] This was not done until a second Pennamite-Yankee war had been waged in 1784, the aftermath of which continued to raise the issue of the rights of Connecticut settlers in Pennsylvania territory. In this connection it is of interest to note that when Connecticut ceded certain western lands in 1786 to the Confederation, it withheld an area equal in extent to the Susquehannah Company or Wyoming Valley area lost to Connecticut by the Decree of Trenton—the territory known as the "Western Reserve." The idea for such a reserve had been raised by Eliphalet Dyer during the Trenton Court of Arbitration in 1782,[213] but it was only consummated when his friend William Samuel Johnson succeeded him as delegate to Congress.[214] The creation and recognition of the Western Reserve was at least a partial recognition of the sea-to-sea charter claims, on which the whole Connecticut position rested in its dispute with Pennsylvania over the Wyoming Valley. Nevertheless, it must be pointed out that such a step may also have been a salving of the corporate conscience of the Congress in the face of the tragic sufferings of the Connecticut settlers during the Revolution as the result of the absence of their main source of manpower—the Westmoreland Independent Companies attached to the Continental Army. James Madison later hinted that the session of the Western Reserve was in a sense a bribe for acquiescence in the Trenton decree.[215]

The ultimate resolution of the conflict between Pennsylvania and Connecticut only came about with the confirmation of individual claims through a series of acts passed by the Pennsylvania General Assembly in 1799, 1802, 1805, 1807, and 1808, although the land titles had been broadly confirmed in 1787, a year after the disputed territory had been erected into the Pennsylvania county of Luzerne. In the interim, however, the harsh treatment of the Connecticut settlers over such a long period had provoked retaliatory measures,[216] and the troubles had been revived sporadically.

---

[212] *Ibid.*, XVIII, 629–30.

[213] See G. C. Groce, Jr.,: "Eliphalet Dyer: Connecticut Revolutionist," *loc. cit.*, especially pp. 302–3.

[214] See *Journals of the Continental Congress*, XXIV, 6–32; see also G. C. Groce, Jr.,: *William Samuel Johnson*, Chap. 7.

[215] *The Records of the Federal Convention of 1787* (ed. Max Farrand, 3 vols., New Haven and London, 1911), I, 316–17, 326.

[216] For the various steps taken by the government of Pennsylvania to conclude the controversy, see *Pennsylvania Archives*, 2nd ser., XVIII, 629–721, 778–9, which include Dickinson's proclamation of January 6, 1783, the so-called Compromise Act

In the final analysis the constitutional implications of this dispute become clear. The home government, after reviewing the facts and supporting the claims of the Penn family, stood upon a policy of not interfering in a matter which, they deemed, lay solely within the jurisdiction of Pennsylvania authorities. Acting upon this decision, as well as upon its charter rights, the Pennsylvania Assembly condoned the actions of the authorities of Northampton County in their attempt to evict the aggressive Connecticut settlers in order to prevent them from making inroads upon Pennsylvania land. It is clear that the inherent weakness in the Connecticut case was the colony's attempt, after a long period without protest, to exercise its sea-to-sea claims by seeking title to lands within the bounds granted by royal patent to William Penn. Furthermore, Connecticut's long-term official acknowledgment of the eastern boundary of New York as its western boundary, combined with the initial disinterest of its Assembly in the affairs of the Susquehannah Company, helped to negate the suit brought before the Privy Council and to influence the final decision of the Continental Congress. Thus the Decree of Trenton must, in fact, be regarded as legally and equitably proper and just. As to the group of inhabitants who had settled in the Wyoming Valley under the auspices of the Susquehannah Company, those who lived through the hardships ultimately won protection of the ground rights they claimed, but only after they, on their part, finally recognized the authority of the Commonwealth of Pennsylvania.

In summarizing the outcome of the contest over lands between the Proprietors of Pennsylvania and Maryland, it may be affirmed that the Penn family obtained more than it was *legally* entitled to receive, but not more than its *equitable* claims to the city of Philadelphia justified.

Finally, as the issue raised by the claims of the Province of Virginia to the western area of Pennsylvania is more clearly a phase of the trans-Appalachian expansion of British colonials, it has seemed best to reserve consideration of it for the chapter to follow.

---

of 1799, the 1802 "Act to maintain the territorial rights of this State, and protect the property of persons holding lands under the same." Subsequently, with the passage of the Act of 1805, the "Westmoreland Records" embodying the claims of Connecticut settlers became a part of the official public records of Luzerne County; see O. J. Harvey: *op. cit.*, III, 1659 (It should be noted that with Vol. III of the *History of Wilkes-Barré*, E. G. Smith becomes the author). For an extended treatment of activities during the termination of the conflict, see *ibid.*, III, 1304–1673.

CHAPTER XII

Trans-Appalachian Developments: British Policies and Plans for the Management of Western Lands and Indian Affairs

THE two preceding chapters have dealt with intercolonial rivalries over lands and boundaries lying east of the Appalachian mountain barrier. The conflicts that resulted arose out of confusions in interpreting charter rights, out of the lack of a land policy or consistent land system, and out of the land hunger of colonial settlers and land speculators. Speculation in land was practiced by government officials both in England and in the colonial service—as well as by colonial men of wealth and enterprising aspirants to such position—some eager to supplement their meagre official earnings, some motivated by avarice, some by expediency or opportunism, some by foresight and wisdom, but all seeking a common goal in a period when land was the greatest source of prestige, wealth, and power.

The vast area stretching westward beyond the Appalachians to the great Mississippi River had beckoned to these speculators—as it had also to pioneer settlers and merchants and traders eager to exploit the Indian trade—even before the Great War for the Empire.[1] But once that conflict had been successfully concluded with

[1] The problem of controlling trans-Appalachian expansion was the subject of deliberation at the Albany Congress of 1754; see in this connection especially Thomas Hutchinson's "Representation on the Present State of the Colonies," which proposed many of the ideas subsequently incorporated in the establishment of the Indian superintendencies and the Proclamation Line of 1763, as discussed in Chap. 4, Volume V, of this series, especially pp. 132–3. For the early plans for exploiting the lands west of the Appalachians see *Scheme for the Settlement of a New Colony to the Westward of Pennsylvania* (Philadelphia, 1755,) which embodied the ideas

the Peace of Paris of 1763, and the threat of French rivalry thereby removed, the prospects of western expansion presented immediate problems to the British government, already faced with the task of consolidating and bringing under control the new acquisitions of Canada and the French trading posts in the Great Lakes region.[2] Volume IX of this series has emphasized the setting up of the Proclamation Line of 1763 as a measure for protecting the Indians, preserving their hunting grounds, and ensuring them just and fair dealings. It was but a temporary expediency in the face of the restless surge toward the west by those who had staked claims there in the 1740's and 1750's, by army veterans with awards of land patents for their services, by those who had gained in affluence during the war, by people from over-populated areas, and, finally, by that lawless element of the population ready to ignore the Crown restrictions—the squatters and "long hunters." To construct a permanent plan for the management of Indian affairs that could permit westward expansion involved enormous complexities. For it meant that the government in London had to reconcile its policies for preserving certain lands to the Indians with those for opening up for white settlement, through formal treaty and purchase, such lands as the natives were disposed to sell, and all the while preserving regulations for a system of open trade. How difficult it was to implement the basic policies with adequate regulations will be considered in this chapter, while the added problems raised by the activities of land speculators and land company promoters and their lobbyists in London will be reserved for the chapter to follow, although these aspects of the western movement cannot, in fact, be divorced from each other. It must also be borne in mind that trans-Appalachian development should not be examined without reference to the evolving crisis in the relations of the seaboard colonies with the mother country during the 1760's and 1770's,

---

of Samuel Hazard, presumably based on conversations with Franklin, according to L. C. Wroth: *An American Bookshelf, 1755* (Philadelphia, 1934), Chap. 2, especially pp. 56–8. For Thomas Pownall's solutions of 1754 and 1755 to the frontier problem, based upon Archibald Kennedy's *The Importance of Gaining and Preserving the Friendship of the Indians to the British Interest, Considered* (New York, 1751), as was that of Benjamin Franklin of 1756—all of them advocating the centralization of Indian affairs under a superintendent, the regulation of trade with the Indians, and the setting up of "border colonies" as part of a defence system—see J. A. Schutz: *Thomas Pownall: British Defender of American Liberty . . .* (Glendale, Calif., 1951), pp. 38–50.

[2] For the peace treaty of 1763 see the final chapter of Volume VIII of this series. The new acquisitions also included, of course, Spanish Florida and the ceded islands in the West Indies, as is discussed in Volume IX of this series, Chaps. 8–11.

which was producing new colonial attitudes toward parliamentary control of American domestic affairs. Further, the attempts of the British government to formulate sound policies for the new West were complicated not only by the factors of distance and time, which had great bearing on securing clear information upon which to base decisions, but also by the variety of the reports and recommendations facing it on this subject, along with a multitude of other problems involving the far-flung Empire—problems which pressed upon those responsible for making the decisions, and led to additional delays.

Before turning to trans-Appalachian developments after 1763—and more particularly after the conclusion of the great Indian uprising of that year in the Great Lakes and Ohio Valley areas, which was not terminated until toward the close of 1764[3]—we should consider the steps taken to extend British authority into the Illinois country.[4] This was the only important New World area settled by an alien European people that had been ceded to Great Britain but had not been formally taken over by the end of 1763.[5]

Isolated from all other European settlements in North America and hundreds of miles from Pittsburgh, the closest British-American community, the Illinois area could be easily approached only by way of the Ohio River or the Mississippi. During the Indian war the logical access had been by way of the Mississippi. This was also the avenue taken in 1764 when an effort was made early in that year by General Thomas Gage, the Commander-in-Chief of the British Forces in North America, to send a military detachment up the Mississippi River under Major Arthur Loftus. The effort failed due to the hostility of the southern Indian tribes living along the course of the river.[6] However, going overland by way of Choctaw and Chickasaw lands, Lieutenant John Ross and a small party—which included Indian trader Hugh Crawford—crossed what is now Kentucky and reached the lower course of the Ohio. Thence they proceeded down-river to its mouth and, moving up the Mississippi, at length attained Fort Chartres in the spring of 1765. Although the

[3] See, in this series, Volume IX, Chap. 5, "The Great Indian Uprising, 1763."

[4] For an account of the Illinois country in the 1750's see Chap. 5, "The French New World Granary," in Volume IV of this series.

[5] For the consolidation of Canada and East and West Florida into British provinces see, in this series Volume IX, Chaps. 7–9. For the problems of expansion and trade in the old Northwest see Volumes V and IX in this series and N. V. Russell: *The British Régime in Michigan and the Old Northwest, 1760–1796* (Northfield, Minn., 1939); see also Louise P. Kellogg: *The British Régime in Wisconsin and the Northwest* (Madison, 1935).

[6] Gage to Lord Halifax, New York, May 21, 1764, *Gage Correspondence*, I, 29–30.

French officer in charge apparently cooperated fully with Ross in his attempt to reconcile the Indians of the area to the change in sovereignty, the Indians' hatred of the British was so violent that Ross and his party were forced to leave. They returned down the river to New Orleans in April of that year.[7] But even before Lieutenant Ross reached the Illinois country, Sir William Johnson planned that a party should leave Fort Pitt under the leadership of his deputy for Indian affairs, the great Pennsylvania trader George Croghan, and Lieutenant Alexander Fraser of the regular army. They were to bring presents to the Indians of that area, to issue a proclamation to the *habitants,* and to take over the Illinois country formally from the French.

When Croghan was delayed at Fort Pitt, Fraser and a party went ahead, arriving at Fort Chartres shortly after Ross had left. Again, the hostility of the Indians toward the British was so great that, to save his life, Fraser was compelled, like Ross, to descend the Mississippi.[8] Croghan, who left Fort Pitt in May, was stopped short of the Illinois country when his party was attacked by Kickapoo and Mascouten Indians near the mouth of the Wabash River. Wounded and captured, he was carried to the French post at Vincennes and from there to Fort Ouiatenon (Ouiatanon) further up that river.

During some skilful negotiations with Pontiac, Croghan was assured by the great Indian leader that no further resistance to the British would be offered. He then made his way directly to Detroit to attend an important Indian conference, but not before he had sent news to Fort Pitt of his diplomatic victory and assurances that the way was at last open for taking over the Illinois country from the French.[9] The British occupation was accomplished in October 1765, when Captain Thomas Stirling (Sterling, Starling) reached

---

[7] St. Ange, French commander in the Illinois country, to Governor Dabbadie at New Orleans, April 7, 1765, with enclosures relating to the talks with the Indians signed by Ross and others, *The Critical Period, 1763–1765* (eds. C. W. Alvord and C. E. Carter, Illinois State Historical Library *Collections,* X, *British Series,* I, Springfield, Ill., 1915), pp. 468–81. There are two volumes in addition to the above in the *British Series* of the *Collections of the Illinois State Historical Library,* also edited by Alvord and Carter: *The New Régime 1765–1767* (*Collections,* XI, 1916) and *Trade and Politics, 1767–1769 (Collections,* XVI, 1921); all three volumes will be referred to subsequently as *Illinois Historical Collections* (X, XI, XVI).

[8] Fraser to Lieutenant Colonel John Campbell at Detroit, May 20, 1765, *ibid.,* X, 495–7.

[9] See Croghan's Official Journal from May 15 to September 25, 1765, *ibid.,* XI, 38–51. For Croghan's return to Detroit in 1767 once more pacify the Indians, to learn their intents, and to carry the papers recalling Major Robert Rogers from Michilimackinac, see *George Croghan's Journal of His Trip to Detroit in 1767* (ed. H. H. Peckham, Ann Arbor, 1939).

Fort Chartres by way of the Ohio.[10] Stirling was superseded in command early in December when Major Robert Farmar arrived from Mobile, West Florida, by way of the Mississippi.[11] However, the Indian tribes in that area were not fully pacified until the summer of 1766—when Croghan arrived laden with a good supply of presents for the Indians and accompanied by representatives of the Six Nations and the Delawares.[12] As for the some 1,400 *habitants,* to escape British control many of them deserted their homes in the villages and established themselves on the west bank of the Mississippi at St. Louis and other nearby places.[13] With the west bank of the Mississippi now a Spanish possession under a commandant determined to enforce restrictions on trade, many of those who had left were gradually induced to return to the Illinois country, where their activities would be subject to less interference, despite the British military control of the area.[14]

From 1765 to 1774 no official provision was made for the civil government of the Illinois country. What supervision existed came from the commander of the regular troops stationed at Fort Chartres,

---

[10] Stirling to Gage, October 18, 1765, *Illinois Historical Collections,* XI, 107–11.

[11] Farmar (Farmer, Fermar, Firmer) to Gage, December 16–19, 1765, *ibid.,* XI, 131–4.

[12] For Croghan's trip to the Illinois County in 1766 see the new exhaustive study by N. B. Wainwright: *George Croghan: Wilderness Diplomat* (Chapel Hill, N.C., 1959), 230–8; for an earlier biography of Croghan see A. T. Volwiler: *George Croghan and the Westward Movement, 1741–1782* (Cleveland, 1926).

[13] Dabbadie to the French minister, January 10, 1764, *Illinois Historical Collections,* X, 209. It should be pointed out that St. Louis, founded as a trading post by the French in 1764, soon became a great trading centre for Indians on both sides of the Mississippi. As many as twenty-five tribes, including such northern Indians as the Sacs, Foxes, Iowas, Sioux, and Ottowas, were drawn there to trade and receive presents, thus diverting the trade from the Illinois country. See *Spanish Régime in Missouri* (ed. Louis Houck, 2 vols., Chicago, 1909), I, 44–5; also by the same author: *A History of Missouri . . .* (3 vols., Chicago, 1908), I, 7–16. For the Spanish documents see *Spain in the Mississippi Valley, 1765–1794,* Pt. I (American Historical Association *Annual Report, 1945, II,* ed. Lawrence Kinnaird, Washington, 1949).

Captain Harry Gordon, a military engineer who was sent down the Ohio to the Illinois country by General Gage in 1766 at the same time as George Croghan and George Morgan, reported in his "Journal" that the French controlled the Indian trade on the upper Mississippi and that the British "Possession of the Illinois is only useful at present in one respect, it Shews the Indian Nations our Superiority over the French . . . This is dearly bought by the Expence it is to us, and the Inconvenience of Supporting it" ("Journal of Captain Harry Gordon," *Travels in the American Colonies* [ed. N. D. Mereness, New York, 1916], p. 476).

[14] With the departure of the French, the supplying of the British troops in the Illinois country loomed as a major problem for a period of time. Gage therefore proposed in the spring of 1766 that favourable terms should be made on land grants to settlers who would come down the Ohio to cultivate the soil. The grants were to be "held of the King on condition of Military Service" (Gage to Conway, March 28, 1766, *Gage Correspondence,* I, 85–9).

who assumed jurisdiction in the civil realm without authorization by his superiors. Before the British took over, all cases had been tried by two French officials, one the King's commissary and the other the *procureur du Roi,* with the right of appeal to the Governor's Council at New Orleans. But these officials had crossed the Mississippi to continue their functions, at least temporarily, in what was by that time Spanish territory. Therefore, to deal with the *habitants* who remained, Captain Stirling appointed a man of property, Jean Lagrange (La Grange) of Kaskaskia, giving him power to decide all disputes arising among them "According to the Laws and Customs of the Country," with liberty to appeal to the commandant.[15] Lagrange apparently knew little law, and although Stirling urged General Gage, his immediate superior, to see that qualified judges were sent to administer justice, this was not done. In fact, most cases between the *habitants* were settled by arbitration, it would appear, with each side selecting an arbitrator and the two so chosen selecting a third. When the three had reached a decision, based upon their knowledge of French law and custom, it was reported to the commandant and enforced by him.[16] This problem of civil disputes between individuals in the Illinois country was to become much more complicated with the appearance of British-American merchants on the scene.

In 1766 the Pennsylvania partnership firm of John Baynton, Samuel Wharton, and George Morgan, anticipating large profits, sent a series of bateau-convoys down the Ohio.[17] The boats left Pittsburgh loaded with goods for trade. George Morgan went along with one of the convoys.[18] By November he had gathered enough peltry to justify a trip down the Mississippi to meet a chartered vessel waiting to convey the cargo to New York.[19] The prospects for the firm seemed to be excellent. For a time it had virtually a monopoly of the trade in the Illinois country. But difficulties were to arise. Competition appeared, especially from the rival Pennsylvania partnership of Joseph Simon and the brothers Barnard and Michael

---

[15] Stirling to Gage, December 15, 1765, *Illinois Historical Collections*, XI, 124.

[16] C. W. Alvord: *The Illinois Country, 1673–1818* (*Centennial History of Illinois*, I, Springfield, Ill., 1920), p. 266.

[17] Baynton, Wharton, and Morgan to John Irwin, Philadelphia, September 21, 1766, *Illinois Historical Collections*, XI, 383–7.

[18] Morgan to his wife, June 29–July 8, 1766, *ibid.*, XI, 315–17; for Morgan's career see the fine biography by Max Savelle: *George Morgan, Colony Builder* (New York, 1932).

[19] Baynton, Wharton, and Morgan to William Franklin, December 10, 1766, *Illinois Historical Collections*, XI, 447–9, and Morgan's Journal, *ibid.*, XI, 438–47.

Gratz, with whom others were associated.[20] Profits gradually waned. By 1768 some sixty British-American traders were to be found in the Illinois country. However, the trade in furs and peltries was disappointing, as was that in farm produce from the French-speaking settlers. Further, those articles that could not be sold to the troops in garrison had, on account of their weight, to be shipped down the Mississippi to New Orleans, where furs commanded a higher price than in London. Yet, the cost of supporting this trade by means of the garrison at Fort Chartres was very expensive. It amounted to over £10,000 for the year ending September 1767, which General Gage called "monstrous."[21]

Although the Baynton-Wharton-Morgan firm survived a financial crisis in 1767, serious disputes now began to develop between Morgan and the commandant of Fort Chartres. The issues were temporarily settled when the command changed hands, but the problem of collecting debts from the *habitants* remained; for the arbitration system was not adequate to protect the interests of British creditors.[22] To meet the general demand for a proper court for civil cases, action was taken by the new commandant, Lieutenant Colonel John Wilkins, working closely in conjunction with Morgan and apparently sharing in the firm's profits. He created "a Civil Court of Judicatory . . . to Hear and Try in a Summary way all Causes of Debt and Property . . . and to give their Judgement thereon according to the Laws of England to the Best of their Judgement and understanding."[23] The judges—four of English speech and

[20] For an account of the leading competitors of Baynton, Wharton, and Morgan see *B. and M. Gratz, Merchants in Philadelphia, 1754–1798* (W. V. Byars ed., Jefferson City, Mo., 1916). In this connection see C. M. Thomas: "Successful and Unsuccessful Merchants in the Illinois Country," the Illinois State Historical Society *Journal*, XXX, 429–40.

[21] See Gage to Sir William Johnson, April 4, 1768, *Illinois Historical Collections*, XVI, 220–1. Max Savelle (*op. cit.*, Chaps. 2 and 3) throws a flood of light on this subject, especially on the difficulties faced by George Morgan in carrying out the grandiose plans of his firm in the Illinois country.

[22] Although Baynton, Wharton, and Morgan got into financial difficulties by 1767, they continued to operate under trustees until their partnership ended in 1776. Addressing Lauchlin Macleane, secretary to the Earl of Shelburne, on October 9, 1767, the firm wrote: "Our Speculation has been attended with the most favorable Circumstances to his Majesty's Interest, As we are the only English Merchants Who have ventured to forward British Merchandize to the Illinois Country . . ." (P.R.O., C.O. 323:24, T. 46; see also *Illinois Historical Collections*, XVI, 84). The activities of the firm are embodied in the Baynton, Wharton, and Morgan Papers in the Pennsylvania Public Record Office at Harrisburg. These show that the company did not confine its interests to the Illinois country but extended them to the region of the upper Allegheny River and beyond. However, as indicated by Max Savelle (*op. cit.*, p. 75), their Illinois venture finally failed.

[23] See C. W. Alvord: *The Illinois Country*, p. 267; see also C. E. Carter: *Great Britain and the Illinois Country, 1763–1774* (Washington, 1910), p. 66.

two of French, with Morgan as presiding judge—were commissioned by Wilkins on his own authority. They acted without a jury. Early in 1770 their jurisdiction was extended to criminal cases, with the membership of the court now divided equally between French-speaking and English-speaking judges. Since the court was merely the creation of the commandant and existed therefore only at his will, it could not survive his displeasure. This became evident during the spring of 1770 when an open break occurred between Wilkins and Morgan. By June of that year the court of judicature had apparently ceased to function.[24]

The civilian community was now left without a system of justice other than that of the military arm. Nor was any better provision made for the spiritual needs of the Roman Catholic *habitants.* No priest was settled among them during this period and only twice a year did an elderly but devoted Spanish priest, Father Sebastian Meurin, cross the Mississippi to perform his sacred offices. It was not until 1774, with the passing of the Quebec Act, that Parliament provided at last for the civil administration of law, and for the protection and encouragement of the Roman Catholic religion. Only then was the military relegated to its proper function in the Illinois country. Finally, in accordance with the plan of the government of Great Britain to reduce the expenses involved in maintaining a large number of posts in the interior of North America, a decision was reached late in 1771 to destroy Fort Chartres, already heavily undermined by the waters of the Mississippi, and to withdraw most of the troops stationed there. Seven companies of the 18th Regiment were withdrawn; the remainder, some fifty men, were then removed to a picketed fort at Kaskaskia.[25]

But other aspects of trans-Appalachian developments were of

[24] It would appear that in the controversies with Lieutenant Colonel Wilkins, Morgan was supported by most of the inhabitants and that he maintained good relations with the Indians. Wilkins, however, became convinced that Morgan had been involved in "very scandalous and iniquitous Proceedings," and in the spring of 1771 wrote a series of letters to Gage which the latter described as "full of Dirt, Invectives, Law and Indecencies, many of them . . . dressed up with great Art and Plausability to prove Assertions." In writing to Hillsborough about this episode, Gage was impelled to voice his "Strong Disapprobation of some parts of the Commanding Officers Conduct," and to note the lack of any judicial power in the Illinois country "to try and determine." See Gage to Hillsborough, August 6, 1771, *Gage Correspondence*, I, 306.

[25] Lieutenant Colonel Wilkins by the spring of 1771 had reached the conclusion that Fort Chartres served no useful purpose, nor did a large garrison in the Illinois country. He therefore recommended the destruction of the fort. See Wilkins to Gage, May 1, 12, 13, 1771, Gage Papers, Clements Library; see also Gage to Hillsborough, August 6, 1771, and September 2, 1772, and Hillsborough to Gage, December 4, 1771, *Gage Correspondence*, I, 306 and 332; II, 137.

equal, if not of greater importance than the Illinois country, for they concerned matters more nearly related to the desires and ambitions of most British-Americans in 1763.

In Volume IX of this series the Cherokee War waged from 1759 to 1761 and the even more formidable Indian uprising in the Ohio and Great Lakes region that took place from 1763 to 1764, were examined in some detail.[26] Perhaps the chief importance of these Indian wars was that they had put a temporary check upon western expansion by British colonials ready to press into the great basin of the Mississippi from the more settled areas at the conclusion of the Great War for the Empire.

With peace re-established throughout the West by the end of 1764, the lure of trans-Appalachian lands led to the movement of thousands of people into the region beyond the bounds laid down for white settlement by the Proclamation Line of 1763.[27] Writing of the fertile area lying about the upper Ohio and its tributaries, Governor Fauquier of Virginia affirmed to the Earl of Shelburne in 1766 that those lands were "so very good" that people would run all risks to get possession of them.[28] Moreover, to the problem of the unlawful entry of new settlers into the region west of the Line was added the dilemma presented by the return there of hundreds of pioneers seeking to regain their former holdings. Before the Proclamation Line had set a temporary barrier to western settlement, and even before the outbreak of the two Indian wars, these frontier people had established perfectly valid claims under Virginia grants and had already begun to make improvements on the land. They took the position that as British subjects their individual rights were not, and could not be, adversely affected by any subsequent measure taken by the government. At the same time, in view of the precariousness of the situation, they refused to pay quit-rents until they should be assured of protection so as to enjoy their property.[29] Joined with them in opposition to the British regulations creating the vast trans-Appalachian Indian reserve, were those who had no proper equity and were virtually nothing more than squatters. Ignoring the prohibition against encroachment upon the Indian territory, these newcomers proceeded to appropriate land at favoured spots,

[26] See Volume IX of this series, Chaps. 4 and 5.

[27] For a consideration of the Proclamation Line of 1763 see *ibid.*, Chap. 3.

[28] Fauquier to Shelburne, December 18, 1766, C.O. 5:1345, p. 339.

[29] Fauquier to Shelburne, November 18, 1766, C.O. 5:1345, pp. 313–16; see also his letter of December 18 to Shelburne of the same year in which he stressed "the anxiety of those settled under Authority to the west of the Line," C.O. 5:1345, pp. 338–40.

particularly in the neighbourhood of Redstone Creek and the Cheat River, which flow into the Monongahela from the west and east respectively. Not only did these early "long hunters" erect rude cabins but they also proceeded to destroy the game in that region. This wanton action led the Indians to complain bitterly to the commanding officer at Fort Pitt against such infringement of their hunting grounds.

Acting on orders from General Gage, Captain James Murray, temporarily in charge at Pittsburgh, in June 1766 sent Alexander MacKay (McKee) with a small detachment of regulars to Redstone Creek. Upon arrival, MacKay, acting according to instructions, issued a summons to the new settlers. Having censured them for "the Lawless and Licentious manner" in which they had behaved "in violation of the Proclamation," he threatened that, should they not leave, the Commander-in-Chief would order an armed force to drive them out of the country west of the mountains.[30] Nor could these squatters look to the government of Virginia for support. For Fauquier, like General Gage, was bound by royal instructions to enforce the prohibition against unauthorized settlement beyond the Appalachians.[31]

Although the Virginia Governor had already released two earlier proclamations against this movement, he proceeded on July 31, 1766, to issue a third, calling upon all settlers in forbidden areas to evacuate their lands immediately and warning them that, unless they did, they would receive no protection or mercy from the vengeance of the Indians.[32] However, in writing to Governor John Penn—who was concerned that many Virginians were moving in upon lands

---

[30] For the "Summons to the illegal settlers" June 22, 1766, see C.O. 5:1345, pp. 343–4; see also Fauquier to the Board of Trade, July 26, 1766, C.O. 5:1331, pp. 305–6.

[31] Fauquier's particular instruction on the above point was dated October 24, 1765. For this instruction see *Royal Instructions to British Colonial Governors, 1670–1776* (ed. L. W. Labaree, 2 vols., New York and London, 1935), II, 473–4; see also Fauquier to Governor John Penn, December 11, 1766, Gunther Manuscripts, Chicago Historical Society, which is printed in *Pennsylvania Colonial Records*, IX, 349–50. On September 13, 1766, Shelburne sent a circular letter to the Governors in North America calling upon them to deal with the violence of the white intruders in the Indian country beyond the Proclamation Line and also commanding them in the name of the King to support the Commander-in-Chief in enforcing obedience to this proclamation. For a copy of this letter see *Documents relating to the Colonial History of the State of New Jersey, New Jersey Archives*, 1st ser., IX, 569–70; a letter of similar import, written that same day, went to General Gage, Sir William Johnson, and John Stuart. See Shelburne Papers, 53:97, pp. 87–8, 281–4, 287–9; see also *Gage Correspondence*, II, 44–6; and *The Papers of Sir William Johnson* (eds. James Sullivan, A. C. Flick, and M. W. Hamilton, 13 vols. +, Albany, 1921–62 +), V, 374–5, cited subsequently as *Sir William Johnson Papers.*

[32] For this proclamation see C.O. 5:1331, p. 337.

which, as was ultimately established, belonged to the proprietary of Pennsylvania—Fauquier was obliged to admit: "I find . . . no Regard is paid to Proclamations, and I can expect no great good from them."[33] Some of the Redstone people, meanwhile, had found themselves in so uncomfortable and exposed a position that they temporarily left the country; but the Cheat River settlers, farther to the east, felt more secure and doggedly remained.[34]

Relations between the trans-Appalachian settlers and the Indians remained tense. As Governor Fauquier of Virginia wrote to Shelburne on May 24, 1767 (when news reached him that one Ryan had killed a chief warrior of the Delawares), "the Inhabitants of the Frontier are the Persons who secrete and screen these Miscreants . . . they wish for nothing so much as an Indian war and have used every Method in their Power to promote it."[35] That same year Gage, in his letter of August 20 to the Earl, also stressed the disorders in the Indian country. Pointing out the bad effect of the large number of licensed traders from the different provinces, he referred to the request made by John Stuart, Superintendent of the Southern District, that he (as Commander-in-Chief of the British Forces in North America) should urge the Governors to conform to the system for granting licences provided in the Proclamation of 1763.[36] In this connection the General indicated the difficulties of enforcing such regulations in the face of the attitude, for example, of Virginia, the Assembly of which, according to Fauquier, "*Jealous of the Liberty of the Subject, have Appointed Commissioners to manage the Indian Trade, and will not Suffer the Traders to be Subjected to any [other] Regulations, or Restrictions whatsoever*"—

---

[33] Fauquier to Penn, December 11, 1766, *Pennsylvania Colonial Records*, IX, 349–50. See also Fauquier to Shelburne, December 18, 1766, Shelburne Papers, 52:23–5, and C.O. 5:1345, pp. 338–40.

[34] Gage to Shelburne, April 29 and June 13, 1767, *Gage Correspondence*, I, 137–9, 142.

[35] Shelburne Papers, 52:62–3. Gage, writing to the Board of Trade on October 10, 1767, confirmed the Governor's views of the impossibility of doing justice to the Indians. "Since the Peace was concluded with them in 1764, Many of their People have been killed and wounded, and . . . no Satisfaction has been given them. . . . The People of Virginia are those who have been chiefly concerned in the Outrages. . . . Some were Apprehended & lodged in Gaol, but the Country People rose, forced the Jail & rescued them. And it is a Fact, that all the People of the Frontiers from Pennsylvania to Virginia inclusive, openly avow, that they will never find a Man guilty of Murder, for killing an Indian. These People must of Course be impannelled upon every Jury, the Law directing the Tryal to be held where the Fact is committed" (C.O. 323:24, T. 35). See also Gage to Shelburne on the same date, *Gage Correspondence*, I, 151–4.

[36] See Stuart to Shelburne, April 11, 1767, Shelburne Papers, 51:163–4.

an attitude which Gage called "Most extraordinary."[37] In line with this view, Sir William Johnson likewise pointed out to Lord Shelburne that "the Indians have no reason to expect Redress here, on the score of Lands, abuses in Trade, or Insults, Murders and Robberies on the Frontiers, which are their principal Grievances."[38]

Much of the violence on the frontiers was due largely to the presence of lawless men in that area, but the many peaceable people also established there now pressed their claims to rights acquired prior to the disturbances, in view of the restrictions created by the Proclamation of 1763.[39] To the south of the Cheat on the upper waters of the Holston River and close to the Cherokee country, scattered settlements had been made before 1755 upon lands previously applied for to the Council of Virginia. But it was not until about 1770 that people again moved into this area—well to the west of the Proclamation Line. A settlement made in the area of Chiswell's Mine on the upper New River, before the Indian wars had engulfed the region, was restored even sooner.[40] Moreover, as early as 1768, families from the central part of North Carolina as well as from Virginia began to migrate into what is now the northeastern part of Tennessee, settling in the valley of the Watauga River.[41] By 1772 it was estimated that there were some three hun-

[37] Shelburne Papers, 51:115–17, and *Gage Correspondence*, I, 144–5. The italicized portion of Gage's letter conforms to underlining in the original. In view of the fact that Fauquier seemed to be ignorant of the Proclamation of 1763, Stuart sent him abstracts from it, pointing out that "a Provincial Law can not possibly operate beyond the Limits of the Province where it is enacted, or reach Indian Countrys" (*ibid.*). See also Stuart to Shelburne, July 28, 1767, in which Stuart refers to Fauquier's letter to him, dated May 6, stating that he could not subject Virginia traders to any regulations or lay down any boundary line between Virginia and the Indian country without His Majesty's orders for that purpose, as he knew nothing "of any Proclamation or Instruction on that head" (Shelburne Papers, 51:169–73).

[38] For the address to the King by the Virginia Burgesses, December 13, 1766, urging the rescinding of the Proclamation of 1763 in order to permit Virginia settlers to retain their holdings in the West and to continue to promote settlements there, see *Journal of the House of Burgesses, 1766–1769*, p. 69; for the action on this address taken in June 1768 by the Board of Trade at the request of the Privy Council, ordering the strict enforcement of the Proclamation provisions until a new boundary with the Indians had been established, see C.O. 5:1346, pp. 25–36; see also Board of Trade *Journal, 1768–1775*, pp. 28–32.

[39] Johnson to Shelburne, August 14, 1767, C.O. 323:24, T. 46; *New York Colonial Documents*, VII, 946–8.

[40] T. P. Abernethy: *Western Lands and the American Revolution* (New York, 1937), p. 79.

[41] *Colonial Records of North Carolina* (ed. W. L. Saunders, 10 vols., Raleigh, 1886–90), VII, 652, cited hereafter as *North Carolina Colonial Records*; for a treatment of early settlements in what is now Tennessee see T. P. Abernethy: *From Frontier to Plantation in Tennessee* (Chapel Hill, N.C., 1932), pp. 1–18, and especially S. C. Williams: *Dawn of Tennessee Valley and Tennessee History* (Johnson City, Tenn., 1937).

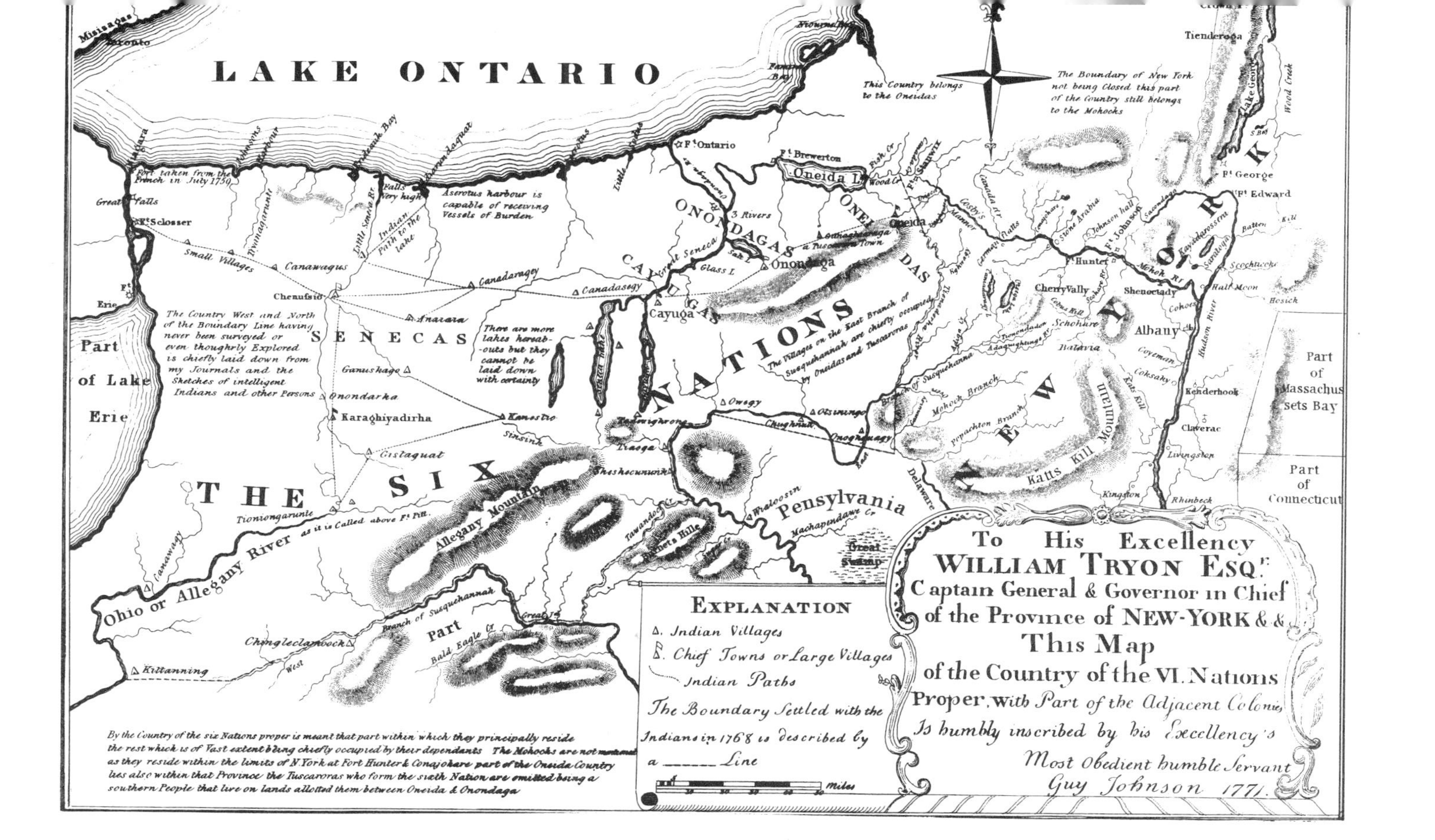

Map of the country of the Six Nations, inscribed by Guy Johnson to Governor William Tryon, 1771.

(From *Documentary History of the State of New York*, Vol. IV)

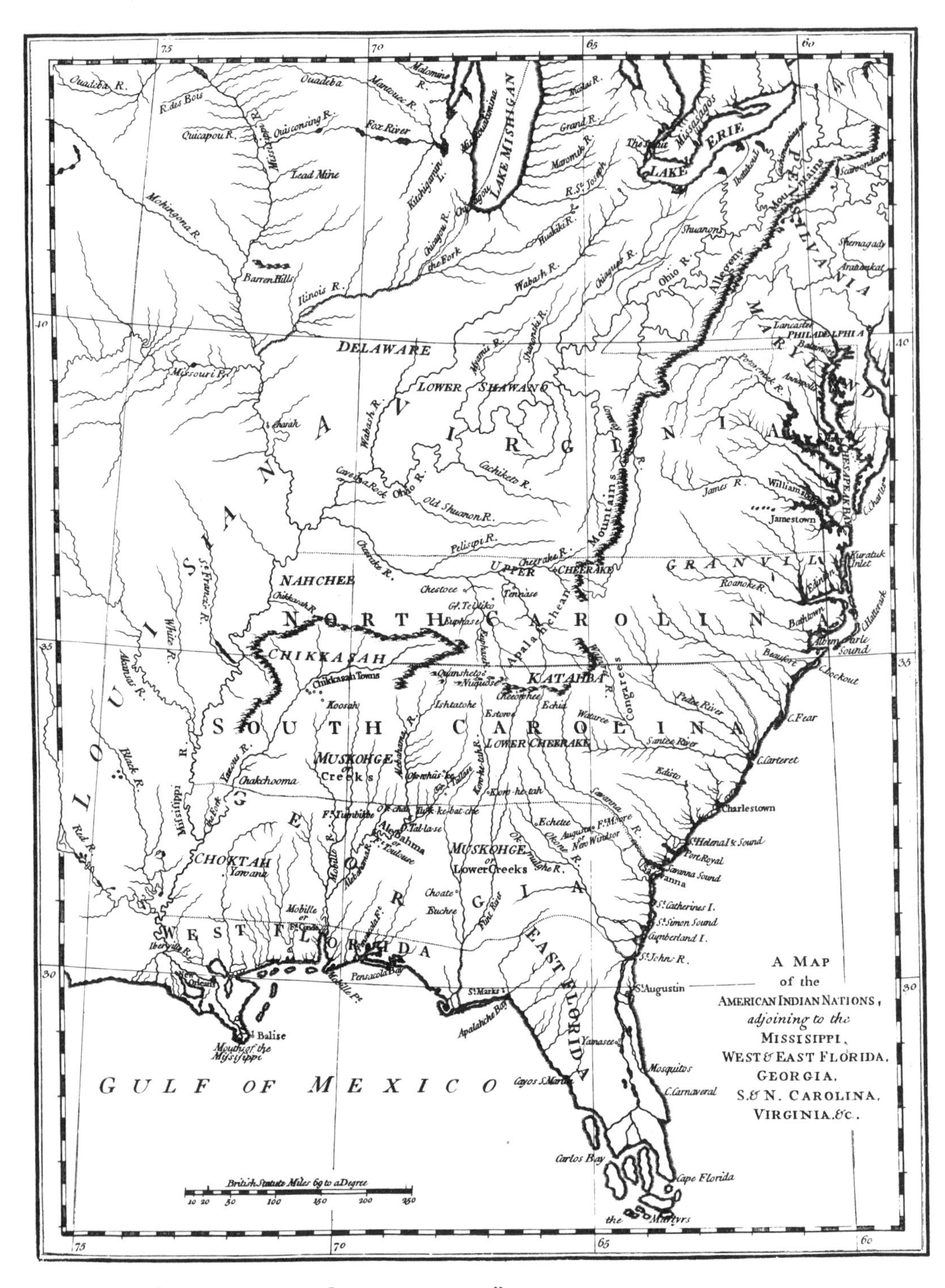

"A Map of the American Indian Nations . . ."

(From James Adair's *History of the American Indians*, 1775, Henry E. Huntington Library)

dred men capable of bearing arms in the Watauga settlement and by 1776 the number of riflemen living there was placed at between seven and eight hundred.[42] With this area as a nucleus, a movement was launched in 1774 to colonize what is now Kentucky, as will be stressed in the chapter to follow. It is therefore clear that by the outbreak of the American War for Independence large numbers of people were established without legal authorization within the vast region south of the Ohio that had been reserved to the Indians.

As to the strength of the Indian tribes of the Great Lakes region and the eastern Mississippi basin, Colonel Bouquet in 1764 reported that twenty-eight tribes listed were supposed to have somewhat over 23,000 members; while in 1768 the numbers were placed by Captain Hutchins at some 25,000.[43] These figures, however, must have included only warriors, if Sir William Johnson's report of 1773 has any validity; for he estimated that in the Northern Indian Department alone there were over 25,000 warriors or possibly 130,000 Indians in all living east of the Mississippi[44]—a figure far beyond that presented by any other contemporary, although not to be lightly dismissed on that account. In 1776 it was also reported that there were 15,000 warriors among the Southern tribes,[45] or about 70,000 Indians in all—assuming that the same proportion of fighters to non-combatants held for the Southern Indians as for the Northern Indians. This would have made a total of almost 200,000 natives embraced within the Northern and Southern Indian departments or districts. If one assumes that an actual census might have reduced the figures by one-half or even one-fourth, the potential strength and importance of the trans-Appalachian Indian population would still have been very impressive.

The Indian policy of the British government from 1763 to 1775 was based upon the idea that, on the one hand, there was to be no extirpation of the aborigines, nor, on the other, were they to be systematically Europeanized. Rather, they were to be permitted to

---

[42] Massachusetts Historical Society *Collections*, 2nd ser., VII, 58 and 60.

[43] E. B. Greene and Virginia D. Harrington: *American Population before the Federal Census of 1790* (New York, 1932), pp. 197–9.

[44] Johnson to Governor Tryon, October 22, 1773, *New York Colonial Documents*, VIII, 459. It may be noted that such groups as the Sioux of the Forest, living to the east of the upper waters of the Mississippi, had had little contact as yet with either the French or the English.

[45] Greene and Harrington: *op. cit.*, p. 206. John Stuart, some ten years earlier, had estimated the warriors in his Indian district, including some tribes living within the territory ceded by France to Spain and two other tribes more closely identified with the Illinois country, at about 14,000. See the "Observations of Superintendent John Stuart . . ." (ed. C. E. Carter), *American Historical Review*, XX, 815–31, especially pp. 825–6.

live their lives, under proper protection and controls, much after the manner of their forefathers. The only exception was that efforts were to be made to bring Christianity to them and wars among them were to be discouraged. It was anticipated that by following orderly procedures Indian lands no longer needed as hunting grounds would from time to time be purchased by the Crown in order to permit white settlement upon them under peaceful conditions; accordingly, sales were not to be forced or carried out with trickery.

In an earlier attempt to safeguard the interests of the western tribes, the office of Indian Superintendent had been created at the recommendation of the Board of Trade, then headed by Lord Halifax. Its mission was to do away with the confusion that had previously attended the competitive activities of colonial governments in their contacts with the red men, and to promote harmonious relations between them and the English settled in North America. Two departments or districts, one for the Northern Indians and the other for the Southern Indians, thus came into existence between 1755 and 1756. William Johnson,[46] not as yet a baronet, was appointed Superintendent of Indian Affairs for the Northern Department—a post he held for the rest of his life—and Edmund [Edmond] Atkin, for the Southern.[47] Atkin passed away in the fall of 1761 and John Stuart was selected early the following year to take his place.[48] The duties of the Superintendents included making treaties, purchasing lands, and setting up boundary lines between the Indian country and that of the white men, in addition to other activities encompassing the authority of the Crown.[49] However, not until 1765—despite the Halifax plan of a decade earlier—were the Superintendents given control of the Indian trade (in accordance with the terms of the Proclamation of 1763); until then it had remained in the hands of the Governors, who had continued to issue licences to those seeking to barter with the Indians. As a result, men had

[46] See *New York Colonial Documents*, VI, 957–8, 961; see also W. L. Stone, Jr.: *The Life and Times of Sir William Johnson, Bart.* (2 vols., Albany, 1865), Arthur Pound and R. E. Day: *Johnson of the Mohawks* (New York, 1930), and, most recently, the colourful *Mohawk Baronet: Sir William Johnson of New York* by J. T. Flexner (New York, 1959). See also, for the cultural level of Sir William's life at Johnson Hall, M. W. Hamilton: *New-York Historical Society Quarterly*, XL, 209–51.

[47] See *Indians of the Southern Colonial Frontier: The Edmond Atkin Report and Plan of 1755* (ed. W. R. Jacobs, Columbia, S.C., 1954) and J. R. Alden: *John Stuart and the Southern Colonial Frontier . . . 1754–1775* (University of Michigan *Publications*, History and Political Science, XV, Ann Arbor and London, 1944), pp. 41–2 and 69–70, referred to hereafter as *Southern Colonial Frontier*; see also by the same author: "The Albany Congress and the Creation of the Indian Superintendencies," *Mississippi Valley Historical Review*, XXVII, 193–210.

[48] J. R. Alden: *Southern Colonial Frontier*, pp. 135–6.

[49] *New York Colonial Documents*, VII, 637; for Stuart's activities before 1766 see also Volume IX of this series, pp. 51 *et seq.*

crowded into the Indian country with goods to exchange for skins and furs, and many of them had engaged in such sharp practices that the resentment of the natives and the indignation of the Superintendents had ultimately been aroused.[50]

The suitable regulation of the Indian trade was obviously a problem that had to be dealt with at the highest level. The ideas conceived by Lord Halifax when he was President of the Board of Trade in the 1750's had not been fully implemented; however, in 1763, as Secretary of State for the Southern Department, he again had the problem very much at heart, and had, together with Secretary of State Lord Egremont, helped to effect the Proclamation of 1763. But the Proclamation of 1763 failed to produce adequate regulations for the Indian trade, among its other defects as a temporary measure. Thus, in reply to the request of Indian Superintendent Stuart for instructions on the future management of Indian Trade, Halifax drew up a brief outline of a plan for its regulation,[51] which was later submitted to the Board of Trade, now under the presidency of the Earl of Hillsborough. As a result of this, as well as certain reactions to the Proclamation of 1763, the Board—taking into consideration the reports and recommendations previously submitted to the Lords Commissioners at their request[52]—prepared an elaborate plan "for the future management and direction of Indian affairs." In July 1764 the plan was forwarded to North America for the consideration not only of the two Superintendents but also of the Governors of those provinces directly concerned with western Indian relations.[53]

The Board of Trade plan comprehended, among its forty-three clauses, the following features: (1) the repeal of all colonial laws

[50] General Gage to the Earl of Shelburne, August 20, 1767, Shelburne Papers, 51:115–17.

[51] Halifax to General Amherst, October 19, 1763, *Gage Correspondence*, II, 5. By January 14, 1764, Halifax was writing to Gage (*ibid.*, II, 10) that when the royal proclamation should have reached the Indians it would not only quiet their concerns over encroachments on their lands but assure them of a fair and well-regulated trade.

[52] See Board of Trade to Johnson, August 5, 1763, and his reply of November 13 [18], 1763, *New York Colonial Documents*, VII, 535–6 and 575–81; for Stuart to the Board of Trade, March 9, 1764, see P.R.O., C.O. 323:17. See also Board of Trade *Journal, 1764–1767*, pp. 65 and 67.

[53] *Ibid.*, pp. 70–1, 98. For detailed analyses of the plan of 1764, which reflected the ideas of both Johnson and Stuart, see J. R. Alden: *Southern Colonial Frontier*, Chap. 14, and J. M. Sosin: *Whitehall and the Wilderness: The Middle West in British Colonial Policy, 1760–1775* (Lincoln, Nebr., 1961), Chap. 3. Johnson's recommendations were put before the Board in person by his deputy, George Croghan, who also presented his own supporting views; see *ibid.*, pp. 73–5, and J. R. Alden: *op. cit.*, p. 244. It may be noted that Alden confirms the view of V. W. Crane (*The Southern Frontier, 1670–1732* [Durham, N.C., 1929], p. 137) that the influence of Stuart's recommendations have sometimes been underestimated.

relating to the Indian trade; (2) the concentration of this trade in the Indian towns of the Southern Department and, within the Northern Department, at posts or other specified points, so that all of it would be under direct supervision of the deputies or commissaries or interpreters appointed by each of the Superintendents and empowered to act without interference from either the military or the civil authorities in America; (3) the support of good order, by giving the Superintendents and their commissaries—the latter residing within the particular tribes—the powers of justices of the peace, also by bestowing on certain chosen Indians appointments as war captains and other distinctions, and by making provision for the permanent residence of a blacksmith within each tribe and of a chosen chief at the headquarters of each commissary; (4) the issuance by the colonial Governors of licences to traders for a one-year period with specification on the licence of the fort or "truckhouse" where each trader should maintain his dealings; (5) the supervision of all trade under the general authority of the commissaries; (6) provision in detail for protecting the rights of the Indians to their lands.[54]

The ambitious Board of Trade plan, with its many excellent features, was strongly approved by Johnson and Stuart among others,[55]

[54] "Plan for the future Management of Indian Affairs," *New York Colonial Documents*, VII, 637–41.

[55] Board of Trade *Journal, 1764–1767*, p. 271; and J. R. Alden: *Southern Colonial Frontier*, pp. 245–6. For Johnson's detailed observations on the plan see Johnson to the Board of Trade, October 8, 1764, *New York Colonial Documents*, VII, 657–66; for the "Observations of Superintendent John Stuart . . ." see *American Historical Review*, XX, 815–31; for correspondence of the Governors and others on this subject see P.R.O., C.O. 323:19 and 20.

Sir Jeffrey Amherst at the request of the Earl of Shelburne made a report on the plan in the fall of 1766 under title "Answers & Remarks to A Plan for the future Management of Indian Affairs." Although approving most of the Board of Trade proposals, he was critical of the effect upon the Indians of requiring the repeal of all colonial laws regulating Indian affairs; he also questioned the soundness of excluding the Commander-in-Chief of the British Forces and the colonial Governors from all public affairs relating to the Indians; and, finally, he was strongly opposed to the idea of giving favoured Indians the proposed military distinctions. Rather, he recommended, "let the Indians have every help that is necessary for their hunting, a fair Trade and Protection, and treat them with tenderness; [for] to instil in their minds their Consequence as Warriours, may be productive of much Evil & can tend to no Good" (Amherst to Shelburne, October 6, 1766, Amherst Papers, 14:2–6, Canadian Archives transcripts).

Benjamin Franklin was also generally favourable to the plan, although he doubted the wisdom of repealing the colonial laws regulating the trade without careful consideration; he also thought the districts were too large, especially the Northern Department, and questioned the desirability of trying criminals in the Indian country and the attempt to set schedules of prices without regard to the quality of goods. See *Writings of Benjamin Franklin* (ed. A. H. Smyth, 10 vols., New York, 1905–7), IV, 467–71.

but it was destined never to go into effect as a whole. To have implemented it, or any other comprehensive unified plan, would have entailed vast expenses, and by 1765 the Ministry had become deeply concerned with the great cost of supporting and governing the American possessions.[56] The growing cost of maintaining the Indian departments[57]—even without any such elaboration as that proposed by the Board of Trade—was of especial concern to the Earl of Shelburne, who in 1766, as Secretary of State for the Southern Department, was seeking to bring the departments under better control. To him the failure of the plan of 1764 in West Florida—the only colony where an attempt had been made to implement it fully—was evidence of its weakness. The only feasible means of financing any plan of Indian relations, he thought, was by "an American Fund to defray American Expenses, in part, or in the whole." Such a fund, he believed, could be secured "by taking proper care of the [colonial] Quit Rents and by turning the Grants of Lands to real benefit. . . ."[58] This proposal, however, was never to be implemented, nor was it a practical one, since the lands in a number of colonies were not subject to the control of the Crown and the system would therefore have placed an unfair burden on a few of the royal colonies. Nevertheless, Shelburne determined to bring about a greater degree of coordination between the Indian departments and the office of Commander-in-Chief of the British Forces in North America. Writing to Johnson and Stuart in December of that year, he directed that their "regular & fixed correspondence . . . be with the Commander in chief of His Majesty's Forces," and then declared that

> "The System of Indian Affairs as managed by Superintendents must ultimately be under his [the Commander-in-Chief's] Direction. . . . It is therefore Necessary that the Superintendents should take the Orders of the Commander in Chief on all material Occasions . . . and as he will be very particularly instructed by Administration he must be looked upon as a proper Medium of material intelligence either to or from England or the Colonies. . . ."[59]

[56] The estimates of total ordinary charges for administering the colonies in that year amounted to the high sum of £463,313, with extraordinaries bringing the total to £558,313; see "Annual Expense of America," Shelburne Papers, 57:255–8.

[57] For a list of those employed in 1766 by the Northern Department of Indian Affairs, including deputies, commissaries, interpreters, and blacksmiths, at a total cost of £3,299, see *Gage Correspondence*, II, 385–6 .

[58] Shelburne to Gage, December 11, 1766, *ibid.*, II, 47–51.

[59] Shelburne to Johnson, December 11, 1766, *Sir William Johnson Papers*, V, 447–9, and Shelburne to Stuart, December 11, 1766, *Illinois Historical Collections*, XI, 451–4. There are slight variations in the two letters in phraseology. The styling of the Johnson letter has been followed.

While the significance of these instructions is a matter of dispute among scholars, it appears that the Indian Superintendents continued to have direct access to the Ministry.[60]

In an effort to introduce more regularity and good order into the Indian trade, and protect the natives from the sharp practices employed by the white traders from which so many evils had arisen, Sir William Johnson early in 1767 issued certain regulations for his Northern Department of Indian Affairs. These came "in consequence of his Majesty's Orders signified to him by the Secretary of State." By these the trade was to be strictly confined to the posts where one of his commissaries resided—except in the case of "the peculiar Situation of the Indians North of Lake Huron," which might justify granting permission for the traders from Michilimackinac to go among these tribes. Every trader was expected to have a pass from the Governor of his colony and to enter into a bond to observe all regulations. For example, he was not to trade along the way to the post where he was going to dispose of his goods. To insure that this rule was observed, he was expected to present to the commissary of the post in question an invoice of all goods that he had carried into the Indian country. He was also obliged to have just weights and measures, was strictly forbidden to abuse any Indian or to hold meetings or send belts among the natives, and he was to observe the tariff on goods as established each spring by the commissary.[61]

Despite the apparently sensible and salutary nature of these regulations, strong objections were voiced to some of them, especially by the merchants and traders of Montreal. They took the position that "to oblige a free Citizen to give an entire Knowledge of his Trade . . . to a Commissary often partial and interested is to rob him entirely of the Advantages of a British Subject"; to have him confine his operations to a single post would "entirely destroy the Fur Trade," for the trader—as the result of an accident, such as damage to a canoe—might find it absolutely necessary "to trade upon the Road." They also objected to rigid tariffs being set, on the grounds that prices fluctuated depending on the quantity of goods available and offered. However, their major position was "that

[60] C. E. Carter, in his article "The Significance of the Military Office in America, 1763–1775," *American Historical Review*, XXVIII, 475–88, and his essay "The Office of Commander in Chief: a Phase of Imperial Unity on the Eve of the Revolution," in *The Era of the America Revolution* (ed. R. B. Morris, New York, 1939), affirms that the office of the Indian Superintendent was under the control of the Commander-in-Chief, while J. R. Alden argues (*Southern Colonial Frontier*, Chap. 9) that it enjoyed a very large measure of freedom from such control. Each view seems to be correct, with theory contrasted to practice.

[61] For a copy of these "Orders and Regulations" see *Sir William Johnson Papers*, XII, 246–8.

the Trade with the Indians should be free to all" and that "restraining of it to Posts that are Garrisoned will entirely destroy it."[62]

Realizing the strong opposition of many traders and merchants to control of the Indian trade by the Superintendents, their deputies, and the commissaries, Johnson at this juncture put forth a great effort to convince the government at home of the soundness of his plan. The result was a most exhaustive survey of the changing course of Anglo-Indian relations during the period from 1744 to 1767. Johnson entitled his recommendations "A Review of the progressive State of Trade, Politics and Proceedings of the Indians in the Northern district, with some Hints humbly offered towards Establishing such Regulations as may be enforced for preventing Abuses, and securing Tranquility of the Colonies."[63] In the course of this analysis he strongly recommended both laying down a boundary line that would, as a substitute for the Proclamation Line, separate the frontier settlements from the Indian country, and the re-establishment of a number of deserted trading posts in the Great Lakes region formerly maintained to advantage by the French. He proposed that all colonial laws—consistent with the Board of Trade plan of 1764—relating to the Indians be repealed, and that the authority of the Superintendent be clarified and increased "as may be deemed necessary to the due execution of his Office." Further, his plan urged that the powers of justice of the peace be granted to the respective divisional deputy agents and to the commissaries at the various posts; they would thus be empowered to deal with Indian matters lying beyond the jurisdiction of a particular colony and to summon

[62] See the objections of the Montreal merchants, January 15, 1768, to "Sir Wm. Johnson's Regulations for the Indian Trade, and the Observations of the Quebec Merchants thereon," March 1768, *ibid.*, XII, 409–14. For the importance of the Indian trade in Canada and the Great Lakes frontier area see Volume V of this series, Chaps. 1–2, especially the section on the fur trade, pp. 42–61. See in this connection Governor James Murray's famous "Report" of 1762 giving the value of fur exports under the French regime in 1754 and 1755 as close to £140,000 sterling, William Smith: *History of Canada . . .* (2 vols., Quebec, 1815, issued in 1826), I, Appendix, pp. 66–7, and *Canadian Archives, Sessional Papers No. 18: Documents Relating to the Constitutional History of Canada, 1759–1791* (eds. Adam Shortt and A. G. Doughty, 2nd edn., Ottawa, 1918), Pt. I. 76. This report was transmitted by Amherst to the Board of Trade, among other reports submitted for their information in preparing a plan for the administration of the new acquisitions; see also *ibid.*, Pt. I, 231–6.

On December 29, 1766, the merchants of Montreal addressed a long letter to the committee of London merchants for Indian affairs indicating how impossible it was to carry on trade with the more distant Indian tribes under the new regulations; see Hardwicke Papers, B.M. Add. Mss. 35,915: 228–32. See also "The memorial of the Sundry Merchants of the City of London interested in the Trade of the Province of Quebec," addressed to the Earl of Shelburne, which endorsed the position of the Montreal merchants, P.R.O., C.O. 42:26, p. 705.

[63] For this "Review" see C.O. 323:24, T. 48; see also *New York Colonial Documents*, VII, 953–78, and *Illinois Historical Collections*, XVI, 24–66.

juries on which Indians who had embraced the Christian faith could serve. Johnson also advocated that the testimony of all Indians, whether Christian or not, should be admitted in writing (presumably by an interpreter) in all civil actions. In the case of a trader committing a crime not cognizable by the commissary or any of his superiors in the Department of Indian Affairs, this should be reported to the Governor who had issued the trader's pass, and all evidence against the offender should, at the expense of the Crown, be sent back to the colony so that its attorney general could proceed against the accused. Finally, missionaries should be established among the Indian tribes.

In other words, what Sir William visualized as necessary to establish effective Indian relations were certain changes in the Board of Trade plan of 1764 that would add to the powers conferred by it on the Superintendents and their subordinates and would eliminate all colonial laws that attempted to control the activities of traders within the Indian country. Thus Johnson's proposed regulations meant the strengthening of the plan of 1764 to the formulation of which he had contributed so much. But the implementation of his recommendations would involve very considerable additional expenditures at a time when those demanding a retrenchment of American expenses had become quite vocal in Parliament, and this was a matter of deep concern to Shelburne, as well as to the Board of Trade. Indeed, no evidence has come to light that the Johnson proposals were ever seriously considered, not only because of the costs involved but also because of the opposition they would have encountered in those colonies deeply involved in the Indian trade.

Superintendent Stuart in 1765 had also evolved a set of regulations for the Indian trade, based on the plan of 1764, but found during the course of the next few years that he could not make them effective without further action on the part of the government. He, too, therefore sought additional government legislation.[64] It may be re-emphasized at this juncture that those on the spot most affected by the problems of regulating trade up to 1768 were General Gage and his military commanders and Indian Superintendents Johnson and Stuart and their deputies and commissaries. For his part, Gage allowed the superintendents a free hand and gave them the support which enabled them to take initiative. As for the superintendents, they were both men of forcefulness and decision. Loyal

---

[64] For Stuart's attempts to implement the plan of 1764 in West Florida see Volume IX in this series, pp. 219–24; see also J. R. Alden: *Southern Colonial Frontier*, pp. 209–14, 247–56, and especially 341–3, Appendix A, for Stuart's Trade Regulations of 1765.

to the Crown as well as to their Indian charges—although both managed to amass vast fortunes and land holdings in following their feudal propensities—they were unquestionably the best-informed men in the colonies on Indian affairs and sought to treat the Indians with fairness.[65]

Shelburne, as well as the Board of Trade, was giving active consideration during the second half of 1767 to the problems facing the colonial administrators involved with North American Indian relations.[66] As a result of his investigations he felt that he had a proper solution to the formulation of a western policy. His plan, as finally reported to the Cabinet Council in the fall of 1767, took into consideration the representations of the Indian Superintendents, the memorials of "Merchants both in America and at home," as well as the recommendations of Amherst and Gage, among others. It was "a very simple System which would answer every intention of Government, and cut off every unnecessary Expence, . . . by the Erection of two new Governments, the Establishment of a few principal Posts, and the leaving the Indian Affairs to the Provinces, subject to such general Regulations as the Board of Trade should think expedient for the Interest of Great Britain."[67] On September 11 the Cabinet Council resolved that Shelburne's recommendations should be referred to the Board of Trade so that a plan could be devised that would reduce expenses in the management of Indian affairs.[68]

But, despite additional efforts on the part of Shelburne and the hearty endorsement of his plan by merchants trading to North America and the London agents for several provinces,[69] no final action was taken until 1768, by which time American affairs had been with-

---

[65] For the office of superintendent see J. R. Alden: *op. cit.*, Chap. 9; for a characterization of Stuart see *ibid.*, Chap. 10; for Johnson see the biographies previously cited.

[66] See Shelburne's correspondence with the Board of Trade concerning the Indian superintendents, October 5, 1767, Shelburne Papers 50:173–83, and "The Substance of what passed between L[d] Shelburne and Mr. Dyson [a member of the Board of Trade] about the Superintendants . . . , Nov. 1767," as well as additional notes on this subject, ibid., 50:219–31; see also "Plan for the Future Management of Indian Affairs proposed when Lord Hillsborough was at the head of the Board of Trade," bearing Shelburne's comment: "Remarks upon which are grounded the Minutes submitted by me to the Cabinet in Summer 1767," *ibid.*, 50:257–84, and "Observations upon a Plan for the Future Management of Indian Affairs," *ibid.*, 60:135. In this connection the student should also consult R. A. Humphreys: "Lord Shelburne and British Colonial Policy, 1766–1768," *English Historical Review*, L, 257–77.

[67] "Minutes submitted to the Cabinet . . . , 1767, relative to the System of Indian Traffick," *Illinois Historical Collections*, XVI, 12–21, especially p. 18.

[68] *Ibid.*, XVI, 21.

[69] For a letter addressed to the Lords Commissioners on October 30, 1767, by the influential London alderman, merchant, and colonial agent Barlow Trecothick, reflecting the sentiments of eighteen of the most influential London merchants trad-

drawn from the office of the Secretary of State for the Southern Department and turned over to the new American Department headed by the Earl of Hillsborough. Nevertheless, it is clear that the best features of Shelburne's programme were finally embodied in the plan devised by the Board of Trade for the management of Indian affairs in March.[70] This representation provided that the governments of the individual colonies should regulate the Indian trade, while leaving other matters affecting the Indians in the hands of the Superintendents, who were to retain responsibility for all land purchases from the Indians, for holding Indian congresses, for making treaties, and for laying down boundaries between the Indian country and the white settlements. Approved by the Cabinet Council on March 18, 1768,[71] the decision was communicated to the Governors in circular letters of April 15, 1768, from Hillsborough, as well as to Gage and the Indian Superintendents. Thus the plan that he himself had helped to formulate in 1764 as President of the Board of Trade was now laid aside. This reversal of British policy, it was stated in the circular, was due to the great expense of maintaining the various establishments far exceeding "the Value of the Object," the difficulties attendant upon executing the plan "for Want of due Authority in the Superintendent," and the decision that the colonial assemblies were after all "the best Judges of what their several Situations & Cercumstances may require."[72]

One of the greatest items of expense faced by Great Britain in North America was the maintenance of a series of forts and posts extending from Cape Breton Island on the North Atlantic to Pensacola on the Gulf of Mexico and ultimately to Fort Chartres in the distant Illinois country. Many of these military bases undoubtedly had strategic value, while others were merely posts of communication between the outlying and the more settled areas. But to maintain strength in each of them meant that the some fifteen battalions of troops allotted for the security of British North America had to be deployed in such small detachments that in case of emergency it would have been difficult to assemble as many as 500 men at any one point without great delay. In 1766 Viscount Barring-

ing to America and carrying the endorsement of such other agents as Benjamin Franklin, Richard Jackson, and Edward Montague, see C.O. 323:24, T. 34; see also *Illinois Historical Collections*, XVI, 102.

[70] *Ibid.*, XVI, 183–204.

[71] *Ibid.*, XVI, 219–20.

[72] *Ibid.*; XVI, 245; see also *New York Colonial Documents*, VII, 55–6, which prints the Board of Trade "Representation," together with the letter of transmittal to Hillsborough of March 17, 1768, *ibid.*, VIII, 19–31.

ton, Secretary at War, had made an effort to deal with the situation after corresponding with colonial officials, especially with General Gage and Sir William Johnson. In the spring of that year the Secretary at War formulated a tentative plan for the interior, which he sent to Gage for comment.[73] It was then circulated among the members of the Cabinet Council. Barrington, with Gage's sanction, made clear the point that—on account of the expenses involved and the relative meagreness of the returns from the fur trade—many of the interior posts situated "to the Westward of the Limits settled by the Proclamation in 1763" should be abandoned and the troops removed to the new provinces of East Florida, West Florida, Nova Scotia, and Canada. In his argument, the Secretary at War reasoned that:

> If it be right policy that the Indians should come to us, not we to them, wandering trade should be discouraged & disavowed. The Indians can at least come as easily to our back Settlements as we can go to their towns. . . . If we had no Forts, Garrisons or Settlements, in Indian Country, it is probable we would never be in a State of National Hostility with those People, should any of our Colonies by Misconduct get themselves into War with the Indians let them get themselves out of it as they always used to do when they were not so strong; or else let them beg for Military Assistance; acknowledge their want of it, be thankful for it & pay its Expence."[74]

Certain forts, such as those at Oswego, Niagara, Detroit, and even Michilimackinac in the Great Lakes region, as well as Fort Chartres in the Illinois country, should, Barrington thought, be held, in view of the recommendations not only of Gage but also of Lieutenant Colonel James Robertson, who had served in America. In this connection he admitted that Sir William Johnson opposed the idea but added that "his Reasonings do not appear to me either Clear or conclusive."[75]

---

[73] See "L[d] Barrington's Plan relative to the Out Posts, Indian Trade etc.," dated May 10, 1766, and printed in the *Illinois Historical Collections*, XI, 234–43. Gage's comments on the plan were written on the manuscript copy of the Barrington plan opposite each paragraph that called for comment. They have been separated and printed as a whole by Alvord and Carter in *ibid.*, XI, 243–5. For the manuscript see Shelburne Papers, 50:45.

[74] *Illinois Historical Collections*, XI, 237–8.

[75] *Ibid.*, XI, 239. Gage seems to have been influenced in his attitude toward the abandonment of many of the weak military posts by the military engineer Captain Harry Gordon, who had inspected them. See his "Memorial concerning the back Forts in N. America Dec: 17, 1765," printed in *Military Affairs in North America, 1748–1765, Selected Documents from the Cumberland Papers in Winsdor Castle* (ed. S. M. Pargellis, New York and London, 1936), pp. 464–70. The student should at this point refer—as a correction to C. W. Alvord's interpretation in *The Mississippi Valley in British Politics* (2 vols., Cleveland, 1917), I, 246–9—to the excellent study by J. M. Sosin: "The French Settlements in British Policy for the North American

Barrington was mistaken in his view that it was possible or desirable to have the Indians, living no matter how far distant, come to the nearest settlements with their furs; he was also mistaken in his understanding that the British then enjoyed "the whole Indian Trade except just about New Orleans."[76] Nevertheless, the plan, together with Gage's supporting comments, was destined to influence British policy in North America. The most searching criticism of it seems to have come from Sir Jeffrey Amherst. To him the Barrington plan meant nothing less than leaving the great trans-Appalachian West a vast waste. As a counter-proposition, he urged that the greatest benefit to Great Britain would come "by taking Possession of our Conquests to their utmost Extent", and establishing three "Governments," one at Detroit, another on the upper Mississippi River, and a third on the lower part of that waterway. He also favoured the retention of all posts and forts in the interior as a means of keeping the Indians under control, unless the Commander-in-Chief of the British Forces in North America should no longer consider certain ones necessary for that purpose. As for the expense involved, he thought that under the circumstances it was not only unavoidable but proper.[77] Amherst's "Remarks to Barrington's Plan" was placed at the disposal of the Earl of Shelburne, after he became Secretary of State later in 1766. Therefore, upon considering Lord Barrington's proposals "for a disposition of troops and reduction of forts" in North America, Shelburne noted that "Sr Jeffrey Amherst entirely disapproved this plan."[78]

One consideration that remained paramount in the development of a policy toward the American West was the need for laying down at least temporary boundaries to separate the Indian tribes dwelling

Interior, 1760–1774," *Canadian Historical Review*, XXXIX, 185–208, especially pp. 196–202; see also the same writer's previously cited *Whitehall and the Wilderness*, pp. 114–20.

[76] *Illinois Historical Collections*, XI, 237. Gage's remarks on the Barrington plan stress the fact that an illicit trade in furs secured in the Illinois country was centered at New Orleans, where tenpence more a pound was given for them than "at any of our Markets" (*ibid.*, XI, 244). For a recent study of the fur trade in connection with western expansion see P. C. Phillips: *The Fur Trade* (2 vols., Norman, Okla., 1961), I, Chap. 27, "The Imperial Plan"; for an earlier study see M. G. Lawson: *Fur: A Study in English Mercantilism, 1700–1775* (Toronto, 1943), Chap. 4.

[77] See Amherst's "Remarks to Lord Barrington's Plan. Private," Amherst Papers, 14:9–15, *loc. cit.* General William Amherst, who led the expedition against the French after the invasion of Newfoundland in 1762, was also opposed to the Barrington proposals. His views, outlined in a long, undated report, were more detailed than those of Sir Jeffrey. As they are to be found among the Amherst papers (Bundle 63), one may surmise that they were used by the former Commander-in-Chief of the British Forces in North America in framing his "Remarks."

[78] See "Things to be considered of in North America," Shelburne Papers, 49:17; this memorandum is printed in C. W. Alvord: *The Mississippi Valley in British Politics*, I, 277–8.

to the west of the Proclamation Line from the white settlements now located on either side of it.[79] As early as November 10, 1763, to satisfy the Lower Creeks with claims on Georgia lands, a line was agreed upon at a congress held at Augusta. Present were the Governors of Georgia, South Carolina, North Carolina, and Virginia, as well as Superintendent Stuart of the Southern Indian District, together with representatives of the Lower Creeks and other Indian tribes. The line laid down ran up the Savannah River to a certain point, from there to the Ogeechee, down it to a certain point, thence to the Altamaha, and southward to the Georgia line.[80] Again, on March 26, 1765, at a congress held at Mobile, West Florida, with the Chickasaws and Choctaws, a line was agreed upon involving lands on either side of the Tombigbee River and north of the Gulf of Mexico.[81] Late that same year, on November 15, a treaty was signed at Picolata in East Florida by the Lower and Upper Creeks laying down the bounds that would limit white settlement.[82] Somewhat earlier, by another treaty signed with the Cherokee at Fort Prince George on October 19, part of the boundary between these Indians and the South Carolina settlements was established at a line drawn for some ten miles from a brook called Dewitt's [Dewiss's] Corner to the Long Canes. This was supplemented by an additional agreement with the Cherokee, arrived at on May 10, 1766, also at Fort Prince George, which extended the line fifty miles northeast from Dewitt's Corner to the Reedy [Rudy] River, thus completing the separation of the South Carolina settlements from the Cherokee country.[83]

In the course of the last treaty the Cherokee indicated their readiness to extend the line northward so as to comprehend all the

[79] For a challenge to Turner's thesis that the frontier was one continuous line at various periods, and an analysis of the plurality of frontier lines created by the settled areas at different periods, see Fulmer Mood: "Settled Areas and Frontier Lines, 1625–1790," *Agricultural History*, XXVI, 16–34.

[80] See *Colonial Records of Georgia*, IX, 666–7; see also, for an extract of the Augusta Congress, *Pennsylvania Archives*, 1st ser., IV, 322. This extract and the extracts that follow it relating to boundary treaties (*ibid.*, IV, 323–31) were presumably taken from the official records sent to the Board of Trade, forwarded by them to Lord Hillsborough, and by him to Governor John Penn. For Hillsborough to Penn, April 15, 1768, see *Pennsylvania Colonial Records*, IX, 552–3.

[81] For an extract from this treaty see *Pennsylvania Archives*, IV, 320–1.

[82] For this treaty see *ibid.*, IV, 321–2; see also Superintendent John Stuart to the headman of the Cherokee, February 11, 1766, stating: "I had a Meeting with the Lower Creek Nations' Warriors at Picolata, near St Augustine . . . I have settled a Boundary line between their and our Grounds all round the Two *Floridas & Georgia*. The Line between the Chactaws and us is also settled, so that henceforward we can never have any Dispute about Lands with any Nation of Red Men" (*New York Colonial Documents*, VIII, 34).

[83] Extract of treaty, *Pennsylvania Archives*, IV, 323–4; see also J. R. Alden: *op. cit.*, p. 219.

North Carolina back country. The Governor of North Carolina was equally anxious that this should be done. However, due to an epidemic in the Cherokee towns, the running of the line had to be postponed to the following spring.[84] In view of the importance attached to this event, in May 1767, Tryon himself set out with a military escort for the Reedy River to participate in the transaction, but delays prevented him from carrying out his plan to trace the line in person.[85] Nevertheless, the line was run, based upon the agreement arrived at on October 19, 1765, between Stuart and the headmen of the Cherokee. It was to begin at the Reedy where the South Carolina line terminated "and . . . run a North Course into the Mountains whence a Straight Line to the Lead Mines of Col. Chiswell should Fix the Boundary."[86] As the work was being concluded, the Indians permitted the line to be surveyed so as to avoid the mountains and, moving slightly to the west of them, to include the people settled within the then western limits of Rowan and Mecklenberg counties.[87] By July 16, the day the boundary had been completed, Tryon issued a proclamation "strictly requiring all Persons settled within the Indian Lands to remove from thence by the first day of January next" and giving due notice that no white man should "presume to Hunt thereon."[88]

Now came the difficult problem of the boundary between the Indian country and Virginia, a matter of special concern to the Cherokee. Writing to Lieutenant Governor Fauquier on November 26, 1766, Stuart conveyed the hopes of these Indians that "the Governor & beloved men of Virginia will agree to settle the line in the back country so as to make a final conclusion of the matter."[89] But Fauquier was not disposed to be hurried into any agreement on a boundary that might adversely affect Virginia interests;[90] nor did

---

[84] John Stuart to Governor Fauquier, November 26, 1766, with the substance of a "talk" by the Cherokee chieftain Kittagusta on September 26, 1766, C.O. 323:24, T. 19.

[85] John Stuart to Tryon, May 14, 1767, C.O. 5:310, p. 485; Tryon to Stuart, May 20, 1767, Tryon to the Earl of Shelburne, July 8, 1767, and Tryon's dispatches, *North Carolina Colonial Records*, VII, 460–1, 500–1, 991–1008.

[86] "An Agreement between Governor Tryon and the Indians in regard to the Western boundary," *ibid.*, VII, 469–71. Upon this basis the surveyors John Rutherford, Robert Palmer, and John Frohock ran the line. *Ibid.*, VII, 468–70.

[87] See Stuart to President Blair of the Virginia Council, October 17, 1768, C.O. 5:1347, pp. 25–7; Tryon to Lord Hillsborough, December 12, 1768, C.O. 5:301, p. 59.

[88] *North Carolina Colonial Records*, VII, 502–3.

[89] For this letter see C.O. 323:24, T. 19.

[90] In writing to the Board of Trade on December 2, 1766, with reference to this problem, Stuart said that the Lieutenant Governor of Virginia had not enabled him "to give them [the Indians] any answer to their request of continuing the Line behind his Province" (C.O. 323:24, T. 19).

he feel that he had been empowered to lay down a boundary; thus, when writing to the Earl of Shelburne early in 1767, he indicated that he was favourable to the idea but desired specific authorization.[91] The matter therefore remained in abeyance for a period of time. Then, at a gathering of the principal Cherokee leaders in the month of October 1768, at a place called Hard Labour, Stuart entered into an agreement on the 14th with them on a boundary line that would run northward from Chiswell's Mine to the mouth of the Great Kanawha, which flows into the Ohio. As Stuart pointed out to President Blair this was but "confirming the boundary Line mark'd by the Lords Commissioners of Trade and Plantations. . . ."[92]

In order to understand the implication of Stuart's statement to Blair it is now necessary to consider the similar problem of laying down a boundary between the Indians and the white settlements north of the Ohio. From the point of view of the Board of Trade there must be one continuous line separating the Indian country from those western lands open to exploitation by the whites.

The Iroquoian Confederation had long maintained a claim to the upper Ohio Valley—a claim based not only upon its early conquest of the area and the destruction of the Shawnee settlements on the lower waters of the Ohio, but also upon the acknowledgment of its superior rights to this region by the Delawares, Shawnee, and Mingo settled there, and the recognition accorded in 1744 at the Treaty of Lancaster by the governments of Pennsylvania and Virginia. Subsequently, in 1754, it was with representatives of the Confederation that Connecticut and Pennsylvania commissioners to the Albany Congress negotiated for the release of western lands.

Early in 1765 the Confederation was induced to accept the ultimate responsibility for having plundered the Pennsylvania traders operating in the Ohio Valley during the years 1750 and 1755 and again in 1763.[93] What is more, as a gesture of restitution, these Indians agreed on May 6 to make a cession of all the lands to the east of a boundary line that they themselves now proposed. This line, beginning at a place called Owego on the east branch of the Susquehanna River, would run down to its juncture with the west branch, where Fort Augusta (Shamokin) was located, then up the west branch a considerable distance and thence by a straight line westward to the Indian town of Kittanning on the Allegheny River

[91] Fauquier to Shelburne, February 2, 1767, C.O. 5:1345, pp. 355–6.

[92] Stuart to President Blair of the Virginia Council, October 17, 1768, *Journals of the House of Burgesses, 1766–1769*, pp. xxvi–xxvii.

[93] For the negotiations of Johnson with the Iroquois and Delawares at Johnson Hall in April and May 1765, see *New York Colonial Documents*, VII, 718–41.

and from there, via the Allegheny and the Ohio, down to the Cherokee River (later called the Tennessee) and up to its source.[94] But nothing was done at the time, as Johnson did not feel that he was prepared or authorized to enter into a formal treaty involving land cessions. Writing to the Earl of Shelburne on September 22, 1767, he stressed, among other things, that the failure of the government to determine a boundary line, "as was promised," gave the Northern Indians no small concern.[95] The following month, he reported that in view of "the grievances concerning Lands, Murders and intrusion of the frontier inhabitants," the Indians had become increasingly anxious about the settlement of "the intended boundary line" by the government.[96] When Johnson brought the urgency of this matter to the attention of General Gage,[97] the Commander-in-Chief was sceptical that the laying down of any general line could possibly be effective: "The People would go beyond the Limits, tho' they were fixed at the Ohio"; nor could the Governors be prevailed upon to use force to keep them back.[98]

As for the Secretary of State for the Southern Department, Lord Shelburne, his attitude toward a permanent boundary was by no means clear in 1767. In October, in support of his own earlier proposal, he had sent to the Board of Trade some letters from General Gage and Sir Jeffrey Amherst recommending the establishment "of further new Governments on the Mississippi, the Ohio, and at Detroit" and had suggested to the Lords Commissioners that in case they "should think it right to advise His Majesty to establish these new Governments," they should try to fall upon some plan that would avoid the expense incurred by the establishment of the new governments of East Florida, West Florida, and Quebec after the peace of 1763.[99] Yet little more than a month later he wrote to Governor Fauquier:

> "The Boundary Line having been compleated between the Indians and the Provinces of South and North Carolina, as also between them and the Provinces of Pennsylvania and Maryland; it is very necessary that the same should be continued along the back of Virginia, taking it up Southward at Col. Chiswell's Mines, . . . and running it behind

[94] *Ibid.*, VII, 728–9.

[95] *Ibid.* VII, 951–2.

[96] Johnson to Shelburne, October 26, 1767, *ibid.*, VII, 985–6, and *Sir William Johnson Papers*, V, 762–4.

[97] Johnson to Gage, October 22, 1767, *Documentary History of . . . New York* (ed. E. B. O'Callaghan, 4 vols., Albany, 1849–51), II, 511–12.

[98] Gage to Johnson, November 9, 1767, *Sir William Johnson Papers*, XII, 376–8.

[99] Shelburne to the Board of Trade, October 5, 1767, *New York Colonial Documents*, VII, 981–4; see also *Illinois Historical Collections*, XVI, 77–81.

your Settlements till it falls in with that Point from whence the [line of the] Northern Provinces set out."[100]

What Shelburne was implying was that the establishment of the line between Virginia and the Indian country would close the boundary gap, without realizing that the survey made by Mason and Dixon between 1763 and 1767 was to define the line separating the provinces of Pennsylvania and Maryland and was not concerned with a western boundary. Nor would this closing of the gap have been consonant with the assumption that new governments might be established in the heart of Indian territory.

Shelburne's error soon became evident to him when, in reply to his letter of October 5, the Board of Trade indicated on December 23 that, with reference to the complaints by the Northern Indians of encroachments upon their lands, "the expediency of the establishing a boundary line" had long been urged by the Superintendent, but was not as yet laid down. Further, the Lords Commissioners—referring to the offer of the Indians in 1765 to make a cession of lands east of the Ohio (in reality the Allegheny River) and east of the length of the Cherokee River—recommended that "as the line settled with the Cherokees falls in with a part of the Conohway [the Great Kanawha] River, communicating with the Ohio, it does seem . . . unadvisable, that the line now proposed to be settled with the six Nations and their allies, should be extended lower down the Ohio, than the mouth of the said Conohway River," since this land, while claimed by the Iroquoian Confederation, was actually used as the hunting grounds of the Cherokee.[101] In conformity with this recommendation, Shelburne early in 1768 wrote to Johnson that by His Majesty's command "the Boundary line between the several Provinces and the various Indian Tribes [should] be compleated without loss of time, conformable to a report of the Lords Commissioners for Trade and Plantations." In carrying out this important assignment the Superintendent was to act in concert with the Commander-in-Chief of the British Forces in North America and was also to consult with the various Governors on points that might affect the provinces concerned.[102] When the Earl of Hillsborough took over American affairs, as the occupant of the newly created office of

[100] Shelburne to Fauquier, November 14, 1767, *Sir William Johnson Papers,* V, 793.

[101] Board of Trade to Shelburne, December 23, 1767, *New York Colonial Documents,* VII, 1004–5. It should be added that the western policy produced on March 7, 1768, by the Lords Commissioners for Trade and Plantations supported its position for using the mouth of the Great Kanawha rather than the Cherokee River as the western boundary. See *ibid.,* VIII, 19–31.

[102] Shelburne to Johnson, January 5, 1768, *ibid.,* VIII, 2.

Secretary of State for the Colonies, he reinforced Shelburne's injunction to Johnson as to the importance of laying down the boundary and enclosed a map, "whereon is delineated the Boundary Line proposed by the Board of Trade to be Settled with the Six Nations, . . . and also those lines [already] settled with the Choctaws, Creeks, and Cherokees by the Superintendent for the Southern District."[103] Writing to Johnson a month later, Hillsborough confirmed his earlier letter by stating that His Majesty had determined "That the line described in the Report of the Board of Trade shall be ratified and confirmed in every part, and the Colonies required to enact the most effectual laws for preventing all Settlement beyond such line."[104]

There were delays before the holding in 1768 of the Indian congress that was to ratify the 1765 offer by the Six Nations of a cession of western lands. Johnson himself was ill and was obliged to go to the Atlantic coast to recuperate; also, other Indian problems not related to the Indian boundary line had to be dealt with first. Nevertheless, commissioners representing Virginia and Pennsylvania were appointed to meet the Indians at Fort Stanwix on the Mohawk River and negotiate with the natives in conjunction with Superintendent Johnson, acting in the dual capacity of Indian Superintendent and representative for New York as an appointee of Governor Moore. Various presents for the Indians were sent up the Mohawk from Albany in twenty boats. On September 19 Johnson and his party appeared at the fort, but the Indians continued to arrive in groups until October 30. By then, they numbered over three thousand, including representatives of not only the Iroquoian Confederation but also the ten other so-called "dependent" tribes—such as the Shawnee and Delawares—in friendly relations with the Six Nations.

While a consideration of certain aspects of the Fort Stanwix Congress must be reserved for the chapter to follow, it should be pointed out here that, as a result of the deliberations that took place and the liberal distribution of gifts, the Indians signed over a cession of land on November 6 in the presence of Johnson, the commissioners from Pennsylvania[105] and Virginia, and Governor William Franklin and Chief Justice Smith of New Jersey. This deed released

[103] Hillsborough to Johnson, March 12, 1768, *ibid.*, VIII, 35–6.

[104] Hillsborough to Johnson, April 15, 1768, *ibid.*, VIII, 57–8.

[105] The Pennsylvania delegation was initially headed by Governor John Penn, Attorney General Benjamin Chew, Secretary James Tilghman of the Land Office, and Richard Peters, who had earlier been secretary of the Land Office and of the provincial Council, but the Governor and the Attorney General left the negotiations in the experienced hands of Peters and Tilghman and returned to Philadelphia. See Hubertis Cummings: *Richard Peters: Provincial Secretary and Cleric, 1704–1776* (Philadelphia, 1944), pp. 297–9, 333.

to the Crown all the lands in New York east of the line that began at Canada Creek east of Lake Oneida and ran southward to the New York-Pennsylvania boundary; to the Proprietors of Pennsylvania it gave all the lands to the east and south of the line that, striking the east branch of the Susquehanna River, ran in an irregular fashion down the west branch to Kittanning [Kittaning] on the Allegheny, and thence, following this river, along the Ohio to the Cherokee or Tennessee River.[106] As to the lands to the eastward of the Cherokee River and south of the Ohio, in which the Virginians had a primary interest, the deed was silent. It did, however, at least serve to bar further claims of the Six Nations to those hunting grounds claimed by the Cherokee.[107]

In accepting this deed, Sir William Johnson acted contrary to the definite instructions that should have bound him. All he could plead, when writing to Hillsborough after the Congress, was that he found "the Six Nations insisting on their right to the Lands as far South as the Cherokee River . . . and notwithstanding that the Report of the Board of Trade spoke of the Great Kanhawa as their Southern bounds, I found . . . that I could not deny them the liberty of asserting their pretensions to the Southward without highly disobliging them, and preventing the Settlement of the rest [of the boundary]."[108] It is clear, however, that the extension of the southern boundary was introduced as the result of the demands of land speculators, who had their eyes on the vast expanses of country south of the Ohio and as far west as the mouth of the Tennessee and who denied that the Cherokee had any interest in it.[109]

---

[106] For the Fort Stanwix Congress see *Sir William Johnson Papers,* XII, 617–29, and *New York Colonial Documents,* VIII, 111–37; for the deed of release of lands signed by the leaders of the Six Nations see *ibid.,* VIII, 135–7; see also Johnson to Thomas Penn, August 24, 1768, *Sir William Johnson Papers,* VI, 335–6. For a map of the lands granted see *ibid,* VI, opposite p. 450; for a map of the Board of Trade's proposed boundary line, see *ibid.,* V, 286. For an excellent study of this treaty see R. A. Billington: "The Ft. Stanwix Treaty of 1768," *New York History,* XXV, 182–94.

[107] The deed covering the above point reads: that "we [the Six Nations] have now agreed upon and do hereby establish as the Boundary between us and the British Colonies in America [a line] beginning at the mouth of Cherokee or Hogohego River where it emptys into the River Ohio and running from thence upwards along the South side of said River to Kittaning which is above Fort Pitt . . ." (*New York Colonial Documents,* VIII, 136).

[108] Johnson to Hillsborough, November 18, 1768, *ibid.,* VIII, 110–11.

[109] The land speculators' demands, also previously noted, will be emphasized in the chapter to follow. See T. P. Abernethy: *Western Lands and the American Revolution,* p. 34. The student is further referred to R. A. Billington's careful analysis in *New York History,* XXV, 185–96, of the motivations—supposed as well as real—that animated Johnson in the extension of the line to the Tennessee. In referring to this aspect of the treaty Professor Billington calls it "one of the worst treaties in the history of Anglo-Indian relations."

Returning once again to the Treaty of Hard Labour consummated on October 14, 1768, between the Cherokee and Superintendent Stuart, acting for the Crown, it should be pointed out that this agreement was quite in line with the instructions sent by the Board of Trade.[110] Nevertheless, when its terms were presented to the Governor's Council of Virginia there were strong protests against Stuart's action.[111] The Virginians sought a new survey in harmony with the Treaty of Fort Stanwix from the Southern Indian Superintendent, and the demand was supported by Lord Botetourt, the newly arrived Governor-in-Chief.[112] Moreover, the latter in writing on December 24 to Lord Hillsborough insisted that the line agreed upon between Stuart and the Cherokee would deprive numerous settlers west of it of lands which they had secured before the war with the encouragement of the Assembly and the approval of the King.[113] In fact, the Virginia Assembly now demanded a western extension of the province's accepted southern boundary. A line running westward 36° 30′ north latitude, consistent with the Fort Stanwix settlement, was the province's idea of a proper boundary to separate it from the Cherokee country to the south. All of this led to a heated controversy between Stuart and the Virginia authorities, with each appealing to Hillsborough.[114]

The Secretary of State for the Colonies, although initially unwilling to recognize the extreme demands of the people of the Old Dominion, at length agreed to a modification of the Board of Trade plan so as to protect the rights of legitimate settlers. As a result, with Hillsborough's consent,[115] a new line was agreed upon in a treaty negotiated in the fall of 1770 at Lochaber plantation in South Carolina, whereby the southern boundary of Virginia was to be extended westward to a point near the upper waters of the Holston and from

[110] Stuart to President Blair of the Council of Virginia, October 17, 1768, C.O. 5:1347, pp. 25–7, and *Journals of the House of Burgesses, 1766–1769,* pp. xxvi–xxviii.

[111] Minute of the Virginia Council of December 16, 1768, C. O. 5:1347, p. 87.

[112] See "Instructions to the Virginia Indian Commissioners," December 20, 1768, C.O. 5:1347, pp. 95–7; see also the *Virginia Magazine of History and Biography,* XIII, 28–30. The commissioners appointed to arrange for the new survey, Colonel Andrew Lewis and Dr. Thomas Walker, both with interests in western lands, reported to Governor Botetourt on February 2, 1769, on the results not only of their visit to Stuart in Charleston but also of their talks with the Cherokee, whose leaders were anxious that a boundary line be drawn sufficiently far west to exclude any white settlements from the Indian lands. They also mentioned Stuart's attitude that "the Boundary between the Cherokees and Virginia was fully settled and ratified in Great Britain." See *ibid.,* XIII, 30–6.

[113] C.O. 5:1347, pp. 59–61.

[114] See Stuart to Lord Botetourt January 13 and July 12, 1770, and Botetourt to Stuart, February 8 and June 21, 1770, C.O. 5:1348, pp. 149–51, 153, 157, 231, 269–70.

[115] Hillsborough to Botetourt, March 1 and May 13, 1769, C.O. 5:1347, pp. 111–12 and 135–6.

there northward to the confluence of the Great Kanawha and the Ohio.[116]

But even the new line was soon changed to the advantage of the Old Dominion. For when the Virginia commissioner Colonel John Donelson and the Indians began the survey in the spring of 1771, they found the country between the Holston and the mouth of the Kanawha so mountainous and difficult of access that the Cherokee themselves suggested that for a small consideration they would accept a new line. This, avoiding the mountains, ran across the country from the Holston northwest to the upper waters of the Kentucky and then down that stream to the Ohio.[117]

While this so-called Donelson Line (sometimes called the "Ministerial Line") was a wide deviation from the Board of Trade western boundary for Virginia, it was at length given the blessing of the Earl of Dartmouth, who took over the office of Secretary of State for the Colonies in 1772 when Hillsborough resigned over the issue of granting lands to the Vandalia Company for the establishment of a proposed new colony.[118] In fact, Dartmouth was committed to western expansion.[119]

The final extension of the Virginia boundary up to the Cumberland River was achieved without the blessing of the government of Great Britain. It came as the result of the purchase of the land west of the Kentucky and up to that river on March 17, 1775, by Judge Richard Henderson of North Carolina for the so-called Transylvania Company, in connection with the Cherokee Treaty concluded at Sycamore Shoals (a subject to be considered in the chapter that

---

[116] For the minutes of the Treaty of Lochaber of October 18, 1770, see C.O. 5:72, pp. 43–68; see also Stuart to Lord Botetourt, October 25, 1770, C.O. 5:1349, pp. 39–42. The Cherokee Indians thereby secured the inclusion in their territory of a favourite camping ground, Long Island on the Holston. The treaty is printed in *Virginia Magazine of History and Biography*, IX, 360–4.

[117] Dunmore to Hillsborough, March 1772, C.O. 5:1350, pp. 37–41. In the map of the survey Donelson called the Kentucky River the Louisa, and Dunmore in his letter uses the latter name for the new treaty boundary of Virginia.

[118] The Donelson Line was approved by the King in Council several days after Dartmouth took office, August 14, 1772; see Board of Trade *Journal, 1768–1775*, p. 316. The Vandalia Colony is dealt with in the next chapter of this volume.

[119] Stuart, writing to Lord Dartmouth on February 25, 1773, makes the following cryptic statement about the Louisa (that is, the Kentucky) River: "What Coll. Donalson the Virginian Surveyour calls Louisa River in his report, and which forms the present boundary, is in Mitchell's map called the Catawba or Cuttawa River, by which map Louisa River is made to fall into the Kenhaway" (C.O. 5:74, p. 123). With his letter, he enclosed a map covering the area of his superintendency. Dartmouth's reply to Stuart of May 5, 1773, stated that the "map of North America with the Indian boundary line marked upon it and the separate plan of that line enclosed in your letter, . . . will be of great use, and I am happy to find that the Cherokees, in finally fixing the line . . . have chosen a natural boundary which will prevent future disputes . . ." (C.O. 5:74, p. 191).

follows). It also resulted from the failure of the plan of the North Carolinians to establish their new colony of Transylvania in the face of Virginia claims to the area.[120]

But Virginia's exploitation of the lands released by agreement with the Six Nations and the Cherokee—not to mention claims extending westward beyond the Kentucky River—presented perplexing problems that had still not been solved in 1772.

At the same time that Virginians were flooding into the region about the forks of the Ohio and southward to join North Carolinians from the Watauga settlement who were penetrating into the Kentucky country, Pennsylvanians also began to press westward along the Forbes Road and its subsidiary paths to settle west of the Alleghenies. To meet this situation the county of Westmoreland was erected in 1773 to comprehend fast-growing Pittsburgh and the country immediately adjacent to it,[121] and Governor Penn proclaimed his jurisdiction over it. Countering this move, Lord Dunmore the following year confirmed the view held by most Virginians that Pittsburgh was within Augusta County and proceeded to set up a military government under Dr. John Connolly for the District of West Augusta, which embraced the town. Writing to the Earl of Dartmouth soon after, Dunmore defended his action of extending the jurisdiction of the Old Dominion to the forks of the Ohio by stating that the bounds of Virginia, as "understood by all the people of this Colony, include Fort Pitt or Pittsburgh." He further pointed out that there were at least ten thousand settlers at or about the forks who had begged him to appoint magistrates, which he had finally agreed to do, to their great joy.[122]

The conflict of jurisdiction involving the forks of the Ohio led to a test of strength between Pennsylvania and Virginia, with each side contending that it was simply acting to uphold its proper charter rights.[123] The Old Dominion, however, enjoyed two great temporary

[120] *Journals of the House of Burgesses, 1770–1772*, pp. xxxiv–xxxv. The settlement of the Kentucky country will be considered in the chapter to follow.

[121] See S. J. and Elizabeth H. Buck: *The Planting of Civilization in Western Pennsylvania* (Pittsburgh, 1939), pp. 139–70, and C. M. Bomberger: *A Short History of Westmoreland County* (Pittsburgh, 1939), Chap. 1.

[122] Dunmore to Dartmouth, March 18, 1774, C.O. 5:1352, pp. 31–9.

[123] See Connolly's "Address to the People of Pittsburgh," January 1, 1774; Connolly to Dunmore, January 28, 1774; Governor Penn to Lord Dunmore, January 31, 1774; and Dunmore to Dartmouth, March 18 and May 2, 1774, C.O. 5:1352, pp. 31–9, 41, 43–6, 51–4, 165–9. For other printed documents on this controversy see *Documentary History of Dunmore's War, 1774* (eds. R. G. Thwaites and L. P. Kellogg, Wisconsin Historical Society, Madison, 1905), and Peter Force: *American Archives*, 4th ser., I, 252–83, 454–85; see also P. B. Caley: "Lord Dunmore and the Pennsylvania-Virginia Boundary Dispute," *Western Pennsylvania Historical Magazine*, XXII, 87–100, and, for a brief but excellent treatment of the controversy, S. J. and E. H. Buck: *op. cit.*, pp. 156–68.

advantages: most of the settlers—as well as the garrison, made up of local militia that now occupied decayed Fort Pitt (renamed Fort Dunmore)—favoured its claim; what is more, these claims were supported by the Secretary of State for the Colonies, the Earl of Dartmouth.[124] It is therefore quite possible that had the War for American Independence not intervened, the western limits of the Province of Pennsylvania might have fallen short of the five degrees from the Delaware River assigned to the founder by charter. For there was some validity to the reasoning of Virginians and others that this right had lapsed as the result of conquest by the French and reconquest by His Majesty's arms and that the claims of Virginia to the trans-Appalachian region were, after all, prior to those of the Penn family.

However, the opposition of the authorities of Pennsylvania to the claims of the Old Dominion in the trans-Appalachian region was not the only difficulty facing the Virginians. The Shawnee—who, although represented at Fort Stanwix, apparently had not been consulted on the terms of the treaty signed there[125]—were especially incensed at the appropriation of their hunting grounds south of the Ohio by the "long hunters" and settlers. In fact, it appears that these Indians had continued to be restive, even after the peace contracted with them by Colonel Bouquet in 1764, and had, it was claimed, murdered white men in the region to the south of the Ohio during the following ten years.[126] Nevertheless, it is clear that this violence had not erupted without provocation.[127] The Mingo now began to

[124] Dartmouth to Dunmore, June 1, 1774, C.O. 5:1352, pp. 93–5. In a later letter, written on August 3, 1774 (C.O. 5:1352, p. 223), with reference to the western limits of Pennsylvania, Dartmouth told Dunmore that this must be determined by a commission appointed by the King for that purpose and went on to say that should His Majesty think fit to establish a government on the Ohio, it would be to the interest of the proprietors of the new colony jointly with the Proprietors of Pennsylvania to employ such a commission, for "it will not be, I conceive, in the power of the Crown, of its own Authority, to decide the Controversy. . . ." Governor Fauquier, nevertheless, in answering queries sent by the Board of Trade in 1763, had warned that with the running of the boundary line between Pennsylvania and Maryland and the extension of this line to the western limits of Pennsylvania, the "Pennsylvanians will be found to have a right to a large Tract of Land now reputed to be in the Colony of Virginia" (H.M. 572, p. 5, Huntington Library, San Marino, Calif.).

[125] It should be noted that the only Indians who signed the deed releasing lands to the English were members of the Six Nations. *New York Colonial Documents,* VIII, 137.

[126] Lord Dunmore to the Indians, 1774, *The Olden Time* (ed. N. B. Craig, Pittsburgh, 1848, and Cincinnati, 1876), II, 26–9.

[127] That the Shawnee were guilty of much violence against the whites is indicated in Sir William Johnson's address to the Six Nations and Western Confederacy on January 13, 1774: "The Conduct of the Shawanese by your, and all accounts, plainly shew their Insincerity, and Contempt of all the solemn engagements they have for several years past entered into with the English . . ." (*Sir William Johnson Papers,* XII, 1056). Alexander McKee wrote in his "Journal" under dates of February 27

take part in the Shawnee hostilities as the result of the shocking murder of a number of their tribe by corrupt and abandoned whites early in May 1774.[128] By July the Virginia frontier was ablaze with a new Indian war, some of the young Delawares joining the warriors of the two other tribes in making reprisals—killing, burning, and looting. Yet the Indian aggressions were not directed against all the whites, nor even against the Pennsylvania traders in their midst; they were launched at the "Big Knife," as they called the Virginians.[129]

Against this threat Lord Dunmore now moved into action,[130] taking personal command of the punitive campaign that was to become known as Dunmore's War. As early as June he had ordered the western settlers to place themselves in a defensive position. As a result, there was a concentration of Virginia militia at three places: Pittsburgh, Wheeling, and Camp Union in Greenbrier County. The first troops to take the offensive were those gathered at Wheeling. With Major Angus MacDonald (McDonald) at their head, 400 men crossed the Ohio and, late in July, destroyed an important Shawnee town on the Muskingum together with five Mingo towns.[131] In September the troops at Camp Union, some 1,100 under command of Colonel Andrew Lewis, began moving down to the mouth of the Great Kanawha in order to cross it and unite with the forces under Lord Dunmore, presumed to be descending that river from Pittsburgh for the rendezvous. However, when Lewis reached the south

---

and March 1, 1774, of the outrages committed by these Indians against the Virginia settlers. See *ibid.*, XII, 1080. However, the Shawnee chiefs, at a meeting with McKee at Pittsburgh on March 8, pointed out "the very great Numbers of your people going down this River [the Ohio] beyond the bounds fixed for them and over spreading the Hunting Country of our Young Men." They added that "from this Cause proceeds at present all our Disturbances; . . . for when they [the Indians] . . . find the Woods cover'd with white people & their Horses where they used to find their Game, they are foolish enough to make Reprisals . . ." (*ibid.*, XII, 1084–5). R. C. Downes in his "Dunmore's War: An Interpretation," *Mississippi Valley Historical Review*, XXI, 311–30, places the chief blame for the war upon the conduct of the lawless whites who, in pressing westward, would not be bound by any governmental regulations; to a lesser extent he also blames Lord Dunmore and the British authorities at home. See also the same author's chapter on "Dunmore's War" in his *Council Fires on the Upper Ohio . . .* (Pittsburgh, 1940).

[128] *The Olden Time*, II, 49–67.

[129] Arthur St. Clair to Governor John Penn, May 29, 1774, *American Archives*, 4th ser., I, 286–7.

[130] Writing to the Earl of Dartmouth from Frederick County on August 14, 1774, Dunmore stated that "the Shawnees, Mingoes, and some of the Delawares, have fallen on our frontiers, killed, scalped, and most cruelly murdered, a great many men, women, and children . . . but I hope in eight or ten days to march with a body of men over the Alleghany Mountains, and then down the Ohio to the mouth of the Sciota . . ." (*Documentary History of Dunmore's War, 1774*, pp. 149–50).

[131] *American Archives*, 4th ser., I, 722–4.

bank of the Ohio early in October, Dunmore had not arrived. The Indians, to prevent the joining of the two Virginia forces, now attempted to destroy Lewis's little army. Under Chief Cornstalk they attacked with great fury at Mount Pleasant on the 10th. The fight continued all that day with heavy losses on both sides. That night, having failed of their objective and realizing that the Virginians were holding firm, the natives retreated.[132]

Dunmore, meanwhile, had loaded his troops into about 100 canoes and other small craft and dropped down the Ohio from Pittsburgh. After stopping at Wheeling, he had moved down to the mouth of the Hocking (then called the Hockhocking)—rather than, as earlier contemplated, halting for the rendezvous with Colonel Lewis at the mouth of the Great Kanawha.[133] He then struck across country to the neighbourhood of the Shawnee town of Chillicothe on the Scioto.

Even before Dunmore neared his destination, the hostile Indians began capitulating. Peace was therefore consummated in November, at Dunmore's fortified Camp Charlotte, without further loss of life. The Shawnee and Mingo assembled there not only agreed to surrender the prisoners they had failed to give up in 1764 but also to refrain from crossing the Ohio to hunt and from molesting the whites who used the river.[134] That Dunmore's own officers highly approved the Governor's conduct of the campaign and the manner of its termination, is evident from their declaration drawn up at a meeting held on November 5. For they affirmed that he had conducted the operations "with Honour and Advantage to the Colony and ourselves," and they resolved:

---

[132] *Pennsylvania Gazette,* November 16, 1774.

[133] See Dunmore's order to Colonel Lewis, July 24, 1774, *Documentary History of Dunmore's War, 1774,* pp. 97–8; see also Andrew Lewis to William Preston, September 8, 1774, William Fleming to Adam Stephen, October 8, 1774, and William Christian to William Preston, October 15, 1774, *ibid.,* pp. 191, 236–8, 263–4.

[134] *The Olden Time,* II, 41–2. Colonel Lewis had originally been ordered by Dunmore to join him at Chillicothe; but the order was countermanded. This was deeply resented by Lewis and his men, who at first disregarded the new order. In fact, the Governor's changes in the plan of campaign have been the subject of much discussion and adverse criticism since that time on the part of various writers. It seems, however, that the men under the Colonel were thirsting for revenge and were bent upon "the total destruction of the Indians and their towns along the Scioto and Sandusky rivers" (*ibid.*). Dunmore, it appears, realizing that such punishment of the Shawnee and Mingo would doubtless lead to a general Indian war involving all the Delawares and the Six Nations, felt disposed, as had Bouquet in 1764, to lay aside his earlier, more drastic plan in favour of milder treatment that would at the same time attain the larger objective—something that could, he reasoned, be achieved more easily in the absence of the men gathered from the region of the Holston and New rivers who nursed a bitter hatred of the Indians.

"That we entertain the greatest Respect for his Excellency the Right Hon. Lord Dunmore, who commanded the Expedition against the Shawanese; and who, we are confident, underwent the great Fatigue of this singular Campaign from no other Motive than the true Interest of this Country."[135]

He was also highly commended by the Council of Virginia upon his return.[136] The following year, in the Convention of Delegates for the Counties and Corporation . . . of Virginia, it was, on March 25, "*Resolved unanimously*, That the most cordial thanks of the people of this Colony are . . . due to our worthy Governor, Lord Dunmore, for his truly noble, wise, and spirited conduct on the late expedition against our Indian enemy. . . ."[137]

However, neither Dunmore's expedition nor his entire Indian policy was to escape the severe criticism of other people involved in the disputed territory around the forks of the Ohio. The charge that the Virginians had provoked the war, made by various Pennsylvania traders, merchants, and agents, did not fail to reach the ears of Lord Dartmouth through the complaints of the Pennsylvania Proprietor.[138] As a result of Governor Penn's representations, the Secretary of State for the Colonies rebuked Lord Dunmore and forced him into the position of defending his actions.[139] But the outbreak of the War for Independence also postponed settlement of this aspect of the dispute between Pennsylvania and Virginia until it was no longer a concern of the British government.

As to the problems of primary importance, neither the regulation of the Indian trade nor the placing of some sort of limits on the encroachment by whites upon Indian territory west of the Appalachians was ever achieved during the colonial period in view of the land hunger of the white settlers, hunters, trappers, traders, merchants, and land speculators.

---

[135] *Pennsylvania Gazette*, January 4, 1775.

[136] For this commendation see *American Archives*, 4th ser., I, 1043–4.

[137] *Ibid.*, 4th ser., II, 170.

[138] See *ibid.*, 4th ser., I, 454–85, 506; see also [Samuel Wharton]: *Facts and Observations* (London, 1775), pp. 79–107; this important pamphlet will be discussed in further detail in the next chapter.

[139] See the copy of Dartmouth's letter to Dunmore of September 8, sent to Governor Penn, *American Archives*, 4th ser., I, 774. For Dunmore's official report defending his policy, which resulted in his expedition against the Shawnee, see his very long letter to Dartmouth of December 24, 1774, C.O. 5:1353, 13–78, especially pp. 15–58, which is printed in full in *Documentary History of Dunmore's War*, pp. 368–95 (in the introduction of which may also be found an attempt to make an objective defense of Dunmore's action), and in part in *American Archives*, 4th ser., I, 1061–3. For a more recent strong defence of Dunmore see R. D. Curry: "Lord Dunmore and the West: A Re-evaluation," *West Virginia History*, XIX, 231–43.

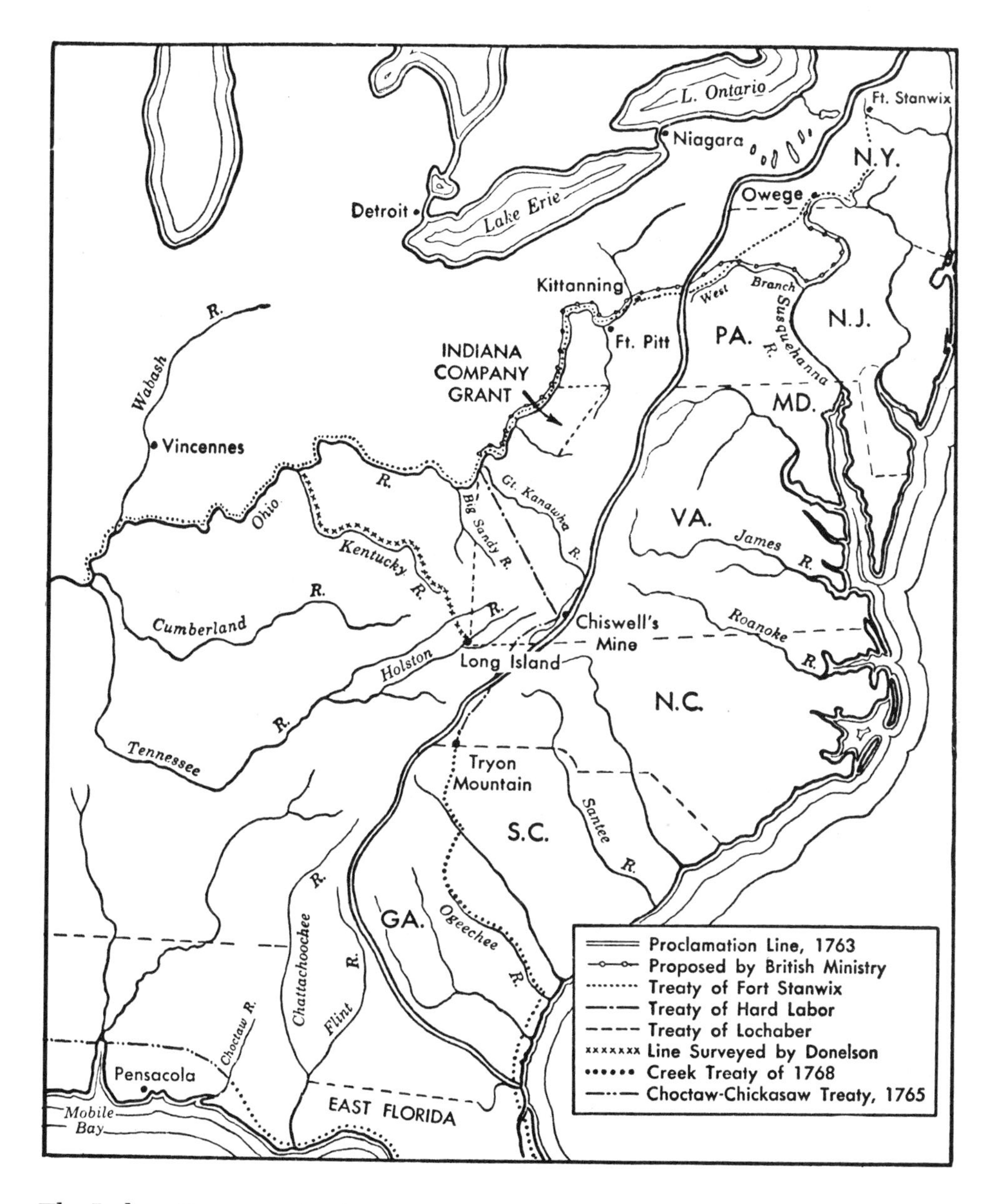

The Indian Demarcation Lines.

(From Ray A. Billington's *Westward Expansion: A History of the American Frontier*, 1960)

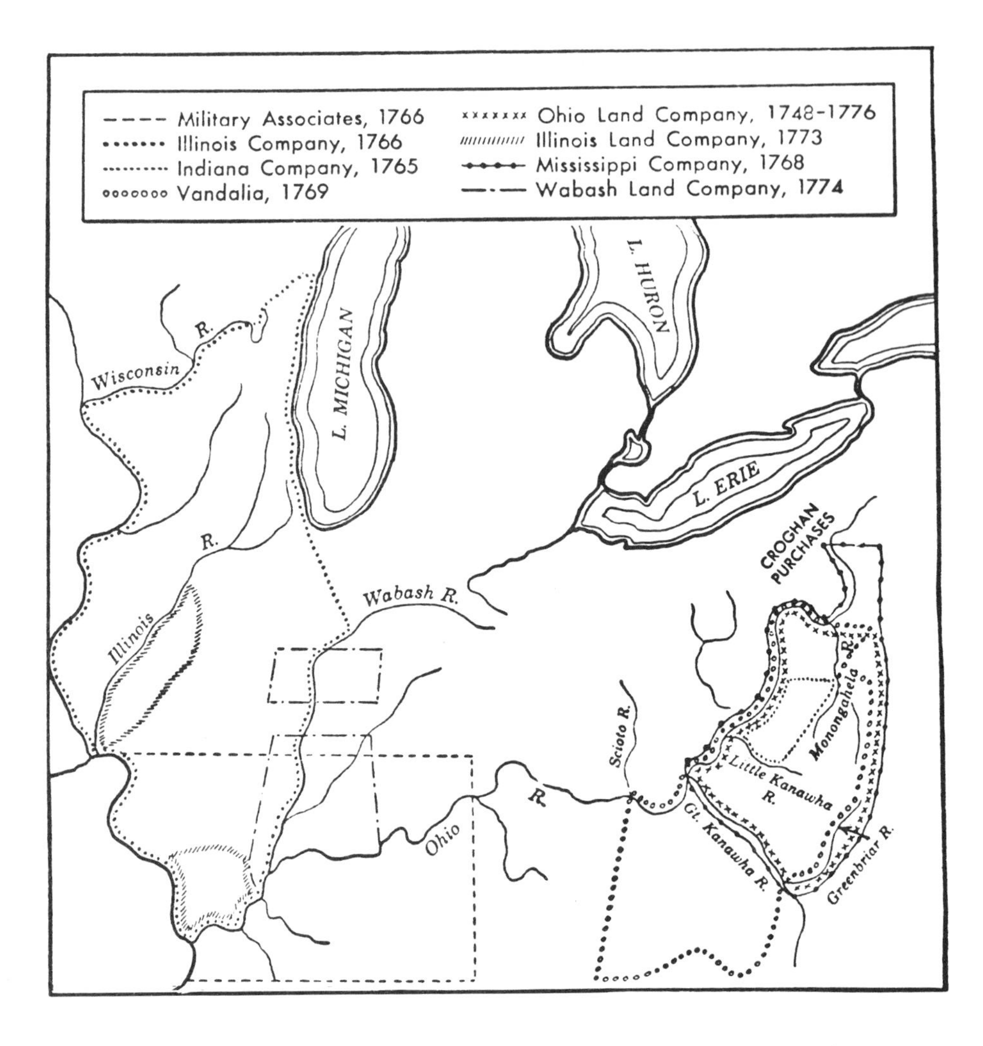

"Land Speculation, 1763–1776."

(From Ray A. Billington's *Westward Expansion: A History of the American Frontier*, 1960)

CHAPTER XIII

Trans-Appalachian Developments: The British Ministry Faces the Failure of Imperial Regulation

THE introductory paragraphs to the previous chapter will serve also as an introduction to the present one. For in that chapter the treatment of trans-Appalachian developments was confined to the problems that faced the British government in providing policies and plans for the administration of the Illinois country, for the general management of Indian affairs—especially the regulation of Indian trade—and for making provision, by means of formal treaties, for the pioneer settlers pushing ever westward. During the Great War for the Empire, the mountain barrier had been breached by military roads, with traders and frontiersmen following close behind the heels of the army. Then, with the French threat removed and the Indian rebellion put down, the western movement gathered momentum and land jobbers and speculators saw their opportunity to profit from the situation by forming land companies or fostering the setting up of new interior colonies.

The Mississippi Company of 1763 and Plans for the Charlotina and New Wales Colonies

The chief obstacle to western settlement was the line marking the beginning of the great Indian reserve as laid down by the Proclamation of 1763. This line, as has already been emphasized, was never designed to be permanent. Indeed, hardly had the Proclamation been issued when a proposal was made in a pamphlet published in Scotland[1] that a new colony, to be known as Charlotina,[2] should be erected in the Illinois country bounded in the east by the Maumee (called the Miamis) and Wabash (called the Waback) rivers, in the south by the Ohio to its juncture with the Mississippi, and in the west by the Mississippi northward from that point to the area west of the Great Lakes.[3] Moreover, even before this proposal was made, a group of Virginia and Maryland men, including George Washington and members of the Lee family, organized in 1763 as the Mississippi Company to secure and settle lands on the Mississippi "and its Waters." Each of fifty members was to be entitled to 50,000 acres of land. In 1768 their plan was changed, and they petitioned the Crown for an area lying well to the east of the Mississippi and including not only much of the land embraced within the proposed colony of Charlotina but also most of what is now Kentucky.[4] Further, a number of New York land speculators likewise conceived the idea of a colony, to be called New Wales in honour of the Prince of Wales, which would lie in the same general area. The extent of this

---

[1] *The Expediency of Securing our American Colonies by Settling the Country adjoining the River Mississippi, and the Country upon the Ohio, Considered,* reprinted from the original Edinburgh edition of 1763 in *Illinois Historical Collections,* X, 134–61.

[2] Not "Charlotiana," as given in most works of reference and on most maps. See *ibid.,* X, 139*n.*

[3] *Ibid.,* X, 139. In this connection see G. H. Alden: *New Governments West of the Alleghanies before 1770* (University of Wisconsin *Bulletin,* Madison, Wis., 1897), pp. 12–14.

It is of interest that William Pulteney, Earl of Bath, was a strong advocate of the creation of new colonies in the West. In his pamphlet *Reflections on the Domestic Policy . . .* (London, 1763, pp. 65–6), he wrote: "The apprehensions of some, that if we suffer our colonies to spread over North America, they will soon shake off their dependance upon their mother country, seem weak and groundless. On the contrary . . . the wider we spread our colonies on that continent, there is the less reason to fear their being disunited from us. While they enjoy the same liberties and privileges as other Britons, we need not apprehend a universal confederacy, and it would not be the interest of any one colony to be disunited from the British Empire, or of others to suffer such a dismemberment. The different governments are mutual checks upon each other; if we shall therefore form two or three colonies on the Ohio and Mississippi, we thereby add so many new pledges for securing the fidelity of the whole."

[4] For the articles of agreement of the Mississippi Company see the *Ohio Archaeological and Historical Publications,* XVII, 439 *et seq.* In 1768 the Company decided to ask for a grant about the upper Ohio between the thirty-eighth and forty-second parallels of north latitude. For the Mississippi Company see C. W. Alvord: *The Mississippi Valley in British Politics* (2 vols., Cleveland, 1917), I, 95–6, 315; II, 93–4, 123, 172. For documents relating to the Mississippi Company from 1763 to 1769, edited by the late C. E. Carter, see *American Historical Review,* XVI, 311–19. The papers themselves are among the Chatham Collection in the Public Record Office; they are all in the handwriting of William Lee, secretary of the Company.

proposed grant was to be "nine degrees of N. latitude and nine degrees of W. longitude, beginning nine degrees from Philadelphia, and ending at the seventeenth degree of western longitude, from 36 to 44 [degrees of north latitude]."[5] But the project was apparently not promoted.

The Company of Military Adventurers

Another group that seemed to have an excellent claim to royal indulgence, the "Company of Military Adventurers," was made up of retired colonial officers who held promises of western land bounties as a result of their service in the Great War for the Empire. These military associates and some thousands of other people with claims to western lands dating back to 1755 were represented by Major General Phineas Lyman of Connecticut,[6] who in 1766 petitioned the King in Council in their name. The petition sought a grant that would stretch some six hundred miles along the eastern bank of the Mississippi River, both north and south of the Ohio.[7] Nothing, however, was accomplished by Lyman for his "Military Adventurers," although he himself, as a highly deserving and distinguished veteran of the late war, finally received a mandamus grant to 20,000 acres in the Natchez area of West Florida.[8]

The Illinois Company of 1766

Also in 1766 a group of Pennsylvanians and others, including Governor William Franklin of New Jersey, Joseph Galloway, Sir William Johnson, George Croghan, John Baynton, and Samuel Wharton, conceived the Illinois Company.[9] The aim of this group

[5] The outline of the project for the colony of New Wales is given in a communication to the *Gentleman's Magazine* (XXXIII, 287–8), under the date-line New York, April 21, 1763; it refers to the creation of "a very extensive colony upon the fairest part of the Ohio. . . ."

[6] For the fullest account of the "Military Adventurers" see Shaw Livermore: *Early American Land Companies* . . . (New York, 1939), pp. 97–102.

[7] The Lyman petition was for a "Tract of Land situate on the East side of the River Mississippi from about 300 miles south of the mouth of the Ohio to as far north of the Same & for a great Extent Eastward. . . ." For the petition see the *Illinois Historical Collections,* XI, 260–4. See Lyman to Shelburne, October 28, 1766, Shelburne Papers, 48:13, 121–2, Clements Library.

[8] *Acts of the Privy Council, Col. Ser., 1766–1783,* p. 594.

[9] G. H. Alden (*op. cit.,* pp. 16–19) presents the correspondence of Benjamin Franklin with his son relating to the prospect of securing the British government's approval of the Illinois Company plans.

was to purchase the rights of the French *habitants* and to colonize the "Terrestial Paradise" after securing a huge grant, which, they envisaged, would extend from the mouth of the Wisconsin River down the east bank of the Mississippi to the mouth of the Ohio, then eastward up the Ohio to the Wabash and up that river northward and then down the Maumee to Lake Erie, with a northern boundary designated by certain natural features from the Maumee westward to the mouth of the Wisconsin.[10] In order to give the Company an effective leverage with the British government its members proposed to associate with it "two or three Gentlemen of fortune & Influence in England. . . ."[11] But the Illinois Company had at least one major defect—the proposal to rid the Illinois country of its French settlers by the purchase of their lands. Such action had not been contemplated or favoured by the British government for dealing with any of the former French territories ceded under terms of the Peace of Paris. Then, too, both the Illinois Company and the Lyman "Military Adventurers" Company faced the hostility of those in the British government who still felt that the rights of the western Indians should be protected.

The Indiana Company

A much more important colonization enterprise was that of the so-called Indiana Company. This group was seeking western lands as compensation for losses suffered by traders in 1763 in the Ohio Valley at the hands of the Indians. Late in that year a number of the sufferers appealed to General Gage to support their efforts to secure reimbursement from the Indians for their losses.[12] The following year the Indian trader and western land speculator George Croghan went to England to press their claims.[13] In 1765 the Company was transformed into what one might call a syndicate, which included not only the "Suffering Traders" but also merchants who had given the traders credit. Shares were allotted according to the

[10] For articles of agreement signed March 29, 1766, and the reasons put forward by the Illinois Company, see *Illinois Historical Collections*, XI, 203–4, 248–57.

[11] See George Croghan to Sir William Johnson on March 30, 1766, *ibid.*, XI, 205–7.

[12] *The Papers of Sir William Johnson* (ed. James Sullivan, M. W. Hamilton, *et al.*, 13 vols.+, Albany, 1921–62+), X, 922–3; to be cited hereafter as *Sir William Johnson Papers*.

[13] G. E. Lewis: *The Indiana Company, 1763–1798: A Study in Eighteenth Century Frontier Land Speculation and Business Venture* (Old Northwest Historical Series, IV, Glendale, Calif., 1941), pp. 38–41; for a brief account of the Indiana Company see Shaw Livermore: *op. cit.*, pp. 113–19; see also Max Savelle: *George Morgan: Colony Builder* (New York, 1932), Chap. 5.

amount of the losses.[14] Apparently to give the enterprise—which was largely confined to Pennsylvania people—greater prestige and influence, Governor William Franklin of New Jersey, the natural son of Benjamin Franklin, was also given a block of shares. In that year, at a meeting of Iroquois and Delawares at his home, Johnson Hall on the Mohawk, Sir William Johnson brought about an agreement whereby the Indians would make a grant of land covering the traders' losses.[15] William Trent, acting for the Indiana Company, immediately set to work to gather evidence. From those who had been despoiled he secured affidavits covering the years 1753 to 1763 and also powers of attorney to act for them.[16] As a result of his efforts, at the Treaty of Fort Stanwix in 1768 the Indians, among other things, ceded a specific tract of land in what is now West Virginia as full recompense for the traders' losses.[17] This was in the form of a separate deed, distinct from the deeds they made to the Crown or to the Pennsylvania Proprietors.[18]

On the face of it, the prospects of the shareholders of the Indiana Company were very bright at the end of 1768. One thing, however,

[14] Two rival Pennsylvania firms suffered the heaviest losses: that of Simons, Trent, Franks, and Company and that of Baynton, Wharton, and Morgan. See G. E. Lewis: *op. cit.*, pp. 45–6.

[15] *New York Colonial Documents*, VII, 724, 729, 740.

[16] G. E. Lewis: *op. cit.*, pp. 49–50. Most of the materials collected by Trent are to be found among the misnamed "Ohio Company Papers," in the Etting Collection of the Historical Society of Pennsylvania. Many of these papers have been published by K. P. Bailey under the title of *The Ohio Company Papers, 1753–1817, Being Primarily Papers of the "Suffering Traders" of Pennsylvania* (Arcata, Calif., 1947), pp. 33–228, cited hereafter as *Ohio Company Papers.*

[17] G. E. Lewis: *op. cit.*, pp. 61–2 and Appendix A, p. 302; see also K. P. Bailey, *op. cit.*, pp. 190–7. The land was actually granted to William Trent, under his powers of attorney to act for the twenty-two persons named in the deed. The name of the Indiana Company does not appear, nor was there any mention of acreage, but the bounds of the ceded land ran from the mouth of the Little Kanawha southeast to Laurel Hill, along that mountain to the Monongahela River and following that river to the southern boundary line of Pennsylvania, thence west along the provincial boundary to the Ohio River, which formed the western line. This grant, estimated variously at 1,800,000 to 2,500,000 acres, was in compensation for the losses of the traders specified at close to £86,000 in the grant. See in this connection Max Savelle: *George Morgan*, p. 79; see also N. B. Wainwright: *George Croghan: Wilderness Diplomat* (Chapel Hill, N.C., 1959), p. 256–8. For the Treaty of Fort Stanwix, see also the preceding chapter in this volume.

[18] "Saturday, November 5, 1768: The Deed to His Majesty, that to the Proprietors of Pensylvania, with that to the Traders being then laid on the Table were executed in the presence of the Govr Commissioners [appointed by New York, Pennsylvania, and Virginia], & the rest of the Gentlemen after which the Cheifs of each Nation received the Cash which was piled on a Table for that purpose and then proceeded to divide the Goods amongst their People which occupied the remainder of that day" (*New York Colonial Documents*, VIII, 134). For the deed see [Samuel Wharton and Edward Bancroft]: *View of the Title to Indiana, . . .* (Philadelphia, 1776), pp. 15–22, and [Samuel Wharton]: *Plain Facts . . .* (Philadelphia, 1781), pp. 82–8.

was considered essential to give validity to the grant: the approval of the Crown. To secure it William Trent and Samuel Wharton of Baynton, Wharton, and Morgan, the firm with the heaviest claim for losses, felt it imperative to go to England. Soon after reaching London and coming in contact with the leading men there, the plans of the two men became greatly enlarged. But, before taking up the transformation of the Indiana Company project into the greatly enlarged Grand Ohio Company, it is important to review the history of the Ohio Company of Virginia after 1763. For, like the Indiana Company, it was, at least in the eyes of the British Ministry, temporarily embraced within a still greater project relating to the Ohio Valley.

The Ohio Company of Virginia

The Ohio Company of Virginia, among all the enterprises for the settlement of trans-Appalachian lands before the outbreak of the Great War for the Empire, was the only one to receive royal permission to patent land.[19] It was also the only one that—preliminary to securing a patent to 200,000 acres reserved for it by the Virginia Council—had invested a good deal of money in preparation for peopling the granted land against the promise of 300,000 more acres when the first increment of land should be occupied under specified terms.[20] Its efforts in this direction had been frustrated in 1754 by the advance of French forces down the Allegheny River and the overwhelming of the Company's servants busy with the construction of a fort at the forks of the Ohio.[21] From that time on until the Peace of Paris was signed, there was little that the Company could do to secure its trans-Appalachian land claims. Late in 1759, or early in 1760, it did draw up an extended "Case of the Ohio Company, 1754," which told in great detail the steps taken, before the events of 1754, to fulfil its plans for the colonization of lands about the Ohio. This was later sent to one of its members in London, John

---

[19] For the Ohio Company petition for 500,000 acres of land and the Privy Council's action on it see *Acts of the Privy Council, Col. Ser., 1745–1766*, pp. 55–8.

[20] For the early history of the Ohio Company see Volume IV in this series, Chap. 8, "The Ohio Company"; see also *The George Mercer Papers Relating to the Ohio Company of Virginia* (ed. Lois Mulkearn, Pittsburgh, 1954), pp. 1–40, cited hereafter as *George Mercer Papers*, and A. P. James: *The Ohio Company. Its Inner History* (Pittsburgh, 1959), 9–110, together with an earlier pioneering study by K. P. Bailey: *The Ohio Company of Virginia and the Westward Movement . . .* (Glendale, Calif., 1939), cited hereafter as *The Ohio Company of Virginia.*

[21] See Volume IV in this series, pp. 302–6.

Hanbury,[22] was subsequently redrafted as a petition to the King, and was ultimately referred to the Board of Trade. Also, the following year, to secure the support of Lieutenant Colonel Henry Bouquet, commanding at Fort Pitt, the Company offered him a share of stock, which he refused.[23] Indeed, in October of 1761 he issued a proclamation against the settlement of trans-Appalachian lands and his position was supported by Lieutenant Governor Fauquier and the Virginia Council in an open advertisement prohibiting the survey of such lands until permission had been received from the British government.[24]

With the conclusion of the peace between Great Britain and France in 1763 the Ohio Company was stirred into new activity. A memorial to George III was drawn up asking the Crown to instruct the government of Virginia to implement the earlier conditional grant of trans-Appalachian land. What is more, it was decided to send George Mercer to England with instructions to work intimately with former Lieutenant Governor Dinwiddie and John Hanbury and his sons, Capel and Osgood.[25] Circumstances, however, were unfavourable in that year for the Company's success in attaining its immediate objective. For its demands were in direct opposition to principles relating to western lands enumerated by the government on October 7 in the Proclamation of 1763 setting up, at least temporarily, a vast trans-Appalachian Indian reserve.[26] In fact, it was not until June 1765 that Mercer felt he was in a position to present to the Crown the petition prepared two years earlier by the committee of the Company—that is, in 1763 before his departure from Virginia. This petition was accompanied by a memorial of his own writing.[27] These embodied the view that the Proclamation Line laid down in 1763 was merely temporary and not designed to prevent the Ohio Company from acting upon the royal instructions of 1749, authorizing settlement of lands allotted to it by the Virginia Council. If this were not to be the case, the memorial went on, then it was

[22] For the "Case of the Ohio Company, 1754," see the *George Mercer Papers*, pp. 233–86; see also A. P. James: *op. cit.*, pp. 88–9 and 113–16.

[23] *George Mercer Papers*, pp. 614–15.

[24] A. P. James: *op. cit.*, p. 118.

[25] *George Mercer Papers*, pp. 182–3. See also A. P. James: *George Mercer of the Ohio Company: A Study in Frustration* (Pittsburgh, 1963).

[26] For an analysis of the Proclamation of 1763 with an account of the events that led to it, see Volume IX, in this series, Chap. 3, "The Proclamation of 1763."

[27] For these memorials see K. P. Bailey: *The Ohio Company of Virginia*, pp. 253–6 and 310–13; see also A. P. James: *op. cit.*, p. 130. For the originals of these documents in the Public Record Office see C.O. 5:1331, pp. 413–18, 421–30.

the hope of the members of the Company that they would receive compensation for their large expenditures.

Not until two years later, on June 26, 1767, were the memorials taken up for consideration. At that time the Board of Trade recommended to the Privy Council that a full report on the activities of the Company be requested from the Governor of Virginia. This was done on October 8, when the Earl of Shelburne, Secretary of State for the Southern Department, called upon Governor Fauquier to transmit "an Exact Account of the Nature of the Claim which the Ohio Company have to the Lands petitioned for. . . ."[28] All this meant a further postponement on the part of the British government of action on the Company's claim.

While the Company's case was pending in London, a proposal for a change in the boundaries of the 1749 grant was presented by the leading member of the Company, George Mason, at its meeting held in Virginia during February 1768. The new boundaries proposed were designed to avoid the inclusion of lands claimed by the Proprietors of Pennsylvania, since—as a result of the recent running of the boundary line between Maryland and Pennsylvania—it was foreseen that the extension of the southern boundary line of Pennsylvania westward to its charter limits would "cross the Monongahaly, and strike the Ohio many Miles below Pitsburg [and would] consequently include all Lands the Ohio Company had settled . . ." Mason therefore recommended that the Ohio Company grant should take in the lands south and west of Pennsylvania described as follows: Beginning with the Monongahela "where the Pennsylvania Line crosses the said River; and running with the Pennsylvania Line a due West Course to the Ohio River," then skirting its right bank down to the mouth of the Great Kanawha and up that river to the mouth of the Greenbrier River "and from thence by a streight Line to the Beginning of the River Monongahaly."[29] However, later in 1768, as has already been stated, the Indians in the Treaty of Fort Stanwix, ceded the same lands to the "Suffering Traders," then represented by the Indiana Company. Furthermore, with the arrival in London of this company's most influential supporter, Samuel Wharton, and later in the year of William Trent, who was strongly recommended to the Earl of Shelburne by Sir

[28] Shelburne Papers, 54:67–70, Clements Library, Ann Arbor, Mich.

[29] These limits of the grant were proposed to the Company on February 26, 1768; the proposal was sent as an enclosure in John Mercer's letter to George Mercer of March 3, 1768. See *George Mercer Papers,* pp. 229–32.

William Johnson,[30] the prospects of a successful outcome to George Mercer's negotiations with the Ministry in behalf of the Ohio Company rapidly declined. Because Shelburne's office of Secretary of State for the Southern Department was no longer concerned with American affairs, Samuel Wharton at first thought that the Earl and his friends were opposed to the establishment of new settlements in the American interior; he later discovered that he was mistaken.[31]

Before the arrival of Trent, Wharton wrote to George Croghan on May 18, 1769, that Lord Hillsborough and his secretary "have formed an injurious Opinion respecting the Terms on Which the Cessions [that is, the land cessions to Croghan and the "Suffering Traders"] has been obtained and have expressed Dissatisfaction among other Things that Sr William [Johnson] suffered the Six Nations to make a Grant of Confirmation to you and a Deed to the Traders." At the same time Wharton assured Croghan that "a powerfull Body have their Eyes fixed on the conduct of [Hillsborough and his secretary], and have declared that If any fatal Consequences should arise from their not ratifying the Promises of Sr William to the S[ix] N[ation]s, they shall answer for it." Hillsborough's chief objection to the land cessions, according to Wharton, was that Johnson did not have the King's permission to allow the Six Nations to make them.[32] Writing to Croghan on June 16 of the same year, Wharton confided to him that Mr. Walpole, "a member of Parliament, Brother to Lord Walpole, & a most intimate acquaintance of Lord Chatham's—sent to me and informed me that the Lord Ch[ancello]r [that is, Camden] had . . . told Him, that there was not one member in all the [Cabinet Council] But that thought L^d^ H[illsborough] *mad* in his Objection to the Bo[un]d[ar]y . . . and therefore it as the *unanimous Opinion and Determination of them* to Confirm *it in all its parts.*"[33] In his letter to Croghan of August 12 he was able to report that he was "on the best of terms with . . . the first ruling Characters in the Adm[inistratio]n and in Parliament . . ."[34]

---

[30] Johnson to Shelburne, February 16, 1769, *Sir William Johnson Papers*, VI, 627–8.

[31] Writing to George Croghan on May 18, 1769, Wharton declared that Shelburne's plan "was first to establish the *interior Governments* and that after they were fixed, as they would be in the heart of the Indian Country, the Regulation of the Indian Commerce was to be committed to Them; But that, Sir William etc. were to be provided for, in a very generous honorable Manner . . . (George Croghan Papers, Cadwalader Collection, Box 37, Historical Society of Pennsylvania, to be cited hereafter as Cadwalader Collection of Croghan Papers).

[32] *Ibid.*

[33] *Ibid.*

[34] *Ibid.*

Trent, who arrived in England on May 25, wrote on June 10 to Croghan:

> "With respect to my particular Business here, it is not necessary for me to say much, As Mr Wharton and Doctor Franklin has wrote you so fully; But the Doctor told Me yesterday that if Sir William [Johnson] did not suffer Himself nor the Six Nations to be intimidated by the ministerial Letters . . . the whole Transactions, as wisely settled by Him at Fort Stanwix, would be undoubtedly ratified."[35]

The Formation of the Grand Ohio Company

Standing behind and supporting Wharton were such leading men of influence in London as Benjamin Franklin, whose son was involved in the Company and whose many British connections were considered invaluable. As a result of consultations with them, Wharton apparently came to the conviction that the only hope for the Indiana Company shareholders was to leave their concerns in abeyance in favour of pursuing an expanded project that would include a group of leading British political and business figures and would enlarge its objectives.[36] At the same time both Franklin and Lord Camden, according to William Trent's later testimony, advised that the grant received from the Indians on November 6, 1768, at Fort Stanwix need not be confirmed by the Crown. It was therefore decided not to press the Privy Council for a confirmation of the Indiana Company grant.[37] Instead, men like the Hon. Thomas

[35] *Pennsylvania Magazine of History and Biography,* LXXXIV, 48. Governor William Franklin, writing to his friend William Strahan in London on June 18, 1771, said in appreciation of Samuel Wharton's efforts: "I have not any doubt of Mr. Wharton's activity, sagacity or perseverance in this business. He is very capable and has certainly every inducement to excel all his abilities in carrying it through" ("William Franklin Letters," *ibid.,* XXXV, 449).

[36] By the summer of 1769, as a result of connections that Wharton had made, a new plan for western development had taken shape. This is indicated by his letter to Croghan of August 12, in which he says that the latter and Johnson will have a share but "I am under a solemn Engagement not to disclose the Plan untill the publick offices open again [in the fall] . . ." (Cadwalader Collection of Croghan Papers).

[37] See William Trent's testimony given at a meeting of the "Suffering Traders" on September 21, 1775, in Bailey's *Ohio Company Papers,* pp. 288–9. It should be borne in mind that Lord Camden, although Chancellor until January 1770, was in bitter opposition to the administration's policies, especially those having to do with the American colonies. Therefore, there is no reason to question the veracity of Trent's statement on Camden's attitude toward the land purchased from the Indians, especially in view of the Lord Chancellor's earlier opinion supporting the competence of the United East India Company to secure lands from the native princes of India without letters patent, a matter which will be discussed later in this chapter.

Walpole, banker and merchant, Thomas Pownall, former Governor of Massachusetts Bay, Lord Hertford, brother of General Conway, and Grey Cooper, a joint secretary of the Treasury, were approached.[38] The result was a decision to erect a new company, to be called officially the Grand Ohio Company (also known as the Walpole Company and the Vandalia Company), that would, incidentally, protect the land interests of the "Suffering Traders."[39]

Accordingly, a committee of five, consisting of Wharton, Franklin, Thomas Pownall, Thomas Walpole, and John Sargent, petitioned in June 1769 for 2,400,000 acres of land which included the tracts granted to the traders and Croghan at Fort Stanwix. Referred by the Lords of the Committee of the Council for Plantations on November 20 to the Board of Trade, the petition came up for consideration by the Lords Commissioners in the presence of the Earl of Hillsborough on December 20.[40] Hillsborough on this occasion reportedly encouraged the petitioners "to purchase a Quantity [of land] large enough for a separate Government," and suggested, as Wharton wrote, that "if we approved of his Hint, He kindly offered to step down to the Lords of the Treasury . . . & know whether they would treat with us." This Hillsborough did and reported "that their Lordships were ready to treat."[41]

Thus encouraged, sixteen members of the new company held a meeting on December 27 at the Crown and Anchor Tavern in London.[42] It was there proposed by Samuel Wharton that in consequence of the attitude displayed by Lord Hillsborough, the Company should purchase not 2,400,000 acres but all the land within certain suggested boundaries, or an estimated 20,000,000 acres,[43] on which they would set up a proprietary colony to be called Vandalia. The limits of the proposed purchase were as follows: Starting from a

---

[38] Wharton to Croghan, August 12, 1769, Cadwalader Collection of Croghan Papers.

[39] Wharton to Croghan, June 12, 1770, *ibid.* For the formation of the Grand Ohio Company see A. P. James, *op. cit.*, Chap. 10, and K. P. Bailey, *op. cit.*, p. 14.

[40] *Acts of the Privy Council, Col. Ser., 1766–1783,* p. 202; Board of Trade *Journal, 1768–1775,* pp. 152, 154–5; K. P. Bailey: *The Ohio Company of Virginia,* pp. 239–40.

[41] Samuel Wharton to George Croghan, September 4, 1770, Cadwalader Collection of Croghan Papers; see also Samuel Wharton: *Statement of the Petitioners in the Case of the Walpole Company Grant* (published in 1771), p. 12, and Board of Trade *Journal, 1768–1775,* pp. 154–5.

[42] Among those present were Benjamin Franklin, Thomas and Richard Walpole, Governor Thomas Pownall, Samuel Wharton, and William Trent.

[43] See the minutes of the meeting of the so-called Indiana Company held at Pittsburgh on September 22, 1775, at which William Trent produced the minutes of the Grand Ohio Company covering the meeting of December 27, 1769, with a list of those present, in K. P. Bailey: *Ohio Company Papers,* pp. 289–91.

point on the Ohio opposite the mouth of the Scioto River, the boundary line of the enlarged grant would run southward through the pass of the Quasioto (Wasioto) Mountains, following their south side in an easterly direction to where the Greenbrier and the New River join to create the Great Kanawha. The line would then continue up the east side of the Greenbrier to the termination of its northeast branch and from that point in an easterly direction to the Allegheny Mountains and the beginning of Lord Fairfax's estate. Skirting this, it would run to the head spring of the north branch of the Potomac and then along the western boundary of Maryland to the southern boundary of Pennsylvania, which it would follow until the western boundary of that province and the Ohio River were reached. The line would then run along the left bank of the Ohio to the starting point.[44]

Since both the traders who suffered losses in 1763 and George Croghan had received grants from the Six Nations for parcels of land in this same area, Wharton also embodied in his proposal the provision that as soon as the Company obtained a title for the whole tract from the Crown it should release their respective grants to the traders and to Croghan. This proposal "being fully considered by the Company was unanimously agreed to by them."[45]

The Ohio Company of Virginia and the Grand Ohio Company—Rivalry and Merger

On January 4, 1770, the Company petitioned the Lords Commissioners of the Treasury for the purchase of "a large Tract of Land on the River Ohio," offering the Crown immediate payment of the sum of £10,460.7.3, "being the whole of the Money paid by Government for all the Lands purchased of the Six Nations at Fort Stanwix" (actually this sum was simply the value of the presents to the Indians), and further offering to pay a quit-rent of two shillings on every one hundred acres of "Cultivatable Land within the said Tract, praying an Exemption from the payment of the said Quit Rent for the space of twenty years." On April 7 the petitioners

[44] *Acts of the Privy Council, Col. Ser., 1766–1783*, p. 208; see also *Ohio Company Papers*, pp. 290–1. For the location of the Quasioto Mountains see Lewis Evans: "A General Map of the Middle British Colonies in America" (1755) in L. H. Gipson's *Lewis Evans* (Philadelphia, 1939), p. 23; see also *George Mercer Papers*, p. 524, note 250.

[45] *Ibid.*, p. 291.

were informed that the Lords Commissioners of the Treasury had no objections to accepting their proposition "if it should be thought adviseable by those departments of Government to whom it belonged to Judge of the propriety of the Grant both in point of Policy and Justice." Upon renewing the application for a grant the petitioners expressly agreed to respect "the rights of occupiers [of lands] within the tract prayed for."[46]

This memorial for land in the Ohio country struck squarely at the rights claimed by Virginia in this region. In fact, shortly after the January 4 petition of the Grand Ohio Company, Edward Montague, the London agent for Virginia, submitted a counter-petition against "a Grant of certain Lands in & part of his Majestys Colony & Dominion of Virginia. . . ." In it he pointed out that "no less than 1,350,000 Acres of such Land have already been granted, partly to a Society of Gentlemen called the Ohio Company."[47] To counter this, at least so far as the Grand Ohio Company was concerned, on February 7 Thomas Walpole by letter assured Osgood Hanbury, one of the London members of the earlier company, that, pursuant to a meeting of the Grand Ohio Company, he was authorized to state that there was "no Intention to interfere with any Persons who have had any *legal Grants* from Government." The letter concluded: "if the Ohio Company think it right to prosecute their Pretentions, Mr. Walpole & those concerned with him can have no Objection thereto."[48]

Early in the year George Mercer had issued in printed form *The Case of the Ohio Company*, tracing the history of the Virginia Company's activities down to December 18, 1769.[49] It is quite clear, however, that soon afterwards he himself became convinced that the fate of the Company was sealed unless steps were taken to incorporate with its powerful rival, "formed by Mr. Walpole & others, stiled The Grand Company, who having petitioned for a Tract of Country including Lands desired by the Ohio Comp^{y} and being united with such of the nobility & Ministry as promised Success, left little hopes of the Ohio Company's succeeding in their Claim upon

---

[46] *Acts of the Privy Council, Col. Ser., 1766–1783*, pp. 202–3 and 208–9.

[47] See Montague to the Board of Trade [January 1770], C.O. 5:1332, p. 323; see also Montague to the Virginia committee of correspondence, January 18, 1770, *Virginia Magazine of History and Biography*, XII, 159–61.

[48] *George Mercer Papers*, p. 311.

[49] A copy of this interesting and rare pamphlet, which contains a collection of important documents, is in the Rufus King Collection at the New-York Historical Society; it has also been reproduced in facsimile by Mrs. Mulkearn in the *George Mercer Papers*, pp. 329–90.

so slight an Interest. . . ."[50] Therefore, on May 7, 1770, Mercer entered into an agreement, without previous authorization from the other Ohio Company members, to merge the two companies. In the merger two shares out of a total of seventy-two equal shares were allotted to the older company.[51]

The Virginia Government Grants and the Vandalia Scheme of the Grand Ohio Company

Despite the fact that Mercer—again without authorization—from those who had appointed him their agent—subsequently took steps to withdraw the petition of the Ohio Company for a re-grant of lands as well as the caveat against any grant to the Grand Ohio Company,[52] all was not clear sailing for the new company. The petition of Virginia London agent Montague against the Walpole application —which had come before the Board of Trade on January 31, 1770, and had then been referred to the Lords Commissioners of the Treasury for consideration—was still pending.[53] On June 7, the Grand Ohio Company's memorial was reviewed by the Board of Trade; it was again up for consideration on July 2. On the 18th the Lords Commissioners, after mature consideration, arrived at the unanimous decision that it would be highly improper for them to make any report to the Lords of the Committee of the Privy Council on the Walpole application until light had been shed on the extent to which the Governor and Council of Virginia had made grants in the same area. It was also their view that as the government of

---

[50] James Mercer to several members of the Ohio Company, January 9, 1772, *ibid.*, pp. 312–15. It will be noted that the above is the statement of James Mercer in Virginia based upon letters received from his brother George in England which have disappeared, yet giving the substance of them, one may rest assured.

[51] The agreement reads as follows: "We the Committee of the Purchasers of a Tract of Country for a new Province on the Ohio in America, do hereby admit the Ohio Company as a Co-Purchaser with us for two shares of the said Purchase, in Consideration of the Engagement of their Agent, Col. Mercer, to withdraw the Application of the said Company, for a separate Grant within the Limits of the said Purchase. Witness our Hands this 7th Day of May 1770. Thomas Walpole, T. Pownall, B. Franklin, Sam[l] Wharton. [Note] The whole [purchase] being divided into Seventy two equall Shares . . ." (*The American Historical Record* . . . [ed. B. J. Lossing, 3 vols., Philadelphia, 1872–4], III, 205).

[52] For Mercer's memorial to the Board of Trade, May 8, 1770, see C.O. 5:1332, p. 353, to be found printed in the appendix of Bailey's *The Ohio Company of Virginia*, p. 319; see also Board of Trade *Journal, 1768–1775*, p. 188.

[53] *Ibid.*, p. 166.

Virginia had in other respects a very direct interest in this matter, their case should be heard before any decision was reached.[54]

Moreover, the Earl of Hillsborough had now come to view plans for trans-Appalachian colonization in a new light. On July 31, he wrote a letter to Lord Botetourt, the Governor of Virginia, containing enclosures having to do with the Grand Ohio Company's petitions. In the letter Hillsborough made clear that the King not only had supported the position of the Board of Trade but had ordered him to signify to Governor Botetourt that no further grants of land beyond the Proclamation Line of 1763 should be made until His Majesty's pleasure was made known.[55] Prior to receiving this letter, Botetourt had sent the Board of Trade a list of the Virginia land grants west of the Appalachians. Included were thirty-two orders in council issued by the provincial government for grants of land, as well as petitions for grants that had not been acted upon.[56]

On October 15, 1770, a change took place in the government of Virginia. On this date, after a painful illness, Botetourt passed away. William Nelson, as President of the Council, then took upon himself all executive duties permitted by his office[57] until Lord Dunmore should take control. Three days later he signed a long letter to Hillsborough that undoubtedly influenced the latter's growing opposition to the plan for the proposed colony of Vandalia[58] which was to be

---

[54] *Ibid.*, pp. 192, 194, 201–2. It may be added that Major General Sir Jeffrey Amherst, Governor-in-Chief of Virginia between 1763 and 1768, whose influence in Great Britain carried great weight, was also a strong advocate of the colonization of lands up to the Mississippi River. Writing, apparently early in 1768, he upheld the proposals to establish a distinct government at Detroit, one in the Illinois country, and another on the lower Mississippi between the Iberville and Ohio rivers which could be supported by regular troops. See Amherst Papers, Bundle 63, Canadian Archives transcripts.

[55] C.O. 5:1348, p. 225.

[56] Botetourt to the Board of Trade, July 31, 1770, C.O. 5:1333, pp. 137–59. An addition to this list of grants made before the year 1761 was later sent to the Board. See C.O. 5:1348, pp. 345–6. In this connection see also "An account of Virginia land grants reported December 6, 1769," drawn up by Nathaniel Walthoe, Clerk of the Virginia Council, which was laid before the Virginia House of Burgesses, and other papers dated 1770, in K. P. Bailey: *Ohio Company Papers*, pp. 232–46.

[57] Nelson to Hillsborough, October 18, 1770, C.O. 5:1348, p. 305.

[58] The first use of the name Vandalia—outside of marginal notations—in any official document is in the Board of Trade representation to the Privy Council of May 6, 1773. This is printed in Bailey's *Ohio Company Papers*, pp. 263–79, but is wrongly ascribed to be a report from the Privy Council. See Board of Trade *Journal, 1768–1775*, p. 356. See in this connection J. M. Sosin: *Whitehall and the Wilderness*, Chap. 8, "Vandalia: an Interior Colony," for an illuminating discussion that goes beyond that by T. P. Abernethy in Chap. 3 of his *Western Lands*. See also the succinct statement on this subject by R. A. Billington: *Westward Expansion* (2nd edn.), pp. 150–3.

carved out of the trans-Appalachian lands previously held to be a part of Virginia by earlier patents.

To answer certain charges that the Virginia Council had made many large grants of these lands subsequent to the Proclamation of 1763, Nelson showed that not one such grant had been approved. However, in this connection, he cited the grant of 200,000 acres to the Ohio Company in 1749 which had been conditionally approved by George II. As to the Ohio Valley lands that had been promised by Governor Dinwiddie in 1754 to the officers and soldiers who would volunteer to defend the frontiers against the French and Indians, he pointed out that these lands were currently being surveyed. These would comprehend, he declared, another 200,000 acres, and at least 200,000 more were destined for new volunteers and the King's Service in America.

While admitting that he had not had access to any authentic copy of the Treaty of Fort Stanwix, Nelson went on to state that George Croghan had been given 100,000 acres by the Indians at the Stanwix Congress, as had the Pennsylvania traders. In other words, according to Nelson, all the acreage granted "to the northward," amounted to 800,000 acres. Of the other Virginia grants in question, many of the earlier ones had lapsed or were about to lapse, but two were being settled; one to John Lewis and associates (the so-called Loyal Company)[59] for 800,000 acres and another to James Patton and others for 100,000 acres. Both of these grants lay in the area stretching from the Greenbrier River to the branches of the Holston River, well within the limits of the territory which the Cherokee Indians were in the process of ceding for £2,500 sterling appropriated for this purpose by the Virginia Assembly, and where many hundreds of families were actually settled. These pioneers, he claimed, had refused to abandon the lands on which they had made improvements before the Proclamation. In fact, they had no other place to go, "having expended their little all under the grants from this Government." Other people were also settling these lands "under the equitable right they derived from the grant to John Lewis and others," while "James Patton's grant is also pretty full of inhabitants. . . ." Thus, according to Nelson, there were 1,700,000 acres of land granted to individuals, whose rights, "whether *Equitable or legal*," should be preferred before the claims of any new adventurers.[60]

---

[59] See Archibald Henderson: "Dr. Thomas Walker and the Loyal Company of Virginia," American Antiquarian Society *Proceedings* (new ser., XLI, 77–178); see also Volume IV in this series, p. 257.

[60] Nelson to Hillsborough, October 18, 1770, C.O. 5:1348, pp. 221–30; this is printed in the *Journals of the House of Burgesses, 1770–1772,* pp. xxii–xxv.

When the Nelson letter arrived, it and its enclosures were sent to the Board of Trade, which made the contents available to the Walpole group. They, in turn, prepared a reply. At a meeting of the Lords Commissioners on March 24, 1771, the letter and the reply of the petitioners were taken up for detailed consideration.[61] The petitioners' reply, dated March 5, made clear that the land claims of the Virginia Ohio Company had been recognized and cared for in the plan for the new colony. It also stated that Colonel Mercer—London representative not only of the earlier Ohio Company but also of the officers and soldiers with bounties for western lands pledged by the Council of Virginia and Governor Dinwiddie in the 1750's—had been given assurances that by joining with the Grand Ohio Company these equitable interests would also be protected. The petitioners further pledged that the claims of all those who actually had made settlements on the lands in question before the Proclamation of 1763 would be respected.[62]

The Government Crisis over the Grand Ohio Company

But action on the petition was delayed. The new Governor of Virginia, Lord Dunmore, even before leaving his post in New York to enter upon his duties at Williamsburg, had voiced bitter opposition to the proposed new colony at the back of Virginia. Writing to Hillsborough on November 12, 1770, he had declared: "The scheme alarms extremely all the settled parts of America, the people of property being justly apprehensive of consequences that must inevitably ensue. . . ." For the draining of people out of the older colonies would, he advised, be accompanied by the fall of land values and default of quit-rents, in addition to which there was the probability that an attempt to colonize the Ohio country would lead to another Indian war.[63]

In view of such warnings it is not difficult to understand why the Board of Trade should have shared Hillsborough's misgivings as to

[61] Board of Trade *Journal, 1768–1775,* p. 293.

[62] For this reply see *Statement of the Petitioners in the Case of the Walpole Company Grant* [London, 1771], Appendix 3, John Carter Brown Library; see also George Mercer to George Washington, December 18, 1770, *Letters to Washington . . .* (ed. S. M. Hamilton, 4 vols, Boston and New York, 1901), IV, 39–40. For George Washington's opposition to plans of the Walpole Associates, see his letter to Lord Botetourt, October 5, 1770, *Writings of George Washington* (ed. J. C. Fitzpatrick, 39 vols., Washington 1931–44), III, 26–9; see also *Journal of the House of Burgesses, 1770–1772,* pp. xx–xxii.

[63] For Dunmore's letter see *Journals of the House of Burgesses of Virginia, 1770–1772,* p. xxvi.

the wisdom of the Grand Ohio Company enterprise. Not until the spring of 1772 did the Board finally issue its report.[64] Drawn up in the form of a representation to the Lords of the Committee of the Privy Council, it was delivered to them on April 29, but the Privy Council hearing was not held until June 5.[65] At this time the petitioners were permitted to appear and to reply in person to President Nelson's objections to the grants, as expressed in his letter written in the fall of 1770. In their rebuttal they took the surprising position that they did not conceive the petitioned lands to be a part of the Province of Virginia, but to be vested in the Crown by reason of the Treaty of Fort Stanwix with the Six Nations. As to the question of any Cherokee rights, the petitioners took the position that only recently had these Indians put forth any claims to ownership of lands lying north of Chiswell's Mine. As for white claimants of trans-Appalachian lands, however, the petitioners professed themselves willing to continue to make the concession of including a clause in their grant "to take into consideration any legal Rights" that others might have within the limits of the Vandalia lands.[66]

The attitude of the Lords of the Committee of the Council toward the Walpole Associates petition was in striking contrast to that of the Board of Trade.[67] Indeed, the prospects for success of the plan to establish a new trans-Appalachian colony were never brighter, for after hearing the petitioners, the Committee on July 1, 1772, returned a favourable report to the Privy Council.[68]

By the time the petition had reached this stage, at least fifty-four people—a number of them men of influence in public life—had

---

[64] See *Writings of Benjamin Franklin* (Smyth) v, 467–78.

[65] For the action on the report see *Acts of the Privy Council, Col. Ser., Unbound Papers,* pp. 512–18. It should be noted that one of the principal objections of the Board of Trade to the petition for the grant was that "part of the Lands prayed for lie beyond the Line which has in consequence of His Majesty's orders been settled by Treaty as well with the Tribes of the Six Nations and their Confederates as with the Cherokee Indians as the boundary line between His Majesty's Territories and their hunting grounds" (Thomas Walpole to Secretary John Pownall, May 14, 1772, C.O. 5:1333, pp. 431–2).

[66] *Acts of the Privy Council, Col. Ser., 1766–1783,* pp. 203–8; see also *Report of the Lords Commissioners . . . on the Petition of . . . Walpole . . . and . . . Associates . . . With Observations and Remarks* (London, 1772); this report on the promotion tract issued by the Grand Ohio Company was written by Lord Hillsborough and the "Observations," by Samuel Wharton, according to R. W. G. Vail: *Voice of the Old Frontier* (Philadelphia, 1949), p. 294.

[67] Samuel Wharton wrote to George Croghan on November 9, 1771: "There is the best Disposition in all the M[iniste]rs, except L[d] H[illsborough] to do it [that is, carry out the plans of the Grand Ohio Company]; and he will not oppose the whole of his Friends" (Cadwalader Collection of Croghan Papers).

[68] See *Acts of the Privy Council, Col. Ser., Unbound Papers,* p. 518.

become identified with the Grand Ohio Company as members. They included such men as Lord Rochford, Secretary of State for the Northern Department, and Lords Gower and Camden; other important British members were Thomas Pitt, brother of William, and John Robinson, later to become Under-Secretary of the Treasury.[69]

When the Earl of Hillsborough was forced to realize that his opposition to the project could not sway the Privy Council, he reluctantly resigned on August 1 out of conviction that he should not be a party to an unwise governmental decision for setting up colonies in the trans-Appalachian region.[70] In the words of Lord North, the King's chief minister: "He was not prompted to his resignation either by love of action or repose, but purely by notion of necessity he was under of resigning. . . ."[71] In his place, William Legge, the Earl of Dartmouth, was chosen as Secretary of State for the Colonies.[72] In this connection Benjamin Franklin wrote to his son:

[69] For a list of members as of 1773, all of whom seem to have been identified with the Grand Ohio Company in 1772, see C.O. 5:1336, p. 575; see also C. W. Alvord: *The Mississippi Valley in British Politics,* II, 98–102. It may also be noted that on July 3, 1770, Samuel Wharton wrote to Thomas Pitt: "I have the pleasure to inform you, That I have secured a Share in Our purchase [of lands from the] Government for Mr. Grenville, and I beg you will do me the Favor to make Him acquainted therewith" (Stowe Americana, Miscellaneous File, 1670–1813, Huntington Library). It would appear that at the reorganization meeting forming the Grand Ohio Company on December 7, 1769, seventy-two shares were created which allowed for proportional shares to go to Croghan and the "Suffering Traders." See Alvord: *op. cit.,* II, 103. It should also be recalled that among the prominent American members of the Grand Ohio Company were Joseph Galloway, Sir William Johnson, George Mercer, William Trent, Benjamin Franklin and his son William, Samuel Wharton and others of his family, and several of the Franks family.

[70] Peter Livius wrote from London to Hutchinson on August 3, 1772, as follows: "The Establishment of a Government on the Ohio is a measure at this time much talk'd of, & patronized by the greater part of the Administration, but Lord Hillsborough is much set against it, on the same principles that he opposes all internal Colonization . . . ; he declares if the measure is adopted he will resign, & I believe considers himself about to quit. Lord Chatham is talk'd of as his successor, & it is said he is to be brought in, in order to regulate the Colonies" ("Hutchinson Family Correspondence, 1740–1780," Egerton Manuscripts, 2659:22, British Museum). Obviously the writer did not know that Hillsborough had already resigned. Livius, it may be added, had gone to England to complain against the action of Governor John Wentworth of New Hampshire in depriving him and other grantees of lands which Wentworth's uncle, Benning Wentworth, had granted when occupying the Governor's chair. See *Acts of the Privy Council, Col. Ser., Unbound Papers,* pp. 526, 529–36.

[71] Reginald Lucas: *Lord North, Second Earl of Guilford . . . 1732–1792* (2 vols., London, 1913), I, 353.

[72] Writing to Lord Dartmouth on August 3, 1772, Lord North commented on "the petition for a grant of land in the Ohio, in consequence of which Lord Hillsborough has seen fit to send in his resignation." He then asked Dartmouth's permission to recommend him to the King as Hillsborough's successor, giving his reasons for this decision. See *The Manuscripts of the Earl of Dartmouth,* Vol. II (*American Papers*), *Historical Manuscripts Commission, Fourteenth Report, Appendix, Part* X (1895), p. 86; cited hereafter as *Dartmouth Manuscripts.*

"At length we have got rid of Lord Hillsborough, and Lord Dartmouth takes his place, to the great satisfaction of all the friends of America. You will hear it said among you, I suppose, that the interest of the Ohio planters had ousted him; but the truth is, what I wrote you long since, that all his brother ministers disliked him extremely, and wished for a fair occasion of tripping up his heels; so, seeing that he made a point of defeating our scheme, they made another of supporting it, on purpose to mortify him, which they knew his pride could not bear. I do not mean they would have done this, if they had thought our proposal bad in itself, or his opposition well founded; but I believe, if he had been on good terms with them they would not have differed with him for so small a matter. The King, too, was tired of him and of his administration, which had weakened the affection and respect of the colonies for a royal government. . . . The King's dislike made the others more firmly united in the resolution of disgracing Hillsborough, by setting at nought his famous report. . . ."[73]

That North's leadership was not very vigorous at this juncture is attested in George III's account of the crisis to Lord Suffolk, Secretary of State for the Southern Department. To the Secretary, the King reported the events following North's letter to Lord Gower, President of the Council, desiring that the Lords of the Committee postpone their report "on the Ohio business."[74] In reply, Gower stated his willingness to do so, provided the Cabinet Council, and more particularly Suffolk and Lord Rochford, would agree. But Rochford took the position that it would represent a constitutional departure for the Cabinet even to debate the question "whether a report directed by the Privy Council should remain dormant . . ." and wrote to Gower that the two Secretaries of State were opposed to the North proposal. Thereupon Gower, in his official capacity, directed Rochford to report the Council's favourable decision. This not only brought about Hillsborough's resolution to resign, but also left North, as the King's chief minister, in a most embarrassing position from which he extricated himself only by sacrificing Hillsborough.[75]

With Hillsborough out of the way and the Privy Council con-

---

[73] Benjamin Franklin to William Franklin, August 17, 1772, *Writings of Benjamin Franklin* (Smyth), V, 410.

[74] George III to Lord Suffolk, July 22, 1772, *Letters of King George III* (Bonamy Dobrée, London, 1935), pp. 83–4.

[75] *Ibid.* Among the William Knox Papers is one dated August 15, 1772, the day Hillsborough resigned, which gives in great detail the circumstances surrounding the resignation. See *The Manuscripts of Captain H. V. Knox* (ed. Mrs. S. C. Lomas, 1909), *Historical Manuscripts Commission, Report on . . . Various Collections,* VI, 253–5, cited hereafter as *Knox Manuscripts.* Knox was Under-Secretary for the Colonies from 1770 to 1782.

trolled by supporters of the Walpole Associates, the Vandalia project seemed to be near consummation. On August 14, 1772, an order in council was issued.[76] It pointed out that the two most material arguments in favour of the project had not been presented to the Board of Trade. These were: first of all, that the lands in question were not mere wild Indian hunting grounds but, on the contrary, had for some time been in process of settlement with numbers of families continuously moving to them, and should therefore be subject to some definite type of control; secondly, these same lands did "*not* lie beyond the reach of advantageous Intercourse with this Kingdom."

After reciting the proposed limits of the new colony, the order in council then referred to the opinion of the Lords of the Committee that, in case the King should be pleased to make a grant of any of the lands in question, the petitioners should have preference, as the first to make definite proposals for purchase and to agree, moreover, to assume the whole expense of the civil government of the colony. Among the Committee's recommendations included in the order were: the Superintendent of Indian Affairs for the Northern District should be directed to apprise the Six Nations and their confederates of the proposed settlement; the Board of Trade should draw up a proper clause among the terms of the grant that would protect the prior claims of actual occupiers of lands within its limits; further, the Board should make clear to the petitioners that only those lands petitioned for should be subject to their immediate exploitation rather than all the lands that might be included within the bounds of the colony; and finally—to the end that persons settled or settling on the lands should be protected and the grant be properly governed—the district should be erected into a separate government "in such Form and Manner as to your Majestys Wisdom shall seem meet, and under such . . . Regulations as the Lords Commissioners for Trade and Plantations shall advise."[77]

On September 2, 1772, Dartmouth forwarded a copy of the order to Sir William Johnson, the Indian Superintendent, calling upon him to make clear to the Six Nations and their allies that the King expected to establish a colony to the south of the Ohio.[78] Several months later Johnson reported back to Dartmouth that he had demonstrated to the Indians how the establishment of a government

[76] For a copy of the order in council see C.O. 5:1333, pp. 85–92; see also K. P. Bailey: *Ohio Company Papers*, pp. 257–62.

[77] *Ibid.*

[78] *New York Colonial Documents*, VIII, 311.

on the Ohio would be much to their advantage, since those white people who had acted in an unfriendly manner toward the Indians would now be placed under control. His report also stated that he had reason to believe the Six Nations viewed the prospect of a new colony in a favourable light.[79]

On November 2 the Board of Trade received the order in council, which charged its members with reporting their opinion "on the terms of settlement and the reservations necessary to be inserted in the grant of land to be made to Mr. Walpole and others," and with preparing "a plan for establishing a separate government upon the said tract" to be laid before His Majesty.[80] But the Lords Commissioners were in no hurry. As for the new Secretary for the Colonies, although he was favourable to British expansion into the interior of America, he was doubtless more inclined to let things unfold than to put pressure on the Board to hurry its work [81] He was unquestionably swayed by the fact that the Secretary of State for the Northern Department, Lord Suffolk—the man of chief influence in American affairs at this juncture—was a confidant of the King and therefore was not to be challenged.[82] Nevertheless, on April 1, 1773, the Lords Commissioners at last took into consideration the order in council referring to the new colony, as well as to the tentative grant to the Grand Ohio Company, and directed the petitioners to appear on the 5th. At this meeting Samuel Wharton was present as agent for the Company. After some discussion it was agreed to prepare a repre-

---

[79] Johnson to Dartmouth, November 4, 1772, *ibid.*, VIII, 314–17.

[80] Board of Trade *Journal, 1768–1775,* p. 316.

[81] In October 1772 Dartmouth received an anonymous communication on the Ohio settlement plan in which the writer insisted that a colony of this nature would face such great difficulties in attempting to carry on trade that, instead of engaging in silk culture, as some had suggested would be the case, the settlers would become "tartars or savages," and would be utterly lost to Great Britain from a "commercial view" (*Dartmouth Manuscripts,* II, 103–4). This type of communication, taken together with the influence on public issues still exerted by Hillsborough (now promoted to the House of Lords as Viscount Fairford and Earl of Hillsborough of the British peerage) and others, may have caused Dartmouth to have doubts about pushing the Vandalia project to completion. At least Horace Walpole felt Dartmouth was responsible for the delay. See *The Last Journals of Horace Walpole during the Reign of George III from 1771–1783* (ed. A. F. Steuart, 2 vols., London, 1910), I, 305. With reference to the production of silk in the trans-Appalachian area, it may be noted that, at the meeting with the Lords of the Committee on Plantation Affairs on June 5, 1772, a Mr. Paterson, concerned in the manufacture of silk, gave an account of some 150 pounds of silk "Imported from the Lands in Question" in 1770, a part of which he had purchased, had worked up in the mills, and had found to be of excellent quality. See *Acts of the Privy Council, Col. Ser., 1766–1783,* pp. 205–6.

[82] John Pownall to William Knox, July 23, 1773, *Knox Manuscripts,* p. 110. See C. W. Alvord: *The Mississippi Valley in British Politics,* II, Chaps. 4–6, for an extended treatment of the Grand Ohio Company.

sentation to the King embodying propositions for the establishment of the new colonial government and the proposed grant of lands. By May 6 it was approved and signed.[83]

The representation of the Board of Trade recommended boundary lines for the new colony far beyond the limits applied for by the Grand Ohio Company in 1769, previously described. It was to be bounded on the north by the Ohio River; on the west by the Kentucky River (called by Colonel John Donelson, who laid down the Cherokee cession lines, "the Louisa River" and designated on John Mitchell's map as the Catawba or Catawa River), from its mouth to its spring-head, and then by a straight line to the point on the Holston River where it intersected the North Carolina northern boundary line. On the south, the boundary should run along a straight line to the point intersecting the Great Kanawha River, otherwise called Woods River or New River. The eastern boundary would be determined by a line running north from the North Carolina boundary to the mouth of the Greenbrier River, then east to the Allegheny Mountains and, following them northward to the head of the north branch of the Potomac River, along the western boundary line of Maryland to the southern boundary of Pennsylvania, which it would follow west to a point where it reached the Ohio.[84]

This area, it was recommended, should be erected into a separate colony with a well-rounded royal type of government, the general and local officials of which were designated, but not by name. Also laid down were the freehold and religious qualifications for the franchise. Within the colony the Anglican Church was designated as the religious establishment and the means for its support specified. The cost of supporting the general government, with salaries and allowances to the chief officers, amounting to £2,500 a year, was also outlined.[85]

As the Grand Ohio Company had covenanted not only to pay £10,460.7.3, pursuant to the agreement of April 7, 1772, but also to provide the expense of supporting the new colony, the Board in its representation recommended the appointment of five Company members to be responsible for these payments. These five, after having given security to the amount of £10,000 sterling, should make semi-annual payments to a royal Receiver General against the

[83] Board of Trade *Journal, 1768–1775,* pp. 351, 352, 354, 356.

[84] For a copy of the representation of the Board of Trade of May 6, 1773, see K. P. Bailey: *The Ohio Company Papers,* pp. 263–79. Dr. Bailey calls this incorrectly "The Report of the Privy Council on Vandalia Grant, May 6, 1773." See also note 58 in this chapter.

[85] *Ibid.*

annual expense and up to £500 in addition as a contingent fund until such a time as, by some act of the General Assembly of the new province, this responsibility could be assumed by the inhabitants. The lands within the new colony to be specifically granted to the Company were to conform to the area requested on January 4, 1770, by its members in their second petition, with the important proviso that all those who already had "equitable or legal Titles" to lands should be protected in their holdings. Likewise, the grant of 200,000 acres made by Virginia to the officers of the regiment in 1754 were to be recognized by the Company.[86]

This representation came before the Privy Council on May 19 and was automatically referred to the Lords of the Committee, who on July 3 directed the Attorney General and Solicitor General to prepare the draft of a grant to Walpole and his associates along the lines proposed by the Board of Trade.[87] With the great grant of lands to the Grand Ohio Company all but accomplished, the need for its members to raise a fund without delay became apparent. On July 10 William Walpole, a banker and member of the Company, gave receipts to forty subscribers or their agents for sums of from £200 to £400, amounting in all to £8,200 sterling.[88]

---

[86] *Ibid.* The Council of Virginia on October 31, 1771, with the support of Governor Dunmore, had agreed that, in fulfilment of the promise made to the 1st Virginia Regiment in 1754, each field officer should have 15,000 acres of western land; each captain, 9,000; subalterns, 6,000; cadets, 2,500; sergeants, 600; corporals, 500; and private soldiers, 400. Thereupon, Captain William Crawford, by appointment, made surveys of 127,899 acres in thirteen distinct tracts. These, designated as the "first surveys," were laid before the Council. On November 6 it was agreed that out of one tract of 13,532 acres George Mercer should be free to patent 12,000 acres (6,000 in his own right, as a subaltern, and 6,000 acres as heir to his brother John Mercer, also a subaltern), and that four tracts of 10,990 acres, 4,395 acres, 2,448 acres, and 2,314 acres, respectively, amounting to 20,147 acres, should be immediately patented in the name of George Washington, which, with a shortage of 453 acres to be allotted at the next distribution, totalled 20,600 acres (15,000 acres as his allowance as a field officer, and the remainder as purchase rights). See *Virginia Gazette* (Rind), January 14, 1773, for the order of the Virginia Council, December 9, 1772, and for George Washington's announcement from Mount Vernon dated December 23, 1772. These surveys, one may rest assured, were of choice tracts. As the soldiers were entitled to 200,000 acres, tracts up to 72,101 acres remained to be surveyed and allotted. For Washington's interest in western lands see C. H. Ambler: *George Washington and the West* (Chapel Hill, N.C., 1936), R. B. Cook: *Washington's Western Lands* (Strasburg, Va., 1930), and D. S. Freeman: *George Washington* (6 vols., New York, 1948–57), III, 215–16, and *passim,* especially Chap. 13 and pp. 333–5; for Washington's correspondence with Colonel William Crawford, who was to survey western lands for him, see also *The Washington-Crawford Letters* (ed. C. W. Butterfield, Cincinnati, 1877) and the Fitzpatrick *Writings,* II and III, *passim.*

[87] *Acts of the Privy Council, Col. Ser., 1766–1783,* p. 210.

[88] Benjamin Franklin, for example, acted not only for his friend Joseph Galloway in Pennsylvania, but also for his son, Governor William Franklin of New Jersey. "List of Receipts signed by Mr. Walpole, July 10th, 1773," in K. P. Bailey: *Ohio Company Papers,* p. 280.

The Collapse of the Vandalia Scheme

But unexpected obstacles now arose. On July 16 Edward Thurlow, Attorney General, and Alexander Wedderburn, Solicitor General, made their report to the Lords of the Committee.[89] The opinion of the two chief law officers was that the grant, as held in joint-tenancy by members of the Company, would probably render it impossible to give purchasers of land "Complete Titles"; further, that the description of the area to be granted was "much more loose and uncertain than hath been usual in Royal Grants"; and finally, that payment of the royal quit-rent was not well secured. Their chief criticism was centred on the boundary description of the region, which seemed to be "wholly unknown" to the petitioners: "The bounds are described to cross an indeterminate number of mountains, and then to run *by the side* of such mountains, and *along* other mountains, and by the *north branch* or *north-easterly branch* of rivers, which in maps appear to have several branches corresponding to those descriptions." They ended their report by observing: "We take it to be of the essence of his Majesty's grants that his Majesty should appear to be informed of what he bestows."[90]

Subsequently, Lord Dartmouth took the position that the bounds of the proposed colony were "as clearly and distinctly ascertained as the knowledge of the country will admit of."[91] At the same time the Lords of the Committee directed the Attorney General and the Solicitor General to redraft the grant so as to provide that the quit-rents (after twenty years) would be payable not only by those who sought the grant of lands but also by the under-tenants, thus obviating one of the basic criticisms.[92] However, beyond the Privy Council's approval on October 28, 1773, of the action of its committee,[93] no further steps were taken toward establishing the new colony or making the grant to the Grand Ohio Company.

Many factors doubtless contributed to the collapse of the Grand Ohio Company project. Among them, apparently, was the fear that the older American colonies were now controlled by those seeking freedom from ties with the mother country. For example, early in

[89] *Dartmouth Manuscripts,* II, 172.

[90] *Acts of the Privy Council, Col Ser., 1766–1783,* p. 210, and *ibid., Unbound Papers,* p. 543.

[91] Dartmouth to the Earl of Rochford, September 9, 1773, *Dartmouth Manuscripts,* II, 172–3.

[92] *Acts of the Privy Council, Col. Ser., 1766–1783,* p. 210.

[93] *Ibid.*

1773 General Gage had written from New York to Lord Barrington:

> "The Boston Assembly has now thrown off all Dependence upon the Supreme Legislature [Parliament], and done it deliberately, without being prompted to it by any Sudden Heat or Passion. The Principle is not yet generally adopted in the other Provinces, tho' there may be many who Maintain it, and there is no knowing how soon it may become general: I really fear a small Matter might make it so."[94]

The ominous rioting over the Tea Act later that year at the chief American seaports upon the appearance of the tea ships confirmed this observation. If the Atlantic seaboard colonies were in danger of slipping out of the control of the government of Great Britain, how much more difficult would it be to maintain the proper relationship with a colony located hundreds of miles in the great interior of North America? Gage, as Commander-in-Chief of British Forces in America, later in 1773 returned to England to report on the American situation. He was no friend of western colonization. In fact he had written to Barrington from America during the summer of 1772:

> "People have long expected that new Governments would be formed in this Country upon the back of the old Provinces, and some of the chief Projectors of the Scheme have been a long time on your side of the Water, it's said to prove the advantage of such a measure to the Kings Ministers, but I apprehend rather to deceive them. . . . I [think it would] be for our interest to keep the Settlers within reach of the Sea-Coast as long as we can; and to cramp their Trade as far as it can be done prudentially. Cities flourish and increase by extensive Trade; Artisans and Mechanicks of all Sort's are drawn thither, who teach all sorts of handicraft work before unknown in the Country and they soon come to make for themselves what they used to import. I have seen this Increase, and I assure your Lordship that Foundations are laid in Philadelphia, that must create Jealousy in an Englishman."[95]

One may assume therefore that Gage, before returning to America in the spring of 1774, used his influence against the plan for a western colony. In the light of his high position, his views must have carried great weight. At least this seems to have been the opinion of Americans, according to Major General Frederick Haldimand, who, as acting commander during Gage's absence in England, reported to the General on November 4, 1773: "It is published here

---

[94] Gage to Barrington, February 8, 1773, *Correspondence of General Thomas Gage . . .* (ed. C. E. Carter, 2 vols., New Haven, 1931, 1933), II, 636–7.

[95] Gage to Barrington, August 5, 1772, *ibid.*, II, 615–16.

that there will be no government on the Ohio and that you are the cause of it."[96]

At the very moment the fate of the project hung in the balance, there were published, both in Boston and in London, certain confidential letters written by Governor Thomas Hutchinson to an unnamed private person in England, referring to the developing crisis in Massachusetts Bay. In the midst of charges and counter-charges involving the reputation of prominent Englishmen, Benjamin Franklin, one of the leading promoters of the Grand Ohio Company, publicly acknowledged that he had obtained possession of these letters in 1772 and had sent them to Boston for the enlightenment of the members of the General Court under stipulation that they were to be neither copied nor published. This admission led to his dismissal from his post of deputy postmaster-general in America and his denunciation by certain members and supporters of the government. Summoned to appear before the Privy Council on January 29, 1774, he was castigated in the most public manner by Solicitor General Wedderburn,[97] one of the two legal advisers of the King, who had the responsibility of implementing the order in council of 1772 by preparing the final draft for setting up the colony and making the grant of land. It does not require much historical imagination to realize that after the Franklin episode, Wedderburn—always hostile to the enterprise—could never have been brought to take any further steps in his official position or otherwise to support the Grand Ohio Company plan for the colony of Vandalia.

Parenthetically, it may be pointed out that there had been a break in the relationship of both Samuel Wharton and William Trent with Franklin and his son, the Governor. Writing to George Croghan on February 3, 1773, Wharton remarked:

> "I am no way surprised at Governor F[ranklin]'s Behaviour to you. He has treated Mr. Trent and myself as ill, and as ungratefully as He possibly could do. But I despise him and all his sunshine, pretended Friends in Philadelphia—If I have never informed you, let me now tell you that his Father has had no more Interest, Trouble or Concern in affecting the negociation about the Ohio Colony, than the smallest Farmer in Cumberland County. In short, I have not seen Him six Times, in the last two years, and I have not once conversed with him, since last June, till four days ago. In one word, neither Father nor

---

[96] "Haldimand Papers," B.M., Add. Mss. 21665:177.

[97] *Writings of Benjamin Franklin* (Symth), V, 448; VI, 188–93 and 258–89; X, 258–72. For a fuller discussion of the episode involving the Hutchinson-Oliver letters see Volume XII in this series, Chap. 4.

> Son has the smallest Share of Interest with Administration, and all we were thought to believe, before I left America was meer piff and Declamation."[98]

Wharton was obviously expecting to be appointed Governor of the new colony, for in the same letter he referred to the destruction of the "Governor's House" at Fort Pitt and then went on to remark confidentially that since he would soon be appearing in the above capacity, "I must have a suitable House provided for me." Authorizing Croghan to hire or buy such a house for him, he added: "Two of the best Houses in Pittsburgh . . . at a Distance of eight or ten or even twelve feet from each other" might perhaps be secured and joined together by a wide entry-way. However, if this could not be done, Croghan was to set about building a house according to a plan sent with the letter.[99]

Meanwhile, on August 8, 1774, the Hon. Thomas Walpole presented a very lengthy memorial to the King in Council on behalf of himself, ten others designated by name, and their associates. The name of Franklin was conspicuously absent, but notably present were the names of Lord Camden, Earl Temple, and Richard Jackson. The memorial, after tracing the steps that had been taken by the Company to secure the grant of land and the delays that had been faced, "most humbly prayed his Majesty that the establishment of the Government of the new Colony of Vandalia, may be no longer delayed,—and that the Grant to your Memorialists of the Lands agreed for, may be expedited."[100] But nothing came from the memorial nor from the ably penned *Facts and Observations . . .*[101] that, embodying it as well as the background of the history of the enterprise, was published in London in the spring of

[98] Cadwalader Collection of Croghan Papers. Governor Franklin had agreed to underwrite the expenses of Wharton and Trent in London to the extent of two-tenths of the whole, but apparently did not live up to his promise; other underwriters were Croghan, Baynton, and Morgan, Wharton's partners, and Robert Callender. See Etting Collection, "Ohio Company Papers," pp. 49–50.

[99] Cadwalader Collection of Croghan Papers.

[100] *Acts of the Privy Council, Col. Ser., 1766–1783*, p. 210 For the memorial see [Samuel Wharton]: *Facts and Observations . . .* (London, 1775), pp. 136–70, where Wharton speaks of the memorial as presented by "Walpole, in Behalf of himself and eleven others named and their Associates."

[101] Wharton was the anonymous author of the pamphlet which appeared without divulging the name of the printer. Its full title is, *Facts and Observations, respecting the country granted to His Majesty by the Six Nations of Indians, on the Southwest Side of the river Ohio, in North America; the establishment of a new colony there; and the causes of the Indian War, which last year desolated the frontier settlements of the provinces of Pennsylvania, Maryland, and Virginia.* In the latter pages of the pamphlet (pp. 107–31), arguments were marshalled to demonstrate not merely the desirability but the necessity of establishing a colony in the area of the upper Ohio Valley to control the settlers and to appease the Indians.

1775. In fact, it is clear that even before this pamphlet came from the press Wharton and his associates had come to the conclusion that the prospect for the creation of the Vandalia colony was slight—especially in view of the crisis then developing in the relations of the mother country with the colonies. They therefore decided to revive the Indiana Company project[102]—without any plan for the creation of a colony, since this could be done only by royal letters patent—hoping to acquire the lands that had been granted to the so-called "Suffering Traders" by special deed from the Six Nations at the Treaty of Fort Stanwix in 1768. It must be borne in mind that each member of the Walpole Associates had contributed at least £200 to further the Vandalia enterprise, anticipating handsome returns on their investment. By 1775 a good deal of their money had been expended for supporting Wharton and Trent in London and for other promotional purposes, including the entertainment of prominent members of the government.[103] However, Wharton undoubtedly must have assured the contributors that, even if the Vandalia colony could not be realized, every effort would be taken to protect them from losses.

The Indiana Company as an Alternate Plan

Preparations were now made with great care to overcome any reluctance on the part of officials in America toward supporting the plan to take over the Indiana Company grant. Writing to George Croghan on April 17, 1775, Wharton informed him that the opinions of two very eminent counsellors had been solicited—Counsellor Henry Dagge of Lincoln's Inn, who had written "a most accom-

[102] See G. E. Lewis: *The Indiana Company, 1763–1798* (previously cited), pp. 149–51.

[103] On August 12, 1769, Wharton wrote to Croghan that he was "much drained of cash" and begged him to remit £200 sterling. But Croghan himself was in straightened financial circumstances, as he pointed out in his letters of July 20 and September 10, 1769. On December 6 Wharton's reply to Croghan's letters noted "the air of Distress," but went on to say: "To my astonishment a Number of Bills came presented to me of your Draft and as I had no money . . . nor any Advices from you, I was cruely constrained to note them for non acceptance." On September 4, 1770, he wrote to Croghan: ". . . I have involved some of the first noblemen & members of Parliament . . . in the Business of obtaining a great Grant and thereby, effectualy securing yours & our property"; on the 21st of that month he again wrote that he had not received a shilling from America since he left that country and that he and Trent were "in the greatest distress for money." However, by November 9, 1771, he was able to report that he had been in the country to recover his health and that Major Trent "is very polite and accomplished and drives twice or thrice a week with the best Company in the Kingdom." From this time forward there is no note of distress in Wharton's letters to Croghan. For this correspondence see the Cadwalader Collection of Croghan Papers.

plished treatise upon the criminal Laws of England,"[104] and the famous Serjeant-at-law John Glynn, a Wilkes supporter, who held the important and well-paid post of Recorder of London as well as a seat in Parliament for Middlesex. Both men gave the opinion that the title held by the Indiana Company to the lands ceded by Indian deed was "*good, lawful and sufficient*,"[105] an opinion confirmed by Lord Camden.[106]

Camden, it will be recalled, was one of the Walpole Associates and an investor in their land speculation. What is more, there would seem to be every likelihood—in view of the phrasing of Dagge's opinion—that Camden was involved in the opinion given by the counsellors, or that he at least called Dagge's attention to his own opinion rendered as Charles Pratt, the King's Attorney General, in collaboration with Charles Yorke, His Majesty's Solicitor General, in 1757. This opinion had been given in connection with the territorial claims of the United East India Company. In that year the Company had petitioned the King that in the new charter—which it was seeking to secure—a claim should be inserted enabling the Company to hold and enjoy, subject to the King's right of sovereignty, all districts and other territories it had acquired or might thereafter acquire in the Far East from any nation, state, or people by treaty, grant, or conquest. When this petition had been submitted to them, Pratt and Yorke had advised the King in Council:

> "In respect to such Places as have been or shall be acquired by [the Company through] treaty or Grant from the Mogul or any of the

[104] *Considerations on Criminal Law* first appeared in London in 1772, and in 1774 was republished in a greatly expanded form in three volumes.

[105] Dagge's opinion, signed on March 20, 1775, after reviewing the legal points involved, stated: "Upon the whole, I am of the opinion, that Mr. Trent, in his own right and as attorney for the traders, *hath a good, lawful and sufficient title to the land* granted by the said deed of conveyance, subject *only* to the King's sovereignty over the settlements to be established thereon, and over the inhabitants, as English subjects." Glynn, after summarizing his own views of the legality of the transfer of the lands, declared in an opinion written on April 13: "I entirely concur with Mr. Dagge in his opinion on *this* case." For these opinions see [Samuel Wharton and Edward Bancroft]: *View of the title to Indiana, a Tract of Country on the River Ohio. Containing Indian Conferences at Johnson-Hall, in May, 1765; the Deed of the Six Nations to the Proprietors of Indiana; the Minutes of the Congress at Fort Stanwix, in October and November, 1768; the Deed of the Indians, settling the Boundary Line between the English and Indians Lands, and the Opinion of Counsel on the Title of the Proprietors of Indiana* (Philadelphia, 1776), pp. 40–6. It is interesting to note that Benjamin Franklin on July 12 wrote: "I concur fully with Counsellor Dagge and Serjeant Glynn in their opinions" (*ibid.*, p. 46), and even Virginian Patrick Henry on July 19, while in Philadelphia, stated: "From principles which appear to me very clear, I concur in the above opinions" (*ibid.*, p. 46).

[106] See Samuel Wharton to Croghan, April 17, 1775 (Cadwalader Collection of Croghan Papers), in which Wharton states: "Lord Camden entirely agrees in opinion with these Gentlemen . . . and this is also, the real opinion of every sound Lawyer in Westminster Hall."

Indian Princes or Governments[,] Your Majestys Letters Patent are not necessary, the property of the soil vesting in the Company by the Indian Grants subject only to your Majestys Right of Sovereignity over the Settlements as English Settlements & over the Inhabitants as English Subjects who carry with them your Majestys Laws wherever they form Colonies & receive your Majestys protection by virtue of your Royal Charters."[107]

Having secured these important legal opinions in support of the Indiana Company claims, Wharton decided to send Major Trent back to America with them. The "*Chief* Causes of his Return, *before* me," wrote Wharton to Croghan "is to join with you, in endeavouring, *immediately,* to accomplish the *Purchase,* which you so positively wrote me, you *could* make. . . ." No time was to be lost, he warned, "as you may depend upon it, that an Act of Parliament, or an Act of Quebeck will be made *soon,* to declare all Purchases of the Natives made, *after* that act, by private Persons, illegal & void."[108] However, when Trent arrived in America prepared to use the opinions to push Croghan into action, the situation was so changed that nothing effective could be done. Croghan, in fact, had quietly proceeded to purchase from the Six Nations some six million acres on the upper waters of the Allegheny. Nevertheless, on September 21, 1775, a two-day meeting of nine of the stockholders of the Indiana Company was held at Pittsburgh. There it was agreed not only to locate the grant and provide for its survey but also to open a land office.[109] An advertisement was also framed which, after specifying the particular lands granted on November 3, 1768, by

[107] For this opinion see Shaw Livermore: *Early American Land Companies,* p. 106*n*. The above opinion, in slightly different form, is given in [Samuel Wharton]: *Plain Facts: being an examination into the rights of the Indian nations of America to their respective countries; and a vindication of the grant from the six united nations of Indians to the proprietors of Indiana against the decision of the legislature of Virginia; together with authentic documents proving that the territory westward of the Allegany mountain never belonged to Virginia etc.* (Philadelphia, 1781), p. 9. The opinion in *Plain Facts* was "that in respect to such territories as have been, or shall be acquired by treaty or grant from the Great Mogul or any of the Indian princes or governments, your Majesty's letters patent are not necessary; the property of the soil vesting in the Company by the Indian grant, subject only to your Majesties right of sovereignty over the settlements, as English settlements, and over the inhabitants, as English subjects, who carry with them your Majesties laws wherever they form colonies, and receive your Majesties protection by virtue of your royal charters." As this was declared to be among the "authentic documents," and was published as such, its variation from the document submitted to the King in Council and on file among the India Office (London) "Charters and Treaties," Charters 7:103–5, calls for explanation. The one that comes most naturally to mind is that Camden—not having at hand the final draught—supplied to Wharton the draught he himself had made in 1757 before submitting it to Yorke for revision that same year.

[108] Samuel Wharton to Croghan, April 17, 1775, Cadwalader Collection of Croghan Papers.

[109] "Indiana Company Papers," in K. P. Bailey: *Ohio Company Papers,* pp. 288–95.

the Six Nations to the traders (as recompense for the plundering in 1763 of their goods to the amount of £85,916.10.8 lawful money of New York), went on to state:

> "Whereas we understand there are numbers of Families settled on the said Land We do hereby give Notice that they may be Assured of Peaceable possession on Complying with the Terms of our General Land Office, which will be shortly opened for the Sale of the said Lands in behalf of all the Grantees, & that the purchase will be made easy."[110]

Before adjourning, it was agreed that a second meeting of the "Suffering Traders" be held at Carlisle, Pennsylvania, in order "to agree on such Matters & things as may be esteem'd most beneficial for the Grantees, & to encourage the Settlement of the Land Contain'd within their Grant."[111] When the meeting took place at Carlisle, in November, William Trent was conspicuously absent, so that nothing could be done. In fact, some other important shareholders did not appear either. But the chief obstacle to implementing the Indiana Company claims was the opposition of Virginia. Two years later—that is, in 1777—the Company petitioned the Virginia Assembly for recognition of its claims;[112] the following year the House of Delegates resolved "that all Purchases of Lands made or to be made of the Indians within the Charter'd Boundaries of this Common Wealth, as prescribed by the Constitution or Form of Government, by any Person or Persons not authorized by public Authority, are void."[113] A memorial submitted by Trent to the Congress of the United States in 1779, in behalf of the stockholders, was no more effective.[114] In fact, no redress or compensation was ever received by them. [115]

Nor was the fate of the old Ohio Company any kinder in the eyes of the members who sought recognition of their land claims.

---

[110] *Ibid.*, pp. 298–9. It should be noted that Thomas Wharton, as a member of the Indiana Company, wrote to Trent protesting the action taken at Pittsburgh. See *ibid.*, pp. 301–2. For a list of the chief stockholders in the Indiana Company in 1776 see Shaw Livermore: *op. cit.*, p. 116*n*.

[111] K. P. Bailey: *Ohio Company Papers*, p. 301.

[112] For a draught of the petition see *ibid.*, pp. 307–8.

[113] *Virginia Gazette*, November 13, 1778, as printed in *ibid.*, p. 315. In 1779, the Virginia Assembly declared that all deeds and cessions of land by the Indians to the Crown of Great Britain should inure to the benefit of the Commonwealth of Virginia. See *The Statutes at Large: being a Collection of all the Laws of Virginia, from . . . 1619* (ed. W. W. Hening, 13 vols., Richmond, 1809–23), X, 35–71; cited hereafter as Hening: *Laws of Virginia*. See also George Mason to Richard Henry Lee, June 19, 1779, quoted in A. P. James: *op. cit.*, p. 169.

[114] *Ohio Company Papers*, pp. 324–30.

[115] See Livermore: *op. cit.*, pp. 117–19; see also G. E. Lewis, *op. cit.*, pp. 234–93.

By 1773 this company, under the guidance of its treasurer, George Mason, had shifted its interests away from the upper Ohio region and toward the Kentucky area, and by 1775 had surveyed 200,000 acres of these lands and possibly more. Several years later the Company presented an able memorial to the Virginia Assembly in support of its rights, but this, too, failed to win its objective.[116] With the intervention of the War for Independence the original Ohio Company disappeared into oblivion as did the Grand Ohio Company and the Indiana Company along with the Vandalia colony project.

While trans-Appalachian expansion continued, it was in spite of the attitude of the government of Great Britain. For example, on July 31, 1770, the Earl of Hillsborough wrote to Lord Botetourt that he was under orders from the King to direct the Governor and Council of Virginia to desist from making any further grants of land beyond the limits described in the Proclamation of 1763 until His Majesty's pleasure had been signified.[117] This prohibition was reiterated on October 5, 1774, when Lord Dartmouth emphasized to Lord Dunmore that the Proclamation Line still remained in force.[118]

But such restrictions did not prevent land speculators and prospective settlers from purchasing lands from the Indians and forming plans for settlements on their own initiative. This they felt free to do under the sanction of the distorted and deceptive version of the 1757 Pratt-Yorke opinion[119] concerning the right of the East India Company to obtain lands by treaty from the local rulers in East India; this garbled version reads:

> "In respect to such places as have been or shall be acquired by Treaty or Grant from any of the Indian Princes or Governments; Your Majesty's Letters Patents *are not necessary,* the *property of the soil vesting in the Grantees by the Indian Grants;* Subject only to your Majesty's Right of Sovereignty over the Settlements as English Settlements and over the Inhabitants as English *Subjects who carry with them your Majesty's Laws wherever they form Colonys* and receive your Majesty's Protection by Virtue of your Royal Charters."[120]

---

[116] For the activities of the Ohio Company of Virginia in 1778–9 see A. P. James: *op. cit.,* pp. 159–85, and K. P. Bailey: *The Ohio Company of Virginia,* especially Appendix, pp. 320–27, for the memorial presented to the Virginia Assembly in 1779. By this year, according to Professor James, the Ohio Company had surveyed 400,000 acres of Kentucky lands; see James: *op. cit.,* p. 470.

[117] C.O. 5:1348, p. 225.

[118] For this letter see C.O. 5:1352, pp. 289–92; it is given in *Ohio Company Papers,* pp. 282–3.

[119] The original Pratt-Yorke decision of 1757 is given earlier in this chapter.

[120] This altered version of the opinion, with the particular phrases underlined as shown in italics above, was sent by Lord Dunmore while Governor of Virginia to the Earl of Dartmouth, Secretary of State for the Colonies. This was annexed to

This wording makes the opinion seem to apply directly to the situation in America and it was so used by those who sought grants from the Indians without royal confirmation. Certainly by the fall of 1770 this view had become prevalent among those Americans in London interested in western lands. Samuel Wharton, writing to George Croghan on September 4, after explaining that it would be futile to seek confirmation of the Indiana Company 1768 grant, in view of Lord Hillsborough's hostility, had added:

> "Dr. F[ranklin] says, that if the property was his, he would not seek for any other title, But sell and settle on it, as was most agreeable to Him & if the King would annex it [the land grant] to any of his Governments he [Franklin] would subject it thereto and pay a *Beaver* skin or small quit Rent or other acknowledgement expressing of its being under the protection and government of the Crown."[121]

Again, in 1771, Wharton expressed the same idea in connection with the general agreement of the legal minds he consulted on this subject; writing to Croghan on July 21, he said:

> "I am rejoiced to find that the Settlers on the Ohio are as chearfully disposed to buy Lands under some Indian Title as they are from the King or Mr. Penn. It shews their good Sense, and that they reason naturaly and justly upon the Subject; for King Charles the first could not grant to William Penn Esq. any *other* Right, than the Power of buying in *preference* of his other Subjects, from the native Proprietors. This is so well understood in this Kingdom, that from the lowest to the highest Counselor and Personage in it, it is not pretended the King has or can have any Degree of Right to Lands, which he has not bought from the natural Original Proprietors. . . . Go therefore and sell for the best price you can, and I shall bring over with me, the ablest & most learned Counsellors Opinions in this Kingdom, in favor of you and our Rights. In short, Every judicious Man smiled at me, when I formerly talked of applying to the Crown for a *Confirmation* and they have asked me, What would you apply for? Had the Crown any Right to Lands on the Ohio, until such Time as it bought and paid for them? Surely not—and was not your Deed made Two Days before the Natives made one to the King? And is not your Grant made one of the express Conditions, on which the King actualy holds his Lands [granted at the same treaty with the Six Nations]?"[122]

Dunmore's letter of May 16, 1774. For the letter and the annex see C.O. 5:1352, pp. 141–7, and 155. The most extended analysis of the origin of this altered Pratt-Yorke opinion is given by J. M. Sosin: "The Yorke-Camden Opinion and American Land Speculators," *Pennsylvania Magazine of History and Biography*, LXXXV, 38–49, and in his *Whitehall and the Wilderness*, pp. 229–34 and Appendix, pp. 259–67; see also T. P. Abernethy: *Western Lands and the American Revolution*, pp. 116–20, for an interpretation of the origin of the altered opinion that is challenged by Dr. Sosin.

[121] Cadwalader Collection of Croghan Papers, *loc. cit.*

[122] *Ibid.*

The Illinois and Wabash Companies

Acting on the basis of the deceptive Yorke-Pratt decision, a group of Pennsylvania speculators with trading interests in the Illinois country—among them William Murray, David and Moses Franks, and Barnard and Michael Gratz—organized the Illinois Company for the purpose of purchasing Indian land in the Illinois country.[123] Murray, already acquainted with the region, was sent out in 1773 furnished with a copy of the opinion.[124] Upon arriving in June he indicated the purpose of his mission to the British commandant at Kaskaskia, Captain Hugh Lord, who felt, however, that he was bound by earlier orders forbidding land purchases from the Indians. Nevertheless, Murray moved ahead with his plans, and on July 5, at a gathering of Indians and in the presence of Lord, who witnessed the deed, he was able to purchase not only a large tract of land lying between the lower Ohio and the upper Mississippi River but also one on the Illinois River. As these purchases lay beyond the territorial charter limits of Pennsylvania, but were included in those of Virginia, the members of the Company petitioned Governor Dunmore "to be received into the participation of the Laws and

[123] For the membership of the Company when first organized see "The Illinois and Wabash Land Company Minutes, 1778–1812," Historical Society of Pennsylvania; see also *B. and M. Gratz, Merchants of Philadelphia, 1754–1798* (W. V. Byars ed., Jefferson City, Mo., 1916. For the Illinois Company of 1766, see the beginning pages of this chapter and note 10.

[124] It should be noted that when on December 21, 1810, the United Illinois and Wabash Companies presented a memorial to the Congress of the United States in support of its claim, it was argued that the Illinois Indians before 1763 either were not British subjects, and consequently no acts of the British government could affect them, or, if British subjects, had full rights as such that the Proclamation of 1763 could not and did not alter. This, the memorial went on to state: "is further manifest from an opinion given officially to the King, nine years after its date, by three of the greatest lawyers that England ever produced, Pratt, Yorke, and Dunning, who were then the Crown lawyers, and two of whom, Yorke and Pratt, (afterwards the famous Lord Camden,) became Chancellors of England. Being consulted by the King in council, in the year 1772, as to the legal effects of Indian grants and royal patents, they gave the following answer, on the 1st of August, 1772." There follows a version identical to the spuriously worded Pratt-Yorke opinion quoted earlier in the text. The adding of Dunning's name to the opinion under the date of August 1, 1772, makes it clearly a figment of the imagination of whoever wished to bolster the claims of the United Illinois and Wabash Land Companies. For, although John Dunning may have agreed with Serjeant Glynn and Lord Camden as to the right of Indians to sell lands, he stood clearly in opposition to the government by 1770, after resigning the post of Solicitor General held under the Grafton administration, and would not have been consulted by it. Furthermore, it was in 1770 that Yorke died and Camden was dismissed from the Lord High Chancellorship. See again Sosin's detailed study on this subject (*Whitehall and the Wilderness*, Appendix, pp. 259–67). For this memorial see *American State Papers. Documents Legislative and Executive, Class VIII, Public Lands* (Washington, 1834), II, 108–20, especially p. 114.

Government of Virginia." In this connection they sent not only a copy of the deed of purchase filed at Kaskaskia but also a copy of "the opinions of Lord Chancellors Cambden and York, who held, as it appears, that purchases made by His Majesty's Subjects of the Indians are good, and His Majesty's Letters Patent not necessary to Such purchases."[125]

Meanwhile, Lord Dunmore urged the Earl of Dartmouth to give sympathetic consideration to the petitioners. "Whatever may be the law with respect to the title," he wrote, "there are, I think, divers reasons which should induce His Majesty to comply with the petition, [and] seeing there is no possibility of setting bounds to the settlements of the Americans, it would tend most to the advantage of His Majesty and to preserve peace and order in the back countries, that his Majesty should indulge the views of adventurers like the present, who willingly conform to government."[126] On July 6, in reply to Dunmore, Dartmouth referred to the petition of the Illinois Company without indicating that it was improper, but he warned the Governor against admitting this area to the protection of the government of Virginia.[127] In fact, by the time that Dartmouth had written, the Illinois country had been embodied by act of Parliament into the extended Province of Quebec.[128] Nevertheless, it would appear that Dunmore, desirous of securing a tract of land in America upon which to settle with his family, had come to the conviction, "from every authority that the law knew, that a purchase from the natives gave as full and ample a title as could be obtained, [and] that they had Lord Camden and Mr. Yorke's opinion on that head. . . ."[129]

---

[125] See *Illinois-Wabash Land Company Manuscript* (ed. C. W. Alvord, Chicago, 1915), p. 14; see also C. W. Alvord: *The Illinois Country*, pp. 301–3, Shaw Livermore: *op. cit.*, pp. 106–8, and J. M. Sosin: *op. cit.*, pp. 231–5. For a copy of the deed and affidavit see the memorial of the United Illinois and Wabash Land Companies, *American State Papers, Class VIII, Public Lands*, II, 117–19. The purchase was made in goods which were specified; the names of the purchasers were also specified, as were the bounds of the purchase.

[126] See Dunmore to Dartmouth, May 11, 1774, C.O. 5:1352, pp. 141–7. For the petition which recites that at an expense of several thousand pounds and very great fatigues, and in an open and fair purchase, the petitioners purchased lands of the Indians and prayed the protection of the government of Virginia, see C.O. 5:1352, pp. 151–4; the copy of the deed forwarded by Dunmore is in C.O. 5:1352, pp. 157–60.

[127] Dartmouth to Dunmore, July 6, 1774, C.O. 5:1352, pp. 175–7; see also the Secretary's letter to the Governor, under date of September 8, 1774, in which he now called upon Dunmore to repudiate the activities of the speculators. For this letter see C.O. 5:1352, pp. 231–8.

[128] This act, 14 Geo. III, c. 83, "An Act for making more effectual Provision for the Government of the Province of Quebec in North America," was given the King's approval on June 22, 1774. See *Statutes at Large*, VIII, 405–7.

[129] This is the testimony of Patrick Henry, who affirmed to Thomas Wharton that he overheard Lord Dunmore make the above statement in the presence of Dr. John

To satisfy Dunmore's desire for land and doubtless also to strengthen the position of the Illinois Company, Murray now organized the Ouabache (Wabash) Company, in which the Governor was a shareholder. On October 18, 1775, by using the Frenchman Louis Viviat—active previously in the Illinois country—as agent, it purchased from the Piankashaw Indians, living about the deserted Fort Vincennes, "two several tracts or parcels of land . . . lying and being on both sides of the Ouabache (Wabash) river. . . ."[130] These two companies, it may be added, on March 13, 1779, were welded together under the title "United Illinois and Ouabache Land Companies."[131] But efforts of the companies to secure recognition from either Virginia or the Continental Congress were unavailing.[132]

The Final Pre-Revolutionary Speculation Activities

There were at this period other unauthorized purchases of Indian land, based upon the altered Pratt-Yorke opinion of 1757. On July 10, 1775, with the War for American Independence already under way, George Croghan purchased from the Six Nations, for himself and others, 6,000,000 acres of land lying about the western tributaries of the Allegheny.[133] Farther to the south—beyond the Donelson Line and therefore within the Cherokee country—settlers were moving into the valleys of the Watauga and Clinch rivers and were leasing lands from the Indians.[134] Although a group of Virginia land speculators, including William Byrd and Patrick Henry, had in mind the purchase of these lands and had made preliminary negotiations with the Cherokee early in 1774, nothing came of their plans.[135]

Connolly and himself. Thomas Wharton in turn relayed it to Thomas Walpole in a letter dated September 23, 1774. For the letter see the *Pennsylvania Magazine of History and Biography,* XXXIII, 444–8.

[130] In the deed the name of Lord Dunmore follows that of Viviat. The purchasers, some eighteen in number, are given. It may be noted that the only people concerned in both companies were William Murray and the three Franks: Moses, Jacob, and David. While the Illinois Company was made up predominantly of Pennsylvania people, the Wabash Company was chiefly of Maryland people. Outside of Lord Dunmore, the royal Governor, no one from Virginia was a member of either company. For the deed, which indicates the consideration for the purchases, the bounds, and the grantees, and which was executed at Post St. Vincent (Vincennes), see *American State Papers,* II, 119–20; see also "Articles of Agreement of the Illinois-Wabash Land Company," Shaw Livermore: *op. cit.,* Appendix C, pp. 305–8.

[131] *Ibid.,* p. 306.

[132] For the fate of the Illinois and Wabash Companies see *ibid.,* pp. 108–11.

[133] A part of this land was in turn sold to Dr. Thomas Walker, the Virginia land speculator, for five thousand Spanish dollars. See N. B. Wainwright: *George Croghan, Wilderness Diplomat,* p. 296.

[134] T. P. Abernethy: *From Frontier to Plantation in Tennessee,* pp. 5–9.

[135] J. R. Alden: *John Stuart and the Southern Colonial Frontier,* p. 290.

However, later in that year, as indicated in the preceding chapter, a number of North Carolinians—the most prominent of whom was Judge Richard Henderson—organized a company first known as the Louisa Company,[136] but later called the Transylvania Company.[137] In November its representatives entered into an agreement with a number of Cherokee chiefs to buy all the lands lying south of the Ohio and between the mouth of the Great Kanawha and that of the Tennessee.[138] Although proclamations were issued against the enterprise by both Governor Josiah Martin of North Carolina and Lord Dunmore, the purchase was consummated on March 17, 1775, at a great gathering of Indians at Sycamore Shoals on the banks of the Watauga. The deed included the lands lying between this river and the Cumberland Mountains as well as those between the Ohio and Kentucky rivers and the upper waters of the Cumberland—some 20,000,000 acres in all, and all for the sum of £10,000. There followed the establishment of the towns of Harrodsburg and Boonesborough (named after Daniel Boone), the swarming of people into the fertile country, and the setting up by Henderson of the government of the short-lived Transylvania colony—but these events occurred beyond the chronological limits of this account of trans-Appalachian developments.[139]

---

[136] For the "Articles of Association of the Louisa Company," signed August 27, 1774, see Shaw Livermore: *op. cit.*, Appendix A, p. 299.

[137] For the "Articles of Association of the Transylvania Company," signed January 6, 1775, see *ibid.*, Appendix B, pp. 300–4.

[138] Colonel William Preston, writing from Fincastle County, Virginia (roughly, what is now the state of Kentucky), to Governor Dunmore on January 23, 1775, stated that a few days earlier Henderson and followers with six wagons of goods had passed through the county on the way to Watauga to complete the treaty. According to Preston, Judge Henderson planned to sell the lands secured by the treaty for twenty shillings sterling per hundred acres and intended to give deeds to the land "in his own and Companys names . . . as the Sole Proprietors . . . and . . . does not propose paying quit-rents, unless his Majesty will recognize his title" (C.O. 5:1353, pp. 185–6). Dunmore, writing to the Earl of Dartmouth on March 14, 1775, about Henderson's militant colonization plans, indicated that the Judge "expects to have his purchase ratified by the Crown, or [if not], declares he will set up an independent Government, and that he will never otherwise suffer the Officers of the King's Government to exercise any Authority within his purchase" (C.O. 5:1353, pp. 215–20). The Governor added that he had issued a proclamation against the Henderson enterprise.

[139] The most extensive accounts of the Kentucky enterprise are from the pen of Archibald Henderson. These are as follows: "The Creative Forces in American Expansion: Henderson and Boone," *American Historical Review,* XX, 86–107; "Richard Henderson and the Occupation of Kentucky, 1775" and "A Pre-Revolutionary Revolt in the Old Southwest," both printed in the *Mississippi Valley Historical Review,* I, 341–65, XVII, 191–212; and *The Conquest of the Old Southwest* (New York, 1920). The student should also consult W. S. Lester: *The Transylvania Colony* (Spencer, Ind., 1935), T. P. Abernethy: *Western Lands and the American Revolution,* pp. 123–35, Shaw Livermore: *op. cit.*, pp. 90–7, and J. R. Alden: *Southern Colonial Frontier,* pp. 290–3, and his *History of the South, 1763–1789* (Baton Rouge, 1957),

Meanwhile, Virginia had begun to assert control of its trans-Appalachian lands. "An Act for dividing the County and Parish of Augusta . . ." was signed by the Governor on December 21, 1769. All the area south of Mary's River, extending to the westernmost limit of Virginia, was erected into the new county of Botetourt.[140] The following day thirteen gentlemen were commissioned justices of the peace for the county with instructions to enforce "all ordinances & statutes of the Kingdom of Great Britain and Laws of the Colony & Dominion aforesaid made for the Good of the Peace . . . & for the quiet Rule & Government of his People . . . in the said County . . ."[141] On February 13, 1770, they met and organized as a county court. Seven of them were authorized as justices of the quorum to hear and determine all suits, and to punish offenders and law breakers. That same day Richard Woods, Gent., produced before the court his commission from the Governor as sheriff of Botetourt County; other officers, such as surveyor of the county and coroners, likewise were installed, after taking the prescribed oath of office.[142] The following day a number of constables and surveyors were selected, and prices to be observed at taverns were established for drink, food, and lodging.[143] Gradually the county government began functioning smoothly.[144]

Just as it had seemed desirable to create Botetourt County out of the southwestern part of Augusta County, so some three years later, on April 11, 1772, the new county was again divided and the area west of the New or Great Kanawha River became Fincastle County.[145] Early the following year the court of this additional county was organzied and the various officials were installed in their posts, each commissioned by the government of Virginia.[146]

Despite the outbreak of the War for American Independence in

Chap. 8, "Advance into the Old Southwest"; a recent volume by J. A. Caruso: *The Appalachian Frontier: America's First Surge Westward* (Indianapolis, 1959) presents a series of well-executed vignettes of Henderson, Boone, and other trans-Appalachian pioneers involved in the Transylvania Company enterprise and in the founding of the future states of Kentucky and Tennessee. The expansion southwest into the area of the Floridas will be dealt with in Volume XIII of this series.

[140] *Journals of the House of Burgesses, 1766–1769*, pp. 298, 353; Hening: *Laws of Virginia*, VIII, 395.

[141] L. P. Summers: *Annals of Southwest Virginia, 1769–1800* (Abingdon, Va., 1929), p. 58.

[142] *Ibid.*, pp. 58–61.

[143] *Ibid.*, pp. 62–5.

[144] For the records of Botetourt County from February 15, 1770, to 1800 see *ibid.*, pp. 66–587.

[145] *Journals of the House of Burgesses, 1770–1772*, p. 316, and Hening: *Laws of Virginia*, VIII, 600.

[146] L. P. Summers: *op. cit.*, pp. 588–600.

1775 and the launching of Indian expeditions against the trans-Appalachian settlements by Lieutenant Governor Henry Hamilton, the British commander at Detroit, settlers streamed into various parts of the new Virginia county. The extensiveness of the area encompassed by Fincastle County made it desirable in 1777 to subdivide it and drop the name Fincastle.[147] Accordingly, three new counties were created, Montgomery, Washington, and Kentucky[148]—with the third one practically coterminous with what was in 1792 to become the state of Kentucky. By this extension of the local government of Virginia throughout the very area that Judge Henderson and his associates were seeking to make into the state of Transylvania, these men were forced to renounce their project but not their claim to the lands they had purchased from the Indians.[149]

Before concluding this account of trans-Appalachian lands, reference should be made of the attempt on the part of the King in Council to introduce a new land policy for the royal colonies in 1773. Throughout this series abundant evidence has been presented to demonstrate the need of a fundamental alteration in the methods by which individuals acquired land rights, both to the east and to the west of the Appalachians. Among other things, it had become clear that the Crown was being deprived of substantial amounts of revenue in the form of quit-rents and purchase rights. In the case of New York particularly, land patents had been issued at a low consideration for modest amounts of land designated only roughly by certain land marks, but these had subsequently been expanded by the patentees into vast claims. For example, a patentee holding title to 300 acres of land later claimed that his grant included 60,000 acres.[150] Moreover, in a colony such as North Carolina the royal land system was particularly in need of reform both to control the prevalent practice of squatting on land in the frontier area and to remedy the chaotic condition of the quit-rent rolls which

---

[147] Both Fincastle, the county seat of Botetourt County, and Fincastle County were named in honour either of George, Lord Fincastle, eldest son of the Earl of Dunmore, or of the family estate in England. By 1777, with the War for American Independence in progress, Governor Dunmore was a declared enemy of the state of Virginia; thus it is understandable why the Fincastle name disappeared from the county.

[148] Hening: *Laws of Virginia,* IX, 257–61.

[149] Ultimately, when Henderson agreed to recognize the jurisdiction of Virginia over the area that he claimed by purchase and decided to accept a compromise, he was awarded 200,000 acres of land on Green River in Kentucky. See *Journal of the House of Delegates of the Commonwealth of Virginia 1776–1790* (ed. T. W. White, Richmond, 1828), pp. 28, 31, 36, 42, 79, 105. For an extensive treatment of trans-Appalachian developments to the south of the Ohio in the 1770's and 1780's see T. P. Abernethy's *Western Lands . . . ,* pp. 123–369.

[150] See Volume III, revised, in this series, p. 105.

had resulted from the lax system of granting lands and the consequent failure of quit-rent collection.[151]

In view of the fact that other schemes for bolstering the royal revenues in America had failed by the 1770's, it is perhaps not surprising that consideration was given to the possibility of increasing these by a more careful disposition of royal lands. This had, in fact, been the Earl of Shelburne's idea in 1766 when, in writing to General Gage on December 11, he declared: "The forming of an American Fund to support the Exigencies of Government . . . is what is so highly reasonable that it must take place sooner or later. The most obvious manner of laying the Foundation for such a Fund seems to be by taking proper care of the Quit Rents and by turning Grants of Land to real benefit, and which might tend to encrease rather than diminish the Powers of Government in so distant a Country."[152] On April 7, 1773, as a necessary preliminary measure to this desirable end, the Privy Council sent out instructions pursuant to the decision that no order for a survey of land or for any patent of land, or for any licence for the purchase by private persons of lands from the Indians, should be issued by any Governor or his deputy until the King's pleasure should be further known. Meanwhile, the Board of Trade was to study the question of alternative methods for granting the King's land and report on their findings.[153]

By the summer of 1773 the Board of Trade had drawn up certain so-called additional instructions to the Governors of the royal colonies. Submitted to the Privy Council, these were then referred to the Lords of the Committee on Plantation Affairs. Late in October the Committee recommended the adoption by the Privy Council of the proposed instructions, but with the proviso that they were not to apply to the Province of Quebec, where the French method of granting lands was to be continued.[154] After some further modification the instructions were finally approved on February 3, 1774,[155]

---

[151] See Volume II, revised, pp. 106–7; see also B. W. Bond, Jr.: *The Quit-Rent System in the American Colonies* (New Haven, 1919), p. 300*n*.

[152] *Gage Correspondence,* II, 49–50. For comment on the Shelburne plan for a revenue see J. M. Sosin: *op. cit.,* pp. 124–5; see also C. W. Alvord: *op. cit.,* I, 347.

[153] *Acts of the Privy Council, Col. Ser.,* V, 360–1. One exception was embodied in the above prohibitory instruction in order to protect the rights of officers and soldiers and permit the granting of land to them under terms of the Proclamation of October 7, 1763.

[154] Ibid.; see also the Board of Trade *Journal, 1768–1775,* pp. 353, 356–7, 361, 372.

[155] The Board of Trade had embodied in the instructions a table of fees to be paid by those who sought to patent lands, as applicable in all colonies where unappropriated royal lands were located, except in the Province of Quebec. For this table of fees see *New York Colonial Documents,* VIII, 412*n*. On January 25, 1774,

and copies were directed to the Governors of every royal colony except Quebec and New Jersey.[156] Plans which were under careful consideration for providing for the Canadian western lands resulted in the Quebec Act, as will be discussed more fully in Volume XIII of this series. The additional instructions of 1774 provided, among other things, that prior to any grant or patent all lands to be sold were to be surveyed. After this was done a map of the area within the survey was to be prepared and displayed in the office of the secretary of the province. Thereafter, the Governor, with the advice of the Council, was to advertise the time and place of the sale at least four months prior to disposal of specific plots of land. The terms included sale to the highest bidder, unless otherwise clearly specified by the King. Further, the price of the land was to be fixed according to its quality, with a minimum price of sixpence per acre, to be paid at the time of the sale, with the further proviso that all lands thus sold were to carry an annual quit-rent of a halfpenny sterling per acre—in other words, no longer the customary two shillings per hundred acres, but over twice that amount.[157]

The fact that the most desirable lands lying within the limits of the Southern colonies of Virginia, the Carolinas, and Georgia had been appropriated, and that only less choice lands in small isolated plots were unappropriated, made it evident that the new regulations would not be applied there, at least not without unwarrantable expense and almost universal dissatisfaction.[158] However, enforcement in the vast trans-Appalachian area with its boundless fertile, unappropriated lands presented even greater difficulties. There, as has been noted, in utter disregard of the regulations laid down in the Proclamation of 1763 and in those of 1774, purchases of lands from the Indians by individuals and groups without royal authority—

the Lords of the Committee on Plantation Affairs recommended that the table be dropped, since the fees in a number of colonies had already been settled by provincial law and the use of the table would therefore result in confusion and dissatisfaction. See *Acts of the Privy Council, Col. Ser.*, V, 361.

[156] For Dartmouth's circular letter to the Governors of February 5, 1774, see C.O. 5:75, pp. 53–4, see also *New York Colonial Documents*, VIII, 409–10. With respect to New Jersey, all of the unpatented lands belonged to the Proprietors of East and West New Jersey. See Volume III, revised, of this series, pp. 138–9, for the land system of New Jersey. For the Quebec Act in connection with the problems of western lands see J. M. Sosin: *Whitehall and the Wilderness*, pp. 236–8, and Chap. 10, "The Quebec Act: the Final Decision."

[157] For the additional instructions addressed to Governor Tryon on February 3, 1774, see *New York Colonial Documents*, VIII, 410–13.

[158] See the illuminating article by S. G. L. Sioussat: "The Breakdown of the Royal Management of Lands in the Southern Provinces, 1773–1775," *Agricultural History*, III, 67–98, particularly pp. 78–81.

even in defiance of it—took place, as in the case of the vast land purchase consummated by Richard Henderson and his associates early in 1775.

Thus, even before the outbreak of the War for American Independence, the British land policy for North America proved unworkable and with this administrative failure went the last prospect of gaining a revenue from the colonies. How much influence this failure of the land policy had upon the steps taken by the Ministry in dealing with North America up to the outbreak of hostilities is not clear. What is clear is that the Ministry did attempt to make better provision for the lands to the west of the Province of Quebec with the passage of the Quebec Act—which extended the boundaries previously limited by the Proclamation of 1763—and that, despite the adverse reaction to it of the thirteen older American colonies, this act was a statesmanlike effort at wise administration of a specific area with its special problems of French nationals holding to the Catholic faith. On the whole, however, the government's policies for the west in general or, in particular, for the management of the Indian population and regulation of trade with these natives, were no more effective than had been the land policy developed in the 1770's. Yet it cannot be said that British trans-Appalachian policy was among the prime causes for the coming of the Revolution.[159] Actually, its principal connection with the revolutionary movement lay in the fact that—like other governmental actions deemed by the colonials to be an interference with their natural or charter rights—it represented a restriction upon their freedom of action. Resentment of this, on the part of the generality of people seeking western lands or on the part of the wealthy or privileged speculators, undoubtedly added somewhat to the spirit of discontent, but only in certain areas and instances. Rather, the impasse facing the mother country and the American colonies was the result of the inability of leaders on both sides to negotiate or to reconcile the differences between, on the one hand, the aspirations of colonials for increased autonomy in their local legislatures and, on the other, the confirmed belief of the King, his ministers, and the majority of members of Parliament and the British public at large, in the supreme sovereign power of Parliament to legislate for the colonies.

[159] For the relationship of British western policy to the coming of the Revolution in the opinion of J. M. Sosin, see his *Whitehall and the Wilderness*, pp. 250–5. For the views of other specialists on this subject see also T. P. Abernethy: *Western Lands and the American Revolution*, pp. 363–4 and *passim*, J. R. Alden's *History of the South*, pp. 138–9, and R. A. Billington: *Westward Expansion* (2nd edn.), pp. 174–5.

CHAPTER XIV

The Struggle for Political Equality: North Carolina

THE problems of intercolonial rivalries and conflicts over charter rights and boundaries have been discussed in some detail in preceding chapters of this volume, as have the problems of boundaries between white and Indian territory and the urge to create trans-Appalachian colonies that arose after the Great War for the Empire, when the new surge of westward expansion pushed beyond the mountains into the Old West, then bounded by the Mississippi River. What remains to be examined, in order to gain a more fully rounded picture of the colonial America that engaged in the events leading to open hostilities with the mother country in the 1770's, are some of the issues that produced intracolonial conflicts during the same period. For—while the constitutional crisis that brought about an impasse between Great Britain and the Thirteen Colonies resulted, on the colonial side, chiefly from the drive of the lower houses of assembly to gain more autonomy and from the determination of dissatisfied groups to achieve full political equality as British subjects within the Empire—there existed at the same time in certain of the colonies such serious political inequalities that they ended in open sectional clashes.[1]

---

[1] In his *Rebels and Democrats: The Struggle for Equal Political Rights and the Majority Rule During the American Revolution* (Chapel Hill, N.C., 1955), E. P. Douglass has presented an excellent account of various intracolonial issues and conflicts. His description of conditions in North Carolina in Chap. 6, "Protest and Rebellion in North Carolina, 1765–1771," is particularly to be commended. Douglass's book should be read in conjunction with the brief but important study by R. B. Morris: "Class Struggle and the American Revolution," *William and Mary Quarterly*, 3rd ser., XIX, 3–29, in which a careful distinction is made between the political reforms that were the *avowed* objectives of those who promoted the American Revolution and the social and economic reforms that were not, but that flowed from it. As a correction to the thesis underlying J. F. Jameson's *The American Revolution Considered as a Social Movement* (Princeton, 1926), Professor Morris affirms (*op. cit.,*

Within the framework of this volume it is impossible to do more than indicate by specific examples the nature of either the intercolonial or the intracolonial disunion or friction that existed in British North America in the revolutionary period. Therefore, just as the colonies of New York and Pennsylvania were selected in previous chapters as most suitable to illustrate the intercolonial rivalries, so the Carolinas will perhaps best typify the intracolonial conflicts.[2]

Although the Carolinas stemmed from the same parentage, and in some respects remained singularly alike, after their separation in the early part of the eighteenth century they developed some marked differences.[3] They were alike in that in each colony the older coastal area dominated the backcountry by possession of the capital, the focal point of political influence within the province.[4] As royal colonies, each of them had a Governor, appointed by the King under the Great Seal, who in turn dominated the colony's Council. In each, the effective power of the Assembly rested in the weighted membership from the seaboard counties while the newer interior counties chafed under the lack of equitable representation.[5] However, there

---

p. 26): "We did not declare our independence of George III in order to reform the land laws, change the criminal codes, spread popular education, or separate church and state . . . [but] to achieve political independence, freedom from external controls, emancipation, if you will, of the bourgeoisie from mercantilist restraints." Attention will be given in the concluding volume of this series to the principal writings of the specialists concerned with other forces and objectives that motivated the revolutionists.

[2] For an excellent new study of the local issues that arose in the Carolinas, as well as in Georgia, after 1763 see J. P. Greene: *The Quest for Power: The Lower Houses of Assembly in the Southern Royal Colonies, 1689–1776* (Chapel Hill, N.C., 1963), Chap. 21.

[3] For the Carolinas in the 1750's and early 1760's see Volume II, revised, of this series, Chaps. 4 and 5; see also, Volume X, *passim.*

[4] The conflict of interest between these areas did not end until after the War for American Independence. The capital of North Carolina shifted from New Bern in 1788, when it was established in the heart of the Regulator country at the Wake County court house, where the city of Raleigh was to arise. Meanwhile, Charleston was deserted in 1786 in favour of a site on the eastern bank of the upper waters of the Congaree River, far inland where the South Carolina Regulators had held sway and where the city of Columbia made its appearance.

[5] In 1767 North Carolina representation was based upon the twenty-nine counties and five towns that enjoyed the right to elect representatives to the House of Assembly; in South Carolina the parish within the county was the unit for representation. With respect to the weighted representation of the older North Carolina counties as against the newer western counties, one may take the example in 1767 of Pasquotank and Currituck counties, both to the north of Albemarle Sound, and Orange and Rowan counties in the area of the Piedmont. Pasquotank had but 792 taxables and Currituck but 889; yet each sent five representatives to the Assembly; whereas Orange County with 4,300 taxables and Rowan County with 3,643 taxables had only two each. See *North Carolina Colonial Records* (cited in full in n. 3, Chap. 6 of this volume) VII, 342–3 and 539. For the rivalry between the Albemarle and Cape Fear sections see L. F. London: "The Representation Controversy in Colonial North Carolina," *North Carolina Historical Review*, XI, 255–70.

were important differences between the two colonies. During the period under consideration, the House of Assembly recognized the North Carolina Council as a second branch of the legislature,[6] but in South Carolina the Commons House of Assembly exerted every effort to strip the Council of all its legislative powers, as will be noted in the chapter to follow. In North Carolina the judicial system was broadly conceived to take into account the need of the people living in all parts of the province for local courts of law. For example, in 1762 the province was divided by law into five districts, in each of which the chief justice of the colony, on circuit, held a superior court twice a year, generally supported by an associate judge assigned to the district in question.[7] Moreover, the sheriff, one appointed for each county, possessed very considerable powers both as an officer of the peace and as a fiscal officer.[8] In South Carolina before 1769, except for those held by the justices of the peace for petty cases, the only courts were concentrated at Charleston, where a provost marshal serving through a deputy also had his headquarters and attempted to execute many of the functions assigned to the county sheriff in North Carolina.

In still other respects the two colonies differed from one another. Whereas in North Carolina there was no town of importance in 1767, much less a metropolis, South Carolina's capital and chief seaport was the largest city south of Philadelphia and all activities within the province, whether of a political, economic, or cultural nature, centred there. Moreover, the economy of South Carolina was far superior to that of its northern neighbour. The most profitable export staples of North Carolina were naval stores: tar, turpentine, and pitch; in 1768 these articles were exported to Great Britain to the amount of 127,679 barrels valued at £73,164, thus placing the colony far ahead of any other naval-store-producing

[6] It is true that—perhaps with the example of South Carolina before it—the North Carolina House of Assembly late in 1766, in an address to the Governor, raised the question of the propriety of the Council's acting as a part of the legislature. The Council commented: ". . . as [to] what may be contained in the said Address relative to the rights of the Members of this Board constituting a Branch of the Legislature, . . . they will take proper notice thereof in their Journals as an upper House of Assembly" (*North Carolina Colonial Records,* VII, 272); see also Governor William Tryon's "A View of the Polity of the Province of North Carolina, in the Year 1767," *ibid.,* VII, 472–91, particularly pp. 472–3.

[7] Because the Salisbury District, which included the western counties of Mecklenburg, Anson, and Rowan, was so far from the coast, the chief justices seldom presided at courts held there. As a result the associate judge in this district had to be a lawyer by profession. See *ibid.,* VII, 477. In 1766 an act divided the province into six districts: Wilmington, New Bern, Edenton, Halifax, Hillsborough, and Salisbury. See *Laws of North Carolina, 1715–1776, State Records . . . ,* XXIII, 688–703 and 765–6.

[8] *North Carolina Colonial Records,* VII, 474–88.

colony.[9] But in total value these products represented but a fraction of the export value of rice, the great staple sent from South Carolina to the European markets. In other words, North Carolina in 1767 must be rated as a "poor" colony, despite the very considerable prosperity that had come to people in the settlements and plantations in the neighbourhood of the Cape Fear River and, to a lesser extent, to the inhabitants of such towns as Edenton and New Bern.

If the political structure of North Carolina was far superior to that of South Carolina, the colony contained the same, if not a greater degree of sectionalism. There seems to have been little of common interest and less of daily contact between the people of the seaboard and those of the Piedmont. Settled to a great extent by Ulster Scots and Germans who had moved into the Piedmont chiefly from Pennsylvania by means of the Great Valley Road of Virginia, the area in what is now central North Carolina was almost isolated from the coastal settlements by a wide band of sandy pine barrens. This natural barrier made travel so difficult that the inhabitants had little opportunity to visit the seaboard towns. Nor did the Piedmont people desire to adopt the institutions of the seaboard people. Most of them neither owned nor desired to own slaves.[10] They were not eager to give up the particular Christian faith—whether Presbyterian, German Reformed, Lutheran, or Moravian—that they had brought with them and accept the officially established Church of England, which was particularly strong in the coastal towns.[11] Moreover, the trade of the Piedmont with the outside seems to have gone by convenient roads leading into South Carolina to the metropolis of Charleston by way of such valleys as the Yadkin

[9] See H. T. Lefler and A. R. Newsome: *The History of a Southern State: North Carolina* (Chapel Hill, N.C., 1954), p. 92, for a table of North Carolina exports of naval stores, 1752–77. By contrast, Charleston in 1768 exported merely 14,163 barrels of naval stores. See *Historical Statistics of the United States . . .* (Washington, D.C., 1960), p. 770.

[10] In 1767, out of 869 taxables in Anson County, there were but 173 blacks and mulattoes, and in Orange County out of 4,300 taxables only 729 were blacks and mulattoes; by contrast, in Brunswick County in the Cape Fear region, out of 1,309 taxables, 1,085 were blacks and mulattoes, and in adjacent New Hanover County there were 1,492 blacks and mulattoes out of 2,003 taxables. See *North Carolina Colonial Records,* VII, 539.

[11] See Sarah M. Lemmon: "The Genesis of the Protestant Episcopal Diocese of North Carolina, 1701–1823," *North Carolina Historical Review,* XXVIII, 439; Paul Conkin: "The Church Establishment in North Carolina, 1765–1776," *ibid.,* XXXII, 5; Spencer Ervin: "The Anglican Church in North Carolina," *Historical Magazine of the Protestant Episcopal Church,* XXV, 102–61; Alice M. Baldwin: "Sowers of Sedition . . . ," *William and Mary Quarterly,* 3rd ser., V, 52–76; and Elizabeth H. Davidson: *The Establishment of the English Church in Continental American Colonies* (*Historical Papers of the Trinity College Historical Society,* Ser. XX, Durham, N.C., 1936), pp. 47–57.

and the Catawba.[12] Then, too, to most men of the Piedmont the old settled part of North Carolina stood for officialdom—for quit-rents and tax-collectors, for the Granville District land office,[13] whose jurisdiction covered the northern half of the colony, and for judges and lawyers who came from the east with the opening of the district courts and departed with the winding up of the court docket.

What is more, the spirit of sectionalism increased as a result of the large numbers of people who had settled in the western part of the province on lands they did not own. They were simply squatters. John Rutherford, the receiver general of quit-rents, when reporting on the collection of quit-rents to Governor Tryon in 1769, pointed out: ". . . for many years past the people in Lord Granville's district of this province pay no Quitrents; vast numbers in that district, have no manner of title to the lands they occupy, many of whom pay no taxes for defraying the charges of this government. . . ."[14] He went on to say that if the Earl of Granville's agents were to attempt to collect back rents or to ignore the claims of squatters in the sale of land to which they had no title, "all that part of this gov[t] (by far the most populous and the best lands) would be thrown into confusion. . . ."[15] In short, it may be said that many of these Piedmont people lived outside the law and were opposed to its enforcement. Rather they adhered to a private doctrine of natural rights and popular sovereignty which they regarded to be above the law.

Unhappily, for a long period of time local county government in North Carolina had been corrupt. The sheriffs, who were the dominating figures in the county, collected the taxes in addition to other duties and were only too apt, as Governor Arthur Dobbs pointed out in an address to the Assembly in 1755, to keep this

[12] For example, among the records of the Moravians settled within their Wachovia land purchase at the town of Bethabara in Rowan County, repeated references are made to the movement of supplies by wagon from Charleston. See *Records of the Moravians in North Carolina* (ed. Adelaide L. Fries, 8 vols., *Publications of the North Carolina Historical Commission,* Raleigh, 1922–54), I, 234, 237, 241, *passim,* II, 593, 594, 603, *passim.* The distance was some three hundred miles; it took about three weeks in 1768 by loaded wagon to make the journey from Charleston to Bethabara. See *ibid.,* II, 603.

[13] During the period under consideration the Granville District land office was closed. In the July 15, 1774, edition of the *North Carolina Gazette* Governor Martin inserted a notice to the effect that since the closing of the land office in 1763 no one had been authorized to make any survey of land within the Granville District, and that anyone attempting to survey lands without authorization would be prosecuted.

[14] Rutherford to Tryon, January 19, 1769, P.R.O., C.O. 5:312, p. 481. For the currency shortage in Granville County see Nannie M. Tilley: "Industries of Colonial Granville County," *North Carolina Historical Review,* XIII, 286–7.

[15] *Ibid.*

public money in their own hands "and lay it out for their [own] benefit."[16] What made this situation difficult to remedy was that the local representatives in the Assembly—the justices of the peace, the county treasurer, the clerk of the county court, and other local officials—were all closely connected with the sheriff, who himself had to be a justice of the peace in order to serve. Furthermore, there existed in all the counties what has been described as a "county court ring," which controlled the election of the sheriff but made little effort to control his bad practices. Its power in the Assembly also prevented the creation of a more efficient and honest system of local government.[17] Thus, when an act of the Assembly passed in 1766 sought to remedy this situation, it recited that "many of the Sheriffs of this Province, have . . . embezzled considerable Sums of the Public Money, in Hopes of replacing the same when called for."[18] By the following year, with the condition unchanged, Governor Tryon declared to the Earl of Shelburne:

> ". . . the Sheriffs have embezzled more than one half of the public money ordered to be raised and collected by them. It is estimated that the sheriffs arrears to the publick amount to forty thousand pounds proclamation money, not five thousand of which will possibly ever come into the treasury as in many instances the sheriffs and their securities are either insolvent or retreated out of the province."[19]

It is true that the Assembly made repeated efforts to impose controls on the sheriffs and other officials by various laws passed between 1755 and 1774, but these, too, were without much success.[20] Up to the end of the colonial period, effective influence remained concentrated in a county group which included those freeholders who held no office but whose utilization of their franchise kept certain office-holders in power. This created in the counties—and particularly in the Piedmont—a division between the contented and the malcontents, between those who were at least reasonably well satisfied with the treatment given them by the county officials and those who were increasingly dissatisfied. Perhaps a line could also be drawn between the industrious and successful and those who

[16] *North Carolina Colonial Records,* V, 497.

[17] See Julian P. Boyd's illuminating article "The Sheriff in Colonial North Carolina," *North Carolina Historical Review,* V, 151–80. For the role of the local justices of the peace as members of the Assembly see *ibid.,* p. 161.

[18] *Laws of North Carolina, 1715–1776, State Records . . . ,* XXIII, 722.

[19] Tryon to Shelburne, July 4, 1767, *North Carolina Colonial Records,* VII, 497.

[20] See *Laws of North Carolina, 1715–1776, State Records . . . ,* XXIII, 424–32, 505, 526–31, 713–23, 789, 905, 970. The laws are analyzed by J. P. Boyd: *op. cit.,* V, 162–5.

could not get ahead. The first group of people—those who could meet their obligations, whether public or private—undoubtedly had some social connections with local office-holders. Those in the second category—people who were apt to be in a position of facing obligations beyond their means, especially in view of the scarcity of money, and who were deeply resentful of pressures brought upon them as a result of this situation—were quick to detect what they felt, sometimes with good reason, was evidence of extortion. It was against this background that the so-called Regulator Movement developed in the 1760's.

From the earliest days of its settlement North Carolina had had a turbulent history. There had been successive rebellions—the one in the Albemarle District in 1677, called the Culpepper Rebellion, the one in 1683 against Governor Seth Sothel of that same district, and that of 1710, known as the Cary Rebellion; these were followed by the activities of the infamous North Carolina pirates of such terrible reputation as Edward Teach, or "Blackbeard," and Stede Bonnet. In addition, the early part of the century saw the war of the Tuscarora Indians, which lasted from 1710 to 1714. By 1721, as a result of reports from the province, the Board of Trade made the following statement in a representation to the King in Council on September 8, 1721: "The Government of this Province having for many years been a very disorderly one . . . [now] becomes a place of Refuge for all the Vagabonds whom either Debt or Breach of the Laws have driven from the other Colonies on the Continent. . . ."[21] Some ten years later Colonel William Byrd of Virginia warned the newly installed Governor of North Carolina, George Burrington, that "people accustomed to live without law or gosple will with great Reluctance Submit to either"; at the same time Byrd wished him success "in bringing the chaos into form and reducing that Anarchy into a regular Government."[22] After three years of struggle, Burrington, ruined in health and fortune, begged His Majesty to give him leave to return to England.[23] Gabriel Johnston, a Scot, thereupon took over the administration and spent the next twenty years attempting to introduce order and equity into the affairs of the colony. Despite these efforts, Corbyn Morris, who ap-

[21] *North Carolina Colonial Records,* II, 419–20.

[22] Byrd to Burrington, July 20, 1731, *ibid.,* III, 194–5. On January 1, 1731/2, in a letter home, Burrington told of his trials "in resettling the Authorities of the Judicatures, and restraining profligate lawless men from unruly actions." See Shelburne Papers, 45:192–6, Clements Library, Ann Arbor, Mich.

[23] Burrington to the Duke of Newcastle, June 1, 1734, *North Carolina Colonial Records,* III, 625.

peared before the Board of Trade in 1749 to complain against Johnston, stated that "the Colony was in great distress and confusion and scarce better than an asylum for fugitives. . . ."[24]

With the outbreak of the Great War for the Empire and the thrust at the frontier settlements in Virginia by hostile Indians and their French allies, people from that province poured into what is now central North Carolina to settle where they could. This only added to the prevailing confusion over ownership of the land, especially as such vast acreage in that area was held by great absentee landowners, such as Lord Granville, Henry Eustace McCulloh, and George A. Selwyn, whose grants had not even been surveyed. Early in 1759 Halifax County rioters at Edenton seized the Granville District land agent, Francis Corbin, and carried him to Enfield, where they exacted a promise from him to stand trial on the grounds of "extortionate practices." In March, Reuben Searcy and others petitioned the Granville County court against what they claimed were the illegal and extortionate charges made by Robert Jones, Jr., attorney general of the province.[25] And in May of that year some rioters who had been arrested and placed in gaol at Enfield were rescued by fellow rioters. By 1762 Governor Dobbs found it necessary to issue a proclamation to quell disorders on the frontier.

Still the troubles continued. In the spring of 1765, when attempts were made to survey some of the Selwyn lands in Mecklenburg County in the area of Sugar Creek north of the South Carolina boundary, the squatters drove the surveyors off, after whipping and otherwise mistreating them. Yet none of the perpetrators of these acts of violence could be discovered, nor were they ever brought to justice.[26] In June of that same year the local schoolmaster, George Sims, in an address to the people living along Nutbush Creek in Granville County, denounced the county clerk, the sheriff, and the

---

[24] Board of Trade *Journal, 1712–1749*, p. 374. For the bitter controversy that divided the colony as a result of the county representation law of 1746, see Volume II, revised, of this series, pp. 116–20.

[25] For the Searcy petition see *Some Eighteenth Century Tracts Concerning North Carolina* (ed. W. K. Boyd, Raleigh, N.C., 1927), pp. 180–1, to be cited hereafter as Boyd's *Tracts;* see also Archibald Henderson: "The Origin of the Regulation in North Carolina," *American Historical Review*, XXI, 320–3.

[26] See the memorial of Henry Eustace McCulloh to Lieutenant Governor William Tryon, April 25, 1765, and McCulloh to Edmund Fanning, May 9, 1765, *North Carolina Colonial Records*, VII, 12–34. For the career of Fanning, who was appointed judge of the superior court for Orange County in the place of Maurice Moore in 1766 and subsequently became a much-hated figure in North Carolina, see *ibid.*, VIII, xl–xlii. For Fanning's connection with McCulloh see C. A. Sellers, Jr.: "Private Profits and British Colonial Policy: The Speculations of Henry McCulloh," *William and Mary Quarterly*, 3rd ser., VIII, 535–51.

lawyers for "the notorious and intolerable abuses which have crept into the practice of the law in this county." In this connection he paid special attention to Samuel Benton, a member of the Assembly, chief clerk of the county court, and lieutenant colonel of the local regiment, who was described as intent on "plundering his County to enrich" himself. Sims announced that he would pay no more fees until Benton produced the law that permitted the county clerk to exact them. He called upon all others to follow his example.[27]

In the summer of 1766, as the result of a gathering at Sandy Creek in Orange County, an "Advertisement" appeared calling upon the good people of the colony to save themselves from the "rogues" who were oppressing them by abusing their trust. In another "Advertisement," each neighbourhood in the county was called upon to send one or more representatives to a general meeting to be held on October 10, 1766, at Maddox (Maddock's) Mill; with the assurance that this gathering "will certainly cause the wicked men in power to tremble. . . ." But the officials who were expected to be present and to tremble failed to appear—except for one, who came late in the day with a message from Colonel Edmund Fanning. In it, Fanning, a colonel in the local militia and register of deeds of Orange County, took the position that the meeting was not only illegal but had the character of "an Insurrection."[28] Before the meeting was over, those attending drew up an address attempting to vindicate the holding of such gatherings. This was for the purpose of enlightening their representatives in the Assembly and, although a copy was accordingly sent to the legislature, it received no reply. Moreover, according to Hermon [Herman] Husband[s], a leader

[27] For Sims's "Nutbush Paper" (also called "The Granville Paper") or address of June 6, 1765, see Boyd's *Tracts,* pp. 182–92; see also Archibald Henderson: *op. cit.,* XXI, 324–32.

[28] See [Hermon Husband]: *An Impartial Relation of the First Rise and Cause of the Recent Differences in Publick Affairs, In . . . North-Carolina, etc.* (1770), pp. 10–13. The printer and place of publication of *An Impartial Relation* . . . are unknown. Nevertheless, as the most important published presentation of the point of view of the Regulators, it is to be found in Boyd's *Tracts,* pp. 247–333; see also *North Carolina Colonial Records,* VII, 249–52. The student should also consult the second part of Husband's document, published as *A Continuation of the Impartial Relation* . . . (1770), which may be found reprinted in *North Carolina Historical Review,* XVIII, 48–81, edited by Archibald Henderson. For a reprinting of another primary source, *A Fan for Fanning* (Boston, 1771), often attributed to Hermon Husband, see *North Carolina University Magazine,* VIII, 193, 289, and Boyd's *Tracts,* pp. 335–92. In this connection see also D. L. Swain: "The War of the Regulation," *North-Carolina University Magazine,* IX, 121–61, 327–45, 456–69, X, 17–35, 129–38. It may be noted that Hermon Husband's name is spelled in a variety of ways in the several documents or publications concerning him (Hermon, Herman, Harmon, Harmand, and Husband, Husbands, Husbans, etc.), but he appears to have signed himself Hermon Husband, which is therefore chosen as the preferred spelling in this text.

in this movement against the "rogues" in office, the sheriff and his deputies began to utter such "menaces" against the most active protesters that they were forced to drop their agitation.[29]

The following year, however, Orange County again became the centre of agitation when the issue of excessive fees[30] was once more raised in open court by Husband and a fellow agitator, after they had access to the list of fees established by law.[31] Although they were silenced by the court, resistance to the payment of fees and taxes became widespread. The opposition to taxation came to a head in 1766 and in 1767, when the Assembly passed several acts to provide funds for building a residence for the Governor as well as for other provincial purposes. This calls for comment and explanation.

As has already been stressed in this chapter, North Carolina had no capital. In 1748 Governor Johnston complained: "The Publick Records lye in a miserable condition[:] one part of them at Edenton near the Virginia Line in a place without Lock or Key; a great part of them in the Secretarys House at Cape Fear above Two Hundred Miles Distance from the other[;] Some few of 'em at the Clerk of the Council's House at Newbern, so that in whatever part of the Colony a man happens to be, if he wants to consult any paper or record he must send some Hundred of Miles before he can come at it."[32] Such was still the situation in 1766. It is true that in 1746/7 a bill had been passed to fix the capital at New Bern and to erect government buildings by means of a special tax. But no buildings had been erected and in 1748, on the basis of Governor Johnston's recommendation, the provincial council took the position that because of the unhealthfulness of New Bern it would be best to place the government buildings somewhere on the Trent River. Although no provincial buildings had been constructed ten years later, New Bern remained the titular capital, as was made clear in

[29] *An Impartial Relation . . .*, pp. 12–14.

[30] In 1745 the fees to be received by the various officers within the province were fixed. See "An Act for regulating the several Officers' Fees within this Province . . . ," *State Records . . .*, XXIII, 275–84.

[31] *An Impartial Relation . . .*, pp. 14–15. Husband mentions that "there happened to come out a new Collection of the Laws in one Book; two of us took a Copy of the Fees out of it . . . and carried it to the Court in *August* Term, 1767." The last known edition before the complete revision of the laws that appeared in 1773 is the *Collection of all the Acts of Assembly of the Province of North-Carolina, now In Force and Use*, published in 1764 by the local New Bern printer James Davis.

[32] Johnston to the Board of Trade, December 28, 1748, *North Carolina Colonial Records*, IV, 1165. For a history of New Bern see A. T. Dill, Jr., "Eighteenth Century New Bern . . . ," *North Carolina Historical Review*, XXII, 1–21, 152–75, 293–319, 460–89; XXIII, 47–78, 142–71, 325–59.

an address of the Council on May 28, 1757, which referred to the fact that it was "the present seat of Government where all Publick Business is transacted and Assemblies, Councils, Courts of Chancery and Courts of Claims for lands are held. . . ." Yet, there was still indecision. For the following year it was decided to place the capital at Tower Hill on the Neuse River. This was, however, found to be a very inaccessible region and the Council and Assembly on December 8, 1762, addressed the King to secure his approbation of New Bern

> "as a proper place . . . to Erect a Suitable House for the residence of your Majestys Governor. And such other Edifices as may be requisite for the safe keeping of the Public Records and for other Public Uses."[33]

But not until the latter part of 1766 was a bill finally passed "for erecting a convenient building within the Town of New Bern for the residence of the Governor or Commander in Chief for the time being."[34] By this time William Tryon, who had arrived in the province as Lieutenant Governor in 1764, had succeeded Arthur Dobbs as Governor.[35] The act provided that £5,000 proclamation money should be issued to Governor Tryon for that purpose by the treasurer of the province. To replace this fund, which had been earmarked in 1754 for "erecting Public Schools, and purchasing Glebes," an annual poll tax of eightpence proclamation money was levied for two years and also an additional import duty of twopence on all distilled liquors.[36] When it was later found impossible to complete the structure within the financial limitations laid down, the Assembly agreed to provide the Governor with the further sum of £10,000 proclamation money. To cover this expenditure a poll tax of two shillings and sixpence was voted for three years to begin when the earlier tax had run its course, that is, in 1769.[37]

Tryon, born in England and married to a kinswoman of Secretary of State Hillsborough, is said to have received his appointment as

---

[33] *North Carolina Colonial Records,* IV, 844, 898, V, 760–1, VI, 832, 835, 877–9. It may be noted that three members of the Council entered a protest at the action of December 8, 1762, in favouring New Bern as a permanent capital; see *ibid.,* VI, 878–9.

[34] *Ibid.,* VII, 420.

[35] Tryon's commission as Governor is to be found in Patent Roll 5 Geo. III, pt. 5:17; it is dated July 19, 1765; his instructions dated December 24, 1765, are in C.O. 5:325, pp. 257–405.

[36] *Laws of North Carolina, 1715–1776, State Records . . . ,* XXIII, 664–5; see also Governor Tryon to Shelburne, July 21, 1767, enclosing a financial report including the £5,000, Shelburne Papers, 56:187.

[37] *State Records of North Carolina,* XXIII, 711–13.

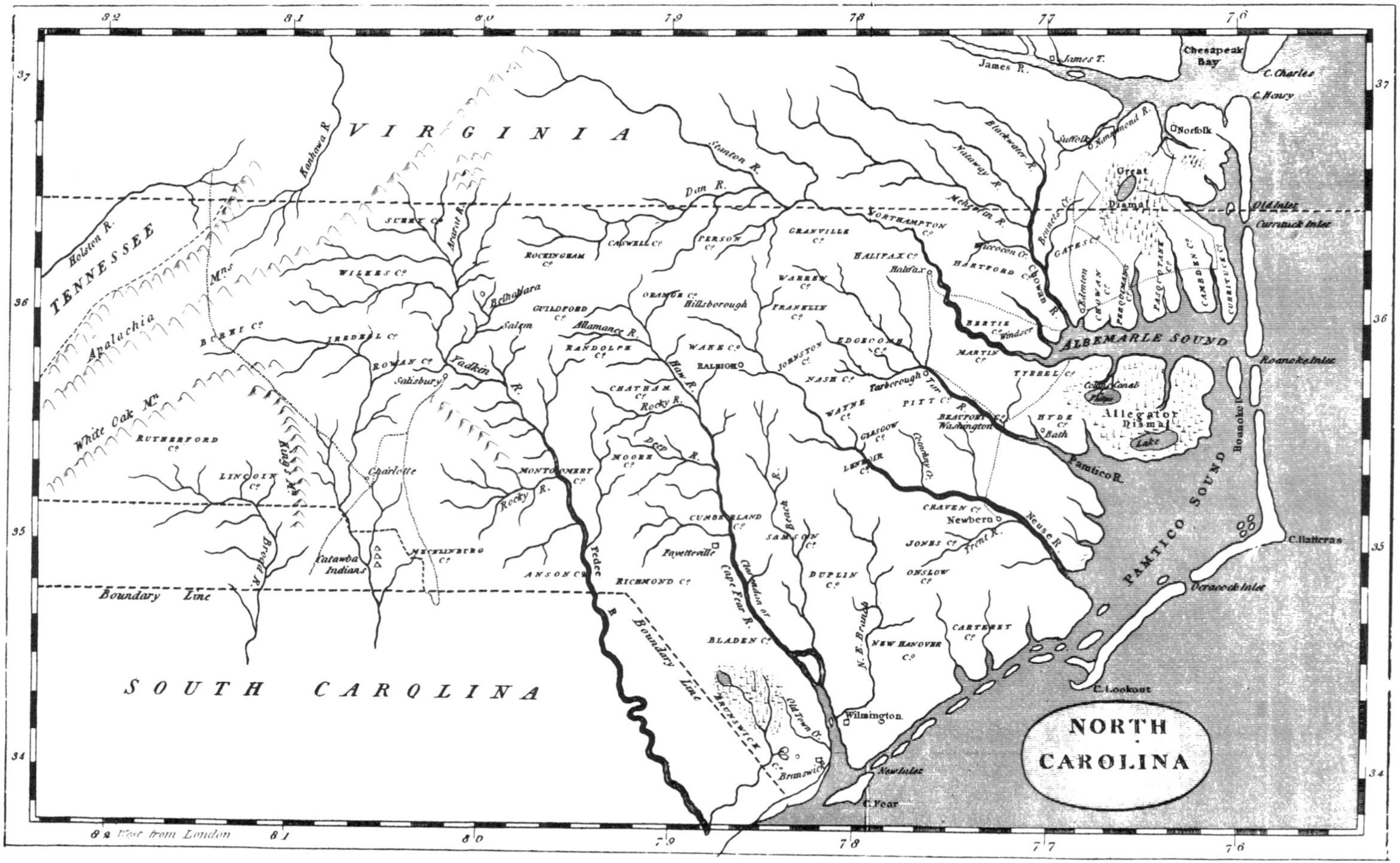

A map of North Carolina, post 1792.

(From Hugh Williamson's *History of North Carolina*, 1812, Vol. I)

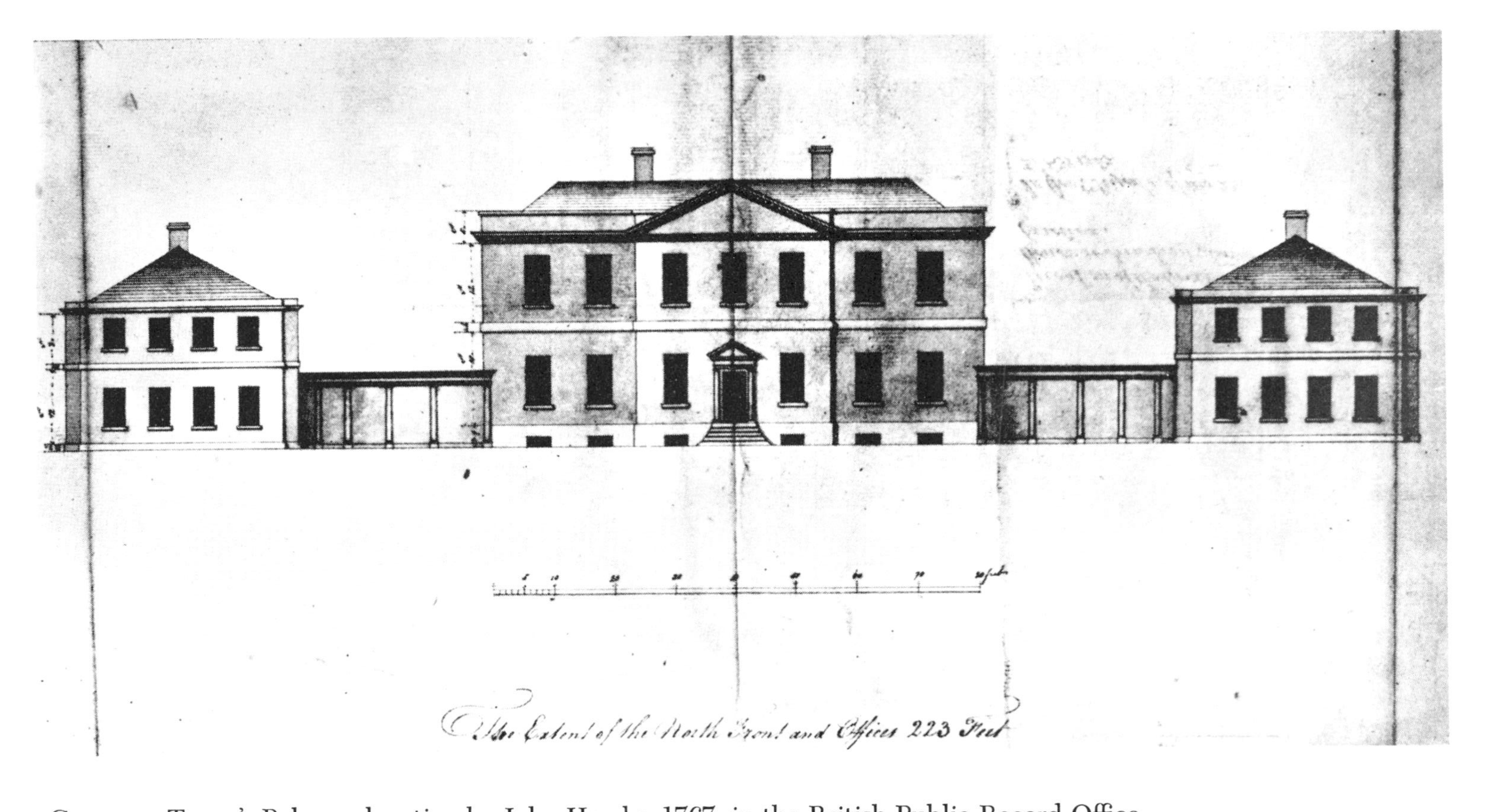

The Extent of the North Front and Offices 223 Feet

Governor Tryon's Palace, elevation by John Hawks, 1767, in the British Public Record Office.

(From Alonzo T. Dill's *Governor Tryon and His Palace*, 1955)

Lieutenant Governor through his family connections. Prior to his arrival in North Carolina he had been a professional military man. He was also an ardent churchman. He therefore seems to have come naturally by his love of pomp and ceremony. His sense of tact and diplomacy served him well, not only in achieving success in the building of the Governor's palace, but in winning a broad popularity that would rally men to his cause in the war of the Regulators and in his subsequent efforts to administer the province within the framework of the law.[38]

When completed in 1770 the government building at New Bern, popularly called "Tryon's Palace," became a symbol of North Carolina's stature as a colony no longer merely a hideout for runaway debtors or the home of agitators hostile to all effective government, but one now qualified to assume a self-respecting place of equality beside its neighbours, Virginia and South Carolina. The structure provided the Governor with a residence of dignity and also offered suitable accommodations for other provincial officers and for meetings of the Council and the Assembly.[39] That its construction did not lay a heavy burden of taxation upon a people already heavily taxed is evident from the fact that in 1767 the tax was seven shillings and fourpence per taxable;[40] in 1768 it was seven shillings "besides the County and Parish Taxes. . . ."[41] The cost of West India rum or Madeira wine in frontier Rowan County at this period was sixteen shillings per gallon and a gallon of whiskey was ten shillings. But men had money to spend on such luxuries, as is apparent from the evidence that between 1753 and 1772 over 140 licenses were granted within the county for the sale of liquors, and of this number 30 were granted to the small community of Salisbury. Moreover, for a loaded wagon and team to cross the ferry over the Catawba the charge made by its licensed owner was six shillings,[42] in accordance with court-established rates.

Where and when the movement in the 1760's against the pay-

[38] For an early study of Tryon during the period under consideration see M. D. Haywood: *Governor William Tryon and His Administration in the Province of North Carolina, 1765–1771* (Raleigh, 1903).

[39] See A. T. Dill, Jr.: *Governor Tryon and his Palace* (Chapel Hill, N.C., 1955), Chap. 5, "Palace on the Trent: 1766–1770"; see also by the same author: "Tryon's Palace. A Neglected Niche of North Carolina History," *North Carolina Historical Review*, XIX, 119–67.

[40] See the Bethabara Diary for August 14, 1767, in which the statement is made that Francis Lock came to Bethabara to collect the taxes levied in 1766, which "were 7 sh. 4 d. per Taxable" (*Records of the Moravians in North Carolina*, I, 360).

[41] Governor Tryon to the Regulators, June 21, 1768, Boyd's *Tracts*, p. 372.

[42] For the tables of rates covering 1769 and 1772 see J. S. Brawley: *The Rowan Story, 1753–1953* . . . (Salisbury, N.C., 1953), pp. 38–9.

ment of taxes actually began is not clear. As early as May 28, 1768, according to an entry in the Moravian Bethabara Diary, the settlers living along the Yadkin met at the home of one Isaac Free and signed "a Contract against the Public Taxes and other grievances." The diarist went on to note: "Many of them do not know what they want; it is a contrivance of certain rebellious heads."[43] But the anger of large numbers of frontier people was certainly directed against paying for the construction of the New Bern government building. This was especially true in Orange County, where the Haw River settlers declared in March 1768 they would not pay any taxes "till an act granting an enormous sum for building a house for the Governor be repealed."[44] Under the terms of a law passed by the Assembly the sheriff in every county was expected to spend two days at each of five different places within his county between January and March to receive taxes, with the penalty for non-payment of these obligations during the specified period set at two shillings and eightpence. Furthermore, if taxes were not paid before March 10 of each year the sheriff was empowered to sell at auction slaves, goods, and chattels that had been distrained to satisfy said taxes.[45] To the rage of those who determined not to pay taxes until the act for constructing the New Bern provincial house had been repealed, the sheriffs began to levy upon the goods of delinquents and to sell these at public auction at a low rate.[46]

The formal organization of the North Carolina Regulators took place at a general meeting of dissatisfied settlers held in Orange

---

[43] *Records of the Moravians in North Carolina,* I, 378; see also Ruth Blackwelder: "The Attitude of the North Carolina Moravians toward the American Revolution," *North Carolina Historical Review,* IX, 1–21, especially pp. 7–8.

[44] *Virginia Gazette,* October 27, 1768, Supplement. As this position appeared to some of the more sober agitators "too hot and rash, and in some Things not legal," it was modified by Hermon Husband and other leaders in the Sandy Creek area of the county, with the consent of Haw River agitators, to read: "1st. That we will pay no more Taxes until we are satisfied they are agreeable to Law, and applied to the Purposes therein mentioned; unless we cannot help it, or are forced" (*An Impartial Relation . . . ,* p. 17); see also *North Carolina Colonial Records,* VII, 671. The *Boston Chronicle,* edition for November 7–14, 1768, printed a letter from Mecklenburg County which referred to the failure of the Cider Tax that bore chiefly on one section of England and compared this levy with the "enormous sum" granted to build a house for the Governor—a grant which chiefly affected the western North Carolina counties because of their greater population, and was also unfair in that, as a poll tax, it bore equally upon a person worth £10,000 and one having nothing but the labour of his hands for his daily support. This letter is reprinted in *North Carolina Colonial Records,* VII, 864–5.

[45] "An Act for appointing Sheriffs and directing their Duty in Office," *Laws of North Carolina, 1715–1776, State Records . . . ,* XXIII, 718; see also Sheriff Tyree Harris's notice, *North Carolina Colonial Records,* VII, 771–2.

[46] *An Impartial Relation . . . ,* p. 15.

County on April 4, 1768.[47] As the name implies, they were organized to regulate local affairs. This was to be done by calling upon the sheriff of the county and a vestryman of the parish to produce before their committee of twelve "a copy of the list of Taxables for each year and a list of the . . . Insolvents returned each year with an account how the money was applied, to whom paid and to what uses . . . and to request our representatives to confer with them in our behalf and to show us law for the customary fees that have been taken. . . ." What is more, the Regulators agreed to hold meetings four times a year "until the business be completed to satisfaction. . . ."[48]

Here was a plan to ignore the recognized means of securing relief from alleged abuses in government. Instead of recourse to petitions to the Governor or Assembly or appeals to the courts, authority was placed in an extra-legal body designed, in the final analysis, to override the legal instrumentalities of the government. A clash between the two was therefore inevitable.

When one of the Orange County Regulators refused to pay the levy, Sheriff Hawkins seized the man's horse, bridle, and saddle, all of which, following the terms of the law, were required to be sold to the highest bidder in order to pay the tax. On April 8, 1768, according to Lieutenant Colonel John Gray's letter to Colonel Edmund Fanning of the following day, a crowd of almost a hundred Regulators converged on Hillsborough, the county seat of Orange County, took the horse from Hawkins, after binding him, "and treated sundry of the Inhabitants of the Town very ill & crowned the whole by shooting two or three Bullets through your House." In view of the determination of the mob to take the law into its own hands, Gray recommended that the militia be raised and that everyone connected with the raid be apprehended and placed in gaol.[49] Upon receipt of this letter, Fanning—who was in Halifax County while Chief Justice Howard was presiding at a meeting of the superior court—secured a warrant from the Justice for the arrest of three of the most active rioters: William Butler, Peter Craven, and Ninian Bell Hamilton; Fanning also ordered the captains of seven militia companies of the county to raise as many men as appeared necessary

---

[47] For the adoption of the term "Regulator," see "Regulators' Advertisement No. 6," *North Carolina Colonial Records,* VII, 702–3. It is the view of J. S. Bassett, in "The Regulators of North Carolina," Amercan Historical Association *Annual Report for 1894,* p. 164*n,* that the term was adopted from South Carolina, where it had been used earlier.

[48] *North Carolina Colonial Records,* VII, 702–3.

[49] *Ibid.,* VII, 705–6.

to check the spirit of "riotousness and rebellion and to enforce a full obedience to the Civil Officers of Government and the execution of Laws."[50] Yet when summoned to appear, not more than 120 militiamen out of the seven companies answered the call. Many of them were "in favour of the Mob or . . . chose to stand neutral," with the result that it seemed best to Adjutant Francis Nash to recommend that forces be brought to the county from elsewhere to restore order.[51]

When Fanning returned to Hillsborough he sent an appeal to Governor Tryon informing him that people

> "in every part and Corner of the County [were] meeting, conspiring, and confederating by solemn oath and open violence to refuse the payment of Taxes and to prevent the execution of Law, threatening death and immediate destruction to myself and others, requiring . . . Clerks, Sheriffs, Registers, Attornies and all Officers of every degree and station to be arraigned at the Bar of their Shallow Understanding and to be punished and regulated at their Will, and in a word, for them to become the sovereign arbiters of right and wrong."[52]

It may be pointed out that the Regulators bore deep resentment against Fanning, for his activities as a member of the Assembly in encouraging the erection of the government building and for his presumed position "at the head of affairs" in the county.[53] According to Fanning, the resistance to authority first started in Anson County, then spread to Orange, and "encouraged by some of the principal men of Cumberland . . . became considerable."[54]

After Tryon had placed before the Council various dispatches and the members had reached the conclusion that "an absolute Insurrection of a dangerous tendency has broke out in Orange County," he issued a proclamation on April 27 calling upon all people concerned "in such Insurrections to disperse" and, in case of their refusal to comply with his request, directing all civil and

[50] Fanning to Gray, April 13, 1768, *ibid.*, VII, 706–7.

[51] Adjutant Nash and Captain Thomas Hart to Fanning, April 17, 1768, *ibid.*, VII, 710–12.

[52] Fanning to Tryon, April 23, 1768, *ibid.*, VII, 713–16.

[53] *Ibid.*, VII, 711.

[54] *Ibid.*, VII, 713. In Anson County at the time of the opening of the superior court late in April, about forty men armed with clubs and fire-arms took possession of the court house and sought to prevent the court from entering upon its business. The next day, an even larger group of rioters forced the judges off the bench and proceeded to displace the authorized representative of the county, John Crawford, by electing a popular figure, Charles Robinson, in his stead, although no writ of election had been issued. See Samuel Spencer to Governor Tryon, April 28, 1768, *ibid.*, VII, 722–6. For the resolves of the Anson rioters and the oath they took see *ibid.*, VII, 726.

military officers to take every lawful means to suppress the riots.[55] That same day he also sent warrants by express to the commanding officers of eight western counties for calling out the militia to oppose the insurrections.[56] Tryon also commissioned by name all members of the Council as justices to see to the execution of the laws and to the confinement of those "who have Committed any Treasons, Felonies, . . . Trespasses and Extortions whatsoever within our said Province . . ." who could not or would not give security.[57] When the proclamation was posted in Orange County, Fanning placed under it his own "Advertisement" pointing out the Governor's promise that "if any Grievance subsists, in this County, if the same is made known by a suitable Petition, to the legislative Body it shall meet with his support if they make themselves the deserving Objects, of the legislative notice, by . . . paying a due and proper Obedience to the Laws. . . ."[58]

The formation of the extra-legal government in Orange County was advanced a step farther at a convention of Regulators held on April 30 at Rocky River, when detailed "Instructions" were issued to the committee of "Settlers appointed by the County." They were to procure a list of all taxables, insolvents, and delinquents and a fair account of all money paid during the past two years together with the use to which it had been put and the citation of every law authorizing the expenditure, especially the tax for 1767; in addition the committee was to examine "the true Cost by Law" for recording deeds and for procuring letters of administration and letters testamentary and the payment of "Fees in Common Law."[59] At this same meeting some 450 Regulators or their supporters, including Hermon Husband, signed petitions to the Governor and Council asserting that the people of Orange County were obliged to pay larger fees for recording deeds than those in any of the adjacent counties "and many other Fees more than the Law allows," pointing out at the same time that the application of protest sent to their representatives in the Assembly had been disregarded; and they therefore begged that their wrongs be redressed.[60]

Apparently in reply to this petition, Edmund Fanning on May 1

---

[55] *Ibid.*, VII, 720–1.
[56] *Ibid.*, VII, 718.
[57] *Ibid.*, VII, 730–1.
[58] *Ibid.*, VII, 739–40.
[59] *Ibid.*, VII, 732.
[60] That the people who signed the petition were literate is indicated by the fact that but one person signed with a cross. For the petition see *ibid.*, VII, 733–7, in which Husband's name also appears as Husbans.

entreated by letter three prominent residents of Orange County—Jacob Fudge, who had signed the foregoing petition, Richard Cheek, "a Dutchman," and Benjamin Saxon, neither of whom had signed it—to meet him at Hillsborough, and guaranteed them not only kindly treatment, but all information at his disposal on why taxes had been laid and for what purposes. He also suggested that if the people of the county laboured under public grievance, a few of them should come to him so that he might draw up a petition for relief, to the Governor, Council, and Assembly, which he himself would present at the next meeting of the Assembly. Fanning also gave the assurance that if any who had suffered a private injury were to apply to him, they would find certain and sure redress through the laws of the land.[61] Unfortunately, that very day a warrant was issued by Justice of the Peace Thomas Lloyd for the arrest of the chief penman for the insurgents, Hermon Husband, who was not technically one of the Regulators, never having taken the prescribed oath because of his Quaker scruples (although he had been disowned by the Society of Friends in 1764). Husband was accused of "Traterously and feloniously Conspiring with others in stirring up an Insurrection among his Majesty's Liege Subjects of the County . . . and endeavouring by seditious libellous and Traterous practices to withdraw divers Inhabitants . . . from their Natural Obediences to our said Lord the King and Excite them to act in open Rebellion to his Government & Laws."[62] Early the following day Husband was arrested at his home in Sandy Creek, as was William Butler, who was accused of being a leader in the Hillsborough riot early in the year. Although the prisoners were to have been sent to the New Bern gaol, they were admitted to bail when it became apparent to the authorities that a gathering mob was determined to rescue the two.[63]

Later in May, the earlier petition to the Governor and Council ("Regulators' Advertisement No. 9") was adopted by the Regulators ("Advertisement No. 10") and joined to it was a narrative of events from 1766 to the time of the petition ("Advertisement No. 11"). The account painted a picture of "the wretched Poor" being exploited by court officers, described as "nefarious & designing men" and "Monsters in iniquity," whose fees were "exorbitant, oppressive

[61] For this letter see *ibid.*, VII, 741.

[62] For the warrant see *ibid.*, VII, 742, in which Husband's name is given as Harmond Husband.

[63] *Ibid.*, VII, 765; see also Hermon Husband's "Narrative" (J. H. Hill: *Reminiscences and Memoirs of North Carolina* [4 parts, Washington, D.C., and Columbus, Ohio, 1883–4], Part II, 316–17), and also his *An Impartial Relation . . .*, pp. 41–5.

and extra-legal." As evidence of this, these officials were accused of requiring for the recording of deeds two shillings more than was paid in other counties and of demanding a head tax of ten shillings and eightpence instead of eight shillings and fourpence.[64]

Tryon was in Brunswick when he received the Regulators' petition. After consulting with the Council, he ordered the exact rate of taxes to be published and directed the attorney general to proceed against all officials who had given evidence of being extortionists. He also warned the rioters of the dangers they faced and charged them to disperse and repudiate the title of Regulators.[65] His decision to go into the western area of discontent himself, at the head of regiments from Rowan, Mecklenburg, and Granville counties, brought him to Hillsborough on July 6. There, by proclamation, he ordered officers to post all lawful fees and called upon the people to pay the 1767 tax, but these steps brought little response on the part of the mutinous settlers.[66]

Early in August reports were brought to the Governor, who was

[64] For the list of items for which taxes, amounting to ten shillings and eightpence, were to be paid by residents of Orange County, see *North Carolina Colonial Records*, VII, 772–3. It may be noted that among other items there was a shilling tax for sinking £21,350 granted by the Assembly in 1748, a shilling for sinking £40,000 granted in 1754, two shillings for sinking £20,000 granted in 1761, and eightpence for building the province house with the £5,000 granted in 1766. For the "Advertisements" covering the petition and narrative of the Regulators see *ibid.*, VII, 733–7 and 758–66. Rednap Howell, a prominent Regulator of Granville County, was apparently the author of this petition, although Husband had been chiefly responsible for earlier protest papers. See *ibid.*, VIII, xxvi. Before the Regulators' petition was sent, a resident of Orange County, Ralph McNair, an associate of Fanning—later a member of the Assembly and still later a Loyalist—framed a petition to the Governor and Council and, as promised, sent it to Hermon Husband for his approval. In a covering letter to Husband he pointed out that—in view of the adoption by the North Carolina Assembly in 1749 of a great body of English statutes, among which was 7 Wm. III, c. 3, relating to treason and misprison of treason—the people, in opposing the government by force, were liable to the most serious penalties. He also begged Husband to believe that those seeking redress had a sincere friend in Edmund Fanning. The McNair petition was therefore expressed in terms of petitioners who imagined that they had for a long time "been imposed and exacted upon by Sheriffs and other Persons" not only with respect to fees charged but in the collecting of the public levies as well, and apprehended there had been "many enormities . . . committed under colour of their Offices," and therefore sought redress for the grievances "where found real and where only imaginary kindly excuse the trouble in compassion to our ignorance . . ." The balance of the petition also sought pardon for the error of the illegal steps already taken based on a compassionate view of the errors made by the aggrieved parties as being "ignorant men, and at the same time in such necessitous Circumstances that their utmost industry could scarce afford a wretched subsistance to their Families, much less enable them to engage in uncertain law Suits, with the rich and powerful. . . ." For the McNair letter to Husband and the enclosed petition see *ibid.*, VII, 767–71. The McNair petition was rejected as designed to place the blame on the petitioners.

[65] Tryon to the Regulators, June 21, 1768, Boyd's *Tracts*, pp. 271–3.

[66] Tryon to the Regulators, Hillsborough, August 1, 1768, *ibid.*, pp. 274–5.

still at Hillsborough, that large numbers of people were assembled, that they had unanimously agreed not to pay taxes and that (according to the eye-witness deposition of Ransom Sutherland, later a member of the North Carolina Provincial Congress) they threatened to "kill any Person that should distrain [property] for their levies. . . ."[67] On the 10th Tryon received the intelligence that over 400 men had gathered at a place called Peed's, forty miles from the county seat, with the intention of moving upon Hillsborough, and that "if the requisitions they should make to the Governor, were not complied with, they would then burn the Town, and take satisfaction their own way." According to report, by the 11th the "Insurgents" had advanced twenty miles. Thereupon orders were sent to eight captains to march as many men as possible to Hillsborough. Within Orange County, Colonel Fanning mustered some 250 men to defend the town. To gather additional troops, Tryon moved to Salisbury in Rowan County—where "a great many gentlemen . . . welcomed his arrival with expressions of great satisfaction"—and then into Mecklenburg County, where a regiment of 900 men had gathered.[68] On August 26 he received a joint letter from four Presbyterian ministers of the backcountry expressing their "abhorrence of the present turbulent and disorderly spirit that shows itself in some parts of this Province," together with a copy of a letter that they had sent out to "the Presbyterian Inhabitants of North Carolina" calling upon those who had taken an oath to oppose the government to disregard it as a "greater guilt will lie upon them if they keep it" and to "return immediately to your Duty and Loyalty. . . ."[69]

By August 26 eleven companies of the Rowan County regiment had gathered. In reviewing them, Tryon called upon those who would freely volunteer to serve to come forward to take their stand with the "King's Colours," the standard of which he held. All but one of the companies responded. Preparations proceeded for the movement to Hillsborough during the early part of September. On the 5th Judge Richard Henderson informed the Governor that "the whole Body of Militia of Granville County was ready to march in support of Government." The little army left Salisbury on the 12th or 13th for Hillsborough, arriving there on the 19th. In all about 1,400 men rallied to the King's colours. On the 22nd, according to

[67] Deposition of Ransom Sutherland, August 3, 1768, *North Carolina Colonial Records,* VII, 799.

[68] "Governor Tryon's Journal," *ibid.,* VII, 819–20.

[69] Letter of Hugh McCaddon, James Creswell, Henry Patillo, and David Caldwell to Tryon, August 23, 1768, with copy of letter addressed to all North Carolina Presbyterians, *ibid.,* VII, 813–16.

Tryon, some 800 "Insurgents" from Anson, Rowan, and Orange counties approached within a mile of the town. Then, apparently in view of the force that Tryon had mustered, they sent a letter to the Governor asking for the terms of pardon. Tryon now held a "Council of War" at which it was agreed that a free pardon would be extended to all the insurgents (except five from the Hillsborough district and two each from Rowan and Anson counties, to be named by the Governor) under condition that those excepted from pardon be delivered up to be tried according to the laws of the country, that the whole body of insurgents lay down their arms, and, finally, that they make a declaration to pay all taxes whenever required. When the insurgents received these conditions they asked for time to consider them. The night of the 23rd, without replying to the Governor's offer, they dispersed, each man to his home.[70]

On September 22 the superior court opened in Hillsborough. Hermon Husband and William Butler—both of whom had previously been accused of inciting the public to riot but had been released on bail—now appeared among others for trial. Husband was finally discharged with the jury returning the verdict *ignoramus*. Butler, however, was sentenced as a leader of the Regulators to pay a fine of £50 and to serve six months in gaol; two other Regulators were also tried and convicted, but they were soon released on Tryon's orders. True also to the Governor's pledge to the people, the clerk and the register of deeds of the county court were indicted by the attorney general and were "found guilty of taking too high fees." The register, Edmund Fanning, was fined a penny and costs in six cases.[71] As "extortionate" fees figure so largely in the

[70] "Tryon's Journal," *ibid.*, VII, 826–33, and "Proceedings and Resolutions of the Council of War . . . the 22nd and 23d September 1768," *ibid.*, VII, 840–2. It may be noted that whereas Tryon's account states that 800 insurgents appeared before Hillsborough under arms, Husband gave the figure as 3,700 Regulators, adding that these men would pay their taxes as usual, if permitted to come into town peaceably "to Complain of our Officers, and [were granted a] Pardon for all past Breaches of the Peace, (except the two under Bail, who would Stand their Trials) . . ." (*An Impartial Relation* . . . , p. 41).

[71] Proceedings of the Hillsborough Superior Court, September 22–October 1, 1768, *North Carolina Colonial Records*, VII, 842–7, and *An Impartial Relation* . . . , pp. 49–59. Writing to the Earl of Hillsborough on December 24, 1768, Tryon stated: "It manifestly appearing that Colonel Fanning, the Register, had acted with the utmost candor to the people and that his conduct proceeded from a misconstruction of the fee bill, he was in court honorably acquitted of the least intentional abuse in office[;] Colonel Fanning however immediately after the above verdict resigned up to me his commission of Register" (*North Carolina Colonial Records*, VII, 884–6). That Fanning felt deeply that a grave injustice had been done to him is manifest from the evidence that he sought, through the London agent for North Carolina, Henry E. McCulloh, to secure the opinion of legal counsel in England. The facts of the case were laid before John Morgan of the Inner Temple. These included the fee act of

grievances of the Regulators, it may be noted in passing that the six shillings which Fanning thought he was justified in taking for a deed to land does not seem to have been out of line with the usual charges made for a deed in Pennsylvania at the same period. A Pennsylvania recorder of deeds was entitled to receive, for recording or copying any deed, three farthings for every line of at least twelve words; for every search, one shilling; for every acknowledgment on the margin of satisfaction of a mortgage on land, one shilling; for affixing the seal to every exemplification, a shilling and sixpence; and for every seal of office and endorsement of certificate on each deed, a shilling and sixpence.[72]

For a period after the trials there was relative quiet in North Carolina. According to the Governor, writing to the Earl of Hillsborough late in 1768, the real objective of most of the rioters in the western counties was "an abolition of taxes and debts," which the concentration of the militia at Hillsborough led them to put aside, at least for the moment.[73] It may also be noted that of 1,461 militiamen who came to the support of the government at this contingency, 602 were from the Orange County battalion, 253 were from the Mecklenburg County battalion, 147 from the Rowan County bat-

---

1748, the indictment and conviction of Fanning as register for extortion in taking six shillings for a deed in place of two shillings and sixpence, and the evidence presented in the trial that, upon taking office as register, he had sought the advice of the county court and had been informed that he was entitled to "6s. and odd pence at least for every Deed whatsoever, with probate, order for Registering, and Registers certificate of the due Registering, & in case of other instrum[t]: more, as by Bill drawn up by the Court & delivered to the s[d] Register." Moreover, the "opinion of the late Atty Gen[l] of No. Carolina was likewise taken on this matter, who declared that the Register was intitled to demand Fees to the amount of 8s. 7d. on any Deed." Fanning also presented as evidence bills furnished by other county registers for fees taken for the same service that were "considerably more than 6s." However, to be within the law, as he conceived it, he testified that he never took more than six shillings for the various duties involved in providing the owner of property with a deed. In giving his opinion dated May 1, 1769, Morgan concluded that Fanning was not guilty of any wrongdoing, acting as he did on the advice of the judges of the county court; if he erred it was "an involuntary mistake . . . consequently he is not a criminal" (*ibid.*, VIII, 33–6). But, doubtless as the result of aroused public opinion regarding fees, Fanning did not prevail on the court to alter its judgment. Consequently, to secure a vindication he wrote to McCulloh on April 23, 1770, asking him to secure the opinion of two of the greatest English lawyers and liberals, John Dunning and Serjeant John Glynn. As they were both on circuit court duty, McCulloh once more turned to John Morgan, who on August 6, 1770, again wrote: "I do not see the least foundation for criminating the Defendant, and I am therefore clearly of opinion, he ought, in every respect, to be Exculpated" (McCulloh to Fanning, London, August 4, 1770, enclosing Morgan's opinion, *ibid.*, VIII, 224–6).

[72] *The Statutes at Large of Pennsylvania from 1682 to 1801* (eds. J. T. Mitchell and Henry Flanders, 17 vols., Harrisburg, 1896–1915), VIII, 414.

[73] Tryon to Hillsborough, December 24, 1768, *North Carolina Colonial Records*, VII, 885.

talion, and 90 from the Granville County battalion.[74] Moreover, Tryon testified that "His Majesty's presbyterian subjects as well as those of the church of England, showed themselves very loyal on this service. . . ."[75] This seems to indicate that even in those counties where the Regulators had their greatest strength there were large numbers of men willing to demonstrate their loyalty by taking up arms against the insurgents. With the disbanding of the Regulators, the Governor's troops were discharged. But the day before this event took place, Tryon, after informing the Council of his intention and securing its consent, issued a proclamation granting pardon to all except thirteen of those who had committed "many Acts of violence contrary to Law being led on by some evil, wicked and designing men."[76] The sheriff of Orange County, Tyree Harris, reported late in October—apparently acting upon instructions issued by the Governor on the 10th granting further pardon to all, except Husband, who would submit to the government and pay their tax debts—that he had been to see many of the Regulators, who either paid him or his deputy the taxes that were due or promised to do so as quickly as they could produce the money.[77] That there was a great scarcity of currency in the newer counties is indicated by a petition to the Governor signed by sixty-seven residents of Halifax County that "the grait Scarcity of Money laye Us Under Very grait hardships In so much as not to be able to Pay Our Taxes which has been the Real Cause of all the Disturbance that leatly Hapned. . . ." They therefore begged his Excellency to grant an act of the Assembly to provide more money or an act to pay taxes in commodities "which would Enable Us to Chearfully pay as Useual."[78]

When the General Assembly met at New Bern on November 7 the Governor addressed the members on the necessity of and the means taken for stopping the "licentious and tumultous Meetings . . . held by a large body of Insurgents . . . , Insurrections, destructive of the good order of Government and dangerous to the Constitution of this country." In reply, the Assembly expressed its thanks that the militia had been raised "to oppose the intentional outrages of a set of men who forgetful of their duty . . . and in defiance of the

[74] "A General Return of the Troops assembled under His Excellency's Command. Hillsborough Camp 22nd September 1768," *ibid.*, VII, 889.

[75] Tryon to Hillsborough, December 24, 1768, *ibid.*, VII, 886.

[76] For the proclamation of October 1, 1768, see *ibid.*, VII, 850–1.

[77] Harris to Tryon, October 29, 1768, *ibid.*, VII, 863–4. For Tryon's query to Hillsborough seeking extension of the proclamation of pardon to make it general, "both with respect to persons and fines," except for Hermon Husband, see *ibid.*, VII, 886.

[78] For the above petition see *ibid.*, VII, 866–7.

Laws under which they lived, were pursuing measures . . . dangerous to the Constitution of their Country."[79] At the same session efforts were made, especially by Edmund Fanning, representing Orange County, to meet some of the difficulties facing the settlers in the western areas. On November 11 he presented a petition from inhabitants of Orange living in the neighbourhood of Cumberland County asking that, to relieve them from going a great distance to the court house, a new county be erected out of portions of Orange and Cumberland.[80] He also presented another petition that same day praying for a law that would empower a single justice of the peace to try and determine all causes to the amount of £5.[81] While neither bill became law, it may be noted that the bill for small debts passed its required readings in the Assembly, in the process of which it was amended and then sent to the Council for action.[82] There it ran into difficulty of such a nature that the Assembly was unwilling to approve the Council amendment attached to it which restored a clause "relative to the trial of rioters, etc." The clause introduced by the Council would not only have permitted appeals on judgments involving twenty shillings and upwards but would have allowed those accused by the Attorney General of promoting the "late many wicked and dangerous Riots & Insurrections," to be tried in other districts beyond the one in which the offence had been committed—provided that this change of venue should be approved by one of the judges of the superior court.[83] The Assembly was quite prepared to accept the clause permitting appeals involving any sum above twenty shillings but very properly opposed altering the jurisdiction of the Superior Court "in particular instances" as foreign to the bill and "expressly contrary to the sentiments of this House."[84] Nor did Fanning have any better success with a bill "for lessening the number of public claims, diminishing the public debts and relieving the present burden of taxation on the poor," which he presented on November 28. It was rejected on the second reading.[85] However, he did succeed in securing relief from public taxes for certain residents of Orange County—undoubtedly

[79] For Tryon's address and the reply of the Assembly see *ibid.*, VII, 890–3 and 930–2.

[80] *Ibid.*, VII, 929.

[81] *Ibid.*

[82] *Ibid.*, VII, 944, 947, 959.

[83] *Ibid.*, VII, 911–12 and 965–6.

[84] *Ibid.*, VII, 966.

[85] *Ibid.*, VII, 961 and 962.

hardship cases—upon presentation of certificates from the local court.[86]

When the end of the 1768 Assembly session was reached without the provision of any important remedial measures for the relief of the inhabitants of the backcountry, these people continued to feel a deep sense of grievance against both the provincial and the county government. For example, on October 9, 1769, 260 inhabitants of Anson County signed a petition to the Assembly which was ably framed even if pitched in a highly emotional tone. In it the people of the western part of the province asserted: "We . . . have too long yielded ourselves slaves to remorseless oppression." Under seven headings the petitioners listed their chief criticisms of the conduct of those in power. Among the grievances complained of were that the poor in general paid disproportionate taxes, especially in the western counties; that there was no method in those counties for paying taxes in produce in lieu of currency, such as existed in the east with tobacco notes; that lawyers, clerks, "and other pentioners" exploited the western people by extorting exorbitant fees, unreasonably instituting law-suits, and otherwise evading "the intention of the law." Thereupon, under seventeen additional headings, the reformers sought for redress and relief; these included the use of ballots in elections, the payment of proportionate taxes based upon individual profits, the substitution of commodities for money in laying the taxes until the currency be expanded, the creation of a Western District with a treasurer, the setting up of a loan office, the trial of civil debt cases under £10 without lawyers by a single justice and six jurymen whose decision should be final, the payment to the chief justice of a salary in place of fees, and the curbing of clerks and lawyers respecting fees.[87]

At the same period came the petition to the Governor and General Assembly from a combined Orange and Rowan group, significantly without signatures. It was directed chiefly against the "heavy Exactions, Oppressions and Enormity, committed on us by Court Officers, in every Station: the Source of which our said Calamity, we impute to the Countenance and Protection they receive from such of our Lawyers and Clerks, as have obtained seats in the House of Representatives, and who intent on making their own fortune, . . . regardless of their Country's Interest: are ever . . . projecting such

[86] *Ibid.*, VII, 963.

[87] "The Petition of the Inhabitants of Anson County, being part of the Remonstrance of the Province of North Carolina," *ibid.*, VIII, 75–80.

Laws as may best Effect their wicked purposes." The petitioners therefore asked the Assembly to pass an act that would prevent any lawyer or county clerk from being a candidate in provincial elections. They were especially bitter against the "Summons and petition Act: an Act replete with Misery and ruin to the lowest Class of people throughout the province" and called for its repeal; they also asked for a division of Orange County to save the expense of attending courts of justice at a great distance.[88]

In the elections of 1769 the counties of Anson, Granville, Halifax, and Orange were carried by the Regulators, who sent to the Assembly Hermon Husband of Orange County, their chief penman, and Thomas Person of Granville County, a man of ability and wealth as well as a member of the Anglican Church, a leading Regulator, and an outstanding member of the Assembly in 1764.[89] However, nothing outstanding was accomplished before the termination of the 1769 session. But in his final speech before dissolving the Assembly and thanking the members for their cooperation, Tryon turned again to discuss his plan for the careful management of the public funds, which he had earlier presented to the legislature. Affirming that, if carried, his plan would prove to be exceptionally beneficial to the colony, he added:

> "But this blessing is not to be obtained for the Country, while the Treasurers, late Sheriffs, and their sureties, can command a majority in the lower House, and while a Treasurer [of the northern district] is suffered to absent himself, and withhold his public accounts from the General Assembly, let the pretence of his absence be ever so urgent."

[88] *Ibid.*, VIII, 81–4. The so-called "Summons and petition Act" was "An Act for Establishing County Courts, for enlarging their Jurisdiction, and Setting the Proceedings therein"; this was passed in 1754 and provided that all causes in common law involving amounts from 25 shillings to £40 proclamation money should be heard by the justices of the peace at a place and period of the year laid down in the law itself. The law was a very long and complex one utilizing the terms "Petition" and "Summons"; it also set up an expensive procedure as, among other things, it provided for appeals to the superior court of the district in which the county court lay. For this law see *State Records . . .*, XXV, 287–95.

[89] It may be noted that John Ashe, who among other posts had been Speaker of the Assembly and was in 1771 a leader of the forces that put down the Regulators, as a member of the Assembly informed the House on October 31, 1769, that Person "hath been frequently charged with perjury and if guilty thereof is unworthy of a seat in this House" (*North Carolina Colonial Records,* VII, 118). The following year, while still a member of the House, Person was charged by Thomas Macknight "with extortion, usury, and exacting illegal fees, and under colour of his office unduly oppressing the people" (*ibid.*, VIII, 326). Although it was Judge Richard Henderson who appeared before the committee appointed to investigate Person to present these charges against him, the committee reported to the House that the accusations were made as the result of "malice and envy" (*ibid.*, VIII, 448–9).

As to the accounts of the treasurer of the southern district, Tryon found them "so very irregular, and negligently kept, that the Public must be abused if an amendment is not made to the mode there pursued."[90] From this statement and previous messages delivered to the Assembly, it is clear that the Governor was as anxious to achieve a reform of the government as were the Regulators, but only by proceeding within the framework of the law.

Turning to the events of 1770, it should be noted that Edmund Fanning had been rejected by the voters of Orange County as a representative in the Assembly, in favour of Hermon Husband. To meet the charge directed against him that he was "a mere dependant on the Crown" and therefore unworthy to represent Orange, "several" freemen of the county drew up a counter-charge in vindication of his character, asserting that this attitude against him came "from malice and a jealousy of his superior abilitys and interest with the people." The statement went on to affirm that "Colonel Fanning's generosity, public spirit & zeal for the good of Orange and Hillsborough are notorious even to his enemies."[91] Moreover, that he was not without many friends in Hillsborough is shown by the fact that when the town was incorporated in July 1770 and thus became entitled to a seat in the Assembly, its freeholders chose Fanning to represent them.[92] Nevertheless, his popularity did not save him from abuse and indignity at the hands of rioters in connection with the September meeting of the superior court of justice with Judge Richard Henderson presiding.

The depth of feeling displayed by the Regulators at the time the court assembled at Hillsborough may be judged from a petition addressed to the justices of this court by 174 signers. The petition was based upon the maxim "that no Law[,] Statute or Custom which are against Gods Law or principalls of nature can be of any validity but are all null." Then followed a statement, based on this premise, that it was "against Justice, Reason and Equity to exact Taxes and extort Fees that are unlawful for the poor industrious Farmers." In this connection the petition charged that, to defeat justice, juries were chosen made up of men "prejudiced in favor of extortionate Officers" and sheriffs who were delinquent in their accounts. In fact, the only crime that those opposed to this system were guilty of, the petition went on to state, was "vertue in the very highest degree[;] namely to risque our all to save our Country from Rapine and

[90] *Ibid.*, VIII, 104–5.
[91] *Ibid.*, VIII, 230–1.
[92] *Ibid.*, VIII, 215–17, 304, 314.

Slavery in our detecting of practices which the Law itself allows to be worse than open Robbery."[93] It was in this frame of mind that on September 24 the Regulators gathered in force at Hillsborough court house under the leadership of Husband, James Hunter, Rednap Howell, William Butler, and others. The court room became jammed with people. A man by the name of Fields (apparently the Jeremiah Fields prosecuted later for riotous conduct in the court), when given permission to speak, took charge of the proceedings in the name of all the Regulators and warned the judge that if he were to adopt their plan of clearing the docket by trying all the insurgents' cases "it might prevent much mischief."[94]

Seeking to soften "the fury of this mad people" and maintain the dignity of the court, Henderson addressed some pacifying remarks to them, but to no avail. According to his later report to the Governor concerning the events of the riot that followed, when an attorney of the court, a Mr. Williams, advanced past the mob to the door of the court room,

> "they fell upon him in a most furious manner with Clubs and sticks of enormous size and it was with great difficulty he saved his life by taking shelter in a neighbouring Store House. Mr. Fanning was next the object of their fury, him they seized . . . and with hideous shouts of barbarian cruelty dragged him by the heels out of doors, while others were engaged in dealing out blows with such violence that I made no doubt his life would instantly become a sacrifice to their rage and madness."

Fortunately for Fanning, he broke loose from his attackers and "jumped into a door that saved him from immediate dissolution." Not content with the manhandling of Fanning, the mob then moved to his "Mansion House," destroyed all its contents, and then wrecked it with axes. In the midst of this disorder, which lasted for two days. Judge Henderson managed to escape from the town, as did certain of the merchants and other settled inhabitants.[95]

When Judge Henderson's report of the riot reached Tryon, together with one from the inhabitants of Hillsborough, he called a meeting of the Council to consider the matter. Asked for his opinion on what should be done to restore law and order in Orange County,

---

[93] *Ibid.*, VIII, 231–4.

[94] For the court docket with cases listed and comments on each case entered, manifestly, by the rioters, as in the case of John McMund vs. William Courtney, in which the comment is "Damn'd Rogues," see *ibid.*, VIII, 236–40.

[95] Judge Henderson to Governor Tryon, September 29, 1770, *ibid.*, VIII, 241–4. For the depositions of others regarding the riot see *ibid.*, VIII, 245–7.

Attorney General Thomas McGuire on October 18 stated that in his view the assaulting of persons and the pulling down of Fanning's house at Hillsborough amounted "only to a riot" and the treatment of Judge Henderson "only to a misdemeanour, though of the highest nature." As to the steps to be taken to bring the offenders to punishment, he could see none that was feasible except to convene the Assembly so that appropriate laws could be made. He also recommended that the militia be mustered in specific counties to determine what number of men could be relied upon as volunteers. All these steps were taken by the Governor on the advice of the Council.[96] By proclamation he also ordered the justices of the peace to make diligent inquiry into the riot and take depositions which might be laid before the Assembly. Before it met in the latter part of November, however, the hatred of the Regulators was again directed against Judge Henderson. On November 12 his barns and stables in Granville County were burnt, together with several horses and a quantity of corn; two days later his house was consumed by fire. Tryon at once issued a second proclamation, offering a reward of £100 proclamation money to anyone who could apprehend the offenders.[97]

In addressing the Assembly on December 5, Tryon dealt with many matters of general concern. Among other things he referred to his plan already before that body to place proper controls on the provincial treasurers so that revenues would not be unlawfully diverted to the prejudice of the people; he called upon the members "to make the most scrupulous enquiries into complaints" about fees so as to place them "beyond the possibility of doubt or abuse"; he warned of the flooding of the province with counterfeit money, and asked the Assembly to take steps to bring to justice "the Authors of this iniquity"; finally, he referred to "the late outrages at Hillsborough" as the work of "a seditious mob" who have "torn down justice from her Tribunal and renounced all Legislative authority." To remedy this situation, Tryon recommended that the members provide him with the means to raise a sufficient body of troops "under the rules and discipline of War to march into the settlements of those Insurgents" and protect the magistrates in the execution of existing laws or laws that it might be found expedient to enact.[98]

[96] For the attorney general's opinion and the recommendation of the Council see *ibid.*, VIII, 251–3.

[97] For the proclamation of October 18 and November 19, 1770, see *ibid.*, VIII, 253–4 and 258–9.

[98] For Tryon's address see *North Carolina Colonial Records*, VIII, 282–6.

The Governor's recommendations were speedily taken into consideration by the Assembly. On December 15, Samuel Johnston of Chowan County[99] introduced a bill for preventing riotous assemblies of people and for "the more speedy and effectually punishing the rioters. . . ." The law, passed on January 15, 1771, was a severe one.[100] It provided: (1) that, after February 1, if ten or more people were to gather for the purpose of disturbing the peace and would not disperse when called upon by a justice of the peace or a sheriff, they should be adjudged felons, should "suffer Death as in Case of Felony" and be denied benefit of clergy upon conviction; (2) that, were such a group to refuse to disperse within one hour when called upon to do so, the justice of the peace or sheriff and those called upon to aid him should seize such persons, and if any of them were killed or hurt in the process, the justice of the peace or sheriff and those aiding him should be, if arrested, discharged and indemnified; (3) that, after March 1, if ten or more people were to gather to obstruct the sitting of the courts or were to beat or wound any officer of a court, or any officer charged with collecting the taxes, or pull down any public building or private dwelling or barn, the offenders should be guilty of felony and, if convicted, suffer death; (4) that persons accused of felony could be tried in any superior court or court of oyer and terminer, wherever situated, regardless of where the crime was committed; (5) that, to prevent the escape from justice of "enormous Offenders," it would be lawful for the judges of the superior court to issue proclamations commanding any person against whom a bill of indictment were found to surrender himself within sixty days under penalty that thereafter it would be lawful "for any Person or Persons to kill and destroy such Offender" and anyone killing such offenders should "be free discharged and indemnified" and, further, the lands and chattels of offenders so killed should be forfeited and sold by the sheriff at

[99] Johnston was one of the most eminent of North Carolinians. His uncle was Gabriel Johnston, Governor of the Province of North Carolina (1734–52), and he himself was destined to be Governor of the state of North Carolina and to play a leading civilian role in the course of the War for American Independence and thereafter as one of the more conservative patriots.

[100] *Ibid.*, VIII, 319, 428, 481–6. It is of interest to note that James Iredell, destined to become attorney general in North Carolina and a leading revolutionary figure, wrote on December 21, 1770, to John Harvey, recently Speaker of the Assembly and soon again to take that post: "The day I left Town (Newbern) Mr. Johnston presented a spirited Bill to the House upon the subject of punishing the Regulators—The substance . . . was this—to enforce in effect, tho' not in express words, the Riot Act as it is in England. . . . This Bill, I believe Sir, you would have thought expedient tho' severe—but desperate diseases must have desperate Remedies." (For the letter see *ibid.*, VIII, 270–1.)

public vendue after due notice, and the money arising from such sale should be paid to the treasurer of the district; (6) that, since it was apprehended that efforts would be made to protect those found guilty of riots and insurrections, the Governor was fully authorized to draft from the regiments of militia, at the public expense, a sufficient number of soldiers to assist in the execution of the law; (7) that, should any body of men be embodied "in an armed and hostile manner, to withstand or oppose any military Forces" and should when commanded refuse to lay down their arms and surrender, such persons should be considered "Traitors and may be treated accordingly." The act was to be in force for one year and no longer.[101]

An act of such harsh nature could only have come from an Assembly deeply frightened at the anarchy which seemed to be enveloping a number of the western counties. This same sense of fear had also been manifested in December 1770 at the time of the expulsion from his seat in the Assembly of Hermon Husband as "a principal mover and promoter of the late Riots and seditions in the County of Orange and other parts of this Province," as well as for "gross prevarication and falsehood" at his examination before a committee of the Assembly, and his veiled threat that "in case he should be confined [at New Bern] by order of the House he expected down a number of People to release him."[102] Again the Assembly on January 25, 1771, took into account charges directed against Colonel Fanning "in the Public papers." After enquiring into the facts, they came to the resolution that the aspersions thrown upon his character were "groundless, base, and scandalous, and that . . . his conduct has been fair, just and honorable both as a Member of this

[101] *Ibid.*, VIII, 481–6. The act was sent over for approval of the King in Council. Grave objection was found to the fifth clause. In the words of Richard Jackson, legal counsel for the Board of Trade: "Altho' the Circumstances of the province may excuse the inserting such Clause in this Act Yet . . . it is altogether unfit for any part of the British Empire and therefore . . . the said Act is fit to be repealed." Although by order in council the act was permitted to expire without repeal, yet the Privy Council declared: ". . . we cannot but think this Clause highly Exceptionable, as being full of Danger in it's operation, and irreconcileable to the principles of the Constitution, depriving withal the Crown of it's prerogative of extending Mercy to Offenders, by committing the Execution of the Law into the hands of the Subject. . . ." An instruction to the Governor was thereupon framed that any future law must be free of such objections. See *Acts of the Privy Council, Col. Ser., 1766–1783*, pp. 336–8. For the instructions given to Tryon's successor, Governor Josiah Martin, see *North Carolina Colonial Records*, VIII, 515–16.

[102] At the advice of the Council, Husband was placed under arrest by order of Chief Justice Howard and placed in confinement in the New Bern gaol. The reason for so doing was the fear that his return to the western settlements "might be attended with fatal consequences. . . ." For the resolutions taken by the Assembly on December 20, 1770, to expel Husband see *ibid.*, VIII, 268–70 and 330–1.

House in particular, and of the community in general."[103] In fact, it was Fanning who on January 19 asked leave to present a bill which would amend the law governing suits for small debts that involved "great Costs and Expence to the Parties," by providing an economical and speedy method for recovering obligations under £5 proclamation money—something that the backcountry settlers had much at heart. This bill finally became law. Under its terms, all debts of forty shillings or less were to be determined by a single justice of the peace and debts of over forty shillings by two justices of the peace; safeguards were also set up against undue pressure upon the debtor for prompt payment.[104]

But the small debts act was but one of the beneficial acts passed at the Assembly session of 1770 to 1771 and approved by the Governor on January 26, 1771, to relieve the discontented settlers. By "An Act to Ascertain Attornies Fees," a definite scale of fees was established under penalty of £50 proclamation money should any lawyer demand or receive any sum above the stipulated amount.[105] Another act clarified in great detail earlier acts respecting fees for public services, so as to do away with complaints that unjust fees were demanded, and obliged clerks of all courts to give bonds to the sum of £500 for the faithful discharge of their respective offices under penalty of dismissal should they be twice convicted of charging any greater fee than the one stated.[106] Further, to meet the public demand that judges be salaried rather than depend upon fees, the chief justice of the superior court was now provided with suitable compensation out of the public funds in lieu of all fees or perquisites of office.[107] Moreover, in view of bitter complaints about the disposal of lands, goods, and chattels by sheriffs in levying executions, especially for lack of currency, an act was passed which offered a large measure of protection to the owner against unfair appraisal of the value of the property offered for sale, with a penalty of £1,000 against any sheriff guilty of disposing of it at less than two-thirds its value.[108] Finally, in order to clarify an act passed in 1770 respecting the collection of taxes for sinking £12,000 granted in 1760 and £12,000 granted in 1761, it was stated that in those

[103] For the above resolution see *ibid.*, VIII, 461.

[104] *Ibid.*, VIII, 441–2, 447, 448, 478; see also *Laws of North Carolina, 1715–1776, State Records . . .*, XXIII, 846–9.

[105] *Ibid.*, XXIII, 788–9.

[106] "An Additional and Explanatory Act to an Act, entitled, An Act for regulating the several Officers Fees within this Province . . . ," *ibid.*, XXIII, 814–18.

[107] *Ibid.*, XXIII, 818–19.

[108] "An Act to direct Sheriffs in levying Executions, and the Disposal of Lands, Goods and Chattels, taken thereon," *ibid.*, XXIII, 833–5.

cases in which these taxes had continued to be collected by the sheriffs, persons who had paid them should be reimbursed.[109] Meanwhile, acting on an earlier petition, the legislature also voted the creation of a number of new western counties out of over-large counties, so as to permit people to do business at the county seat without traveling excessive distances.[110]

The above measures tend to show that the Assembly, while determined to restore law and order throughout the province, was also aware of the nature of the deep discontent behind the Regulator Movement and had set itself to remedy every abuse in government that could make the lot of the people as favourable as possible.[111] In fact, it is hard to reject the conviction that, had more of the disaffected western farmers been fully apprised of the nature of the new laws, the Regulator Movement would have collapsed. Such was obviously the Governor's hope when he wrote soon after the prorogation of the Assembly on January 26, 1771: "As soon as the many beneficial laws that were enacted last session are published through the province they will tend much to quiet the general discontents of the inhabitants and probably make it less difficult for administration to suppress the insurgents in the back frontiers. . . ."[112]

But hand in hand with measures of reform went the necessity of impressing upon the rioters that the colony was governed by laws all must obey. This had certainly not been the case at the time of the court hearings held at Hillsborough in September 1770, which ended in open riot, as has been related. Nor was there any real evidence that the insurgents would remain law-abiding colonials when a special court of oyer and terminer and general gaol delivery opened at New Bern on February 2, 1771, with Chief Justice Martin Howard presiding. For, when a bill of indictment against Hermon Husband for libel was presented to the grand jury on February 8, no true bill

[109] *Ibid.*, XXIII, 840–1. It will be noted that the law, as cited in this source, also gives the figure of £20,000 for the sum granted in 1761, but speaks of £12,000 in the title of the act.

[110] For example, Wake County was erected out of portions of Johnston, Cumberland, and Orange counties; Guilford County was created out of portions of Orange and Rowan counties; Chatham County was also set up out of the southwestern part of Orange County. See *ibid.*, XXIII, 819–31. It may be noted in this connection that most of the Orange County rioters lived in the area that was separated to create Guilford County. See Tryon to Hillsborough, March 12, 1771, *North Carolina Colonial Records,* VIII, 527.

[111] Tryon, in his letter to Hillsborough of January 31, 1771, affirmed that the Assembly had taken every step "that the circumstances of the country would admit of, toward the reformation of the abuses in the government, and the restoration of the public tranquility" (*ibid.*, VIII, 494–5).

[112] *Ibid.*

was found and he was therewith discharged and released from gaol. That the acquittal of Husband was influenced by the threat that the insurgents "were making preparations to come down to New Bern to release Husband, and to lay the town in ashes, if opposed in their design," is suggested in a later report of the events made by Tryon to Hillsborough. The only other activity of this court before its adjournment on the 28th was the trial and discharge of David Butler.[113]

When a new special court of oyer and terminer and general gaol delivery met at New Bern from March 11 to 16, 1771, Chief Justice Howard again presided. On the 15th the grand jury made the presentment on the basis of the outrages committed against the September court by "wicked, seditious, evil, designing and disaffected persons" called Regulators and of their current moves to assemble themselves "in great numbers armed and arrayed in warlike manner and publickly avowing their intention of Marching to Newbern and of carrying into execution by Force their hostile measures." That same day true bills were found against some sixty leading rioters.[114] Under terms of the new law against riots and insurrections, those indicted were given sixty days (after due posting of a proclamation in the locality of their crimes) to surrender and submit to trial, under penalty of outlawry. According to the new act against riots and insurrections, as outlaws they were subject to be shot on sight by anyone choosing to uphold the law.[115] Despite this threat, not only were the indictments ignored, but many of

[113] For the court minutes of February 2–28, 1771, see *ibid.*, VIII, 507–10. For Tryon to Hillsborough, April 12, 1771, see *ibid.*, VIII, 546, in which Tryon makes clear that he had ordered several regiments to be prepared to protect the town of New Bern, if necessary. That the threats of the Regulators were not idle ones is attested by an intercepted letter which the Governor laid before the Council in March. Written on February 16, 1771, by Rednap Howells, a leader of the Regulators in Halifax County, and addressed to James Hunter of Rowan County, recognized head of all the Regulators, it states: "I had certain information that Herman was at liberty; so that I found it needless to raise the Country but I am satisfied it would be easily done if occasion required. . . . I understand Butler and you are to be outlawed; despise it, laugh at it . . . I give out here that the Regulators are determined to whip every one who goes to Law or will not pay his just debts or will not agree to leave his cause to men where disputes [arise?]; that they will choose Representatives but not send them to be put in jail [as was Husband]; in short to stand in defiance and as to thieves [meaning the officers of the court and lawyers, also called rascals] to drive them out of the Country" (*ibid.*, VIII, 536–7).

[114] For the minutes of the court, March 11–16, 1771, see *ibid.*, VIII, 528–32. The grand jury was made up of jurors chosen from other counties as well as from Craven County, where New Bern was located. Moreover, true bills on the indictment were returned only after fifteen witnesses had been brought from Hillsborough "under the confidence of the protection of government" (*ibid.*, VIII, 547); see also *ibid.*, VIII, 696.

[115] *Ibid.*, VIII, 484.

those indicted busied themselves seeking recruits to the Regulator army.[116]

As the judges of the superior court felt it impossible to hold court at Hillsborough in view of the previous serious disturbances and the present distractions in the district,[117] Tryon, on the advice of the Council, determined to raise a force and march with it "into the settlements of the Insurgents to reduce . . . to Obedience [those] who by their rebellious Acts and Declarations have set the Government at defiance." Accordingly, on March 19 he ordered the commanding officers of several of the militia regiments to recruit volunteers for this service.[118] At the same time the Governor repudiated an agreement entered into under great pressure in March between certain Rowan County officials—John (Frohawk) Frohock, clerk of the court, Alexander Martin, justice of the peace, Griffith Rutherford, sheriff, among others—and the Regulators, some 400 to 500 of whom were encamped near Salisbury. The agreement had been for submitting to the arbitration of parties chosen by both sides any claims over exorbitant fees previously taken by the county officers. Upon receiving a letter from Frohock and Martin about the necessity of making the agreement (because "the Spirit of sedition has been propagated with much industry among the lower class of Inhabitants here"), Tryon wrote, very properly, to these officers:

> "If you have abused Your Public Trust it is Your Duty to give satisfaction and make restitution to the injured. As for my own part I entertain a just Abhorrence of the Conduct of that Man who is guilty of Extortion in the execution of his public Character. The mode however of Your Agreement with the insurgents, by including Officers who are amenable only for their public conduct to the Tribunal of their Country is unconstitutional, Dishonorable to government and introductive of a practice the most dangerous to the peace and happiness of society."[119]

No colonial Governor who wished to remain in power could possibly have yielded to means so unconstitutional in the face of armed threats.

In making his military preparations, Tryon appointed Hugh Wad-

---

[116] *Ibid.*, VIII, 538.

[117] Judges of the Superior Court to Tryon, March 18, 1771, *ibid.*, VIII, 538–9 and 542.

[118] See *ibid.*, VIII, 540–2, 697–8, and especially p. 697 for a list of the number of volunteers to be raised in each county, to a total of 2,550.

[119] See "Agreement for restitution by Rowan County officials to the Regulators," March 7, 1771; Frohock and Martin to Tryon, March 18, 1771; and Tryon to Frohock and Martin, April 5, 1771, *ibid.*, VIII, 521–2, 533–6, 545.

dell—a seasoned wilderness fighter who, before settling in Bladen County, had lived in Rowan County and was much beloved by the frontiersmen—to be joint commander with himself of the armed forces. While General Waddell went from the Cape Fear region to the backcountry to enlist volunteers for his rangers, Tryon proceeded to organize the volunteer companies that arrived at New Bern in detachments from the militia regiments of Carteret, Beaufort, Pitt, New Hanover, Onslow, Dobbs, Johnston, and Orange counties, as well as one Craven County regiment. On May 5 the troops began their march westward; on the 8th the detachment from the new county of Wake joined the troops, and on the 11th the army reached Hillsborough, where two of the four companies of Orange County volunteers were detached to guard Hillsborough from possible destruction at the hands of the Regulators, while the main army marched on to encamp by Great Alamance Creek on the 14th. In order to engage the insurgents assembled five miles away in the direction of Salisbury, the army was ordered to march at break of day on the 16th. Leaving behind all baggage and supply wagons and their tents standing, the troops set forth at the appointed hour with no beat of drums.[120]

Meanwhile General Waddell, with an artillery company supported by volunteer detachments from the militia regiments of Anson, Rowan, Mecklenburg, and Tryon counties,[121] assembled his forces on the bank of the Yadkin River on May 5 and slowly moved forward expecting to join forces with Tryon.[122] But on the 9th his small force of 250 volunteers, having marched only two miles east of the Yadkin, was obliged to retreat to Salisbury when the troops were all but surrounded by the Regulators in greatly superior numbers, "threatening to cut them to pieces" if they attempted to join the army under Tryon. Waddell had also had the misfortune of having two of his powder wagons blown up by Regulators in Mecklenburg County; short of powder, he was therefore immobilized on the day of the engagement.[123]

It is exceedingly difficult to reconstruct with accuracy what took place in the so-called Battle of the Alamance on May 16, 1771.

---

[120] See *ibid.*, VIII, 548, and "Tryon's Order Book in Campaign against the Regulators," *ibid.*, VIII, 574–84; see also *ibid.*, VIII, Appendix, 659–77 and 696–718.

[121] In 1779 Tryon County disappeared and in its place appeared Lincoln and Rutherford counties.

[122] See Tryon to Waddell, June 7, 1771, *ibid.*, VIII, 673–4 and 717.

[123] "General Waddell's Order Book," May 5–16, 1771, *ibid.*, VIII, 601–4; Tryon to Hillsborough, May 18, 1771, *ibid.*, VIII, 610; *Records of the Moravians in North Carolina,* II, 652–3.

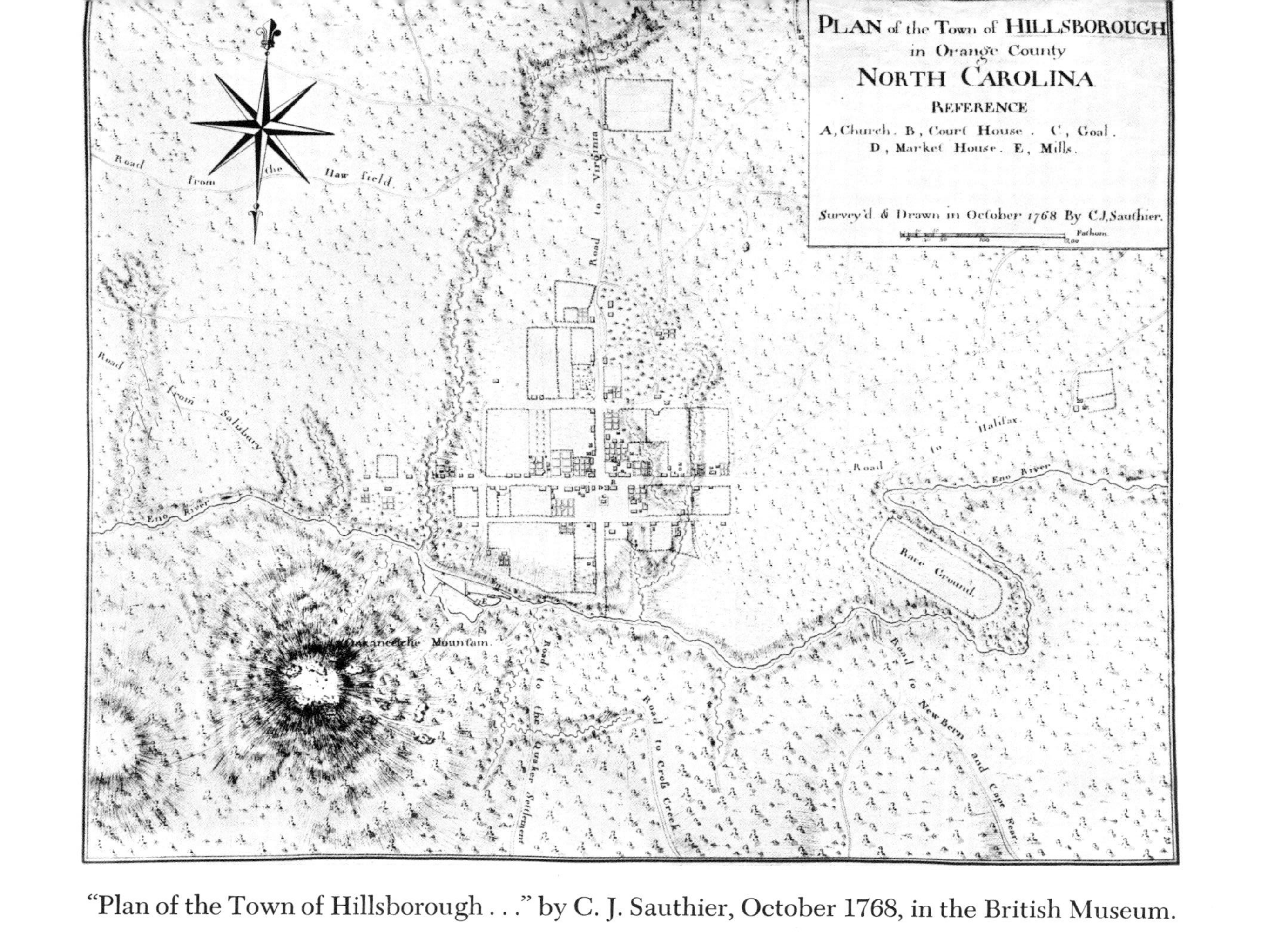

"Plan of the Town of Hillsborough . . ." by C. J. Sauthier, October 1768, in the British Museum.

(From the Map Division, Library of Congress)

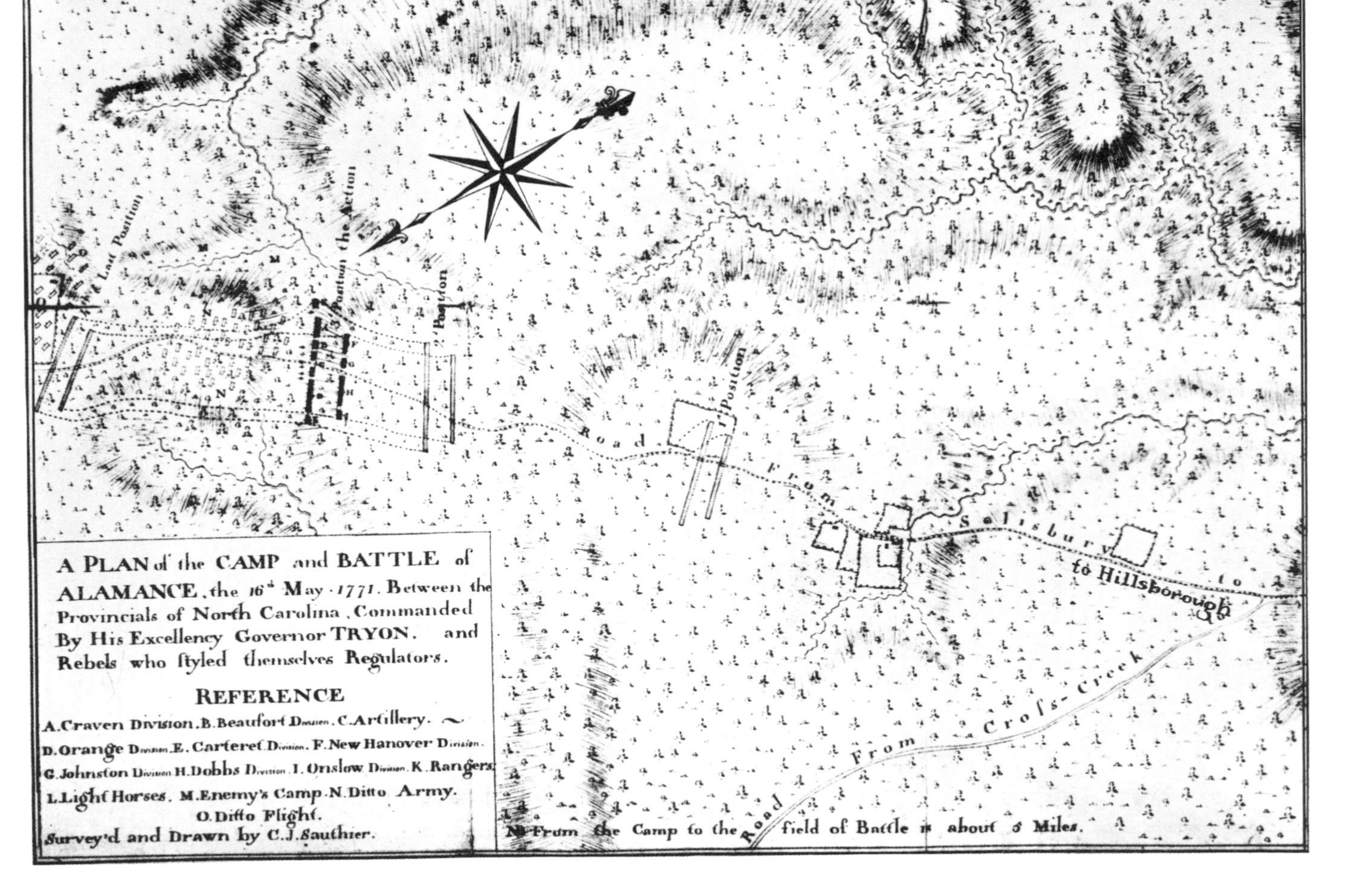

"A Plan of the Camp and Battle of Alamance, the 16th May 1771," by C. J. Sauthier.

According to an account sent to New Bern from Tryon's headquarters immediately after the engagement,[124] the Governor had under his command some 1,300 troops. His objective in marching from his camp at Great Alamance Creek was to attack the Regulators (who numbered at least 2,500 men under arms) unless they accepted his terms. His conditions were: to surrender for trial their "principals"—that is, those leading Regulators against whom true bills of indictment had been found by the special grand jury on March 11, which they had ignored at the peril of their lives—to lay down their arms, and to swear allegiance to the King. When the army had arrived within a mile of the insurgents, the Regulators sent a messenger requesting counter-terms. These the Governor considered "wholly inadmissible."[125] He therewith marched his army within a "small distance" of the Regulators, who "immediately formed within 20 or 30 paces distance, and behaved in a most daring and desperate manner. His Excellency again proposed terms to them, which they spurned at, and cried out for battle."[126] Tryon, when his

---

[124] This account, under a New Bern date-line of May 24, appeared in the *Pennsylvania Gazette* of June 20, 1771.

[125] *Ibid.* The petition asked for a redress of grievances, especially "to having roguish [civil] Officers discarded, and others more honest propagated in Stead" with sheriffs and other officers who have abused their trust "brought to a clear, candid, and impartial Account for their past Conduct, and other Grievances of the like Nature, we have long laboured under without any apparent Hope of Redress." Then, referring to the men who had been indicted and ordered by proclamation to surrender themselves but who had not done so at their peril, the petition affirmed that they were "Men of the most remarkable honest Characters of any in our Country"; it then asked the Governor "whether your Excellency will lend an impartial Ear to our Petition or no. . . ." The petition made no reference to the series of laws passed by the Assembly early in the year that were designed to meet all genuine grievances of the people against their local governments. Nor could the Governor possibly agree to the request to remove roguish Officers," until it had been established in a court of law that the accused officials were actually "roguish." On every ground the petition —especially as it came from the Regulators at the very time they were under arms against their government—must be considered to have been inadmissible. The terms requested are embodied in "The Petition of us the Inhabitants of Orange County . . . ," *North Carolina Colonial Records,* VIII, 640–1.

[126] *Pennsylvania Gazette,* June 20, 1771. "A letter from a gentleman in North Carolina to a friend in New Jersey," dated July 24, 1771, which appeared in the *Pennsylvania Journal* of October 3, 1771, gives an account of the battle highly sympathetic to the Regulators. According to it, there were "4,000 rebels," who sent James Hunter and Benjamin Merrill to bear their petition to the Governor with "orders to treat with his Honour for peace." Tryon replied that the people must "deliver up their arms, pay off their taxes, swear to be subject to all the laws of this country, and deliver such men as he should name to be put to death, otherwise there would be bloodshed in one hour and ten minutes." An aide-de-camp then promised the insurgents an additional two hours to come to terms. Meanwhile, the army continued to march forward "and the people moved off to give them room; and as soon as the Aid-de-camp returned, a field piece was fired in the midst of the people, which killed one man, & frightened 3,700 from off the ground, leaving only 300 to settle the

terms were rejected, immediately gave the signal for the troops to open battle, which began with a discharge of the artillery,

> "when instantly ensued a very heavy and dreadful firing on both sides, for near two hours and an half; when the Regulators, being hard pressed by our men, and sorely galled by the artillery, which played incessantly on them with grape shot, gave way on all sides, and were pursued to the distance of a mile thro' the woods and bushes, our troops making great slaughter among them, as they did not make a regular retreat, but ran in great confusion to all quarters from whence they apprehended the least danger."[127]

According to this report, Tryon's losses showed as not above ten killed and only about sixty wounded, whereas on the Regulators' side "300 were found dead on the field next day, and a very great number wounded; about 20 or 30 were made prisoners."[128]

The back of the Regulator Movement had been broken by the resolute action of Governor Tryon. James Iredell, who was to play

---

matter who returned the fire . . . about two hours and a quarter, when [James] Hunter and his men fled, and left the field to the Governor."

A more detailed account of many aspects of the battle, some of them not contained in any other report, was given in a long letter that Samuel Cornell, a member of the North Carolina Council, wrote to the New York merchant Elias Debrosses on June 6, 1771. For example, Cornell stated that Tryon's immediate objective in moving forward was to join forces with Waddell, after receiving news that the General did not have enough strength to advance from the Yadkin; again, he mentioned the fact that he and the other members of the Council present unanimously advised Tryon to attack the rebels who stood in the way of his making contact with Waddell; he further added that there were not more than 1,100 troops available to take the field against some 3,000 Regulators, that some of the Regulators were so impatient for a fight as to move to the mouths of the cannons and others "were so bold & hardened in their Villainy, as to run up to our first Line before the Battle began & wounded some of our men with Cutlasses," and, finally, that the chief agency for demoralizing the rebels was the possession by the army of eight pieces of artillery. He gave the number of Regulators killed and wounded in the battle as "upwards of 300." For a copy of this letter, sent back to England by Lord Dunmore, Governor of New York at the time, in his private letter of June 20, 1771, see P.R.O., C.O. 5:154.

[127] *Pennsylvania Gazette,* June 20, 1771. The Moravian Bethabara Diary for June 1, 1771, records the statement of Colonel Martin Armstrong, a Tryon officer, that the bodies of some of the Regulators were found half burnt in the woods which the Governor had ordered to be fired in the course of the battle; Gideon Wright, who was also in the battle, mentioned the loss of life suffered by the insurgents who sought the protection of the woods. See *Records of the Moravians in North Carolina,* I, 460, and J. H. Clewell: *History of Wachovia in North Carolina* (New York, 1902), p. 110. Tryon's letter to Hillsborough, written two days after the battle, stated that "the enemy took to tree fighting and much annoyed the men who stood at the guns, which obliged me to cease the artillery for a short time and advance the first line to force the rebels from their covering, this succeeded and we pursued them half a mile beyond their camp . . ." (*North Carolina Colonial Records,* VIII, 609–10).

[128] *Pennsylvania Gazette,* June 20, 1771. Two days after the battle, the Governor listed his own losses "in killed wounded and missing . . . about sixty men." He did not list the rebel losses. *North Carolina Colonial Records,* VIII, 609–10.

a most distinguished role in American political life, doubtless expressed the apprehension of many law-abiding North Carolinians when, after the Battle of the Alamance, he wrote to his father on June 15: "How horrid are the miseries of civil war, but how much more horrid to have property insecure, and lives held at the will of a parcel of banditti!"[129] Undoubtedly there were many lawless men of the bandit type among the Regulators who were such a scourge in the western Carolinas at this period. But the impression one gets in studying the records is that most of the recruits to the movement were impoverished and dissatisfied farmers labouring to make an honest living off the land, who felt that they, or at least their neighbours, had been thwarted by the sharp practices of unscrupulous public officials.[130] What is more, the leaders of the Regulators were mostly men of substance and also of some education, such as Hermon Husband, Rednap Howell, Thomas Person, and James Hunter.[131] They threw themselves into the struggle for reforms because their sense of justice had been outraged; perhaps some of them were also motivated by the desire to satisfy secret ambitions. Unhappily, they misled the common people who had faith in their leadership. For at best their plans were uniformly hazy and at worst any attempt to apply them under the given conditions would have plunged the province into indescribable anarchy.[132] They persuaded

[129] For this letter see G. J. McRee: *Life and Correspondence of James Iredell* (2 vols., New York, 1857–8, reprinted 1949), I, 89. The account from Tryon's headquarters, written immediately after the battle, referred to the "glorious and signal victory of this day, gained over a formidable body of lawless desperadoes" (*Pennsylvania Gazette,* June 20, 1771).

[130] Governor Martin, who succeeded Tryon in office, after making a trip through the backcountry in the summer of 1772, wrote to the Earl of Hillsborough on August 30: "I now see most clearly that they [the inhabitants] have been provoked by insolence and cruel advantages taken of the peoples ignorance by mercenary tricking Attornies, Clerks and other little Officers who have practiced upon them every sort of rapine and extortion . . ." (*North Carolina Colonial Records,* IX, 330). It is true that Martin seems to have heard but one side of the story, that of the former Regulators; nevertheless, he was convinced that the Regulators had a strong case against a system they felt they could not alter. Yet, the legislation enacted early in 1771 largely answered their chief demands.

[131] William L. Saunders, secretary of state and editor of the *North Carolina Colonial Records,* contributes a warm defence of the Regulators and particularly their leaders in his Introductory Notes to Vol. VIII; see especially pp. xiv–xxxiv.

[132] How far the insurgents had actually intended to go in overturning the government, had they been victorious over Tryon, is not clear. The *Pennsylvania Gazette* of July 11, 1771, printed the following under a Wilmington, North Carolina, date-line of June 19: "Sundry papers and letters have been found in the house of Hermon Husbands (the Cataline of this province) by which it appears, the Insurgents were confident they should defeat the Governor, and were determined to put every man in his army to death—that they looked upon themselves so much masters of the province, that many of the public offices had been already disposed of among themselves—such were the views—such were the designs of these people, of whom it was

the people that it was proper to refuse to obey the laws of the land, although made by their own representatives, and to oppose the appointed law-enforcement officers when these officials seemed to them to limit freedom of action, which all men had a right to enjoy under what they chose to call natural law and the law of God. In taking this position they encouraged violence and the virtual overthrow of a type of government the English-speaking people had peacefully evolved over the centuries and had come to respect and obey. Perhaps without fully realizing the implication of their acts, they were seeking to turn back the clock to the days of peasant violence under the leadership of such earlier-century champions of natural justice as Wat Tyler and Jack Cade. Moreover, they chose to ignore the series of wholesome laws passed in the last session of their own Assembly to protect the interests of the people; they were thus guilty of sending many of their trusting followers to an untimely death on the battlefield for a cause that had already been won.[133]

The day after the battle of Alamance the Governor issued a proclamation giving notice that everyone—except those who had been outlawed and those now held prisoners in the camp—who would come to the camp, lay down his arms, take the oath of allegiance, promise to pay taxes due now or hereafter, and promise to submit to the laws of the country, should be pardoned "for all Treasons, Insurrections and Rebellion done or committed before this day. . . ."[134] Within twelve days after this proclamation from

iniquitously reported, 'that they wanted only to obtain justice for their POOR OPPRESSED BRETHREN.' But these diabolical schemes are now happily defeated, and Alamance is made their court of record." The writer then went on "to lament the fate of those unhappy people, who, through their own ignorance, have been persuaded by a few artful and designing men, to join with them, and impiously attempt to subvert the constitution of the province." For a fundamentally different impression of the objectives of the Regulators see E. W. Caruthers: *A Sketch of the Life and Character of the Rev. David Caldwell . . .* (Greensborough, N.C., 1842), pp. 144–77, and W. D. Cooke: "Battle of the Alamance and War of the Regulation," *Revolutionary History of North Carolina . . .* (Raleigh, N.C., and New York, 1853), pp. 13–41.

[133] For the heated discussion in the colonial press, attacking and defending Governor Tryon's actions in the War of the Regulators, see "Historical Notes," ed. D. L. Corbitt, *North Carolina Historical Review*, III, 477–505. Among several letters to the publishers of the *Virginia Gazette* (Purdie and Dixon) is one in the issue of September 26, 1771, deprecating remarks made by Husband in Wilmington on the Delaware and stating: "The least Reflection must compel a Belief that Something was wrong, Something amiss . . . especially when among the Provincial Laws of the Province, . . . are to be found Acts for redressing and removing every Grievance that could possibly have an Existence among them."

[134] For the proclamation of May 17, 1771, see *North Carolina Colonial Records*, VIII, 608–9. By it people who had rebelled were required to make their submission on or before May 21; the time for submission was gradually extended to July 10 by proclamations issued on May 21, 24, and 31 and June 11. See *ibid.*, VIII, 610–11, 613, 617–18.

1,300 to 1,400 of the Regulators brought in their arms, made the proper submission, and were pardoned; by June 19 the number of those who had submitted totalled 3,300, and by the end of the year the total was 6,409.[135] The Regulator Movement was at an end. This came about not only as the result of the actual battle of May 16, but also as the psychological after-effect of the destruction of the property of certain insurrection leaders, such as James Hunter, "the General of the Rebels and an Outlaw," and Hermon Husband, the chief propagandist of the Regulators.[136] An additional impact on the minds of the insurgents was made by the offer of rewards for the capture of the escaped and outlawed leaders—especially Husband, Hunter, Rednap Howell, and William Butler.[137] Finally, there was the effect of the execution of one of the outlaws, James Few, the day following the battle,[138] and the trial by special court of oyer and terminer of twelve of the Regulators, all of whom were convicted of treason and six of whom—including Captain Benjamin Merrill, a man of prominence—were hanged, while the rest were reprieved.[139]

---

[135] *Pennsylvania Gazette,* June 27 and July 11, 1771; *North Carolina Colonial Records,* VIII, 615, 649, 715–16; Governor Josiah Martin to Hillsborough, December 26, 1771, *ibid.,* IX, 78.

[136] "Journal of the Expedition Against the Insurgents . . . ," *State Records of North Carolina,* XIX, 846–7, and *North Carolina Colonial Records,* VIII, 615. James Hunter, as an outlaw, appeared before Governor Martin in the summer of 1772 to beg for pardon; he was supported by two petitions by friends; he took the required oath on September 6, 1776. See *ibid.,* IX, 85–7, 329; X, 826. Hermon Husband escaped into Pennsylvania and settled in the western part of that province and later became a leader in the so-called Whiskey Rebellion. See *ibid.,* IX, 37, and the article by the late J. G. deR. Hamilton, "Hermon Husbands," *Dictionary of American Biography,* IX, 427–8.

[137] See Tryon's proclamation of June 9, 1771, *North Carolina Colonial Records,* VIII, 617.

[138] Few was an advocate, it would seem, of some very revolutionary ideas; not only would he do away with all lawyers but even all governments, which he considered the root of all mankind's evils. See A. D. Vinton: "The First American Anarchist," *Magazine of American History with Notes and Queries,* XVI, 443–5. For the death of Few see Tryon to Hillsborough, August 1, 1771, *North Carolina Colonial Records,* VIII, 651. In the official "Journal of the Expedition" the statement is made that Few was hanged on May 17 after the burial of the soldiers killed in battle because the army was "importunate that public justice should be immediately executed against some of the outlaws" (*State Records of North Carolina,* XIX, 845).

[139] The trial of the twelve men accused of treason lasted from May 30 to June 20. On the 19th six were executed, including Captain Merrill. In sentencing Merrill to death Chief Justice Howard had the following to say: "*Benjamin Merrill,* you have been indicted and found guilty by your Country of High Treason, which is the greatest Crime that any Man can commit, . . . because thereby he would overturn that State of Order and Civil Government, which secures us every Thing that is valuable or desirable in Life. To complain of Grievances, and to endeavour a Redress of them in a lawful Way, is not only justifiable, but Praise-worthy; but to snatch the Sword from the Magistrate, and to refer to the Decision of Arms . . . is a most detestable Crime; for it brings on the Miseries of an intestine War, which is perhaps the greatest Evil that any Nation or People can suffer" (New Bern advices, June 28,

By August 1 the Governor was able to report to the Earl of Hillsborough: "The inhabitants chearfully pay their taxes, are satisfied that Husband, Hunter and a few others have by misrepresentations misled them, and are convinced that they are much happier by losing the victory, than they would have been had they defeated his Majesty's forces."[140]

Nevertheless, there were many people so deeply dissatisfied with conditions in North Carolina after the collapse of the Regulator Movement that they moved farther westward into the areas that later became the states of Tennessee and Kentucky. Morgan Edwards, who went through the province in 1772 to gather materials for his history of the Baptists in North Carolina wrote: "It is said 1,500 families departed since the battle of Alamance and to my knowledge a great many more are only waiting to dispose of their plantations in order to follow them."[141] Yet, it is obvious that many of the frontiersmen settled in western North Carolina were restless people, who had left settlements to the north because of dissatisfaction with conditions there and who would always be looking for greener pastures as they or their children shifted from place to place, ever lured to new frontiers with the opening up of new lands in Kentucky, Tennessee, or elsewhere in the vast and appealing West. For the great majority that remained, efforts were made by Josiah Martin (who took over the government when Tryon left to head the government of New York in the summer of 1771) to see that the legislation governing fees was strictly adhered to by officials. He ordered them to display tables of fees in all public offices—with a warning to them that they would answer "at their Peril for failure to do so."[142] In 1772, the Governer travelled through the communi-

---

Pennsylvania Gazette, July 18, 1771). In a repentant speech before his execution Merrill declared that his "first seducers" were James Hunter of Orange County and Daniel Gillespie (spelled Gelaspie in the account) of Guilford County, who pressed him to join the Regulators, promising that all things would be settled without bloodshed. He was led, he said, to take up arms as the result of false reports that the country was to be laid waste and the inhabitants destroyed, rumors propagated, he now realized, "to screen old offenders from justice" (*North Carolina Colonial Records,* VIII, 656). Tryon wrote to the Earl of Hillsborough on August 1, 1771: "Benjamin Merril a Capt[n] of militia . . . died under a thorough conviction of his crime and the justice of the sentence . . ." (*ibid.,* VIII, 650). Tryon's recommendation to Hillsborough, that in view of Merrill's repentance his forfeited estate be returned to his widow and children, was later approved by the King. See *ibid.,* VIII, 650, IX, 65–6. For the effects of the royal pardon granted, as the result of Governor Martin's efforts, to five of the six men convicted of treason but not executed (the sixth had meanwhile died), see *ibid.,* IX, 340.

[140] *Ibid.,* VIII, 650.

[141] Quoted in *ibid.,* VIII, 655.

[142] For the proclamation of August 22, 1771, see *ibid.,* IX, 25.

ties where disaffection had been rife and while there sought to make clear to the inhabitants that they could count on his full support in rectifying errors in government. At the same time he sent a full report of his estimate of the Regulator troubles to Hillsborough in a masterly summary of the situation.[143] He also sought the advice of the chief law officers of the province on the expediency of healing the wounds by a general amnesty, in the belief that a "cordial union can never take place until the victors forget to exult on the last years triumph at Alamance."[144]

A gradual change in the attitude of many of the one-time Regulators appears to have led them to support the government. At least Governor Martin, writing to the Earl of Dartmouth in the spring of 1775, when the revolutionary fever had taken hold in the coastal counties of the province, was able to report:

> "The Inhabitants of the Western Counties who were for the most part concerned in the late Insurrections remember very properly the correction they received for their offences from Governor Tryon and the solemn Oath of Allegiance they took at that time[,] nor do I think they will be reduced [seduced?] from their duty by any means. I have received the fullest assurances of their devotion to His Majesty and of their readiness to support me in maintaining the constitution and Laws of their Country upon all occasions, and I have no doubt that I might command their best services at a word on any emergency."[145]

---

[143] Martin to Hillsborough, August 30, 1772, *ibid.*, IX, 329–33; see also his letter to Dartmouth of November 28, 1772 (*ibid.*, IX, 357–8), in which he reiterated his thoughts on the Regulator crisis and urged that either the Earl of Granville look to his lands or they be bought by the Crown in order to obviate the evils taking place there.

[144] *Ibid.*, IX, 332. For the opinions of Chief Justice Howard, Judge Henderson, Judge Moore, and Attorney General Thomas McGuire see *ibid.*, IX, 333–9.

[145] Martin to Dartmouth, April 20, 1775, *ibid.*, IX, 1228. In his "The Regulators of North Carolina" (*Annual Report of the American Historical Association for the Year 1894*, p. 211), the late John Spencer Bassett wrote in confirmation of this view: "It is true that some Regulators were in the armies of the Revolution, but the great majority of them were Tories." On the other hand, H. T. Lefler and A. R. Newsome (*The History of a Southern State: North Carolina*) challenge the Bassett statement, as a myth, by the following statement (p. 178): "An examination of the records reveals that of 883 of the known Regulators, 289 were Whigs, 34 Tories, and 560 Revolutionary status unknown." The question arises, under what conditions was this census taken? These authors very properly also emphasize the "East-West" controversy as a continuing factor in the sectional struggle in North Carolina that lasted until the "West" finally achieved victory in the Constitutional Convention of 1835. In 1775 loyal addresses were sent to Governor Martin from Rowan, Surry, Guilford, and Anson counties, signed by hundreds of people. See *North Carolina Colonial Records*, IX, 1160–4. R. O. DeMond in his *The Loyalists in North Carolina . . .* (Durham, N.C., 1940, pp. 46–50) takes the position that most of the Regulators

There is no doubt that the War of the Regulators in North Carolina was the most dramatic event in the history of the South before the outbreak of the War for American Independence, but it cannot be considered a part of this war.

---

never departed from the oath of loyalty taken by over 6,000 of them. For the joint action in 1776, of Loyalist Regulators and Scottish Highlanders in an assault on the patriots in the battle of Moore's Creek Bridge, see I. C. C. Graham: *Colonists from Scotland: Emigration to North America, 1707–1783* (Ithaca, 1956), pp. 150, 154, 157–9; see also Duane Meyer: *The Highland Scots of North Carolina, 1732–1776* (Chapel Hill, N.C., 1961).

CHAPTER XV

The Struggle for Political Equality: South Carolina

SOUTH CAROLINA was regarded as a highly prosperous colony during the decade preceding the year 1771. Its staples, rice and indigo, were in high demand. What is more, the price per barrel of rice, which in 1761 was forty shillings, in 1771 had risen to seventy shillings (£3.10); and indigo, which sold in 1761 for two shillings a pound, brought three shillings ten years later. As a result, the value of exports in 1771 was £756,000 sterling as compared with the annual average of almost £400,000 sterling between 1763 and 1766.[1] In 1765 it required 424 vessels to export from the province the 111,310 barrels of rice and 545,020 pounds of indigo, together with the other produce of the land.[2]

The prosperity of the colony was reflected in the trade and civic improvement of its principal city. In 1752 a committee of the

[1] [Alexander Hewat]: *An Historical Account of the Rise and Progress of the Colonies of South Carolina and Georgia* (2 vols., London, 1779), II, 300–1. Writing on November 30, 1770, to the Earl of Hillsborough, Lieutenant Governor William Bull stated that agriculture was in "a very prosperous state"; that rice would yield between 120,000 and 140,000 barrels, and indigo about 500,000 pounds, plus another 150,000 pounds if the destruction of the plants by grasshoppers and locusts could be prevented. See P.R.O., C.O. 5:394. It is therefore not surprising that Bull could state at this period that the rate of exchange—700 currency to 100 sterling—had remained quite constant during the past fifty years, indicating the high standing of both public and private credit in the province. See Bull to Hillsborough, November 30, 1770, *ibid.* For the importance of deerskins as a leading export product, together with a detailed study of the export trade in rice, indigo, and deerskins, see Leila Sellers: *Charleston Business on the Eve of the Revolution* (Chapel Hill, N.C., 1934), Chap. 8; for her figures of £341,727 for the value of South Carolina's exports to England in 1763 and £579,549 in 1775, see p. 11. For the state of manufactures in South Carolina, see Governor Bull's letter of September 6, 1768, C.O. 5:379, which may be found printed in *English Historical Documents*, IX, *American Colonial Documents to 1776* (ed. Merrill Jensen, New York, 1955), pp. 422–3.

[2] Lieutenant Governor Bull to the Board of Trade, March 15, 1765, George Chalmers Manuscript Collection (25 vols.), "Papers Relating to Carolina, 1662–1795," New York Public Library, cited hereafter as Chalmers Collection.

Commons House of Assembly asserted that Charleston "for the number of its inhabitants carrys on as great, if not a greater trade than any Town in America or perhaps in the King's Dominions";[3] this was also doubtless true during the period under consideration. Peter Timothy, the publisher and editor of the *South-Carolina Gazette,* declared in 1768: "I do not suppose there is a Colony on this Continent in so flourishing and promising a Situation as So. Carolina at present. Private and public Works are every where carrying on with Spirit." He then listed the near completion of a lighthouse and beacon in Charleston Harbour, the erection of new fortifications on White Point, progress on the new Watch House which would contain various offices, the beginning of construction of an exchange which would be "an elegant Structure," the work on a new hospital, the stone bridge all but finished at the north end of town, the plan for the construction of a canal "at the Head of our principal street," opposite the exchange, and the drainage of a large body of marsh land for a city common. He also stressed private initiative:

> "At the same Time very elegant Buildings are raising in almost every Street by private Gentlemen. The Lawyers, Doctors, and Planters get rich apace, the Merchants do not in general so well. Our staple Rice is in a fine way. The enormous Crop made last Year will be exceeded this."[4]

In describing the churches of Charleston in 1765 the Rev. Charles Woodmason wrote that St. Philip's of Charleston "is allow'd to be the most elegant Religious Edifice in British America," while in the newly built St. Michael's, boasting "a Tower and Steeple 196 feet high, and a Ring of 8 Bells lately hung," he found the "Plate and Ornaments . . . superb."[5]

As has already been emphasized in this series,[6] Charleston (Charles Town as it was called in the eighteenth century) was the political, social, and economic centre of South Carolina and dominated the life of the province. There, or nearby, resided the

[3] Journal of Commons House of Assembly (ms.), 28, Part I:115, South Carolina Historical Commission Archives, Columbia, S.C., cited hereafter as Commons House Journals.

[4] Peter Timothy to Benjamin Franklin, September 3, 1768, *South Carolina Historical Magazine,* LV, 161–4; see also "Charleston in 1774 as described by an English Traveler," *South Carolina Historical Magazine,* XLVII, 179–80.

[5] *The Carolina Backcountry on the Eve of the Revolution. The Journal and Other Writings of Charles Woodmason, Anglican Itinerant* (ed. R. J. Hooker, Chapel Hill, N.C., 1953), pp. 70–1; cited hereafter as *Woodmason Writings.*

[6] See Volume II, revised, pp. 144–9.

Governor, the Lieutenant Governor, the members of the Council, the judges of the court of common pleas and general sessions, and a majority of the members of the Commons House of Assembly; there also were to be found all the amenities of a highly civilized society. Unhappily, these advantages were limited to those who, by living in the coastal areas of South Carolina, were in a position to resort to the metropolis without too much effort. While the vast backcountry was theoretically included inside the bounds of Craven, Berkeley, Colleton, and Granville counties and, up to 1767, the nineteen parishes within them, the western limits of these counties and parishes were not defined. In the course of the eighteenth century the interior of the province had begun filling up until by the 1760's it contained fully one half the white people of South Carolina.[7]

Yet the backcountry settlers had little influence on the political life of the province. This was the result of the South Carolina voting system. Those qualified to vote for parish representatives in the Commons House of Assembly[8] were obliged, as a rule, to go to the parish church where the polls were held. Few of the backcountry inhabitants living any distance from the church would make the effort to get there, even if they knew in which parish they lived (and apparently many of them did not). With the parish churches located largely in the tidewater areas, those living adjacent to them had a decisive advantage in determining who would be their representatives and what were to be the important issues. Furthermore, the

---

[7] Lieutenant Governor Bull to the Earl of Hillsborough, September 10, 1768, Chalmers Collection. For the settlement of the interior of South Carolina in the eighteenth century to 1765 see R. L. Meriwether: *The Expansion of South Carolina, 1729–1765* (Kingsport, [Tenn.], 1940); see also R. M. Brown: *The South Carolina Regulators* (Cambridge, Mass., 1963), Chaps. 1 and 2, especially pp. 3 and 182 for population figures.

[8] From 1759 to 1776 the following were the qualifications for exercising the franchise: the voter was to be a white male, twenty-one years of age or over, who had resided for one year in the parish, was of the Protestant faith, and who had a " 'Settled' plantation, or 100 acres 'unsettled' land paying taxes or property valued at £60 proclamation money or [paid] taxes amounting to 10s. proclamation money." To be qualified to sit in the Commons House of Assembly in 1759 one had to be a Protestant white male British subject, twenty-one years of age, who had "resided one year in the province, . . . and owned 500 acres in a 'settled' plantation, and 20 slaves" or was possessed of "property valued at £1,000 in the province." For an interesting, tabular view of the changing qualifications between the 1670's and 1770's for the franchise and for membership in the General Assembly, see W. C. Schaper: "Sectionalism and Representation in South Carolina," *Annual Report of the American Historical Association for the Year 1900* (2 vols., Washington, 1901) I, 350–1. For the law of 1759, which reduced the amount of unsettled land required from 300 acres to 100, see *Statutes at Large of South Carolina* (eds. Thomas Cooper and Daniel McCord, 10 vols., Columbia, S.C., 1836–41), IV, 98–9.

representation itself was weighted. In 1765 the parishes within Berkeley County, where Charleston was located, returned twenty-three members; those of Craven County to the north, nine; those of Colleton to the south, twenty; and those of Granville still further south along the coast, six.[9] It is true that St. Mark's Parish, Craven County, had been created in 1757 out of the western part of Prince Frederick Parish on the upper Santee River and had been accorded two members in the Assembly, but it lacked a minister and the vestry was still struggling in 1768 with the problems of the church;[10] and by 1766 the parish of St. Matthew, on the upper waters of the Edisto, also in the backcountry, had been laid out, but not until 1768 was it ready to function as a unit of government and as an ecclesiastical centre.[11] Not only were the settlers in the backcountry without representation in the Assembly, where they might have aired their grievances, but they laboured under the great disadvantage of having neither courts capable of dealing with crime nor yet gaols for imprisoning criminals. In other words, all those accused of crimes had to be taken to Charleston for incarceration and trial; witnesses also were obliged to journey a great distance, often at the sacrifice of their interests at home, and sometimes at the risk of hardship and even peril for members of the family obliged to remain behind. These handicaps had produced a serious sectional issue by 1767.[12]

There is little doubt that by the 1750's the South Carolina backcountry was overrun with lawless men. In a petition to the Council in 1752 settlers on the Pedee River asked for the erection of a county court on the grounds that the area had become "a place of refuge for many evil-disposed people . . . crowding in among us—Such as Horse Stealers and other Felons, having made their escape from North Carolina, and other parts. . . ."[13] On January 16, 1754, Governor James Glen, in an address to the two houses of the General Assembly, stated that there were thousands of settlers living about the Wateree, Saluda, and Broad rivers and Stevens Creek who, to-

[9] For the distribution of representation by parishes in 1765 see *Woodmason Writings*, pp. 67–8; Lieutenant Governor Bull gave the representatives of the parishes in 1770 somewhat differently, with a total of 48 members; for his letter to the Earl of Hillsborough of November 30, 1770, see P.R.O., C.O. 5:394; see also D. D. Wallace; *Constitutional History of South Carolina from 1725 to 1775* (Abbeville, S.C., 1899), pp. 9–10.

[10] *Woodmason Writings*, p. 40.

[11] Writing in 1766, Woodmason noted: "St. Matthew Is a Parish just laid out—Has as yet no Church built, or Parsonage House or Glebe laid out" (*ibid.*, p. 71).

[12] See W. A. Schaper: *op. cit.*, I, 334–8.

[13] For the petition of the Pedee River settlers see Alexander Gregg: *History of the Old Cheraws* (Columbia, S.C., 1925), pp. 131–2.

gether with those in such long-settled townships as Amelia, Saxe Gotha, and New Windsor, had never had a minister or a schoolmaster; he also stressed the fact that courts of judicature were located too far from them. Moreover, he emphasized his fear that unless the situation were relieved these people "would be driven from those places where they have planted at so much care and at so great an expence to this Public!"[14] That same month the Commons House agreed to provide two ministers of the Established Church for the more settled parts of the backcountry. In addition, an elaborate plan for the erection of three circuit courts was drawn up.[15] But certain basic features of the plan were disapproved after the first reading and the plan was never implemented.[16] Nor did a bill, submitted later in the year, to establish inferior courts in Granville and Craven counties and on the upper Congaree fare any better.[17] Then came the Great War for the Empire, followed by the revolt of the Cherokee Indians. When peace with the Indians was at length restored along the frontiers, the settlers were faced with waves of bandits and other criminals coming from the north, many of them doubtless fleeing from justice in their old haunts.[18]

By 1767 the situation in the South Carolina backcountry had become so bad that in November the "Upper Inhabitants of the said Province"[19] sent a remonstrance to the Governor, Lord Charles Greville Montagu, the Council, and the Assembly calling for protection from "an infernal Gang of Villains." The picture they painted of lawlessness was such as to demand action:

> "Our large Stocks of Cattel are either stolen or destroyed—our Cow Pens are broke up—and All our valuable Horses are carried off—Houses have been burned by these Rogues, and families stripp'd and turn'd naked into the Woods. . . . Married Women have been Ravished—Virgins deflowered, and other unheard of Cruelties committed by those barbarious Ruffians."

What was equally serious was the charge that the magistrates[20] "conniv'd at" the crimes of the lawless bands. Referring to the fact

[14] Commons House Journals, 29:19–20.

[15] For the plan for circuit courts submitted February 26, 1754, see *ibid.*, 29:137–140.

[16] *Ibid.*, 29:186–9.

[17] *Ibid.*, 29:262–3, 336–9, 342–50.

[18] For the Cherokee War and its aftermath see John Alden: *John Stuart and the Southern Colonial Frontier . . . 1754–1775* (Ann Arbor, Mich., 1944); see also Volume IX of this series, Chap. 4, and R. M. Brown: *op. cit.*, Chap. 1.

[19] That is, those living to the north of the Santee River.

[20] The reference here is to the justices of the peace. In 1765 there were 250 of them in South Carolina. Though their powers were very limited, two justices, pro-

that the welfare of the frontier settlers was ignored by the government, the remonstrance pointed out that the northern part of the province was unequally represented, with the "South Side of Santee River electing 44 members, and the North Side, with these Upper Parts of the Province (containing ⅔ of the White Inhabitants) returning but Six. . . ." It also demonstrated that neglect of the back-country was reflected by the failure to create parishes there—a situation, it was charged, that arose from the "Selfish Views" of those living in or near Charleston, who desired all things to centre there, however detrimental to the rest of the province. The remonstrance embodied, in all, twenty-three requests to the government of the province. The first was for circuit or county courts "for the Due and speedy Administration of Justice . . . as is in the Neighbouring Provinces"; then followed pleas for "some subordinate Courts," for court houses and gaols, for coercive laws to punish idleness, for revision of the laws for stealing and branding cattle and horses, for a digest of the laws, laying out parishes in the interior part of the province, erecting churches within them and providing resident ministers, for running the lines of the several counties from the sea westward to the Cherokee boundary line, and finally, for the Assembly to make provision for "a Quantity of Bibles, Common Prayers, and Devotional Tracts, to be distributed by the Ministers among the Poor, which will be of far greater Utility to the Province, than erecting the Statue of Mr. Pitt."[21]

But the peaceful settlers did not stop with a remonstrance. They organized to drive out the gangs of criminals,

> "burning their Cabbins and Camps—taking away the Goods and Horses, and Young Girls they had carried off. Many Battles were fought, and Persons killed on both Sides—While the Government did nothing—Silently look'd on—Publishing Proclamations—Some against the Rogues—Others against the Mobb. The Rogues at length began to Fire Houses likewise. This brought the Mobb to consider of some Order in their Proceedings Who chose a thousand Men, to

---

vided that one was of the quorum, could at least bind people for trial. See *South-Carolina Gazette,* October 19–31, 1765, and D. D. Wallace: *Constitutional History,* p. 23. The Rev. Charles Woodmason, in framing "Notes" for the remonstrance after it had been submitted, charged: "Most of the magistrates are Tavern Keepers—which occasions great Licentiousness and Prophaneness thro' the Country—for they are Breakers and Perverters of the Laws, instead of Conversators [Conservators?]" (*Woodmason Writings,* p. 241).

[21] For this remonstrance see *ibid.,* pp. 213–33. It was framed by Woodmason, who strongly supported the cause of the Regulators. See *ibid.,* p. 28. The erection of a statue of Pitt by vote of the General Assembly in 1766 has been dealt with in Chap. 1 of this volume.

execute the Laws against all Villains and Harbourers of Villains—These Men assum'd the Title of Regulators—They pull'd down the Houses of all who had entertain'd, secreted, abetted, and supported these Gangs of Theives [and] Whipped the Magistrates Who went Snacks with them in their Plunder, and protected them."[22]

It would appear that the government of the province was ignorant of the true state of affairs in the backcountry and of the imperative need for providing protection to the law-abiding people. Writing to the Earl of Shelburne on October 8, 1767, Governor Montagu disclosed that he had received information of some riots and unlawful assemblies of the inhabitants dwelling about 150 miles from Charleston, revealing that some 1,500 persons had risen in the country and were supposed to "have signed a paper to support one another in defiance of the Civil Magistrates and against the Laws of the Country."[23] By the spring of 1768 sufficient interest in the plight of the backcountry people had been aroused to bring about the passage in April of a circuit court act that was, apparently, acceptable only to its formulators.[24] It provided among other things that courts of general sessions of the peace, oyer and terminer, assize and general gaol delivery, should be held at times designated in the statute at Charleston, Orangeburg, Camden, Ninety-Six, Cheraws, Georgetown, and Beaufort, respectively; the fees for authorized court actions were also stated in the statute; the office of provost marshal of

---

[22] *Ibid.*, p. 234. For the rise of the Regulation Movement, see R. M. Brown: *op. cit.*, Chap. 3.

[23] Shelburne Papers, 52:188–9, Clements Library. Lieutenant Governor Bull, as a native of South Carolina, had a much deeper understanding of frontier conditions than had Governor Montagu. His sympathies were with the peaceful settlers. Reporting to England the following year, he emphasized the point that the Regulators were not lawless men but were merely seeking—in the absence of local courts—to put an end to lawlessness by the only means at their disposal. See Bull to Hillsborough, September 10, 1768, Chalmers Collection.

[24] In a letter to his son Arthur, Henry Middleton (later the moderate second President of the Continental Congress) wrote on September 22, 1768, from Goose Creek: "They are a good deal dissatisfied with the act lately passed for establishing of Circular Courts and seem determined not to suffer it to take place amongst them; and among other things they complain much of the want of County Courts and of the exorbitant and insupportable charges of the Law: with respect to the last their complaint is most certainly well founded, for it is a grievance generally complained of, and which, I believe, everybody wishes to see remedied, except the dealers in the Law themselves. How it will end is uncertain, but they give a good deal of uneasiness, and people in these lower parts seem to be much alarmed, and are apprehensive that such a formidable body of lawless people got together will not disperse themselves without doing mischief. . . . A Spirit of Sedition seems also to have spread itself in the neighbouring province to the northward of us, and by what we hear they must be in great confusion there." See "Correspondence of Hon. Arthur Middleton," ed. J. W. Barnwell, *South Carolina Historical and Genealogical Magazine,* XXVII, 110.

the province was abolished and in place of this office a sheriff for Charleston and each of the six districts was authorized, with the mode of his appointment specified, as well as the powers he should exercise; further, the judges of the court of general sessions who were to go on circuit were to receive definite salaries upon their appointment by His Majesty and were to have tenure during good behaviour.[25] The Act was to go into force after it had been approved by the King in Council and as soon as court houses and gaols had been erected. However, this approval could not be obtained because the statute, while "founded in wisdom and propriety and of the greatest importance to the happiness and prosperity of the people," was held to be seriously defective in some respects.[26]

Nevertheless, the groundwork had been carried out for a court that could be approved by the Privy Council. The need for this was reinforced by a long letter written by Lieutenant Governor Bull on September 10, 1768, to the Earl of Hillsborough, the new Secretary of State for the Colonies. In it he made clear how essential it was to bring order out of the anarchic conditions on the frontiers and how defective was the present system of administering justice within

---

[25] *Acts of the General Assembly of South-Carolina, Passed the 12th of April, 1768* (Charleston, 1768), pp. 3–15. For an excellent analysis of the Circuit Court Act of 1768 see W. H. Smith: *South Carolina as a Royal Province, 1719–1776* (New York, 1903), pp. 134–5, and R. M. Brown: *op. cit.*, Chap. 5. See also the very long letter from Charles Garth to the South Carolina committee of correspondence, August 14, 1768, *South Carolina Historical and Genealogical Magazine*, XXX, 218–23.

[26] *Acts of the Privy Council, Col. Ser., 1766–1783*, p. 171. The Lords of the Committee of the Privy Council on July 22, 1767, referred the Circuit Act to the Board of Trade, which in turn sought the opinion of its legal adviser, Sir Matthew Lamb. Although Lamb found the law to contain useful things "for Ease and benefit of the people there," he objected, among other things, to the fact that the office of provost marshal, held by patent from the Crown, was to be abolished without directions from the King, and to the clause providing salaries for the judges whenever it pleased His Majesty that they should hold office during good behaviour. For Lamb's report see *ibid.*, pp. 166–8. Lamb was apparently unaware that, with the King's approval in 1768, permission had been given to abolish the office of provost marshal and to appoint sheriffs for the several counties, provided that compensation were given to the holder of the patent for the office. See Shelburne Papers, 54:84–5. In fact, on November 11, 1767, the Assembly had agreed to pay patent-holder Richard Cumberland, an absentee serving by deputy, the sum of £5,000 sterling. For these negotiations, which had been going on since 1766, and the action of the Assembly see Commons House Journals, 37:238–9, 469; see also "Garth Correspondence" (ed. J. W. Barnwell), *South Carolina Historical and Genealogical Magazine*, XXIX, 115–16, 214–16, XXX, 168–84, 217–24.

The Board of Trade representation of September 15, 1768, brushed aside much of Lamb's criticism, approved certain clauses of the Act, agreed with Lamb that the provision for judges to hold tenure during good behaviour was "both unnecessary and Improper," and in addition found inadmissible the fact that the Governor could have no part in the appointment of sheriffs. On the basis of their representation the Privy Council rejected the Act on October 8. See *Acts of the Privy Council, Col. Ser., 1766–1783*, pp. 166–71, and Board of Trade *Journal, 1768–1775*, pp. 44 and 48.

the province. In this same letter Bull mentioned that the backcountry settlers—"at least 4000 sensible men half the Strength of the province," who hitherto had not voted since there was uncertainty in which parish they lived—had lately resolved to make use of this right and had been running the dividing lines of the parishes westward to ascertain where their settlements were situated. "Many of the voters," he wrote, "will ride 150 miles to the parish church at which the elections are made."[27] On this subject Peter Timothy wrote to Benjamin Franklin on September 3, 1768:

> "They are at last in Arms, and refuse Submission to every Law or Act of Government that to them is oppressive. . . . They call themselves Regulators, and intend to regulate our ensuing Election by marching down 100 or 150 Men to every Parish where they have a Right (which they never exercised before) to vote. . . . these People extend from the Sea on one Side, to Savannah River on the other; 45 miles deep."[28]

Soon after the dissolution of the Commons House on November 19, 1768, new elections were held. To what extent the Regulators were able to influence them is not clear. At any rate it was not until June of the following year that the Assembly was allowed to meet. It was then, in 1769, that Governor Montagu—who had recently visited the frontiers—appealed to the legislators to take action to improve the intolerable backcountry situation, at the same time informing them of the reasons for the disapproval of the law of 1768 as reported by the Board of Trade.[29] After a committee of the House had submitted a revised plan for a circuit court act which the Governor refused to accept, as not meeting all the objections of the government at home, a new version of the act was framed. This the Governor signed on July 29 and personally carried to England.[30] The "Act

---

[27] See Bull to Hillsborough, September 10, 1768, Chalmers Collection. In August, while Governor Montagu was summering in the Northern colonies, Bull issued a proclamation against the rioters. See *South-Carolina Gazette,* August 15, 1768.

[28] *South Carolina Historical Magazine,* LV, 163; see also *South-Carolina Gazette,* August 28 and September 2, 1768, for the organization of the Regulators. Edward McCrady, in his *History of South Carolina under the Royal Government, 1719–1776* (New York and London, 1899), pp. 593–5 and 637–90, gives an account of the 1768 disturbances in the backcountry; see also the thorough account of R. M. Brown: *op. cit.,* Chaps. 4 and 8.

[29] For the Moderator Movement and the end of the Regulation see *ibid.,* Chap. 6. For Governor Montagu's appeal see Commons House Journals, 38:11.

[30] See J. F. Grimké: *The Public Laws of the State of South Carolina* (Philadelphia, 1790), pp. 268–73. This copy of the statute is defective, as brought up to date to the time of Grimké's compilation. For where a clause was obsolete he generally left it out, simply noting that it no longer held; however Clause 8, having to do with the

for establishing Circuit Courts, building Gaols, and appointing Sheriffs . . . ," strongly supported by Lieutenant Governor Bull,[31] came before the Board of Trade on November 17 and, after being considered and appearing to be free of objections, was approved by the Privy Council on November 29.[32] With the confirmation of the law, announced to the Assembly in February of the following year, it was now necessary to implement it by the erection of court houses and gaols.[33] This was not accomplished until the spring of 1772, at which time the circuit courts began to function.[34] The results of the new act were salutary in quieting the minds of the people of the backcountry. Lieutenant Governor Bull, writing to the Secretary of State for the Colonies in 1773, affirmed:

> "the operation of the Circuit Court Act produced the most happy effects in the interior parts of the Province. Many had conceived terrible apprehensions of the arbitrary behaviour of the Judges and the rapaciousness of the Lawyers, but by the experience of the circuits, the impartiality, prudence and affability of the former and the moderation of the latter render them most acceptable visitors, which with [the execution of the] law will introduce civility among them, and in a few years give a different face to the country."

Yet, he pointed out, there was still an absence of parish churches and schools among most of these people, despite his attempt in 1770 to provide for a system of free schools in Charleston and eight other places.[35] While it was true that the churches in the parishes of St. Matthew and St. Mark were located in the interior, eighty miles distant from Charleston, none of the other churches was situated more than thirty miles from the seacoast.[36]

The steps that followed were not to prove so favourable. With the approval by the Crown of the Circuit Court Act, it was decided to send out from England an entire bench of judges, consisting of a chief justice and four associate justices, all provided with substantial

abolition of the office of provost marshal, was included. See also R. M. Brown: *op. cit.*, Appendix B (pp. 148–58), for the Circuit Court Act of 1769 as it appears in *Acts of the General Assembly of South-Carolina, ... 1769* (Charleston, 1769).

[31] See Bull to Hillsborough, September 7, 1769, Chalmers Collection.

[32] Board of Trade *Journal, 1768–1775*, pp. 107 and 113; *Acts of the Privy Council, Col. Ser., 1766–1783*, p. 584.

[33] Commons House Journals, 38:273–5.

[34] *Ibid.*, 39, Part II:69.

[35] For Lieutenant Governor Bull's message on January 30, 1770, to the Commons House on a free school system see "The South Carolina Education Bill of 1770," ed. J. H. Easterby, *South Carolina Historical and Genealogical Magazine*, XLVIII, 95–111. The Education Bill, sponsored by the Governor, was set aside, together with all bills involving the appropriation of public funds, because of the controversy over the Wilkes fund, an issue that will be dealt with later in this chapter.

[36] Bull to Dartmouth, May 5, 1773, Chalmers Collection.

fixed salaries,[37] thus ignoring South Carolinians who had been thoroughly trained in the law at the London Inns of Court and were well qualified for the posts.[38] The psychological impact of filling all the best-paid provincial offices with placemen from Great Britain cannot be ignored in dealing with the sources of the growing spirit of alienation from the parent country among the leaders of South Carolina. The appointment in 1762 of Charles Shinner [Skinner] as chief justice of the court of common pleas and of the court of common sessions illustrates the point.

When Shinner took his place on the bench he was unfamiliar with the laws of South Carolina. During the Stamp Act crisis he supported the government of Great Britain but was overruled by the four associate judges on the question whether the business of the courts could proceed without stamps; they even refused to record his opinions.[39] By the end of 1766 Shinner was isolated by the overwhelming opposition that had developed against him in South Carolina. On April 20 of the following year the Commons House presented an address to Governor Montagu asking that he immediately suspend Shinner from office for reasons stated in an accompanying report. Although the Chief Justice made an extended and able answer to the charges on May 3, the Council, when called upon to advise the Governor, came to the unanimous opinion that Shinner should be suspended on the grounds that he was "unacquainted with law and entirely unfit for the Office of Chief Justice." This the

---

[37] Transcripts of records relating to South Carolina in the British Public Records Office, 33:40–1, 113–16, South Carolina Archives Department, Columbia, S.C.; these transcripts will be cited hereafter as South Carolina Public Records in conformity with the short title used by earlier scholars, but should not be confused with P.R.O. numbering or that of the Commons House Journals. It may be noted that J. P. Greene—in his authoritative article on the Wilkes fund controversy (to be cited later) and in the section on South Carolina local issues in his *The Quest for Power: The Lower Houses of Assembly in the Southern Royal Colonies, 1689–1776* (Chapel Hill, N.C., 1963), pp. 399–416—cites this source as "Transcripts of South Carolina Records," in preference to citation of P.R.O., C.O. 5:394, 395, 396, correspondence of the South Carolina governors.

The appointments of the judges were made in 1770 but, as previously indicated, it was not until 1772 that the justices could go on circuit; see Commons House Journals, 39, Part II:69.

[38] Between 1731 and 1774 forty-eight persons from South Carolina studied at the Inns of Court—the highest number that went from any colony; Virginia sent thirty-seven, North Carolina, ten. See J. G. de Roulhac Hamilton: "Southern Members of the Inns of Court," *North Carolina Historical Review*, X, 273–86; see also E. A. Jones: *American Members of the Inns of Court* (London, 1924).

[39] See "An Account of the proceedings of the Chief Justice, Assistant Judges, and Lawyers of South Carolina on the Stamp Act," included in the letter of Governor Montagu to the Board of Trade of August 6, 1766, with other supporting documents, South Carolina Public Records, 31:86–230.

Governor did on May 11.[40] To the Earl of Shelburne, the step was an unprecedented one. Writing to the Governor on October 8, 1767, he pointed out that since the chief justice had been given no opportunity to be heard in his own defence, "His Majesty can never consent to a Proceeding which is so Contrary to the Maxims of general Justice & the practice and Fundamental Principles of the English Constitution. . . ."[41] With the appointment of the Earl of Hillsborough to the newly created office of Secretary of State for the Colonies, however, Shelburne was no longer in a position to follow up the issue, and the suspension stood. The office of chief justice remained vacant until it was filled by Thomas Knox Gordon, one of the British judges appointed in 1771 to carry out the purposes of the Circuit Court Act.

The impact on local opinion of ignoring South Carolina legal talent is also illustrated in the case of the Leigh family. First of all, in 1753 Peter Leigh was appointed chief justice rather than Charles Pinckney, the most distinguished lawyer in South Carolina, who had earlier been given a temporary appointment to that post by Governor Glen with the recommendation that he become permanent holder of this office.[42] This action inevitably created resentment. Leigh's son, Egerton, who accompanied his father to South Carolina, was admitted to the bar there at the age of twenty, two years later was appointed to the lucrative office of surveyor general of lands, became a member of the South Carolina Council in 1759, in 1762 was appointed judge of the South Carolina Court of Vice-Admiralty, and in 1765 received the office of attorney general of the province.[43] Nor was Leigh alone in the enjoyment of a number of South Carolina offices; another placeman, Thomas Skottowe, not only was a member of the Council, clerk of both that body and the Commons House of Assembly, but also held the important post of secretary of the province. It was therefore not surprising that the committee of correspondence, at the request of the Commons House, should lay

[40] See Montagu to the Board of Trade, May 12, 1767, Shelburne Papers, 52:177–8. For Shinner's defence of his conduct and recommendations for improving the judicial system of the province see "Observations of Charles Skinner, Esq., Chief Justice of South Carolina," transmitted with Montagu's letter to the Board of Trade of August 6, 1766, *ibid.*, 52:157–8.

[41] For this letter see *ibid.*, 54:81–5.

[42] Board of Trade *Journal, 1749–1753*, p. 382; see H. H. Bellot: "The Leighs of South Carolina," Royal Historical Society *Transactions*, 5th ser., VI, 170–7. Peter Leigh held office until his death in 1759 and fulfilled his duties in an acceptable manner.

[43] Board of Trade *Journal, 1759–1763*, p. 45; P.R.O., Admiralty 2:1057; H. H. Bellot: *op. cit.*, pp. 175–6.

the matter before the London agent of the province, Charles Garth, emphasizing "the incompatability of some of the Offices held by Mr. Leigh and Mr. Skottowe, Members of His Majesty's Council, which is so striking that it cannot escape your notice."[44] Upon receipt of this letter Garth waited upon the Earl of Shelburne, then in control of colonial affairs, but Shelburne could hold out little prospect of remedying the situation because most of those offices were held "under patents from the Crown, and no Representation [had been made] of Misbehaviour or Omission of Duty against the Patentees."[45] Nevertheless, a situation was to arise in 1768 which would compel Leigh to surrender his office of judge of the South Carolina Court of Vice-Admiralty. As this situation affected the interests of the merchants and planters of the province and bulked much larger in the minds of the people than the problem of the monopolization of offices, it warrants consideration in detail.

Henry Laurens, merchant prince, ship-owner, and landed magnate, was rightly regarded during the Stamp Act crisis as an opponent of the South Carolina Sons of Liberty and a loyal supporter of the government of Great Britain;[46] at the same time he felt so strongly that the Council of the province was being down-graded by royal placemen that in 1764 he refused a seat in it, preferring to remain a member of the Commons House of Assembly.[47] His conversion from loyal subject to one of the most powerful opponents of British control of American affairs[48] had its beginnings in the year 1767, when one of his vessels, the *Active*, was seized by Daniel Moore, the new collector of customs at Charleston, for violation of the trade and navigation acts.

The Charleston collector had already aroused the animosity of the merchants by his rigid enforcement of the trade laws and had

[44] South Carolina committee of correspondence to Charles Garth, July 2, 1766, *South Carolina Historical and Genealogical Magazine*, XXVIII, 228.

[45] Garth to the committee of correspondence, September 26, 1766, *ibid.*, XXIX, 45. In fact Garth, writing to the committee on January 31, 1767, pointed out that strong solicitations had been made in behalf of both Leigh and Skottowe that nothing should be done to their prejudice unless there was an application that would charge them with "Faults of Commission or of Omission . . ." (*ibid.*, XXIX, 131).

[46] See Volume X of this series, pp. 319–20, 361. For Laurens see D. D. Wallace: *The Life of Henry Laurens* (New York and London, 1915).

[47] See *ibid.*, pp. 112–14. For the decline in prestige of the Council with the increase of placemen up to 1774, see M. C. Sirmans: "The South Carolina Royal Council, 1720–1763," *William and Mary Quarterly*, 3rd ser., XVIII, 373–92.

[48] By 1769 the once-conservative Laurens had become so firm in support of the patriot program for American rights that the three years, 1771 to 1774, that he spent in England while his sons were pursuing their education there and in Geneva did not change his attitude. See, in this connection, D. D. Wallace: *Henry Laurens*, Chap. 15.

been accused, with good reason, of seeking to enrich himself. He was also suspect because he had received this post as a result of his activities as stamp collector. What was worse in the eyes of the trade was that, contrary to precedent and the practice of his predecessor in office, he demanded fees for signing certificates for the export of indigo to England and insisted that every decked vessel going to another river within the province should register and take out bonds with him for which he received fees that were divided with the local comptroller of the customs; further, he exacted much higher fees for ship papers than those previously paid.[49]

Although the *Active* was released because no law had been violated, when the case came before Judge Leigh of the vice-admiralty court, Laurens had to divide the costs of the trial. What is more he had won the hostility of Moore. Soon after the trial involving the *Active,* Laurens's schooner *Wambaw* was seized and libeled. Late in May 1767 it had gone to the owner's plantation on the Altamaha in Georgia with supplies. Since there was no custom house within forty miles of the Altamaha the Charleston collector had taken no bond for non-enumerated goods and had left Laurens with the impression that the schooner did not need clearance papers before returning to Charleston. On the return voyage the *Wambaw* was loaded with cypress shingles valued at about £6 sterling, "partly for Ballast . . . and partly in hopes of paying a small Part of the very heavy Expenses attending such a Voyage," as neither stones nor sand suitable for ballast was available. Upon the schooners arrival at Charleston, the collector refused to admit it except under terms that were unacceptable to Laurens and his friends, who were requested to seek permission from the collector "as a great Favour." The *Wambaw* was therefore "condemned as forfeited," and it cost Laurens £175 current money to repurchase it.[50]

Again, about the middle of June, another of Laurens's schooners, the *Broughton-Island Packet,*[51] was ready to sail to the same Georgia plantation. Upon receiving the manifest, Moore spoke insultingly to Laurens, who retorted "that he heartily despised him, and that he

[49] *A Representation of Facts, Relative to the Conduct of Daniel Moore, Esquire; Collector of . . . Customs at Charles-Town . . . Transmitted by the Merchants of Charles-Town to Charles Garth, Esquire* [South Carolina London agent] (Charleston, 1767), p. 3. With respect to the illegal demand for payment for an export certificate on indigo produced in South Carolina, in order to ship it to Great Britain, see the testimony on oath of John Champneys, merchant, on September 23, 1767, concerning Moore's demand on May 15, *ibid.*, p. 20.

[50] See *ibid.*, p. 7; Laurens to Richard Oswald of London, October 10, 1767, Henry Laurens Letter Book, South Carolina Historical Society, Charleston.

[51] The schooner's name is spelled in a variety of ways in the proceedings.

had heard his Fame Twenty-five Years ago." With these words Laurens was also impelled to pull the collector's nose. The enraged Moore immediately challenged the merchant to a duel, but neither then nor later did he name a date or place.[52] Meanwhile, the schooner sailed to Georgia and returned loaded with firewood for ballast. It was seized late in July and subsequently prosecuted in the vice-admiralty court for lack of clearance papers, as had been true of the *Wambaw*.[53] But Leigh released the vessel. Further, the costs of the trial were levied against the prosecutor, who in this case was the searcher, George Roupell.[54] When Laurens sued for damages in the civil court, the judge and jury awarded him £1,400, plus costs.[55] But the collector's career in South Carolina had come to an end by the time of this trial.

The Charleston merchant John Logan charged Moore in the

[52] In connection with the above incident see the long letter of October 14, 1767, from Laurens to James Habersham of Savannah, Laurens Letter Book. Laurens felt the need to go into detail because reports of the incident made it appear that he had acted in a manner that Habersham considered "exceptionable."

[53] That Moore acted from spite in the case of the two vessels is indicated in a letter written by Laurens to Governor James Grant of Florida on October 13, 1767, in which he stated "that a Vessel came in yesterday in exactly the same circumstances of my vessels as to the Custom House documents, from a place where none was to be had, having therefore none—but with the remarkable difference as to her lading, that she had on board a full Cargo of Logwood from Bahama & Florida & yet was admitted to an entry without Let or demur . . ." In this same letter, while referring to "European-American affairs," he said, interestingly enough in view of his later attitude, "I am in no dread about them; there may possibly be some disagreeable work, but [it] must be soon at an end & produce an establishment of union to endure for ages; there are mistaken men on both sides, [but] the eyes of the nation will be opened & Men on either part who do not want Wisdom & who can see the compatibility of freedom & subordination will arise with healing under their wings & build an everlasting Bridge from Britain to British America—God grant it may be soon!" (Laurens Letter Book).

[54] *A Representation of Facts Relative to the Conduct of Daniel Moore . . .*, p. 8. It should be noted that the collector was also inconsistent in the fees charged for clearing Laurens's schooners with "no Difference in the Circumstances of the two Vessels; the charges for the *Wambaw* was £3.15 currency and for the *Boughton-Island Packet*, it was £5.12.6" *(ibid.)*.

[55] The *Broughton-Island Packet* was a new schooner that had cost £4,200, South Carolina currency. Laurens at first sued for £5,000 currency damage because, as he stated, the vessel was faced with danger on account of the tempestuous season when it was seized. But when the issue came to court in May 1768, he asked only for £469.10 damages since the schooner was now safe and he desired, again following his statement, to recover only such damage as had been done to the bottom and for loss of the use of it. Nevertheless, the judge and jury gave him £1,400 currency (or some £200 sterling), plus £89.15.7 for costs. As George Roupell had been obliged to defend the seizure of the vessel in court, in the absence of Collector Moore, the damages were assessed against him. Roupell, a poor man, could not possibly pay such a sum without ruining his family. Laurens not wanting this to happen, gave the searcher time to apply to the London Customs Commissioners for the sum levied against him. This money was paid in March 1769, apparently out of the American customs fund. It was then that Roupell sent Laurens a challenge,

common law court with extortion in the case of the ship *Nelson;* a grand jury found a true bill against the collector. With the entire body of merchants arrayed against him, Moore fled to Georgia early in the fall of 1767 and soon afterwards sailed for England, despite his pledge to give security against his appearance at the trial.[56] The way was now open for an agreement between the custom house and the merchants as to the fees that should be charged at the port of Charleston. On September 15, 1767, after the merchants had exhibited the list of fees charged respectively by Thomas Gadsden and Hector Berenger De Beaufain, Moore's predecessors, Deputy Collector R. P. H. Hatley, a young man of twenty-two, signed such an agreement.[57]

This abuse in levying fees, as practiced arbitrarily by Moore, once corrected, was no longer, it appears, a matter of concern to the trading public down to the outbreak of the War for American Independence. However, the corrections of Moore's malpractice did not mean that the officers of the custom house at Charleston would not pursue their efforts to bring about strict enforcement of the trade and navigation acts. In fact, in 1768 Laurens again became concerned in a case involving the ship *Ann,* of which he was a part owner. Loaded with rice, deerskins, and also some non-enumerated articles, the *Ann* was prepared to sail for England on June 20, 1768, when it was libeled and seized for failure to give bond *before* taking on board the non-enumerated articles, as provided by law[58] Techni-

---

which the latter accepted; happily, this was as far as the matter went, as had been true of Moore's challenge. See [Henry Laurens]: *Extracts from the Proceedings of the High Court of Vice-Admiralty in Charles-Town . . . with an Appendix* (2nd edn., Charleston, 1769), Appendix, pp. 53–4. The only copy of this very rare pamphlet now available is a badly damaged one in the South Carolina Historical Society Library. It contains much more material than Laurens's *Extracts from the Proceedings . . .* reputedly published in Philadelphia in 1768. For the official record of the trial see P.R.O., Treas. 1:465, Library of Congress transcripts.

[56] See *A Representation of Facts Relative to the Conduct of Daniel Moore . . . ,* pp. 39–40; see also the South Carolina committee of correspondence to Charles Garth, September 29, 1767, *South Carolina Historical and Genealogical Magazine,* XXIX, 304–5, and Governor Montagu to the Earl of Shelburne, October 5, 1767, Shelburne Papers, 52:187–8. For Moore's explanation for his reason for leaving South Carolina see P.R.O., Treas. 1:468, pp. 230–1.

[57] For the list of fees charged respectively by Gadsden and De Beaufain, and the list that Hatley agreed to levy as "established by Act of Parliament and Acts of Assembly of this Province," see *A Representation of Facts Relative to the Conduct of Daniel Moore . . . ,* pp. 21–2 and 24.

[58] All these facts are set forth at large in Laurens's long letter to William Cowles & Co. and William Freeman, both of Bristol, under date of July 13, 1768, Laurens Letter Book. "An Act for granting certain Duties in the British Colonies" of 1764, generally called the Sugar Act (4 Geo. III, c. 23), has the following to say about

cally, Laurens and his agent were guilty of violating the law, although a manifest of the cargo, presented after all articles were on board, included the non-enumerated ones. Roupell again represented the custom house in the trial that took place before Leigh in the Charleston Vice-Admiralty Court.[59] In the course of the proceedings the point was emphasized that the day before the *Ann* was to sail another ship had been permitted to clear and had sailed, although loaded under similar conditions.[60] In other words, it was clear that Laurens had not intended to commit fraud and yet was singled out for different and harsher treatment than was accorded to others. As these facts were public property, Leigh's decision was to release the *Ann* to its owners; at the same time, however, he ruled that there was probable cause for the seizure. This meant that Laurens, as well as the co-owners, not only were obliged to pay part of the cost of the trial but were unable to carry the case to the civil court, as had been possible before the passing of the provisions of the Townshend Act relating to the vice-admiralty courts.[61] As a result, the great merchant-planter turned to his pen to wage a bitter

the shipping of non-enumerated goods: ". . . and if any . . . non-enumerated Goods shall be laden on board any such Ship . . . before such Bond shall be given, The Goods so laden, together with the Ship . . . and her Furniture shall be forfeited, and shall and may be seized by any Officer of the Customs, and prosecuted in the Manner herein after directed." This statement in the Act was preceded by one to the effect that there had been great abuses in the colonial trade "to the Prejudice of the Revenue, and the great Detriment of the Trade of this Kingdom, and its American Plantations."

[59] Roupell, according to Laurens's statement in *Extracts from the Proceedings . . . with an Appendix* (1769 edn., p. 20 or 21), offered to give up the case of the *Ann* if Laurens would renounce the verdict he had won against the searcher in the common law court. This offer was declined when made by Deputy Collector Hatley, acting for Roupell.

[60] For the case of the *Ann* see P.R.O., Treas. 1:463 and especially 465, which is a complete transcript of the trial covering thirty-two folios; see also Leila Sellers: *op. cit.*, pp. 198–201, D. D. Wallace: *Henry Laurens*, pp. 142–5, O. M. Dickerson: *The Navigation Acts and the American Revolution* (Philadelphia, 1951), pp. 227–9, and Carl Ubbelohde: *The Vice-Admiralty Courts and the American Revolution* (Chapel Hill, N.C., 1960), pp. 109–40.

[61] *Ibid.* Laurens, writing to Governor Wright on August 8, 1768, mentioned his great uneasiness over the terms of the acquittal of the *Ann* and added: "it opened my eyes to see that the judge hath not acted altogether with that candour & purity in proceeding & judgment that I am willing to believe he would have acted had he been disengaged from another office [that is, the office of attorney general]" (Laurens Letter Book). On the other hand, the searcher, George Roupell, and the American Customs Commissioners, after hearing from Roupell, were equally certain that the judge of the vice-admiralty court was biased against the customs service and were equally anxious that Leigh should be required to give up one of his offices. See George Roupell to the Commissioners of Customs in America, July 11, 1768, and John Temple, Henry Hutton, and John Robinson to the Lords Commissioners of the Treasury, Boston, December 16, 1768, P.R.O., Treas. 1:465.

war on both the American customs and vice-admiralty officers.[62] Although Leigh had warned Laurens not to publish the proceedings of his cases in the court of vice-admiralty,[63] the need for caution was removed when in September 1768 Leigh gave up the office of judge, preferring to retain that of attorney general.[64] In the latter part of that year there appeared anonymously, both as to author and publisher, his *Extracts from the Proceedings of the Court of Vice-Admiralty in Charleston . . .*,[65] which was Laurens's indictment of the South Carolina customs and vice-admiralty court services. But he limited his criticism to the period after the year 1767—he lauded the collectors of customs who preceded Moore, and he cast no reflection on the conduct of Judge Leigh from the time he received his appointment to the vice-admiralty post in 1762 until 1767. In fact, the impression is gained that the relations of the two men had been friendly.[66] Furthermore, the language in the pamphlet is more restrained than normally used by Laurens in his correspondence and more clearly designed to appeal to general American sentiment.[67] Under his own name Leigh published an answer in Charleston in 1769, *The Man Unmasked: or, the World Undeceived,*

[62] In this connection see D. S. Lovejoy: "Rights Imply Equality: The Case Against Admiralty Jurisdiction in America, 1764–1776," *William and Mary Quarterly,* 3rd ser., XVI, 459–84.

[63] See Laurens to William Fisher of Philadelphia, one of the joint owners of the *Ann,* August 1, 1768, Laurens Letter Book.

[64] On May 9, 1768, the Admiralty Board wrote to Governor Montagu that there was an incompatibility in Leigh occupying the two posts of attorney general and judge of the court of vice-admiralty, since the attorney general should, when cases arose, "support the Officers of the Revenue in the discharge of their duty." See P.R.O., Admiralty 2:1057, folio 384. It may be noted that the Board also had taken the position that John Randolph, who succeeded his brother Peyton to the same two offices in Virginia in 1767, must also resign one of his offices. See Carl Ubbelohde: *op. cit.,* pp. 113–14 and 162–3, and Royal Historical Society *Transactions,* 5th ser., VI, 178–9.

[65] Previously cited, this pamphlet appeared as published in "America"; it was probably published in Philadelphia in 1768 and was undoubtedly the work of Henry Laurens.

[66] It should be pointed out that Leigh had married the daughter of Laurens's sister and was therefore a kinsman by marriage. Leigh, it may also be mentioned, was guilty, shortly before receiving a baronetcy in 1772 for his services in America, of seducing his wife's sister—Laurens's niece. This matter was apparently kept secret, for Leigh remained not without supporters. As was true of his father, he was a member of the Charleston Masonic Lodge; moreover, in 1768 and again in 1770 he was elected provincial Grand Master, and still held this high fraternal office in 1774. See *South-Carolina Gazette,* June 4, 1768, and *South Carolina Historical and Genealogical Magazine,* III, 145, IV, 313, LIII, 213. These facts must be kept in mind in dealing with the Laurens-Leigh controversy.

[67] In his letter to William Fisher on August 1, 1768, Laurens referred to the customs and vice-admiralty court officials, adding: "The avidity of these Locusts . . . should be rectified by wholesome Medicine, nothing less than a Halter will cure some of them" (Laurens Letter Book).

in the Author of a late Pamphlet, intitled, "Extracts from the Proceedings of the High Court of Vice-Admiralty in Charlestown, South-Carolina," etc. with Suitable Remarks on that Masterly Performance. To this Laurens replied, again anonymously, with a very much expanded second edition of *Extracts,* which was also provided with an appendix.[68]

The judicial-minded student who reads these pamphlets is apt to arrive at the same conclusion as did the lawyer-historian Edward McCrady, who stated that Laurens,

> "considering himself aggrieved by a judicial decision of Sir Egerton, adopted the unwise and improper course of publishing a pamphlet calling the judgment in question. Instead of treating this attack upon his judicial conduct as a contempt of court, or passing it by in dignified silence, Sir Egerton, with still greater impropriety, answered it in another pamphlet, entitled *The Man Unmasked,* the forthcoming of which was advertised in the *Gazette* of the day in conspicuous type and with flaming notices."[69]

With the resignation of Moore as collector of customs and of Leigh as judge of the court of vice admiralty, quiet again reigned in the Charleston port, although it is true that in 1769 a seizure "of Considerable consequence" was made by the new collector, Roupell, and the case was brought before the newly appointed judge of the court of vice-admiralty, James Simpson, a young man of ability.[70] In fact, conditions of trade were in general so harmonious in 1771 that in February of that year some seventy Charleston merchants joined in an address to Captain Mark Robinson, commander of the South Carolina district naval patrol—a part of the naval patrol system established in 1763 along the Atlantic seaboard to enforce a strict observation of the trade acts. The address reads as follows:

> "Sir, Your regard to the welfare of this Country, and the constant attention you have shewn during your command here, to our naviga-

[68] See D. D. Wallace: *Henry Laurens,* pp. 145–9, especially Appendix 2, which prints Laurens's "A Few General Observations on American Custom-house Officers and Courts of Vice-Admiralty," which appeared in the 1769 edition of *Extracts from the Proceedings.* When this version is compared with the "Observations" in the 1768 edition, it will be noted that some changes were made to sharpen the attack against the Crown officers regulating trade. For example, when referring to these officers it was stated that "the Spirit of Industry and Commerce must either submit to them and in the End be entirely extinguished, or by a vigorous Exertion of all its Faculties such baneful Harpies must be expelled" ("Observations," p. 2, *Extracts . . . ,* 2nd edn., 1769).

[69] See Edward McCrady's *History of South Carolina* previously cited, pp. 471–2.

[70] See Carl Ubbelohde: *op. cit.,* p. 150.

tion, entitle you to the warmest thanks of your fellow-subjects, and to the approbation of government. . . ."

As a further mark of their admiration for Captain Robinson, who was about to leave this station, the merchants presented him with a piece of plate valued at £90 sterling. To the next in command, Lieutenant George Robertson, they offered a sword "with their thanks for his care and attention while on this station." Replying to the address, Robinson declared: "It has ever been my study to execute my trust, agreeable to His Majesty's gracious Intentions, with the least possible inconvenience to his loving subjects. . . ."[71]

Yet such amenities must not obscure the fact that South Carolina was slipping away from the moorings that earlier had tied it firmly to the mother country. The Commons House of Assembly had already tested its strength in the 1760's in a controversy of a constitutional nature with Governor Thomas Boone over his efforts to curb the Assembly's power to determine the validity of the election of its members.[72] Then in July 1769, under the influence of the same Christopher Gadsden who had been the subject of the election controversy, the Commons House had adopted a non-importation agreement reflecting the action taken in Boston.[73] This steady rise in power of the Commons had been taking place at a time when the Council was so declining in prestige that prominent men refused appointments as councillors and Lieutenant Governor Bull characterized it as "a dependent body, removeable at pleasure," adding that he could wish it "were on a more respectable footing."[74]

Late in 1769 a constitutional issue arose involving the right of the executive branch of the government—along with the Council, acting in its legislative capacity—to be consulted about expenditures. What exacerbated the problem was that money was appro-

---

[71] See Advices, Charleston, January 21, in the *Pennsylvania Journal,* February 21, 1771.

[72] See J. P. Greene's definitive study of this early constitutional crisis, "The Gadsden Election Controversy and the Revolutionary Movement in South Carolina," *Mississippi Valley Historical Review,* XLVI, 469–92.

[73] See Chap. 6 in this volume. For Lieutenant Governor Bull's remark to Hillsborough of July 16, 1770, that "We are too apt to cast our eyes to the North Star of Boston in our political navigation . . . ," see "Papers Relating to Carolina 1662–1769," Chalmers Collection.

[74] Bull to Hillsborough, November 30, 1770, South Carolina Public Records, 32:373; see also M. E. Sirmans: *op. cit., William and Mary Quarterly,* 3rd ser., XVIII, 390–1. For an analysis of the decline in power and prestige of the South Carolina Council during the late 1750's and early 1760's as the result of the struggle for power between the Assembly and the Council (especially over the issue of a colonial agent in 1756) and resentment over the appointment of placemen, see *ibid.,* 373–92.

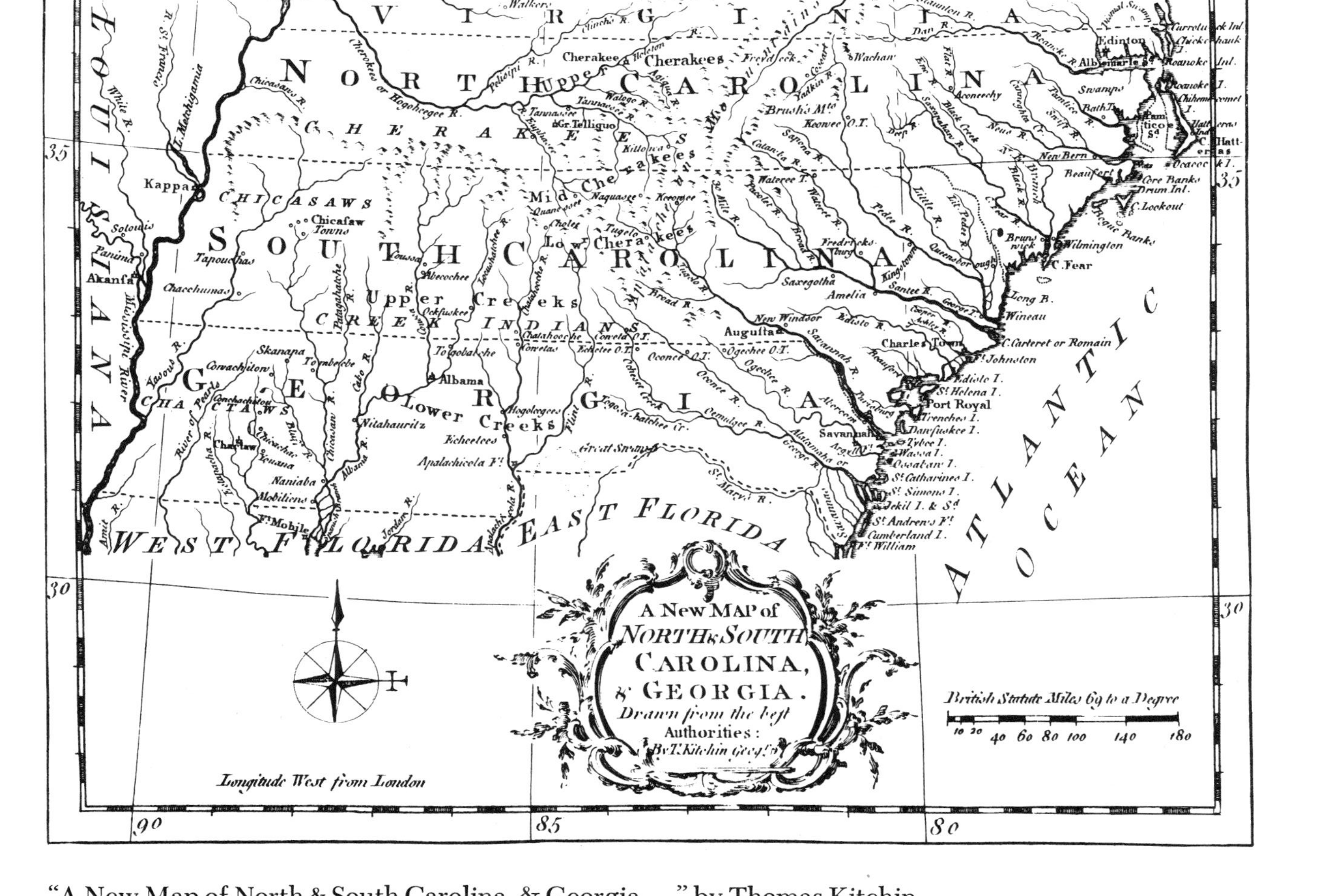

“A New Map of North & South Carolina, & Georgia . . .” by Thomas Kitchin.

(From *London Magazine*, 1765, William L. Clements Library)

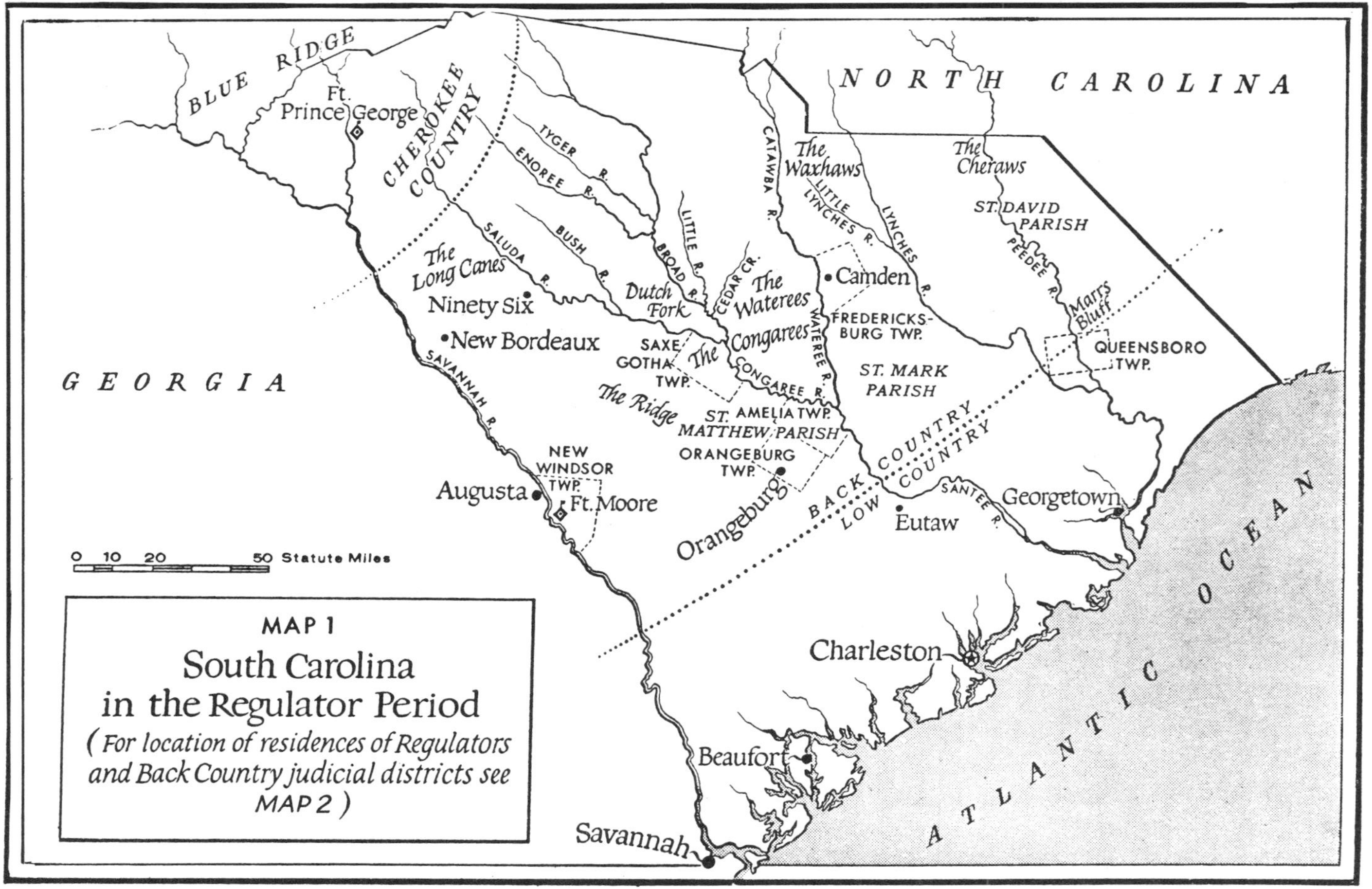

MAP 1

South Carolina in the Regulator Period

(For location of residences of Regulators and Back Country judicial districts see MAP 2)

"South Carolina in the Regulator Period."

(From Richard Maxwell Brown's *The South Carolina Regulators*, 1963)

priated by the Commons House of Assembly for an end foreign to the purposes of the provincial government and one designed to place Parliament in contempt before all the world. On December 8, the House ordered the treasurer of the province to advance the sum of £10,500 province currency out of the public treasury to a committee made up of Commons House members who would, in turn, remit £1,500 sterling to the Bill of Rights Society in Great Britain "for the support of the just and Constitutional Rights of the People of Great Britain and America"; at the same time it resolved to make provision to reimburse the treasurer for this advance.[75] Writing the following day to Robert Morris, secretary for the Society of the Supporters of the Bill of Rights (a society organized in February 1769 to pay the political expenses and debts of John Wilkes),[76] the committee of the House informed him that this branch of the South Carolina legislature was convinced of how greatly Americans must be affected "by any Attacks upon the constitutional Rights and Liberties of their fellow Subjects residing in Great Britain, and . . . that the Oppressions they and the Colonists actually suffer, proceed from the same Cause; . . . the whole collected Fury of Ministerial Vengeance. . . ." In other words, they implied that the attempt of the government of Great Britain to secure a revenue in America under the terms of the Townshend Revenue Act was a part of "the Fury of Ministerial Vengeance."[77]

That the gift to the Bill of Rights Society was planned in secrecy and sprung by surprise, and the order on the provincial treasurer designedly given an indefinite character, was stated by Lieutenant Governor William Bull in his letter of December 12 to the Earl of Hillsborough. Discussing the peculiar plan chosen by the House for appropriating the money to an end they knew he could not approve, Bull wrote:

---

[75] Commons House Journals, 38:215. For the latest and most complete study of this constitutional crisis see J. P. Greene: "Bridge to Revolution: The Wilkes Fund Controversy in South Carolina, 1769–1775," *Journal of Southern History,* XXIX, 19–52.

[76] See Chap. 7 in this volume.

[77] For this letter see *South Carolina Historical and Genealogical Magazine,* XXXI, 132–3. See also the letter by the committee to the London bankers of the same date remitting bills of exchange to the amount of £10,500 currency or £1,500 sterling to be turned over to Morris. *Ibid.,* p. 134. Who fathered the project of the gift in the Commons House in the first instance is not clear; nor is it clear who wrote the letter to Morris, at the end of which the name of Christopher Gadsden stands next to that of the Speaker of the Commons House, Peter Manigault, among the signatures of the committee members. As an extreme Son of Liberty, Gadsden doubtless played a leading part in these matters; others on the committee were John Rutledge, James Parsons, Thomas Ferguson, Benjamin Dart, and Thomas Lynch.

> "No particular use or agent is mentioned in the Journals. It is therefore probable that it is applicable to the purposes of the Supporters of the Bill of Rights in London from whose committee a solicitation for some aid was sent to this province and kept secret till the moment it was moved in Assembly. Whether this solicitation is circular or particular to this province your Lordship will soon be informed from the respective governors. . . ."

In accounting for the undercover way in which the vote was taken in the House, he added that this method was followed "that it might have its effect with more secrecy as well as expedition. . . ."[78]

The question that immediately comes to mind is: why had the South Carolina Commons House of Assembly assumed the powers over the distribution of public funds that neither the British House of Commons nor any other colonial assembly had ever attempted to exercise in the eighteenth century? Bull explained to Lord Hillsborough that the standard practice in any emergency had been an order on the provincial treasurer "concurred to by the Governor, Council, and Assembly to issue the sum wanted," with the Commons House of Assembly resolving at the time to make provision to replace the money. He then went on to say: "But, since the late unhappy discontents and the universal extension of the claims of the American Commons, their power hath risen to a great height, and lately in this province, as your Lordship may see in our Journals, the mode of an order in the Commons house to the Treasurer to advance Money has been adopted, as less liable to any Obstruction from the Governor or Council to their pursuing any favourite object."[79] Indeed, the committee of correspondence of the Commons House of Assembly, in a letter to its London agent on the subject, admitted that in Britain "Votes of Credit only follow a Royal Requisition"—that is, the inclusion of all items involving the expenditure of public money in the budget of the Chancellor of the Exchequer. The excuse offered by the Commons House for having assumed this extraordinary power was that the distance between Great Britain and America "must make the King's immediate Requisition impracticable on emergent Occasions, and if it were left to the Governor, a weak, ignorant or Corrupt one, might suffer the Public safety to be greatly endangered. . . ."[80]

It is true that before 1737 there were instances when the Com-

---

[78] See P.R.O., C.O. 5:379.

[79] *Ibid.*

[80] The committee of correspondence to Charles Garth, September 6, 1770, *South Carolina Historical and Genealogical Magazine*, XXXI, 244–6.

mons House had acted alone to order the treasurer of the province to hand over funds upon promise of reimbursement, but thereafter the practice was discontinued until 1751, when there were two instances of the Commons House acting alone. Later the practice varied, with some orders being sent up for concurrence by the Council while others were not.[81] But before 1769 no order for disbursing money was ever made with the design of indirectly attacking the government of the mother country by the method pursued in connection with the support of the Wilkes fund. It is therefore not surprising that when Lieutenant Governor Bull's letter of December 12, 1769, was received by the Secretary of State for the Colonies, he immediately submitted it as a matter of first importance to the Privy Council, which in turn passed it along to its committee and then to the Board of Trade.[82]

On February 23, 1770, the Lords Commissioners, after consulting with the Attorney General, made their report. This was concerned with the constitution of South Carolina and the limits which it placed upon the power of the Commons House of Assembly. Going back to the creation of a distinct province of South Carolina in 1719, the representation of the Board stated that, by the commission and instructions issued at that time to the Governor, a new form of constitution for the colony was introduced which provided a legislative body composed of the Governor, the Upper House of Assembly of twelve (the members of which were also to assist the Governor as a Council of State), and a "lower House of Assembly, or House of Representatives." Further, with regard to the mode of granting, raising, and issuing money, the constitution provided that, in all acts and orders for levying money, express mention should be made that such funds were granted to the King "for the Publick Uses of that Province and the support of the Government thereof," and

[81] For a list of precedents for orders on the South Carolina treasurer from the Commons House of Assembly acting alone, covering the years 1752 to 1770, extracted from the Journal of the House, see *ibid.*, XXXI, 246–53. In going over these items it may be noted that not one of them relates to other than the routine business of the province having no political overtones. The first item on the list presented by the committee of the House to the London agent is dated May 13, 1752, and is an order on the treasurer to pay £250 currency to send certain Indians to Albany; the last order given, dated February 2, 1770, was for paying the commissioners for encouraging the silk industry in the colony the sum of £1,000 currency toward a filature for winding silk.

[82] When the Earl of Hillsborough appeared at the Board of Trade on February 19, 1770, he referred to "a late very extraordinary Order of the Commons House of Assembly" relative to the remittance to Great Britain of £10,500 South Carolina currency "for the support of the Constitution of Great Britain and America" (Board of Trade *Journal, 1768–1775,* p. 171).

that "no publick Money whatever should be issued or disposed of otherwise than by Warrant under the Hand of the Governor, by and with the advice and Consent of the Council." The representation went on to state that from the time the constitution went into effect in 1721 until 1731, its provisions were observed and money was only granted by the "General Assembly, that is to say, by all three Branches of the Legislature"; that about the year 1732, however, the method of granting money was altered so that instead of its being based upon estimates of the cost of services for the ensuing year, these services were performed on credit and at the end of the year an act was passed to cover the public debts thus incurred. Yet for years after this change, the evidence in the journal of the Commons House showed that all orders on the treasurer were concurred in by the Governor, Council, and Commons House of Assembly, and that the practice of one branch of the legislature acting alone had "obtained only of late years," which in any case represented a violation of the constitution of the province. For under the constitution the Commons House could not "without the Concurrence of the Governor and Council legally direct the Treasurer of the Colony to issue out . . . any Sums of Money. . . ." This report of the Board of Trade was approved by the King in Council on April 5, 1770.[83]

Upon the basis of the above decision an additional instruction was issued to Governor Montagu by the King in Council under date of April 14, 1770. In it reference was made to the remission of money to Great Britain "for the support of the just and constitutional rights and liberties of the people of Great Britain and America," and the necessity of "putting a stop to such dangerous and unwarrantable practices and for guarding for the future against such unconstitutional application" of funds granted by the people of South Carolina for the public uses of the province and for the support of government. Montagu was therefore commanded, on pain of being removed from his government, not to give his assent to any bill passed by the lower house whereby any sum of money should be appropriated by the Commons House under the following terms:

> ". . . for services or purposes not immediately arising within or incident to our said province of South Carolina, unless upon special requisition from us . . . , nor to any bill or bills for granting any sum of money . . . , in which . . . it shall not be provided in express words that the money so to be granted, . . . shall not be issued or applied to any other services than those to which it is by the said bill appro-

[83] *Acts of the Privy Council, Col. Ser., 1766–1783,* pp. 229–35; Board of Trade *Journal, 1768–1775,* p. 172.

priated, unless by act . . . of the general assembly of our said province; and it is our further will and pleasure . . . not to give your assent to any bill . . . passed by our said lower house of assembly, . . . unless there be a clause . . . in the said bill . . . providing that the said money so to be granted shall remain in the treasury subject to such appropriation . . . by act . . . of the general assembly and not otherwise; and it is our further will and pleasure that . . . every bill and bills so to be passed by you . . . for raising and granting public moneys a clause or clauses be inserted therein subjecting the public treasurer . . . in case he . . . shall issue or pay any such money otherwise than by express order contained in some act or ordinance of the general assembly, to a penalty in treble the sum so issued contrary thereto, and declaring him . . . *ipso facto* incapable of holding the said office of treasurer or any other office civil or military within our said province. . . ."

The instruction ended with the request that its contents be communicated by the Governor to the Council and lower House of Assembly.[84]

Here now were clearly stated the constitutional limits within which the government of South Carolina was to operate. For the constitutions of all royal colonies were determined by royal commissions held by the Governors, royal instructions sent to the Governors, those fundamental acts passed by the assemblies that were approved by the King in Council, and finally by decisions delivered by the Privy Council, acting in its judicial capacity, on appeals made to it from a colony.

Turning now to observe developments in South Carolina concerning the appropriation of money by the Commons House of Assembly acting alone, we find that this body, when framing the annual tax bill in the spring of 1770, introduced an item covering the sum voted the preceding year for Treasurer Jacob Motte to turn over to the committee for transmittal to England. The Council, when this tax bill was submitted to it, returned the bill to the Commons House on April 5, 1770, declaring that they did not wish to weaken the harmony which existed between the two houses, but reminding the Commons of their mutual legislative duty to work in "happy Combination . . . for the public good," keeping in mind that

"in attending to one principle of policy, we do not at the same time violate another. . . . Fully sensible that we live under a kind and

[84] For this instruction see South Carolina Public Records, 32:236–40; for a printed copy see *Royal Instructions to British Colonial Governors, 1670–1776* (ed. L. W. Labaree, 2 vols., New York and London, 1935), I, 208–9.

gracious prince, and are blessed with a Constitution, which has perhaps, arrived at as great a state of perfection as human wisdom can extend to. We cannot persuade ourselves, that a grant of such a sum, is in any sense honourable, fit, or decent, nor fit or honourable, as we conceive your Jurisdiction to Grant is local and merely for Provincial purposes, and not Decent, as the Grant by the Tax Bill . . . is especially declared to be to His Majesty. . . ."[85]

Two days after he received the additional royal instruction of April 14, Lieutenant Governor Bull duly laid the document before the Commons House of Assembly, which promptly referred it to a committee. On the 29th of August this committee reported a series of resolutions. These resolves, adopted therewith, denied that the King could place any restrictions on the exclusive right of the House to grant money or that the action of the House on December 8 was unconstitutional. They refused to acknowledge the clauses of the instruction relating to restrictions to be placed upon the provincial treasurer. Further, while not repudiating the power of the King to regulate the affairs of the colony, they in essence denied the authority of the King in Council to accept and act on the advice of a minister with respect to the disposition of South Carolina public money as the basis for framing an instruction. The last of the resolutions read:

"That it is the opinion of this Committee that a Minister's dictating how a Money Bill shall be framed is an Infringement of the Privileges of this House, to whom alone it belongs to Originate and prepare the same for the concurrence and assent of the Governor and Council without any alteration or amendment whatsoever."[86]

This outright denial of the authority of the King in Council and of his ministers to interfere in the action on monetary matters taken by the Commons House of Assembly—even when providing financial support to one under a sentence of outlawry (an action doubtless held to be so irresponsible in nature that no other colonial assembly saw fit to emulate it)—was inconsistent with the very principle that the popular leaders in the several colonies were beginning to formulate. This principle, fast taking shape as a doctrine, held that while Parliament had no right to interfere in any colonial matters except those having to do with trade and navigation, the colonies were, nevertheless, subject to the King and obedient to the royal authority. Indeed, what the House of Assembly virtually said to the King's

[85] Commons House Journals, 38:387–8.
[86] See Commons House Journals, 38:403–5 and 430–3.

minister was: that it had the right, if its members saw fit, to appropriate money for any cause, and that it alone could determine what was constitutional and what was not. This was revolutionary language.[87]

That the popularly elected chamber of the General Assembly of South Carolina should have taken the steps it did, may well cause surprise and puzzlement. No colony had had less cause to feel that the authority of the mother country had been used to thwart its development, no colony was more prosperous in 1769, no colony on the mainland of North America fitted in more harmoniously or more to its own advantage with the British trade and navigation system. Finally, no colony had consistently received greater support financially and militarily in its relations with powerful, potentially dangerous Indian tribes living near its western settlements. However, having decided to repudiate the royal instruction, the Commons House held to its position with consistent firmness.[88] Upon the death of Treasurer Motte late in the summer of 1770, it framed a bill for filling the vacancy so created. The Council amended the bill so as to embody the principles embraced in the royal instruction of April 14; but these amendments were eliminated by the Commons. The result was that the Council on September 7 refused to approve the bill;[89] nor would it accept a general tax bill that provided among other things for a reimbursement of the treasurer for the £10,500 currency advanced to aid John Wilkes. So the matter stood on September 8 when the General Assembly was prorogued until the new year.[90]

When the Assembly met on January 16, 1771, Lieutenant Gov-

---

[87] Henry Laurens, writing from London on November 28, 1771, to William Williamson of Charleston, took the following position respecting the unrestrained power in money matters claimed by the Commons House: "I do not maintain the Propriety of the [Wilkes] Gift, . . . but I insist on the Right of giving—and if the Representatives of the Inhabitants of South Carolina, without instructions from their Constituents had given Money to levy Arms against the King—such an Act would not work the Loss of the Constitutional Rights of the People nor authorize the Ministry to advise his Majesty to give such Instructions . . . " (Laurens Letter Book).

[88] Writing to the London agent on September 6, 1770, the committee of correspondence declared: "The House look upon their Right to grant the Money of their Constituents to the Crown, to stand upon the same ground as that of the House of Commons . . ." (*South Carolina Historical and Genealogical Magazine,* XXXI, 245). Yet, it should be borne in mind that even the House of Commons could not grant money by its sole authority. Its members were restrained by the Crown to limiting their appropriations to stated ends specifically requested by the Crown.

[89] It may be noted that the assistant treasurer, Henry Peronneau, temporarily took over the duties of the treasurer's office until he and Benjamin Dart were elected joint treasurers on February 23, 1771; see Commons House Journals, 38:494.

[90] Commons House Journals, 38:453-8; see also W. R. Smith: *op. cit.,* pp. 371–5.

ernor Bull addressed the members. This wise, humane man announced that he had ordered the acting treasurer to lay before them the public accounts in order that these could be speedily settled; at the same time he recommended that they pay due attention to the King's recent additional instruction and thus facilitate obtaining his assent to a bill to provide the treasury funds. This instruction was designed "to set a guard on your Provincial Treasure," he pointed out, and imposed no restraint on the granting of money for the service of the province, except in so far as it prevented the Governor, the Council, or the Commons House from acting independently of each other or from diverting public money to uses other than those for which it was granted. Concluding his address, Bull stated: "I think it my duty to assure you, that I shall pay a most strict obedience to the Royal Instruction, in exercising my negation to every money-bill, not agreeable thereto, which may be presented to my assent."

On January 23 the Commons House returned its answer. The message stressed the "outrageous behaviour" of the Council in refusing to pass tax bills framed in the usual manner; thus any delay in paying the public debts could not be imputed to the Assembly. As to the additional instruction, it was branded as being as unnecessary as it was unconstitutional and founded on misinformation. Indeed, the message went on to say, some instructions sent to Governors were "diametrically opposite to reason, law, and the constitutions of the colonies" which received them. Then, replying to Bull's declaration that he would pay strict obedience to the instructions that bound him, the House message informed the Lieutenant Governor that he could not "be more devoted to the will of the Ministers, than this House is, to their duty to their most gracious Sovereign, and to the interest, rights and privileges of their constituents," but the framing of money bills was held to be an essential right of the House, which "would not suffer the interposition of any person or power whatsoever in that matter without basely betraying the trust reposed in them by the people, and consequently injuring the interest of his Majesty. . . ."[91]

Such was the stand taken early in 1771 by the South Carolina Commons House of Assembly over the binding power of an instruction that had been deliberately approved by the King in Council before it was sent. On January 31, an attempt was made by the Commons House to prove its unlimited power to dispose of public funds by passing a bill to place in the Lieutenant Governor's hands

[91] Commons House Journals, 38:464–5.

a trifling fund for the purpose of providing temporary aid to certain newly arrived immigrants. Bull refused to honour the grant since it was not the united act of the General Assembly.[92] The following month the House sought to make a distinction between surpluses in the treasury not granted specifically to the King's use and funds that had been so specified. They claimed the sole right of disposing of the former while agreeing that the latter were to be paid out only by vote of the General Assembly. This, it was claimed, was the true intent of the additional instruction and as such was accepted as binding.[93] But the Lieutenant Governor could not be swayed from the position he had taken.

Meanwhile in support of the position of the Commons House, London agent Garth had on November 22, 1770, presented a petition to the King for the withdrawal of the additional instruction, resting his case especially on past practices in granting public money.[94] But when writing to the committee of correspondence on December 17, 1770, he was forced to advise them that before the instruction had been prepared, the King in Council had taken great pains "to be fully apprised and informed of the Power [of the Commons House of Assembly], its Rise, and Progress," and therefore he held out little "hope of . . . a withdrawing of the said Instruction."[95] Garth was right in his apprehensions. His petition was referred to the Board of Trade and, although he was permitted to defend it in person, the Board nevertheless opposed the petition in a representation framed on March 27, 1771, which was subsequently accepted by the Privy Council.[96]

Meanwhile the struggle continued between the Commons House of Assembly and the Council.[97] In the fall of 1771 a tax bill sub-

---

[92] *Ibid.*, 38:476.

[93] *Ibid.*, 38:497–9; W. R. Smith (*op. cit.*, pp. 377–9) stresses the distinction between the broad interpretation of the provincial constitution held by the Commons House and the narrow interpretation maintained by the ministers of the Crown.

[94] For the petition see *South Carolina Historical and Genealogical Magazine*, XXXIII, 120–3; it may be noted that in the copy of C.O. 5:380 in the Public Record Office the place and date given is "Picadilly, Novr 29, 1770."

[95] *South Carolina Historical and Genealogical Magazine*, XXXIII, 123–4.

[96] Board of Trade *Journal, 1768–1775*, pp. 233, 239, 240, and *Acts of the Privy Council, Col. Ser., 1766–1783*, p. 235. For the representation of the Board of Trade dated March 27, 1771, and enclosed in Garth's letter to the South Carolina committee of correspondence signed April 5, 1771, see *South Carolina Historical and Genealogical Magazine*, XXXIII, 130–1.

[97] Governor Montagu, writing to the Earl of Hillsborough on September 26, 1771, made the following comment respecting the donation to the Wilkes fund: "In regard to the Fifteen Hundred Pounds which were sent to England in 1769 by a particular order of the House of Assembly only, there are scarcely above Two Members in the House but what in Private condemn the Measure. Yet from a certain kind of Pride

mitted by the Commons House to the Council included an item of £28,123.14.8 as reimbursement to the estate of the late treasurer for sums advanced on specific orders from the House; among these amounts appeared the sum of £10,500 disguised under the general term "for other services." When this bill was rejected by the Council, on the ground that it did not conform to the terms of the additional instruction, the House replied that it would never be bound by any instruction that called into question its right freely to frame money bills. Acting on this position, the House on October 2 ordered the joint treasurers, Henry Peronneau and Benjamin Dart, to put into the hands of the commissioners some £3,000 currency to be used for encouraging the production of silk. When the treasurers refused to do so, because of the instruction, they were arrested and placed in the "Publick Jail." In the face of this situation, Governor Montagu —who meanwhile had returned to South Carolina—immediately dissolved the House.[98]

That feelings in general were running high in South Carolina on the subject of the rights of the Commons House, is evident from the actions of the Assembly. Nor were specific individuals hesitant about expressing their opinions on the importance of the issue at stake. For example, Henry Laurens—who, although a member of the Commons House, was in England at the time—wrote to a friend in South Carolina on November 28, 1771:

> "I wish from the Center of my Heart for a continued Opposition [to the additional instruction]—because I am sure that our Perseverance will command Success. I would not myself, nor would I wish that others should perservere in obstinately maintaining an unconstitutional or wrong measure, but the Subject now before us is of the first Importance in which Posterity is more concern'd than we are and the Point which we contend for is not unconstitutional[;] it is a point which we must gain, or we must never hereafter preface our Tax Bills with 'freely and voluntarily Give and Grant.'"

Hoping the House would keep it in mind, Laurens then made a distinction "between the Propriety of a Gift hastily made, for good

find it very difficult to recede from the Orders they have so Publicly made" (see P.R.O., C.O. 5:394). Hillsborough's reply to this letter expressed the hope that not more than the same number would oppose the instructions, "the sole object of which is to restore to the Constitution of the Colony those barriers against like Attempts for the future" which had been set up at an earlier period. See Hillsborough to Montagu, December 4, 1771, *ibid.*

[98] See Montagu to Hillsborough, November 10, 1771, *ibid.*, and Commons House Journals, 38:377–8 and 574–84.

Purposes in the View of the Givers—which will admit much to be said on both Sides—and the *Right* of the people to give and grant voluntarily in mode and in Quantity free from the Fetters of Ministerial Instructions, restrictive or obligatory—which it is indubitable."[99]

But Laurens was wrong in his estimate that perseverance in prolonging the issue would command success. For, when the news of the conduct of the Commons House reached the government in London, Hillsborough was directed to express the displeasure of the King and his ministers in the following terms: "The manner in which the Assembly has attempted to support their unwarrantable claim to dispose of and issue public Money without the consent and concurrence of the other two Branches of the Legislature, after being apprized of the King's instruction . . . is such a mark of disrespect to the Crown, and so unconstitutional a proceeding as could not fail of being very displeasing to the King." This lack of respect for the King on the part of the Commons House, the Secretary for the Colonies continued, was also evident in its attitude toward providing a suitable home for the chief representative of the Crown in the colony. As was well known, the Governors of Virginia and North Carolina enjoyed handsome residences by 1770, yet highly prosperous South Carolina, Hillsborough complained, by refusal of the Commons House to provide similar amenities for its Governor, exposed him "to the disgraceful situation of either taking up his Lodging at a Public Tavern, or in a fort, at a distance from the Capital, and very ill fitted for his reception."[100]

After the elections of February 1772 the new House met on April 2. Again Montagu appeared before the Assembly simply to warn the members that he would be required to dissolve the House should it persist in the course previously followed. This he did on the 10th when the Commons refused to accept such restrictions.[101] The attitude of the Commons House was expressed in the following statement embodied in the letter of the committee of correspondence to Charles Garth signed that same day:

---

[99] Laurens Letter Book. Writing to his brother James on December 12 of that same year, Laurens expressed his feelings even more frankly. "If the House of Assembly," he declared, "ever submit to insert such Clauses [as required by the royal instruction], they will sell their Birth Right and dearest Privilege of their Constituents, and will incur the Hatred and Detestation of the present Age, and their name will be branded in all future Ages with the infamous Character of Betrayers of the Trust reposed in them by the People." At the same time he admitted that the "Gift was an unlucky Act—those who prompted it I am sure must be sorry for it . . ." (*ibid.*).

[100] See Hillsborough to Montagu, January 11, 1772, P.R.O., C.O. 5:394.

[101] South Carolina Public Records, 33:140, 142.

> ". . . We can never be persuaded to think any House that can be convened in this province, will ever submit to so unconstitutional a remedy as that insisted on by the Instruction, and how an Opposition to a proposal of such extraordinary and pernicious tendency can be deemed 'an Encroachment upon His Majesty's just Prerogative' We are not only amased to think, but totally at a loss to imagine."[102]

When the new elections were held in the fall of 1772, the Governor decided to have the General Assembly meet in Beaufort at the spacious Port Royal harbour some distance south of Charleston, doubtless in the hope that most of the members from that city, to save their private affairs, would be obliged to be absent while the members living in the southern part of the province—willing to conform to the King's instructions, and anxious to have the capital in Beaufort—would be there in force and thus a tax bill could be passed in harmony with the additional instruction.[103] However, when the House assembled on October 8, the Charleston members were on hand in force and took control by once again electing as speaker a strong defender of the great power claimed by the House, Peter Manigault. On the 10th, after Manigault had taken office, Montagu addressed the Commons House. He stressed his obligation "to preserve the Laws of this Province from Violation." In this connection he pointed out that "as there is not any Instance of a Lawful House of Commons [of Great Britain] having ever appropriated and caused Money to be issued for Publick Services, of their Sole Authority, and against the Consent of the other Branches of the Legislature [that is, the House of Lords and the King], or even having, at any Time, claimed such a Power; so upon Principles of our Constitution, of Law and of Reason, it cannot be

[102] *South Carolina Historical and Genealogical Magazine*, XXXIII, 136.

[103] Writing to the Earl of Hillsborough on July 27, 1772, Governor Montagu elaborated as follows on his proposal to summon the Assembly to meet at Beaufort, Port Royal: "I am now, my Lord, in daily expectations of receiving directions from you in regard to calling a new Assembly. I have not been able to procure a House in Town, neither do the Gentlemen of the Province at all interest themselves in procuring of one. I have been advised by some of the Gentlemen of His Majesty's Council, to call the Assembly at Port Royal, as the Gentlemen of Charles Town would then become more sensible of the great inconveniences arising from the want of a Governor's House at or near the Metropolis. This is a measure I shall by no means hastily adopt, as I have always made it my study to remove every obstacle to Publick Business and to avoid whatever might unnecessarily tend to increase the too general prejudice against His Majesty's Officers in this Province, but unless a House in Charles Town is provided for me, I shall of necessity be compelled to follow the above advice and I think, My Lord, I foresee a probability of many advantages arising to the Publick from it, as the principal promoters of the opposition reside in or near Charles Town, whose Private Interests will not allow their being long absent from it" (C.O. 5:394).

allowed that any Commons House of Assembly of this Province can or ought to have any such Power." For the House to claim such a right, he maintained, could destroy and overturn "every Fundamental Principle of that Constitution of Government which is the envy of admiring Nations."[104] At the end of his speech he prorogued the General Assembly to October 22 to meet at the usual place in Charleston.[105]

Far from giving up its stand that the King in Council was usurping power over money matters in violation of the constitution of South Carolina, the leaders of the Commons House of Assembly now turned upon the Governor. A committee on grievances, appointed on October 22, reported on the 29th. Among its recommendations was one stating that an effort should be made to remove Lord Montagu. This resulted in a series of resolutions protesting his conduct in causing the General Assembly to meet at Beaufort, and in delaying his acceptance of the Speaker.[106] Suspecting that some move was to be made against him, the Governor called for the journal of the House and, when his suspicions had been confirmed, demanded the immediate attendance of the mem-

---

[104] *South-Carolina Gazette,* October 15, 1772. Later Montagu wrote to Dartmouth, November 4, 1772, that "to allow Houses of Assembly to proceed, as it were daily, in altering the usage of Parliament [is] thereby taking the power of the King in the most alarming manner and changing the very Nature of the Constitution" (South Carolina Public Records, 33:188–92).

[105] Montagu's letter to Lord Hillsborough (apparently word had not yet reached the Governor of Dartmouth's appointment in August as successor to Hillsborough) of September 24, 1772, showed his uneasiness over the indication of the Secretary for the Colonies that the King disapproved of some of the measures the Governor had adopted in dealing with the leaders of the opposition to the royal instruction. He explained that the opposition had already entered into resolutions (1) never to pass a tax bill without the £10,500 (£1,500 sterling) being included in it, (2) never to pass a bill which recognized the binding power of the additional instruction, and (3) never on any account to approve "any Declaratory Act." In view of this determination, the Governor went into additional detail regarding his reasons for calling the Assembly at Beaufort and holding it there if need be by frequent adjournments. However, in light of the views expressed by the Secretary for the Colonies, Montagu indicated that he would give up the "system" he had in mind for getting a tax bill and would prorogue the Assembly to meet in Charleston, well realizing "I must encounter anger for having summoned the Assembly in a different place . . ." (P.R.O., C.O. 5:394). See also Montagu to Hillsborough, October 20, 1772, in which he indicated "that in consequence of the conciliating measures recommended in your Letter . . . I prorogued them in my Speech to meet at Charles Town the 22[d] instant" (*ibid.*). That the Governor continued to feel that his own system was the best is shown by his letter to the new Secretary for the Colonies, of January 4, 1773, in which he said: "I am sorry the measure I adopted of calling the Assembly to Port Royal does not meet with your approbation, tho' I must confess I still remain of the same opinion that I was of at that time in regard to the utility of it" (*ibid.*).

[106] Commons House Journals, 39, Part I:1–2 and 20–1; see also the committee of correspondence to Charles Garth, March 27, 1773, enclosing their letter of November 20, 1772, *South Carolina Historical and Genealogical Magazine,* XXXIII, 273–80.

bers in the Council chamber. However, before appearing they hurriedly passed the resolutions recommended in the committee's report. The House was then immediately prorogued until November 9. By this time the exasperated Montagu declared his desire to relieve "the long distressed situation of our public affairs" and added: "I warned you against the danger of innovating against the constitution of your country," but instead of "annihilating the former innovations upon the constitution, the Commons House of Assembly have proceeded to make other innovations"—those of withholding the journal from the Governor's inspection by the action of its Speaker, Rawlins Lowndes, until shortly before the House met and of continuing to carry on business after they had been summoned to appear before His Excellency without delay.[107] The Governor therefore on November 10 pronounced the dissolution of the Assembly.[108]

Again, new elections were held. The General Assembly met early in 1773 and the Commons House proceeded to re-elect Lowndes as Speaker, despite the obstructionist tactics he had used in October to prevent the Governor from having access to the journal and his conduct in the Council chamber at the time of the dissolution, which had given offence to the Council and the Governor. Montagu therefore disapproved of the election and called upon the House to choose another. This the members refused to do, asserting their right to choose their own Speaker without interference from the Crown. In view of this attitude, Montagu again prorogued, and soon after dissolved the Assembly, after issuing writs of election for a meeting to be held on February 23, 1773.[109] In reporting on the situation to the Earl of Dartmouth, the Governor pointed out that as a result of his attempts to perform his duty in line with his instructions, both his fortune and his health were depleted; therefore, following his physician's advice, he proposed to return to England the following month, availing himself of what he con-

[107] Commons House Journals, 39, Part I:27–8; see also Montagu to the Secretary of State for the Colonies, November 4, 1772, P.R.O., C.O. 5:394. It should be pointed out that the committee of correspondence, writing to Garth in London on November 20, presented a different version. See *South Carolina Historical and Genealogical Magazine*, XXXIII, 276–7.

[108] Commons House Journals, 39, Part I:29. Upon hearing of this situation the new Secretary of State for the Colonies, Lord Dartmouth, who was appointed upon the resignation of the Earl of Hillsborough, wrote to Lord Montagu that the conduct of the Commons House was both "unprecedented and unwarrantable" and was "highly disrespectful . . . of the King's representations," but did not choose to go further into the matter except to say that the whole proceedings would come before the Privy Council. See Dartmouth to Montagu, January 6, 1773, C.O. 5:395.

[109] Commons House Journals, 39, Part II:1.

sidered to be a special leave of absence granted by the King.[110] When the new Assembly members gathered in February, the House was prorogued to March 8, but did not organize until the 11th, the day after the Governor had sailed for England.

Upon his arrival in London early in April, Lord Montagu was made aware that the ministers were much displeased with his sudden unauthorized appearance. As a result, disheartened and sick, he resigned his post.[111] In his place Lord William Campbell, brother of the Duke of Argyle, was selected.[112] At the time of his appointment he was Governor of Nova Scotia. Although Lord William Campbell's commission was presented to the Privy Council for approval on June 10, 1773, it was not until August 11 that it received the Privy Seal, and it was not until June 17 that the new Governor appeared in South Carolina to be sworn into office.[113] Meanwhile, Lieutenant Governor Bull once again undertook the administration of the colony and as a gesture of good will permitted Lowndes to assume the office of Speaker.

Nevertheless, if the leaders of the opposition to the Governor were under the impression that the departure of Lord Montagu would clear the way for passing a tax bill in accordance with their desires, they were soon to be disabused; for the Council still felt bound by the royal instruction. Thus, when the 1769–70 tax bill was sent up for approval with the £10,500 for the Wilkes fund included, the Council rejected it. Thereupon Lieutenant Governor Bull granted the Commons House its requested leave to adjourn to the beginning of July.[114] Dartmouth wrote to Bull on June 10, approving his conduct and that of the Council in face of "the unwarrantable claim of the House of Representatives respecting the issue of public revenue." He also expressed the hope that the very disagreeable situation would soon be accommodated.[115] But this hope was not destined to be gratified. When the time came for the

[110] Montagu to Dartmouth, January 21, 1773, C.O. 5:395.

[111] On May 1, 1773, Montagu wrote from Bath, England, to B. Elliott, Esq.: "You must certainly know by this time that I am no longer your Governor; upon my arrival here, I understand the Ministers were displeased with my coming over without leave, as soon therefore [as possible] . . . I went up to London and resign'd my Government" (*South Carolina Historical and Genealogical Magazine,* XXXIII, 261).

[112] Board of Trade *Journal, 1768–1775,* p. 361.

[113] For the commission as submitted on June 10 and as dated July 8, 1773, see P.R.O., C.O. 5:404, pp. 464–95, and C.O. 5:408, pp. 100–18; for his instructions submitted June 20 and as dated August 5, 1774, see C.O. 5:405, pp. 7–99, and C.O. 5:206, No. 1.

[114] Bull to Dartmouth, March 30, 1773, C.O. 5:395; Commons House Journals, 39, Part II:4–6.

[115] C.O. 5:395.

General Assembly to meet in July, so few were present and so firm seemed to be the disposition not to do business under the circumstances that it was prorogued until August 9.[116] At that time a serious breach in the Council took place. Two of the members, John Drayton and his son, William Henry Drayton, opposed postponing consideration of the two money bills before it. Their opposition became news when a copy of their protest appeared in Thomas Powell's *South-Carolina Gazette* on August 30. The majority of the Council ordered Powell's arrest and commitment in the city gaol for breach of privilege. But the Speaker of the Commons House, Rawlins Lowndes, and another member, George Gabriel Powell, both acting as justices of the peace, gave the printer his freedom upon the presentation of a writ of *habeas corpus*.[117] This event reopened the whole question of whether the Council was an upper house of the Assembly.[118] As Lieutenant Governor Bull stated in his letter of September 18 to Lord Dartmouth, "a spirit of degrading the Council in various ways has prevailed more or less in the Assembly for 28 years." In 1745, he pointed out, an attempt had been made by the Commons House to ignore the Council as a lawmaking body by seeking, through two members acting in a private capacity, to secure from the incumbent Governor an opinion as to whether he would ratify a bill sent from the Commons House without previously submitting it to the Council as usual for its concurrence. Since such bypassing of the Council would surely have brought the King's heavy displeasure, the Governor, who was then Gabriel Johnston, had stated that he would not receive such a bill. Bull further asserted that by reason of the powers invested in it by royal commissions and instructions, the Council had "a share in Legislature, which has been confirmed by an usage of 54 years." Undeterred by these precedents, the Commons House now sought to undermine the position of the Council as part of the General Assembly by demanding the suspension of all Council members guilty

[116] Bull to Dartmouth, July 24, 1773, C.O. 5:395.

[117] Bull to Dartmouth, September 18, 1773, C.O. 5:395.

[118] Governor James Wright of Georgia saw the claim of the South Carolina Commons House of Assembly as bearing profoundly on the whole system of British colonial government. Writing to the Earl of Dartmouth on October 30, 1773, he declared that he could not keep silent on the subject of the action of the Assembly of South Carolina in denying the right of the Council to sit as an upper house, as the decision over that issue would affect not only Georgia but other colonies as well. For "if that very useful and necessary check of the Middle Branch of Power is lost . . . the consequences may prove of a very serious nature, Probably Worse than may be apprehended at the first View . . ." (Wright to Dartmouth, October 30, 1773, Transcripts of papers relating to Georgia from the British Public Record Office, 38, Part I:98–9, Georgia Archives).

of ordering the commitment of the printer; but this the Lieutenant Governor refused to do.[119] Further, an effort was made to bring suit against the Council President for having, in the name of the Council, ordered the commitment of the printer, but the court of common pleas refused to do so.[120] Both the Council and the Commons House, the latter through its London agent, Garth, now turned to the Privy Council for support of their positions.[121]

Meanwhile Lieutenant Governor Bull sought to ease the tension that had developed between the Commons House of Assembly and the Council. Upon the death of Justice John Murray, of the court of common pleas, Bull persuaded the Council to fill the vacancy by appointing his nephew, William Henry Drayton, a member of the Council known to be in opposition to its policy and therefore in opposition to the Crown.[122] Yet this did little or nothing to heal the breach between the two bodies, in view of the determination of the Commons House to hold firmly to "the two grand Points":

---

[119] Commons House Journals, 39, Part II:77–88. Bull to Dartmouth, September 18, 1773, C.O. 5:395; with this letter is enclosed among other documents a long statement by the President of the Council of South Carolina, Sir Egerton Leigh, addressed to the King, stressing the unconstitutional conduct of the Commons House in ignoring the prerogative powers of the Crown.

[120] Bull to Dartmouth, October 30, 1773, C.O. 5:395 which also includes Leigh's letter of October 6 to Bull. See also South Carolina Public Records, 33:325–33, for the statement of the judges that the Council was an upper house of the Assembly and as such had the right to commit for contempt. It should be noted that, under the Circuit Court Act of 1769, the judges were the panel sent out from England.

[121] See Garth to the Privy Council, December 15, 1773, Bull to Dartmouth, December 24, 1773, and Dartmouth to Bull, January 8, 1774, C.O. 5:395 and 396.

[122] Bull to Dartmouth, February 11, 1774, C.O. 5:396. The appointment of Drayton —a temporary one for which he volunteered until a placeman could be sent from England to fill the judgeship, after other colonials with legal training refused to give up their lucrative practices to fill the vacancy in the interim—resulted in confirming him as a bitter opponent of the British administration of colonial affairs. His experiences in the post, one for which he had applied unsuccessfully in 1771, gave him the opportunity to observe the non-native judges and convinced him that these placemen were inadequate both professionally and in concern for the welfare of the colony. He took pains to discourse upon this grievance in his pamphlet *A Letter from 'Freeman' of South Carolina to the Deputies of North America, Assembled in the High Court of Congress at Philadelphia* (Charleston, 1774)—a lengthy statement of American grievances which included "The American Claim of Rights." As a result of this publication he was relieved of his assistant-judgeship and later dismissed from the Council. For Drayton's account of these events see his *Memoirs of the American Revolution . . . to the year 1776 . . . as Relating to the State of South-Carolina* (written by Drayton during the years 1773–6 and published by his son John, 2 vols., Charleston, 1821), I, 149–53 and 157–61. For Drayton's statement of American grievances and other documents concerning his suspension from the Council see R. W. Gibbes: *Documentary History of the American Revolution . . . 1764–1776* (New York, 1855), pp. 11–82. For writings on Drayton see W. M. Dabney: "Drayton and Laurens in the Continental Congress," *South Carolina Historical Magazine*, LX, 74–82, and especially W. M. Dabney and Marion Dargan: *William Henry Drayton & the American Revolution* (Albuquerque, 1962), pp. 53–64.

the payment of the £1,500 sterling advanced by the late provincial treasurer on its orders, and the decision not to recognize the binding power of the royal additional instruction.[123]

When Bull reported this continued defiance of the Crown by the Commons House of Assembly to the Secretary of the Colonies, Dartmouth replied: "The King's Governor never must consent to any Act by which the money sent over by the Assembly to the Society of the Bill of Rights shall be replaced in the Treasurer's Hands out of any Revenue granted to the Crown nor to any other Act for replacing in his Hands any Public Money whatever issued by the Authority of the Lower House of Assembly alone."[124] Nevertheless, the Commons House—faced with the Council's rejection of a bill to provide for the defence of the frontier by calling for an enlistment of additional companies of rangers—now, in the words of the Lieutenant Governor, "fell upon an expedient to relieve the pressing wants and distresses of many of the Public Creditors by ordering their Clerk to issue Certificates of sums equal to the several demands of the Creditors, certifying that such Sum was due and should be provided for in the next Tax Bill that should pass."[125] In view of the fact that all agreed that when the certificates were issued they would receive them in lieu of money, the bills circulated freely within the province, especially as, in order to guard against counterfeiting, five members of the House signed every certificate. At the same time there was full realization that the certificate was imperfect and its redemption, precarious, so that, according to report, "the People shift it from hand to hand almost like a hot iron."[126] In line with the general acceptance of the certificates, the attorney general and the President of the Council as well as other officers of the government went along with the expedient, but the Lieutenant Governor refused to follow their example.

[123] Bull to Dartmouth, March 10, 1774, C.O. 5:396.

[124] Dartmouth to Bull, May 4, 1774, *ibid.*

[125] Bull to Dartmouth, May 3, 1774, *ibid.*, Commons House Journals, 39, Part II:162–4.

[126] Bull to Dartmouth, May 3, 1774, C.O. 5:396. It may be pointed out that the so-called "General Duty Law" provided, among other things, for the support of the clergy and the judges. The Commons House was determined not to continue or revive this law before the passing of a tax bill. However, by means of issuing the certificates to these groups their immediate needs were met. For the problem of the passing of the General Duty Act see Bull to Dartmouth, July 24, 1773, C.O. 5:395. In this connection it may be noted that the members of the Commons House of Assembly were not influenced to provide the certificates by considerations of their own personal benefit. As Lieutenant Governor Bull wrote to Hillsborough on November 30, 1770: "Members of Assembly disdain taking any pay for their attendance, tho the members of North Carolina and Virginia [Assemblies] receive eight or nine shillings sterling a day" (C.O. 5:394).

His position, simply stated, was: "I view this matter as dangerous to the Public."[127] By this device it was possible to reimburse the estate of the late treasurer with certificates covering the amount that Motte had advanced for the Wilkes fund on order of the Commons House. Nevertheless, the internecine conflict in South Carolina continued.

The fundamental constitutional issue over the right of the Commons House to assume the power to act alone in making appropriations of money for whatever object it saw fit was never settled before the outbreak of the War for American Independence. After 1769 no tax bill was passed in the colony and after 1771 no legislation was enacted at all. The emergency measures just described were accomplished by resolutions of the House. To the government of Great Britain the claim of the Commons House to the authority to act unilaterally in issuing money from the treasury was unconstitutional and an attempt to arrogate powers that had never been granted to one branch of the legislature in any colony. Although—at Garth's insistence, and at the request of Lord William Campbell, successor to Montagu—the authorities in London were taking steps to modify the offensive instruction to the Governor so as to permit the assemblymen to frame their money bills as they saw fit, the new Governor's commission and instructions were so worded that he was prohibited from passing any bill that implied recognition of the Commons' power to order money from the treasury without executive approval,[128] or from approving the repayment of the Wilkes fund money.

To deny the binding power of the Governor's commission and instructions was, in essence, to deny that the King could any longer determine the nature of the government or constitution of South Carolina. Such a denial was revolutionary in nature.[129] Moreover, the general colonial trend in the 1770's was revolutionary. Therefore, by the end of 1773, the internal problem raised in South Carolina over the powers vested in the Commons House of Assembly, important as it was, disappeared into the background as more serious issues arose to threaten the relations of the mother country with the thirteen older North American colonies. These issues will be considered in the next volume of this series.

---

[127] C.O. 5:394. At the time there was owing to Bull over £2,000 sterling. South Carolina Public Records, 34:21–2, 24, 36–40.

[128] Campbell's commission and instructions are cited earlier in this chapter. See also, in this connection, J. P. Greene's *Quest for Power*, pp. 413–16.

[129] See D. D. Wallace: *Constitutional History of South Carolina*, pp. 88–92.

Index

A NOTE ABOUT THE AUTHOR

LAWRENCE HENRY GIPSON is Research Professor of History, Emeritus, at Lehigh University. After receiving a bachelor of arts degree from the University of Idaho, he entered Oxford as the first Rhodes Scholar from the state of Idaho, and gained a degree in the Oxford Honour School of Modern History. He was later a Bulkley Fellow in the graduate school at Yale, where his doctoral dissertation, *Jared Ingersoll: A Study of American Loyalism in Relation to British Colonial Government,* received the Porter Prize as the best work in literary form presented by a student in any division of the University during the preceding year; it was also awarded the Justin Winsor Prize by the American Historical Association. Since then he has written and published many works relating to colonial history (including twelve volumes of his *magnum opus;* the final volume is in preparation). During the academic year 1951–2 he occupied the Harmsworth Chair in American History at Oxford; he also has been a member of the board of editors of the *American Historical Review,* was a founder of the Conference on Early American History, and is a past president of both the Conference on British Studies and the Pennsylvania Historical Association. He is the Honorary Consultant in American Colonial History to the Library of Congress for the period 1965 through 1967. Many prizes and honors have come to him as a result of his writing, including the Pulitzer Prize in History for 1962 for Volume X of *The British Empire before the American Revolution* and, most recently, his election as Honorary Fellow of Lincoln College, Oxford University.

July 1965

A NOTE ON THE TYPE

THE TEXT of this book is set in *Caledonia,* a typeface designed by W(ILLIAM) A(DDISON) DWIGGINS for the Mergenthaler Linotype Company in 1939. Dwiggins chose to call his new typeface Caledonia, the Roman name for Scotland, because it was inspired by the Scotch types cast about 1833 by Alexander Wilson & Son, Glasgow type founders. However, there is a calligraphic quality about this face that is totally lacking in the Wilson types. Dwiggins referred to an even earlier typeface for this "liveliness of action"—one cut around 1790 by William Martin for the printer William Bulmer. Caledonia has more weight than the Martin letters, and the bottom finishing strokes (serifs) of the letters are cut straight across, without brackets, to make sharp angles with the upright stems, thus giving a "modern face" appearance.

W. A. Dwiggins (1880–1956) was born in Martinsville, Ohio, and studied art in Chicago. In 1904 he moved to Hingham, Massachusetts, where he built a solid reputation as a designer of advertisements and as a calligrapher. He began an association with the Mergenthaler Linotype Company in 1929, and over the next twenty-seven years designed a number of book types for that firm. Of especial interest are the Metro series, Electra, Caledonia, Eldorado, and Falcon. In 1930, Dwiggins first became interested in marionettes, and through the years made many important contributions to the art of puppetry and the design of marionettes.

Composed by The Haddon Craftsmen, Inc., Scranton, Pa.,
printed and bound by The Kingsport Press, Kingsport, Tenn.
Typography and binding design by
W. A. DWIGGINS